Analytic Information Theory

Through information theory, problems of communication and compression can be precisely modeled, formulated, and analyzed, and this information can be transformed by means of algorithms. Also, learning can be viewed as compression with side information. Aimed at students and researchers, this book addresses data compression and redundancy within existing methods and central topics in theoretical data compression, demonstrating how to use tools from analytic combinatorics to discover and analyze precise behavior of source codes. It shows that to present better learnable or extractable information in its shortest description, one must understand what the information is, and then algorithmically extract it in its most compact form via an efficient compression algorithm. Part I covers fixed-to-variable codes such as Shannon and Huffman codes, variable-to-fixed codes such as Tunstall and Khodak codes, and variable-to-variable Khodak codes for known sources. Part II discusses universal source coding for memoryless, Markov, and renewal sources.

MICHAEL DRMOTA is Professor for Discrete Mathematics at TU Wien. His research activities range from analytic combinatorics over discrete random structures to number theory. He has published several books, including *Random Trees* (2009), and about 200 research articles. He was President of the Austrian Mathematical Society from 2010 to 2013, and has been Corresponding Member of the Austrian Academy of Sciences since 2013.

WOJCIECH SZPANKOWSKI is the Saul Rosen Distinguished Professor of Computer Science at Purdue University where he teaches and conducts research in analysis of algorithms, information theory, analytic combinatorics, random structures, and machine learning for classical and quantum data. He has received the Inaugural Arden L. Bement Jr. Award (2015) and the Flajolet Lecture Prize (2020), among others. In 2021, he was elected to the Academia Europaea. In 2008, he launched the interdisciplinary Institute for Science of Information, and in 2010, he became Director of the NSF Science and Technology Center for Science of Information.

Analytic Information Theory

From Compression to Learning

Michael Drmota
TU Wien

Wojciech Szpankowski
Purdue University

 CAMBRIDGE
UNIVERSITY PRESS

Shaftesbury Road, Cambridge CB2 8EA, United Kingdom

One Liberty Plaza, 20th Floor, New York, NY 10006, USA

477 Williamstown Road, Port Melbourne, VIC 3207, Australia

314–321, 3rd Floor, Plot 3, Splendor Forum, Jasola District Centre,
New Delhi – 110025, India

103 Penang Road, #05–06/07, Visioncrest Commercial, Singapore 238467

Cambridge University Press is part of Cambridge University Press & Assessment,
a department of the University of Cambridge.

We share the University's mission to contribute to society through the pursuit of
education, learning and research at the highest international levels of excellence.

www.cambridge.org
Information on this title: www.cambridge.org/9781108474443
DOI: 10.1017/9781108565462

First published 2023

A catalogue record for this publication is available from the British Library

A Cataloging-in-Publication data record for this book is available from the Library of Congress

ISBN 978-1-108-47444-3 Hardback

Cambridge University Press & Assessment has no responsibility for the persistence or accuracy of
URLs for external or third-party internet websites referred to in this publication
and does not guarantee that any content on such websites is, or will remain,
accurate or appropriate.

To Gabi

Contents

Preface

Information and computation are two of the defining concepts of the modern era. Shannon laid the foundation of information (theory), demonstrating that problems of communication and compression can be precisely modeled, formulated, and analyzed. Turing, on the other hand, formalized the concept of computation, defined as the transformation of information by means of algorithms. In this book, we focus on information (or better, learnable/extractable information) that we hope to present in its most compact form (i.e., shortest description). To achieve this goal, we need first to understand what information is, and then algorithmically extract it in its most compact form (i.e., find an efficient compression algorithm).

Let us start with a general discussion of information. We adopt here a definition of information as that which can be used to *distinguish* one set of data samples from another. This process of "distinguishing" involves an "observer function" that maps a dataset to an observed object. The observer function in traditional information theory may correspond to a *channel*. In a more general setting, the observer function may be an arbitrary function, such as a learning operator, formulated as an optimization procedure. For example, a given dataset can be "observed" through a classifier (e.g., a logistic regression function). In this case, two datasets have the same information content if they yield the same classifier relative to the learning method that produces that classifier.

Another fundamental question of information theory and statistical inference probes how much "useful or learnable information" one can actually extract from a given dataset. We would like to understand how much useful information, structure, regularity, or summarizing properties are in a database or sequence. We will argue in this book (see Section 10.4) that learnable information is not so much related to entropy, the beloved quantity of information theory, but rather the excess of the shortest database description over the entropy, which is known as the redundancy of regret. This book is devoted to studying redundancy via some powerful analytic tools that allow us to analyze it with the utmost precision.

The basic problem of *source coding*, better known as (lossless) *data compression*, is finding a (binary) code that can be unambiguously recovered with the shortest possible description either on average or for individual sequences. Thanks to Shannon's work, we know that on average the number of bits per source symbol cannot be smaller than the source entropy rate. There are many codes asymptotically achieving the entropy rate, therefore our attention turns to *redundancy*. The average redundancy of a source code is the amount by which the expected number of binary digits per source symbol for that code exceeds entropy. One of the goals in designing source coding algorithms is to minimize redundancy. Redundancy can be viewed as the rate of convergence to the entropy, and only those compression algorithms that converge fast enough (with small redundancy) are of interest. In this book, we discuss various classes of source coding and their corresponding redundancy for known sources (Part I) and some classes of unknown sources (Part II).

We can view data compression as a probability assignment. Then, source coding and prediction are special cases of the *online learning problems* that we briefly discuss in the second part of this book.

Lossless compression comes in three flavors: fixed-to-variable (FV) length codes, variable-to-fixed (VF) length codes, and finally variable-to-variable (VV) length codes. In FV codes, a fixed length block (sequence) is mapped into a variable length code. In VF codes, a variable length block is represented by a fixed length code, usually an entry to a dictionary. The VV codes include the previous two families of codes and are the least studied among all data compression schemes. Over the years, there has been a resurgence of interest in redundancy rates for *fixed-to-variable* coding as seen in Dembo and Kontoyiannis (1999, 2001, 2002), Jacquet and Szpankowski (1995), Kontoyiannis (1999, 2000, 2001), Linder, Lugosi, and Zeger (1995), Louchard and Szpankowski (1995), Rissanen (1984a, 1996), Savari (1997, 1998), Savari and Gallager (1997), Shields (1996), Shtarkov (1987), Szpankowski (1998, 2000), Weinberger et al. (1994), Wyner (1972), Xie and Barron (1997, 2000), Yang and Kieffer (1998). Surprisingly, there are only a handful of results for variable-to-fixed codes as witnessed by Jelinek and Schneider (1972), Krichevsky and Trofimov (1981), Merhav and Neuhoff (1992), Savari (1999), Savari and Gallager (1997), Schalkwijk (1972), Tjalkens and Willems (1992), Visweswariah, Kulkurani, and Verdu (2001) and Ziv (1990). There is almost no existing literature on variable-to-variable codes with the exception of a few such as Fabris (1992), Freeman (1993), Khodak (1972), Krichevsky and Trofimov (1981). While there is some work on universal VF codes, such as Tjalkens and Willems (1992), Visweswariah et al. (2001) and Ziv (1990), to the best of our knowledge redundancy for universal VF and VV codes was not studied with the exception of some work of the Russian school, Krichevsky (1994), and Krichevsky and Trofimov (1981).

Throughout this book, we shall study various intriguing trees describing Huffman, Tunstall, Khodak, and Boncelet codes and other advanced data structures such as graphs, by analytic techniques of analysis of algorithm as discussed in Flajolet and Sedgewick (2008), Knuth (1997, 1998a, 1998b), Szpankowski (2001). The program of applying mathematical techniques from analytic combinatorics (which have been successfully applied to analysis of algorithms) to problems of source coding and in general to information theory lies at the crossroad of computer science and information theory. It is also known as *analytic information theory*: see, for example, Jacquet and Szpankowski (1999) and Szpankowski (2012). We study source coding algorithms using tools from the analysis of algorithms and analytic combinatorics to discover precise and minute behavior of such code redundancy.

Let us mention that the interplay between information theory and computer science/machine learning dates back to the founding father of information theory, Claude E. Shannon. His landmark paper "A Mathematical Theory of Communication" is hailed as the foundation for information theory. Shannon also worked on problems in computer science such as chess-playing machines and computability of different Turing machines. Ever since Shannon's work on both information theory and computer science, the research at the interplay between these two fields has continued and expanded in many exciting ways. In the late 1960s and early 1970s, there were tremendous interdisciplinary research activities, exemplified by the work of Kolmogorov, Chaitin, and Solomonoff, with the aim of establishing algorithmic information theory. Motivated by approaching Kolmogorov complexity algorithmically, A. Lempel (a computer scientist) and J. Ziv (an information theorist) worked together in the late 1970s to develop compression algorithms that are now widely referred to as Lempel–Ziv algorithms. Analytic information theory is a continuation of these efforts. Furthermore, recently we have seen efforts to apply analytic combinatorics to learning theory, in particular, online regret as witnessed by Jacquet et al. (2021) and Shamir and Szpankowski (2021b, 2021a).

Contents of the Book

The preliminary Chapter 1 introduces some notation and definitions. Chapter 2 is focused on fixed-to-variable codes in which the encoder maps fixed-length blocks of source symbols into variable-length binary code strings. Two prominent fixed-to-variable length coding algorithms are the Shannon code and the Huffman code. We first discuss precise analyses of Shannon code redundancy for memoryless and Markov sources. We show that the average redundancy either converges to an explicitly computable constant, as the block length increases, or it exhibits very erratic behavior fluctuating between 0 and 1. We also observe similar behavior for the worst-case or maximal redundancy. Then we move to the Huffman code. Despite the fact that Huffman codes have been so well known for so long, it was only relatively recently that their redundancy was fully understood. Abrahams (2001) summarizes much of the vast literature on fixed-to-variable length codes. Here, we present a precise analysis as discussed in Szpankowski (2000) of the Huffman average redundancy for memoryless sources. Again, we show that the average redundancy either converges to an explicitly computable constant, as the block length increases, or it exhibits a very erratic behavior fluctuating between 0 and 1. Then we discuss similar results for Markov sources.

In Chapter 3, we study variable-to-fixed codes. A VF encoder partitions the source string into variable-length phrases that belong to a given dictionary $\mathcal{D}$. Often a dictionary is represented by a complete tree (i.e., a tree in which every node has maximum degree), also known as the *parsing tree*. The code assigns a fixed-length word to each dictionary entry. An important example of a variable-to-fixed code is the Tunstall (1967) code. Savari and Gallager (1997) present an analysis of the dominant term in the asymptotic expansion of the Tunstall code redundancy. In this book, we describe a precise analysis of the phrase length (i.e., path from the root to a terminal node in the corresponding parsing tree) for such a code and its average redundancy. We also discuss a variant of Tunstall code known as VF Khodak code.

In Chapter 4, we continue analyzing VF codes due to Boncelet (1993). Boncelet's algorithm is computationally fast and its practicality stems from the *divide-and-conquer* strategy: it splits the input (e.g., parsing tree) into several smaller subproblems, solving each subproblem separately, and then knitting together to solve the original problem. We use this occasion to present a careful analysis of a divide-and-conquer recurrence that is at the foundation of several divide-and-conquer algorithms such as heapsort, mergesort, discrete Fourier transform, queues, sorting networks, compression algorithms, and so forth, as discussed in depth in Flajolet and Sedgewick (2008), Knuth (1998a) and Szpankowski (2001). Here we follow Drmota and Szpankowski (2013).

In Chapter 5 we consider variable-to-variable codes. A variable-to-variable (VV) code is a concatenation of variable-to-fixed and fixed-to-variable codes. A VV-length encoder consists of a *parser* and a *string encoder*. The parser, as in VF codes, segments the source sequence into a concatenation of phrases from a predetermined dictionary $\mathcal{D}$. Next, the string encoder in a VV scheme takes the sequence of dictionary strings and maps each one into its corresponding binary codeword of variable length. Aside from the special cases where either the dictionary strings or the codewords have a fixed length, very little is known about VV-length codes, even in the case of memoryless sources. Khodak (1972) described a VV scheme with small average redundancy that decreases with the growth of phrase length. He did not offer, however, an explicit VV code construction. We will remedy this situation and follow Bugeaud, Drmota and Szpankowski (2008) to give an explicit construction of the VV code.

In Chapter 6, we discuss redundancy of one-to-one codes that are not necessarily prefix or even uniquely decodable. Recall that nonprefix codes are codes that are not prefix free and do not satisfy Kraft's inequality. In particular, we analyze binary and nonbinary one-to-one codes whose average lengths are smaller than the source entropy in defiance of the Shannon lower bound.

The last two chapters in Part I, Chapters 7 and 8, deal with more advanced data structures. Information theory traditionally deals with conventional data almost exclusively represented by sequences, be it textual data, images, or video data. Over the last decade, repositories of various data have grown enormously. Most of the available data is no longer in conventional form. Instead, biological data (e.g., gene-expression data, protein-interaction networks, phylogenetic trees), topographical maps (containing various information about temperature, pressure, etc.), medical data (cerebral scans, mammograms, etc.), and social network data archives are in the form of *multimodal* data structures; that is, multitype and context-dependent structures, often represented by trees and graphs. In Chapter 7, we present compression algorithms and precise analysis of various trees: from plane binary trees to non-plane general trees. In Chapter 8, we discuss a harder problem, namely how many bits are needed to describe a graph. In fact, we focus on nonlabeled graphs that we call structures. First we discuss standard Erdős–Rényi graphs and, after designing a structural compression, we precisely analyze it using analytic tools such as Mellin transform, and analytic depoissonization. Then we study dynamic graphs in which nodes and vertices may be added or deleted. We focus on the *preferential attachment graphs*. We first discuss its symmetry in detail and then derive the graph and structural entropies. Finally, we present asymptotically optimal structural compression for such graphs.

The second part of the book is about universal compression and online learning in which the encoder receives a sequence generated by an unknown source with potentially additional information known as feature data. We start with a preliminary Chapter 9, in which we precisely define worst-case and average minimax redundancy and regret. We then show that worst-case redundancy can be studied through the so-called Shtarkov sum, while for average minimax redundancy we have to resort to Bayesian methods. Finally, we compare worst-case and average minimax redundancies and provide a constructive method to estimate one from the other.

Chapter 10 deals with worst-case and minimax redundancy for the memoryless class of sources. We first observe that due to the integer nature of the code length, we need to split the redundancy into two parts called the coding part and the noninteger part. The coding part is studied using tools developed in Chapter 2. The noninteger part depends on the statistics and structure of the source. We first consider sources with finite alphabets as well as constrained sources in which the symbol probability belongs to a bounded set. For such sources we provide precise asymptotic expansion of the average and maximal redundancy. We apply here special generating functions called tree-function and singularity analysis. In the last part of the chapter, we consider sources over unbounded alphabets that may grow with the sequence length. We also turn our attention to online minimax regret, which can be viewed as source coding with side information.

In Chapter 11, we study minimax redundancy for Markov sources. We first discuss Markov types, counting the number of sequences of a given type and the number of Markov type. This allows us to provide a precise asymptotics of the minimax redundancy, the coding part and the noncoding part.

Finally, in Chapter 12, we consider non-Markovian sources with unbounded memory. For clarity, we only discuss renewal sources introduced by Csiszar and Shields (1996) and prove precise asymptotics for the worst-case minimax regret for renewal sources of order 1, and discuss the average minimax regret, suggesting that they are not asymptotically equivalent.

We end the book with six Appendices. They cover probability, generating functions, and special functions, as well as more esoteric topics like complex analysis, Mellin transforms, exponential sums, and Diophantine approximations.

Acknowledgments

There is a long list of colleagues and friends from whom we benefited through their encouragement and constructive comments. They have helped us in various ways during our work on the analysis of algorithms and information theory. We mention here only a few: Alberto Apostolico, Yongwook Choi, Luc Devroye, Ananth Grama, H.-K. Hwang, Philippe Jacquet, Svante Janson, John Kieffer, Chuck Knessl, Yiannis Kontoyiannis, Tomasz Luczak, Abram Magner, Ralph Neininger, Arun Padakandal, Yuriy Reznik, Bob Sedgewick, Gadiel Seroussi, Gil Shamir, Krzysztof Turowski, Brigitte Vallée, Sergio Verdu, Mark Ward, Marcelo Weinberger. We are particularly in debt to Philippe Jacquet for his friendship and collaboration. This book could not have happened without the Herculean job in analytic combinatorics done by our late friend and mentor Philippe Flajolet. We thank all of them.

This book has been written over the last five years, while we have been traveling around the world carrying (electronically) numerous copies of various drafts. We have received invaluable help from the staff and faculty of the Institute of Discrete Mathematics and Geometry of TU Wien and the Department of Computer Sciences at Purdue University. The first author thanks the Austrian Science Fund (FWF) for their support. The second author is grateful to the National Science Foundation, which has supported his work over the last 30 years. We have also received support from institutions around the world that have hosted us and our book: INRIA, LINCS, Paris; the Gdańsk University of Technology, Gdańsk; Jagiellonian University, Kraków; the University of Hawaii; and ETH, Zurich. We thank them very much.

Finally, no big project like this one can be completed without help from our families. We thank Heidemarie, Johanna, and Peter as well as Mariola, Lukasz, Paulina, and Olivia from the bottoms of our hearts. This book is dedicated to Gabi, who passed away too early.

Part I

Known Sources

1

Preliminaries

In this chapter we introduce some notation, including definitions and basic properties of source coding, entropy, and redundancy. In particular, we define the average redundancy and the worst-case redundancy for prefix codes.

1.1 Source Code and Entropy

Let us start with some notation. Throughout, we write $x = x_1 x_2 \ldots$ for a nonempty sequence of unspecified length over a finite alphabet $\mathcal{A}$. We also write $x_i^j = x_i, \ldots, x_j \in \mathcal{A}^{j-i+1}$ for a consecutive subsequence of length $j - i + 1$. Sometimes we use the abbreviation $x^n = x_1^n$. Finally, throughout we write $\mathbb{Z}$, $\mathbb{Q}$, and $\mathbb{R}$ for integer, rational, and real numbers respectively.

A *(binary) code* is a one-to-one (or injective) mapping:

$$C \colon \mathcal{A} \to \{0, 1\}^+$$

from a finite alphabet $\mathcal{A}$ (the *source*) to the set $\{0, 1\}^+$ of nonempty binary sequences (where we use the notation $S^+ = \cup_{i=1}^{\infty} S^i$) One can extend this concept to *m*-ary codes $C \colon \mathcal{A} \to \{0, 1, \ldots, m-1\}^+$, if needed. We write $L(C, x)$ (or simply $L(x)$) for the length of $C(x)$. Finally, a code is a prefix code if no codeword is a prefix of another codeword.

In this book, we mostly deal with a sequence of codes:

$$C_n \colon \mathcal{A}_n \to \{0, 1\}^+,$$

where $\mathcal{A}_n$ is a sequence of alphabets. In particular, if this sequence is of the form $\mathcal{A}_n = \mathcal{A}^n$, where $\mathcal{A} = \{0, \ldots, m-1\}$, the code is called a fixed-to-variable (FV) code, discussed in Chapter 2. If $\mathcal{A}_n \subseteq \mathcal{A}^+$ and $\{0, 1\}^+$ is replaced by $\{0, 1\}^M$ for some M, we deal with variable-to-fixed (VF) codes; otherwise we have a general variable-to-variable (VV) code. We discuss VF codes in Chapters 3 and 4 and VV codes in Chapter 5.

We denote by P a probability distribution on the alphabet $\mathcal{A}$. The elements of the source can be then interpreted as a random variable X with probability distribution $P(X = x) = P(x)$. Such a source is also called *probabilistic source*. For example, the code length $L(X)$ is then a random variable too, and the expected code length $\mathbf{E}[L(X)]$ is an important parameter of a probabilistic source code.

The source *entropy* of a probabilistic source is defined by

$$H(X) := H(P) = -\mathbf{E}[\log P(X)] = -\sum_{x \in \mathcal{A}} P(x) \log P(x),$$

3

where we write log for the logarithm of unspecified base; however, throughout the book, the base is usually equal to 2, unless specified otherwise.

Finally, we introduce a few other concepts related to entropy that we will use throughout the book.

Definition 1.1 (i) Let $\mathcal{A}$ and $\mathcal{A}'$ be two finite alphabets and P a probability distribution on $\mathcal{A} \times \mathcal{A}'$, and (X, Y) a random vector with $P(X = a, Y = a') = P(a, a')$. Then the Joint Entropy $H(X, Y)$ is defined as

$$H(X, Y) = -\mathbf{E}[\log P(X, Y)] = -\sum_{a \in \mathcal{A}} \sum_{a' \in \mathcal{A}'} P(a, a') \log P(a, a'). \tag{1.1}$$

(ii) The Conditional Entropy $H(Y|X)$ is

$$H(Y|X) = -\mathbf{E}[\log P(Y|X)] = \sum_{a \in \mathcal{A}} P(a) H(Y \,|\, X = a)$$

$$= -\sum_{a \in \mathcal{A}} \sum_{a' \in \mathcal{A}'} P(a, a') \log P(a'|a), \tag{1.2}$$

where $P(a'|a) = P(a, a')/P(a)$ and $P(a) = \sum_{a' \in \mathcal{A}'} P(a, a')$.

(iii) The Relative Entropy or Kullback Leibler Distance or Kullback Leibler Divergence between two distributions P and Q defined on the same probability space (or finite alphabet $\mathcal{A}$) is

$$D(P\|Q) = \mathbf{E}\left[\log \frac{P(X)}{Q(X)}\right] = \sum_{a \in \mathcal{A}} P(a) \log \frac{P(a)}{Q(a)}, \tag{1.3}$$

where, by convention, $0 \log(0/Q) = 0$ and $P \log(P/0) = \infty$.

(iv) The Mutual Information of X and Y is the relative entropy between the joint distribution of X and Y and the product distribution $P(X)P(Y)$; that is,

$$I(X; Y) = \mathbf{E}\left[\log \frac{P(X, Y)}{P(X)P(Y)}\right] = \sum_{a \in \mathcal{A}} \sum_{a' \in \mathcal{A}'} P(a, a') \log \frac{P(a, a')}{P(a)P(a')}. \tag{1.4}$$

(v) Rényi's Entropy of order b $(-\infty \le b \le \infty, b \ne 0)$ is defined as

$$H_b(X) = -\frac{\log \mathbf{E}[P^b(X)]}{b} = -\frac{1}{b} \log \sum_{a \in \mathcal{A}} P^{b+1}(a), \tag{1.5}$$

provided $b \ne 0$ is finite, and by

$$H_{-\infty} = \min_{i \in \mathcal{A}}\{P(i)\}, \tag{1.6}$$

$$H_{\infty} = \max_{i \in \mathcal{A}}\{P(i)\}. \tag{1.7}$$

Observe that $H(X) = \lim_{b \to 0} H_b(X)$.

If P_n is a sequence of probability measures on $\mathcal{A}^n$ (for $n \ge 1$), we also define the entropy rate h, if it exists, as

$$h = \lim_{n \to \infty} \frac{H(P_n)}{n} = \lim_{n \to \infty} \frac{-\sum_{x^n \in \mathcal{A}^n} P_n(x^n) \log P_n(x^n)}{n}.$$

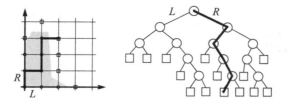

Figure 1.1 Lattice paths and binary trees.

1.2 Prefix Codes and Their Properties

As discussed, a *prefix code* is a code for which no codeword $C(x)$ for $x \in \mathcal{A}$ is a prefix of another codeword. For such codes, there is mapping between a codeword $C(x)$ and a path in a tree from the root to a terminal (external) node (e.g., for a binary prefix code, a move to the left in the tree represents 0 and a move to the right represents 1), as shown in Figure 1.1. We also point out that a prefix code and the corresponding path in a tree define a lattice path in the first quadrant also shown in Figure 1.1. Here left L and right R traversals in the binary tree correspond to "left" or "up" movement in the lattice. If some additional constraints are imposed on the prefix codes, this translates into certain restrictions on the lattice path indicated as the shaded area in Figure 1.1. (See Section 3.4 for some embellishments on this topic.)

The prefix condition imposes some restrictions on the code length. This fact is known as Kraft's inequality discussed next.

Theorem 1.2 (Kraft's inequality) *Let* $|\mathcal{A}| = N$. *Then for any binary prefix code C we have*

$$\sum_{x \in \mathcal{A}} 2^{-L(C,x)} \leq 1.$$

Conversely, if positive integers $\ell_1, \ell_2, \ldots, \ell_N$ *satisfy the inequality*

$$\sum_{i=1}^{N} 2^{-\ell_i} \leq 1, \tag{1.8}$$

then there exists a prefix code with these codeword lengths.

Proof This is an easy exercise on trees. Let $\ell_{\max}$ be the maximum codeword length. Observe that at level $\ell_{\max}$, some nodes are codewords, some are descendants of codewords, and some are neither. Since the number of descendants at level $\ell_{\max}$ of a codeword located at level ℓ_i is $2^{\ell_{\max} - \ell_i}$, we obtain

$$\sum_{i=1}^{N} 2^{\ell_{\max} - \ell_i} \leq 2^{\ell_{\max}},$$

which is the desired inequality. The converse part can also be proved, and the reader is asked to prove it in Exercise 1.7. ∎

Using Kraft's inequality we can now prove the first theorem of Shannon (which was first established by Khinchin) that bounds from below the average code length.

Theorem 1.3 *Let C be a prefix code on the alphabet $\mathcal{A}$, P a probability distribution on $\mathcal{A}$, and X a random variable with $P(X = a) = P(a)$. Then the average code length $\mathbf{E}[L(C,X)]$ cannot be smaller than the entropy $H(P)$; that is,*

$$\mathbf{E}[L(C,X)] \geq H(P),$$

where the expectation is taken with respect to the distribution P and the logarithms in the definition of $H(P)$ are the binary logarithms.

Proof Let $K = \sum_x 2^{-L(x)} \leq 1$ and $L(x) := L(C,x)$. Then by Kraft's inequality, $K \leq 1$. Furthermore, by using the inequality $-\log_2 x \geq \frac{1}{\ln 2}(1-x)$ for $x > 0$ we get (recall that $\log = \log_2$)

$$\mathbf{E}[L(C,X)] - H(P)] = \sum_{x \in \mathcal{A}} P(x)L(x) + \sum_{x \in \mathcal{A}} P(x)\log P(x)$$

$$= -\sum_{x \in \mathcal{A}} P(x)\log \frac{2^{-L(x)}/K}{P(x)} - \log K$$

$$\geq \frac{1}{\ln 2}\left(\sum_{x \in \mathcal{A}} P(x) - \frac{1}{K}\sum_{x \in \mathcal{A}} 2^{-L(x)}\right) - \log K$$

$$= -\log K \geq 0,$$

as proposed.   ∎

Observe that this theorem implies the existence of at least one element $\widetilde{x} \in \mathcal{A}$ such that

$$L(\widetilde{x}) \geq -\log P(\widetilde{x}). \tag{1.9}$$

Furthermore, we can complement Theorem 1.3 by the following property.

Lemma 1.4 (Barron)   *Let C be a prefix code and $a > 0$. Then*

$$P(L(C,X) < -\log P(X) - a) \leq 2^{-a}.$$

Proof We argue as follows (again $\log = \log_2$):

$$P(L(X) < -\log P(X) - a) = \sum_{x:\, P(x) < 2^{-L(x)-a}} P(x)$$

$$\leq \sum_{x:\, P(x) < 2^{-L(x)-a}} 2^{-L(x)-a}$$

$$\leq 2^{-a}\sum_x 2^{-L(x)} \leq 2^{-a},$$

where we have used Kraft's inequality.   ∎

What is the best prefix code with respect to code length? We are now in a position to answer this question. One needs to solve the following constrained optimization problem:

$$\min_L \sum_x L(x)P(x) \quad \text{subject to} \quad \sum_x 2^{-L(x)} \leq 1. \tag{1.10}$$

This optimization problem has an easy *real-valued* solution through Lagrangian multipliers, and one finds that the optimal code length is $L(x) = -\log P(x)$, provided the *integer character of the length is ignored* (see Exercise 1.8). If it is not ignored, then interesting things happen. First, the excess of the code length over $-\log P(x)$ is called the redundancy and is discussed in this book, in particular in Chapter 2. Furthermore, to minimize the redundancy, that is, to make $-\log P(x)$ as close to an integer as possible, ingenious algorithms were designed, which we will discuss in Part I of this book, in particular in Chapter 5.

In this book, we mostly deal with prefix codes, with the exception of Chapter 6 where we discuss nonprefix one-to-one codes.

To start with, we just mention a very simple prefix code, namely the Shannon code. It assigns to $x \in \mathcal{A}$ a codeword with code length

$$L(x) = \lceil -\log P(x) \rceil.$$

By Theorem 1.2, such a prefix code always exists, since

$$\sum_{x \in \mathcal{A}} 2^{-\lceil -\log P(x) \rceil} \leq \sum_{x \in \mathcal{A}} P(x) = 1.$$

1.3 Redundancy

In general, one needs to round the length to an integer, thereby incurring some cost. This cost is usually called *redundancy*. More precisely, redundancy is the excess of real code length over its ideal (optimal) code length, which is assumed to be $-\log P(x)$. There are several possible specifications of this general definition. For a *known* distribution P, which we assume throughout Part I, the *pointwise redundancy* $R^C(x)$ for a code C and the *average redundancy* $\overline{R}^C$ are defined as

$$R^C(x) = L(C,x) + \log P(x),$$
$$\overline{R} = \mathbf{E}[L(C,X)] - H(P)].$$

Furthermore, we define the *maximal* or *worst-case* redundancy R^* as

$$R^* = \max_{x \in \mathcal{A}}[L(C,x) + \log P(x)] = \max_{x \in \mathcal{A}} R^C(x).$$

The pointwise redundancy can be negative, but the average and worst-case redundancies cannot due to the Shannon theorem (Theorem 1.3) and (1.9), respectively.

For example, for the Shannon code we have

$$0 \leq \overline{R} \leq R^* = \max_{x \in \mathcal{A}}[\lceil -\log P(x) \rceil + \log P(x)] < 1.$$

1.4 Exercises

1.1   Establish the following properties:

$$H(X,Y) = H(X) + H(Y|X),$$
$$H(X_1, X_2, \ldots, X_n) = \sum_{i=1}^{n} H(X_i|X_{i-1}, \ldots, X_1),$$
$$I(X;Y) = H(X) - H(X|Y) = H(Y) - H(Y|X),$$
$$I(X;X) = H(X).$$

1.2   Prove that the following inequalities hold:

$$D(P\|Q) \geq 0, \tag{1.11}$$

$$I(X;Y) \geq 0, \tag{1.12}$$

$$H(X) \geq H(X|Y), \tag{1.13}$$

$$H(X_1,\ldots,X_n) \leq \sum_{i=1}^{n} H(X_i), \tag{1.14}$$

with equality in (1.11) if and only if $P(a) = Q(a)$ for all $a \in \mathcal{A}$, equality in (1.12) and (1.13) if and only if X and Y are independent, and equality in (1.14) if and only if $X_1,\ldots,X_n$ are independent.

1.3   Let $Y = g(X)$ where g is a measurable function. Prove

- $h(g(X)) \leq h(X)$;
- $h(Y|X) = 0$.

1.4   Random variables X, Y, Z form a Markov chain in that order (denoted by $X \to Y \to Z$) if the conditional distribution of Z depends on Y and is independent of X; that is,

$$P(X = x, Y = y, Z = z) = P(X = x)P(Y = y|X = x)P(Z = z|Y = y)$$

for all possible x, y, z. Prove the *data processing inequality* that states

$$I(X;Y) \geq I(X;Z)$$

if $X \to Y \to Z$.

1.5   Consider a probability vector $\mathbf{p} = (p_1,\ldots,p_n)$ such that $\sum_{i=1}^{n} p_i = 1$. What probability distribution $\mathbf{p}$ minimizes the entropy $H(\mathbf{p})$?

1.6   (Log sum inequality) (i) Prove that for nonnegative numbers $a_1,\ldots,a_n$ and $b_1,\ldots,b_n$,

$$\sum_{i=1}^{n} a_i \log \frac{a_i}{b_i} \geq \left(\sum_{i=1}^{n} a_i \right) \log \frac{\sum_{i=1}^{n} a_i}{\sum_{i=1}^{n} b_i}$$

with equality if and only if $\frac{a_i}{b_i} = const$.

(ii) Deduce form (i) that for $p_1,\ldots,p_n$ and $q_1,\ldots,q_n$ such that $\sum_{i=1}^{n} p_i = \sum_{i=1}^{n} q_i = 1$, we have

$$\sum_{i=1}^{n} p_i \log \frac{1}{q_i} \geq \sum_{i=1}^{n} p_i \log \frac{1}{p_i};$$

that is,

$$\min_{q_i} \sum_{i=1}^{n} p_i \log \frac{1}{q_i} = \sum_{i=1}^{n} p_i \log \frac{1}{p_i}.$$

(iii) Show that the following (potential) extension of (ii) is **not true**:

$$\sum_{i=1}^{n} p_i \left\lceil \log \frac{1}{q_i} \right\rceil \geq \sum_{i=1}^{n} p_i \left\lceil \log \frac{1}{p_i} \right\rceil,$$

where $\lceil x \rceil$ is the smallest integer greater than or equal to x.

1.7   Prove the converse part of the Kraft inequality in Theorem 1.2.
1.8   Consider the optimization problem (1.10). Show that the optimal length is $L(x) = -\log P(x)$.

Bibliographical Notes

Information theory was born in 1948 when Shannon (1948) published a monumental work wherein he presented three theorems: on source coding, channel coding, and distortion theory. There are many good books discussing information theory. We recommend Gallager (1968) and Cover and Thomas (1991).

Lemma 1.4 was first proved by Barron (1985). The worst-case redundancy was introduced by Shtarkov (1987).

2

Shannon and Huffman FV Codes

We now turn our attention to fixed-to-variable length codes, in particular to Shannon and Huffman codes. In this chapter, we assume that a known source with distribution P generates a sequence $x^n := x_1^n = x_1 \ldots x_n$ of *fixed* length n, that is, the alphabet $\mathcal{A}$ is of the form $\mathcal{A}_n = \mathcal{A}^n$, where we write $\mathcal{A} = \{0, 1, \ldots, m-1\}$, however, we mostly discuss the binary case ($m = 2$). The codewords $C(x_1^n)$ may be of a variable length. We first analyze the average redundancy for Shannon and Huffman codes for memoryless sources. Then we study the Shannon code redundancy for Markov sources. Finally, we consider a code that optimizes the worst-case redundancy which turns out to be a generalized Shannon code.

2.1 Average Redundancy for Memoryless Sources

We now assume that a sequence of fixed length n, denoted $x^n = x_1^n$, is generated by a binary memoryless source with p being the probability of emitting 0, that is, $P(x^n) = p^k(1-p)^{n-k}$, where $k = |\{1 \leq j \leq n : x_j = 0\}|$. We also write $q := 1 - p$. We also observe that the entropy rate $h = -p \log p - (1-p) \log(1-p)$.

2.1.1 Shannon Code

Recall that the Shannon code is a prefix code that is as close as possible to the *optimal* (real-valued) codeword length $- \log P(x^n)$. It assigns to $x^n \in \mathcal{A}_n = \{0, 1\}^n$ a codeword with code length

$$L(x^n) = \lceil - \log P(x^n) \rceil.$$

As mentioned above, Kraft's inequality (Theorem 1.2) assures that such a code always exists.

For a memoryless source, we have $P(x^n) = p^k q^{n-k}$ where k is the number of 0s in x^n. Hence, its average redundancy $\overline{R}_n^S$ is then

$$\overline{R}_n^S = \sum_{k=0}^n \binom{n}{k} p^k q^{n-k} \left(\lceil - \log(p^k q^{n-k}) \rceil + \log p^k q^{n-k} \right).$$

We rewrite it in a slightly different form. We denote by $\langle x \rangle = x - \lfloor x \rfloor$ the fractional part of real number x. It is easy to see that

$$\lceil -x \rceil + x = \langle x \rangle \tag{2.1}$$

for any real x. Hence, we have

$$\bar{R}_n^S = \sum_{k=0}^{n} \binom{n}{k} p^k q^{n-k} \langle \alpha k + \beta n \rangle, \qquad (2.2)$$

where

$$\alpha = \log \left(\frac{p}{1-p} \right) \quad \text{and} \quad \beta = \log (1-p). \qquad (2.3)$$

We are interested in the asymptotic behavior of $\bar{R}_n^S$ given by (2.2). In order to handle the function $\langle x \rangle$ (that is periodic with period 1), at least heuristically, we start with a Fourier series:

$$\langle x \rangle = \frac{1}{2} - \sum_{h=1}^{\infty} \frac{\sin 2\pi hx}{h\pi}$$

$$= \frac{1}{2} + \sum_{h \in \mathbb{Z} \setminus \{0\}} c_h e^{2\pi ihx}, \qquad c_h = \frac{i}{2\pi h}. \qquad (2.4)$$

Hereafter, we shall write

$$\sum_{h \neq 0} := \sum_{h \in \mathbb{Z} \setminus \{0\}}.$$

Observe that for $x = 0$ and $x = 1$, the right-hand and the left-hand sides of (2.4) do not agree. These are the points of discontinuity of $\langle x \rangle$.

We now continue to try to evaluate the average redundancy $\bar{R}_n^S$ as expressed in (2.2). Observe that its behavior depends on the rationality or irrationality of α. Indeed, if α is rational, say $\alpha = 1/2$, and $\beta = 0$, then $\langle \alpha k + \beta n \rangle$ takes only two values (i.e., 0 or 1/2), and hence the average redundancy oscillates. This is not the case when α is irrational.

Let us first deal with the case when α is irrational. Using (2.4) in (2.2) and by neglecting the discontinuities of $\langle x \rangle$, we obtain

$$\bar{R}_n^S = \frac{1}{2} + \sum_{k=0}^{n} \binom{n}{k} p^k q^{n-k} \sum_{h \neq 0} c_h e^{2\pi ih(\alpha k + \beta n)}$$

$$= \frac{1}{2} + \sum_{h \neq 0} c_h e^{2\pi ih\beta n} \left(p e^{2\pi im\alpha} + q \right)^n. \qquad (2.5)$$

If α is irrational then $|p e^{2\pi ih\alpha} + q| < 1$, which implies that $\left(p e^{2\pi ih\alpha} + q \right)^n \to 0$. Hence, it is very likely that the infinite sum $\sum_{h \neq 0}$ is $o(1)$ as $n \to \infty$, or equivalently $\bar{R}_n^S \to \frac{1}{2}$ as $n \to \infty$. Unfortunately, it seems to be cumbersome to prove this fact directly from the representation (2.5) since the Fourier series does not converge absolutely. However, we can deal with the sum (2.2) rigorously by applying the theory of *sequences distributed modulo 1* (see Appendix E) and obtain the following result.

Theorem 2.1 *Let $\overline{R}_n^S$ denote the average redundancy of the Shannon code over a binary memoryless source $\mathcal{A}_n = \{0,1\}^n$ of length n with parameter $p \in (0,1)$. If $p = \frac{1}{2}$, then $\overline{R}_n^S = 0$. If $p \neq \frac{1}{2}$ and α and β are defined in (2.3), then as $n \to \infty$,*

$$
\overline{R}_n^S = \begin{cases} \frac{1}{2} + o(1) & \textit{if } \alpha \quad \textit{is irrational,} \\[2mm] \frac{1}{2} + \frac{1}{M}\left(\langle Mn\beta \rangle - \frac{1}{2}\right) + O(\rho^n) & \textit{if } \alpha = \frac{N}{M}, \ \ \gcd(N,M) = 1\,, \end{cases}
$$

where $\rho < 1$.

The rest of this section is devoted to the proof of Theorem 2.1. We start with the irrational case. We set

$$
p_{n,k} = \binom{n}{k} p^k q^{n-k},
$$

and observe that $\sum_k p_{n,k} = (p+q)^n = 1$. We then apply Theorem E.4 from Appendix E (see also Exercises 2.1 and 2.2), which says that the condition

$$
\sum_{k=0}^{n} \binom{n}{k} p^k q^{n-k} e^{2\pi i h(\alpha k + \beta n)} \to 0 \tag{2.6}
$$

(for all nonzero integers h) implies that

$$
\lim_{n \to \infty} \sum_{k=0}^{n} \binom{n}{k} p^k q^{n-k} f(\alpha k + \beta n) = \int_0^1 f(y)\, dy
$$

for all Riemann-integrable functions f with period 1. We will apply this property for $f(y) = \langle y \rangle$ with integral $\int_0^1 \langle y \rangle\, dy = \frac{1}{2}$.

We just have to check the condition (2.6). By the binomial theorem, we have

$$
\sum_{k=0}^{n} \binom{n}{k} p^k q^{n-k} e^{2\pi i h(\alpha k + \beta n)} = e^{2\pi i h\beta n} \left(p e^{2\pi i h\alpha} + q \right)^n. \tag{2.7}
$$

As already observed, we have $|p e^{2\pi i h\alpha} + q| < 1$ if α is irrational. Thus, (2.6) is satisfied for all nonzero integers h. Consequently Theorem 2.1 holds if α is irrational.

Now, we turn our attention to the case when α is rational. Here we use a discrete Fourier analysis: see also Lemma 2.5. We assume $\alpha = M/N$ where M, N are nonzero integers such that $\gcd(N,M) = 1$. (If $\alpha = 0$ – which is equivalent to $p = \frac{1}{2}$ – we trivially have $\overline{R}_n^S = 0$.) We proceed as follows:

$$
\overline{R}_n^S = \sum_{k=0}^{n} \binom{n}{k} p^k q^{n-k} \left\langle k\frac{N}{M} + \beta n \right\rangle = \sum_{k=0}^{n} p_{n,k} \left\langle k\frac{N}{M} + \beta n \right\rangle
$$

$$
= \sum_{\ell=0}^{M-1} \sum_{k \equiv \ell \bmod M} p_{n,k} \left\langle \ell\frac{N}{M} + \beta n \right\rangle
$$

$$= \sum_{\ell=0}^{M-1} \sum_{k \equiv \ell \bmod M} p_{n,k} \left\langle \frac{\ell}{M} + \beta n \right\rangle$$

$$= \sum_{\ell=0}^{M-1} \left\langle \frac{\ell}{M} + \beta n \right\rangle \sum_{k \equiv \ell \bmod M} \binom{n}{k} p^k (1-p)^{n-k}. \tag{2.8}$$

To evaluate the last sum we need the following simple lemma. It asserts that if one picks every Mth term of the binomial distribution, then the total probability of this sample is "well" approximated by $1/M$.

Lemma 2.2 *For fixed M, there exist $\rho < 1$ such that*

$$\sum_{k \equiv \ell \bmod M} \binom{n}{k} p^k (1-p)^{n-k} = \frac{1}{M} + O(\rho^n) \tag{2.9}$$

for all $\ell \le M$.

Proof Let $\omega_k = e^{2\pi i k/M}$ for $k = 0, 1, \ldots, M-1$ be the Mth root of unity. It is well known that

$$\frac{1}{M} \sum_{k=0}^{M-1} \omega_k^n = \begin{cases} 1 \text{ if } M|n, \\ 0 \text{ otherwise,} \end{cases} \tag{2.10}$$

where $M|n$ means that M divides n. In view of this, we can write

$$\sum_{k \equiv \ell \bmod M} \binom{n}{k} p^k q^{n-k} = \sum_{k=0}^{n} \binom{n}{k} p^k q^{n-k} \frac{1}{M} \sum_{r=0}^{M-1} \omega_r^{k-\ell}$$

$$= \frac{1 + (p\omega_1 + q)^n \omega_1^{-\ell} + \cdots + (p\omega_{M-1} + q)^n \omega_{M-1}^{-\ell}}{M}$$

$$= \frac{1}{M} + O(\rho^n), \tag{2.11}$$

since $|(p\omega_r + q)| = p^2 + q^2 + 2pq \cos(2\pi r/M) < 1$ for $r \ne 0$. This proves the lemma. ∎

By (2.8) we thus have

$$\overline{R}_n^S = \frac{1}{M} \sum_{\ell=0}^{M-1} \left\langle \frac{\ell}{M} + \beta n \right\rangle + O(\rho^n).$$

Now set

$$g(y) = \frac{1}{M} \sum_{\ell=0}^{M-1} \left\langle \frac{\ell}{M} + y \right\rangle.$$

Then by definition we have $g\left(y + \frac{1}{M}\right) = g(y)$. So let us assume first that $0 \le y < \frac{1}{M}$. In this case, we obtain

$$g(y) = \frac{1}{M} \sum_{\ell=0}^{M-1} \left\langle \frac{\ell}{M} + y \right\rangle$$

$$= \frac{1}{M} \sum_{\ell=0}^{M-1} \left(\frac{\ell}{M} + y \right)$$

$$= \frac{1}{M^2} \frac{M(M-1)}{2} + y$$

$$= \frac{1}{2} - \frac{1}{2M} + y.$$

In general, we find

$$g(y) = g\left(\frac{1}{M} \langle My \rangle \right) = \frac{1}{2} - \frac{1}{2M} + \frac{1}{M} \langle My \rangle = \frac{1}{2} - \frac{1}{M} \left(\frac{1}{2} - \langle My \rangle \right).$$

Summing up, we arrive at

$$\overline{R}_n^S = \frac{1}{2} - \frac{1}{M} \left(\frac{1}{2} - \langle \beta n M \rangle \right) + O(\rho^n)$$

in the rational case. This completes the proof of Theorem 2.1.

2.1.2 Huffman Codes

It is known that the following optimization problem over all prefix codes C,

$$\overline{R}^H = \min_C \mathbf{E}[L(C, X) + \log P(X)],$$

is solved by the *Huffman code*. Recall that the Huffman code is a recursive algorithm built over the associated Huffman tree, in which the two nodes with lowest probabilities are combined into a new node whose probability is the sum of the probabilities of its two children.

We assume again that P is a memoryless source on $\mathcal{A}_n = \{0, 1\}^n$ with parameter p, where we also assume that $p < \frac{1}{2}$, and we continue to write

$$P(x^n) = p^k q^{n-k}$$

for the probability of generating a binary sequence consisting of k zeros and $n - k$ ones. The expected code length $\mathbf{E}[L_n]$ of the Huffman code is

$$\mathbf{E}[L_n] = \sum_{k=0}^{n} \binom{n}{k} p^k q^{n-k} L(k), \tag{2.12}$$

where

$$L(k) = \frac{1}{\binom{n}{k}} \sum_{j \in \mathcal{S}_k} l_j$$

with $\mathcal{S}_k$ representing the set of all inputs having probability $p^k q^{n-k}$, and l_j being the length of the jth code in $\mathcal{S}_k$. By the sibling property of Gallager (1978) we know that code lengths in $\mathcal{S}_k$ are either equal to $l(k)$ or $l(k) + 1$ for some integer $l(k)$. If n_k denotes the number of codewords in $\mathcal{S}_k$ that are equal to $l(k) + 1$, then

$$L(k) = l(k) + \frac{n_k}{\binom{n}{k}}.$$

Clearly, $l(k) = \lfloor -\log(p^k q^{n-k}) \rfloor$. Stubley (1994) analyzed carefully n_k and showed

$$\overline{R}_n^H = \sum_{k=0}^{n} \binom{n}{k} p^k q^{n-k} \left(\log(p^k q^{n-k}) + \lfloor -\log(p^k q^{n-k}) \rfloor \right) \tag{2.13}$$

$$+ 2 \sum_{k=0}^{n-1} \binom{n}{k} p^k q^{n-k} \left(1 - 2^{(\log(p^k q^{n-k}) + \lfloor -\log(p^k q^{n-k}) \rfloor)} \right) + o(1).$$

In Exercise 2.3 we ask the reader to establish (2.13).

As before, using $\langle x \rangle = x - \lfloor x \rfloor$ we find

$$\log(p^k q^{n-k}) + \lfloor -\log(p^k q^{n-k}) \rfloor = -\langle \alpha k + \beta n \rangle,$$

where for convenience we restate (cf. (2.3))

$$\alpha = \log \left(\frac{1-p}{p} \right), \quad \beta = \log \left(\frac{1}{1-p} \right). \tag{2.14}$$

Thus we arrive at the following:

$$\overline{R}_n^H = 2 - \sum_{k=0}^{n} \binom{n}{k} p^k q^{n-k} \langle \alpha k + \beta n \rangle - 2 \sum_{k=0}^{n} \binom{n}{k} p^k q^{n-k} 2^{-\langle \alpha k + \beta n \rangle} + o(1). \tag{2.15}$$

This is our starting formula for the average Huffman redundancy that can be asymptotically evaluated. In the rest of this section we prove the following result.

Theorem 2.3 (Szpankowski, 2000) *Consider the Huffman block code of length n over a binary memoryless source. Suppose that $0 < p < \frac{1}{2}$ and define α and β by (2.14). Then as $n \to \infty$ the average redundancy is given by*

$$\overline{R}_n^H = \begin{cases} \frac{3}{2} - \frac{1}{\ln 2} + o(1) \approx 0.057304, & \alpha \notin \mathbb{Q}, \\ \frac{3}{2} - \frac{1}{M} \left(\langle \beta M n \rangle - \frac{1}{2} \right) - \frac{1}{M(1 - 2^{-1/M})} 2^{-\langle n \beta M \rangle / M} + o(1), & \alpha = \frac{N}{M}, \end{cases}$$

where $\mathbb{Q}$ is the set of rational numbers, and N, M are relatively prime integers; that is, $\gcd(N, M) = 1$.

Before we present a proof, we plot in Figure 2.1 the average redundancy $\overline{R}_n^H$ presented in (2.15) as a function of n for two values of α, one *irrational* (Figure 2.1(a)) and one *rational* (Figure 2.1(b)). The two modes of behavior are clearly visible. The function in Figure 2.1(a) converges to a constant (≈ 0.057) for large n as predicted by Theorem 2.3, while the curve in Figure 2.1(b) is quite erratic.

In the rational case, we observe that the redundancy swings from almost zero to about 0.086. In order to be more precise (and reproving the upper bound of Gallager (1978)), we

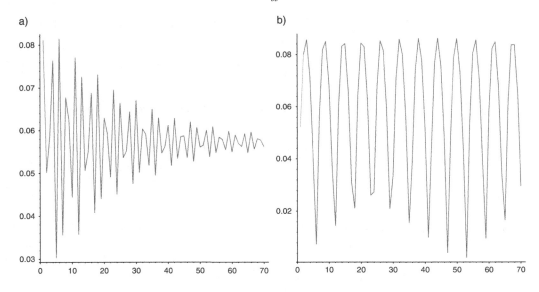

Figure 2.1 The average redundancy of Huffman codes (2.15) versus block size n for (a) irrational $\alpha = \log((1-p)/p)$ with $p = 1/\pi$; (b) rational $\alpha = \log((1-p)/p)$ with $p = 1/9$.

set $x = \langle Mn\beta \rangle$ and observe that $\overline{R}_n^H$ can only be maximal if $M = 1$. In this case we, thus, have

$$\overline{R}_n^H(x) \sim 2 - x - 2^{-x+1}, \tag{2.16}$$

which satisfies

$$\max_{0 \le x < 1} 2 - x - 2^{-x+1} = 1 - \frac{1 + \ln\ln 2}{\ln 2} = \log(2(\log e)/e) = 0.08607\ldots \tag{2.17}$$

and corresponds to the Gallager upper bound. We formulate it as a corollary.

Corollary 2.4 *Let $\overline{R}_n^H$ denote the average redundancy of a Huffman block code of length n over a binary memoryless source. Then*

$$\limsup_{n \to \infty} \overline{R}_n^H \le 1 - \frac{1 + \ln\ln 2}{\ln 2} = \log(2(\log e)/e) \sim 0.08607\ldots. \tag{2.18}$$

Proof of Theorem 2.3 To establish Theorem 2.3 we must only deal with the asymptotics of the following sum:

$$T_n = \sum_{k=0}^{n} \binom{n}{k} p^k q^{n-k} 2^{-\langle \alpha k + \beta n \rangle}. \tag{2.19}$$

Here, too, we consider the rational and irrational case. For the irrational case, we simply use Theorem E.4 from Appendix E with $f(t) = 2^{-t}$ and $\delta_n = \beta n$; recall that the exponential sums (2.7) tend to 0 if α is irrational.

For the rational case, we can use Lemma 2.5 (with $f(y) = 2^{-\langle y \rangle}$) from which Theorem 2.3 follows. The proof follows in the footsteps of our derivations in (2.8). We ask the reader to prove it in Exercise 2.4.

Lemma 2.5 *Let $0 < p < 1$ be a fixed real number and suppose that $\alpha = \frac{N}{M}$ is a rational number with $\gcd(N, M) = 1$. Then, for every bounded function $f : [0, 1] \to \mathbb{R}$, we have*

$$\sum_{k=0}^{n} \binom{n}{k} p^k (1-p)^{n-k} f(\langle k\alpha + y \rangle) = \frac{1}{M} \sum_{l=0}^{M-1} f\left(\frac{l}{M} + \frac{\langle My \rangle}{M}\right) + O(\rho^n)$$

uniformly for all $y \in \mathbb{R}$ and some $\rho < 1$.

2.1.3 Golomb Code

In this section we give a short account of Golomb's code that can be viewed as a special case of Huffman's code adapted to infinite alphabets. Our analysis in this section will differ from other sections since we perform asymptotics not with regard to the block length but rather at the limit of a code parameter.

More precisely, let

$$P(i) = (1-\theta)\theta^i, \quad i \in \mathbb{Z}_{\geq 0} \tag{2.20}$$

be the probability assignment on the set of nonnegative integers where $0 < \theta < 1$. Golomb (1996) proposed the following optimal binary code. Let ℓ be an integer such that

$$\theta^\ell = \frac{1}{2}, \tag{2.21}$$

which means that we restrict on θ that are roots of $1/2$. In Golomb's code an integer i is represented as $i = \ell j + r$, where $j = \lfloor i/\ell \rfloor$ and $0 \leq r < \ell$. We encode j by a unary code (i.e., j zeros followed by a one) while r is encoded by a Shannon code (for a uniform distribution on ℓ symbols).

In Exercise 2.5, we ask the reader to show that the average Golomb code length $\mathbf{E}[L]$ is

$$\mathbf{E}[L] = \lceil \log \ell \rceil + \frac{\theta^{2^{\lfloor \log \ell \rfloor + 1}}}{\theta^\ell - 1}. \tag{2.22}$$

Roughly speaking, the first term corresponds to the Shannon code while the second term represents the unary coding. The average redundancy $\overline{R}_\ell^G$ of the Golomb code becomes

$$\overline{R}_\ell^G = \mathbf{E}[L] - H(\theta), \tag{2.23}$$

where the entropy $H(\theta)$ of the geometric distribution (2.20) can be computed as

$$H(\theta) = -\log(1-\theta) - \frac{\theta}{1-\theta} \log \theta. \tag{2.24}$$

We will estimate $\overline{R}_\ell^G$ as $l \to \infty$ or equivalently as $\theta \to 1$.

The result on the behavior of the average redundancy is presented next. Observe that, in this case, there is *only* the oscillatory mode behavior of $\overline{R}_\ell^G$ as illustrated in Figure 2.2.

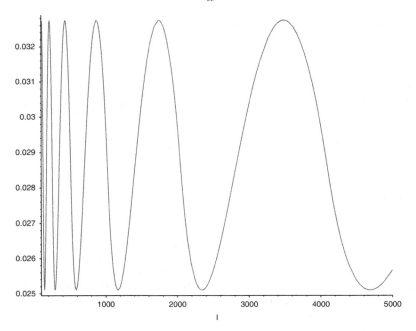

Figure 2.2 The average redundancy of Golomb codes versus ℓ.

Theorem 2.6 *Consider the Golomb code over the nonnegative integers generated by a geometric source Geometric(θ) such that there exists an integer ℓ with $\theta^\ell = \frac{1}{2}$. Then as $\ell \to \infty$, so that $\theta \to 1$,*

$$\overline{R}_\ell^G = 1 - \langle \log \ell \rangle + 4 \cdot 2^{-2^{1-\langle \log \ell \rangle}} - \log(\log e) - \log e - \frac{1}{2\ell} + O(\ell^{-2}). \tag{2.25}$$

Furthermore, the average redundancy $\overline{R}_\ell^G$ oscillates around $2 - \log(\log e) - \log e = 0.028538562 \ldots$ with

$$\liminf_{\ell \to \infty} \overline{R}_\ell^G = 0.0251005712 \ldots, \tag{2.26}$$

$$\limsup_{\ell \to \infty} \overline{R}_\ell^G = 0.0327344112 \ldots. \tag{2.27}$$

Proof We assume that $\theta^\ell = 1/2$ as in (2.22), and estimate the entropy $H(\theta)$ (cf. (2.24)) as $\ell \to \infty$ (i.e., $\theta = 2^{-1/\ell} \to 1$). Using the following Taylor expansion,

$$\log(1 - 2^{-x}) = \log(\ln(2)) + \log(x) - \frac{1}{2}x + \frac{\ln(2)}{24}x^2 + O(x^3), \quad x \to 0, \tag{2.28}$$

we arrive at

$$H(\theta) = \log \ell + \log(\log e) + \frac{1}{2\ell} + O(\ell^{-2}). \tag{2.29}$$

The average redundancy $\overline{R}_\ell^G = \mathbf{E}[L] - H(\theta)$, where $\mathbf{E}[L]$ is given by (2.22), follows after some simple algebra:

$$\overline{R}_\ell^G = 1 - \langle \log \ell \rangle + 4 \cdot 2^{-2^{1-\langle \log \ell \rangle}} - \log(\log e) - \log e - \frac{1}{2\ell} + O(\ell^{-2}), \tag{2.30}$$

as $\ell \to \infty$ or $\theta \to 1$. This proves (2.25) of Theorem 2.6. We should also point out that by using this approach, we can get a full asymptotic expansion of $\overline{R}_\ell^G$ as $\ell \to \infty$.

To compute the magnitude of the oscillation, let us define $C = \log(\log e) + \log e = 1.971461414\ldots$. We set

$$g(x) = 1 - x + 4 \cdot 2^{-2^{1-x}} - C \tag{2.31}$$

for $0 \le x \le 1$. (Observe that $g(x)$ is asymptotically equal to R_ℓ^G when $x = \langle \log \ell \rangle$.) One derives that $g(x)$ achieves its maximum value $g(x_1) := \max\{g(x)\} = 0.327344112\ldots$ at

$$x_1 = \log\left(\frac{-2\ln(2)}{W(-0.25 \log e)}\right) \tag{2.32}$$

where $W(x)$ is the Lambert-W function defined as $W(x)e^{W(x)} = x$ (see Corless et al. (1996) or Appendix C). Similarly, the function $g(x)$ achieves its minimum value $g(x_2) := \min\{g(x)\} = 0.251005712\ldots$ at

$$x_2 = \log\left(\frac{-2\ln(2)}{W(-1, -0.25 \log e)}\right), \tag{2.33}$$

where $W(-1, x)$ is a branch of the Lambert-W function (see Appendix C). It is also easy to see that the average redundancy oscillates around $g(0) = g(1) = 2 - C = 0.0285385862\ldots$. This proves Theorem 2.6. ∎

We should remark that since $\langle \log n \rangle$ is dense in $(0, 1)$ it follows by (2.30) that the average redundancy $\overline{R}_\ell^G$ asymptotically oscillates within a certain interval without reaching a limit, as observed in Figure 2.2.

2.2 Shannon Code Redundancy for Markov Sources

In this section, we study the average redundancy of the Shannon code for Markov sources; that is, the probability distribution on the alphabet $\mathcal{A}_n = \{0, 1, \ldots, m-1\}^n$ is given by a first-order Markov process $X_1, X_2, \ldots$. The transition matrix will be denoted by $\mathbf{P} = (p(j|k))_{j,k=0}^{m-1}$ and the initial state probabilities by $p_k = P(X_t = k)$ ($k = 0, 1, \ldots, m-1$). Furthermore, we write π_k ($k = 0, 1, \ldots, m-1$) for the stationary state probabilities. Thus, the probability of a given source string $x^n = (x_1, \ldots, x_n) \in \mathcal{A}_n = \mathcal{A}^n$, under the given Markov source, is

$$P(x^n) = p_{x_1} \prod_{t=2}^{n} p(x_t | x_{t-1}). \tag{2.34}$$

The average redundancy of the Shannon code is then

$$\overline{R}_n = \mathbf{E}[\lceil -\log P(X^n) \rceil + \log P(X^n)] = \mathbf{E}[\langle \log P(X^n) \rangle]. \tag{2.35}$$

Our main result in this section is the following theorem.

Theorem 2.7 *Consider the Shannon code of block length n for a Markov source with initial state probabilities $p_0, \ldots, p_{m-1}$ and a positive transition matrix* **P**. *Define*

$$\alpha_{jk} = \log\left[\frac{p(j|0)p(j|j)}{p(k|0)p(j|k)}\right], \quad j, k \in \{0, 1, \ldots, m-1\}. \tag{2.36}$$

Then the average redundancy $\overline{R}_n$ is characterized as follows:
(a) If not all α_{jk} are rational, then

$$\overline{R}_n = \frac{1}{2} + o(1). \tag{2.37}$$

(b) If all α_{jk} are rational, then for every $j, k \in \{0, \ldots, m-1\}$, let

$$\zeta_{jk}(n) = M[(n-1)\log p(0|0) - \log p(j|0) + \log p(k|0) + \log p_j], \tag{2.38}$$

and

$$\Omega_n = \frac{1}{2}\left(1 - \frac{1}{M}\right) + \frac{1}{M}\sum_{j=0}^{m-1}\sum_{k=0}^{m-1} p_j\pi_k\langle\zeta_{jk}(n)\rangle, \tag{2.39}$$

where M is the smallest common integer multiple of the denominators of $\{\alpha_{jk}\}$, when each one of these numbers is represented as a ratio between two relatively prime integers. Then

$$\overline{R}_n = \Omega_n + O(\rho^n) \tag{2.40}$$

for some $\rho < 1$.

Before we prove Theorem 2.7, we give some comments. Theorem 2.7 tells us that, as in the memoryless case, $\overline{R}_n$ has two modes of behavior. In the convergent mode, which happens when at least one α_{jk} is irrational, $\overline{R}_n \to 1/2$. In the oscillatory mode, which happens when all $\{\alpha_{jk}\}$ are rational, $\overline{R}_n$ oscillates and it asymptotically coincides with Ω_n.

The expression of the oscillatory case, Ω_n, is not quite intuitive at first glance, therefore we make an attempt to give some quick insight that captures the essence of the main points. The arguments here are informal and nonrigorous (see Section 2.2.1 for a rigorous proof). The Fourier series expansion of the periodic function $\langle u \rangle$ is given by

$$\langle u \rangle = \frac{1}{2} + \sum_{h \neq 0} c_h e^{2\pi i h u}. \tag{2.41}$$

The important fact about the coefficients $c_h = i/(2\pi h)$ is that they are inversely proportional to h, so that for every two integers k and h, $c_{h\cdot k} = c_h/k$. Now, when computing $\overline{R}_n = \mathbf{E}[\langle \log P(X^n)\rangle]$, let us take the liberty of exchanging the order between the expectation and the summation; that is,

$$\overline{R}_n = \frac{1}{2} + \sum_{h \neq 0} c_h \mathbf{E}[e^{2\pi i h \log P(X^n)}]. \tag{2.42}$$

It turns out that under the conditions of the oscillatory mode, $\mathbf{E}[e^{2\pi i h \log P(X^n)}]$ tends to zero as $n \to \infty$ for all h, except for multiples of M, namely, $h = \ell M, l = \pm 1, \pm 2, \ldots$. Thus, for large n, we have

$$\bar{R}_n \approx \frac{1}{2} + \sum_{\ell \neq 0} c_{\ell M} \mathbf{E}[e^{2\pi i \ell M \log P(X^n)}]$$

$$= \frac{1}{2} + \frac{1}{M} \sum_{\ell \neq 0} c_\ell \mathbf{E}[e^{2\pi i \ell M \log P(X^n)}]$$

$$= \frac{1}{2} + \frac{1}{M} \left[\mathbf{E}[\langle M \log P(X^n) \rangle] - \frac{1}{2} \right]$$

$$= \frac{1}{2} \left(1 - \frac{1}{M} \right) + \frac{1}{M} \mathbf{E}[\langle M \log P(X^n) \rangle]. \tag{2.43}$$

Now, consider the set of all x^n that begin from state $x_1 = j$ and end at state $x_n = k$. Their total probability is about $p_j \pi_k$ for large n since X_n is almost independent of X_1. It turns out that all these sequences have exactly the same value of $\langle M \log P(x^n) \rangle$, which is exactly $\langle \zeta_{jk}(n) \rangle$ (or, in other words, $\langle M \log P(x^n) \rangle = \langle \zeta_{x_1 x_n}(n) \rangle$ independently of $x_2, \ldots, x_{n-1}$) and this explains the expression of Ω_n. The reason for this property of $\langle M \log P(x^n) \rangle$ is the rationality conditions $\langle M \cdot \alpha_{uv} \rangle = 0$, $u, v \in \{0, 1, \ldots, m-1\}$, which imply that $\langle M \log p(x_t|x_{t-1}) \rangle = \langle M \log[p(x_t|1)p(0|0)/p(x_{t-1}|0)] \rangle$, and so,

$$\langle M \log P(x^n) \rangle = \langle M \log p_j \rangle + \sum_{t=2}^n \langle M \log p(x_t|x_{t-1}) \rangle \mod 1$$

$$= \langle M \log p_j \rangle + \sum_{t=2}^n \langle M \log[p(x_t|1)p(0|0)/p(x_{t-1}|0)] \rangle \mod 1,$$

which, thanks to the telescopic summation, is easily seen to coincide with the fractional part of $\zeta_{jk}(n)$, and of course, $\langle \zeta_{jk}(n) \rangle$ depends on $\zeta_{jk}(n)$ only via its fractional part.

We will illustrate Theorem 2.7 in one example.

Example 2.8 Consider a Markov source for which the rows of **P** are all permutations of the first row, which is $\mathbf{p} = (p_0, \ldots, p_{m-1})$. Now, assuming that $\alpha_j := \log(p_1/p_j)$ are all rational, let M be the least common multiple of their denominators (i.e., the common denominator) when each one of them is expressed as a ratio between two relatively prime integers. Then,

$$\langle \zeta_{jk}(n) \rangle = \langle M(n-1) \log p(0|0) - M \log p(j|0) + M \log p(k|0)$$
$$+ M \log p_j \rangle$$
$$= \langle M(n-1) \log p_0 - M \log p_j + M \log p_k + M \log p_j \rangle$$
$$= \langle M(n-1) \log p_0 + M \log p_k \rangle$$
$$= \langle Mn \log p_0 - M \log p_0 + M \log p_k \rangle$$
$$= \langle Mn \log p_0 \rangle,$$

where in the last step, we have used the fact that $(M \log p_0 - M \log p_k)$ is an integer and that $\langle u \rangle$ is a periodic function with period 1. We have

$$R_n = \frac{1}{2}\left(1 - \frac{1}{M}\right) + \frac{1}{M}\sum_{j=0}^{m-1}\sum_{k=0}^{m-1} p_j \pi_k \langle \zeta_{jk}(n)\rangle + o(1)$$

$$= \frac{1}{2}\left(1 - \frac{1}{M}\right) + \frac{1}{M}\sum_{j=0}^{m-1}\sum_{k=0}^{m-1} p_j \pi_k \langle nM \log p_1\rangle + o(1)$$

$$= \frac{1}{2}\left(1 - \frac{1}{M}\right) + \frac{1}{M}\langle nM \log p_0\rangle + o(1). \tag{2.44}$$

If not all α_j are rational, then $\overline{R}_n \to 1/2$, as predicted by Theorem 2.7.

To see why the conditions of Theorem 2.7 lead to the rationality condition herein, let us denote

$$u_{jk} = \langle h \log[p(j|0)/p(k|0)]\rangle,$$
$$v_{jk} = \langle h \log[p(j|j)/p(j|k)]\rangle.$$

Then, the conditions of Theorem 2.7 mean that $u_{jk} + v_{jk} = 0$ and for all pairs j and k. Therefore, the number of constraints here is of the order of m^2, whereas the number of degrees of freedom that generate these variables, in this example, is $m-1$ the variables $\langle h \log(p_1/p_j)\rangle$, $j = 1, 2, \ldots, m-1$. Thus, we can think of this as an overdetermined set of homogeneous linear equations whose only solution is zero, meaning that all $\langle h \log(p_1/p_j)\rangle, j = 1, 2, \ldots, m-1$, vanish. Note that the memoryless source is a special case of this example, where the rows of **P** are all identical to the first row, $(p_0, \ldots, p_{m-1})$. Indeed, (2.44) coincides with the expression of the memoryless case as discussed in the first subsection of this chapter.

2.2.1 Proof of Theorem 2.7

The main idea behind the analysis of $\overline{R}_n = \mathbf{E}[\langle \log P(X^n)\rangle]$ is to approximate the periodic function $\langle \cdot \rangle$ by a sequence of trigonometric polynomials, and then to commute the expectation with the summation and analyze the various terms of the series. Actually, this is the same idea that is used in Appendix E for the proof of Lemma E.3. The main Fourier analytic tool that we use is an approximation lemma by Vaaler (1985) (see also Theorem E.2 in Appendix E). The following analysis is very close to the proof of Lemma E.3.

Define the functions ϱ_H^- and ϱ_H^+ as

$$\varrho_H^-(y) = C_H(y) - D_H(y) \tag{2.45}$$

and

$$\varrho_H^-(y) = C_H(y) + D_H(y), \tag{2.46}$$

where the functions $C_H(y)$ and $D_H(y)$ are given as finite Fourier series

$$C_H(y) = \sum_{|h|\leq H} c_h(H)e^{2\pi ihy}, \quad D_H(y) = \sum_{|h|\leq H} c_h(H)e^{2\pi ihy}$$

for which the coefficients satisfy

$$c_0(\alpha, H) = \frac{1}{2}, \quad |c_h(H)| \leq \frac{1}{2\pi |h|}, \quad |d_h(H)| \leq \frac{1}{2H+2}.$$

As stated in Theorem E.2 in Appendix E, the functions ϱ_H^- and ϱ_H^+ satisfy

$$\varrho_H^-(y) \le \langle y \rangle \le \varrho_H^+(y).$$

We now proceed to establish upper and lower bounds for $\overline{R}_n$, however, we only present details for the lower bound. We have

$$
\begin{aligned}
\overline{R}_n &= \mathbf{E}\left[\langle \log P(X^n) \rangle\right] \\
&\ge \mathbf{E}\left[\varrho_H^-(\log P(X^n))\right] \\
&= \frac{1}{2} + \sum_{1 \le |h| \le H} c_h(H)\mathbf{E}\left[e^{2\pi ih \log P(X^n)}\right] \\
&\quad - d_0 - \sum_{1 \le |h| \le H} d_h(H)\mathbf{E}\left[e^{2\pi ih \log P(X^n)}\right].
\end{aligned}
\tag{2.47}
$$

We next show that in the irrational case we have

$$\lim_{n \to \infty} \mathbf{E}\left[e^{2\pi ih \log P(X^n)}\right] = 0 \tag{2.48}$$

for all integers $h \ne 0$. Clearly, if (2.48) holds then it follows that

$$\liminf_{n \to \infty} \overline{R}_n \ge \frac{1}{2} - \frac{1}{2H+2} \quad .$$

for all integers $H \ge 1$ and thus $\liminf_{n \to \infty} \overline{R}_n \ge \frac{1}{2}$. We ask in Exercise 2.6 to complete the derivation and establish an upper bound. Consequently we have $\overline{R}_n = \frac{1}{2} + o(1)$ (as $n \to \infty$) in the irrational case.

In order to show (2.48) in the irrational case, we define the $m \times m$ complex matrix A_h whose entries are

$$a_{jk}(h) = p(k|j)\exp\left[2\pi ih \log p(k|j)\right], \quad j,k = 0,\ldots,m-1. \tag{2.49}$$

We also define the m-dimensional column vectors:

$$\mathbf{c}_h = (p_0 \exp[2\pi ih \log p_0)],\ldots,p_{m-1}\exp[2\pi ih \log p_{m-1}])^T, \tag{2.50}$$

and $\mathbf{1} = (1,1,\ldots,1)^T$, where the superscript T denotes vector/matrix transposition. Then, according to (2.34), it follows that

$$\mathbf{E}\left[e^{2\pi ih \log P(X^n)}\right] = \mathbf{c}_h^T A_h^{n-1}\mathbf{1}. \tag{2.51}$$

Let $\mathbf{l}_{j,h}$ and $\mathbf{r}_{j,h}$ be, respectively, the left eigenvector and the right eigenvector pertaining to the eigenvalue $\lambda_{j,h}$ $(j = 0,1,\ldots,m-1)$ of the matrix A_h. Here, we index the eigenvalues of A_h according to a nonincreasing order of their modulus; that is,

$$|\lambda_{1,h}| \ge |\lambda_{2,h}| \ge \cdots \ge |\lambda_{m,h}|. \tag{2.52}$$

Since $\mathbf{P}$ is a stochastic matrix (so, its maximum modulus eigenvalue is 1) and its elements are the absolute values of the corresponding elements of A_h, it follows from theorem 8.4.5 of Noble and Johnson (1985) that $|\lambda_{1,h}| \le 1$ (and hence $|\lambda_{j,h}| \le 1$ for all $j = 0,1,\ldots,m-1$). Also, the systems of left and right eigenvectors form a bi-orthogonal system; that is, $\mathbf{l}_{j,h}^T\mathbf{r}_{k,h} = 0, j,k = 0,1,\ldots,m-1, j \ne k$. We scale these vectors such that $\mathbf{l}_{j,h}^T\mathbf{r}_{j,h} = 1$ for all $j = 0,1,\ldots,m-1$. For a quadratic matrix A, the spectral radius is denoted by $\rho(A)$.

By the spectral representation of matrices, we have

$$A_h^{n-1}\mathbf{1} = \sum_{j=0}^{m-1} \lambda_{j,h}^{n-1} \cdot \mathbf{l}_{j,h}^T \mathbf{1} \cdot \mathbf{r}_{j,m}, \tag{2.53}$$

and so,

$$\mathbf{c}_h^T A_h^{n-1}\mathbf{1} = \sum_{j=0}^{m-1} \lambda_{j,h}^{n-1} \cdot \mathbf{l}_{j,h}^T \mathbf{1} \cdot \mathbf{c}_h^T \mathbf{r}_{j,h}. \tag{2.54}$$

Now the following lemma, which appears in Noble and Johnson (1985) (with minor modifications in its phrasing), is useful to show that $|\lambda_{1,h}| < 1$ in the irrational case.

Lemma 2.9 (see Noble and Johnson (1985) theorem 8.4.5) *Let $F = \{f_{kj}\}$ and $G = \{g_{kj}\}$ be two $m \times m$ matrices. Assume that F is a real, nonnegative and irreducible matrix, G is a complex matrix, and $f_{kj} \geq |g_{kj}|$ for all $k, j \in \{0, 1, \ldots, m-1\}$. Then, $\rho(G) \geq \rho(F)$ with equality if and only if there exist real numbers s, and $w_0, \ldots, w_{m-1}$ such that $G = e^{2\pi i s} D F D^{-1}$, where*

$$D = diag\left(e^{2\pi i w_0}, \ldots, e^{2\pi i w_{m-1}}\right).$$

The proof of the necessity of the condition $G = e^{2\pi i s} D F D^{-1}$ appears in Noble and Johnson (1985). The sufficiency is obvious since the matrix DFD^{-1} is similar to F and hence has the same set of eigenvalues.

We wish to apply Lemma 2.9 in order to distinguish between the two aforementioned cases concerning the spectral radius of A_h. Consider the state transition probability matrix $\mathbf{P}$ in the role of F of Lemma 2.9 (i.e., $f_{kj} = p(j|k)$) and the matrix A_h in the role of G. Since $\mathbf{P}$ is assumed positive in this part, it is obviously nonnegative and irreducible. Since it is a stochastic matrix, its spectral radius is, of course, $\rho(P) = 1$. Also, by definition of A_h, as the matrix $\{p(j|k) \cdot \exp[2\pi i h \log p(j|k)]\}$, it is obvious that the elements of $\mathbf{P}$ are the absolute values of the corresponding elements of A_h, and so all the conditions of Lemma 2.9 clearly apply. The lemma then tells us that $\rho(A_h) = \rho(P) = 1$ if and only if there exist real numbers s and $w_0, \ldots, w_{m-1}$ such that for some integer h,

$$h \log p(j|k) = (s + w_k - w_j) \bmod 1, \quad j, k = 0, \ldots, m-1, \tag{2.55}$$

where $x = y \bmod 1$ means that the fractional parts of x and y are equal; that is, $\langle x \rangle = \langle y \rangle$.

To find a vector $\mathbf{w} = (w_0, \ldots, w_{m-1})$ and a number s with this property (if exists), we take the following approach. Consider first the choice $k = j$ in (2.55). This immediately tells us that s, if exists, must be equal to $h \log p(j|j) \pmod 1$ for every $j = 0, \ldots, m-1$. In other words, one set of conditions is that $h \log p(j|j)$ are all equal (mod 1), or equivalently,

$$\left\langle h \log \frac{p(j|j)}{p(0|0)} \right\rangle = 0, \quad j = 0, 1, \ldots, m-1, \tag{2.56}$$

and then s is taken to be the common value of all $\langle h \log p(j|j) \rangle$. Thus, (2.55) becomes

$$-h \log \frac{p(j|j)}{p(j|k)} = (w_k - w_j) \bmod 1, \quad j, k = 0, \ldots, m-1, \tag{2.57}$$

and it remains to find the vector $\mathbf{w}$, if possible. To this end, observe that if $\mathbf{w}$ satisfies (2.57), then for every constant c, $\mathbf{w} + c$ also satisfies (2.57). Taking $c = -w_0$, the first component of $\mathbf{w}$, is arbitrary. It is apparent that if (2.57) can hold for some $\mathbf{w}$, then there is such a vector whose first component vanishes, and then by setting $k = 0$ in (2.57), we learn that

$$w_j = \left\langle -h \log \frac{p(j|0)}{p(j|j)} \right\rangle, \quad j = 0, \ldots, m-1, \tag{2.58}$$

is a legitimate choice. Thus, (2.57) becomes

$$\left\langle -h \log \left[\frac{p(j|0)p(j|j)}{p(k|0)p(j|k)} \right] \right\rangle = 0, \quad j, k = 0, \ldots, m-1. \tag{2.59}$$

Note that by setting $k = 0$ in (2.59), we get (2.56) as a special case, which means that (2.59), applied to all $j, k \in \{0, 1, \ldots, m-1\}$, are all the necessary and sufficient conditions needed for $\rho(A_h) = 1$. Now, a necessary and sufficient condition for (2.59) to hold for *some* integer h, is that the numbers

$$\alpha_{jk} = \log \left[\frac{p(j|0)p(j|j)}{p(k|0)p(j|k)} \right] \tag{2.60}$$

would be all rational.

Summing up, it follows that $\rho(A_h) < 1$ if at least one α_{jk} is irrational. Hence, as explained above, it follows in this case that $\overline{R}_n \sim \frac{1}{2} + o(1)$. This establishes the first part of Theorem 2.7.

If all α_{jk} are rational, then we have to argue in a different way. We have already done some heuristic calculations indicating what kind of result we can expect. Actually, we can use a method similar to the calculations of (2.8) and Lemma 2.2, properly adapted to Markov sources, that cover the rational case.

In order to simplify the presentation, we consider just the binary case $m = 2$. The general case is just notationally more involved. First, we split up the sum according to the initial and final states:

$$\mathbf{E}\left[\langle \log P(X^n) \rangle \right] = \sum_{x_1, \ldots, x_n} P(x^n) \langle \log P(x^n) \rangle$$

$$= \sum_{j=0}^{1} \sum_{k=0}^{1} \sum_{x_1=j, x_n=k} P(x^n) \langle \log P(x^n) \rangle.$$

Let us consider (first) the case $j = k = 0$ and denote by k_{ij} the number of pairs (ij) in x^n. Clearly, $k_{00} + k_{01} + k_{10} + k_{11} = n - 1$. But also $k_{01} = k_{10}$ since the number of pairs ending at 1 must be equal to the number of pairs starting with 1 (for in-depth discussion of Markov types, see Section 11.2 of Chapter 11). We then can write $P(x^n)$ as

$$P(x^n) = p_0 P(0|0)^{k_{00}} P(0|1)^{k_{01}} P(1|0)^{k_{10}} P(1|1)^{k_{11}},$$

$$= p_0 [P(0|0)]^{n-1} \left[\frac{P(0|1)P(1|0)}{P(0|0)P(0|0)} \right]^{k_{01}} \left[\frac{P(1|1)}{P(0|0)} \right]^{k_{11}}.$$

Hence, using (2.36), we can represent $\log P(x^n)$ as

$$\log P(x^n) = (n-1) \log P(0|0) + \log p_0 - k_{01}\alpha_{01} + k_{11}\alpha_{10}.$$

By assumption, we can write $\alpha_{01} = L_0/M$ and $\alpha_{10} = L_1/M$, assuming that $\gcd(L_0, L_1, M) = 1$. Thus, $\langle \log P(x^n) \rangle$ is constant if $-k_{01}L_0 + k_{01}L_1$ is in a fixed residue class mod M. With the help of the following lemma, which generalizes Lemma 2.2 to Markov sources, we are then able to asymptotically evaluate the sum

$$\sum_{x_1 = x_n = 0} P(x^n) \langle \log P(x^n) \rangle.$$

Lemma 2.10 *Suppose that $M \geq 1$ and that L_0 and L_1 satisfy $\gcd(L_0, L_1, M) = 1$. Then, for every $0 \leq \ell < M$ and $0 \leq j, k \leq 1$, there exists $\rho < 1$ such that*

$$\sum_{x_1 = j, x_n = k, -k_{01}L_0 + k_{01}L_1 \equiv \ell \bmod M} P(x^n) = \frac{p_j \pi_k}{M} + O(\rho^n). \tag{2.61}$$

Proof We start with the case $j = k = 0$. Let $G_{00}(z)$ and $G_{01}(z)$ be the generating function:

$$G_{00}(z) = \sum_{n \geq 1} \sum_{x_1 = x_n = 0} P(x^n) z^n, \quad G_{01}(z) = \sum_{n \geq 1} \sum_{x_1 = 0, x_n = 1} P(x^n) z^n.$$

Then these generating functions satisfy the following system of linear equations:

$$G_{00}(z) = G_{00}(z)p(0|0)z + G_{01}(z)p(1|0)z + p_0 z,$$
$$G_{01}(z) = G_{00}(z)p(0|1)z + G_{01}(z)p(1|1)z.$$

In particular, it follows that

$$G_{00}(z) = \frac{\begin{vmatrix} p_0 z & -p(1|0)z \\ 0 & 1 - p(1|1)z \end{vmatrix}}{\begin{vmatrix} 1 - p(0|0)z & -p(1|0)z \\ -p(0|1)z & 1 - p(1|1)z \end{vmatrix}}$$

$$= \frac{p_0 z(1 - p(1|1)z)}{1 - (p(0|0) + p(1|1))z + (p(0|0)p(1|1) - p(0|1)p(1|0))z^2}.$$

Note that this identity is also true if the $p(j|k)$ are treated as formal variables. However, if we assume that $p(0|0) + p(0|1) = p(1|0) + p(1|1) = 1$, then we have

$$G_{00}(z) = \frac{p_0 z(1 - p(1|1)z)}{(1 - z)(1 - (p(0|0) + p(1|1) - 1)z)},$$

which implies that

$$[z^n]G_{00}(z) = \frac{p_0(1 - p(1|1))}{2 - p(0|0) - p(1|1)} + O(|1 - p(0|0) - p(1|1)|^n) = p_0 \pi_0 + O(\rho^n)$$

for $\rho = |1 - p(0|0) - p(1|1)| < 1$.

Furthermore, by setting $\omega_r = e^{2\pi i r/M}$ and by using (2.10), we have

$$\sum_{x_1=j,\, x_n=k,\, -k_{01}L_0+k_{01}L_1 \equiv \ell \bmod M} P(x^n) \tag{2.62}$$

$$= [z^n]\frac{1}{M}\sum_{r=0}^{M-1}\omega_r^{-\ell} \cdot \frac{p_0 z(1 - p(1|1)\omega_r^{L_1}z)}{1 - (p(0|0) + p(1|1)\omega_r^{L_1})z + (p(0|0)p(1|1)\omega_r^{L_1} - p(0|1)\omega_r^{L_0}p(1|0))z^2};$$

that is, we replace $p(0|1)$ by $p(0|1)\omega_r^{L_0}$ and $p(1|1)$ by $p(0|1)\omega_r^{L_1}$, $r = 0, \ldots, M-1$. Note that for $r = 0$, we already observed that $[z^n](1/M)G_{00}(z) = (1/M)p_0\pi_0 + O(\rho^n)$. Thus it remains to show that the corresponding contributions for $r = 1, \ldots, M-1$ are negligible. For this purpose we consider the matrix

$$A^{(r)} = \begin{pmatrix} p(0|0) & p(0|1)\omega_r^{L_0} \\ p(1|0) & p(1|1)\omega_r^{L_1} \end{pmatrix}.$$

For $r = 0$, we clearly have $\rho(A^{(0)}) = 1$ for the spectral radius. If we can show that $\rho(A^{(r)}) < 1$ for $r = 1, \ldots, M-1$, then the polynomial

$$\begin{vmatrix} 1 - p(0|0)z & -p(0|1)\omega_r^{L_0}z \\ -p(1|0)z & 1 - p(1|1)\omega_r^{L_1}z \end{vmatrix}$$

$$= 1 - (p(0|0) + p(1|1)\omega_r^{L_1})z$$
$$+ (p(0|0)p(1|1)\omega_r^{L_1} - p(0|1)\omega_r^{L_0}p(1|0))z^2 \tag{2.63}$$

has no zeros of modulus $|z| \leq 1$ (see Exercise 2.9). Hence, both poles of the corresponding generating function have modulus > 1, which implies that the nth coefficient can be bounded by $O(\rho^n)$ for some $\rho < 1$.

In order to show that $\rho(A^{(r)}) < 1$, we just have to apply (again) Lemma 2.9 and directly observe that $\rho(A^{(r)}) = 1$, would imply that $\omega_r^{L_0} = \omega_r^{L_1} = 1$, which can only occur for $r = 0$ (here we have to use the assumption $\gcd(L_0, L_1, M) = 1$).

The other cases (where $j = 1$ or $k = 1$) can be handled in the same way. ∎

Summing up, this shows that

$$\overline{R}_n = \sum_{j=0}^{1}\sum_{k=0}^{1}p_j\pi_k \frac{1}{M}\sum_{\ell=0}^{M-1}\left\langle \frac{\ell + \zeta_{jk}(n)}{M} \right\rangle + O(\rho^n).$$

We should observe that the term $p_j\pi_k$ is approximately the probability of $X_1 = j$ and $X_n = k$ since for large n, X_1 and X_n are almost independent. Thus we immediately obtain (2.40) completing the proof of Theorem 2.7.

2.2.2 Extension to Irreducible Aperiodic Markov Sources

We now discuss some extensions of Theorem 2.7. In particular, we drop the assumption that all transition probabilities must be strictly positive and assume that $\mathbf{P}$ corresponds to an irreducible aperiodic Markov source.

When some of the entries of the matrix $\mathbf{P}$ vanish, then, obviously, Theorem 2.7 cannot be used as the corresponding parameters α_{jk} are no longer well defined. Lemma 2.9, which stands at the heart of the proof of Theorem 2.7, can still be used as long as **P** is irreducible, but more caution should be exercised. The key issue is still to determine whether there exist parameters s and $\mathbf{w}$ that satisfy

$$h \log p(j|k) = (s + w_k - w_j) \bmod 1, \tag{2.64}$$

but now these equations are imposed only for the pairs (j, k) for which $p(j|k) > 0$ (as for the other pairs, $a_{jk}(h) = p(j|k) = 0$ satisfy the conditions of Lemma 2.9 automatically anyway).

For example, if one or more diagonal element of **P** is positive, and for all positive $p(j|j)$, the numbers $\langle h \log p(j|j) \rangle$ are equal, then s can still be taken to be the common value of all these numbers. If, in addition, at least one row of **P** is strictly positive, say, row number l, then w_j can be taken to be $\langle -h \log[p(l|l)/p(j|l)] \rangle$, and then the rationality condition of Theorem 2.7 is replaced by the condition that

$$\alpha'_{jk} = \log \left[\frac{p(j|0)p(0|0)}{p(k|0)p(j|k)} \right] \tag{2.65}$$

must be rational for all (j, k) with $p(j|k) > 0$.

For a general nonnegative matrix **P**, however, it may not be a trivial task to determine whether (2.64) has a solution, and if so, what this solution is. In fact, it may be simpler and more explicit to check directly if A_h has an eigenvalue on the unit circle (which thereby dictates s) and then to find $\mathbf{w}$ using Lemma 2.9. This leads to the following generalized version of Theorem 2.7.

Theorem 2.11 *Consider the Shannon code of block length n for an irreducible aperiodic Markov source. Let M be defined as the smallest positive integer h such that*

$$\rho(A_h) \equiv |\lambda_{1,h}| = 1 \tag{2.66}$$

and set $M = \infty$ if (2.66) does not hold for any positive integer h. Then, $\overline{R}_n$ is characterized as follows:
(a) If $M = \infty$, then

$$\overline{R}_n = \frac{1}{2} + o(1). \tag{2.67}$$

(b) If $M < \infty$, then the asymptotic representation of Theorem 2.7, part (b), holds with $\zeta_{jk}(n)$ being redefined according to

$$\zeta_{jk}(n) = -M[(n-1)s + w_j - w_k - \log p_j], \tag{2.68}$$

where

$$s = \frac{\arg(\lambda_{1,M})}{2\pi} \tag{2.69}$$

and

$$w_j = \frac{\arg(x_j)}{2\pi}, \quad j = 0, 1, \ldots, m-1, \tag{2.70}$$

x_j being the jth component of the right eigenvector $\mathbf{x}$ of A_M, which is associated with the dominant eigenvalue $\lambda_{1,M}$.

The proof of Theorem 2.11 is very similar to that of Theorem 2.7 and hence we will not provide it here. In a nutshell, we observe that the Perron–Frobenius theorem and Lemma 2.9 are still applicable. Then, we use the necessity of the condition $A_h = e^{2\pi i s} DPD^{-1}$ and the fact that once this condition holds, the vector

$$\mathbf{x} = D \cdot \mathbf{1} = (e^{2\pi i w_0}, \ldots, e^{2\pi i w_{m-1}})^T$$

is the right eigenvector associated with the dominant eigenvalue $\lambda_{1,m} = e^{2\pi i s}$. We again have to prove a corresponding analogue of Lemma 2.10.

Finally, we present an example with a *reducible* Markov source for which our results do not apply. In particular, in this case, there is only one convergent mode of behavior.

Example 2.12 Consider the case $m = 2$, where $p(0|1) = 0$ and $\alpha := p(1|0) \in (0, 1)$; that is,

$$P = \begin{pmatrix} 1 - \alpha & \alpha \\ 0 & 1 \end{pmatrix}. \tag{2.71}$$

Assume also that $p_0 = 1$ and $p_1 = 0$. Since this is a *reducible* Markov source (once in state 1, there is no way back to state 1), we cannot use Theorems 2.7 and 2.11, but we can still find an asymptotic expression of the redundancy in a direct manner. Note that the chain starts at state '0' and remains there for a random duration, which is a geometrically distributed random variable with parameter $(1 - \alpha)$. Thus, the probability of k 0's (followed by $n - k$ 1's) is about $(1 - \alpha)^k \cdot \alpha$ (for large n) and so the argument of the function $\langle \cdot \rangle$ should be the logarithm of this probability. Taking the expectation with regard to the randomness of k, we readily have

$$\overline{R}_n = \sum_{k=0}^{\infty} \alpha(1 - \alpha)^k \langle \log \alpha + k \log(1 - \alpha) \rangle + o(1). \tag{2.72}$$

We see then that there is *no oscillatory mode* in this case, as $\overline{R}_n$ always tends to a constant that depends on α, in contrast to the convergent mode of Theorems 2.7 and 2.11, where the limit is always $1/2$, independent of the source statistics. To summarize, it is observed that the behavior here is very different from that of the irreducible case, characterized by Theorems 2.7 and 2.11.

2.3 Maximal Redundancy for a Generalized Shannon Code

In this section we switch from the average redundancy to the worst-case or maximal redundancy. For a given probability distribution P on an alphabet $\mathcal{A}$, we are looking for a prefix code that minimizes the maximal redundancy $R^*(P)$; that is,

$$R^*(P) = \min_C \max_{x \in \mathcal{A}} [L(C, x) + \log P(x)]. \tag{2.73}$$

To solve this optimization problem, we introduce a generalized Shannon code denoted as C^{GS}. We write the code length of a generalized Shannon code as

$$L(x, C^{GS}) = \begin{cases} \lfloor \log 1/P(x) \rfloor & \text{if } x \in \mathcal{L}, \\ \lceil \log 1/P(x) \rceil & \text{if } x \in \mathcal{U}, \end{cases}$$

where $\mathcal{L} \cup \mathcal{U} = \mathcal{A}$ is a partition of the alphabet $\mathcal{A}$. In addition, we shall postulate that Kraft's inequality holds; that is, we have (for the binary case)

$$\sum_{x \in \mathcal{L}} P(x) 2^{\langle - \log P(x) \rangle} + \frac{1}{2} \sum_{x \in \mathcal{U}} P(x) 2^{\langle - \log P(x) \rangle} \leq 1.$$

Our main result of this section is to prove that there exists a generalized Shannon code that is optimal with respect to the maximal redundancy as formulated in (2.73).

Theorem 2.13 (Drmota and Szpankowski 2004) *If the probability distribution P is dyadic, that is, $\log P(x) \in \mathbb{Z}$ for all $x \in \mathcal{A}$, then $R_n^*(P) = 0$. Otherwise, let $t_0 \in T = \{ \langle - \log P(x) \rangle : x \in \mathcal{A} \}$ be the largest t such that*

$$\sum_{x \in \mathcal{L}_t} P(x) 2^{\langle - \log P(x) \rangle} + \frac{1}{2} \sum_{x \in \mathcal{U}_t} P(x) 2^{\langle - \log P(x) \rangle} \leq 1, \tag{2.74}$$

where

$$\mathcal{L}_t := \{ x \in \mathcal{A} : \langle - \log P(x) \rangle < t \}$$

and

$$\mathcal{U}_t := \{ x \in \mathcal{A} : \langle - \log P(x) \rangle \geq t \}.$$

Then

$$R^*(P) = 1 - t_0 \tag{2.75}$$

and the optimum is obtained for a generalized Shannon code with $\mathcal{L} = \mathcal{L}_{t_0}$ and $\mathcal{U} = \mathcal{U}_{t_0}$.

Proof If P is dyadic then the numbers $l(x) := - \log P(x)$ are positive integers satisfying

$$\sum_x 2^{-l(x)} = 1.$$

Kraft's inequality holds and consequently there exists a (prefix) code C with $L(C, x) = l(x) = - \log P(x)$ for all $x \in \mathcal{A}$, and this $R^*(P) = 0$.

Now assume that P is not dyadic and let $\mathcal{C}^*$ denote the set of optimal codes:

$$\mathcal{C}^* = \{ C \in \mathcal{C} : R^*(C, P) = R^*(P) \}.$$

The idea of the proof is to establish several properties of an optimal code. In particular, we will show that there exists an optimal code $C^* \in \mathcal{C}^*$ with the following two properties:

(i) For all x,

$$\lfloor - \log P(x) \rfloor \leq L(C^*, x) \leq \lceil - \log P(x) \rceil. \tag{2.76}$$

(ii) There exists $s_0 \in (0, 1]$ such that

$$L(C^*, x) = \lfloor \log 1/P(x) \rfloor \quad \text{if} \quad \langle \log 1/P(x) \rangle < s_0 \tag{2.77}$$

and

$$L(C^*, x) = \lceil \log 1/P(x) \rceil \quad \text{if} \quad \langle \log 1/P(x) \rangle \geq s_0. \tag{2.78}$$

Observe that without losing generality, we may assume that $s_0 = 1 - R^*(P)$. Thus, in order to compute $R^*(P)$ we just have to consider codes satisfying (2.77) and (2.78). As already mentioned, (2.74) is just Kraft's inequality for codes of that kind. The optimal choice is $t = t_0$, which also equals s_0. Consequently $R^*(P) = 1 - t_0$.

In view of this, it suffices to prove properties (i) and (ii). Assume that C^* is an optimal code. First of all, the upper bound in (2.76) is obviously satisfied for C^*. Otherwise we would have

$$\max_x [L(C^*, x) + \log P(x)] > 1,$$

which contradicts a simple bound applied to a regular Shannon code. Second, if there exists x such that $L(C^*, x) < \lfloor \log 1/P(x) \rfloor$, then (in view of Kraft's inequality) we can modify this code to a code $\widetilde{C}^*$ with

$$L(\widetilde{C}^*, x) = \lceil \log 1/P(x) \rceil \quad \text{if } L(C^*, x) = \lceil \log 1/P(x) \rceil,$$
$$L(\widetilde{C}^*, x) = \lfloor \log 1/P(x) \rfloor \quad \text{if } L(C^*, x) \leq \lfloor \log 1/P(x) \rfloor.$$

By construction, $R^*(\widetilde{C}^*, P) = R^*(C^*, P)$. Thus, $\widetilde{C}^*$ is optimal too. This proves (i).

Now consider an optimal code C^* satisfying (2.76) and let $\widetilde{x} \in \mathcal{A}$ with $R^*(P) = 1 - \langle -\log P(\widetilde{x}) \rangle$. Thus, $L(C^*, x) = \lfloor \log 1/P(x) \rfloor$ for all x with $\langle -\log P(x) \rangle < \langle -\log P(\widetilde{x}) \rangle$. This proves (2.77) with $s_0 = \langle -\log P(\widetilde{x}) \rangle$. Finally, if (2.78) is not satisfied, then (in view of Kraft's inequality) we can modify this code to a code $\widetilde{C}^*$ with

$$L(\widetilde{C}^*, x) = \lceil \log 1/P(x) \rceil \quad \text{if } \langle \log 1/P(x) \rangle \geq s_0,$$
$$L(\widetilde{C}^*, x) = \lfloor \log 1/P(x) \rfloor \quad \text{if } \langle \log 1/P(x) \rangle < s_0.$$

By construction, $R^*(\widetilde{C}^*, P) = R^*(C^*, P)$. Thus, $\widetilde{C}^*$ is optimal too. This proves (ii) and the lemma. ∎

We apply the above now to a binary memoryless source on the alphabet $\mathcal{A}_n = \{0, 1\}^n$ with parameter p.

Theorem 2.14 *Let P be a binary memoryless source on the alphabet $\mathcal{A}_n = \{0, 1\}^n$ with parameter p and let $R_n^*(p)$ denote the corresponding maximal redundancy.*
(i) If $\log \frac{1-p}{p}$ is irrational then, as $n \to \infty$,

$$R_n^*(p) = -\frac{\ln \ln 2}{\ln 2} + o(1) = 0.5287 \ldots + o(1). \tag{2.79}$$

(ii) If $\log \frac{1-p}{p} = \frac{N}{M}$ (for some coprime integers $M, N \in \mathbb{Z}$) is rational and nonzero, then as $n \to \infty$,

$$R_n^*(p) = o(1) +$$

$$-\frac{\lfloor M \log(M(2^{1/M} - 1)) - \langle Mn \log 1/(1-p) \rangle \rfloor + \langle Mn \log 1/(1-p) \rangle}{M}. \tag{2.80}$$

Finally, if $\log \frac{1-p}{p} = 0$ then $p = \frac{1}{2}$ and $R_n^*(1/2) = 0$.

Proof As before, we set

$$\alpha = \log \frac{1-p}{p}, \qquad \beta = \log \frac{1}{1-p}.$$

Then

$$-\log(p^k(1-p)^{n-k}) = \alpha k + \beta n.$$

Since α is irrational, we know from the previous section that for any Riemann integrable function f,

$$\lim_{n\to\infty} \sum_{k=0}^{n} \binom{n}{k} p^k (1-p)^{n-k} f(\langle \alpha k + \beta n \rangle) = \int_0^1 f(x)\, dx. \qquad (2.81)$$

Now set $f_{s_0}(x) = 2^x$ for $0 \le x < s_0$ and $f_{s_0}(x) = 2^{x-1}$ for $s_0 \le x \le 1$. We find

$$\lim_{n\to\infty} \sum_{k=0}^{n} \binom{n}{k} p^k (1-p)^{n-k} f_{s_0}(\langle \alpha k + \beta n \rangle) = \frac{2^{s_0-1}}{\ln 2}.$$

In particular, for

$$s_0 = 1 + \frac{\ln \ln 2}{\ln 2} = 0.4712\ldots$$

we obtain $\int_0^1 f(x)\, dx = 1$, so that Kraft's inequality becomes equality. This implies that

$$\lim_{n\to\infty} R_n^*(p) = 1 - s_0 = 0.5287\ldots,$$

which proves (2.79).

Now we establish the second part of Theorem 2.14; that is, $\log \frac{1-p}{p} = \frac{N}{M}$ is rational and nonzero (with coprime integers N, M). We use Lemma 2.5 applied to $f_{s_0}(x)$ and obtain

$$\sum_{k=0}^{n} \binom{n}{k} p^k (1-p)^{n-k} f_{s_0}(\langle \alpha k + \beta n \rangle) = \frac{1}{M} \sum_{m=0}^{M-1} f_{s_0}\left(\left\langle \frac{mN}{M} + \beta n \right\rangle\right) + o(1)$$

$$= \frac{1}{M} \sum_{m=0}^{M-1} f_{s_0}\left(\frac{m + \langle M\beta n \rangle}{M}\right) + o(1).$$

We suppose that s_0 is of the form

$$s_0 = \frac{m_0 + \langle M\beta n \rangle}{M}$$

and choose m_0 maximal such that

$$\frac{1}{M} \sum_{m=0}^{M-1} f_{s_0}\left(\frac{m + \langle M\beta n \rangle}{M}\right) = \frac{2^{\langle M\beta n \rangle}/M}{M}\left(\sum_{m=0}^{m_0-1} 2^{m/M} + \sum_{m=m_0}^{M-1} 2^{m/M-1}\right)$$

$$= \frac{2^{(\langle M\beta n \rangle + m_0)/M - 1}}{M(2^{1/M}-1)}$$

$$\le 1.$$

Thus,

$$m_0 = M + \lfloor M \log(M(2^{1/M} - 1)) - \langle Mn \log 1/(1-p) \rangle \rfloor,$$

and consequently

$$
\begin{aligned}
R_n^*(p) &= 1 - s_0 + o(1) \\
&= 1 - \frac{m_0 + \langle M\beta n \rangle}{M} + o(1) \\
&= -\frac{\lfloor M \log(M(2^{1/M} - 1)) - \langle Mn \log 1/(1-p) \rangle \rfloor + \langle Mn\beta \rangle}{M} + o(1).
\end{aligned}
$$

This completes the proof of Theorem 2.14. ∎

2.4 Exercises

2.1   We say that a real-valued sequence x_n is B-uniformly distributed if $D_N^{(p_{n,k})}(x_n) \to 0$ for $p_{n,k} = \binom{n}{k}p^k(1-p)^{n-k}$. Provide a detailed proof of the following theorem.

Theorem 2.15   *Let $0 < p < 1$ be a fixed real number and suppose that the sequence x_n is B-uniformly distributed modulo 1. Then for every Riemann integrable function $f : [0, 1] \to \mathbb{R}$, we have*

$$\lim_{n \to \infty} \sum_{k=0}^{n} \binom{n}{k} p^k (1-p)^{n-k} f(\langle x_k + y \rangle) = \int_0^1 f(t)\, dt, \tag{2.82}$$

where the convergence is uniform for all shifts $y \in \mathbb{R}$.

See Appendix E for more details.

2.2   Prove the Weyl criteria presented below.

Theorem 2.16 (Weyl's Criterion)   *A sequence x_n is B-u.d. mod 1 if and only if*

$$\lim_{n \to \infty} \sum_{k=0}^{n} \binom{n}{k} p^k (1-p)^{n-k} e^{2\pi i m x_k} = 0 \tag{2.83}$$

holds for all $m \in \mathbb{Z} \setminus \{0\}$.

2.3   Provide all details to prove Stubley's formulas (2.12) and (2.13).

2.4   Prove Lemma 2.5, which we repeat here.

Lemma 2.17   *Let $0 < p < 1$ be a fixed real number and suppose that $\alpha = \frac{N}{M}$ is a rational number with $\gcd(N, M) = 1$. Then, for every bounded function $f : [0, 1] \to \mathbb{R}$, we have*

$$
\sum_{k=0}^{n} \binom{n}{k} p^k (1-p)^{n-k} f(\langle k\alpha + y \rangle) = \frac{1}{M} \sum_{l=0}^{M-1} f\left(\frac{l}{M} + \frac{\langle My \rangle}{M}\right) \\
+ O(\rho^n)
$$

uniformly for all $y \in \mathbb{R}$ and some $\rho < 1$.

2.5   Establish the following formula:

$$\mathbf{E}[L] = \lceil \log \ell \rceil + \frac{\theta^{2^{\lfloor \log \ell \rfloor + 1}}}{\theta^\ell - 1}, \quad \theta^\ell = 1/2,$$

for the average length of the Golomb code.

2.6   Derive the corresponding upper bound to (2.47).

2.7   Prove Lemma 2.9.

2.8   Provide details for the derivation of (2.62).

2.9   Prove that the polynomial defined in (2.63) has no zeros of modulus $|z| \leq 1$.

2.10   Provide a proof of Lemma 2.11.

2.11   Consider the following generalization of the average and worst-case redundancy. Let r be a real number and define the r-redundancy as follows:

$$R_r(P) = \max_{\mathcal{C}} \left(\sum_x P(x)[l(x) + \log P(x)]^r \right)^{1/r}.$$

Notice that for $r = 1$, it reduces to the average redundancy while for $r = \infty$, it becomes the worst-case redundancy. Find the optimal code.

2.12   Extend Theorem 2.14 to Markov sources.

Bibliographical Notes

Since the appearance in 1952 of Huffman's classical paper (Huffman 1952) on optimal variable length source coding, Huffman coding still remains one of the most familiar topics in information theory. A good survey on this topic can be found in Abrahams (2001). Over more than 60 years, insightful, elegant, and useful constructions have been set up to determine tighter bounds on the Huffman code redundancy: see Capocelli and de Santis (1989, 1991), Gallager (1978), Manstetten (1980), and Stubley (1994). Formulas (2.12) and (2.13) were first derived in Stubley (1994). To the best of our knowledge, the first precise asymptotics of the Huffman redundancy was presented in Szpankowski (2000). We base our presentation of the Huffman redundancy on this work. The Markov case discussed in Section 2.2 is based on Merhav and Szpankowski (2013).

The worst-case (maximum) redundancy was introduced by Shtarkov (1987). The optimization problem (2.73) was likely presented for the first time in Drmota and Szpankowski (2002) (see also Drmota and Szpankowski (2004)), however, some earlier work can also be found in Campbell (1965), Nath (1975), and Parker (1980), where conditions for optimality of the Huffman and other codes were given for a class of weight function and cost criteria.

Golomb code was introduced in Golomb (1996), however, we follow here the description from Gallager and van Voorhis (1975) and Merhave, Seroussi, and Weinberger (2000).

The theory of sequences distributed modulo 1 is well explained in Kuipers and Niederreiter (1974) and Drmota and Tichy (1997). See also Appendix E.

3

Tunstall and Khodak VF Codes

In this chapter and the next we study variable-to-fixed (VF) length codes. Recall that in the VF scenario, the source string x, say over an m-ary alphabet $\mathcal{A} = \{0, 1, \ldots, m-1\}$, is partitioned into nonoverlapping (unique) phrases, each belonging to a given *dictionary* $\mathcal{D}$. In what follows, we will assume that $\mathcal{D}$ is prefix free (no string of $\mathcal{D}$ is prefix of another string in $\mathcal{D}$), which guarantees the uniqueness of the partioning. Such a dictionary $\mathcal{D}$ can be represented by a complete m-ary *parsing tree* $\mathcal{T}$. The dictionary entries $d \in \mathcal{D}$ correspond to the *leaves* of the associated parsing tree, and, of course, the tree representation of $\mathcal{D}$ can be directly algorithmically used to partition the source string. The encoder then represents each element of $\mathcal{D}$ by a fixed length binary codeword. If the dictionary $\mathcal{D}$ has M entries, then the codeword for each phrase has $\lceil \log M \rceil$ bits (recall that log denotes the binary logarithm). The code C is, thus, a mapping $C : \mathcal{D} \to \{0, 1\}^{\lceil \log M \rceil}$. Since the average length of this code is (trivially) $\lceil \log M \rceil$ the redundancy can be only small if the dictionary $\mathcal{D}$ has the property that all $d \in \mathcal{D}$ have *almost* the same probability $P(d) \approx \frac{1}{M}$.

The best known variable-to-fixed length code is the Tunstall code that is (almost) the same as the independently discovered Khodak code. Since the Khodak code can be mathematically described in a more direct way, we focus our analysis mainly on the Khodak code. At the end of the chapter, we also study a Khodak code variant with phrase length constraints.

3.1 Variable-to-Fixed Codes

We start with a description of the Tunstall code for an m-ary memoryless source. In such a code, edges in the m-ary parsing tree correspond to letters from the source alphabet $\mathcal{A} = \{0, 1, \ldots, m-1\}$ and are labeled by the alphabet probabilities, say $p_0, \ldots, p_{m-1}$. Every vertex in such a tree is assigned the probability of the path leading to it from the root, as shown in Figure 3.1. This is, of course, consistent with the assumption that we consider a memoryless source, the probability of a vertex is the product of probabilities of edges leading to it. Clearly the probabilities of the leaves – which correspond to the dictionary $\mathcal{D}$ – add up to 1. The goal of the following algorithm is to construct a parsing tree such that the probabilities of the leaves are as close as possible; that is, the distribution on $\mathcal{D}$ is close to uniform. The algorithm starts with the trivial tree that contains just the root (corresponding to the empty word and) that is labeled by the probability 1. At each iteration one selects a (current) leaf of *highest probability*, say $P_{\max}$, and grows m children out of it with probabilities $p_0 P_{\max}, \ldots, p_{m-1} P_{\max}$. Clearly all these probabilities are smaller than $P_{\max}$. After J iterations, the parsing tree has J nonroot *internal nodes* and $M = (m-1)J + m$ leaves, each representing a distinct dictionary entry.

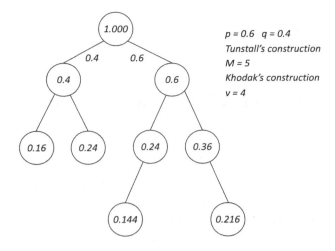

Figure 3.1 Tunstall's and Khodak's Codes for $M = 5$, $v = 4$, binary source with $p = 0.6$ (and $q = 1 - p$). Here the resulting dictionary is $\mathcal{D} = \{00, 01, 10, 110, 111\}$.

Another algorithm was proposed by Khodak (1969) who independently discovered the Tunstall code using a rather different approach. Let us define $p_{\min} = \min\{p_0, \ldots, p_{m-1}\}$. Khodak suggested to choose a real number $v > 1/p_{\min}$ and to grow a complete parsing tree until all leaves $d \in \mathcal{D}$ satisfy

$$p_{\min}/v \le P(d) < 1/v. \tag{3.1}$$

Khodak's and Tunstall's algorithms are illustrated in Figure 3.1 with the dictionary $\mathcal{D} = \{00, 01, 10, 110, 111\}$ corresponding to strings represented by the paths from the root to all terminal nodes.

It is known (see Exercise 3.1) that the parsing trees for the Tunstall and Khodak algorithms are – in most instances – exactly the same; however, they react differently to the probability tie when expanding a leaf. More precisely, when there are several leaves with the same probability, the Tunstall algorithm selects *one* leaf and expands it, then selects another leaf of the same probability, and continues doing this until all leaves of the same probability are expanded. The Khodak algorithm expands *all* leaves with the same probability simultaneously, in parallel; thus, there are "jumps" in the number of dictionary entries M when the parsing tree grows. For example, in Figure 3.1 two nodes marked "0.24" will be expanded simultaneously in the Khodak algorithm, and one after another by the Tunstall algorithm.

Our goal is to present a precise analysis of the Khodak and Tunstall redundancy as well as to provide some insights into the behavior of the parsing tree (i.e., the path length distribution). In particular, we consider the average redundancy *rate* $\bar{r}$, which is defined as

$$\bar{r} = \frac{\log M}{\mathbf{E}[D]} - h, \tag{3.2}$$

where $\mathbf{E}[D] = \sum_{d \in \mathcal{D}} |d| P(d)$ is the average phrase length of the dictionary $\mathcal{D}$ and

$$h := h_S = \sum_{i=0}^{m-1} p_i \log(1/p_i)$$

is the entropy rate of the source; we recall again that log denotes the binary logarithm. We note that $\mathbf{E}[D]$ is also known as the average *delay*, which is actually the average path length from the root to a terminal node in the corresponding parsing tree.

In passing, we should mention here the *Conservation of Entropy Property*, which states that the entropy of the dictionary $h_\mathcal{D}$ is related to the source entropy h_S as follows

$$h_\mathcal{D} = h_S \mathbf{E}[D]. \tag{3.3}$$

We ask the reader to establish this relation in Exercise 3.2.

3.2 Redundancy of the Khodak VF Code

For Khodak's code, it follows from (3.1) that if y is a proper prefix of one or more entries of $\mathcal{D}$ (that is, y corresponds to an internal node of the parsing tree $\mathcal{T}$), then

$$P(y) \geq 1/v. \tag{3.4}$$

It is therefore easier to describe the internal nodes of the parsing tree $\mathcal{T}$ rather than its leaves. We shall follow this approach when analyzing the phrase length D of Khodak's code.

In what follows, we always fix some $v > 0$ and will denote by $\mathcal{D}_v$ the dictionary of the corresponding Khodak code, by M_v the cardinality of $\mathcal{D}_v$, and by D_v the phrase lengths $|d|$ of $d \in \mathcal{D}_v$, considered as a random variable with probability distribution P on $\mathcal{D}_v$.

As mentioned, our goal is to understand the behavior of the dictionary size M_v and the probabilistic behavior of the phrase length D_v (when the source is memoryless). We present our results for a general source alphabet $\mathcal{A} = \{0, 1, \ldots, m - 1\}$ of size m with probability p_i for $0 \leq i < m$; however, most proofs are for a binary source alphabet with $p_0 = p$ and $p_1 = q = 1 - p$.

We first deal with M_v and provide a simple relation between it and parameter v. To find an expression for M_v, we introduce a new function $A(v)$ defined as the number of source strings with probability at least $1/v$; that is,

$$A(v) = \sum_{y:P(y)\geq 1/v} 1. \tag{3.5}$$

Observe that $A(v)$ represents the number of internal nodes in Khodak's construction with parameter v of a Tunstall tree. Equivalently, $A(v)$ counts the number of strings y with the self-information $-\log P(y) \leq \log v$. The function $A(v)$ satisfies the following recurrence:

$$A(v) = \begin{cases} 0 & v < 1, \\ 1 + A(vp_0) + \cdots + A(vp_{m-1}) & v \geq 1. \end{cases} \tag{3.6}$$

Indeed, by definition, we have $A(v) = 0$ for $v < 1$. Now suppose that $v \geq 1$. Since every m-ary string is either the empty string or a string starting with a source letter j where $0 \leq j < m$, we directly find the recurrence $A(v) = 1 + A(vp_0) + \cdots + A(vp_{m-1})$.

Since $A(v)$ represents the number of internal nodes in Khodak's construction with parameter v, it follows that the dictionary size is given by

$$M_v = |\mathcal{D}_v| = (m - 1)A(v) + 1.$$

Therefore, it is sufficient to obtain asymptotic expansions for $A(v)$ for $v \to \infty$.

To present these results succinctly, we need to introduce the concept of *rationally related* numbers.

Definition 3.1 (Rationally/irrationally related) We say that $\log(1/p_0), \ldots, \log(1/p_{m-1})$ are *rationally related* if there exists a positive real number L such that $\log(1/p_0), \ldots, \log(1/p_{m-1})$ are integer multiples of L; that is,

$$\log(1/p_j) = n_j L, \quad n_j \in \mathbb{Z}, \quad (0 \leq j < m).$$

Without loss of generality we can assume that L is as large as possible, which is equivalent to $\gcd(n_0, \ldots, n_{m-1}) = 1$.

For example, in the binary case $m = 2$, this is equivalent to the statement that the ratio $\log(1/p_0)/\log(1/p_1)$ is rational. Similarly we say that $\log(1/p_0), \ldots, \log(1/p_{m-1})$ are *irrationally related* if they are not rationally related.

Now we are ready to present our first result.

Theorem 3.2 *We consider Khodak's VF code with parameter v. If we assume that $\log(1/p_0), \ldots, \log(1/p_{m-1})$ are irrationally related, then*

$$M_v = (m-1)\frac{v}{h \ln 2} + o(v), \tag{3.7}$$

where h denotes the entropy rate of the source.

Otherwise, when $\log(1/p_0), \ldots, \log(1/p_{m-1})$ are rationally related, let $L > 0$ be the largest real number for which $\log(1/p_1), \ldots, \log(1/p_m)$ are integer multiples of L. Then

$$M_v = (m-1)\frac{Q_1(\log v)}{h} v + O(v^{1-\eta}) \tag{3.8}$$

for some $\eta > 0$, where

$$Q_1(x) = \frac{L}{1 - 2^{-L}} 2^{-L\langle \frac{x}{L} \rangle}, \tag{3.9}$$

and, recall, $\langle x \rangle = x - \lfloor x \rfloor$ is the fractional part of the real number x.

Proof We present the proof based on the Mellin transform. Furthermore, for simplicity, we only present it for the binary case $m = 2$. In Exercise 3.3 we ask the reader to provide a detailed proof for $m > 2$.

The Mellin transform $F^*(s)$ of a function $F(v)$ for complex s is defined as (see Appendix D)

$$F^*(s) = \int_0^\infty F(v)v^{s-1}dv,$$

if it exists. Using the fact that the Mellin transform of $F(av)$ is $a^{-s}F^*(s)$, a simple analysis of recurrence (3.6) reveals that the Mellin transform $A^*(s)$ of $A(v)$ is given by

$$A^*(s) = \frac{-1}{s(1 - p_0^{-s} - p_1^{-s})}, \quad \Re(s) < -1.$$

In order to find asymptotics of $A(v)$ as $v \to \infty$ one can directly use the Tauberian theorem by Wiener–Ikehara (properly adapted for the Mellin transform, as discussed in Appendix D), which says that if $F(v) = 0$ for $v < 1$, $F(v) \geq 0$ and nondecreasing for $v \geq 1$, and if $\frac{1}{s}F^*(s)$ can be represented as

$$\frac{1}{s}F^*(s) = G(s) + \frac{A_0}{s - s_0},$$

where $G(s)$ is analytic for $\Re(s) < s_0$ and has a continuous extension to the half plane $\Re(s) \leq s_0$, then it follows that

$$F(v) \sim A_0 v^{-s_0}.$$

In the present context, we can apply this theorem directly in the case where $\log(p_0)/\log(p_1)$ is irrational. In this case, we observe that $s_0 = -1$ is the only (polar) singularity on the line $\Re(s) = -1$ (compare with Lemma D.7), that $A^*(s)$ exists for $\Re(s) < -1$ and that $(s+1)A^*(s)$ can be analytically extended to a region that contains the line $\Re(s) = -1$. In particular, one finds

$$A(v) \sim \frac{v}{h \ln 2}, \qquad (v \to \infty).$$

This proves the first part of Theorem 3.2.

In the rational case, where $\log(1/p_0) = n_0 L$ and $\log(1/p_1) = n_1 L$, for coprime integers n_0, n_1, we just have to analyze the recurrence:

$$G_n = 1 + G_{n-n_0} + G_{n-n_1}, \tag{3.10}$$

where G_n abbreviates $A(2^{Ln})$. Equivalently we have $A(v) = G(\lfloor \log v \rfloor / L)$. By setting

$$G(z) = \sum_{n \geq 0} G_n z^n,$$

we obtain from (3.10) the relation

$$G(z) = \frac{1}{(1-z)(1 - z^{n_0} - z^{n_1})}.$$

This rational function has a dominant simple polar singularity at $z_0 = 2^{-L} < 1$. Since n_0 and n_1 are coprime, there are no other polar singularities on the circle $|z| = 2^{-L}$. Thus, from the representation

$$G(z) = \frac{1}{(1 - z_0)(n_0 z_0^{n_0} + n_1 z_0^{n_1})}\frac{1}{1 - z/z_0} + H(z),$$

where $H(z)$ is analytic for $|z| < z_0 + \kappa$ for some $\kappa > 0$, we directly get

$$G_n = \frac{1}{(1 - 2^{-L})(n_0 2^{-n_0 L} + n_1 2^{-n_1 L})}2^{Ln} + O(2^{Ln(1-\eta)})$$

for some $\eta > 0$ and consequently

$$A(v) = \frac{L 2^{-L\langle \log v/L\rangle}}{(1 - 2^{-L})}\frac{v}{h} + O(v^{(1-\eta)}).$$

As before, $\langle x \rangle$ is the fractional part of x. ∎

Next we deal with our main goal; namely the analysis of the phrase length and Khodak's code redundancy. We start with deriving the moment generating function of the phrase length

D_v and then its moments. Let us define the probability generating function $D(v,z)$ of the phrase length $D := D_v$ for the Khodak code with parameter v as

$$D(v,z) := \mathbf{E}[z^{D_v}] = \sum_{d \in \mathcal{D}_v} P(d)z^{|d|}.$$

However, it is better to work with another generating function describing the probabilities of strings that correspond to *internal nodes* in the parsing tree $\mathcal{T}_v$. Therefore, we also define

$$S(v,z) = \sum_{y:\, P(y) \geq 1/v} P(y)z^{|y|}. \tag{3.11}$$

Lemma 3.3 *The function $S(v,z)$ satisfies the following recurrence:*

$$S(v,z) = \begin{cases} 0 & v < 1, \\ 1 + p_0 z S(vp_0, z) + \cdots + p_{m-1} z S(vp_{m-1}, z) & v \geq 1. \end{cases} \tag{3.12}$$

Furthermore,

$$D(v,z) = 1 + (z-1)S(v,z) \tag{3.13}$$

for all complex z.

Proof The recurrence (3.12) can be derived in the same way as for $A(v)$. The relation (3.13) follows from the following general fact on trees.

Let $\widetilde{\mathcal{D}}$ be a uniquely parsable dictionary (e.g., leaves in the corresponding parsing tree) and $\widetilde{\mathcal{Y}}$ be the collection of strings that are proper prefixes of one or more dictionary entries (e.g., internal nodes). Then for all complex z,

$$\sum_{d \in \widetilde{\mathcal{D}}} P(d) \left(1 + z + \cdots z^{|d|-1} \right) = \sum_{y \in \widetilde{\mathcal{Y}}} P(y)z^{|y|}. \tag{3.14}$$

This can be deduced directly by induction and implies (3.13), as the reader is asked to check in Exercise 3.4.

Alternatively we can use the following result (see Exercise 3.5). For every real-valued function G defined on strings over $\mathcal{A}$,

$$\sum_{d \in \mathcal{D}} P(d)G(d) = G(\emptyset) + \sum_{y \in \mathcal{Y}} P(y) \sum_{s \in \mathcal{A}} \frac{P(ys)}{P(y)}(G(ys) - G(y)), \tag{3.15}$$

where $\emptyset$ denotes an empty string, $\mathcal{D}$ the set of external nodes, and $\mathcal{Y}$ the set of internal nodes. By choosing $G(x) = z^{|x|}$, we directly find

$$\sum_{d \in \mathcal{D}} P(d)z^{|d|} = z^0 + \sum_{y \in \mathcal{Y}} P(y) \sum_{s \in \mathcal{A}} P(s) \left(z z^{|y|} - z^{|y|} \right)$$

$$= 1 + (z-1) \sum_{y \in \mathcal{Y}} P(y),$$

which again proves (3.14). ∎

In view of Lemma 3.3, we conclude that

$$\mathbf{E}[D] = \sum_{y \in \mathcal{Y}} P(y) = S(v,1), \qquad \mathbf{E}[D(D-1)] = 2\sum_{y \in \mathcal{Y}} P(y)|y| = S'(v,1).$$

This allows us to formulate our next result.

Theorem 3.4 *We consider Khodak's VF code with parameter v.*
(i) *If* $\log(1/p_0), \ldots, \log(1/p_{m-1})$ *are irrationally related, then*

$$E[D_v] = S(v, 1) = \frac{\log v}{h} + \frac{h_2}{2h^2} + o(1), \tag{3.16}$$

where $h_2 = \sum_{i=0}^{m-1} p_i \log^2(1/p_i)$, *while in the rational case*

$$E[D_v] = S(v, 1) = \frac{\log v}{h} + \frac{h_2}{2h^2} + \frac{Q_2(\log v)}{h} + O(v^{-\eta}) \tag{3.17}$$

for some $\eta > 0$, *where*

$$Q_2(x) = L \cdot \left(\frac{1}{2} - \left\langle \frac{x}{L} \right\rangle \right) \tag{3.18}$$

for L as defined above.
(ii) *The phrase length D_v in Khodak's construction with parameter v of the Tunstall code with a dictionary of size M_v over a biased memoryless source (i.e., not all symbol probabilities are equal) satisfies a central limit law; that is, as $M_v \to \infty$,*

$$\frac{D_v - \frac{1}{h} \log M_v}{\sqrt{\left(\frac{h_2}{h^3} - \frac{1}{h} \right) \log M_v}} \to N(0, 1),$$

where $N(0, 1)$ denotes the standard normal distribution. Furthermore, we have

$$\mathbf{E}[D_v] = \frac{\log M_v}{h} + O(1),$$

$$\mathrm{Var}[D_v] \sim \left(\frac{h_2}{h^3} - \frac{1}{h} \right) \log M_v,$$

where M_v is as given in Theorem 3.2.

Finally, before presenting a proof of Theorem 3.4, let us discuss its consequences for the redundancy rate of the Khodak code. By combining (3.7) and (3.16) resp. (3.8) and (3.17) we find for the irrational case

$$\mathbf{E}[D_v] = \frac{\log M_v}{h} + \frac{\log(h \ln 2/(m-1))}{h} + \frac{h_2}{2h^2} + o(1),$$

and in the rational case we have

$$\mathbf{E}[D_v] = \frac{\log M_v}{h} + \frac{\log(h/(m-1))}{h} + \frac{h_2}{2h^2}$$
$$+ \frac{-\log L + \log(1 - 2^{-L}) + L/2}{h} + O(M_v^{-\eta}).$$

Recall that $L > 0$ is the largest real number for which $\log(1/p_0), \ldots, \log(1/p_{m-1})$ are integer multiples of L. As a direct consequence, we can derive a precise asymptotic formula for the average redundancy of the Khodak code; that is,

$$\bar{r}_M^K = \frac{\log M}{\mathbf{E}[D]} - h.$$

The following result is a consequence of these derivations.

Corollary 3.5 *Let $\mathcal{D}_v$ denote the dictionary in Khodak's construction of the Tunstall code of size M_v. If $\log(1/p_0), \ldots, \log(1/p_{m-1})$ are irrationally related, then*

$$\overline{r}_{M_v}^K = \frac{h}{\log M_v} \left(-\frac{h_2}{2h} - \log(h \ln 2/(m-1)) \right) + o\left(\frac{1}{\log M_v}\right).$$

In the rational case, we have

$$\overline{r}_{M_v}^K = \frac{h}{\log M_v} \left(-\frac{h_2}{2h} - \log(h/(m-1)) - \log\left(\frac{2^{L/2} - 2^{-L/2}}{L}\right) \right)$$
$$+ O\left(\frac{1}{\log^2 M_v}\right),$$

where $L > 0$ is the largest real number for which $\log(1/p_i)$, $0 \le i \le m-1$ are integer multiples of L.

3.2.1 Proof of Theorem 3.4

Again, we only present the proof of the binary case. In order to prove Theorem 3.4(i), we consider

$$\mathbf{E}[D_v] = \sum_{y:P(y)\ge 1/v} P(y) = S(v, 1).$$

Here the Mellin transform is given by

$$D^*(s) = \int_0^\infty \mathbf{E}[D_v] v^{s-1}\, dv = \frac{-1}{s(1 - p_0^{1-s} - p_1^{1-s})} \qquad (\Re(s) < 0),$$

and it leads (in the irrational case) after applying a proper extension of the Wiener–Ikehara theorem (see Theorem D.3 in Appendix D) to the asymptotic equivalent

$$\mathbf{E}[D_v] \sim \frac{\ln(v)}{h \ln 2} = \frac{\log(v)}{h}.$$

Note that the double pole at $s = 0$ is responsible for the log-factor. Actually a more careful analysis that is based on the inverse Mellin transform (see the last part of Appendix D, properly adapted) determines the second order term as well:

$$\mathbf{E}[D_v] = \frac{\log(v)}{h} + \frac{h_2}{2h^2} + o(1).$$

In the rational case, it is easy to see (similarly to the proof of Theorem 3.2) that

$$\mathbf{E}[D_v] = \frac{\log(v)}{h} + \frac{h_2}{2h^2} + \frac{L}{h}\left(\frac{1}{2} - \left\langle\frac{\log(v)}{L}\right\rangle\right) + O(r^\eta)$$

for some $\eta > 0$, where we recall $\langle x \rangle$ is the fractional part of x.

The analysis of $D(v, z)$ is more involved. Here we do not give a full proof but restrict ourselves to the irrational case and give (only) a heuristic argument based on the Wiener–Ikehara Tauberian theorem discussed in Appendix D and below. The reader is asked to provide a full proof in Exercise 3.3.

We assume that z is a real number close to 1, say $|z - 1| \le \delta$. The Mellin transform $D^*(s, z)$ of $D(v, z)$ with respect to v is

$$D^*(s, z) = \frac{1 - z}{s(1 - zp^{1-s} - zq^{1-s})} - \frac{1}{s} \tag{3.19}$$

for $\Re(s) < s_0(z)$, where $s_0(z)$ denotes the real solution of the characteristic equation:

$$zp^{1-s} + zq^{1-s} = 1, \tag{3.20}$$

where now we write $p := p_0$ and $q := p_1$. It is easy to see that

$$s_0(z) = -\frac{z - 1}{h \ln 2} + \left(\frac{1}{h \ln 2} - \frac{h_2}{2h^3 \ln 2} \right)(z - 1)^2 + O(|z - 1|^3) \tag{3.21}$$

as $z \to 1$.[1]

The next step is to determine the polar singularities of the meromorphic continuation of $D^*(s, z)$ right to the line $\Re(s) = s_0(z)$; that is, we have to analyze the set

$$\mathcal{Z}(z) = \{ s \in \mathbf{C} : zp^{1-s} + zq^{1-s} = 1 \} \tag{3.22}$$

of all complex roots of the characteristic equation (4.14). This can be handled with the help of Lemma D.7 from Appendix D. Since we restrict ourselves to the irrational case, it follows that $s_0(z)$ is the only root on the line $\Re(s) = s_0(z)$. For all other roots $s_k(z)$ ($k \in \mathbb{Z} \subseteq \{0\}$), we have $\Re(s_k(z)) > s_0(z)$. Furthermore, the *additional zero* $s = 0$ is canceled because of the additional term $-1/s$.

From Wiener–Ikehara's Tauberian theorem, we find that (for fixed $z \ne 1$)

$$D(v, z) = \frac{1 - z}{zs_0(z)h(s_0(z) - 1) \ln 2} v^{-s_0(z)}(1 + o(1)), \qquad (v \to \infty), \tag{3.23}$$

where $h(s)$ abbreviates

$$h(s) = p^{-s} \log(1/p) + q^{-s} \log(1/q).$$

Now if we assume that the error term in (3.23) is uniform in z, then we can use the local expansion (3.21) to obtain uniformly for $|z - 1| \le \delta$ as $v \to \infty$, and then

$$\begin{aligned}
D(v, z) &= v^{-s_0(z)}(1 + O(s_0(z)) + o(1)) \\
&= v^{\frac{z-1}{h \ln 2} + \left(\frac{1}{h \ln 2} - \frac{h_2}{2h^3 \ln 2} \right)(z-1)^2 + O(|z-1|^3)} (1 + O(|z - 1|) + o(1)).
\end{aligned}$$

Recall that $D(v, z) = \mathbf{E}[z^{D_v}]$ is the probability generating function of the dictionary length D_v and, therefore, it can be used to derive the limiting behavior. We can use the local expansion (3.21) with $z = e^{t/(\log v)^{1/2}}$ to obtain

---

[1] Note that we now in a similar situation as described in Appendix D. The only difference is that we are considering here the Mellin transform and not the Mellin–Stieltjes transform (which differ only by a proper scaling).

$$v^{-s_0(z)} = \exp\left(\log v\left(\frac{z-1}{h\ln 2} - \left(\frac{1}{h\ln 2} - \frac{h_2}{2h^3\ln 2}\right)(z-1)^2 + O(|z-1|^3)\right)\right)$$

$$= \exp\left(\frac{1}{h}t\sqrt{\log v} + \frac{1}{h}\frac{t^2}{2} - \left(\frac{1}{h} - \frac{h_2}{2h^3}\right)t^2 + O(t^3/\sqrt{\log v})\right)$$

$$= \exp\left(\frac{1}{h}t\sqrt{\log v} + \left(\frac{h_2}{h^3} - \frac{1}{h}\right)\frac{t^2}{2} + O(t^3/\sqrt{\log v})\right).$$

Hence, we arrive at

$$\mathbf{E}\left[e^{t(D_v - \frac{1}{h}\log v)/\sqrt{\log v}}\right] = e^{-(t/h)\sqrt{\log v}}\mathbf{E}\left[e^{D_v t/\sqrt{\log v}}\right] \sim e^{\frac{t^2}{2}\left(\frac{h_2}{h^3} - \frac{1}{h}\right)}. \qquad (3.24)$$

By Laplace's theorem, this would prove the normal limiting distribution as $v \to \infty$ (and also convergence of all (centralized) moments as well as exponential tail estimates).

In order to make this argument rigorous, we have to show that the asymptotic relation (3.23) is uniform for $|z - 1| \leq \delta$. Instead of using a Tauberian theorem, we can also use the inverse Mellin transform,

$$D(v,z) = \frac{1}{2\pi i}\lim_{T\to\infty}\int_{\sigma-iT}^{\sigma+iT} D^*(s,z)v^{-s}\,ds \qquad (3.25)$$

(with $\sigma < s_0(z)$), and proceed as demonstrated at the end of Appendix D.

In the rational case, we reduce the recurrence for $D(v,z)$ to a discrete recurrence (as is the proof of Theorem 3.2), which can be asymptotically solved uniformly in z and provides a central limit theorem by Laplace's theorem. The reader is asked in Exercise 3.7 to provide a detailed proof of this claim.

3.3 Analysis of the Tunstall Code

Let us now return to the Tunstall code. Recall that the parsing tree is the same as for the Khodak code, but in the case of a tie, the Tunstall code adds phrase one at a time, while the Khodak code adds them all at once. Nevertheless, one should expect similar results. Indeed, in the next theorem we present our findings for the Tunstall code.

Theorem 3.6 *Let $\widetilde{D}_M$ denote the phrase length of the Tunstall code when the dictionary size is $M \geq 1$. Then, for a biased source (i.e., when the probabilities p_i are not equal),*

$$\frac{\widetilde{D}_M - \frac{1}{h}\log M}{\sqrt{\left(\frac{h_2}{h^3} - \frac{1}{h}\right)\log M}} \to N(0,1),$$

where $N(0,1)$ denotes the standard normal distribution, and

$$\mathbf{E}[\widetilde{D}_M] = \frac{\log M}{h} + O(1),$$

$$\mathbf{Var}[\widetilde{D}_M] \sim \left(\frac{h_2}{h^3} - \frac{1}{h}\right)\log M$$

for $M \to \infty$.

Proof We shall show that Theorem 3.6 can be deduced from Theorem 3.4. (The converse is obviously true.) This follows, informally, from the fact that Tunstall's code and Khodak's code are "almost equivalent," as discussed In Section 3.1.

Let's be more precise. Suppose that v is chosen in a way that there exists a word x with $P(x) = 1/v$. In particular, the dictionary $\mathcal{D}_v$ contains all external nodes d that are adjacent to internals x with $P(x) = 1/v$. Now let $\widetilde{\mathcal{D}}_M$ be the dictionary (of size M) of any Tunstall code where only some of these internal nodes x with $P(x) = 1/v$ have been expanded. Then $\mathcal{D}_v$ is the Tunstall code where all nodes x with $P(x) = 1/v$ have been expanded. Hence, by this coupling of the dictionaries, we certainly have dictionary lengths $|\widetilde{D}_M - D_v| \le 1$. This also implies that $\mathbf{E}[\widetilde{D}_M] = \mathbf{E}[D_v] + O(1)$ and $\mathbf{Var}[\widetilde{D}_M - D_v] = O(1)$.

We observe that the central limit theorem is not affected by this variation. Since $\mathcal{D}_v$ satisfies a central limit theorem (see Theorem 3.4), we find

$$\frac{\widetilde{D}_M - \frac{1}{h}\log M}{\sqrt{\left(\frac{h_2}{h^3} - \frac{1}{h}\right)\log M}} \to N(0,1).$$

For the expected value and variance, we have $\mathbf{E}[\widetilde{D}_M] = \frac{1}{h}\log M + O(1)$ and

$$\mathbf{Var}[\widetilde{D}_M] = \mathbf{Var}[D_v] + O\left(\sqrt{\mathbf{Var}[D_v]}\right)$$
$$\sim \left(\frac{h_2}{h^3} - \frac{1}{h}\right)\log M.$$

Indeed, more generally, let $Y_n = X_n + Z_n$ and we know that X_n satisfies a central limit theorem of the form

$$\frac{X_n - \mathbf{E}[X_n]}{\sqrt{\mathbf{Var}[X_n]}} \to N(0,1)$$

such that $\mathbf{Var}[X_n] \to \infty$, as well as $\mathbf{Var}[Z_n]/\mathbf{Var}[X_n] \to 0$ as $n \to \infty$. Then also Y_n satisfies a central limit theorem, that is,

$$\frac{Y_n - \mathbf{E}[Y_n]}{\sqrt{\mathbf{Var}[Y_n]}} \to N(0,1),$$

and we have

$$\mathbf{Var}[Y_n] = \mathbf{Var}[X_n] + \mathbf{Var}[Z_n] + O(\sqrt{\mathbf{Var}[X_n]\mathbf{Var}[Z_n]}) \sim \mathbf{Var}[X_n],$$

which follows from the Cauchy–Schwarz inequality

$$\mathbf{E}[(X_n - \mathbf{E}[X_n])(Z_n - \mathbf{E}[Z_n])] \le (\mathbf{Var}[X_n])^{1/2}(\mathbf{Var}[Z_n])^{1/2}.$$

This completes the proof of Theorem 3.6. ∎

Let us offer some final remarks. We already observed that the parsing trees for the Tunstall and Khodak algorithms are the same except when there is a "tie." This situation can occur both for the rational case and for the irrational case, and somewhat surprisingly leads to the cancellation of oscillation in the redundancy of the Khodak code for the rational case. As shown in Savari and Gallager (1997) tiny oscillations remain in the Tunstall code redundancy for the rational case. We ask the reader in Exercise 3.8 to provide details.

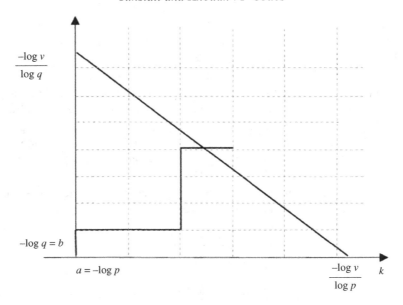

Figure 3.2 A random walk with a linear barrier; the exit time is equivalent to the phrase length in the Khodak algorithm (e.g., the exit time $= 7$).

3.4 Back to Khodak Code with Bounded Phrase Length

Before we discuss a Khodak code with some additional constraints, let us describe another representation of the Khodak code using a random walk in the first quadrant. As already observed in Chapter 1, a path in the parsing tree from the root to a leaf corresponds to a random walk on a lattice in the first quadrant of the plane (see Figure 1.1). Indeed, observe that our analysis of the Khodak code boils down to studying the following sum:

$$A(v) = \sum_{y:P(y)\geq 1/v} f(v)$$

for some function $f(v)$. Since $P(y) = p^{k_1} q^{k_2}$ for some nonnegative integers $k_1, k_2 \geq 0$, we conclude that the summation set of $A(v)$ can be expressed, after setting $v = 2^V$, as

$$k_1 \log(1/p) + k_2 \log(1/q) \leq V. \tag{3.26}$$

This corresponds to a random walk in the first quadrant with the linear boundary condition $ax + by = V$, where $a = \log(1/p)$ and $b = \log(1/q)$ as shown in Figure 3.2. The phrase length D_v of the Khodak code coincides with the *exit time* of such a random walk (i.e., the last step before the random walk hits the linear boundary). This correspondence is further explored in Janson (1986).

This new representation of the Khodak code allows us to analyze a novel version of the code by putting additional constraints on the random walk in the first quadrant. In this section, we consider the Khodak code with *bounded* phrase length; that is, we additionally impose that

$$k_1 + k_2 \leq K \tag{3.27}$$

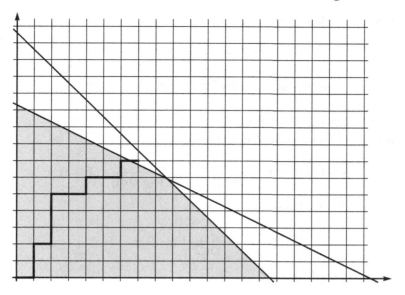

Figure 3.3 Lattice paths in a bounded region.

for some positive integer K. Throughout this section we assume the binary alphabet with $p = p_1$ and $q = p_2$.

We consider here a random walk in the first quadrant with two constraints: (3.26) and (3.27). In other words, we study a Khodak code with phrase length bounded by K; that is, any parsing tree of such a code has no leave beyond level K. This is illustrated in Figure 3.3.

Our goal is to understand the probabilistic behavior of the phrase length $D_{K,V}$ for a Khodak code with bounded phrase length. However, in order to succinctly express these results we need to enumerate the number of paths in the bounded area of the first quadrant. To be more precise, let us define

$$C_{K,V} := \{(x_1, x_2) \in \mathbb{R}^2_{\geq 0} : x_1 + x_2 \leq K, \ x_1 \log(1/p) + x_2 \log(1/q) \leq V\}.$$

Let then $\mathcal{L}_{K,V}$ be the corresponding set of lattice paths within the region $C_{K,V}$ and $T_{K,V}$ be the associated binary tree. In order to present our results, we need to study first the cardinality of $\mathcal{L}_{K,V}$; that is,

$$|\mathcal{L}_{K,V}| = \sum_{k_1 + k_2 \leq K, \ k_1 \log \frac{1}{p} + k_2 \log \frac{1}{q} \leq V} \binom{k_1 + k_2}{k_1}.$$

In this context, it is natural to let K be an integer variable and V a positive real variable.

In the formulation of our results, we will make use of $s_{\mathrm{sp}} = s_{\mathrm{sp}}(K, V)$ defined as the root of

$$R(s_{\mathrm{sp}}) := \frac{p^{-s_{\mathrm{sp}}} + q^{-s_{\mathrm{sp}}}}{p^{-s_{\mathrm{sp}}} \log \frac{1}{p} + q^{-s_{\mathrm{sp}}} \log \frac{1}{q}} = \frac{K}{V}. \tag{3.28}$$

Note that $s_{\mathrm{sp}} > -1$ if and only if $K/V < 1/h$.

We further recall the definition (3.9):

$$Q_1(x) = \frac{L}{1 - 2^{-L}} 2^{-L\langle \frac{x}{L} \rangle}.$$

In the next section, we present a sketch of the proof of our first result.

Theorem 3.7 *Suppose that* $\delta > 0$ *is given.*
(i) *Assume that* K *and* V *satisfy the following constraints:*

$$\frac{V}{h} \cdot (1 + \delta) \le K \le \frac{V}{\min\{\log(1/p), \log(1/q)\}} \cdot (1 - \delta). \tag{3.29}$$

If $\log p / \log q$ *is irrational, then as* $K, V \to \infty$,

$$|\mathcal{L}_{K,V}| = \frac{2^V}{h \ln 2}(1 + o(1)). \tag{3.30}$$

However, if $\frac{\log p}{\log q}$ *is rational, then*

$$|\mathcal{L}_{K,V}| = \frac{Q_1(V)}{h} 2^V + O(2^{V(1-\eta)}) \tag{3.31}$$

for some $\eta > 0$, *where* $L > 0$ *is the largest real number for which* $\log(1/p)$ *and* $\log(1/q)$ *are integer multiples of* L.
(ii) *Next, if*

$$\frac{2V}{\log(1/p) + \log(1/q)} \cdot (1 + \delta) \le K \le \frac{V}{h} \cdot (1 - \delta), \tag{3.32}$$

then

$$|\mathcal{L}_{K,V}| \sim \sum_{\ell \ge 0} \frac{Q_\Delta\left(s_{\mathrm{sp}}, (K - \ell)\ln p - V \ln 2\right)}{(p^{-s_{\mathrm{sp}}} + q^{-s_{\mathrm{sp}}})^\ell} \cdot \frac{(p^{-s_{\mathrm{sp}}} + q^{-s_{\mathrm{sp}}})^K 2^{-V s_{\mathrm{sp}}}}{\sqrt{2\pi K\, T(s_{\mathrm{sp}})}}, \tag{3.33}$$

where $\Delta = \ln q - \ln p$,

$$T(s) = \frac{p^{-s} \ln^2 \frac{1}{p} + q^{-s} \ln^2 \frac{1}{q}}{p^{-s} + q^{-s}} - \left(\frac{p^{-s} \ln \frac{1}{p} + q^{-s} \ln \frac{1}{q}}{p^{-s} + q^{-s}} \right)^2,$$

and

$$Q_\Delta(s, x) = \frac{\Delta}{1 - e^{s\Delta}} e^{s\Delta \langle \frac{x}{\Delta} \rangle}.$$

If $\log p / \log q = d/r$ *is rational then*

$$|\mathcal{L}_{K,V}| \sim \sum_{j=0}^{d-r-1} \frac{e^{2\pi i \frac{l}{\delta}} Q_L\left(s_{\mathrm{sp}} - \frac{2\pi i j}{\delta}, K \ln p - V \ln 2\right)}{1 - \frac{e^{2\pi i \frac{jd}{d-r}}}{p^{-s_{\mathrm{sp}}} + q^{-s_{\mathrm{sp}}}}} \tag{3.34}$$

$$\cdot \frac{(p^{-s_{\mathrm{sp}}} + q^{-s_{\mathrm{sp}}})^K 2^{-V s_{\mathrm{sp}}}}{\sqrt{2\pi K\, T(s_{\mathrm{sp}})}}.$$

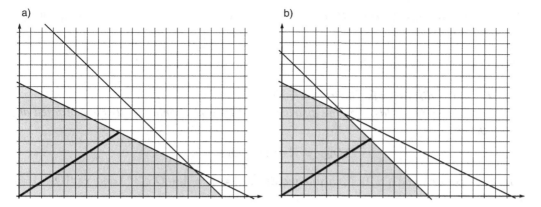

Figure 3.4 The drift in the first and second case of Theorem 3.8.

(iii) *Finally, if*

$$\frac{V}{\max\{\log(1/p), \log(1/q)\}} \cdot (1 + \delta) \leq K \leq \frac{2V}{\log(1/p) + \log(1/q)} \cdot (1 - \delta) \tag{3.35}$$

then (for some $\eta > 0$)

$$|\mathcal{L}_{K,V}| = 2^{K+1} - O(2^{K(1-\eta)}). \tag{3.36}$$

However, the main result of this section deals with the phrase length $D_{K,V}$, which we discuss next. As noticed, the phrase length coincides with the first exit time from $C_{K,V}$. Observe that we assign a natural probability distribution to the lattice paths in $\mathcal{L}_{K,V}$. Recall that if $y \in \mathcal{L}_{K,V}$ consists of k_1 steps of the form R (for right) and k_2 steps of the form L (for left), then we set $P(y) := p^{k_1} q^{k_2}$, and that this is exactly the probability distribution that is induced by a random walk that starts at $(0, 0)$ and is generated by independent steps R and L with probabilities p and q. Further, since every path y eventually leaves $C_{K,V}$ we surely have $\sum_{y \in \mathcal{L}_{K,V}} P(y) = 1$. Certainly, we can also think of the corresponding trees $T_{K,V}$ and their external nodes. Our second result concerns the exit time $D_{K,V}$ of this random walk; that is, the number of steps $|y| = k_1 + k_2$ of $y \in \mathcal{L}_{K,V}$ (see Figure 3.4). In the next subsection we present a brief sketch of the proof.

Theorem 3.8 *Let $D_{K,V}$ denote the exit time of our random walk and the phrase length in the Khodak code with phrase length bounded by K. Fix $\delta > 0$.*
(i) If (3.29) holds, then we have, as $K, V \to \infty$,

$$\frac{D_{K,V} - \frac{1}{h} \log |\mathcal{L}_{K,V}|}{\left(\left(\frac{h_2}{h^3} - \frac{1}{h}\right) \log |\mathcal{L}_{K,V}|\right)^{1/2}} \to N(0, 1),$$

where $N(0, 1)$ denotes the standard normal distribution. Furthermore,

$$E[D_{K,V}] = \frac{\log |\mathcal{L}_{K,V}|}{h} + \frac{\log h}{h} + \frac{h_2}{2h^2} + \frac{-\log L + \log(1 - 2^{-L}) + \frac{L}{2}}{h} \tag{3.37}$$
$$+ o\left(\frac{1}{\log |\mathcal{L}_{K,V}|}\right),$$

where $L = 0$ if $\log p / \log q$ is irrational and $L > 0$ is defined as in Theorem 3.7 if $\log p / \log q$ is rational. Further,

$$\mathbf{Var}[D_{K,V}] \sim \left(\frac{h_2}{h^3} - \frac{1}{h} \right) \log |\mathcal{L}_{K,V}|, \tag{3.38}$$

where $\mathcal{L}_{K,V}$ is as discussed in Theorem 3.7.

(ii) If (3.32) or (3.35) holds, then the distribution of $D_{K,V}$ is asymptotically concentrated at $K + 1$; that is,

$$P(D_{K,V} \neq K + 1) = O(e^{-\eta K}),$$

as $K, V \to \infty$ for some $\eta > 0$. We also have $\mathbf{E}[D_{K,V}] = K + 1 + O(e^{-\eta K})$ and $\mathbf{Var}[D_{K,V}] = O(e^{-\eta K})$.

Let us explain the intuition behind these results. We observe that a random walk (which starts at $(0, 0)$ and is generated by independent steps R and L with probabilities p and q) has an average position (pm, qm) after m steps. Furthermore, by approximating this random walk by a Brownian motion, it is clear that the deviation from the mean is (almost surely) bounded by $O(\sqrt{m \log \log m})$. Thus, if (3.29) holds, then the Brownian motion approximation can be used to derive the central limit theorem (see, for example, Janson (1986)). The bound coming from $k_1 + k_2 \leq K$ has practically no influence (cf. Figure 3.4). However, in the second and third cases ((3.32) and (3.35)), the bound $k_1 \log p^{-1} + k_2 \log q^{-1} \leq V$ is negligible and, thus, the exit time is concentrated at $K + 1$. This also explains the first threshold $K/V \sim 1/h$ of Theorem 3.7. The second threshold $K/V \sim 2/(\log p^{-1} + \log q^{-1})$ comes from the fact that $\sum_{k_1+k_2 \leq K} \binom{k_1+k_2}{k_1} = 2^{K+1} - 1$ and that

$$\sum_{k_1+k_2 \leq K, \, k_1 \log \frac{1}{p} + k_2 \log \frac{1}{q} > V} \binom{k_1 + k_2}{k_1} \tag{3.39}$$

becomes negligible; that is, $O(2^{K(1-\eta)})$ if

$$K/V < (1 - \delta) \cdot 2 / \left(\log \frac{1}{p} + \log \frac{1}{q} \right).$$

The two thresholds $K/V \sim 1/h$ and

$$K/V \sim 2 / \left(\log \frac{1}{p} + \log \frac{1}{q} \right)$$

are not covered by Theorems 3.7 and 3.8. The reader is asked to derive them in Exercise 3.12. In fact, it is possible to characterize the limiting behavior of $|\mathcal{L}_{K,V}|$ and $D_{K,V}$ also in these cases but the statements (and also the derivations) are very involved and are not discussed here.

3.4.1 Proof of Theorem 3.7

For any lattice path y, we set $P(y) = p^{k_1} q^{k_2}$ if y consists of k_1 steps R and k_2 steps L. We further set $v = 2^V$. Then $k_1 \log p^{-1} + k_2 \log q^{-1} \leq V$ is equivalent to $P(y) \geq 1/v$. Observe that

$$A_K(v) = \sum_{y:P(y)\geq 1/v, \, |y|\leq K} 1$$

is the number of lattice paths with endpoints contained in $C_{K,V}$. Due to the binary tree interpretation of these lattice paths, we have

$$|\mathcal{L}_{K,V}| = A_K(v) + 1 = A_K(2^V) + 1,$$

since the number of external nodes of a binary tree exceeds the number of internal nodes by exactly 1.

For the proof of the limit laws of the exit time, we will also make use of the following sum

$$S_K(v,z) = \sum_{y:P(y)\geq 1/v, \, |y|\leq K} P(y)z^{|y|}$$

as already defined (3.11).

First, by definition, it is clear that $A_K(v) = 0$ and $S_K(v,z) = 0$ for $v < 1$ and all $K \geq 0$, however, for $v \geq 1$ we recursively have

$$A_{K+1}(v) = 1 + A_K(vp) + A_K(vq),$$
$$S_{K+1}(v,z) = 1 + pzS_K(vp,z) + qzS_K(vq,z).$$

From this recursive description we immediately obtain the corresponding relations for the Mellin transforms; namely,

$$A^*_{K+1}(s) = -\frac{1}{s} + (p^{-s} + q^{-s})A^*_K(s) \qquad (\Re(s) < -1)$$

and

$$S^*_{K+1}(s,z) = -\frac{1}{s} + (zp^{1-s} + zq^{1-s})S^*_K(s,z) \qquad (\Re(s) < 0).$$

Since $A^*_0(v) = S^*_0(v,z) = -\frac{1}{s}$, we explicitly find

$$A^*_K(s) = -\frac{1 - (p^{-s} + q^{-s})^{K+1}}{s(1 - (p^{-s} + q^{-s}))},$$
$$S^*_K(s,z) = -\frac{1 - (z(p^{1-s} + q^{1-s}))^{K+1}}{s(1 - z(p^{1-s} + q^{1-s}))}.$$

In order to find asymptotics of $A_K(v)$ as $v \to \infty$, we must compute the inverse transform of $A^*_K(s)$:

$$A_K(v) = \frac{1}{2\pi i} \lim_{T\to\infty} \int_{\sigma-iT}^{\sigma+iT} A^*_K(s)v^{-s} \, ds, \qquad (3.40)$$

where $\sigma < -1$. The factor $(z(p^{1-s} + q^{1-s}))^{K+1}$ needs special care and the corresponding part will be handled with saddle point methods.

Case (i) We assume that we are in the first case of Theorem 3.7; that is, the relation (3.29) holds. Then we know that $s_{sp} < -1$. We split up the integral (3.40) into two parts:

$$I_1 = -\frac{1}{2\pi i} \lim_{T \to \infty} \int_{\sigma - iT}^{\sigma + iT} -\frac{1}{s(1 - (p^{-s} + q^{-s}))} v^{-s} \, ds,$$

$$I_2 = -\frac{1}{2\pi i} \lim_{T \to \infty} \int_{\sigma - iT}^{\sigma + iT} \frac{(p^{-s} + q^{-s})^{K+1}}{s(1 - (p^{-s} + q^{-s}))} v^{-s} \, ds.$$

We observe that I_1 is the same expression that occurs in the unconstrained case.

The integral I_2 has to be treated in a completely different way. First of all, we shift the integral to the line $\sigma = s_{sp} < -1$ and observe that

$$(p^{-s_{sp}} + q^{-s_{sp}})^K v^{-s_{sp}} = v^{R(s_{sp}) \log(p^{-s_{sp}} + q^{-s_{sp}}) - s_{sp}},$$

where s_{sp} and $R(s_{sp})$ are defined in (3.28). Notice also that

$$R(s_{sp}) \log(p^{-s_{sp}} + q^{-s_{sp}}) - s_{sp} < 1$$

if $s_{sp} \neq -1$. Hence, I_2 can be estimated by

$$I_2 = O\left(v^{R(s_{sp}) \log(p^{-s_{sp}} + q^{-s_{sp}}) - s_{sp}} \right) = O\left(2^{V(1 - \eta_2)} \right) \tag{3.41}$$

for some $\eta_2 > 0$. In Exercise 3.13, the reader is asked to provide details of this estimate. Again we have to overcome the technical problem that the integral is not absolutely convergent.

Case (ii) Next we assume that we are in the second case of Theorem 3.7; that is, the relation (3.32) holds. Here $s_{sp} > -1$ and we do not split the integral (3.40) into two parts. Of course, we again shift the integral to a line $\sigma > -1$; namely, to $\sigma = s_{sp} > -1$. Note that the zeros of the denominator are not singularities of the function $A_K^*(s)$ since the numerator has the same zeros. Nevertheless, the integral

$$A_K(v) = -\frac{1}{2\pi i} \lim_{T \to \infty} \int_{s_{sp} - iT}^{s_{sp} + iT} \frac{1 - (p^{-s} + q^{-s})^{K+1}}{s(1 - (p^{-s} + q^{-s}))} v^{-s} \, ds \tag{3.42}$$

needs a delicate analysis. It is again not absolutely convergent but this is just a technical question. The second problem comes from the fact that on the line of integration there are infinitely many *saddle points*. First note that $s = s_{sp}$ is a saddle point of the mapping

$$s \mapsto (p^{-s} + q^{-s})^K v^{-s} = e^{K \ln(p^{-s} + q^{-s}) - sV \ln 2}$$

and, thus, the integral from $s_{sp} - iK^{\frac{1}{2} - \varepsilon}$ to $s_{sp} + iK^{\frac{1}{2} - \varepsilon}$ (for some $\varepsilon > 0$) is asymptotically given by

$$\frac{1}{\sqrt{2\pi K \, T(s_{sp})}} \frac{(p^{-s_{sp}} + q^{-s_{sp}})^{K+1} 2^{-s_{sp} V}}{s_{sp}(1 - (p^{-s_{sp}} + q^{-s_{sp}}))}.$$

However, as already noted, this is not the only saddle point on this line of integration. Set $t_h = 2\pi h/(\log p - \log q) = -2\pi i h/\Delta$. Then all points $s = s_{sp} + it_h$, $h \in \mathbb{Z}$, are saddle points. Consequently, the total contribution of the integral is asymptotically given by

$$\sum_{h \in \mathbb{Z}} \frac{1}{\sqrt{2\pi K \, T(s_{sp})}} \frac{(p^{-s_{sp}} + q^{-s_{sp}})^{K+1} 2^{-s_{sp} V} p^{-it_h(K+1)} 2^{-iVt_h}}{(s_{sp} + it_h)(1 - (p^{-s_{sp}} + q^{-s_{sp}}) p^{-it_h})}.$$

The representations (3.33) and (3.34) follow after a few lines of computation by using the Fourier expansion of $Q_\Delta(s, x)$.

Case (iii) If (3.35) holds, then $s_{sp} > 0$. Thus, if we shift the line of integration of the integral (3.42) to $\sigma = s_{sp}$, we have to take into account the residue 2^{k+1} corresponding to the polar singularity $s = 0$. The saddle point machinery for the remaining integral at the line $\sigma = s_{sp}$ provides the error term.

3.4.2 Proof of Theorem 3.8

In order to treat the exit time $D_{K,V}$, we make again use of the corresponding tree $T_{K,V}$ we refer to Lemma 3.3, which we restate as follows: let T be an m-ary tree, let X denote the set of leaves, and Y the set of internal nodes. Furthermore, we assume a probability distribution $p_0, \ldots, p_{m-1}$ on an m-ary alphabet $\mathcal{A}$ and identify a node in T with a word over $\mathcal{A}$ in the usual way. Then we have

$$\sum_{x \in X} P(x) z^{|x|} = (z - 1) \sum_{y \in Y} P(y) z^{|y|} + 1. \tag{3.43}$$

This directly implies that the probability generating function of $D_K(v, z) = \mathbf{E}[z^{D_{K,V}}]$ (where $v = 2^V$) is, as proved in Lemma 3.3, given by

$$D_K(v, z) = (z - 1) S_K(v, z) + 1 \qquad (v \geq 1)$$

and consequently its Mellin transform has the following representation (for $\Re(s) < 0$):

$$D_K^*(s, z) = (z - 1) S_K^*(s, z) - \frac{1}{s} = \frac{(1 - z)(1 - z(p^{1-s} + q^{1-s})^{K+1})}{s(1 - z(p^{1-s} + q^{1-s}))} - \frac{1}{s}.$$

Hence, we have for any $\sigma < 0$,

$$\mathbf{E}[z^{D_{K,V}}] =$$

$$\frac{1}{2\pi i} \lim_{T \to \infty} \int_{\sigma - iT}^{\sigma + iT} \left(\frac{(1 - z)(1 - z(p^{1-s} + q^{1-s})^{K+1})}{s(1 - z(p^{1-s} + q^{1-s}))} - \frac{1}{s} \right) v^{-s} \, ds.$$

In the first case of Theorem 3.8 – that is, if (3.29) holds – we split up the integral into two parts $I_1(z) + I_2(z)$:

$$I_1(z) = \frac{1}{2\pi i} \lim_{T \to \infty} \int_{\sigma - iT}^{\sigma + iT} \left(\frac{(1 - z)}{s(1 - z(p^{1-s} + q^{1-s}))} - \frac{1}{s} \right) v^{-s} \, ds,$$

$$I_2(z) = -\frac{1}{2\pi i} \lim_{T \to \infty} \int_{\sigma - iT}^{\sigma + iT} \frac{(1 - z)(z(p^{1-s} + q^{1-s})^{K+1})}{s(1 - z(p^{1-s} + q^{1-s}))} v^{-s} \, ds.$$

Observe that $I_1(z)$ is again directly related to the unconstrained case. Thus, we get (as above)

$$I_1(z) = v^{-s_0(z)} (1 + O(|z - 1|)),$$

where $s_0(z)$ is the real solution of the equation $z(p^{1-s_0} + q^{1-s_0}) = 1$.

In the second integral, $I_2(z)$, we shift the line of integration to $\sigma = s_{sp} + 1 < 0$ and obtain a negligible exponentially small error term. Consequently we obtain the same kind of central limit theorem as in the unconstrained case.

The derivation of the mean value and variance is asked to be provided in Exercise 3.11.

In the second case of Theorem 3.8 (where (3.32) or (3.35) holds) we do not split up the integral into two parts, which implies that the integrand has no singular points other than $s = 0$. We shift the line of integration to $\sigma = s_{sp} + 1 > 0$ and obtain (again by taking care that there is no absolute convergence)

$$\mathbf{E}[z^{D_{K,V}}] = z^{K+1} + O(|z - 1|v^{-\eta}), \tag{3.44}$$

where $\eta = s_{sp} + 1 > 0$. By construction, we know that $D_{K,V} \leq K + 1$. From (3.44), we can easily deduce that $D_{K,V}$ is in fact concentrated at $K + 1$. By Markov's inequality (for $z < 1$), we directly obtain

$$P(D_{K,V} \leq K) \leq z^{-K} \mathbf{E}\left[z^{D_{K,V}} \mathbf{1}_{\{D_{K,V} \leq K\}}\right]$$
$$= z^{-K}\left(\mathbf{E}[z^{D_{K,V}}] - z^{K+1}\right) + z\,P(D_{K,V} \leq K),$$

which implies (with $z = 1 - \frac{1}{K}$) the estimate $P(D_{K,V} \leq K) = O(v^{-\eta})$. This proves the concentration. We have $v = 2^V$ and, thus, $v^{-\eta} = 2^{-\eta V}$ is exponentially small. By using the corresponding tail estimate of the form $P(D_{K,V} \leq K - r) = O(e^{-r/K}v^{-\eta})$, we can also deal with moments and obtain $\mathbf{E}[D_{K,V}] = K + 1 + O(K^2 v^{-\eta})$ and $\mathrm{Var}\,[D_{K,V}] = O(K^3 v^{-\eta})$.

3.5 Exercises

3.1　Prove that the parsing trees for Tunstall and Khodak algorithms are exactly the same (see Savari and Gallager (1997)).

3.2　Establish the *Conservation of Entropy Property* which states that the entropy of the dictionary $h_{\mathcal{D}}$ is related to the source entropy h_S; that is,

$$h_{\mathcal{D}} = h_S \mathbf{E}[D]$$

(see Savari (1999)).

3.3　Provide detailed proofs of Theorems 3.2 and 3.4 for $m > 2$.

3.4　Prove (3.14).

3.5　Establish the Massey (1983) result; namely (3.15).

3.6　Give a proof of Lemma D.7. See also Drmota, Reznik, and Szpankowski (2010).

3.7　Supply details of the proof of Theorem 3.2 for the rational case using the Mellin transform.

3.8　Consider again the Khodak algorithm for the rational case. Develop precise analysis showing that somewhat surprisingly there is cancellation of oscillation in the redundancy of the Khodak code (see Savari and Gallager (1997)).

3.9　Show that there are tiny oscillations remain in the Tunstall code redundancy for the rational case. See Savari and Gallager (1997).

3.10　Extend our analysis of Tunstall and Khodak codes to Markov sources.

3.11　Complete the proof of Theorem 3.8 by providing a detailed derivations of the average depth (3.37) and the variance (3.38).

3.12　Derive the two remaining thresholds; namely, $K/V \sim (\log 2)/h$ and $K/V \sim 2/(\log_2 \frac{1}{p} + \log_2 \frac{1}{q})$ of Theorem 3.8.

3.13　Provide detailed derivations of the estimation (3.41).

Bibliographical Notes

The Tunstall (1967) algorithm for the construction of a VF code has been extensively discussed in Abrahams (2001). Simple bounds for its redundancy were obtained independently by Khodak (1969) and Jelinek and Schneider (1972). Tjalkens and Willems (1992) were the first to look at extensions of this code to sources with memory. Savari and Gallager (1997) proposed a generalization of Tunstall's algorithm for Markov sources and used renewal theory for an asymptotic analysis of the average codeword length and for the redundancy for memoryless and Markov sources.

The *Conservation of Entropy Property* (3.3) was established in Katona and Tusnady (1967), Savari (1999).

Our presentation of the Khodak and Tunstall algorithms is based on an analytic approach discussed in Drmota et al. (2006), Drmota et al. (2010). Section 3.4 is based on Drmota and Szpankowski (2007); see also Janson (1986). A precise analysis of infinite saddle points is first discussed in Park et al. (2009), but see also Jacquet and Szpankowski (2015) and Jacquet, Milioris, and Szpankowski (2020). A preliminary analysis of a Khodak-like code was presented in Choi and Golin (2001) using a Laplace transform approach.

4

Divide-and-Conquer VF Codes

In this chapter, we consider again a variable-to-fixed code due to Boncelet (1993) who used the *divide-and-conquer principle* to design a practical arithmetic encoding. Boncelet's algorithm is computationally fast and its practicality stems from the divide-and-conquer strategy to build a parsing tree: it splits the input (e.g., parsing tree) into several smaller subproblems, solving each subproblem separately, and then knitting together to solve the original problem.

We first describe Boncelet's algorithm in some detail and present its redundancy analysis. To prove these results, we need precise results about a *discrete* divide-and-conquer recurrence that for some $T(n)$ satisfies

$$T(n) = a_n + \sum_{j=1}^{m} b_j T\left(\lfloor p_j n + \delta_j \rfloor\right) + \sum_{j=1}^{m} \overline{b}_j T\left(\lceil p_j n + \overline{\delta}_j \rceil\right) \tag{4.1}$$

for some known sequence a_n and given $b_j, \overline{b}_j, p_j$ and $\delta_j, \overline{\delta}_j$. The discrete nature of this recurrence (represented by the floor $\lfloor \cdot \rfloor$ and ceiling $\lceil \cdot \rceil$ functions) introduces certain oscillations not captured by traditional analysis of the divide-and-conquer recurrence. In the second part of this chapter, we present a rigorous and precise analysis of the discrete divide-and-conquer recurrence that goes beyond data compression.

4.1 Redundancy of Boncelet's Code

We now describe the Boncelet VF algorithm. To recall, a variable-to-fixed length encoder partitions the source string, say over a binary (or more generally over an m-ary) alphabet, into a concatenation of variable-length phrases. Each phrase belongs to a given dictionary $\mathcal{D}$ of source strings that constitutes a complete prefix-free set. Such a uniquely parsable dictionary is represented by a *complete parsing tree*; that is, a tree in which every internal node has all two (or more generally m) children nodes. The dictionary entries correspond to the *leaves* of the associated parsing tree. The encoder represents each parsed string by the fixed length binary codeword corresponding to its dictionary entry by the code mapping $C: \mathcal{D} \rightarrow \{0, 1\}^{\lceil \log |\mathcal{D}| \rceil}$. Boncelet's algorithm, described next, is a practical algorithm to generate a parsing tree for a VF code, and therefore should be compared to the (asymptotically) optimal Tunstall and Khodak algorithms discussed in Chapter 3.

The main idea of Boncelet's VF code is to construct a parsing tree using a simple divide-and-conquer strategy. More precisely, let $n = |\mathcal{D}|$ denote the number of leaves in the corresponding parsing tree, hence also the size of the dictionary.[1] We construct the parsing tree as follows: to build a tree with n leaves, we split n into $n = n_0 + n_1$ so that there are n_0 leaves in the left subtree and n_1 leaves in the right subtree. We accomplish this using a divide-and-conquer strategy; that is, we set

$$n_0 = \lfloor p_0 n + \delta \rfloor, \quad n_1 = \lceil p_1 n - \delta \rceil$$

for some $\delta \in (0, 1)$ (that satisfies $2p_0 + \delta < 2$) and p_0 is the probability of generating a "0" with $p_0 + p_1 = 1$ (we consider here only the binary case). Then the procedure is recursively applied until only 1 or 2 leaves are left.

Example 4.1 We want to build a tree with $n = 10$ leaves and $p_0 = 1/3$. There are $\lfloor 10/3 \rfloor = 3$ leaves in the left subtree and 7 in the right subtree. Recursively, 7 leaves of the root right subtree we split $7 = 2 + 5$ so that the left subtree of the root right subtree will end up with two leaves, the right subtree of the root right subtree will have 5 leaves, and so on. At the end we will build a complete parsing tree on 10 leaves.

Let $\mathcal{D} = \{v_1, \ldots v_n\}$ denote the set of phrases of the Boncelet code that are constructed in this way, that is, they correspond to the paths from the root to leaves of the Boncelet's parsing tree, and let $\ell(v_1), \ldots, \ell(v_n)$ be the corresponding phrase lengths. Clearly the probabilities p_0, p_1 induce a probability distribution $P(v_1), \ldots, P(v_n)$ on the leaves of the parsing tree and, thus, on the phrases. This fits naturally to a Bernoulli source with probabilities p_0, p_1 when the input string is partitioned according to $\mathcal{D}$.

Our aim is to understand the probabilistic behavior of the phrase length that we denote as D_n and the average redundancy. By definition the probability generating function of D_n is defined as

$$C(n, y) = \mathbf{E}[y^{D_n}] = \sum_{j=1}^{n} P(v_j) y^{\ell(v_j)}.$$

Boncelet's splitting procedure leads to the following recurrence on $C(n, y)$ for $n \geq 2$:

$$C(n, y) = p_0 y C(\lfloor p_0 n + \delta \rfloor, y) + p_1 y C(\lceil p_1 n - \delta \rceil, y), \tag{4.2}$$

with initial conditions $C(0, y) = 0$ and $C(1, y) = 1$. We shall use this representation again in the last section of this chapter when we sketch a proof of a central limit law for the phrase length.

For now, let us focus on the average phrase length and code redundancy. Let $\overline{D}_n$ denote the average phrase length

$$\overline{D}_n = \mathbf{E}[D_n] = \sum_{j=1}^{n} P(v_j) \ell(v_j),$$

which is also given by $\overline{D}_n = C'(n, 1)$ (where the derivative is taken with respect to y) and satisfies the recurrence

$$\overline{D}_n = 1 + p_0 \overline{D}_{\lfloor p_0 n + \delta \rfloor} + p_0 \overline{D}_{\lceil p_1 n - \delta \rceil} \tag{4.3}$$

---

[1] We should mention that in this chapter we use n to denote the number of leaves and the number of dictionary entries. Notice that in the previous chapters we used M for n, which is more convenient in the context of divide-and-conquer recurrences.

with $\overline{D}_0 = \overline{D}_1 = 0$. This recurrence falls exactly under our divide-and-conquer recurrence (4.1).

We will discuss a more general recurrence in the next section where in Theorem 4.6 we give a general solution of (4.1), and in particular recurrence (4.3), discussed in Example 4.13. In Section 4.2 we present a sketch of the proof of our main result regarding the performance of the Boncelet algorithm.

Theorem 4.2 *Consider a binary memoryless source with positive probabilities $p_0 = p$ and $p_1 = q$ and entropy $h = p \log(1/p) + q \log(1/q)$. Let $\overline{D}_n = \mathbf{E}[D_n]$ denote the expected phrase length of the binary Boncelet code with n phrases.*
(i) If the ratio $(\log p)/(\log q)$ is irrational, then

$$\overline{D}_n = \frac{1}{h} \log n - \frac{\alpha}{h} + o(1), \tag{4.4}$$

where

$$\alpha = \frac{\widetilde{E}'(0) - \widetilde{G}'(0)}{\ln 2} - h - \frac{h_2}{2h}, \tag{4.5}$$

$h_2 = p \log^2(1/p) + q \log^2(1/q)$, and $\widetilde{E}'(0)$ and $\widetilde{G}'(0)$ are the derivatives at $s = 0$ of the Dirichlet series defined in (4.26).
(ii) If $(\log p)/(\log q)$ is rational, then

$$\overline{D}_n = \frac{1}{h} \log n - \frac{\alpha + \Psi(\log n)}{h} + O(n^{-\eta}), \tag{4.6}$$

where $\Psi(t)$ is a periodic function and $\eta > 0$.

Recall from Chapter 3 that for variable-to-fixed codes, the average (normalized) redundancy is expressed as

$$\overline{r}_n = \frac{\log n}{\mathbf{E}[D_n]} - h = \frac{\log n}{\overline{D}_n} - h$$

since every phrase of average length $\overline{D}_n$ requires $\log n$ bits to point to a dictionary entry. Our previous results imply immediately the following corollary.

Corollary 4.3 *Let $\overline{r}_n$ denote the (normalized) average redundancy of the binary Boncelet code (with positive probabilities $p_0 = p$ and $p_1 = q$ and n phrases).*
(i) If the ratio $(\log p)/(\log q)$ is irrational, then

$$\overline{r}_n = \frac{h\alpha}{\log n} + o\left(\frac{1}{\log n}\right) \tag{4.7}$$

with α defined in (4.5).
(ii) If $(\log p)/(\log q)$ is rational, then

$$\overline{r}_n = \frac{h(\alpha + \Psi(\log n))}{\log n} + o\left(\frac{1}{\log n}\right) \tag{4.8}$$

where $\Psi(t)$ is a periodic function.

Let us now compare the redundancy of Boncelet's algorithm to the asymptotically optimal Tunstall algorithm. From Corollary 3.5, we know that the redundancy of the Tunstall
/ code is[2]

$$\bar{r}_n^K = \frac{h}{\log n}\left(-\log(h\ln 2) - \frac{h_2}{2h}\right) + o\left(\frac{1}{\log n}\right)$$

(provided that $(\log p)/(\log q)$ is irrational; in the rational case there is also a periodic term in
the leading asymptotics).

Example 4.4 Consider $p = 1/3$ and $q = 2/3$. Then the recurrence for $\overline{D}_n$ is precisely the
same as that of Example 4.13. Consequently, $\alpha \approx 0.0518$ while for the Tunstall code the
corresponding constant in front of $h/\log n$ is equal to $-\log(h\ln 2) - \frac{h_2}{2h} \approx 0.0496$.

It is also interesting to study the asymptotic behavior of the distribution of the phrase
length D_n. Actually a precise analysis of the recurrence (4.2), explained in Section 4.3, leads
to the following result.

Theorem 4.5 *Consider a binary memoryless source with $p \neq q$. Then the phrase length
distribution D_n of the corresponding Boncelet code with n phrases satisfies the central limit
law; that is,*

$$\frac{D_n - \frac{1}{h}\log n}{\sqrt{\left(\frac{h_2}{h^3} - \frac{1}{h}\right)\log n}} \to N(0,1),$$

where $N(0,1)$ denotes the standard normal distribution, and

$$\mathbf{E}[D_n] = \frac{\log n}{h} + O(1), \quad \mathbf{Var}\,[D_n] \sim \left(\frac{h_2}{h^3} - \frac{1}{h}\right)\log n$$

for $n \to \infty$.

4.2 Divide-and-Conquer Recurrence

To prove Theorem 4.2, we will rely quite heavily on a solution of the divide-and-conquer
recurrence that we describe next in some generality.

We shall assume that a problem of size n is split into m subproblems. It is natural to assume
that there is a cost associated with combining subproblems together to find the solution. We
denote such a cost by a_n. In addition, each subproblem may contribute in a different way
to the final solution; we represent this by coefficients b_j and $\bar{b}_j$ for $1 \leq j \leq m$. Finally, we
postulate that the original input n is divided into subproblems of size $\lfloor h_j(n) \rfloor$ and $\lceil \bar{h}_j(n) \rceil$,
$1 \leq j \leq m$, where $h_j(x)$ and $\bar{h}_j(x)$ are functions that satisfy $h_j(x) \sim \bar{h}_j(x) \sim p_j x$ for $x \to \infty$
and for some $0 < p_j < 1$. We aim at presenting precise asymptotic solutions of *discrete*
divide-and-conquer recurrences of the following form for $n \geq 2$:

$$T(n) = a_n + \sum_{j=1}^{m} b_j T\left(\lfloor h_j(n) \rfloor\right) + \sum_{j=1}^{m} \bar{b}_j T\left(\lceil \bar{h}_j(n) \rceil\right). \tag{4.9}$$

---

[2] Recall that we now write n for the dictionary size M.

A popular approach to solve this recurrence is to relax it to a *continuous* version of the following form (hereafter we assume $\bar{b}_j = 0$ for simplicity):

$$T(x) = a(x) + \sum_{j=1}^{m} b_j T(h_j(x)), \quad x > 1, \tag{4.10}$$

where $h_j(x) \sim p_j x$ with $0 < p_j < 1$, and solve it using a master theorem of a divide-and-conquer recurrence. The most general solution of (4.10) is due to Akra and Bazzi (1998) who proved (under certain regularity assumptions, namely that $a'(x)$ is of polynomial growth and that $h_j(x) - p_j x = O(x/(\ln x)^2)$)

$$T(x) = \Theta\left(x^{s_0}\left(1 + \int_1^x \frac{a(u)}{u^{s_0+1}} du\right)\right), \tag{4.11}$$

where s_0 is a unique real root of

$$\sum_j b_j p_j^s = 1. \tag{4.12}$$

Actually, this also leads directly to (see Exercise 4.3)

$$T(n) = \Theta\left(n^{s_0}\left(1 + \sum_{j=1}^{n} \frac{a_j}{j^{s_0+1}}\right)\right) \tag{4.13}$$

in the discrete version provided that $a_{n+1} - a_n$ is at most of polynomial growth.

Discrete versions of the divide-and-conquer recurrence given by (4.9) are more subtle and require a different approach. We will use a Dirichlet series (closely related to the Mellin transform) that better captures the discrete nature of the recurrence, and then apply Tauberian theorems together with the Mellin–Perron formula presented in Appendix D.

We now present asymptotics of the divide-and-conquer recurrence when the sequences a_n of the form $a_n = Cn^a(\ln n)^b$ (with $C > 0$ and $a, b \geq 0$).

Theorem 4.6 (Drmota and Szpankowski 2013) *Let $T(n)$ be the divide-and-conquer recurrence defined in (4.9) with $a_n = Cn^a(\ln n)^b$ ($C > 0$, $a, b \geq 0$) such that the following hold:*

(A1) b_j and $\bar{b}_j$ are nonnegative with $b_j + \bar{b}_j > 0$,

(A2) $h_j(x)$ and $\bar{h}_j(x)$ are increasing and nonnegative functions such that $h_j(x) = p_j x + O(x^{1-\delta})$ and $\bar{h}_j(x) = p_j x + O(x^{1-\delta})$ for positive $p_j < 1$ and $\delta > 0$, with $h_j(n) < n$ and $\bar{h}_j(n) \leq n - 1$ for all $n \geq 2$.

Furthermore, let s_0 be the unique real solution of the equation

$$\sum_{j=1}^{m} (b_j + \bar{b}_j) p_j^{s_0} = 1. \tag{4.14}$$

Then the sequence $T(n)$ has the following asymptotic behavior:

(i) If $a > s_0$, then

$$T(n) = \begin{cases} C'n^a(\ln n)^b + O\left(n^a(\ln n)^{b-1}\right) & \text{if } b > 0, \\ C'n^a + O(n^{a-\delta'}) & \text{if } b = 0, \end{cases}$$

where $\delta' = \min\{a - s_0, \delta\}$ and

$$C' = \frac{C}{1 - \sum_{j=1}^{m}(b_j + \overline{b}_j)p_j^a}.$$

(ii) If $a = s_0$, then

$$T(n) = C''n^a(\ln n)^{b+1} + O\left(n^a(\ln n)^b\right)$$

with

$$C'' = \frac{C}{(b+1)\sum_{j=1}^{m}(b_j + \overline{b}_j)p_j^a \ln(1/p_j)}.$$

(iii) If $a < s_0$ (or if we just assume that $a_n = O(n^a)$ for some $a < s_0$ as long as a_n is a non-negative and nondecreasing sequence), then for $\log p_1, \ldots, \log p_m$ irrationally related (see Chapter 3),

$$T(n) \sim C'''n^{s_0},$$

where C''' is a positive constant. If $\log p_1, \ldots, \log p_m$ are rationally related and if we also assume that (the so-called "small growth property")

$$T(n+1) - T(n) = O\left(n^{s_0-\eta}\right) \tag{4.15}$$

holds for some $\eta > 1 - \delta$, then

$$T(n) = \Psi(\log n) n^{s_0} + O\left(n^{s_0-\eta'}\right)$$

where $\Psi(t)$ is a positive and periodic continuous function with period L and $\eta' > 0$.

We now offer some remarks.

Remark 4.7 The order of magnitude of $T(n)$ can be checked easily using Akra and Bazzi (1998). In particular, if we just know an upper bound for a_n of the form $a_n = O(n^a(\ln n)^b)$ – even if a_n is not necessarily increasing – the Akra–Bazzi theorem provides an upper bound for $T(n)$ of the form stated in Theorem 4.6. Hence, the theorem can be easily adapted to cover a_n of the form

$$a_n = Cn^a(\ln n)^b + O((n^{a_1}(\ln n)^{b_1})$$

with $a_1 < a$ or with $a_1 = a$ but $b_1 < b$. We split up the solution $T(n)$ into $T(n) = T_1(n) + T_2(n)$, where $T_1(n)$ corresponds to $a_n^{(1)} = Cn^a(\ln n)^b$, for which we can apply Theorem 4.6, and $T_2(n)$ corresponds to the error term $a_n^{(2)} = O((n^{a_1}(\ln n)^{b_1})$, for which we apply the Akra–Bazzi theorem.

The same idea can be used for a bootstrapping procedure. Theorem 4.6 provides the asymptotic leading term for $T(n)$ that is (for example, in case (i)) of the form $C'n^a(\ln n)^b$. Hence, by setting $T(n) = C'n^a(\ln n)^b + S(n)$, we obtain a recurrence for $S(n)$ that is precisely of the form (4.9) with a new sequence a_n that is of smaller order than the previous one. At this step we can either apply Theorem 4.6 a second time or the Akra–Bazzi theorem.

Remark 4.8   Theorem 4.6 can be extended to the case

$$a_n = Cn^a(\ln n)^b,$$

where $a > 0$ and b is an arbitrary real number. The same result holds with the only exception $a = s_0$ and $b = -1$. In this case, we obtain

$$T(n) = C''n^a \ln \ln n + O\left(n^a(\ln n)^{-1}\right)$$

with

$$C'' = \frac{C}{\sum_{j=1}^m b_j p_j^a \ln(1/p_j)}.$$

Remark 4.9   The third case (iii): $a < s_0$, is of particular interest. Let us consider first the irrationally related case. Even in this case, it is not immediately clear how to explicitly describe the constant C'''. It depends heavily on a_n and also on $T(n)$ and can be written as

$$C''' = \frac{\widetilde{A}(s_0) + \sum_{j=1}^m b_j(G_j(s_0) - E_j(s_0)) + \sum_{j=1}^m \overline{b}_j(\overline{G}_j(s_0) - \overline{E}_j(s_0))}{s_0 \sum_{j=1}^m (b_j + \overline{b}_j)p_j^{s_0} \ln(1/p_j)} \tag{4.16}$$

with

$$\widetilde{A}(s) = \sum_{n=1}^\infty \frac{a_{n+2} - a_{n+1}}{n^s},$$

and

$$G_j(s) = \sum_{n < n_j(1)} \frac{T\left(\lfloor h_j(n+2)\rfloor\right) - T\left(\lfloor h_j(n+1)\rfloor\right)}{n^s} \tag{4.17}$$

$$+ \frac{T(2) - T\left(\lfloor h_j(n_j(1)+1)\rfloor\right)}{n_j(1)},$$

$$E_j(s) = \sum_{k=1}^\infty (T(k+2) - T(k+1))\left(\frac{1}{(k/p_j)^s} - \frac{1}{n_j(k)^s}\right), \tag{4.18}$$

where $n_j(k) = \max\{n \geq 1 : h_j(n+1) < k+2\}$, and

$$\overline{G}_j(s) = \sum_{n < \overline{n}_j(1)} \frac{T\left(\lceil \overline{h}_j(n+2)\rceil\right) - T\left(\lceil \overline{h}_j(n+1)\rceil\right)}{n^s}$$

$$+ \frac{T(2) - T\left(\lceil \overline{h}_j(n_j(1)+1)\rceil\right)}{n_j(1)},$$

$$\overline{E}_j(s) = \sum_{k=1}^\infty (T(k+2) - T(k+1))\left(\frac{1}{(k/p_j)^s} - \frac{1}{\overline{n}_j(k)^s}\right),$$

where $\overline{n}_j(k) = \min\{n \geq 1 : \overline{h}_j(n+2) > k+1\}$. We will show in the proof of Section 4.2.2 that the series $\widetilde{A}(s_0)$, $E_j(s_0)$ and $\overline{E}_j(s_0)$ actually converge. It should be also mentioned that there is no general error term in the asymptotic relation $T(n) \sim C'''n^{s_0}$.

In the rationally related case, the periodic function $\Psi(t)$ has a convergent Fourier series $\Psi(t) = \sum_k c_k e^{2k\pi i x/L}$, where the Fourier coefficients are given by

$$c_k = \frac{\widetilde{A}(s_k) + \sum_{j=1}^{m} b_j(G_j(s_k) - E_j(s_k)) + \sum_{j=1}^{m} \overline{b}_j(\overline{G}_j(s_k) - \overline{E}_j(s_k))}{s_k \sum_{j=1}^{m}(b_j + \overline{b}_j)p_j^{s_0} \ln(1/p_j)}, \tag{4.19}$$

where $s_k = s_0 + 2k\pi i/L$. In particular, the constant coefficient c_0 equals C'''. Note that it cannot be deduced from this representation that the Fourier series is convergent. This makes the problem really subtle.

Remark 4.10 The *small growth condition* (4.15) is important for the asymptotics. In examples of Section 4.2.1, we discuss several recurrences in which this conditions holds and doesn't lead to different asymptotic behavior.

We next present some applications of our main Theorem 4.6 before presenting a sketch of its proof.

4.2.1 Examples

We first illustrate our theorem on a few simple divide-and-conquer recurrences. Note that we only consider examples for the case (iii) and (ii), since they are more interesting. For more recurrences, see Exercises 4.6–4.9.

Example 4.11 The recurrence

$$T(n) = T(\lfloor n/2 \rfloor) + 2\,T(\lceil n/2 \rceil) + n$$

is related to the Karatsuba algorithm as discussed in Knuth (1998a). Here, after solving the characteristic equation (4.14), we find

$$s_0 = \ln(1/3)/\ln(1/2) = 1.5849\ldots$$

and $s_0 > a = 1$. Furthermore, since $m = 1$, we are in the rationally related case. Here the small growth condition (4.15) is satisfied so that we can apply Theorem 4.6 to obtain

$$T(n) = \Psi(\log n)\,n^{\frac{\ln 3}{\ln 2}} \cdot (1 + o(1)) \qquad (n \to \infty)$$

with some continuous periodic function $\Psi(t)$.

In a similar manner, the Strassen algorithm as discussed in Knuth (1998a) for matrix multiplications results in the following recurrence:

$$T(n) = T(\lfloor n/2 \rfloor) + 6\,T(\lceil n/2 \rceil) + n^2.$$

Here we have $m = 1$, $s_0 = \ln 7/\ln 2 \approx 2.81$ and $a = 2$, and again we get a representation of the form

$$T(n) = \Psi(\log n)\,n^{\frac{\ln 7}{\ln 2}} \cdot (1 + o(1)) \qquad (n \to \infty)$$

with some periodic function $\Psi(t)$.

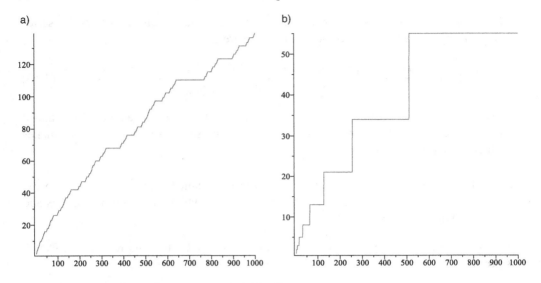

Figure 4.1 Illustration to Example 4.12: (a) recurrence
$T(n) = T(\lfloor n/2 \rfloor) + T(\lceil n/4 \rceil)$, (b) recurrence $T(n) = T(\lfloor n/2 \rfloor) + T(\lfloor n/4 \rfloor)$.

Example 4.12 The next two examples show that a small change in the recurrence might change the asymptotic behavior significantly. First, let

$$T(n) = T(\lfloor n/2 \rfloor) + T(\lceil n/4 \rceil)$$

with $T(1) = 1$. Here we have $s_0 = \ln((1 + \sqrt{5})/2) \ln 2 \approx 0.6942$ and we are in the rationally related case. Furthermore, it follows easily that $T(n+1) - T(n) \le 1$. Hence, the small growth condition (4.15) is satisfied and we obtain

$$T(n) \sim n^{s_0} \Psi(\log n)$$

for a continuous periodic function $\Psi(t)$; see Figure 4.1(a).

However, if we just replace the ceiling function by the floor function, that is,

$$\widetilde{T}(n) = \widetilde{T}(\lfloor n/2 \rfloor) + \widetilde{T}(\lfloor n/4 \rfloor) \qquad \text{for } n \ge 4$$

and $\widetilde{T}(1) = \widetilde{T}(2) = \widetilde{T}(3) = 1$, then the small growth condition (4.15) is not satisfied. We get $\widetilde{T}(n) = F_k$ for $2^{k-1} \le n < 2^k$, where F_k denotes the kth Fibonacci number. This leads to

$$\widetilde{T}(n) \sim n^{s_0} \widetilde{\Psi}(\log n),$$

where $\widetilde{\Psi}(t) = ((1 + \sqrt{5})/2)^{1-\langle t \rangle}/\sqrt{5}$ is discontinuous for $t = 0$; see also Figure 4.1(b).

Example 4.13 Finally, we consider a recurrence for the Boncelet's algorithm with $p_0 = 1/3$ and $p_1 = 2/3$. Then

$$T(n) = \frac{1}{3} T\left(\left\lfloor \frac{n}{3} + \frac{1}{2} \right\rfloor\right) + \frac{2}{3} T\left(\left\lceil \frac{2n}{3} - \frac{1}{2} \right\rceil\right) + 1$$

with initial value $T(1) = 0$. Its asymptotic solution is given by

$$T(n) = \frac{1}{h}\log n + C + o(1),$$

with $h = \frac{1}{3}\log 3 + \frac{2}{3}\log\frac{3}{2}$ and some constant C. We can compute $C = -\alpha/h$, where

$$\alpha = \sum_{m\geq 1} \frac{T(m+2) - T(m+1)}{3}\left(\log\left\lceil 3m + \frac{5}{2}\right\rceil - \log(3m)\right) \tag{4.20}$$

$$+ 2\sum_{m\geq 1} \frac{T(m+2) - T(m+1)}{3}\left(\log\left\lfloor\frac{3}{2}m + \frac{5}{4}\right\rfloor - \log\left(\frac{3m}{2}\right)\right)$$

$$+ \frac{\log 3}{3} - h - \frac{\frac{1}{3}\log^2 3 + \frac{2}{3}\log^2\frac{3}{2}}{2h}.$$

We have used this example for computing the redundancy of the binary Boncelet code in Example 4.4.

4.2.2 Sketch of Proof of Theorem 4.6

We present here only a part of the proof of Theorem 4.6. A complete detailed proof can be found in Drmota and Szpankowski (2013), to which we refer the interested reader.

Let us start with defining some appropriate Dirichlet series whose analysis will lead to asymptotic behavior of $T(n)$. We set

$$\widetilde{T}(s) = \sum_{n=1}^{\infty} \frac{T(n+2) - T(n+1)}{n^s},$$

provided the series is convergent. By partial summation and using a priori upper bounds for the sequence $T(n)$, it follows that $\widetilde{T}(s)$ converges (absolutely) for $s \in \mathbb{C}$ with $\Re(s) > \max\{s_0, \sigma_a, 0\}$, where s_0 is the real solution of Equation (4.14), and σ_a is the abscissa of absolute convergence of $\widetilde{A}(s)$ defined as

$$\widetilde{A}(s) = \sum_{n=1}^{\infty} \frac{a_{n+2} - a_{n+1}}{n^s}. \tag{4.21}$$

To find a formula for $\widetilde{T}(s)$ we apply the recurrence relation (4.9). To simplify our presentation, we first assume that $\overline{b}_j = 0$, that is, we consider only the floor function on the right-hand side of the recurrence (4.9); those parts that contain the ceiling function can be handled in the same way. We thus obtain

$$\widetilde{T}(s) = \widetilde{A}(s) + \sum_{j=1}^{m} b_j \sum_{n=1}^{\infty} \frac{T\left(\lfloor h_j(n+2)\rfloor\right) - T\left(\lfloor h_j(n+1)\rfloor\right)}{n^s}.$$

For $k \geq 1$ set

$$n_j(k) := \max\{n \geq 1 : h_j(n+1) < k + 2\}.$$

By definition, it is clear that $n_j(k+1) \geq n_j(k)$ and

$$n_j(k) = \frac{n}{p_j} + O\left(k^{1-\delta}\right). \tag{4.22}$$

Furthermore, by setting $G_j(s)$, we obtain

$$\sum_{n=1}^{\infty} \frac{T\left(\lfloor h_j(n+2)\rfloor\right) - T\left(\lfloor h_j(n+1)\rfloor\right)}{n^s}$$

$$= G_j(s) + \sum_{k=1}^{\infty} \frac{T(k+2) - T(k+1)}{n_j(k)^s}.$$

We now compare the last sum to $p_j^s \widetilde{T}(s)$:

$$\sum_{k=1}^{\infty} \frac{T(k+2) - T(k+1)}{n_j(k)^s} = \sum_{k=1}^{\infty} \frac{T(k+2) - T(k+1)}{(k/p_j)^s}$$

$$- \sum_{k=1}^{\infty} (T(k+2) - T(k+1))\left(\frac{1}{(k/p_j)^s} - \frac{1}{n_j(k)^s}\right) = p_j^s \widetilde{T}(s) - E_j(s),$$

where $E_j(s)$ is

$$G_j(s) = \sum_{n < n_j(1)} \frac{T\left(\lfloor h_j(n+2)\rfloor\right) - T\left(\lfloor h_j(n+1)\rfloor\right)}{n^s}$$

$$+ \frac{T(2) - T\left(\lfloor h_j(n_j(1)+1)\rfloor\right)}{n_j(1)}, \tag{4.23}$$

$$E_j(s) = \sum_{k=1}^{\infty} (T(k+2) - T(k+1))\left(\frac{1}{(k/p_j)^s} - \frac{1}{n_j(k)^s}\right). \tag{4.24}$$

Defining

$$E(s) = \sum_{j=1}^{m} b_j E_j(s) \quad \text{and} \quad G(s) = \sum_{j=1}^{m} b_j G_j(s),$$

we finally obtain the relation

$$\widetilde{T}(s) = \frac{\widetilde{A}(s) + G(s) - E(s)}{1 - \sum_{j=1}^{m} b_j p_j^s}. \tag{4.25}$$

As mentioned in Theorem 4.2, (almost) the same procedure applies if some of the $\overline{b}_j$ are positive; that is, the ceiling function also appears in the recurrence equation. The only difference to (4.25) is that we arrive at a representation of the form

$$\widetilde{T}(s) = \frac{\widetilde{A}(s) + \widetilde{G}(s) - \widetilde{E}(s)}{1 - \sum_{j=1}^{m} (b_j + \overline{b}_j) p_j^s}, \tag{4.26}$$

with properly modified functions $\widetilde{G}(s)$ and $\widetilde{E}(s)$, however, they have the same analyticity properties as in (4.25).

For the asymptotic analysis we will only consider the irrational case for which we apply Tauberian theory. The analysis of the rational case is based on the inverse Mellin transform and quite involved calculations, see Appendix D. The reader is asked in Exercise 4.10 to provide missing details.

We recall that we have a representation (4.25) of the Dirichlet series $\widetilde{T}(s) = \sum_{n \geq 1}(T(n+2) - T(n+1))n^{-s}$, where $T(n+2) \geq T(n+1)$, and that we are interested in the asymptotic behavior of

$$T(n) = T(2) + \sum_{k=1}^{n-2}(T(k+2) - T(k+1)). \tag{4.27}$$

Hence, it is sufficient to get some information on the partial sums of the coefficient of the Dirichlet series $\widetilde{T}(s)$.

For the asymptotic analysis, we recall the fact that a Dirichlet series $C(s) = \sum_{n \geq 1} c_n n^{-s}$ can be represented as the Mellin–Stieltjes transform of the partial sums $\bar{c}(v) = \sum_{n \leq v} c_n$ (see Appendix D):

$$C(s) = \sum_{n \geq 1} \frac{c_n}{n^s} = \int_0^\infty v^{-s}\, d\bar{c}(v).$$

In our present context we set

$$\bar{c}(v) = \sum_{n \leq v}(T(n+2) - T(n+1))$$

so that we get

$$T(n) = T(2) + \bar{c}(n-2).$$

Hence, the asymptotic behavior of $T(n)$ depends on the asymptotic behavior of $\bar{c}(v)$, which is reflected by the singular behavior of $\frac{1}{s}\widetilde{T}(s)$; see the Wiener–Ikehara Tauberian theorem D.3 from Appendix D. Clearly, the singularities of $\frac{1}{a}\widetilde{A}(s)$ are at least $s = 0$ and the roots of the denominator in (4.26); that is, roots of the *characteristic equation*

$$\sum_{j=1}^{m}(b_j + \bar{b}_j)p_j^s = 1. \tag{4.28}$$

(Note that s_0 is the unique real solution of this equation.) Furthermore, there might be singularities from $\widetilde{A}(s)$, $\widetilde{G}(s)$, and $\widetilde{E}(s)$.

By assumption, we know that $a_n = Cn^a(\ln n)^b$ for some $a > 0$ and some real number b. By Theorem D.5 from Appendix D, we know that $\widetilde{A}(s)$ can be represented as

$$\widetilde{A}(s) = b\frac{\Gamma(b+1)}{(s-a)^{b+1}} + \frac{\Gamma(b+1)}{(s-a)^b} + G(s) \tag{4.29}$$

if b is not a negative integer, or we have

$$\widetilde{A}(s) = \sigma\frac{(-1)^k}{(k-1)!}(s-a)^{k-1}\ln(s-a) \tag{4.30}$$

$$+ \frac{k(-1)^k}{(k-1)!}(s-a)^k\ln(s-a) + G(s)$$

if $b = -k$ is a negative integer. In both cases, $G(s)$ is analytic for $\Re(s) > a - 1$.

We also note that an estimate of the form $a_n = O(n^a)$ implies that the function $\overline{a}(v) = \sum_{n \geq v}(a_{n+2} - a_{n+1})$ satisfies

$$\overline{a}(v) = O(v^a).$$

Consequently the Dirichlet series

$$\widetilde{A}(s) = \sum_{n \geq 1} \frac{a_{n+2} - a_{n+1}}{n^s} = s \int_0^\infty \overline{a}(v)v^{-s-1}\, dv$$

represents an analytic function for $\Re(s) > a$.

By the same reasoning, it follows that the function $\widetilde{E}(s)$ is analytic for $\Re(s) > s_0 - \delta$. For example, by using the Akra–Bazzi theorem we have the a priori upper bound $T(n) = O(n^{s_0})$. Furthermore,

$$\frac{1}{(k/p_j)^s} - \frac{1}{n_j(k)^s} = O\left(\frac{1}{(k/p_j)^{\Re(s)+\delta}}\right).$$

Hence, by partial summation and by the monotonicity of the sequences $T(n)$, it follows that the series

$$\sum_{k \geq 1} (T(k+2) - T(k+1)) \frac{1}{(k/p_j)^{\Re(s)+\delta}}$$

represents an analytic function for $\Re(s) > s_0 - \delta$. Hence, the same holds for the function $\widetilde{E}(s)$.

Summing up, we see that $\widetilde{T}(s)$ is an analytic function for $\Re(s) > \max\{s_0, a\}$. Hence, we have to distinguish three different cases: $a > s_0$, $a = s_0$ and $a < s_0$. These three cases correspond to the different parts of the master theorem for the divide-and-conquer recurrence, Theorem 4.6. In the first case, the (asymptotic) behavior of a_n dominates the asymptotics of $T(n)$, in the second case, there is an *interaction* between the internal structure of the recurrence and the sequence a_n (resonance), and in the third case the behavior of the solution is driven by the recurrence and does not depend on a_n

So let us consider first the case $a > s_0$. From (4.29) and (4.30) it follows that $\frac{1}{s}\widetilde{T}(s)$ has a meromorphic extension to $\Re(s) > s_0$ with polar singularity at $s = a$. Hence, we directly apply the Wiener–Ikehara Theorem D.3 and obtain

$$T(n) = T(2) + \overline{c}(n-2) \sim C'n^a(\ln n)^b$$

for a proper constant $C' > 0$. (By using the inverse Mellin transform it is also possible to obtain the proposed error term.)

Next suppose that $a < s_0$; that is, the third case. Here s_0 is the dominant singularity. Since we are in the irrational case there are no other singularities on the line $\Re(s) = s_0$. Consequently the assumptions of Theorem D.3 are satisfied (with $K = 0$) and it directly follows that

$$T(n) \sim C'''n^{s_0}$$

for some positive constant C'''. Note that we do not require the precise behavior of a_n. We just have to assume that a_n is nondecreasing and that $a_n = O(n^a)$ for some $a < s_0$.

Finally, if $s_0 = a$ then the singularities of $\widetilde{A}(s)$ and that of $\left(1 - \sum_{j=1}^{m} b_j p_j^s\right)^{-1}$ coincide. In particular, the order of the polar singularity at $s = s_0 = a$ is now $b + 2$. Furthermore, in the irrational case, this is the only singularity on the line $\Re(s) = s_0$. Again the assumptions of Theorem D.3 are satisfied so that the result follows:

$$a_n \sim C'' n^a (\ln n)^{b+1}$$

as desired.

4.3 Central Limit Law for Boncelet's Algorithms

We next provide a very brief sketch of the proof of the central limit theorem for the phrase length D_n of the Boncelet algorithm that is stated in Theorem 4.5. Again we only consider the irrationally related case for a binary alphabet.

To deal with $C(n, y)$, we consider the Dirichlet series:

$$C(s, y) = \sum_{n=1}^{\infty} \frac{C(n+2, y) - C(n+1, y)}{n^s}.$$

For simplicity, we just consider here the case $y > 1$. (The case $y \leq 1$ can be handled in a similar way.) Then $C(s, y)$ converges for $\Re(s) > s_0(y)$, where $s_0(y)$ denotes the real zero of the equation (for a binary alphabet)

$$y(p^{s+1} + q^{s+1}) = 1$$

discussed in Lemma D.7. We find

$$C(s, y) = \frac{(y - 1) - \widetilde{E}(s, y)}{1 - y(p^{s+1} + q^{s+1})},$$

where

$$\widetilde{E}(s, y) = py \sum_{k=1}^{\infty} (C(k+2, y)) - C(k+1, y)) \left(\frac{1}{(k/p)^s} - \frac{1}{\left(\left\lceil \frac{k+2-\delta}{p} \right\rceil - 2\right)^s} \right)$$

$$+ qy \sum_{k=1}^{\infty} (C(k+2, y)) - C(k+1, y)) \left(\frac{1}{(k/q)^s} - \frac{1}{\left(\left\lceil \frac{k+1+\delta}{q} \right\rceil - 1\right)^s} \right)$$

converges for $\Re(s) > s_0(y) - 1$ and satisfies $\widetilde{E}(0, y) = 0$ and $\widetilde{E}(s, 1) = 0$.

Then by the Wiener–Ikehara theorem only the residue at $s_0(y)$ contributes to the main asymptotic leading term. (Recall that we consider the case $y > 1$.) We thus have

$$C(n, y) \sim \text{Res} \left(\frac{((y-1) - \widetilde{E}(s, y))(n - 3/2)^s}{s(1 - y(p^{s+1} + q^{s+1}))}; s = s_0(y) \right)$$

$$= \frac{((y-1) - \widetilde{E}(s_0(y), y))(n - 3/2)^{s_0(y)}}{-s_0(y)(\ln(p)p^{s_0(y)+1} + \ln(q)q^{s_0(y)+1})} (1 + o(1)).$$

The essential but non-trivial observation is that this asymptotic relation holds uniform for y in an interval around 1. This can actually be checked in the same way as for the example that is discussed at the end of Appendix D. So let us assume that this uniformity holds. Then we are precisely in the same situation as in the case of the Tunstall code (see Chapter 3) and we obtain a central limit theorem.

As in the previous cases, the rationally related case is even more subtle. In Exercise 4.12, we ask the reader to supply details of the proof.

4.4 Exercises

4.1   Build the Boncelet's parsing tree for $n = 22$ and $p_0 = 1/4$.

4.2   Derive a more precise formula for the oscillating function $\Psi(\log n)$ appearing in (4.6) of Theorem 4.2.

4.3   Derive Akra and Bazzi (1998) formulas (4.11) and (4.13) for the continuous version of the divide-and-conquer recurrence.

4.4   Consider again Examples 4.11–4.13 and consider continuous versions of them; that is, without floor or ceiling function. Apply Akra and Bazzi (1998) formula (4.11) or (4.13) to analyze these recurrences.

4.5   Prove the estimate (4.20) in Example 4.13.

4.6   Consider the recurrence

$$T(n) = 2\,T(\lfloor n/2 \rfloor) + 3\,T(\lfloor n/6 \rfloor) + n \log n.$$

Let $s_0 = 1.402\ldots > 1$ be the solution of the characteristic equation (4.14). Show that

$$T(n) \sim Cn^{s_0} \qquad (n \to \infty)$$

for some constant C.

4.7   Consider the following recurrence

$$T(n) = 2T(\lfloor n/2 \rfloor) + 1 \quad \text{(with } T(1) = 1\text{)}.$$

Show that

$$T(n) = 2^{\lfloor \log n \rfloor + 1} - 1$$

and

$$T(n) = n\Psi(\log n) - 1$$

with $\Psi(t) = 2^{1 - \{t\}}$.

4.8   Consider the recurrence

$$T(n) = 2\,T\left(\left\lfloor \frac{2}{3}n \right\rfloor\right)$$

with $T(1) = 1$. Show that $T(n) = 2^k$ for $n_k \le n < n_{k+1}$, where $n_0 = 1$ and $n_{k+1} = \lceil \frac{3}{2}n_k \rceil$.

4.9   Study the recurrence

$$T(n) = 2\,T\left(\left\lfloor \frac{n + 2\sqrt{n} + 1}{2} \right\rfloor\right) \qquad (n \ge 6)$$

with $T(n) = 1$ for $1 \le n \le 5$. Show that

$$T(n) = 2^k, \quad n_k \le n < n_{k+1},$$

where $n_1 = 6$ and $n_{k+1} = \lceil 2n_k + 1 - 2\sqrt{2n_k} \rceil$. It then follows that n_k is asymptotically of the form $n_k = c_1 2^k - c_2 2^{k/2} + O(1)$ (for certain positive constants c_1, c_2). Show finally that it is not possible to represent $T(n)$ asymptotically as $T(n) \sim n\Psi(\log n)$.

4.10 Establish Theorem 4.6 for the rational cases.

4.11 Prove Theorem D.5. See also Drmota and Szpankowski (2013).

4.12 Provide missing details for the proof of Theorem 4.5 in the rational case.

4.13 Analyze the Boncelet algorithm for Markov sources.

Bibliographical Notes

Divide-and-conquer is a very popular strategy to design algorithms. It splits the input into several smaller subproblems, solving each subproblem separately, and then knitting together to solve the original problem. Typical examples include heapsort, mergesort, discrete Fourier transform, queues, sorting networks, compression algorithms as discussed in Cormen, Leierson, and Rivest (1990), Knuth (1998a), Roura (2001), Szpankowski (2001) and Flajolet and Sedgewick (2008).

It is relatively easy to determine the general growth order of the (continuous) divide and concur recurrence as discussed in Roura (2001). A precise asymptotic analysis is often appreciably more subtle. The most general solution of the continuous version of the divide-and-conquer is due to Akra and Bazzi (1998). The literature on continuous divide-and-conquer recurrence is very extensive. We mention here Akra and Bazzi (1998), Cormen et al. (1990), Roura (2001).

The discrete version of the divide-and-conquer recurrence has received much less attention, especially with respect to precise asymptotics. For example, Flajolet and Golin (1954) and Cheung et al. (2008) studied the recurrence but only for $p_1 = p_2 = 1/2$. Furthermore, Erdős et al. (1987) applied renewal theory and Hwang (2000) (cf. also Grabner and Hwang (2005), Hwang and Janson (2011)) used analytic techniques to analyze similar recurrences. The oscillatory behavior of some divide-and-conquer was observed in Delange (1954, 1975), Grabner and Hwang (2005).

Dirichlet series and the Mellin–Perron formula are discussed in many books. We mention here Apostol (1976). Tauberian theorems are well presented in Korevaar (2002). See also our Appendix C.

The Boncelet's algorithm was introduced by Boncelet (1993). The whole chapter is based on Drmota and Szpankowski (2013) and Drmota et al. (2010).

5

Khodak VV Codes

In the last three chapters, we discussed fixed-to-variables FV codes such as Shannon and Huffman codes (see Chapter 2), and variable-to-fixed VF codes such as Tunstall, Khodak, and Boncelet codes (see Chapters 3 and 4). As a consequence of Theorems 2.1 and 2.3, it follows that the *normalized* redundancy is inversely proportional to the block length n; that is, of order $\Theta(1/n)$. In Theorems 3.4 and 3.6, we analyzed Khodak and Tunstall VF codes and proved that the average redundancy (see in particular Corollary 3.5) decays like $\Theta(1/\mathbf{E}[D])$, where $\mathbf{E}[D]$ is the average phrase length of the input string. In summary, for both FV and VF codes the normalized redundancy (rate) decays inversely proportional to the (average) phrase length (that we will denote by $\overline{D}$).

However, it is an intriguing question whether one can construct a code with normalized redundancy of order $o(1/\overline{D})$. This quest was accomplished by Khodak (1972), who proved that one can find a variable-to-variable VV code with normalized redundancy of order $O(\overline{D}^{-5/3})$. In this chapter, we present a transparent proof and an *explicit algorithm* to achieve this bound. We also will show that the *maximal* normalized redundancy is $O(\overline{D}^{-4/3})$. Finally, in a major extension of Khodak's results we present stronger results for *almost all* sources.

5.1 Variable-to-Variable Codes and Redundancy Rate

A variable-to-variable (VV) length code partitions a source sequence into variable length phrases that are encoded into strings of variable lengths. While it is well known that every VV (prefix) code is a concatenation of a variable-to-fixed length code (e.g., Tunstall code) and a fixed-to-variable length encoding (e.g., Huffman code), an optimal VV code for a given dictionary size has not yet been found.

Let us first briefly describe a VV encoder. A VV encoder has two components, a *parser* and a *string encoder*. The parser partitions the source sequence x into phrases from a predetermined dictionary $\mathcal{D}$. We shall write d or d_i for a dictionary entry, and by $\overline{D}$ we denote the average dictionary (phrase) length also known as the average delay. As argued in previous chapters, a convenient way of representing the dictionary $\mathcal{D}$ is by a complete m-ary tree also known as the *parsing tree*. Next, the string encoder in a VV scheme maps each dictionary phrase into its corresponding binary codeword $C(d)$ of length $|C(d)| = \ell(d)$. Throughout this chapter, we assume that the string encoder is a slightly modified Shannon code and we concentrate on building a parsing tree for which $-\log P(d)$ ($d \in \mathcal{D}$) is close to an integer. This allows us to construct a VV code with redundancy rates (per symbol) approaching zero as the average delay increases.

In (3.2) of Chapter 3, we define the normalized average redundancy rate as

$$\bar{r} = \frac{\sum_{d \in \mathcal{D}} P(d)\ell(d) - h_{\mathcal{D}}}{\mathbf{E}[D]} = \frac{\sum_{d \in \mathcal{D}} P(d)(\ell(d) + \log P(d))}{\mathbf{E}[D]}, \tag{5.1}$$

where P is the probability law of the dictionary phrases and

$$\mathbf{E}[D] = \sum_{d \in \mathcal{D}} |d| P(d) =: \overline{D}.$$

By analogy we define the *maximal* normalized redundancy rate r^* for VV codes as follows:

$$r^* = \frac{\max_{d \in \mathcal{D}}[\ell(d) + \log P(d)]}{\overline{D}}. \tag{5.2}$$

In this chapter, we shall study both, the average redundancy rate and the maximal redundancy rate for VV codes.

5.2 Redundancy of the Khodak VV Code

In this section, we present several results regarding the average and maximal redundancy rates for a VV Khodak code. We also construct an explicit algorithm to achieve these bounds.

We start with the main theorem of this section (which is due to Khodak (1972)).

Theorem 5.1 *Let $m \geq 2$ and consider a memoryless source over an m-ary alphabet. Then for every $D_0 \geq 1$, there exists a VV code with average dictionary length $\mathbf{E}[D] =: \overline{D} \geq D_0$ such that its average redundancy rate satisfies*

$$\bar{r} = O(\overline{D}^{-5/3}), \tag{5.3}$$

and the maximal code length is $O(\overline{D} \log \overline{D})$.

The rest of this section is devoted to the proof of Theorem 5.1. We assume an m-ary source alphabet $\mathcal{A} = \{0, \ldots, m-1\}$ with corresponding probabilities $p_0, \ldots, p_{m-1}$. Let us first give some intuition. For every $d \in \mathcal{D}$, we can represent $P(d)$ as

$$P(d) = p_0^{k_0} \cdots p_{m-1}^{k_{m-1}},$$

where $k_i = k_i(d)$ is the number of times the symbol i appears in d. In what follows, we write type$(d) = (k_0, k_1, \ldots, k_{m-1})$ (see also Chapter 11). Furthermore, the string encoder of our VV code uses a slightly modified Shannon code that assigns to $d \in \mathcal{D}$ a binary word of length $\ell(d)$ close to $-\log P(d)$ when $\log P(d)$ is slightly larger or smaller than an integer. (Kraft's inequality will not be automatically satisfied but Lemma 5.4 takes care of it.) Observe that the average redundancy of the Shannon code is

$$\sum_{d \in \mathcal{D}} P(d)[\lceil -\log P(d) \rceil + \log P(d)] = \sum_{d \in \mathcal{D}} P(d)\langle \log P(d) \rangle$$

$$= \sum_{d \in \mathcal{D}} P(d) \cdot \langle k_0(d)\gamma_0 + k_1(d)\gamma_1 + \cdots + k_{m-1}(d)\gamma_{m-1} \rangle,$$

where $\gamma_i = \log p_i$. In order to build a VV code with $\bar{r} = o(1/\overline{D})$, we have to find integers $k_0 = k_0(d), \ldots, k_{m-1} = k_{m-1}(d)$ such that the linear form $k_0 \gamma_0 + k_1 \gamma_1 + \cdots + k_{m-1} \gamma_{m-1}$ is close to but slightly larger than an integer for almost all d.

Next we discuss some properties of the distribution of $\langle k_0 \gamma_0 + k_1 \gamma_1 + \cdots + k_{m-1} \gamma_{m-1} \rangle$ when at least one of γ_i is irrational.

Some preliminary results Let $\|x\| = \min(\langle x \rangle, \langle -x \rangle) = \min(\langle x \rangle, 1 - \langle x \rangle)$ be the distance to the nearest integer. The *dispersion* $\delta(X)$ of the set $X \subseteq [0, 1)$ is defined as

$$\delta(X) = \sup_{0 \leq y < 1} \inf_{x \in X} \|y - x\|;$$

that is, for every $y \in [0, 1)$, there exists $x \in X$ with $\|y - x\| \leq \delta(X)$. Since $\|y + 1\| = \|y\|$, the same assertion holds for all real y. Furthermore the points of X are at most $2\delta(X)$ apart in $[0, 1]$. Therefore, for every y there exist distinct points $x_1, x_2 \in X$ with $\langle y - x_1 \rangle \leq 2\delta(X)$ and $\langle y - x_2 \rangle \leq 2\delta(X)$.

The following property will be used throughout this chapter. This is a standard result following from Dirichlet's Approximation Theorem F.1. The reader is asked in Exercise 5.2 to prove Lemma 5.2.

Lemma 5.2 (i) *Suppose that θ is an irrational number. Then there exist infinitely many positive integers N such that*

$$\delta \left(\{ \langle k\theta \rangle : 0 \leq k < N \} \right) \leq \frac{2}{N}.$$

(ii) *In general, let $(\gamma_0, \ldots, \gamma_{m-1})$ be an m-vector of real numbers such that at least one of its coordinates is irrational. Then there exist infinitely many integers N such that the dispersion of the set*

$$X = \{ \langle k_0 \gamma + \cdots + k_{m-1} \gamma_{m-1} \rangle : 0 \leq k_j < N \ (0 \leq j < m) \}$$

is bounded by

$$\delta(X) \leq \frac{2}{N}.$$

Crucial lemma The central step of the proof of Theorem 5.1 is the observation that a bound on the dispersion of linear forms of $\log p_j$ implies the existence of a VV code with small redundancy. Clearly, Lemma 5.2 and Lemma 5.3 directly imply Theorem 5.1 by setting $\eta = 1$ if one of the $\log p_j$ is irrational. (If all $\log p_j$ are rational, then the construction is even simpler. We ask the reader to handle this case in Exercise 5.3.)

Lemma 5.3 *Let $p_j > 0$ ($0 \leq j < m$) with $p_0 + \cdots + p_{m-1} = 1$ be given and suppose that for some $N \geq 1$ and $\eta \geq 1$ the set*

$$X = \{ \langle k_0 \log p_0 + \cdots + k_{m-1} \log p_{m-1} \rangle : 0 \leq k_j < N \ (0 \leq j < m) \},$$

has dispersion

$$\delta(X) \leq \frac{2}{N^\eta}. \tag{5.4}$$

Then there exists a VV code with average phrase length $\overline{D} = \Theta(N^3)$, with maximal length of order $\Theta(N^3 \log N)$, and with average redundancy rate

$$\overline{r} \leq c_m \cdot \overline{D}^{-\frac{4+\eta}{3}}$$

where c_m is a constant that may depend on m.

Proof of Lemma 5.3 We now concentrate on the proof of Lemma 5.3. The main thrust of the proof is to construct a complete prefix-free set $\mathcal{D}$ of words (i.e., a dictionary) on m symbols such that $\log P(d)$ is *very close* to an integer $\ell(d)$ with high probability. This is accomplished by growing an m-ary tree $\mathcal{T}$ in which paths from the root to terminal nodes have the property that $\log P(d)$ is close to an integer (for most d).

In the first step, we set $k_i^0 := \lfloor p_i N^2 \rfloor$ $(0 \leq i < m)$ for a large integer N and define

$$x = k_0^0 \log p_0 + \cdots + k_{m-1}^0 \log p_{m-1}.$$

By our assumption (5.4) of Lemma 5.3, there exist integers $0 \leq k_j^1 < N$ such that

$$\langle x + k_0^1 \log p_0 + \cdots + k_{m-1}^1 \log p_{m-1} \rangle$$
$$= \langle (k_0^0 + k_0^1) \log p_0 + \cdots + (k_{m-1}^0 + k_{m-1}^1) \log p_{m-1} \rangle < \frac{4}{N^\eta}.$$

Now consider all paths in a (potentially) infinite m-ary tree starting at the root with $k_0^0 + k_0^1$ edges of type 0, $k_1^0 + k_1^1$ edges of type 1,..., and $k_{m-1}^0 + k_{m-1}^1$ edges of type $m-1$ (cf. Figure 5.1). Let $\mathcal{D}_1$ denote the set of such words. (These are the first words of our prefix-free dictionary set we are going to construct.) By an application of Stirling's formula, it follows that there are two positive constants c', c'' such that the probability

$$P(\mathcal{D}_1) = \binom{(k_0^0 + k_0^1) + \cdots + (k_m^0 + k_m^1)}{k_0^0 + k_0^1, \ldots, k_{m-1}^0 + k_{m-1}^1} p_0^{k_0^0 + k_0^1} \cdots p_{m-1}^{k_{m-1}^0 + k_{m-1}^1}$$

satisfies

$$\frac{c'}{N} \leq P(\mathcal{D}_1) \leq \frac{c''}{N} \tag{5.5}$$

uniformly for all k_j^1 with $0 \leq k_j^1 < N$. In summary, by construction, all words $d \in \mathcal{D}_1$ have the property that

$$\langle \log P(d) \rangle < \frac{4}{N^\eta};$$

that is, $\log P(d)$ is very close to an integer. Note further that all words in $d \in \mathcal{D}_1$ have about the same length

$$n_1 = (k_0^0 + k_0') + \cdots + (k_{m-1}^0 + k_{m-1}') = N^2 + O(N),$$

and words in $\mathcal{D}_1$ constitute the first crop of "good words." Finally, let $\mathcal{B}_1 = \mathcal{A}^{n_1} \setminus \mathcal{D}_1$ denote all words of length n_1 not in $\mathcal{D}_1$ (cf. Figure 5.1). Then

$$1 - \frac{c''}{N} \leq P(\mathcal{B}_1) \leq 1 - \frac{c'}{N}.$$

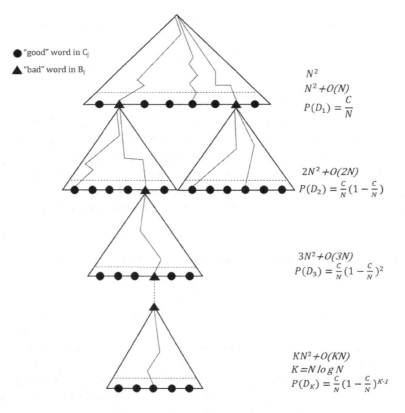

N^2

$N^2 + O(N)$

$P(D_1) = \dfrac{c}{N}$

$2N^2 + O(2N)$

$P(D_2) = \dfrac{c}{N}\left(1 - \dfrac{c}{N}\right)$

$3N^2 + O(3N)$

$P(D_3) = \dfrac{c}{N}\left(1 - \dfrac{c}{N}\right)^2$

$KN^2 + O(KN)$

$K = N\log N$

$P(D_K) = \dfrac{c}{N}\left(1 - \dfrac{c}{N}\right)^{K-1}$

Figure 5.1 Illustration to the construction of the VV code.

In the second step, we consider all words $r \in \mathcal{B}_1$ and concatenate them with appropriately chosen words d_2 of length $\sim N^2$ such that $\log P(rd_2)$ is close to an integer *with high probability*. The construction is almost the same as in the first step. For every word $r \in \mathcal{B}_1$, we set

$$x(r) = \log P(r) + k_0^0 \log p_0 + \cdots + k_{m-1}^0 \log p_{m-1}.$$

By (5.4), there exist integers $0 \le k_j^2(r) < N$ ($0 \le j < m$) such that

$$\langle x(r) + k_0^2(r) \log p_0 + \cdots + k_{m-1}^2(r) \log p_{m-1} \rangle < \frac{4}{N^\eta}.$$

Now consider all paths (in the infinite tree $\mathcal{T}$) starting at $r \in \mathcal{B}_1$ with $k_0^0 + k_0^2(r)$ edges of type 0, $k_1^0 + k_1^2(r)$ edges of type 1, ..., and $k_{m-1}^0 + k_{m-1}^2(r)$ edges of type $m-1$ (that is, we concatenated r with properly chosen words d_2) and denote this set by $\mathcal{D}_2^+(r)$. We again have that the total probability

$$P(\mathcal{D}_2(r)) = P(r)$$

$$\times \binom{(k_0^0 + k_0^2(r)) + \cdots + (k_{m-1}^0 + k_{m-1}^2(r))}{k_0^0 + k_0^2(r), \ldots, k_{m-1}^0 + k_{m-1}^2(r)} p_0^{k_0^0 + k_0^2(r)} \cdots p_{m-1}^{k_{m-1}^0 + k_{m-1}^2(r)}$$

of these words is bounded from below and above by

$$P(r)\frac{c'}{N} \le P(\mathcal{D}_2(r)) \le P(r)\frac{c''}{N}.$$

Furthermore, by construction, we have $\langle \log P(d) \rangle < \frac{4}{N^\eta}$ for all $d \in \mathcal{D}_2^+(r)$.

Similarly, we can construct a set $\mathcal{D}_2^-(r)$ instead of $\mathcal{D}_2^+(r)$ for which we have $1 - \langle \log P(d) \rangle < 4/N^\eta$. We will indicate in the sequel whether we will use $\mathcal{D}_2^+(r)$ or $\mathcal{D}_2^-(r)$.

Let $\mathcal{D}_2 = \bigcup(\mathcal{D}_2^+(r) : r \in \mathcal{B}_1)$ (or $\mathcal{D}_2 = \bigcup(\mathcal{D}_2^-(r) : r \in \mathcal{B}_1)$). Then all words $d \in \mathcal{D}_2$ have almost the same length $|d| = 2N^2 + O(2N)$, their probabilities satisfy

$$\langle \log P(d) \rangle < \frac{4}{N^\eta} \quad \text{or} \quad 1 - \langle \log P(d) \rangle < \frac{4}{N^\eta}$$

and the total probability is bounded by

$$\frac{c'}{N}\left(1 - \frac{c''}{N}\right) \le P(\mathcal{D}_2) \le \frac{c''}{N}\left(1 - \frac{c'}{N}\right).$$

For every $r \in \mathcal{B}_1$, let $\mathcal{B}^+(r)$ (or $\mathcal{B}^-(r)$) denote the set of paths (resp. words) starting with r of length $2(k_0^0 + \cdots + k_{m-1}^0) + (k_1^1 + k_1^2(r) + \cdots + k_{m-1}^1 + k_{m-1}^2(r))$ that are *not* contained in $\mathcal{D}_2^+(r)$ (or $\mathcal{D}_2^-(r)$) and set $\mathcal{B}_2 = \bigcup(\mathcal{B}_2^+(r): r \in \mathcal{B}_1)$ (or $\mathcal{B}_2 = \bigcup(\mathcal{B}_2^-(r): r \in \mathcal{B}_1)$). Observe that the probability of $\mathcal{B}_2$ is bounded by

$$\left(1 - \frac{c''}{N}\right)^2 \le P(\mathcal{B}_2) \le \left(1 - \frac{c'}{N}\right)^2.$$

We continue this construction, as illustrated in Figure 5.1, and in step j we define sets of words $\mathcal{D}_j$ and $\mathcal{B}_j$ such that all words $d \in \mathcal{D}_j$ satisfy

$$\langle \log P(d) \rangle < \frac{4}{N^\eta} \quad \text{or} \quad 1 - \langle \log P(d) \rangle < \frac{4}{N^\eta}$$

and the length of $d \in \mathcal{D}_j \cup \mathcal{B}_j$ is then given by $|d| = jN^2 + O(jN)$. The probabilities of $\mathcal{D}_j$ and $\mathcal{B}_j$ are bounded by

$$\frac{c'}{N}\left(1 - \frac{c''}{N}\right)^{j-1} \le P(\mathcal{D}_j) \le \frac{c''}{N}\left(1 - \frac{c'}{N}\right)^{j-1}, \tag{5.6}$$

$$\left(1 - \frac{c''}{N}\right)^j \le P(\mathcal{B}_j) \le \left(1 - \frac{c'}{N}\right)^j. \tag{5.7}$$

This construction is terminated after $K = O(N \log N)$ steps so that

$$P(\mathcal{B}_K) \le c''\left(1 - \frac{c'}{N}\right)^K \le \frac{1}{N^\beta}$$

for some $\beta > 0$. This also ensures that

$$P(\mathcal{D}_1 \cup \cdots \cup \mathcal{D}_K) > 1 - \frac{1}{N^\beta}.$$

The complete prefix-free set $\mathcal{D}$ on the m symbols is given by

$$\mathcal{D} = \mathcal{D}_1 \cup \cdots \cup \mathcal{D}_K \cup \mathcal{B}_K.$$

By the above construction, it is also clear that the average dictionary phrase length is bounded by

$$c_1 N^3 \leq \overline{D} = \sum_{d \in \mathcal{D}} P(d) |d| \leq c_2 N^3$$

for certain constants $c_1, c_2 > 0$. Notice further that the maximal code length satisfies

$$\max_{d \in \mathcal{D}} |d| = O(N^3 \log N) = O(\overline{D} \log \overline{D}).$$

Now we construct a variant of the Shannon code with $\overline{r} = o(1/\overline{D})$. For every $d \in \mathcal{D}_1 \cup \cdots \cup \mathcal{D}_K$, we can choose a nonnegative integer $\ell(d)$ with

$$|\ell(d) + \log P(d)| < \frac{2}{N^\eta}.$$

In particular, we have

$$0 \leq \ell(d) + \log P(d) < \frac{2}{N^\eta}$$

if $\langle \log P(d) \rangle < 2/N^\eta$ and

$$-\frac{2}{N^\eta} < \ell(d) + \log P(d) \leq 0$$

if $1 - \langle \log P(d) \rangle < 2/N^\eta$. For $d \in \mathcal{B}_K$, we simply set $\ell(d) = \lceil -\log P(d) \rceil$.

The final problem is now to *adjust* the choices of "+" resp. "−" in this construction so that Kraft's inequality is satisfied. For this purpose we use the following easy property.

Lemma 5.4 (Khodak 1972) *Let $\mathcal{D}$ be a finite set with probability distribution P and suppose that for every $d \in \mathcal{D}$ we have $|\ell(d) + \log P(d)| \leq 1$ for a nonnegative integer $\ell(d)$. If*

$$\sum_{d \in \mathcal{D}} P(d)(\ell(d) + \log P(d)) \geq 2 \sum_{d \in \mathcal{D}} P(d)(\ell(d) + \log P(d))^2, \qquad (5.8)$$

then there exists an injective mapping $C \colon \mathcal{D} \to \{0, 1\}^*$ such that C is a prefix-free set and $|C(d)| = \ell(d)$ for all $d \in \mathcal{D}$.

Proof We use the local expansion $2^{-x} = 1 - x \ln 2 + \eta(x)$ for $|x| \leq 1$, where $((\log 4)/4)x^2 \leq \eta(x) \leq (\log 4)x^2$. Hence,

$$\sum_{d \in \mathcal{D}} 2^{-\ell(d)} = \sum_{d \in \mathcal{D}|} P(d) 2^{-(\ell(d) + \log P(d))}$$

$$= 1 - \ln 2 \sum_{d \in \mathcal{D}} P(d)(\ell(d) + \log P(d))$$

$$+ \sum_{d \in \mathcal{D}} P(d) \eta \left(\ell(d) + \log P(d) \right)$$

$$\leq 1 - \ln 2 \sum_{d \in \mathcal{D}} P(d)(\ell(d) + \log P(d))$$

$$+ 2 \ln 2 \sum_{d \in \mathcal{D}} P(d)(\ell(d) + \log P(d))^2.$$

If (5.8) is satisfied, then it follows that

$$\sum_{d \in \mathcal{D}} 2^{-\ell(d)} \leq 1.$$

Consequently, Kraft's inequality is satisfied, and there exists an injective mapping $C \colon \mathcal{D} \to \{0, 1\}^*$ such that C is a prefix free set and $|C(d)| = \ell(d)$ for all $d \in \mathcal{D}$. ∎

We now set

$$E_j = \sum_{d \in \mathcal{D}_j} P(d)(\ell(d) + \log P(d)).$$

Then $E_j > 0$ if we have chosen "+" in our construction and $E_j < 0$ if we have chosen "−". In any case, we have

$$|E_j| \leq P(\mathcal{D}_j) \frac{2}{N^\eta} \leq \frac{2c''}{N^{1+\eta}} \left(1 - \frac{c'}{N}\right)^{j-1} \leq \frac{2c''}{N^{1+\eta}}.$$

Suppose for a moment that we have always chosen "+", that is, $E_j > 0$ for all $j \geq 1$, and that

$$\sum_{j=1}^{K} E_j \leq \frac{8 + 2c''}{N^{1+\eta}}. \tag{5.9}$$

We can assume that N is large enough that $2/N^\eta \leq 1/2$. Hence, the assumptions of Lemma 5.4 are trivially satisfied since $0 \leq \ell(d) + \log P(d) < 1/2$ implies $2(\ell(d) + \log P(d))^2 < \ell(d) + \log P(d)$ for all $d \in \mathcal{D}$. If (5.9) does not hold (if we have chosen always "+"), then one can select "+" and "−" so that

$$\frac{8}{N^{1+\eta}} \leq \sum_{j=1}^{K} E_j \leq \frac{8 + 4c''}{N^{1+\eta}}.$$

Indeed, if the partial sum $\sum_{j=i}^{K} E_i \leq (8 + 2c'')N^{-1-\eta}$, then the sign of E_j is chosen to be "+" and if $\sum_{j=i}^{K} E_i > (8 + 2c'')N^{-1-\eta}$, then the sign of E_j is chosen to be "−". Since

$$\sum_{d \in \mathcal{D}} P(d)(\ell(d) + \log P(d))^2 \leq \frac{4}{N^{2\eta}} \leq \frac{4}{N^{1+\eta}} \leq \frac{1}{2} \sum_{d \in \mathcal{D}} P(d)(\ell(d) + \log P(d)),$$

the assumption of Lemma 5.4 is satisfied. Thus, there exists a prefix-free coding map $C \colon \mathcal{D} \to \{0, 1\}^*$ with $|C(d)| = \ell(d)$ for all $d \in \mathcal{D}$. Applying the lemma, we arrive (after some algebra) at the following bound on the average redundancy rate (see Exercise 5.5):

$$\bar{r} \leq \frac{1}{\overline{D}} \sum_{d \in \mathcal{D}} P(d)(\ell(d) + \log P(d)) \leq C \frac{1}{\overline{D} N^{1+\eta}}. \tag{5.10}$$

Since the average dictionary phrase length $\overline{D}$ is of order N^3, we have

$$\bar{r} = O\left(\overline{D}^{-1 - \frac{1+\eta}{3}}\right) = O\left(\overline{D}^{-\frac{4+\eta}{3}}\right).$$

This proves the upper bound for $\bar{r}$ of Lemma 5.3 and, thus, Theorem 5.1 follows.

5.3 Explicit Construction of a Khodak VV Code

In what follows, we present an algorithm for designing a VV code with arbitrarily large average dictionary length $\overline{D}$ for memoryless sources. More precisely, we construct a code with redundancy $\overline{r} \le \varepsilon/\overline{D}$, where $\varepsilon > 0$ is given and $\overline{D} \ge c/\varepsilon^3$ (for some constant c). In fact, for some large integer N we find that $\overline{D} = N^3$ and $\varepsilon = 1/N$, so that $\overline{r} = O(\overline{D}^{-4/3})$, which does not employ the full strength of Theorem 5.1 that guarantees the existence of a code with the average redundancy smaller than $c\overline{D}^{-5/3}$. This allows some simplification; in particular, we just use a standard Shannon code.

Continued fraction Before we proceed, we need some facts about *continued fractions* (see also Appendix F). A finite continued fraction expansion is a rational number of the form

$$c_0 + \cfrac{1}{c_1 + \cfrac{1}{c_2 + \cfrac{1}{c_3 + \cfrac{\cdot \cdot \cdot}{\cdot \cdot + \frac{1}{c_n}}}}},$$

where c_0 is an integer and c_j are *positive* integers for $j \ge 1$. We denote this rational number as $[c_0, c_1, \ldots, c_n]$. With help of the Euclidean algorithm for gcd, it is easy to see that every rational number has a finite continued fraction expansion. Furthermore, if c_j is a given sequence of integers (that are positive for $j > 0$), then the limit $\theta = \lim_{n \to \infty} [c_0, c_1, \ldots, c_n]$ exists and is denoted by the infinite continued fraction expansion $\theta = [c_0, c_1, c_2 \ldots]$. Conversely, if θ is a real irrational number and if we recursively set

$$\theta_0 = \theta, \quad c_j = \lfloor \theta_j \rfloor, \quad \theta_{j+1} = 1/(\theta_j - c_j),$$

then $\theta = [c_0, c_1, c_2 \ldots]$. In particular, every irrational number has a unique infinite continued fraction expansion.

The *convergents* of an irrational number θ with infinite continued fraction expansion $\theta = [c_0, c_1, c_2 \ldots]$ are defined as

$$\frac{P_n}{Q_n} = [c_0, c_1, \ldots, c_n],$$

where integers P_n, Q_n are coprime. These integers can be recursively determined by

$$P_n = c_n P_{n-1} + P_{n-2}, \quad Q_n = c_n Q_{n-1} + Q_{n-2}, \tag{5.11}$$

which the reader is asked to prove in Exercise 5.6. In particular, P_n and Q_n are growing exponentially quickly. Furthermore, the convergents $\frac{P_n}{Q_n}$ are the best rational approximations of θ in the sense that

$$|Q_n \theta - P_n| < \min_{0 < Q < Q_n, \, P \in \mathbb{Z}} |Q\theta - P|.$$

In particular, one has (see Exercise 5.7)

$$\left| \theta - \frac{P_n}{Q_n} \right| < \frac{1}{Q_n^2}. \tag{5.12}$$

The denominators Q_n are called *best approximation denominators*.

Algorithm Now we present algorithm KHODCODE that constructs a VV code with the normalized redundancy $o(1/\overline{D})$. We will also make the assumption that all symbol probabilities p_j are rational numbers; otherwise we would have to assume that p_j is known to an arbitrary precision. We then know that $\log p_j$ is either irrational or an integer (which means that $p_j = 2^{-k}$). Thus, we can immediately decide whether all $\log p_j$ are rational or not. If all p_j are negative powers of 2, then we can use a perfect code with zero redundancy. Thus, we only have to treat the case where p_{m-1} is not a negative powers of 2. We also assume that the continued fraction expansion of $\log p_{m-1} = [c_0, c_1, c_2, \ldots]$ is given and we determine a convergent

$$[c_0, c_1, c_2, \ldots, c_n] = M/N$$

for which the denominator N satisfies $N > 4/\varepsilon$. The main goal of the algorithms is to construct a prefix-free set of words d with the property that for *most words* $\langle \log P(d) \rangle$ is small. The reason for this philosophy is that if one uses the Shannon code as the string encoder, that is, $\ell(d) = \lceil -\log P(d) \rceil$, then the difference $\ell(d) - \log(1/P(d)) = \langle \log P(d) \rangle$ is small and contributes negligibly to the redundancy.

The main step of the algorithm is a loop of the same subroutine. The input is a pair $\mathcal{D}, \mathcal{B}$ of sets of words with the property that $\mathcal{D} \cup \mathcal{B}$ is a prefix-free set. Words d in $\mathcal{D}$ are already *good* in the sense that $\langle \log P(d) \rangle \leq \frac{3}{4}\varepsilon$, whereas words r in $\mathcal{B}$ are *bad* because they do not satisfy this condition. In the first step of the subroutine, one chooses a word $r \in \mathcal{B}$ of minimal length and computes an integer k with $0 \leq k < N$ that satisfies

$$\frac{1}{N} \leq \langle kM/N + x + \log P(r) \rangle \leq \frac{2}{N}.$$

Here x is an abbreviation of

$$x = \sum_{j=0}^{m-1} k_j^0 \log p_j,$$

where $k_j^0 = \lfloor p_j N^2 \rfloor, 0 \leq j < m$. The computation of k can be done by solving the congruence

$$kM \equiv 1 - \lfloor (x + \log P(r))N \rfloor \bmod N \tag{5.13}$$

(e.g., with the help of the Euclidean algorithm). This choice of k ensures that

$$0 \leq \langle k \log p_m + x + \log P(r) \rangle \leq 3/N \leq \frac{3}{4}\varepsilon.$$

For this k, we determine the set $\mathcal{D}'$ of all words d of type$(d) = (k_0^0, \ldots, k_{m-2}^0, k_{m-1}^0 + k)$. By construction, all $d' \in \mathcal{D}'$ satisfy

$$\langle \log P(r \cdot d') \rangle = \langle k \log p_{m-1} + x + \log P(r) \rangle \leq \frac{3}{4}\varepsilon.$$

We now replace $\mathcal{D}$ by $\mathcal{D} \cup r \cdot \mathcal{D}'$ and $\mathcal{B}$ by $(\mathcal{B} \setminus \{r\}) \cup r \cdot (\mathcal{A}^n \setminus \mathcal{D}')$. This construction ensures that (again) all words in $d \in \mathcal{D}$ satisfy

$$\langle \log P(d) \rangle \leq \frac{3}{4}\varepsilon.$$

The algorithm terminates when $P(\mathcal{D}) > 1 - \varepsilon/4$; that is, *most words* in $\mathcal{D} \cup \mathcal{B}$ are *good*. The proof of Theorem 5.1 shows that this actually occurs when the average dictionary length $\overline{D}$ is of order $O(N^3)$. In particular, the special choice of integers $k_j^0 = \lfloor p_j N^2 \rfloor$ ensures that the probability $P(\mathcal{D})$ increases step by step as quickly as possible; compare with (5.5).

As already mentioned, we finally use the Shannon code $C \colon \mathcal{D} \cup \mathcal{B} \to \{0,1\}^*$; that is, $\ell(d) = \lceil -\log P(d) \rceil$ for all $d \in \mathcal{D} \cup \mathcal{B}$. The redundancy can be estimated by

$$
\begin{aligned}
\bar{r} &= \frac{1}{\overline{D}} \sum_{d \in \mathcal{D} \cup \mathcal{B}} P(d) \left(\ell(d) - \log \frac{1}{P(d)} \right) \\
&= \frac{1}{\overline{D}} \sum_{d \in \mathcal{D} \cup \mathcal{B}} P(d) \, \langle \log P(d) \rangle \\
&= \frac{1}{\overline{D}} \left(\sum_{d \in \mathcal{D}} P(d) \langle \log P(d) \rangle + \sum_{d \in \mathcal{B}} P(d) \langle \log P(d) \rangle \right) \\
&\le \frac{1}{\overline{D}} \left(P(\mathcal{D}) \frac{3}{4} \varepsilon + P(\mathcal{B}) \right) \\
&\le \frac{1}{\overline{D}} \left(\frac{3}{4} \varepsilon + \frac{1}{4} \varepsilon \right) = \frac{\varepsilon}{\overline{D}}.
\end{aligned}
$$

Thus, this algorithm constructs a parsing tree and a VV code with a small redundancy rate. A more formal description of the algorithm follows.

Algorithm KhodCode

Input: (i) m, an integer ≥ 2; (ii) positive rational numbers $p_0, \ldots, p_{m-1}$ with $p_0 + \cdots + p_{m-1} = 1$, p_{m-1} is not a power of 2; (iii) ε, a positive real number < 1.

Output: A VV code, that is, a complete prefix-free set $\mathcal{D}$ on m symbols and a prefix code $C \colon \mathcal{D} \to \{0,1\}^*$, with redundancy $\bar{r} \le \varepsilon/\overline{D}$, where the average dictionary code length $\overline{D}$ satisfies $\overline{D} \ge c(m, p_0, \ldots, p_{m-1})/\varepsilon^3$ (for some constant $c(m, p_0, \ldots, p_{m-1})$).

Notation: For a word $w \in \{0, \ldots, m-1\}^*$ that consists of k_j copies of j ($0 \le j < m$), we set $P(w) = p_0^{k_0} \cdots p_{m-1}^{k_{m-1}}$ for the probability of w and $\mathrm{type}(w) = (k_0, \ldots, k_{m-1})$. By ω, we denote the empty word and set $P(\omega) = 1$.

1. **Calculate** the convergent $\frac{M}{N} = [c_0, c_1, \ldots, c_n]$ of the irrational number $\log p_{m-1}$ for which $N > 4/\varepsilon$.
2. **Set** $k_j^0 = \lfloor p_j N^2 \rfloor$ ($0 \le j < m$), $x = \sum_{j=1}^m k_j^0 \log p_j$ and $n_0 = \sum_{j=1}^m k_j^0$.
3. **Set** $\mathcal{D} = \emptyset$, $\mathcal{B} = \{\omega\}$, and $p = 0$
   while $p < 1 - \varepsilon/4$ **do**
           Choose $r \in \mathcal{B}$ of minimal length
           $b \leftarrow \log P(r)$
           Find $0 \le k < N$ that solves the congruence
           $kM \equiv 1 - \lfloor (x + b)N \rfloor \bmod N$
           $n \leftarrow n_0 + k$
           $\mathcal{D}' \leftarrow \{d \in A^n : \mathrm{type}(d) = (k_0^0, \ldots, k_{m-2}^0, k_{m-1}^0 + k)\}$
           $\mathcal{D} \leftarrow \mathcal{D} \cup r \cdot \mathcal{D}'$

$$\mathcal{B} \leftarrow (\mathcal{B} \setminus \{r\}) \cup r \cdot (\{0, \dots, m-1\}^n \setminus \mathcal{D}')$$
$$p \leftarrow p + P(r)P(\mathcal{D}'), \text{ where}$$

$$P(\mathcal{D}') = \frac{n!}{k_0^0 \cdots k_{m-2}^0! (k_{m-1}^0 + k)!} p_0^{k_0^0} \cdots p_{m-2}^{k_{m-2}^0} p_{m-1}^{k_{m-1}^0 + k}.$$

end while.
4. $\mathcal{D} \leftarrow \mathcal{D} \cup \mathcal{B}$.
5. **Construct** a Shannon code $C \colon \mathcal{D} \to \{0, 1\}^*$ with $\ell(d) = \lceil -\log P(d) \rceil$ for all $d \in \mathcal{D}$.
6. **End.**

Example 5.5 We assume $m = 2$ with $p_0 = 2/3$ and $p_1 = 1/3$. In the first iteration of the algorithm, we assume that both $\mathcal{B}$ and $\mathcal{C}$ are empty. Easy computations show that

$$\log(1/3) = [-2, 2, 2, 2, 3, \dots], \quad \text{and} \quad [-2, 2, 2, 2] = -\frac{19}{12},$$

hence $M = -19$ and $N = 12$. Let us set $\varepsilon = 0.4$ so $4/\varepsilon = 10 < 12 = N$. Therefore, $k_0^0 = 96$, $k_1^0 = 48$ so that $n_0 = 144 = N^2$. Solving the congruence

$$-19k \equiv 1 + 1587 \mod 12$$

gives $k = 8$ and therefore

$$C' = \{d \in \{0, 1\}^{152} : \text{type}(d) = (96, 56)\}$$

with $P(C') \approx 0.04425103411$. Observe that $\mathcal{B} = \{0, 1\}^{152} \setminus \mathcal{C}$.

In the second iteration, we can pick up any string from $\mathcal{B}$, say the string $r = 00 \dots 0$ with 152 zeros. We find, solving the congruence with $b = 152 \log(2/3) \approx -88.91430011$, that $k = 5$. Hence $C' = \{d \in \{0, 1\}^{149} : \text{type}(d) = (96, 53)\}$ and $\mathcal{C} = \{d \in \{0, 1\}^{152} : \text{type}(d) = (96, 56)\} \cup r \cdot C'$. We continue along the same path until the total probability of all "good" strings in $\mathcal{C}$ reaches the value $3/4 \cdot \varepsilon = 0.3$, which may take some time.

5.4 Khodak's Redundancy for Almost All Sources

In this section, we present better estimates for the normalized redundancy rates, however they are valid only for *almost all* memoryless sources. This means that the set of exceptional p_j, those p_j with $\sum_{j=1}^{m} p_j = 1$ and $p_j > 0$ for all $0 \leq j \leq m-1$ that do not satisfy the proposed property, has zero Lebesgue measure on the $(m-1)$-dimensional hyperplane $x_0 + \cdots + x_{m-1} = 1$. From a mathematical point of view, these results are quite challenging.

While Lemmas 5.2 and 5.3 laid the foundation for Theorem 5.1, the next lemma is fundamental for our current considerations.

Lemma 5.6 *Suppose that $\varepsilon > 0$. Then for almost all p_j $(0 \leq j < m)$ with $p_j > 0$ and $p_0 + p_1 + \cdots + p_{m-1} = 1$, the set*

$$X = \left\{ \langle k_0 \log p_0 + \cdots + k_{m-1} \log p_{m-1} \rangle : 0 \leq k_j < N \ (0 \leq j < m) \right\}$$

has dispersion

$$\delta(X) \leq \frac{1}{N^{m-\varepsilon}} \tag{5.14}$$

for sufficiently large N. In addition, for almost all $p_j > 0$ there exists a constant $C > 0$ such that

$$\|k_0 \log p_0 + \cdots + k_{m-1} \log p_{m-1}\| \geq C \left(\max_{0 \leq j < m} |k_j| \right)^{-m-\varepsilon} \tag{5.15}$$

for all nonzero integer vectors $(k_0, \ldots, k_{m-1})$.

We should point out that for $m = 2$, we can slightly improve the estimate of the lemma. Indeed, we will show that for almost all $p_0 > 0, p_1 > 0$ with $p_0 + p_1 = 1$, there exists a constant κ and infinitely many N such that the set $X = \{\langle k_0 \log p_0 + k_1 \log p_1 \rangle : 0 \leq k_0, k_1 < N\}$ has dispersion

$$\delta(X) \leq \frac{\kappa}{N^2}. \tag{5.16}$$

The estimate (5.16) is a little bit sharper than (5.14). However, it is only valid for infinitely many N and not for all but finitely many. We point out that (5.14) and (5.16) are optimal. Since the set X consists of N^m points, the dispersion must satisfy $\delta(X) \geq \frac{1}{2} N^{-m}$.

By combining Lemma 5.3 and Lemma 5.6, we directly obtain the following property.

Theorem 5.7 (Bugeaud, Drmota and Szpankowski 2008) *Let us consider a memoryless source on $m \geq 2$ symbols. Then for almost all source parameters, and for every sufficiently large D_0, there exists a VV code with the average dictionary size $\overline{D}$ satisfying $D_0 \leq \overline{D} \leq 2D_0$ such that its average redundancy rate is bounded by*

$$\bar{r} \leq \overline{D}^{-\frac{4}{3} - \frac{m}{3} + \varepsilon}, \tag{5.17}$$

where $\varepsilon > 0$ and the maximal length is $O(\overline{D} \log \overline{D})$.

This theorem shows that the *typical* best possible average redundancy $\bar{r}$ can be measured in terms of negative powers of $\overline{D}$ that are linearly decreasing in the alphabet size m. However, it seems to be a very difficult problem to obtain the optimal exponent (almost surely). Nevertheless, these bounds are best possible through the methods we applied.

Before we present a proof of Lemma 5.6 and hence prove Theorem 5.7, we complete our analysis with a lower bound for all sources. We start with a simple lemma that follows directly from our proof of Lemma 5.4.

Lemma 5.8 *Let $\mathcal{D}$ be a complete prefix free set with probability distribution P. Then for any code $C \colon \mathcal{D} \to \{0, 1\}^*$, we have*

$$\bar{r} \geq \frac{1}{2} \frac{1}{\overline{D}} \sum_{d \in \overline{D}} P(d) \| \log P(d) \|^2.$$

Proof Suppose that $|x| \leq 1$. Then we have $2^{-x} = 1 - x \ln 2 + \eta(x)$ with $((\ln 4)/4)x^2 \leq \eta(x) \leq (\ln 4)x^2$. Actually we can represent 2^{-x} also for $|x| > 1$ and still have some positive error term $\eta(x)$ that satisfies

$$\eta(x) \geq \min \left(\eta(\langle x \rangle), \eta(1 - \langle x \rangle) \right) \geq \frac{\ln 4}{4} \|x\|^2.$$

Hence, by using the representation

$$x = (1 - 2^{-x} + \eta(x))/\ln 2,$$

we find

$$\bar{r} = \frac{1}{\overline{D}} \sum_{d \in \mathcal{D}} P(d)(\ell(d) + \log P(d))$$

$$= \frac{1}{\overline{D} \ln 2} \sum_{d \in \mathcal{D}} P(d) \left(1 - 2^{-\ell(d) - \log P(d)} + \eta(\ell(d) + \log P(d))\right)$$

$$= \frac{1}{\overline{D} \ln 2} \left(1 - \sum_{d \in \mathcal{D}} 2^{-\ell(d)}\right) + \frac{1}{\overline{D} \ln 2} \sum_{d \in \mathcal{D}} P(d)\eta(\ell(d) + \log P(d)).$$

Hence, by Kraft's inequality and the above observation the result follows immediately. ∎

We are now in a position to present a lower bound on the redundancy rates for almost all sources. Note that the exponent is again linearly decreasing in m, however, with a different rate than in the upper bound (5.17).

Theorem 5.9 *Consider a memoryless source on an alphabet of size $m \geq 2$. Then for almost all source parameters, and for every VV code with average dictionary length $\overline{D} \geq D_0$ (where D_0 is sufficiently large), we have*

$$r^* \geq \bar{r} \geq \overline{D}^{-2m-1-\varepsilon} \tag{5.18}$$

where $\varepsilon > 0$.

Proof By Lemma 5.8, we have

$$\bar{r} \geq \frac{1}{2\overline{D}} \sum_{d \in \overline{D}} P(d) \| \log P(d) \|^2.$$

Suppose that $P(d) = p_0^{k_0} \cdots p_{m-1}^{k_{m-1}}$ holds; that is,

$$\log P(d) = k_0 \log p_0 + \cdots + k_{m-1} \log p_{m-1}.$$

By Lemma 5.6, we conclude from (5.15) that for all p_j and for all nonzero integer vectors $(k_0, \ldots, k_{m-1})$,

$$\| k_0 \log p_0 + \cdots + k_{m-1} \log p_{m-1} \| \geq C \left(\max_{0 \leq j < m} |k_j| \right)^{-m-\varepsilon},$$

and therefore

$$\| \log P(d) \| \geq C \left(\max_{0 \leq j < m} |k_j| \right)^{-m-\varepsilon} \geq C \left(\sum_{0 \leq j < m} k_j \right)^{-m-\varepsilon} = C|d|^{-m-\varepsilon}.$$

Consequently, by Jensen's inequality, we obtain

$$\bar{r} \geq \frac{C}{2\overline{D}} \sum_{d \in \mathcal{D}} P(d)|d|^{-2m-2\varepsilon}$$

$$\geq \frac{C}{2\overline{D}} \left(\sum_{d \in \mathcal{D}} P(d)|d| \right)^{-2m-2\varepsilon}$$

$$\geq \overline{D}^{-2m-1-3\varepsilon}.$$

This completes the proof of Theorem 5.9. ∎

5.4.1 *Proof of Lemma 5.6*

Lemma 5.6 states that for almost all $p_j > 0$ (with $p_1 + \cdots + p_{m-1} = 1$), the set

$$X = \left\{ \langle k_0 \log p_0 + \cdots + k_{m-1} \log p_{m-1} \rangle : 0 \leq k_j < N \ (0 \leq j < m) \right\}$$

has dispersion $\delta(X) \leq N^{-m+\varepsilon}$ for all sufficiently large N (that is, (5.14) holds) and for all nonzero integer vectors $(k_1, \ldots, k_m)$ the relation (5.15) holds for some constant $C > 0$.

These kind of problems fall into the field of *metric Diophantine approximation* that is well established in number theory. One of the problems in this field is to obtain some information about linear forms of type

$$L = k_0 \gamma_0 + \cdots + k_{m-1} \gamma_{m-1} + k_m,$$

where k_j are integers and γ_j are randomly chosen real numbers. In fact, one is usually interested in lower bounds for $|L|$ in terms of $\max |k_j|$.

In our context, we have $\gamma_j = \log p_j$ so that the γ_j's are related by

$$2^{\gamma_0} + \cdots + 2^{\gamma_{m-1}} = 1.$$

This means that they cannot be chosen independently. They are situated on a proper submanifold of the m-dimensional space. It has turned out that metric Diophantine approximation in this case is much more complicated than in the independent case. Fortunately, there now exist proper results that we can use for our purpose.

Theorem 5.10 (Dickinson and Dodson 2000) *Suppose that $m \geq 2$ and $1 \leq k < m$. Let U be an open set in $\mathbf{R}^k$ and, for $0 \leq j \leq m - 1$, let $\Psi_j : U \to \mathbf{R}$ be C^1 real functions. Let $\eta > 0$ be real. Then for almost all $u = (u_0, \ldots, u_{k-1}) \in U$, there exists $N_0(u)$ such that for all $N \geq N_0(u)$ we have*

$$|k_0 \Psi_0(u) + \cdots + k_{m-1} \Psi_{m-1}(u) + k_m| \geq N^{-m+(m-k)\eta} (\log N)^{m-k}$$

for all nonzero integer vectors $(k_0, k_1, \ldots, k_m)$ with

$$\max_{0 \leq j \leq k-1} |k_j| \leq N \quad \text{and} \quad \max_{k \leq j \leq m-1} |k_j| \leq N^{1-\eta}/(\log N).$$

More precisely, let us define a convex body consisting of all real vectors $(y_0, \ldots, y_m)$ with

$$|y_0 \Psi_0(u) + \ldots + y_{m-1} \Psi_{m-1}(u) + y_m| \leq N^{-m+(m-k)\eta} (\log N)^{m-k},$$

$$|y_j| \leq N, \quad (j = 0, \ldots, k-1), \tag{5.19}$$

$$|y_j| \leq N^{1-\eta} (\log N)^{-1}, \quad (k \leq j < m).$$

Dickinson and Dodson (2000), in the course of the proof of their theorem 2, considered the set $S(N)$ that consists of all $u \in U$ for which there exists an integer vector $(k_0, k_1, \ldots, k_m)$ with $0 < \max\limits_{0 \le j \le m-1} |k_j| < N^{1-\eta}$ satisfying (5.19). In particular, they showed that the $S(N)$ has the property that the set

$$\limsup_{N \to \infty} S(N) = \bigcap_{N \ge 1} \bigcup_{M \ge N} S(M)$$

has zero Lebesgue measure. This means that almost no u belongs to infinitely many sets $S(N)$. In other words, for almost every u, there exists $N_0(u)$ such that $u \notin S(N)$ for every $N \ge N_0(u)$. And this is stated in Theorem 5.10.

For $m = 2$, Theorem 5.10 can be improved as shown by Baker (1978).

Theorem 5.11 (Baker 1978) *Let Ψ_0 and Ψ_1 be C^3 real functions defined on an interval $[a, b]$. For x in $[a, b]$, set*

$$k(x) = \Psi_0'(x)\Psi_1''(x) - \Psi_0''(x)\Psi_1'(x).$$

Assume that $k(x)$ is nonzero almost everywhere and that $|k(x)| \le M$ for all x in $[a, b]$ and set $\kappa = \min\{10^{-3}, 10^{-8}M^{-1/3}\}$. Then for almost all x in $[a, b]$, there are infinitely many positive integers N such that

$$|k_0\Psi_0(x) + k_1\Psi_1(x) + k_2| \ge \kappa N^{-2}$$

for all integers k_0, k_1, k_2 with $0 < \max\{|k_0|, |k_1|\} \le N$.

Using Theorem 5.10 and Theorem 5.11 we are now in a position to prove (5.14) and (5.15).

Proof of (5.15) For this purpose we can directly apply Theorem 5.10, where $k = m - 1$ and U is an open set contained in

$$\Delta = \{u = (u_0, \ldots, u_{m-2}) : u_0 \ge 0, \ldots, u_{m-2} \ge 0, u_0 + \cdots + u_{m-2} \le 1\}$$

and $\Psi_j(u) = \log(u_j)$ $(0 \le j \le m - 2)$, resp. $\Psi_{m-1}(u) = \log(1 - u_0 - \cdots - u_{m-2})$. We also know that, for almost all u, the numbers $1, \Psi_0(u), \ldots, \Psi_{m-1}(u)$ are linearly independent over the rationals, hence,

$$L := k_0\Psi_0(u) + \cdots + k_{m-1}\Psi_{m-1}(u) + k_m \ne 0$$

for all nonzero integer vectors $(k_0, k_1, \ldots, k_m)$.

Set $J = \max_{0 \le j \le m-1} |k_j|$ and define N by $N^{1-\eta} = J \log N$. Assume that J is large enough to give $N \ge N_0(u)$. We then have (for suitable constants $c_1, c_2 > 0$)

$$\begin{aligned}
|L| &\ge N^{-m+\eta}(\log N) \\
&\ge c_1 J^{-m-(m-1)\eta/(1-\eta)}(\log J)^{(1-m)/(1-\eta)} \\
&\ge c_2 J^{-m-\varepsilon}
\end{aligned}$$

for $\varepsilon = 2(m - 1)\eta/(1 - \eta)$ and J large enough. This completes the proof of (5.15).

Proof of (5.14) To simplify our presentation, we first apply Theorem 5.11 in the case of $m = 2$ and then briefly indicate how it generalizes. First of all, we want to point out that Theorems 5.10 and 5.11 are lower bounds for the homogeneous linear form

$$L = k_0 \Psi_0(u) + \cdots + k_{m-1} \Psi_{m-1}(u) + k_m$$

in terms of $\max |k_j|$. Using techniques from "geometry of numbers," these lower bounds can be transformed into upper bounds for the dispersion of the set

$$X = \{\langle k_0 \Psi_0(u) + \cdots + k_{m-1} \Psi_{m-1}(u) \rangle : 0 \le k_0, \ldots, k_{m-1} < N\}.$$

In particular, we will use the notion of successive minima of convex bodies. Let $B \subseteq \mathbf{R}^d$ be a 0-symmetric convex body. Then the successive minima λ_j are defined by

$$\lambda_j = \inf\{\lambda > 0 : \lambda B \text{ contains } j \text{ linearly independent integer vectors}\}.$$

One of the first main results of "geometry of numbers" is *Minkowski's Second Theorem* stating that

$$2^d/d! \le \lambda_1 \cdots \lambda_d \operatorname{Vol}_d(B) \le 2^d.$$

Let x and N be the same as Theorem 5.11 and consider the convex body $B \subseteq \mathbf{R}^3$ that is defined by the inequalities

$$|y_0 \Psi_0(x) + y_1 \Psi_1(x) + y_2| \le \kappa N^{-2},$$
$$|y_0| \le N,$$
$$|y_1| \le N.$$

By Theorem 5.11, the set B does not contain a nonzero integer point. Thus, the first minimum λ_1 of B is ≥ 1. Note that $\operatorname{Vol}_3(B) = 8\kappa$. Then from Minkowski's Second Theorem we conclude that the three minima of this convex body satisfy $\lambda_1 \lambda_2 \lambda_3 \le 1/\kappa$. Since $1 \le \lambda_1 \le \lambda_2$ we thus get $\lambda_3 \le \lambda_1 \lambda_2 \lambda_3 \le 1/\kappa$ and consequently $\lambda_1 \le \lambda_2 \le \lambda_3 \le 1/\kappa$. In other words, there exist constants κ_2 and κ_3, and three linearly independent integer vectors (a_0, a_1, a_2), (b_0, b_1, b_2) and (c_0, c_1, c_2) such that

$$|a_0 \Psi_0(x) + a_1 \Psi_1(x) + a_2| \le \kappa_2 N^{-2},$$
$$|b_0 \Psi_0(x) + b_1 \Psi_1(x) + b_2| \le \kappa_2 N^{-2},$$
$$|c_0 \Psi_0(x) + c_1 \Psi_1(x) + c_2| \le \kappa_2 N^{-2},$$
$$\max\{|a_i|, |b_i|, |c_i|\} \le \kappa_3 N.$$

Using these linearly independent integer vectors, we can show that the dispersion of

$$X = \{\langle k_0 \Psi_0(x) + k_1 \Psi_1(x) \rangle : 0 \le k_0, k_1 \le 7\kappa_3 N\}$$

is small.

Let ξ be a real number (that we want to approximate by an element of X) and consider the (regular) system of linear equations

$$-\xi + \theta_a(a_0\Psi_0(x) + a_1\Psi_1(x) + a_2) + \theta_b(b_0\Psi_0(x) + b_1\Psi_1(x) + b_2)$$
$$+ \theta_c(c_0\Psi_0(x) + c_1\Psi_1(x) + c_2) = 4\kappa_2 N^{-2},$$
$$\theta_a a_0 + \theta_b b_0 + \theta_c c_0 = 4\kappa_3 N, \tag{5.20}$$
$$\theta_a a_1 + \theta_b b_1 + \theta_c c_1 = 4\kappa_3 N.$$

Denote by $(\theta_a, \theta_b, \theta_c)$ its unique solution and set

$$t_a = \lfloor \theta_a \rfloor, \quad t_b = \lfloor \theta_b \rfloor, \quad t_c = \lfloor \theta_c \rfloor,$$

and

$$k_j = t_a a_j + t_b b_j + t_c c_j \quad (j = 0, 1, 2).$$

Of course, k_0, k_1, k_2 are integers and from the second and third equation of (5.20) combined with $\max\{|a_i|, |b_i|, |c_i|\} \le \kappa_3 N$ it follows that

$$\kappa_3 N \le \min\{k_0, k_1\} \le \max\{k_0, k_1\} \le 7\kappa_3 N,$$

in particular, k_0 and k_1 are positive integers. Moreover, by considering the first equation of (5.20) we see that

$$\kappa_2 N^{-2} \le -\xi + k_0\Psi_0(x) + k_1\Psi_1(x) + k_2 \le 7\kappa_2 N^{-2}.$$

Since this estimate is independent of the choice of ξ, this implies

$$\delta(X) \le 7\kappa_2 N^{-2}.$$

Clearly, we can apply this procedure for the functions $\Psi_0(x) = \log x$ and $\Psi_1(x) = \log(1-x)$ and for any interval $[a, b]$ with $0 < a < b < 1$.

This also shows that we can choose $\varepsilon = 0$ in the case $m = 2$ for infinitely many N in Lemma 5.6, provided that we introduce an (absolute) numerical constant.

Finally, we discuss the general case $m \ge 2$ (and prove Lemma 5.6). We consider the convex body $B \subseteq \mathbf{R}^{m+1}$ that has volume 2^{m+1} and is defined by (5.19):

$$|y_0\Psi_0(u) + \cdots + y_{m-1}\Psi_{m-1}(u) + y_m| \le N^{-m+(m-k)\eta}(\log N)^{m-k},$$
$$|y_j| \le N, \quad (j = 0, \ldots, k-1),$$
$$|y_j| \le N^{1-\eta}(\log N)^{-1} \quad (j = k, \ldots, m-1).$$

By assumption, the first minimum λ_1 of B satisfies $\lambda_1 \ge N^{-\eta}$, thus, by Minkowski's Second Theorem, its last minimum λ_m is bounded by $\lambda_m \le N^{\eta\eta}$. Consequently, we have $n+1$ linearly independent vectors $\mathbf{q}^{(i)}$, $i = 0, \ldots, m$, such that

$$\|\mathbf{q}^{(i)} \cdot \Psi(u)\| \le N^{-m+(m-k)\eta+m\eta}(\log N)^k, \qquad \|\mathbf{q}^{(i)}\|_\infty \le N^{1+m\eta}.$$

We now argue as before, and consider a system of linear equations analogous to (5.20). Hence, for any real number ξ, there are positive integers $k_0, \ldots, k_{m-1}$ such that

$$\| -\xi + k_0\Psi_0(u) + \cdots + k_{m-1}\Psi_m(u)\| < \frac{1}{N^{m-\varepsilon}}, \qquad \max k_j \le N,$$

where $\varepsilon > 0$ can be made arbitrarily small by taking sufficiently small values of η. Applied to the functions

$$\Psi_j(u) = \log(u_j), \quad 0 \le j \le m - 2$$

and

$$\Psi_{m-1}(u) = \log(1 - u_0 - \cdots - u_{m-2}),$$

this proves (5.14). This completes the proof of Lemma 5.6.   ∎

5.5 Exercises

5.1   Show that every *VV* prefix code is a concatenation of VF and FV codes.
5.2   Prove Lemma 5.2.
5.3   Prove a proper variant of Theorem 5.1 in the case, where all $\log p_i$, $0 \le i < m$ are rational.
5.4   Provide details of (5.6)–(5.7).
5.5   Establish (5.10).
5.6   Derive recurrences (5.11).
5.7   Prove (5.12).
5.8   Solve congruence (5.13).
5.9   Using algorithm KHODCODE construct a VV code for $p_0 = 1/5$ and $p_1 = 4/5$.
5.10 Following the steps of the proof of Lemma 5.3 establish Lemma 5.6.

Bibliographical Notes

There is scarcely any literature on VV codes with a few exceptions such as Fabris (1992), Freeman (1993), Khodak (1972). The most interesting is a 50-year-old work by Khodak (1972). To the best of our knowledge, not much has been done since then, except that Fabris (1992) and also Freeman (1993) analyzed Tunstall–Huffman VV code and provided a simple bound on the redundancy rate. Furthermore, Fabris (1992) also showed that a greedy optimization does not lead to an optimal VV code.

There is much more literature on Diophantine equations and their approximation. We mention here Cassels (1957), Bernik and Dodson (1999), Allouche and Shallit (2008), Sprindzuk (1979). Continued fractions are discussed for example in Cassels (1957) and Allouche and Shallit (2008). Minkowski's Second Theorem is discussed in Cassels (1957), Schmidt (1980).

This chapter is based on Bugeaud et al. (2008).

6

Nonprefix One-to-One Codes

In this chapter, we discuss nonprefix codes; that is, codes which are not prefix free and do not satisfy Kraft's inequality. In particular, we construct a one-to-one code whose average length is smaller than the source entropy in defiance of the Shannon lower bound. To focus, we only consider fixed-to-variable codes over known memoryless sources with block size equal to n. We first present a very precise analysis of one-to-one codes for a binary source alphabet, and then extend it to a general finite source alphabet.

We start with some general comments. Lossless symbol-by-symbol compressors are required to satisfy the condition of "unique decodability" whereby different input strings are assigned different compressed versions. Uniquely decodable nonprefix codes do not offer any advantages over prefix codes since any uniquely decodable code must assign lengths to the various symbols that satisfy Kraft's inequality, while a prefix code is guaranteed to exist with those symbol lengths. Achieved by the Huffman code, an exact expression for the minimum average length of a prefix symbol-by-symbol binary code is unknown; however, in Chapter 2 we provided precise asymptotics.

However, the paradigm of symbol-by-symbol compression is severely suboptimal even for memoryless sources. For example, symbol-by-symbol compression is unable to exploit the redundancy of biased coin flips. Algorithmically, at the expense of a slight penalty in average encoding length, this inefficiency is dealt with in stream codes such as arithmetic coding. To approach the minimum average encoding length, one can partition the source string of length n into blocks of length k and apply the symbol-by-symbol approach at the block level. The resulting average compressed length per source symbol is equal to the entropy of each symbol, $H(X)$, plus at most $1/k$ bits if the source is memoryless, or more generally, equal to the entropy of k consecutive symbols divided by k plus at most $1/k$ bits. Thus, to achieve the best average efficiency without regard to complexity, we can let $k = n$, apply a Huffman code to the whole n-tuple and the resulting average compressed length behaves as

$$L_n = nH(X) + O(1).$$

In Chapter 2, we analyzed precisely the $O(1)$ term, which really constitutes the redundancy of the Huffman code.

It is possible, however, to attain average compressed length lower than the entropy (by, for example, ignoring the unique decodability or Kraft's inequality). The reason is that it is often unnecessary, and in fact wasteful, to impose the prefix condition on a code that operates at the level of the whole file to be compressed. Applying prefix codes to n-block supersymbols is only optimal in terms of the linear growth with n (it attains the entropy rate for stationary ergodic sources); however, as far as sublinear terms, this conventional approach incurs loss of optimality. The optimal fixed-to-variable length code performs no blocking on the source output; instead the optimal length-n compressor chooses an encoding table that lists all source realizations of length n in *decreasing probabilities* (breaking ties using a lexicographical ordering on the source symbols) and assigns code, starting with the most probable.

The fact that the length of the compressed file is unknown a priori is immaterial since the decompressor receives as input the compressed file, including where the file "starts and ends." For example, files stored in a random-access medium (such as a hard disk) do not satisfy the prefix condition: a directory (organized as a so-called *inode pointer structure*), contains the starting and ending locations of the sequence of blocks occupied by each file in the storage medium.

The foregoing code is optimal not just in the sense of average length but in the sense that the cumulative distribution function of its length is larger than or equal to that of any other code. Such optimal codes have been previously considered under the rubric of *one-to-one* codes that we discuss next.

6.1 Binary One-to-One Code

We focus on one-to-one codes for a memoryless source X over the binary alphabet $\mathcal{A} = \{0, 1\}$ with p being the probability of generating a "0." Hence, the sequence $x^n = x_1, \ldots, x_n \in \mathcal{A}^n$ has the empirical probability $P(x^n) = p^k q^{n-k}$, where k is the number of 0's in x^n and p is known. We shall assume that $p \leq q$. We first list all 2^n probabilities in a nonincreasing order and assign the code length $\lfloor \log(j) \rfloor$ to the jth binary string on this list, as shown below:

$$\text{probabilities} \quad q^n \left(\frac{p}{q}\right)^0 \ \geq \ q^n \left(\frac{p}{q}\right)^1 \ \geq \ \cdots \ \geq \ q^n \left(\frac{p}{q}\right)^n$$

$$\text{code lengths} \quad \lfloor \log(1) \rfloor \qquad \lfloor \log(2) \rfloor \qquad \ldots \qquad \lfloor \log(2^n) \rfloor.$$

Observe that there are $\binom{n}{k}$ equal probabilities $p^k q^{n-k}$. Set

$$A_k = \binom{n}{0} + \binom{n}{1} + \cdots + \binom{n}{k}, \quad A_{-1} = 0.$$

Starting from the position $A_{k-1} + 1$ of this list, the next $\binom{n}{k}$ probabilities are the same and equal to $p^k q^{n-k}$. The one-to-one code assigns to x^n the shortest (possibly empty) binary string (ties broken with the ordering $0 < 1$) not assigned to any element y^n with $P(y^n) > P(x^n)$. Thus, for each $j = A_{k-1} + i$, $1 \leq i \leq \binom{n}{k}$, we assign the code length

$$\lfloor \log(j) \rfloor = \lfloor \log(A_{k-1} + i) \rfloor$$

to the jth binary string. Hence the average code length is

$$\mathbf{E}[L_n] = \sum_{k=0}^{n} p^k q^{n-k} \sum_{j=A_{k-1}+1}^{A_k} \lfloor \log(j) \rfloor \qquad (6.1)$$

$$= \sum_{k=0}^{n} p^k q^{n-k} \sum_{i=1}^{\binom{n}{k}} \lfloor \log(A_{k-1} + i) \rfloor.$$

Our goal is to estimate $\mathbf{E}[L_n]$ asymptotically for large n and the average unnormalized redundancy

$$\overline{R}_n = \mathbf{E}[L_n] - nh(p),$$

where $h(p) = -p \log p - q \log q$ is the binary entropy.

Let us first simplify the formula for $\mathbf{E}[L_n]$. We need to handle the inner sum that contains the floor function. To evaluate this sum we apply partial summation (see Exercise 6.1)

$$\sum_{j=1}^{N} a_j = N a_N - \sum_{j=1}^{N-1} j(a_{j+1} - a_j). \tag{6.2}$$

Using this, we easily find an explicit formula for the inner sum of (6.1), namely

$$S_{n,k} = \sum_{j=1}^{\binom{n}{k}} \lfloor \log(A_{k-1} + j) \rfloor$$

$$= \binom{n}{k} \lfloor \log A_k \rfloor - \left(2^{\lfloor \log(A_k) \rfloor + 1} - 2^{\lceil \log(A_{k-1} + 2) \rceil} \right)$$

$$+ (A_{k-1} + 1)(1 + \lfloor \log(A_k) \rfloor - \lceil \log(A_{k-1} + 2) \rceil).$$

After some algebra, using $\lfloor x \rfloor = x - \langle x \rangle$ and $\lceil x \rceil = x + \langle -x \rangle$, we finally reduce the formula for $\mathbf{E}[L_n]$ to the following

$$\mathbf{E}[L_n] = \sum_{k=0}^{n} \binom{n}{k} p^k q^{n-k} \lfloor \log A_k \rfloor \tag{6.3}$$

$$- 2 \sum_{k=0}^{n} \binom{n}{k} p^k q^{n-k} 2^{-\langle \log A_k \rangle}$$

$$+ \sum_{k=0}^{n} \binom{n}{k} p^k q^{n-k} \frac{1 + A_{k-1}}{\binom{n}{k}}$$

$$\times \left(1 + \log\left(\frac{A_k}{A_{k-1} + 2} \right) - \langle - \log(A_{k-1} + 2) \rangle - \langle \log A_k \rangle \right)$$

$$- \sum_{k=0}^{n} \binom{n}{k} p^k q^{n-k} \frac{A_{k-1}}{\binom{n}{k}} \left(2^{-\langle \log A_k \rangle + 1} - 2^{\langle -\log(A_{k-1} + 2) \rangle} \right)$$

$$+ 2 \sum_{k=0}^{n} p^k q^{n-k} 2^{\langle - \log(A_{k-1} + 2) \rangle}.$$

Now we are in the position to present the result on the asymptotic behavior of the average unnormalized redundancy $\overline{R}_n$.

Theorem 6.1 *Consider a binary memoryless source and the one-to-one block code described above. Then for $p < \frac{1}{2}$,*

$$\overline{R}_n = -\frac{1}{2} \log n - \frac{3 + \ln 2}{2 \ln 2} + \log \frac{1-p}{1-2p} \frac{1}{\sqrt{2\pi p(1-p)}}$$

$$+ \frac{p}{1-2p} \log\left(\frac{2(1-p)}{p} \right) + F(n) + o(1). \tag{6.4}$$

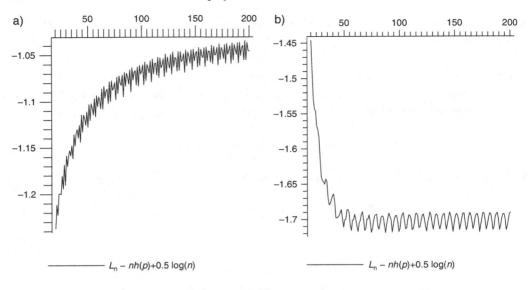

Figure 6.1 Plots of $L_n - nh(p) + 0.5 \log(n)$ (y-axis) versus n (x-axis) for (a) irrational $\alpha = \log(1-p)/p$ with $p = 1/\pi$; (b) rational $\alpha = \log(1-p)/p$ with $p = 1/9$.

Furthermore, if $\alpha = \log(1-p)/p$ is irrational then $F(n) = 0$. Conversely if $\alpha = N/M$ for some integers M, N such that $\gcd(N, M) = 1$, then $F(n) = H_M(\beta n - \frac{1}{2} \log n)$, where $\beta = \log(1/(1-p))$ and $H_M(y)$ is a periodic function with period $1/M$ which is upper bounded by $H_M(y) = O(1/M)$.
Finally, for $p = \frac{1}{2}$, we have

$$\overline{R}_n = -2 + 2^{-n}(n+2) \tag{6.5}$$

for every $n \geq 1$.

We note that the function $H_M(y)$ can be explicitly represented in terms of integrals (see Lemma 6.3).

We continue with some observations. As already discussed in Chapter 2, the redundancy behavior depends on the rationality/irrationality of $\alpha = \log(1-p)/p$. In Figure 6.1, we plot $\overline{R}_n + 0.5 \log(n)$ versus n. We observe a change of "mode" from a "converging mode" to a "fluctuating mode," when switching from $\alpha = \log(1-p)/p$ irrational (cf. Figure 6.1(a)) to rational (cf. Figure 6.1(b)). We saw this behavior already in Chapters 2 and 3 for Huffman, Shannon, and Tunstall codes.

We briefly sketch the proof of Theorem 6.1 and only analyze here part (6.3) of $\mathbf{E}[L_n]$, which we rewrite as follows:

$$\sum_{k=0}^{n} \binom{n}{k} p^k q^{n-k} \lfloor \log A_k \rfloor = \sum_{k=0}^{n} \binom{n}{k} p^k q^{n-k} \log A_k$$
$$- \sum_{k=0}^{n} \binom{n}{k} p^k q^{n-k} \langle \log A_k \rangle,$$

and define

$$a_n = \sum_{k=0}^{n} \binom{n}{k} p^k q^{n-k} \log A_k, \qquad b_n = \sum_{k=0}^{n} \binom{n}{k} p^k q^{n-k} \langle \log A_k \rangle.$$

The other terms can be handled very similarly or are negligible; for example, we have

$$\sum_{k=0}^{n} p^k q^{n-k} 2^{\langle -\log(A_{k-1}+2) \rangle} = O(q^n).$$

We first deal with a_n, for which we need to derive a precise asymptotic estimate for A_n.

Lemma 6.2 *For every sufficiently small $\varepsilon > 0$, there exist $\delta > 0$ such that uniformly for $k = np + O(n^{1/2+\varepsilon})$,*

$$A_k = \frac{1-p}{1-2p} \frac{1}{\sqrt{2\pi np(1-p)}} \left(\frac{1-p}{p}\right)^k \frac{1}{(1-p)^n} \qquad (6.6)$$

$$\times \exp\left(-\frac{(k-np)^2}{2p(1-p)n}\right) \left(1 + O(n^{-\delta})\right)$$

for some $\delta > 0$.

Proof By Stirling's formula and local expansion of the logarithm, it follows that

$$\binom{n}{k} = \frac{1}{\sqrt{2\pi np(1-p)}} \left(\frac{1-p}{p}\right)^k \frac{1}{(1-p)^n} \exp\left(-\frac{(k-np)^2}{2np(1-p)}\right)$$

$$\times \left(1 + O\left(\frac{|k-np|^3}{n^2} + \frac{|k-np|}{n}\right)\right)$$

for $k - np = O(n^{1/2+\varepsilon})$, where $0 < \varepsilon < \frac{1}{6}$. This directly implies (6.6). ∎

We remark that we could have also used the saddle point method applied to the generating function

$$A_n(z) = \sum_{k=0}^{n} A_k z^k = \frac{(1+z)^n - 2^n z^{n+1}}{1-z},$$

with the saddle point $z_0 = p/(1-p)$.

Lemma 6.2 implies that (uniformly for $|k - pn| \leq n^{1/2+\varepsilon}$)

$$\log A_k = \alpha k + n\beta - \log(\omega\sqrt{n}) - \frac{(k-np)^2}{2p(1-p)n \ln 2} + O(n^{-\delta}),$$

where $\omega = (1-2p)\sqrt{2\pi p(1-p)}/(1-p)$ and $\delta > 0$. Consequently we directly obtain

$$a_n = \sum_{|k-pn| \leq n^{1/2+\varepsilon}} \binom{n}{k} p^k q^{n-k} \log A_k + O(n^{-\delta})$$

$$= \alpha pn + n\beta - \log(\omega\sqrt{n}) - \frac{1}{2\ln 2} + O(n^{-\delta}).$$

For b_n we need an extension of Lemma 2.5 from Chapter 2 presented next.

Lemma 6.3 *Let $0 < p < 1$ be a fixed real number and $f : [0,1] \to \mathbb{R}$ be a Riemann integrable function.*

(i) *If α is irrational, then*

$$\lim_{n \to \infty} \sum_{k=0}^{n} \binom{n}{k} p^k (1-p)^{n-k} f \left(\langle k\alpha + y - (k-np)^2/(2pqn \ln 2) + o(1) \rangle \right) \qquad (6.7)$$

$$= \int_0^1 f(t)\, dt,$$

where the convergence is uniform for all shifts $y \in \mathbb{R}$.

(ii) *Suppose that $\alpha = \frac{N}{M}$ is a rational number with integers N, M such that $\gcd(N, M) = 1$. Then uniformly for all $y \in \mathbb{R}$,*

$$\sum_{k=0}^{n} \binom{n}{k} p^k (1-p)^{n-k} f \left(\langle k\alpha + y - (k-np)^2/(2pqn \ln 2) + o(1) \rangle \right) \qquad (6.8)$$

$$= \int_0^1 f(t)\, dt + G_M(y) + o(1),$$

where

$$G_M(y)[f] := \frac{1}{M} \sum_{r=0}^{M-1} \frac{1}{\sqrt{2\pi}} \int_{-\infty}^{\infty} e^{-x^2/2} \left(f \left(\left\langle M \left(y - \frac{x^2}{2\ln 2} \right) \right\rangle \right) - \int_0^1 f(t)\, dt \right) dx$$

is a periodic function with period $\frac{1}{M}$ and satisfies $\lim_{M \to \infty} G_M(y)[f] = 0$. In particular, if f is of bounded variation then $G_M(y)[f] = O(1/M)$.

Proof We consider first the case where α is irrational. In this case, we know that the sequence $x_k = \alpha k$ is uniformly distributed modulo 1. Actually, since $x_{k+k_0} = x_k + x_{k_0}$ is just a shifted version of the sequence x_k, we have uniformly for all k_0 and (additional) shifts s,

$$\sum_{k=0}^{K-1} f(\langle x_{k+k_0} + s \rangle) = K \int_0^1 f(t)\, dt + o(K)$$

as $K \to \infty$. Furthermore we can perturb the sequence x_k slightly to $x_k + o_K(1)$ and still obtain uniformly for all k_0 and shifts s,

$$\sum_{k=0}^{K-1} f(\langle x_{k+k_0} + s + o_K(1) \rangle) = K \int_0^1 f(t)\, dt + o(K)$$

as $K \to \infty$.

Since

$$\binom{n}{k} p^k (1-p)^{n-k} \sim \frac{1}{\sqrt{2\pi np(1-p)}} \exp \left(-\frac{(k-np)^2}{2p(1-p)n} \right)$$

is concentrated in the interval $k \in [np - n^{\frac{1}{2}+\varepsilon}, np + n^{\frac{1}{2}+\varepsilon}] =: I_n$, it is sufficient to restrict ourselves to this interval I_n. We now set $K = \lfloor n^{\frac{1}{2}-2\varepsilon} \rfloor$ and partition the interval

$[np - n^{\frac{1}{2}+\varepsilon}, np + n^{\frac{1}{2}+\varepsilon}]$ into (approximately) $2n^{3\varepsilon}$ subintervals of length K. Next observe that for $k_1, k_2 \in I_n$ with $|k_1 - k_2| \leq K$, we have (uniformly)

$$\exp\left(-\frac{(k_1 - np)^2}{2p(1-p)n}\right) = \exp\left(-\frac{(k_2 - np)^2}{2p(1-p)n}\right)(1 + O(n^{-\varepsilon})).$$

Hence, we have for $k_1 \in I_n$ and the subinterval $[k_1, k_1 + K - 1]$,

$$\sum_{k=k_1}^{k_1+K-1} \binom{n}{k} p^k (1-p)^{n-k} f\left(\langle k\alpha + y - (k - np)^2/(2pqn \ln 2) + o(1)\rangle\right)$$

$$= \frac{1}{\sqrt{2\pi np(1-p)}} \exp\left(-\frac{(k_1 - np)^2}{2p(1-p)n}\right)$$

$$\times \sum_{k=k_1}^{k_1+K-1} (1 + O(n^{-\varepsilon})) f\left(\langle k\alpha + y - (k_1 - np)^2/(2pqn \ln 2 + O(n^{-\varepsilon})) + o(1)\rangle\right)$$

$$= \frac{K}{\sqrt{2\pi np(1-p)}} \exp\left(-\frac{(k_1 - np)^2}{2p(1-p)n}\right) \int_0^1 f(t)\, dt$$

$$+ o\left(\frac{K}{\sqrt{2\pi np(1-p)}} \exp\left(-\frac{(k_1 - np)^2}{2p(1-p)n}\right)\right).$$

Finally, by summing up over all subintervals of I_n, that is, by considering all k_1 of the form $k_1 = \lfloor np - n^{\frac{1}{2}+\varepsilon} \rfloor + rM$ for $0 \leq r < 2n^{3\varepsilon}$, we directly obtain (6.7).

For the rational case, we first partition the sum according to the residue classes modulo M and, hence, obtain by Gaussian approximation

$$\sum_{k=0}^{n} \binom{n}{k} p^k (1-p)^{n-k} f\left(\langle kN/M + y - (k - np)^2/(2pqn \ln 2) + o(1)\rangle\right)$$

$$= \sum_{r=0}^{M-1} \sum_{k \equiv r \bmod M} \binom{n}{k} p^k (1-p)^{n-k} f\left(\langle rN/M + y - (k - np)^2/(2pqn \ln 2) + o(1)\rangle\right)$$

$$= \frac{1}{M} \sum_{r=0}^{M-1} \frac{1}{\sqrt{2\pi}} \int_{-\infty}^{\infty} e^{-x^2/2} f\left(\langle rN/M + y - x^2/(2 \ln 2)\rangle\right) dx + o(1).$$

Since the residue classes $rN \bmod M$, $r = 0, \ldots, M - 1$, are just all residue classes, we complete the proof of (6.8).

Note that the sequence r/M, $0 \leq r \leq M - 1$, has discrepancy $1/M$, even uniformly for a shifted version. Thus, we have uniformly in x,

$$\frac{1}{M} \sum_{r=0}^{M-1} f\left(\langle rN/M + y - x^2/(2 \ln 2)\rangle\right) = \int_0^1 f(t)\, dt + o(1),$$

which implies that $G_M(y)[f] \to 0$ as $M \to \infty$. Furthermore, if f is of bounded variation then by Koksma–Hlawka's inequality (Theorem E.6) we can replace the error term $o(1)$ by $O(1/M)$, which implies that $G_M(y)[f] = O(1/M)$. ∎

This leads us to the asymptotic behavior for

$$b_n = \sum_{|k-pn| \leq n^{1/2+\varepsilon}} \binom{n}{k} p^k q^{n-k} \langle \log A_k \rangle + O(n^{-\delta})$$

$$= \sum_{|k-pn| \leq n^{1/2+\varepsilon}} \binom{n}{k} p^k q^{n-k} \langle Nk/M + n\beta - \log(\omega\sqrt{n}) - \frac{(k-np)^2}{2p(1-p)n \ln 2} + O(n^{-\delta}) \rangle$$

$$+ O(n^{-\delta})$$

$$= \frac{1}{2} + G_M(n\beta - \log(\omega\sqrt{n}))[x] + o(1).$$

As mentioned, the other sums can be handled similarly (see Exercise 6.6 and Szpankowski (2008)). This completes our sketch of the proof of Theorem 6.1.

6.2 Nonbinary One-to-One Code

Finally, we consider a nonprefix code over a general finite alphabet. Consider a probability distribution P on a set of ordered elements $\mathcal{A} = \{0, \ldots, m-1\}$. We define a permutation π on $\mathcal{A}$ by $\pi(a) < \pi(b)$ if $P(a) > P(b)$ or if $P(a) = P(b)$ and $a < b$. Thus, $\pi(x) = \ell$ if x is the ℓth most probable element in $\mathcal{A}$ according to the distribution P, with ties broken according to the ordering in $\mathcal{A}$. It is easy to verify that

$$P(x)\pi(x) \leq 1 \tag{6.9}$$

for all $x \in \mathcal{A}$. Indeed, if (6.9) failed to be satisfied for $x_0 \in \mathcal{A}$, there would be at least $\pi(x_0)$ masses strictly larger than $1/\pi(x_0)$.

The one-to-one code assigns to x the shortest (possibly empty) binary string (ties broken with the ordering $0 < 1$) not assigned to any element y with $\pi(y) < \pi(x)$. Thus, we obtain (the simple but important conclusion) that the length of the encoding of x is $\lfloor \log \pi(x) \rfloor$. We are interested in finding the average code length

$$\overline{L} = \mathbf{E}[\lfloor \log \pi(X) \rfloor].$$

A simple upper bound (first noticed in Wyner (1972)) is obtained as follows:

$$\overline{L} = \mathbf{E}[\lfloor \log \pi(X) \rfloor]$$
$$\leq \mathbf{E}[\log \pi(X)]$$
$$\leq \mathbf{E}\left[\log \frac{1}{P(X)}\right]$$
$$= H(P),$$

where (6.10) follows from (6.9). Note that dropping the prefix condition makes the entropy an upper bound to the minimum average length, rather than a lower bound.

As a simple example, let us compute the average code length when P is uniform over $\mathcal{A} = \{0, \ldots, m-1\}$. Here we have

$$\overline{L} = \frac{1}{m} \sum_{i=1}^{m} \lfloor \log i \rfloor$$

$$= \lfloor \log m \rfloor + \frac{1}{m} \left(2 + \lfloor \log m \rfloor - 2^{\lfloor \log m \rfloor + 1} \right), \tag{6.10}$$

which is quite close to the entropy $H(P) = \log m$. In the second line of (6.10) we apply formula (6.2).

Our goal is to present a general result for the asymptotic behavior of average block code length for memoryless sources over $\mathcal{A}_n = \{0, \ldots, m-1\}^n$.

Theorem 6.4 (Szpankowski and Verdu 2011) *Consider a memoryless source on $\mathcal{A}_n = \{0, \ldots, m-1\}^n$ and assume that the probability distribution $p_0, \ldots, p_{m-1}$ on $\mathcal{A} = \{0, \ldots, m-1\}$ is not uniform. Then the average code length of the one-to-one code is given by*

$$\mathbf{E}[L_n] = nh - \frac{1}{2} \log n + O(1), \tag{6.11}$$

where $h = -\sum_{i=0}^{m-1} p_i \log p_i$ is the entropy. Hence, the average redundancy becomes

$$\overline{R}_n = -\frac{1}{2} \log n + O(1)$$

for large n.

This theorem extends Theorem 6.1 (that was restricted to $m = 2$), however, in contrast to Theorem 6.1, the bounded error term is not specified.

The rest of this section is devoted to the proof of Theorem 6.4. Without loss of generality we assume that

$$p_0 \leq p_1 \leq \cdots \leq p_{m-2} \leq p_{m-1}. \tag{6.12}$$

We set

$$B_i = \log \frac{p_{m-1}}{p_i} \tag{6.13}$$

for $i = 0, \ldots, m - 2$. Note that the entropy h can be expressed as

$$h = \log \frac{1}{p_{m-1}} + \sum_{i=0}^{m-2} p_i B_i. \tag{6.14}$$

Let

$$\mathbf{k} = (k_0, \ldots, k_{m-1}) \tag{6.15}$$

be such that $k_0 + \cdots + k_{m-1} = n$ denote the *type* of an n-string x^n; the probability of each such string is equal to

$$P(x^n) = p^{\mathbf{k}} = p_0^{k_0} \cdots p_{m-1}^{k_{m-1}}. \tag{6.16}$$

Denote the set of all types of n-strings in $\mathcal{A}_n = \{0, \ldots, m-1\}^n$ by

$$\mathcal{T}_{n,m} = \{(k_0, \ldots, k_{m-1}) \in \mathbb{N}^m, k_0 + \cdots + k_{m-1} = n\}.$$

We introduce an order among types:

$$\mathbf{j} \preceq \mathbf{k} \quad \text{if and only if} \quad p^{\mathbf{j}} \geq p^{\mathbf{k}},$$

and we sort all types from the smallest index (largest probability) to the largest. This can be accomplished by observing that $p^{\mathbf{j}} \geq p^{\mathbf{k}}$ is equivalent to

$$j_0 B_0 + \cdots + j_{m-2} B_{m-2} \leq k_0 B_0 + \cdots + k_{m-2} B_{m-2}. \tag{6.17}$$

Therefore, to sort types $\mathbf{k}$, one needs to sort the function $S \colon \mathbb{R}^{m-1} \mapsto \mathbb{R}^+$,

$$S(\mathbf{k}) = k_0 B_0 + \cdots + k_{m-2} B_{m-2}, \tag{6.18}$$

from the smallest value $S(00 \cdots 0) = 0$ to the largest.

There are

$$\binom{n}{\mathbf{k}} = \binom{n}{k_0, \ldots, k_{m-1}} = \frac{n!}{k_0! \cdots k_{m-1}!} \tag{6.19}$$

sequences of type $\mathbf{k}$ and we list them in the lexicographic order. Then, the optimum code assigns length $\lfloor \log i \rfloor$ to the ith sequence ($1 \leq i \leq m^n$) in this list. We denote the number of sequences more probable than or equal to type $\mathbf{k}$ as

$$A_{\mathbf{k}} := \sum_{\mathbf{j} \preceq \mathbf{k}} \binom{n}{\mathbf{j}}.$$

In a first step, we derive an asymptotic property for $A_{\mathbf{k}}$.

Lemma 6.5 *Suppose that $m \geq 2$ and that the probability distribution $p_0 \leq \cdots \leq p_{m-1}$ is not uniform. Then for every sufficiently small $\varepsilon > 0$, there exist positive constants C_1, C_2 such that*

$$C_1 n^{\frac{m-2}{2}} \binom{n}{\mathbf{k}} \leq A_{\mathbf{k}} \leq C_2 n^{\frac{m-2}{2}} \binom{n}{\mathbf{k}}$$

uniformly for $\max_i |k_i - np_i| = O(n^{\frac{1}{2}+\varepsilon})$.

Proof. We consider the case, where $k_i = np_i$, $0 \leq i < m$, and show also that all estimates stay uniform with respect to small perturbation of p_i.

For notational convenience, we write $x_i = j_i - k_i = j_i - np_i$, $0 \leq i < m$. (Note we have $x_0 + \cdots + x_{m-1} = 0$.) Then by applying Stirling's formula and local expansions of the logarithm, we obtain uniformly for $\max_i |j_i - np_i| = O(n^{\frac{1}{2}+\varepsilon})$,

$$\binom{n}{\mathbf{j}} = \frac{2^{nh}}{(2\pi n)^{\frac{m-1}{2}} \sqrt{p_0 \cdots p_{m-1}}} \exp\left(B_0 x_0 + \cdots + B_{m-2} x_{m-2} - \frac{1}{2n} \sum_{i=0}^{m-1} \frac{x_i^2}{p_i} \right)$$
$$\times \left(1 + O(n^{-\delta}) \right)$$

for some $\delta > 0$, where $h = -\sum_{i=0}^{m-1} p_i \log p_i$. Thus, $A_{\mathbf{k}}$ is given by

$$A_{\mathbf{k}} = \sum_{\mathbf{j} \preceq \mathbf{k}} \binom{n}{\mathbf{j}}$$
$$= \frac{m^{nh}}{(2\pi)^{\frac{m-1}{2}} \sqrt{p_0 \cdots p_{m-1}}} \sum_{\mathbf{x} \preceq 0} \exp\left(B_0 x_0 + \cdots + B_{m-2} x_{m-2} - \frac{1}{2n} \sum_{i=0}^{m-1} \frac{x_i^2}{p_i} \right)$$
$$\times \left(1 + O(n^{-\delta}) \right).$$

Clearly we can restrict ourselves to the case, where $x_i = O(n^{\frac{1}{2}+\varepsilon})$, which we assume from now on implicitly. The resulting error is negligible. In this range we also have the property that the term

$$\exp\left(B_0 x_0 + \cdots + B_{m-2} x_{m-2} - \frac{1}{2n} \sum_{i=0}^{m-1} \frac{x_i^2}{p_i}\right)$$

is of the same order of magnitude if the x_i are varied to $x_i \pm 1$. Hence, we can replace the upper sum S over $\mathbf{x}$ by an integral of the form

$$I = \int_{\mathbf{x} \leq 0} \exp\left(B_0 x_0 + \cdots + B_{m-2} x_{m-2} - \frac{1}{2n} \sum_{i=0}^{m-1} \frac{x_i^2}{p_i}\right), \qquad (6.20)$$

so that $C_1 \leq I/S \leq C_2$ for proper positive constants C_1, C_2.

We now estimate the integral (6.20). To simplify our presentation, we focus on the case $m = 3$. We ask the reader in Exercise 6.9 to provide details for all m. So let

$$I = \int_{B_0 x_0 + B_1 x_1 \leq 0} \exp\left(B_0 x_0 + B_1 x_1 - \frac{x_0^2}{2np_0} - \frac{x_1^2}{2np_1} - \frac{(x_0 + x_1)^2}{2np_2}\right) dx_0 dx_1.$$

In a first step we apply a proper linear transformation A_1 to the variables x_0, x_1 such that

$$\frac{x_0^2}{p_0} + \frac{x_1^2}{p_1} + \frac{(x_0 + x_1)^2}{p_2} = y_0^2 + y_1^2.$$

Clearly $B_0 x_0 + B_1 x_1 = B_0' y_0 + B_1' y_1$ for proper real coefficients $(B_0', B_1') \neq (0, 0)$. In a second step, we apply an orthogonal operation A_2 to the variables y_0, y_1 such that $B_0' y_0 + B_1' y_1 = B_0'' z_0$ (and, of course, $y_0^2 + y_1^2 = z_0^2 + z_1^2$). Hence, the integral I is (up to the constant $|\det A_1|$) given by

$$\begin{aligned}
I' &= \int_{B_0'' z_0 \leq 0} \exp\left(B_0'' z_0 - \frac{1}{2n}(z_0^2 + z_1^2)\right) dz_0 dz_1 \\
&= \sqrt{2\pi n} \int_{B_0'' z_0 \leq 0} \exp\left(B_0'' z_0 - \frac{1}{2n} z_0^2\right) dz_0 \\
&= \frac{\sqrt{2\pi n}}{|B|}\left(1 + O(n^{-1})\right).
\end{aligned}$$

Of course, this proves (in the case $m = 3$) that $A_{\mathbf{k}}$ and $\sqrt{n}\binom{n}{\mathbf{k}}$ differ at most by a bounded factor. In the general case, the factor $\sqrt{n}$ is replaced by $n^{\frac{m-2}{2}}$.

Clearly all computations are stable with respect to small perturbation of the p_i. This completes the proof of the lemma. ∎

As a corollary, we obtain the following asymptotic relation for the logarithm

$$\log A_{\mathbf{k}} = nh - \frac{1}{2}\log n + \frac{B_0 x_0 + \cdots + B_{m-2} x_{m-2}}{\ln 2} - \frac{1}{2\ln 2\, n} \sum_{i=0}^{m-1} \frac{x_i^2}{p_i} + O(1) \qquad (6.21)$$

uniformly for $x_i = k_i - np_i = O(n^{\frac{1}{2}+\varepsilon})$, $0 \leq i < m$.

We now turn to the average code length $\mathbf{E}[L_n]$. We use the somewhat informal, but intuitive, notation $\mathbf{k} + 1$ and $\mathbf{k} - 1$ for the *next* and *previous* types, respectively, in the sorted list of the elements of $\mathcal{T}_{n,m}$. Clearly, starting from position $A_\mathbf{k}$ the next $\binom{n}{\mathbf{k}+1}$ sequences have probability $\mathbf{p}^{\mathbf{k}+1}$. Thus the average code length can be computed as follows:

$$
\mathbf{E}[L_n] = \sum_{\mathbf{k} \in \mathcal{T}_{n,m}} \mathbf{p}^{\mathbf{k}} \sum_{i=A_{\mathbf{k}-1}+1}^{A_\mathbf{k}} \lfloor \log i \rfloor
$$

$$
= \sum_{\mathbf{k} \in \mathcal{T}_{n,m}} \mathbf{p}^{\mathbf{k}} \sum_{i=1}^{\binom{n}{\mathbf{k}}} \lfloor \log(A_\mathbf{k} - i + 1) \rfloor
$$

$$
= \sum_{\mathbf{k} \in \mathcal{T}_{n,m}} \binom{n}{\mathbf{k}} \mathbf{p}^{\mathbf{k}} \left(\log A_\mathbf{k} + O\left(\binom{n}{\mathbf{k}} / A_\mathbf{k} \right) \right),
$$

where $\mathbf{p} = (p_0, \ldots, p_{m-1})$ and we have used that $i \le \binom{n}{\mathbf{k}} = O(A_\mathbf{k})$. Actually, we have in the central part, where $|k_i - np_i| = O(n^{\frac{1}{2}+\varepsilon})$,

$$
\binom{n}{\mathbf{k}} = O(n^{-\frac{m-1}{2}} A_\mathbf{k}),
$$

which implies that

$$
\sum_{\mathbf{k} \in \mathcal{T}_{n,m}} \binom{n}{\mathbf{k}}^2 \mathbf{p}^{\mathbf{k}} / A_\mathbf{k} = O\left(n^{-\frac{m-1}{2}} \right).
$$

Furthermore, by (6.21), we have

$$
\sum_{\mathbf{k} \in \mathcal{T}_{n,m}} \binom{n}{\mathbf{k}} p^{\mathbf{k}} \log A_\mathbf{k} = \sum_{\mathbf{k} \in \mathcal{T}_{n,m}} \binom{n}{\mathbf{k}} p^{\mathbf{k}}
$$

$$
\left(nh - \frac{1}{2} \log n + \frac{1}{\ln 2} \sum_{i=0}^{m-2} B_i(k_i - np_i) - \frac{1}{2 \ln 2\, n} \sum_{i=0}^{m-1} \frac{(k_i - np_i)^2}{p_i} + O(1) \right)
$$

$$
= nh - \frac{1}{2} \log n + O(1).
$$

Consequently we obtain $\mathbf{E}[L_n] = nh - \frac{1}{2} \log n + O(1)$ as proposed.

6.3 Exercises

6.1   For any nonnegative sequence a_j, establish the following identity (6.2):

$$
\sum_{j=1}^{N} a_j = N a_N - \sum_{j=1}^{N-1} j(a_{j+1} - a_j).
$$

(see Knuth (1997) ex. 1.2.4–42).

6.2   Establish precise expansion of A_k presented in (6.6) of Lemma 6.2.

6.3   Following our analysis from Chapter 2, prove Lemma 6.3. For details see Drmota, Hwang, and Szpankowski (2002).

6.4   For an unbiased memoryless source with $p = 1/2$ prove (6.5) of Theorem 6.1.

6.5   Establish (6.10).

6.6 Estimate asymptotically the other parts of (6.3).

6.7 Let f be a function of polynomial growth. We seek asymptotics of the so-called *binomial sums*

$$S_f(n) = \sum_{k=0}^{n} \binom{n}{k} p^k (1-p)^{n-k} f(k).$$

Prove that

$$S_f(n) = f(np) + \frac{1}{2} np(1-p) f''(np) + O(nf'''(\xi))$$

for some $\xi \in [0, n]$. For example, show that

$$\sum_{k=0}^{n} \binom{n}{k} p^k (1-p)^{n-k} \log k = \log(np) - \frac{1-p}{2pn} + O(n^{-2}).$$

For more, see Flajolet (1999), Jacquet and Szpankowski (1999). For a multidimensional extension, see Cichon and Golebiewski (2012).

6.8 Compute the precise asymptotic behavior of A_{np} for $m = 3$.

6.9 Estimate the integral (6.20) for all m.

6.10 Consider again the binary one-to-one code but assume now that the source is unknown; that is, p is unknown and needs to be estimated. Analyze the average redundancy in this case (see, e.g., Kosut and Sankar (2017)).

Bibliographical Notes

Unique decipherability was addressed in many papers and books, but most likely for the first time in MacMillan (1956).

The fact that one-to-one codes have average code length smaller than entropy was actually known to Shannon and Huffman. However, Wyner (1972), and then much later Alon and Orlitsky (1994), quantified more precisely this difference. In particular, Alon and Orlitsky (1994) show that

$$L \geq H(X) - \log(H(X) + 1) - \log e.$$

This chapter is based on Szpankowski (2008) and Szpankowski and Verdu (2011). Further extensions can be found in Kontoyiannis and Verdu (2014). A universal scheme with a precise analysis was proposed in Kosut and Sankar (2017).

7

Advanced Data Structures: Tree Compression

Information theory traditionally deals with "conventional data" almost exclusively represented by sequences, be it textual data, images or video data. Over the last decade, repositories of various data have grown enormously. Most of the available data is no longer in conventional form. Instead, biological data (e.g., gene expression data, protein interaction networks, phylogenetic trees), topographical maps (containing various information about temperature, pressure, etc.), medical data (cerebral scans, mammograms, etc.), and social network data archives are in the form of *multimodal* data structures; that is, multitype and context-dependent structures, often represented by trees and graphs.

Unconventional data often contains more sophisticated structural relations. For example, a graph can be represented by a binary matrix that further can be viewed as a binary sequence. However, such a string does not exhibit internal symmetries that are conveyed by the so-called *graph automorphism* (making certain sequences/matrices "indistinguishable"). The main challenge in dealing with such structural data is to identify and describe these structural relations. In fact, these "regular properties" constitute "useful (extractable) information" understood in the spirit of Rissanen (2003) "learnable information."

For efficient compression of such data structures, one must take into account not only several different types of information, but also the statistical dependence between the general data labels and the structures themselves. In Figure 7.1 we show an example of such a multimodal structure representing an annotated protein interaction network in which graphs, trees, DAGs, and text are involved.

In the last two chapters of the first part of this book, we deal with advanced data structures. In this chapter, we discuss various trees (binary tree, d-ary tree, general trees). In the next, Chapter 8, we continue our discussion of advanced data structures focusing on graphs.

7.1 Binary Trees

The most popular data structure are trees, among which binary trees occupy a special position, so we devote this section to such trees. They come in two varieties: *plane-oriented trees*, often simply called (plane) binary trees, and *non-plane-oriented trees*. In plane-oriented trees, the order of subtrees matters, while in non-plane-oriented trees (e.g., representing a phylogenetic tree) all orientations of subtrees are equivalent, as shown in Figure 7.2:

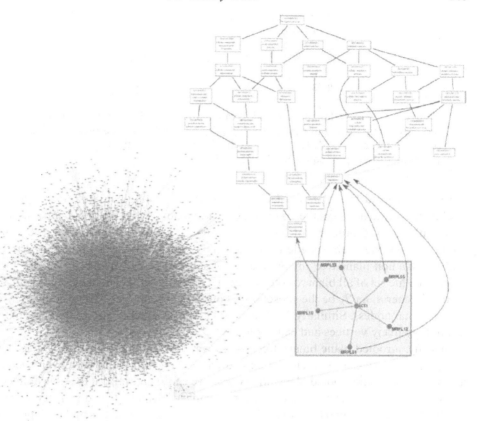

Figure 7.1 Annotated protein interaction network: nodes in the network represent proteins in the human interactome, and there is an edge between two nodes if and only if the two proteins interact in some biological process. Associated with each node is a position in a fixed *ontology* (encoded by a DAG whose nodes represent classes of proteins defined by, say, structural or functional characteristics) known as the gene ontology. Nodes that are connected in the interaction network are often close in the ontology.

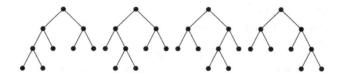

Figure 7.2 Plane-ordered representatives of one non-plane tree.

7.1.1 Plane Binary Trees

In this section, we introduce the concepts of plane binary trees and define two probabilistic models for these types of trees that turn out to be equivalent.

Figure 7.3 A rooted plane tree and its standardization. The left tree can be represented by the list of triples $\{(5, 1, 7), (1, 2, 3)\}$. After standardization, this becomes $\{(1, 2, 5), (2, 3, 4)\}$. Note that this is distinct from the tree $\{(1, 2, 3), (3, 4, 5)\}$ or, equivalently, $\{(5, 1, 7), (7, 2, 3)\}$.

We call a rooted tree a *plane binary tree* when we distinguish the left-to-right-order of the children of the nodes in the embedding of a tree on a plane. To avoid confusion, we call a tree with no fixed ordering of its subtrees a *non-plane* tree (also known in the literature as *Otter trees*). We shall assume throughout this section that every internal node has two children. In a non-plane tree any orientation of subtrees is equivalent.

Let $\mathcal{T}$ be the set of all binary rooted plane trees having finitely many vertices and, for each positive integer n, let $\mathcal{T}_n$ be the subset of $\mathcal{T}$ consisting of all trees with exactly n leaves (and $n - 1$ internal nodes). Similarly, let $\mathcal{S}$ and $\mathcal{S}_n$ be the set of all binary rooted non-plane trees with finitely many vertices and exactly n leaves, respectively.

Formally, a rooted plane binary tree $t \in \mathcal{T}_n$ can be uniquely described by a set of triples (v_i, v_j, v_k), consisting of a parent vertex and its left and right children. Given such a set of triples defining a valid rooted plane binary tree, we can standardize it to a tree defined on the vertex set $\{1, \ldots, 2n - 1\}$ by replacing a vertex v in each triple by the depth-first search index of v. We then consider two trees to be the same if they have the same standard representation; see the example in Figure 7.3.

We now introduce some notation that will be useful in the tree context. Let t be a binary plane tree, and consider a vertex v in t. By $t(v)$, we shall mean the subtree of t rooted at v. We denote by t^L and t^R the left and right subtree of t, respectively. Furthermore, we denote by $\Delta(t)$ the number of leaves in the tree t. Finally, we denote by $root(t)$ the root node of t.

We introduce two models for generating plane binary trees Our first model – the binary increasing tree model – is defined as follows. We start with a tree that consists just of the root (which is also a leaf) and apply then the following steps:

- pick uniformly at random a leaf v in the tree generated in the previous steps,
- append two children v_L and v_R to v,
- repeat this procedure until the tree has exactly n leaves.

Our second model – also known as the binary search tree model – is ubiquitous in science literature, arising, for example, in the context of binary search trees formed by inserting a random permutation of $\{1, \ldots, n - 1\}$ into a binary search tree. Under this model, we generate a random tree $\mathcal{T}_n$ as follows. We start with a tree that is just a leaf and assign to this leaf the number n (indicating that we will finally have precisely a tree with n leaves). Then we recursively apply the following procedure:

- Choose any leaf v of the tree generated in the previous steps, and let n_0 be the integer value assigned to v.

- If $n_0 > 1$, select randomly an integer s_0 from the set $\{1, \ldots, n_0 - 1\}$ with probability $\frac{1}{n_0 - 1}$, and then grow two edges from v with left edge terminating at a leaf of the extended tree with value s_0 and right edge terminating at a leaf of the extended tree with value $n_0 - s_0$.
- Repeat this procedure until all leaves are assigned to the value 1.

Clearly, the recursion terminates with a binary tree having exactly n leaves (in which each leaf has assigned value 1 that can then be deleted). This tree is T_n.

Recall that $\Delta(t)$ is the number of leaves of a tree t, and $\Delta(t(v))$ denotes the number of leaves of a tree t rooted at v. It is easy to see that under the second model

$$P(T_n = t) = \frac{1}{n-1} P(T_{\Delta(t^L)} = t^L) P(T_{\Delta(t^R)} = t^R), \tag{7.1}$$

which leads us to the formula

$$P(T_n = t) = \prod_{v \in \overset{\circ}{V}(t)} (\Delta(t(v)) - 1)^{-1}, \tag{7.2}$$

where $\overset{\circ}{V}(t)$ is the set of the internal vertices of t. It turns out that the probability distribution in the first model (for increasing binary trees) is exactly the same, as we prove in the following.

Theorem 7.1 *Under the increasing binary tree model, it holds that*

$$P(T_n = t) = \prod_{v \in \overset{\circ}{V}(t)} (\Delta(t(v)) - 1)^{-1}, \tag{7.3}$$

where $\overset{\circ}{V}(t)$ is the set of the internal vertices of t.

Proof We use the concept of *labeled histories*: a pair (t, ξ), where $t \in \mathcal{T}_n$ (generated by the first model) and ξ is a permutation of the natural numbers from 1 to $n - 1$, assigned to the *internal* $n - 1$ vertices of t, such that every path from the root forms an ascending sequence. If we think of the internal nodes of t as being associated with their depth-first-search numbers, then the permutation ξ is a function mapping each internal node of t to the time at which its two children were added to it. Thus, for instance, the root always receives the number 1, meaning that $\xi(1) = 1$. Clearly, for each t, each labeled history (t, ξ) corresponds to exactly one sequence of generation, as it defines uniquely the order of the leaves, which are picked during consecutive stages of the algorithm. Moreover, the probability of each feasible labeled history (t, ξ) is equal to $\frac{1}{(n-1)!}$ since it involves choosing one leaf from k available at the kth stage of the algorithm for $k = 1, \ldots, n - 1$. Therefore, denoting $q(t) = |\{\xi : (t, \xi) \text{ is a labeled history}\}|$, we find

$$P(T_n = t) = \frac{q(t)}{(n-1)!}.$$

Note that if $\Delta(t(v)) = k$ for any vertex v of t, then we know that the sequence of node choices corresponding to (t, ξ) must contain exactly $k - 1$ internal vertices from the subtree of v, and that v is the first of them. Moreover, for the subsequence in the sequence corresponding to (t, ξ) of a subtree $t(v)$ rooted at vertex v, the sequences of $\Delta(t(v)^L) - 1$ vertices from its left subtree and of $\Delta(t(v)^R) - 1$ vertices from its right subtree are interleaved in any order. Thus we arrive at the following recurrence for $q(t)$:

$$q(t) = \binom{\Delta(t) - 2}{\Delta(t^L) - 1} q(t^L) q(t^R) = \frac{(\Delta(t) - 2)!}{(\Delta(t^L) - 1)!(\Delta(t^R) - 1)!} q(t^L) q(t^R).$$

This recurrence can be solved by observing that each internal vertex appears exactly once in the numerator, and that each internal vertex not equal to the root r appears exactly once in the denominator. Hence,

$$q(t) = \frac{\prod\limits_{v \in \mathring{V}(t)} (\Delta(t(v)) - 2)!}{\prod\limits_{v \in \mathring{V}(t) \setminus \{r\}} (\Delta(t(v)) - 1)!}.$$

Since $\Delta(t(r)) = \Delta(t) = n$, we thus obtain

$$q(t) = \frac{\prod\limits_{v \in \mathring{V}(t)} (\Delta(t(v)) - 2)!}{\prod\limits_{v \in \mathring{V}(t) \setminus \{r\}} (\Delta(t(v)) - 1)!} = \frac{(n - 2)!}{\prod\limits_{v \in \mathring{V}(t) \setminus \{r\}} (\Delta(t(v)) - 1)}$$

leading finally to

$$P(T_n = t) = \frac{q(t)}{(n - 1)!} = \frac{1}{\prod\limits_{v \in \mathring{V}(t)} (\Delta(t(v)) - 1)}.$$

This completes the proof.   ∎

In conclusion, the models are equivalent for binary trees in the sense that they lead to the same probability distribution on trees.

We should point out that this equivalence does not hold for nonbinary trees. In Exercise 7.3 we ask the reader to analyze m-ary binary search trees while in Section 7.2 we study general d-ary trees for $d \geq 2$.

Remark 7.2   We note that it is possible to extend our tree model by assigning more information to the vertices, for example, by strings/words of given length over an alphabet $\mathcal{A}$. This leads to a *named model* in the spirit of Aldous and Ross (2014). Magner, Turowski, and Szpankowski (2018) considered such binary trees with vertex names, where the names are modeled by a discrete Markov process.

7.1.2 Entropy Evaluation

The next goal is to determine the entropy of the probability distribution $H(T_n)$ of our probability model(s) for plane binary trees. The main result is the following one.

Theorem 7.3   *The entropy of a plane binary tree T_n is given by*

$$H(T_n) = \log(n - 1) + 2n \sum_{k=2}^{n-1} \frac{\log(k - 1)}{k(k + 1)} = h_2 n - \log n + O(1),$$

where

$$h_2 = 2 \sum_{k \geq 2} \frac{\log(k-1)}{k(k+1)} \approx 1.736.$$

Consequently the entropy rate of plane binary trees is

$$\lim_{n \to \infty} H(T_n)/n = h_2 \approx 1.736.$$

The rest of this section is devoted to the proof of Theorem 7.3. We start with the observation that $\Delta(T_n^L)$ is a random variable corresponding to the number of leaves in the left subtree of T_n. From the previous section, we know that $P(\Delta(T_n^L) = k) = \frac{1}{n-1}$. Next, we note that the random variable T_n^L conditioned on $\Delta(LT_n^L) = k$ is identical to the random variable T_k, and the same holds for LT_n^R and T_{n-k}. This leads us directly to the recurrence

$$H(T_n) = H(\Delta(LT_n^L))$$

$$+ \sum_{k=1}^{n-1} P(\Delta(T_n^L) = k) \left(H(T_n^L | \Delta(T_n^L) = k) + H(T_n^R | \Delta(T_n^L) = k) \right)$$

$$= \log(n-1) + \frac{2}{n-1} \sum_{k=1}^{n-1} H(LT_k), \tag{7.4}$$

where we have also used the fact that $H(\Delta(LT_n^L)) = \log(n-1)$.

Such recurrences can be explicitly solved and we present it in the next lemma. A more general version is given in Lemma 7.26.

Lemma 7.4 *For constant α, x_0 and x_1, the recurrence*

$$x_n = a_n + \frac{\alpha}{n} \frac{n!}{\Gamma(n+\alpha-1)} \sum_{k=0}^{n-1} \frac{\Gamma(k+\alpha-1)}{k!} x_k, \qquad n \geq 2 \tag{7.5}$$

has the following solution for $n \geq 2$:

$$x_n = a_n + \alpha(n+\alpha-1) \sum_{k=0}^{n-1} \frac{a_k}{(k+\alpha-1)(k+\alpha)} + \frac{n+\alpha-1}{\alpha+1} \left(x_1 + \frac{x_0}{\alpha-1} \right).$$

Proof Let us multiply both sides of the recurrence by the normalizing factor $\frac{\Gamma(n+\alpha-1)}{n!}$. Define also

$$\hat{x}_n = \frac{x_n \Gamma(n+\alpha-1)}{n!}, \quad \hat{a}_n = \frac{a_n \Gamma(n+\alpha-1)}{n!}.$$

Then (7.5) rewrites

$$\hat{x}_n = \hat{a}_n + \frac{\alpha}{n} \sum_{k=2}^{n-1} \hat{x}_k. \tag{7.6}$$

To solve the recurrence (7.6), we compute

$$n\hat{x}_n - (n-1)\hat{x}_{n-1} = n\hat{a}_n + \alpha\hat{x}_{n-1} - (n-1)\hat{a}_{n-1}.$$

This leads us to

$$\hat{x}_n = \hat{a}_n - \left(1 - \frac{1}{n}\right)\hat{a}_{n-1} + \left(1 + \frac{\alpha - 1}{n}\right)\hat{x}_{n-1},$$

which holds for $n \geq 3$. Then we arrive at

$$\hat{x}_n = \hat{x}_2 \prod_{j=3}^{n}\left(1 + \frac{\alpha - 1}{j}\right) + \sum_{k=3}^{n}\left(\hat{a}_k - \left(1 - \frac{1}{k}\right)\hat{a}_{k-1}\right)\prod_{j=k+1}^{n}\left(1 + \frac{\alpha - 1}{j}\right). \quad (7.7)$$

The product can be rewritten as

$$\prod_{j=k+1}^{n}\left(1 + \frac{\alpha - 1}{j}\right) = \frac{k!\,\Gamma(n + \alpha)}{n!\,\Gamma(k + \alpha)}.$$

Hence, after some standard calculations, we obtain

$$\hat{x}_n = \hat{a}_n + (\hat{x}_2 - \hat{a}_2)\frac{2\Gamma(n + \alpha)}{\Gamma(\alpha + 2)n!} + \frac{\Gamma(n + \alpha)}{n!}\sum_{k=2}^{n-1}\hat{a}_k\frac{k!}{\Gamma(k + \alpha)}\frac{\alpha}{k + \alpha}.$$

Going back from $\hat{x}_n$ and $\hat{a}_n$ to x_n, a_n, respectively, we obtain

$$x_n = a_n + \alpha(n + \alpha - 1)\sum_{k=2}^{n-1}\frac{a_k}{(k + \alpha - 1)(k + \alpha)} + (x_2 - a_2)\frac{n + \alpha - 1}{\alpha + 1}.$$

By observing that $x_2 - a_2 = x_1 + \frac{x_0}{\alpha - 1}$, we have completed the proof. ∎

We can, thus, apply this formula for $\alpha = 2$ and obtain the solution for $x_n = H(T_n)$ and $a_n = \log(n - 1)$:

$$H(T_n) = \log(n - 1) + 2n\sum_{k=2}^{n-1}\frac{\log(k - 1)}{k(k + 1)},$$

where $x_0 = x_1 = 0$.

In order to finish the proof of Theorem 7.3, we just note that

$$\sum_{k=2}^{n-1}\frac{\log(k - 1)}{k(k + 1)} = \sum_{k=2}^{\infty}\frac{\log(k - 1)}{k(k + 1)} - \frac{\log(n)}{n} + O\left(\frac{1}{n}\right).$$

This completes the proof.

7.1.3 A Compression Algorithm for Plane Binary Trees

Clearly, it is now possible to encode a plane binary tree in an (almost) optimal way; that is, the expected code length is close to the entropy. Since the probability distribution of T_n is explicit (see (7.3)), we could use the Huffman code. However, this is not very efficient since we would need all probabilities.

In what follows, we will give an algorithm that computes an arithmetic coding, where we design the codeword directly without computing the whole probability distribution. The idea is to partition the unit interval $[0, 1)$ into subintervals $[a, b)$ such that every tree t of size n corresponds to one of these intervals and that $P(t) = b - a$. We then associate to each interval $[a, b)$ a binary string, namely the first $\lceil -\log(b - a)\rceil + 1$ binary bits of the real number $(a + b)/2$.

It is clear that the redundancy of such an encoding is ≤ 2 since every code-word length differs from $-\log P(t)$ by at most 2. Furthermore, it is clear by construction that all code words are different binary strings (see Exercise 7.1).

More precisely, in the algorithm, we start from the interval $[0, 1)$ and we traverse the tree t to be compressed: at each vertex we split the current interval into parts according to the probability of the number of leaves in the left subtree. That is, if the subtree rooted at v has k leaves and $t(v)^L$ has ℓ leaves, then we split the interval into $k - \ell$ equal parts and pick ℓth subinterval as the new interval. Then, we pick as a new interval, one that represents the value associated with the current vertex (the number of leaves in the left subtree).

After we traverse the whole tree, we obtain an interval $[a, b)$. As mentioned, the crucial idea is that any two intervals corresponding to different trees are disjoint and the length of each interval is equal to the probability of generating its underlying plane tree. We output the first $\lceil -\log(b - a)\rceil$ bits of $\frac{a+b}{2}$. The pseudocode of this algorithm, called COMPRESSPTREE is presented next:

function COMPRESSPTREE(t)

    $[a, b), d \leftarrow CompressPTreeRec(t)$

    $p \leftarrow b - a, x \leftarrow \dfrac{a + b}{2}$

    return $C_n^{(1)} = $ first $\lceil -\log p\rceil + 1$ bits of x

function COMPRESSPTREEREC(t)

    $v \leftarrow root(t)$

    $\ell \leftarrow 0, h \leftarrow 1$

    if v is not a leaf **then**

        $[\ell_{left}, h_{left}), d_{left} \leftarrow CompressPTreeRec(t^L)$

        $[\ell_{right}, h_{right}), d_{right} \leftarrow CompressPTreeRec(t^R)$

        $d \leftarrow d_{left} + d_{right}$

        $range \leftarrow h - \ell$

        $h \leftarrow \ell + range * d_{left}/(d - 1)$

        $\ell \leftarrow \ell + range * (d_{left} - 1)/(d - 1)$

        $range \leftarrow h - \ell$

        $h \leftarrow \ell + range * h_{left}$

        $\ell \leftarrow \ell + range * \ell_{left}$

        $range \leftarrow h - \ell$

        $h \leftarrow \ell + range * h_{right}$

        $\ell \leftarrow \ell + range * \ell_{right}$

    return $[\ell, h), d$

Example 7.5 For the following tree, our algorithm COMPRESSPTREE proceeds as follows:

$$
\begin{array}{ll}
v_5 & \Rightarrow [0,1),\ 1 \\
v_4 & \Rightarrow [0,1),\ 1 \\
v_3 & \Rightarrow [0,1),\ 1 \\
v_2 & \Rightarrow [0,1),\ 2 \\
v_1 & \Rightarrow [0.5,1),\ 3.
\end{array}
$$

Hence, we finally obtain the interval $[0.5,1)$, the probability $p = 0.5$, and the first two digits of $0.75 = (0.11)_2$; that is, $C_3^{(1)} = 11$.

Next we show correctness of the algorithm COMPRESSPTREE.

Lemma 7.6 *Let t denote a given plane binary tree with n external vertices. Then the algorithm COMPRESSPTREE computes an interval whose length is equal to $P(T_n = t)$. Furthermore, the intervals constitute a partition of $[0,1)$.*

Proof First, if t is just a leaf, then the algorithm computes the interval $[0,1)$ and the value $d = 1$.

Second, if t is not a leaf, then the length of the interval $[\ell, r]$ is updated by

$$
r - \ell = \frac{1}{d-1}(r_{left} - \ell_{left})(r_{right} - \ell_{right}),
$$

which corresponds to the recurrence (7.1). Thus, the probability $P(T_n = t)$ is computed correctly. Furthermore, the computed intervals are nested and cover by construction the whole unit interval.   ∎

As mentioned, the redundancy in this arithmetic coding is within at most 2 bits of the entropy.

Lemma 7.7 *The average length of a codeword $C_n^{(1)}$ of COMPRESSPTREE is only within 2 bits from the entropy.*

Proof From this analysis we know that

$$
\mathbf{E}[C_n^{(1)}] = \sum_{t \in \mathcal{T}_n} P(T_n = t)(\lceil -\log P(T_n = t) \rceil + 1)
$$
$$
< \sum_{t \in \mathcal{T}_n} -P(T_n = t) \log P(T_n = t) + 2 = H(T_n) + 2,
$$

which completes the proof.   ∎

7.1.4 Non-plane Binary Trees

As discussed, binary trees come in two flavors, as plane-oriented trees and as non-plane trees. In this section, we discuss non-plane trees, also called unordered trees or Otter trees. These are just rooted trees in the graph theoretic sense – there is no order between subtrees.

Non-plane trees are harder to analyze and less attention has been devoted to them in the literature. Nevertheless, non-plane trees find many important applications, from data compression to biology. For example, in a phylogenetic tree describing n species, there are n leaves representing extant species and $n - 1$ internal nodes. By design, there is no specific order between the two children of a binary node. We will study these trees not in the uniform probability model but rather in a growth model of binary trees.

In data compression and other applications, symmetries of plane and non-plane trees are of interest. In particular, for compression, one needs to know the number of internal nodes that have two isomorphic subtrees, the size of such isomorphic trees, and the entropy of trees. In order to analyze such quantities, we first derive a functional-differential equation for a bivariate generating function from which we compute the average number of nodes with two isomorphic subtrees, as well as the entropy of non-plane trees.

Let $\mathcal{S}$ be the set of all binary rooted non-plane trees having finitely many vertices. Let $\mathcal{S}_n$ be the subset of $\mathcal{S}$ consisting of all trees with exactly n leaves. We recall that $\mathcal{T}$ is the set of all binary rooted plane trees having finitely many vertices and $\mathcal{T}_n$ is the subset of $\mathcal{T}$ consisting of all binary trees with exactly n leaves. For any $s \in \mathcal{S}$ and $t \in \mathcal{T}$, let $t \sim s$ mean that the plane tree t is isomorphic to the non-plane tree s. Furthermore, we define $[s] = \{t \in \mathcal{T} : t \sim s\}$ as a collection of all plane binary trees t that are isomorphic to the same non-plane binary tree s.

From Theorem 7.1, we know that the probability of a tree $t \in \mathcal{T}_n$ is

$$P(T_n = t) = \prod_{v \in \overset{\circ}{V}(t)} (\Delta(v) - 1)^{-1},$$

where $\overset{\circ}{V}(t)$ is the set of internal nodes of t and $\Delta(v)$ is the number of leaves of a tree rooted at v.[1] For any $t_1, t_2 \in \mathcal{T}_n$ such that $t_1 \sim s$ and $t_2 \sim s$, it holds that $P(T_n = t_1) = P(T_n = t_2)$. By definition, s corresponds to $|[s]|$ isomorphic plane trees, so for any $t \in [s]$ we have

$$P(S_n = s) = |[s]| \cdot P(T_n = t), \quad t \in [s]. \tag{7.8}$$

Of course, we can also write

$$P(S_n = s) = \sum_{t \sim s} P(T_n = t).$$

Furthermore,

$$P(T_n = t | S_n = s) = \frac{1}{|[s]|}. \tag{7.9}$$

Let $\mathrm{sym}(t)$ be the number of non-leaf (internal) nodes v of tree t such that the two subtrees stemming from v are isomorphic. Observe that $|\mathcal{S}_1| = |\mathcal{S}_2| = |\mathcal{S}_3| = 1$, and that $|\mathcal{S}_4| = 2$. If $t \in \mathcal{S}_1$, then clearly $\mathrm{sym}(t) = 0$. If $t \in \mathcal{S}_2$ or $t \in \mathcal{S}_3$, then $\mathrm{sym}(t) = 1$. Notice that if t_1 and t_2 are the two subtrees of a tree t whose roots are the two children of the root of t, then

$$\mathrm{sym}(t) = \begin{cases} \mathrm{sym}(t_1) + \mathrm{sym}(t_2) + 1 & \text{if } t_1 = t_2, \\ \mathrm{sym}(t_1) + \mathrm{sym}(t_2) & \text{if } t_1 \neq t_2. \end{cases}$$

Observe also that

$$\mathrm{sym}(s) = \mathrm{sym}(t).$$

---

[1] We use T_n to denote a random variable representing a random tree in $\mathcal{T}_n$; however, we often abuse notation and write T_n for both the set of trees and the random variable.

for all $t \in [s]$. Furthermore, and more interestingly,

$$|[s]| = 2^{n-1-\mathrm{sym}(s)}. \tag{7.10}$$

Indeed, we can form a new tree by rotating both subtrees of a plane tree at every internal node that is *not* symmetric; that is, for those nodes whose subtrees are not isomorphic.

With the help of this notation we can evaluate the entropy $H(S_n)$:

$$
\begin{aligned}
H(S_n) &= -\sum_{s \in S_n} P(S_n = s) \log P(S_n = s) \\
&= -\sum_{s \in S_n} \sum_{t \in [s]} P(T_n = t) \log \left(P(T_n = t)|[s]| \right) \\
&= -\sum_{t \in T_n} P(T_n = t) \log(P(T_n = t)) - \sum_{s \in S_n} P(S_n = s) \log |[s]| \\
&= H(T_n) - \sum_{s \in S_n} P(S_n = s)(n - 1 - \mathrm{sym}(s)) \\
&= H(T_n) - (n - 1) + \sum_{s \in S_n} P(S_n = s)\mathrm{sym}(s). \tag{7.11}
\end{aligned}
$$

Our goal is, therefore, to compute the expected value

$$\mathbf{E}[\mathrm{sym}(S_n)] = \sum_{s \in S_n} P(S_n = s)\mathrm{sym}(s) = \sum_{t \in T_n} P(T_n = t)\mathrm{sym}(t).$$

For this purpose, we first derive a differential equation for the following bivariate generating function:

$$F(u, z) = \sum_{t \in \mathcal{T}} P(T = t)u^{\mathrm{sym}(t)}z^{|t|} = \sum_{n=1}^{\infty} \sum_{t \in \mathcal{T}_n} P(T_n = t)u^{\mathrm{sym}(t)}z^{|t|},$$

where we simplify our notation and write $|t|$ for the size of a tree (i.e., the number of leaves). Define also

$$B(u, z) = \sum_{t \in \mathcal{T}} P(T = t)^2 u^{\mathrm{sym}(t)}z^{|t|-1} = \sum_{t \in \mathcal{T}} p(t)^2 u^{\mathrm{sym}(t)}z^{|t|-1},$$

where we write $p(t) = P(T = t)$.

Lemma 7.8 *Let $f(u, z) = \frac{F(u,z)}{z}$. Then $f(u, z)$ satisfies the following Riccati differential equation:*

$$\frac{\partial f(u, z)}{\partial z} = f(u, z)^2 + (u - 1)B(u^2, z^2). \tag{7.12}$$

Furthermore, after the substitution

$$f(u, z) = -\frac{\frac{\partial g(u,z)}{\partial z}}{g(u, z)}$$

equation (7.12) becomes

$$\frac{\partial^2 g(u, z)}{\partial^2 z} + (u - 1)B(u^2, z^2)g(u, z) = 0, \tag{7.13}$$

which is a second-order linear equation assuming $B(u, z)$ is known.

Proof Observe that

$$F(u,z) = \sum_{n=1}^{\infty} \sum_{t \in \mathcal{T}_n} P(T_n = t) u^{\text{sym}(t)} z^{|t|} = z + \sum_{n \geq 2} \sum_{t \in \mathcal{T}_n} P(T_n = t) u^{\text{sym}(t)} z^{|t|}.$$

Since every tree $t \in \mathcal{T}_n$ for $n \geq 2$ can be divided into two subtrees, we have

$$F(u,z) = z + \sum_{s,t \in \mathcal{T}} \frac{1}{|s| + |t| - 1} p(s) p(t) u^{\text{sym}(s) + \text{sym}(t) + [|s=t|]} \cdot z^{|s| + |t|}$$

$$= z + \sum_{s,t \in \mathcal{T}} \frac{1}{|s| + |t| - 1} p(s) p(t) u^{\text{sym}(s) + \text{sym}(t)} \cdot z^{|s| + |t|}$$

$$- \sum_{t \in \mathcal{T}} \frac{1}{2|t| - 1} p(t)^2 u^{2\text{sym}(t)} \cdot z^{2|t|} + \sum_{t \in \mathcal{T}} \frac{1}{2|t| - 1} p(t)^2 u^{2\text{sym}(t)+1} \cdot z^{2|t|}$$

$$= z + \sum_{s,t \in \mathcal{T}} \frac{1}{|s| + |t| - 1} p(s) p(t) u^{\text{sym}(s) + \text{sym}(t)} \cdot z^{|s| + |t|}$$

$$+ (u - 1) \sum_{t \in \mathcal{T}} \frac{1}{2|t| - 1} p(t)^2 u^{2\text{sym}(t)} \cdot z^{2|t|}.$$

Notice that, from the original definition of $F(u,z)$,

$$F(u,z)^2 = \sum_{s,t \in \mathcal{T}} p(s) p(t) u^{\text{sym}(s) + \text{sym}(t)} z^{|s| + |t|}.$$

Therefore,

$$z \int_0^z \frac{F(u,w)^2}{w^2} dw = \sum_{s,t \in \mathcal{T}} \frac{1}{|s| + |t| - 1} p(s) p(t) u^{\text{sym}(s) + \text{sym}(t)} \cdot z^{|s| + |t|}.$$

We also have

$$B(u,z) = \sum_{t \in \mathcal{T}} p(t)^2 u^{\text{sym}(t)} z^{|t| - 1}$$

and

$$z \int_0^z B(u^2, w^2) dw = \sum_{t \in \mathcal{T}} \frac{1}{2|t| - 1} p(t)^2 u^{2\text{sym}(t)} \cdot z^{2|t|}.$$

Hence,

$$F(u,z) = z + z \int_0^z \frac{F(u,w)^2}{w^2} dw + (u - 1) z \int_0^z B(u^2, w^2) dw.$$

Let $f(u,z) = \frac{F(u,z)}{z}$. From the last equation, we get

$$\frac{\partial f(u,z)}{\partial z} = f(u,z)^2 + (u - 1) B(u^2, z^2).$$

This proves Lemma 7.8. ∎

Remark 7.9   We note that similar considerations can be also done for the uniform model. If we set

$$\widetilde{F}(u,z) = \sum_{s \in \mathcal{S}} u^{\mathrm{sym}(s)} z^{|s|},$$

then this generating function satisfies the functional equation (as shown by Bona and Flajolet (2009))

$$\widetilde{F}(u,z) = z + \frac{1}{2}\widetilde{F}(u,z)^2 + \left(u - \frac{1}{2}\right)\widetilde{F}(u^2, z^2).\tag{7.14}$$

Next, we observe that (7.12) could be viewed as a functional-differential equation. Indeed, let us introduce a special Hadamard product of two generating functions $A(u,z)$, $B(u,z)$, defined by

$$A(u,z) = \sum_{t \in \mathcal{T}} c_A(t) u^{r(t)} z^{s(t)}, \quad B(u,z) = \sum_{t \in \mathcal{T}} c_B(t) u^{r(t)} z^{s(t)},$$

where $r(t)$ and $s(t)$ map combinatorial objects $t \in \mathcal{T}$ to the nonnegative integers. We then define a Hadamard product $A(u,z) \square B(u,z)$ by

$$A(u,z) \square B(u,z) = \sum_{t \in \mathcal{T}} c_A(t) c_B(t) u^{r(t)} z^{s(t)}.$$

We contrast this with the standard bivariate Hadamard product, defined by

$$A(u,z) \odot B(u,z)$$
$$= \sum_{n,m=0}^{\infty} \left(\sum_{t\,:\,r(t)=m,s(t)=n} c_A(t) \right) \left(\sum_{t\,:\,r(t)=m,s(t)=n} c_B(t) \right) u^m z^n.$$

Note that $A(u,z) \square B(u,z)$ is in general not equal to $A(u,z) \odot B(u,z)$, unless $r(t)$ and $s(t)$ uniquely determine t. With this definition in mind, we can rewrite (7.12) as

$$\frac{\partial}{\partial z} f_z(u,z) = f(u,z)^2 + (u-1)(f(u^2,z^2) \square f(u^2,z^2)),\tag{7.15}$$

which is a functional-differential equation.

Let us now evaluate the average $\mathbf{E}[\mathrm{sym}(S_n)]$. For this purpose we set

$$E(z) = \sum_{n=1}^{\infty} \mathbf{E}[\mathrm{sym}(S_n)] z^{n-1}.$$

Using Lemma 7.8, we find the following ordinary differential equation:

$$E'(z) = \frac{2E(z)}{z(1-z)} + B(z^2)\tag{7.16}$$

with $E(0) = 0$, where

$$B(z) = \sum_{t \in \mathcal{T}} p(t)^2 z^{|t|-1} = \sum_{n=1}^{\infty} z^{n-1} \sum_{t_n \in \mathcal{T}_n} p(t_n)^2 = \sum_{n=1}^{\infty} b_n z^{n-1}.$$

with

$$b_n = [z^{n-1}]B(z) = \sum_{t \in \mathcal{T}_n} p(t)^2$$

for $n \geq 1$. It is easy to compute b_n for a few small values of n, namely,

$$b_1 = b_2 = 1, \quad b_3 = \frac{1}{2}, \quad b_4 = \frac{2}{9}, \quad b_5 = \frac{13}{144}, \quad b_6 = \frac{7}{200}. \tag{7.17}$$

Actually, to compute b_n for all values of n, we need a better approach. Define $C(z) = zB(z)$ and notice that

$$b_n = [z^n]C(z) = [z^{n-1}]B(z).$$

We will derive a differential equation for $C(z)$, from which a recurrence for b_n will follow. It is easy to notice that $C(z)$ satisfies the following:

$$C(z) = z + \sum_{u,v \in \mathcal{T}} \frac{1}{(|v| + |u| - 1)^2} p(u)^2 p(v)^2 z^{|u|+|v|}.$$

Furthermore,

$$B'(z) = \sum_{u,v \in \mathcal{T}} \frac{1}{(|v| + |u| - 1)} p(u)^2 p(v)^2 z^{|u|+|v|-2}$$

and

$$C^2(z) = \sum_{u,v \in \mathcal{T}} p(u)p(v) z^{|u|+|v|}.$$

Combining all of these, we arrive at the following Riccati differential equation:

$$C(z) - zC'(z) + z^2 C''(z) = C^2(z). \tag{7.18}$$

By standard tools, we can extract from these a recurrence for $b_n = [z^n]C(z)$. Indeed, for $n \geq 2$ we have

$$b_n = \frac{1}{(n-1)^2} \sum_{j=1}^{n-1} b_j b_{n-j} \tag{7.19}$$

with $b_1 = 1$.

Remark 7.10 In passing, we remark on the generating function $C(z)$ satisfying nonlinear differential equation (7.18) with coefficients $b_n = [z^n]C(z)$. It turns out that applying the method discussed in Chern et al. and Martinez (2012), one can prove the following asymptotic result:

$$b_n = \rho^n \left(6n - \frac{22}{5} + O(n^{-5}) \right)$$

where $\rho = 0.3183843834378459\ldots$.

With the help of b_n, we can now formulate the following result for $\mathbf{E}[\text{sym}(S_n)] = \mathbf{E}[\text{sym}(T_n)]$.

Theorem 7.11 *Consider a binary plane tree and its corresponding non-plane tree. The expected number of internal nodes with two isomorphic subtrees is*

$$E[\text{sym}(S_n)] = n \sum_{\ell=1}^{\lfloor (n+1)/2 \rfloor} \frac{b_\ell}{(2\ell - 1)\ell(2\ell + 1)} \tag{7.20}$$

$$+ b_{\lfloor (n+1)/2 \rfloor} \left((-1)^{n+1} \left(2 - \frac{n+3}{(n+1)(n+2)} \right) + \frac{n}{2(n+1)(n+2)} \right)$$

$$= e_1 n + O(1),$$

where $b_\ell = \sum_{t \in T_\ell} p(t)^2$ and

$$e_1 = \sum_{\ell=1}^{\infty} \frac{b_\ell}{(2\ell - 1)\ell(2\ell + 1)} \approx 0.3725.$$

Proof We now compute $E[\text{sym}(T_n)] = E[\text{sym}(S_n)]$ using the generating function

$$\phi_n(u) = [z^n]F(u,z) = [z^{n-1}]f(u,z)$$

defined previously. We observe that

$$E[\text{sym}(T_n)] = \frac{d\phi_n(u)}{du}\bigg|_{u=1}.$$

Since taking the coefficient commutes with taking the derivative with respect to u, we have

$$\frac{d[z^{n-1}]f(u,z)}{du} = [z^{n-1}]f_u(u,z).$$

Thus, taking the derivative with respect to u in (7.12) gives (using (7.15))

$$f_{z,u}(u,z) = 2f(u,z)f_u(u,z) + (u-1)\frac{\partial}{\partial u}\left[(f(u,z)\square f(u,z)) \bigg|_{(u^2,z^2)} \right]$$

$$+ \left[(f(u,z)\square f(u,z)) \bigg|_{(u^2,z^2)} \right],$$

and setting $u = 1$ results in

$$f_{z,u}(1,z) = 2f(1,z)f_u(1,z) + \left[(f(1,z)\square f(1,z)) \bigg|_{(u^2,z^2)} \right].$$

Now, we use the fact that $\phi_n(1) = 1$ for $n \geq 1$ implies

$$f(1,z) = \frac{1}{(1-z)}.$$

We also note that

$$f_u(1,z) = \sum_{n=1}^{\infty} E[\text{sym}(T_n)]z^{n-1} = E(z).$$

With the notation as outlined, we find

$$E'(z) = \frac{2E(z)}{(1-z)} + (A(z) \boxtimes A(z)) \Big|_{z^2} = \frac{2E(z)}{z(1-z)} + B(z^2), \tag{7.21}$$

with $E(0) = 0$, as needed.

We now solve (7.21). It is easy to see that

$$E(z) = \frac{1}{(1-z)^2} \left(\int_0^z B(x^2)(1-x)^2 dx + C \right).$$

But $E(0) = 0$ implies $C = 0$. Thus

$$\mathbf{E}[\text{sym}(T_n)] = [z^{n-1}]E(z)$$
$$= [z^{n-1}]\frac{1}{(1-z)^2} \int_0^z B(x^2)(1-x)^2 dx.$$

Next, we observe (after some algebra), that

$$\frac{1}{(1-z)^2} \int_0^z B(x^2)(1-x)^2 dx = z + \sum_{n=1}^{\infty} \left(\frac{b_n + b_{n+1}}{2n+1} z^{2n+1} - \frac{b_n}{n} z^{2n} \right).$$

By setting

$$c_k = \begin{cases} 0 & k = 0, \\ 1 & k = 1, \\ -\frac{b_\ell}{\ell} & k = 2\ell, \ \ell \geq 1, \\ \frac{b_\ell + b_{\ell+1}}{2\ell+1} & k = 2\ell + 1, \ \ell \geq 1, \end{cases} \tag{7.22}$$

we have

$$\mathbf{E}[\text{sym}(T_n)] = [z^{n-1}]\frac{1}{(1-z)^2} \sum_{k=0}^{\infty} c_k z^k = \sum_{k=0}^{n} c_k(n-k).$$

It is also easy to see that

$$\sum_{k=0}^{n} k c_k = 1 + \sum_{\ell=1}^{\lfloor n/2 \rfloor} (b_{\ell+1} - b_\ell) = 1 - b_1 + b_{\lfloor n/2 \rfloor+1} = (-1)^{n+1} b_{\lfloor (n+1)/2 \rfloor}.$$

This finally leads to the representation

$$\mathbf{E}[\text{sym}(T_n)] = n \sum_{k=1}^{n} c_k + (-1)^{n+1} b_{\lfloor (n+1)/2 \rfloor}. \tag{7.23}$$

We can further simply this expression by computing $\sum_k c_k$ and obtain (with $L = \lfloor (n+1)/2 \rfloor$)

$$\sum_k c_k = 1 - \frac{2}{3}b_1 + \sum_{\ell=2}^{\lfloor (n+1)/2 \rfloor - 1} b_\ell \left(\frac{1}{2\ell-1} - \frac{1}{\ell} + \frac{1}{2\ell+1} \right) \tag{7.24}$$
$$+ b_L \left(\frac{1}{2L-1} - \frac{1+(-1)^n}{2L} \right).$$

We thus get the following formula:

$$\sum_k c_k = \sum_{\ell=1}^{\lfloor(n+1)/2\rfloor-1} \frac{b_\ell}{(2\ell-1)\ell(2\ell+1)}$$
$$+ b_L\left((-1)^{n+1}\left(1 - \frac{L+1}{2L(2L+1)}\right) + \frac{L-1}{2L(2L+1)}\right).$$

In summary, we have

$$\mathbf{E}[\text{sym}(T_n)] = n\sum_{\ell=1}^{\lfloor(n+1)/2\rfloor} \frac{b_\ell}{(2\ell-1)\ell(2\ell+1)}$$
$$+ b_{\lfloor(n+1)/2\rfloor}\left((-1)^{n+1}\left(2 - \frac{n+3}{(n+1)(n+2)}\right) + \frac{n}{2(n+1)(n+2)}\right)$$
$$= e_1 n + O(1),$$

where we recall that $b_\ell = \sum_{t_\ell} p(t_\ell)^2 = O(1)$. This proves Theorem 7.11. ∎

Remark 7.12   Let us observe that we can use just computed $\mathbf{E}[\text{sym}(S_n)]$ to design and evaluate some compression algorithms on non-plane (and plane) trees. Indeed, let us replace every internal node with two isomorphic subtrees by the second identical subtree with a pointer to the first subtrees. We need about $\approx n \cdot 0.3725$ bits to accomplish it. On the other hand, if we do this, we can save some storage on the replaced subtree. We can quantify that by computing the total size, $\text{size}(S_n)$, of the saved isomorphic subtrees. Similar computations lead to

$$\mathbf{E}[\text{size}(S_n)] = n\sum_{k=1}^{\lfloor(n+1)/2\rfloor} \frac{b_k}{(2k-1)(2k+1)} \approx n \cdot 0.4190. \qquad (7.25)$$

The reader is asked to prove this property in Exercise 7.7.

Finally, we deal with the entropy of the non-plane tree $H(S_n)$ and its rate $h(s) = \lim_{n\to\infty} H(S_n)/n$. Here we just have to collect the results from Theorems 7.3 and 7.11 and the representation (7.11).

Theorem 7.13   *The entropy $H(S_n)$ of non-plane binary trees with n leaves is given by*

$$H(S_n) = \log(n-1) - n + 1 + 2n\sum_{k=2}^{n-1} \frac{\log(k-1)}{k(k+1)} + n\sum_{\ell=1}^{\lfloor(n+1)/2\rfloor} \frac{b_\ell}{(2\ell-1)\ell(2\ell+1)}$$
$$+ b_{\lfloor(n+1)/2\rfloor}\left((-1)^{n+1}\left(2 - \frac{n+3}{(n+1)(n+2)}\right) + \frac{n}{2(n+1)(n+2)}\right)$$
$$= n\left(2\sum_{k=1}^{\infty} \frac{\log(k)}{(k+1)(k+2)} - 1 + \sum_{k=1}^{\infty} \frac{b_k}{(2k-1)k(2k+1)}\right) + O(\log n),$$

where $b_n = \sum_{t\in T_n} p(t)^2$. Consequently the entropy rate $\tilde{h}_2 = \lim_{n\to\infty} H(S_n)/n$ is given by

$$\tilde{h}_2 = 2\sum_{k=1}^{\infty} \frac{\log(k)}{(k+1)(k+2)} - 1 + \sum_{k=1}^{\infty} \frac{b_k}{(2k-1)k(2k+1)} \approx 1.109,$$

which should be compared to the entropy rate h_2 of the plane trees found in Theorem 7.3.

7.1.5 A Compression Algorithm for Non-plane Binary Trees

Next, we present a compression algorithm for non-plane binary trees, again based on an arithmetic encoding. In order to accomplish it, we need to define a total order among non-plane trees and compute efficiently the probability distribution $P(S_n < s)$, where $<$ is the order to be defined. Recall again that S is the set of all non-plane trees and S_n is the set of all non-plane rooted trees of n leaves. Furthermore, $\Delta(s)$ is the number of leaves of the non-plane tree s.

We start with the definition of our total ordering. In what follows, we will denote by subtrees(s) the set of the two subtrees of the tree s rooted at the children of its root; that is, s is not contained in subtrees(s).

Definition 7.14 The relation $<$ on S is defined as follows: $s_1 < s_2$ if and only if one of the following holds:

- $\Delta(s_1) < \Delta(s_2)$,
- or $\Delta(s_1) = \Delta(s_2)$ and $\min\{\text{subtrees}(s_1)\} < \min\{\text{subtrees}(s_2)\}$,
- or $\Delta(s_1) = \Delta(s_2)$, $\min\{\text{subtrees}(s_1)\} = \min\{\text{subtrees}(s_2)\}$ and $\max\{\text{subtrees}(s_1)\} < \max\{\text{subtrees}(s_2)\}$.

Here, min and max are defined recursively in terms of the order relation.

Lemma 7.15 *The relation $<$ is a total ordering on S.*

Proof The reflexivity and antisymmetry are straightforward since either $s_1 < s_2$ or $s_1 = s_2$ or $s_1 > s_2$.

To prove the transitivity, we assume that $s_1 < s_2$ and $s_2 < s_3$. Now, if $\Delta(s_1) < \Delta(s_2)$ or $\Delta(s_2) < \Delta(s_3)$, then $\Delta(s_1) < \Delta(s_3)$ (so $s_1 < s_3$), as from the definition of $<$ we know that $\Delta(s_1) \leq \Delta(s_2) \leq \Delta(s_3)$. The only remaining possibility is that $\Delta(s_1) = \Delta(s_2) = \Delta(s_3)$.

Then, we proceed similarly: if $\min\{\text{subtrees}(s_1)\} < \min\{\text{subtrees}(s_2)\}$ or $\min\{\text{subtrees}(s_2)\} < \min\{\text{subtrees}(s_3)\}$, then we see that $\min\{\text{subtrees}(s_1)\} < \min\{\text{subtrees}(s_3)\}$ (so $s_1 < s_3$) since from the definition of $<$ if $\Delta(s_1) = \Delta(s_2) = \Delta(s_3)$, then $\min\{\text{subtrees}(s_1)\} \leq \min\{\text{subtrees}(s_2)\} \leq \min\{\text{subtrees}(s_3)\}$.

Therefore, the only missing case is when $\Delta(s_1) = \Delta(s_2) = \Delta(s_3)$ and $\min\{\text{subtrees}(s_1)\} = \min\{\text{subtrees}(s_2)\} = \min\{\text{subtrees}(s_3)\}$. Since we know that $s_1 < s_2$ and $s_2 < s_3$, then $\max\{\text{subtrees}(s_1)\} < \max\{\text{subtrees}(s_2)\} < \max\{\text{subtrees}(s_3)\}$ by induction, and this completes the proof. ∎

We denote by less(s) $= \min\{\text{subtrees}(s)\}$ and gtr(s) $= \max\{\text{subtrees}(s)\}$ the minimum and maximum root subtrees of s, respectively, under the ordering just introduced. Moreover, we let T_n denote the (random) plane binary tree from which S_n is generated, and we recall the notation T_n^L and T_n^R for the left and right subtrees of T_n.

The idea is to determine an algorithm that, given a non-plane binary tree s, outputs $P(S_n < s)$ and $P(S_n = s)$. This will allow us to construct an arithmetic coding scheme as follows: we associate to s the half-open interval $[a, b)$, whose left endpoint is given by $P(S_n < s)$ and whose right endpoint is $P(S_n \leq s)$. The length of this interval is clearly $P(S_n = s)$, and, because of our total ordering on non-plane trees, for two trees $s_1 < s_2$, the right endpoint of

s_1 is less than or equal to the left endpoint of s_2. That is, the two intervals do not overlap. Having this interval in hand, we take the midpoint and truncate its binary representation as usual. This will give a uniquely decodable code whose expected length is within 2 bits of the entropy $H(S_n)$.

Let us now consider the probabilities $P(S_n = s)$ and $P(S_n < s)$. First, we derive an expression for $P(S_n = s)$. In the case where s has two nonequal subtrees, we have

$$
\begin{aligned}
P(S_n = s) &= P(\text{less}(S_n) = \text{less}(s), \text{gtr}(S_n) = \text{gtr}(s)) \\
&= P(T_n^L \sim \text{less}(s), T_n^R \sim \text{gtr}(s)) \\
&\quad + P(T_n^L \sim \text{gtr}(s), T_n^R \sim \text{less}(s))
\end{aligned}
\tag{7.26}
$$

where $\sim$ denotes isomorphism. To calculate the first term on the right-hand side, we condition on the number of leaves in the left subtree of T_n taking the correct value:

$$
\begin{aligned}
&P(T_n^L \sim \text{less}(s), T_n^R \sim \text{gtr}(s)) \\
&\quad = P(\Delta(T_n^L) = \Delta(\text{less}(s))) \cdot P(T_n^L \sim \text{less}(s), T_n^R \sim \text{gtr}(s) | \Delta(T_n^L) = \Delta(\text{less}(s))) \\
&\quad = \frac{1}{(n-1)} \cdot P(S_{\Delta(\text{less}(s))} = \text{less}(s)) \cdot P(S_{\Delta(\text{gtr}(s))} = \text{gtr}(s)).
\end{aligned}
$$

Here, we have applied the conditional independence of the left and right subtrees of T_n, given the number of leaves in each. It turns out that the second term of (7.26) is equal to the first, so we get, in this case,

$$
P(S_n = s) = \frac{2}{(n-1)} \cdot P(S_{\Delta(\text{less}(s))} = \text{less}(s)) \cdot P(S_{\Delta(\text{gtr}(s))} = \text{gtr}(s)).
$$

In the case where the two subtrees of s are identical, only a single term in (7.26) is present, and it evaluates to

$$
\begin{aligned}
P(S_n = s) &= \frac{1}{n-1} \cdot P(S_{\Delta(\text{less}(s))} = \text{less}(s)) \cdot P(S_{\Delta(\text{gtr}(s))} = \text{gtr}(s)) \\
&= \frac{1}{n-1} \cdot P(S_{\Delta(\text{less}(s))} = \text{less}(s))^2.
\end{aligned}
$$

Thus, in each case, we have derived a formula for $P(S_n = s)$ (that may be recursively computed with $O(n)$ arithmetic operations in the worst case).

It remains to derive an expression for $P(S_n < s)$. We again first consider the case where s has two nonidentical subtrees. Following the definition of $<$, this event is equivalent to

$$
[\Delta(\text{less}(S_n)) < \Delta(\text{less}(s))]
\tag{7.27}
$$

$$
\cup \left[[\Delta(\text{less}(S_n)) = \Delta(\text{less}(s))] \cap [\text{less}(S_n) < \text{less}(s)] \right]
$$

$$
\cup \left[[\Delta(\text{less}(S_n)) = \Delta(\text{less}(s))] \cap [\text{less}(S_n) = \text{less}(s)] \cap [\text{gtr}(S_n) < \text{gtr}(s)] \right].
$$

The terms of this union are disjoint, so the total probability is the sum of the probabilities of the individual intersection events.

The first event is equivalent to the union of the disjoint events that the left subtree of T_n has $< \Delta(\text{less}(s))$ leaves or more than $n - \Delta(\text{less}(s))$ leaves. The probability of this event is thus

$$P(\Delta(\text{less}(S_n)) < \Delta(\text{less}(s))) = 2 \cdot \frac{\Delta(\text{less}(s)) - 1}{n - 1}.$$

The second and third events can be similarly written in terms of disjoint unions of events involving the left and right subtrees of T_n. This gives recursive formulas for their probabilities. Since the formulas are conceptually simple to derive but tedious to write out explicitly, we do not list them, but we mention that at most 4 recursive tree comparison calls are necessary to evaluate $P(S_n < s)$: we need to know the probability that a tree of the appropriate size is $< \text{less}(s)$, $= \text{less}(s)$, $< \text{gtr}(s)$, and $= \text{gtr}(s)$.

Finally, we compute $P(S_n < s)$ in the case where the two subtrees of s are equal. This happens if $\Delta(\text{less}(S_n)) < n/2$ or $\Delta(\text{less}(S_n)) = n/2$ and either subtree of S_n is less than the tree s' comprising the two subtrees of s.

The probability of the first event is

$$P(\Delta(\text{less}(S_n)) < n/2) = P(\Delta(T_n^L) < n/2) + P(\Delta(T_n^L) > n/2)$$

$$= 1 - \frac{1}{n - 1}.$$

The probability of the second event may be computed by conditioning: the probability that $\Delta(\text{less}(S_n)) = \Delta(T_n^L) = n/2$ is $\frac{1}{n-1}$, and the probability, conditioned on this event, that either subtree of S_n is less than s' is

$$P(T_n^L < s' \cup T_n^R < s' | \Delta(T_n^L) = n/2)$$
$$= 1 - P(T_n^L \geq s' | \Delta(T_n^L) = n/2) \cdot P(T_n^R \geq s' | \Delta(T_n^L) = n/2)$$
$$= 1 - (1 - P(S_{n/2} < s'))^2,$$

where we have used the conditional independence of the two subtrees of T_n given their sizes. Thus, the quantities $P(S_n < s)$ and $P(S_n = s)$ may be recursively computed.

With these results in hand, the aforementioned arithmetic coding scheme, in which the interval corresponding to a tree $s \in \mathcal{S}_n$ is $[P(S_n < s), P(S_n \leq s))$. As in the case of plane binary trees, we encode then the tree s by the digits of the midpoint of the corresponding interval. Again, this leads to a code where the average code length exceeds the entropy at most by 2.

Remark 7.16 It is not difficult to analyze the running time of compression algorithms that are polynomial in n. Indeed, in Exercise 7.2 we ask the reader to prove that the worst case and the average running times of our algorithm are

$$T(n) = O(n^3 \log^2 n \log \log n), \quad A(n) = O(n^2 \log^2 n \log \log n), \tag{7.28}$$

respectively.

7.2 *d*-ary Plane Trees

In this section, we discuss d-ary plane trees that are generated recursively. We derive the entropy and design an arithmetic compression algorithm so that the average code length exceeds the entropy at most by 2 bits.

7.2.1 *d-ary Increasing Trees*

We recall that a rooted tree is a plane tree when the left-to-right order is taken into account. We will also distinguish between labeled trees and unlabeled trees. More precisely, we will start with a recursive process that generates labeled d-ary plane trees; that is, d-ary plane recursive trees. In a second step, we will remove the labels.

The process that generates unlabeled random d-ary plane increasing trees starts with an empty tree; that is, with just an external node (leaf). The first step in the growth process is to replace this external node by an internal one with d successors that are external nodes (see Figure 7.4). Then with probability $\frac{1}{d}$, one of these d external nodes is selected and again replaced by an internal node with d successors. In each subsequent step, one of the external nodes is replaced (with equal probability) by an internal node with d successors. In this process the jth created internal node is by j. Clearly, all labels of all internal successors of any node v are larger than the label of v.

It is clear that this evolution process (without removing the labels) produces random d-ary *plane increasing trees*. We now define the size of the d-ary plane increasing tree by the number of internal nodes. (We need to emphasize here that, unlike in the binary tree case, we measure the size of a tree not in terms of leaves.)

Let $\mathcal{G}$ denote the set of d-ary increasing trees, that is, the set of d-ary trees, with successive labels as described, and $\mathcal{G}_n$ set of d-ary increasing trees with n interval nodes.

Lemma 7.17 *The number $g_n = |\mathcal{G}_n|$ of d-ary increasing trees of size n is given by*

$$g_n = \prod_{j=0}^{n-1}((d-1)j+1) = (-1)^n(d-1)^n\frac{\Gamma(2-\frac{d}{d-1})}{\Gamma(2-\frac{d}{d-1}-n)}. \tag{7.29}$$

Furthermore, conditioned on the size n, the evolution process (just described) generates every element of $\mathcal{G}_n$ with equal probability $1/g_n$.

Proof Clearly we have $g_1 = 1$. Furthermore, if a d-ary tree with k internal nodes has $(d-1)k+1$ external nodes. Thus, there are precisely $(d-1)k+1$ ways to extend a d-ary tree of size k to a d-ary tree of size $k+1$ (by replacing one of the external nodes by a new internal one with label $k+1$ and by attaching d leaves to it). Thus,

$$g_{k+1} = ((d-1)k+1)g_k,$$

which proved (7.29) immediately. Furthermore, this procedure also shows that every tree in $\mathcal{G}_n$ is equally likely to be produced.   ∎

Next, let $\mathcal{F}$ denote the set of all unlabeled d-ary plane trees and, for each integer $n \geq 0$, let $\mathcal{F}_n$ be the subset of $\mathcal{F}$ consisting of all trees that contain exactly n internal nodes. We can consider $\mathcal{F}$ from two different points of view. First, it can be seen as equivalence classes of trees from $\mathcal{G}$, where two trees of $\mathcal{G}$ are considered as equivalent if they represent the same d-ary plane tree after removing the labels. Second, we can also consider the probabilistic construction of d-ary plane trees, where we do not attach labels (but just choose uniformly any external node and extend the tree). Clearly, both points of view lead to the same probabilistic model. Let f be a given d-ary plane tree of size n. In the first case, we just set $P(F_n = f) = |[f]|/g_n$, where $[f]$ denotes the equivalence class of d-ary increasing trees

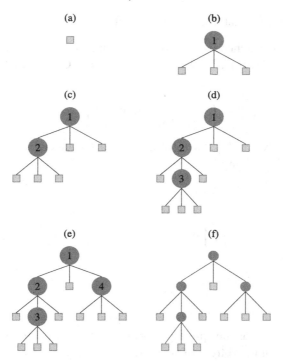

Figure 7.4 Example of the generation process that produces 3-ary plane tree of size 4 and its unlabeled counterpart.

that represent f after deleting the labels. In the second case, we just consider the evolution process and condition on the size n.

Example 7.18 There are

$$\binom{3}{2,0,1}\binom{1}{0,1,0} = 3$$

ways to obtain the resulting tree from Figure 7.4. Thus, the probability of this tree is $3/g_4 = 3/105 = 1/21$.

Remark 7.19 We note that the number of elements in an equivalence class $[f]$ can be also determined by the so-called *hook length formula*. The number of increasing trees induced by an unlabeled plane rooted tree t is

$$\frac{|t|}{\prod_{s \text{ subtree of } t} |s|}, \tag{7.30}$$

where $|\cdot|$ corresponds to the tree size measure.

From this we conclude that the probability of an unlabeled plane rooted tree t obtained by removing labels from a plane increasing rooted tree is

$$P(F_{|f|} = f) = \frac{|f|!}{g_{|t|} \prod_{s \text{ subtree of } t} |s|}. \tag{7.31}$$

In Exercise 7.10, we ask to establish the hook formula.

Next we establish a recurrence relation for the probability distribution $P(F_n = f)$. Suppose that $f \in \mathcal{F}_n$ has the d subtrees $f_1, \ldots, f_d$ of sizes $k_1, \ldots, k_d$. (Clearly we have $k_1 + \cdots + k_d = n - 1$.) Furthermore,

$$|[f]| = \binom{n-1}{k_1, \ldots, k_d} |[f_1]| \cdot |[f_2]| \cdots |[f_d]|$$

since there are precisely $\binom{n-1}{k_1, \ldots, k_d}$ ways to distributed the labels $2, \ldots, n$ to the subtrees $f_1, \ldots, f_d$. Consequently, we have

$$P(F_n = f) = \frac{|[f]|}{g_n} \tag{7.32}$$

$$= \frac{1}{g_n} \binom{n-1}{k_1, \ldots, k_d} \prod_{j=1}^{d} |[f_j]| = \binom{n-1}{k_1, \ldots, k_d} \frac{g_{k_1} \cdots g_{k_d}}{g_n} \prod_{j=1}^{d} P(F_{k_j} = f_j). \tag{7.33}$$

Thus, we can consider the term

$$\binom{n-1}{k_1, \ldots, k_d} \frac{g_{k_1} \cdots g_{k_d}}{g_n},$$

where $n - 1 = k_1 + \cdots k_d$ as the splitting probability; that is, the probability to split at the root of n internal nodes into subtrees of sizes $k_1, \ldots, k_d$, respectively. Note that in the binary case $d = 2$, the splitting probability is uniform: $P(k_1, k_2) = 1/n$.

For later use, it will be convenient to define a random vector $\mathbf{V}_n^{(d)}$ as

$$P\left(\mathbf{V}_n^{(d)} = (k_1, k_2, \ldots, k_d)\right) = \binom{n-1}{k_1, \ldots, k_d} \frac{g_{k_1} \cdots g_{k_d}}{g_n}, \tag{7.34}$$

where $k_1 + \cdots + k_d = n - 1$. The components of $\mathbf{V}_n^{(d)}$ will be denoted by $V_{n,j}$, $1 \leq j \leq d$:

$$\mathbf{V}_n^{(d)} = (V_{n,1}, \ldots V_{n,d}),$$

where $V_{n,1} + \cdots + V_{n,d} = n - 1$.

7.2.2 Entropy for d-ary Plane Trees

Next we derive a formula for the entropy $H(F_n)$. If $n = 0$, we have an empty tree and $H(F_0) = 0$. If $n = 1$, we have one fixed tree and $H(F_1) = 0$ too. By the definition of the trees, for $n > 1$, there is a bijection between a tree F_n and a tuple $(\mathbf{V}_n^{(d)}, F_{V_{n,1}}, \ldots, F_{V_{n,d}})$. Therefore, for $n > 1$, we have

$$H(F_n) = H\left(\mathbf{V}_n^{(d)}, F_{V_{n,1}}, \ldots, F_{V_{n,d}}\right) = H\left(\mathbf{V}_n^{(d)}\right) + H\left(F_{V_{n,1}}, \ldots, F_{V_{n,d}} \mid \mathbf{V}_n^{(d)}\right)$$

$$= H\left(\mathbf{V}_n^{(d)}\right) + \sum_{k_1 + \cdots + k_d = n-1} H\left(F_{k_1}, \ldots, F_{k_d}\right) P(\mathbf{V}_n^{(d)} = \mathbf{k}^{(d)}).$$

Since the subtrees $F_{k_1}, \ldots, F_{k_d}$ are conditionally independent given their sizes, we have

$$H(F_n) = H\left(\mathbf{V}_n^{(d)}\right) + d \sum_{k=0}^{n-1} p_{n,k} H(F_k) \tag{7.35}$$

where

$$p_{n,k} = \sum_{k_2 + \cdots + k_d = n-k-1} P\left(\mathbf{V}_n^{(d)} = (k, k_2, \ldots, k_d)\right). \tag{7.36}$$

The next lemma gives an explicit formula for $p_{n,k}$.

Lemma 7.20 *For $k = 0, \ldots, n-1$ we have*

$$p_{n,k} = \frac{1}{(d-1)n} \frac{n!\,\Gamma\left(k + \frac{1}{d-1}\right)}{k!\,\Gamma\left(n + \frac{1}{d-1}\right)}.$$

Proof Using (7.34), we can rewrite (7.36) as

$$p_{n,k} = \frac{(n-1)!\,g_k}{k!(n-1-k)!\,g_n} \sum_{k_2 + \ldots + k_d = n-1-k} \binom{n-1-k}{k_2, \ldots, k_d} g_{k_2} \cdots g_{k_d}.$$

Let us define the exponential generating function $G(z) = \sum_{n \geq 0} g_n \frac{z^n}{n!}$ with $g_0 = 1$. In Exercise 7.11, we ask to establish the explicit representation

$$G(z) = (1 - (d-1)z)^{-\frac{1}{d-1}}. \tag{7.37}$$

Observe that

$$\sum_{k_2 + \ldots + k_d = n-1-k} \binom{n-1-k}{k_2, \ldots, k_d} g_{k_2} \cdots g_{k_d}$$

is the $(n - 1 - k)$th coefficient of the function $G(z)^{d-1}$ (i.e., $\left[\frac{z^{n-1-k}}{(n-1-k)!}\right] G(z)^{d-1}$). Hence,

$$\begin{aligned}
p_{n,k} &= \frac{(n-1)!\,g_k}{k!(n-1-k)!\,g_n} \left[\frac{z^{n-1-k}}{(n-1-k)!}\right] G(z)^{d-1} \\
&= \frac{(n-1)!\,g_k}{k!\,g_n} \left[z^{n-1-k}\right] \frac{1}{1-(d-1)z} \\
&= \frac{(n-1)!\,g_k}{k!\,g_n} (d-1)^{n-1-k}.
\end{aligned}$$

For $d = 2$, we have $g_n = n!$ and the result is immediate. For $d > 2$, from (7.29), we find (with $\alpha = \frac{d}{d-1}$)

$$p_{n,k} = \frac{(\alpha-1)}{n} \frac{(-1)^n n!\,\Gamma(2-\alpha-n)}{(-1)^k k!\,\Gamma(2-\alpha-k)}.$$

We know that $\Gamma(z-n) = \frac{(-1)^n \pi}{\Gamma(n+1-z)\sin(\pi z)}$, hence,

$$(-1)^n \Gamma(n+\alpha)\Gamma(2-\alpha-n) = \frac{\pi \cdot (n-1+\alpha)}{\sin(\pi(2-\alpha))}, \tag{7.38}$$

and then

$$p_{n,k} = \frac{(\alpha-1)}{n} \frac{n!\,\Gamma(k+\alpha)(n+\alpha-1)}{k!\,\Gamma(n+\alpha)(k+\alpha-1)}.$$

Since $\Gamma(z+1) = z\Gamma(z)$, we get the desired result.   ∎

In summary, by setting $\alpha = \frac{d}{d-1}$, the entropy $x_n = H(F_n)$ satisfies the recurrence

$$x_n = a_n + \frac{\alpha}{n} \frac{n!}{\Gamma(n+\alpha-1)} \sum_{k=0}^{n-1} \frac{\Gamma(k+\alpha-1)}{k!} x_k, \qquad n \geq 2$$

with initial conditions $x_0 = x_1 = 0$. Thus, by applying Lemma 7.4, we obtain the explicit representation

$$x_n = a_n + \alpha(n+\alpha-1) \sum_{k=0}^{n-1} \frac{a_k}{(k+\alpha-1)(k+\alpha)} + \frac{n+\alpha-1}{\alpha+1} \left(x_1 + \frac{x_0}{\alpha-1} \right).$$

This leads us to the following result.

Theorem 7.21 *The entropy of unlabeled d-ary plane tree of size n, generated according to the d-ary plane increasing tree model, is given by*

$$H(F_n) = H\left(\mathbf{V}_n^{(d)}\right) + \frac{d}{d-1} \left(n + \frac{1}{d-1}\right) \sum_{k=0}^{n-1} \frac{H\left(\mathbf{V}_k^{(d)}\right)}{\left(k+\frac{1}{d-1}\right)\left(k+\frac{d}{d-1}\right)}, \qquad (7.39)$$

where

$$H\left(\mathbf{V}_n^{(d)}\right) = - \sum_{k_1+\cdots k_d=n-1} P(\mathbf{V}_n^{(d)} = \mathbf{k}^{(d)}) \log\left(P(\mathbf{V}_n^{(d)} = \mathbf{k}^{(d)})\right)$$

is the entropy of the random vector $\mathbf{V}_n^{(d)}$ that is defined by the probability distribution (7.34).

Example 7.22 Taking a closer look at $H\left(\mathbf{V}_n^{(d)}\right)$ we find

$$H\left(\mathbf{V}_n^{(d)}\right) = \log\left(n\frac{g_n}{n!}\right) - d\sum_{k=0}^{n-1} p_{n,k} \log\left(\frac{g_k}{k!}\right).$$

In particular, $H\left(\mathbf{V}_n^{(2)}\right) = \log(n-1)$, and for $d = 3$ and $n > 0$ we have

$$H\left(\mathbf{V}_n^{(3)}\right) = \log\left(\frac{n}{2^n}\binom{2n}{n}\right) - \frac{3}{2n}\sum_{k=0}^{n-1} \frac{\binom{2k}{k}2^{2n}}{\binom{2n}{n}2^{2k}} \log\left(\frac{\binom{2k}{k}}{2^k}\right).$$

From Theorem 7.21, we can also deduce the asymptotic behavior of $H(F_n)$. However, we have to know something about the order of magnitude of $H\left(\mathbf{V}_n^{(d)}\right)$. Here, we first observe that the range of the random vector $\mathbf{V}_n^{(d)}$ is contained in the set $\{0,\ldots,n-1\}^d$. Since the entropy is upper bounded by the logarithm of the image cardinality, we have

$$H\left(\mathbf{V}_n^{(d)}\right) \leq \log\left(n^d\right).$$

Consequently, the series

$$\sum_{k=0}^{\infty} \frac{H\left(\mathbf{V}_k^{(d)}\right)}{\left(k+\frac{1}{d-1}\right)\left(k+\frac{d}{d-1}\right)}$$

is certainly convergent and we can formulate it as the following corollary.

Corollary 7.23 *The entropy rate* $h_{d,f} = \lim_{n\to\infty} H\,(F_n)\,/n$ *of the unlabeled d-ary plane trees, generated according to the model of d-ary plane increasing tree s, is given by*

$$h_{d,f} = \frac{d}{d-1} \sum_{k=0}^{\infty} \frac{H\,(\mathbf{V}_k)}{\left(k + \frac{1}{d-1}\right)\left(k + \frac{d}{d-1}\right)}. \tag{7.40}$$

For example, for $d = 2$ and $d = 3$, we have $h_{2,f} \approx 1.73638$ and $h_{3,f} \approx 2.470$

7.2.3 A Compression Algorithm for d-ary Plane Trees

Next we provide a compression algorithm for unlabeled d-ary plane trees. As in the previous cases, we will use a proper arithmetic coding method.

We first define a total order $<$ on the set of such trees with a given size n. Having fixed this, we must show how to efficiently compute two quantities, for a given tree f: the probability of all trees $f' < f$ of size n, as well as the probability of f itself. We, thus, produce a subinterval $I(f)$ of $[0, 1)$, unique to f, which has length equal to the probability of f and whose left endpoint is the probability $P(F_n < f)$ of all trees $f' < f$. We than compute the first $\lceil -\log P(F_n = f)\rceil + 1$ binary digits of the mid-point of $I(f)$ and obtain a code for which the expected code length exceeds the entropy $H(F_n)$ at most by 2 bits.

Definition 7.24 The relation $<$ on $\mathcal{F}$ is defined as follows: let $f_1, f_2 \in \mathcal{F}$ with subtrees sizes $(s_1, \ldots, s_d)$, $(k_1, \ldots, k_d)$ respectively, then $f_1 < f_2$ if and only if one of the following holds:

- $(s_1, \ldots, s_d) \prec (k_1, \ldots, k_d)$,
- or if $(s_1, \ldots, s_d) = (k_1, \ldots, k_d)$ and first subtree of $f_1 <$ first subtree of f_2,
- or if $(s_1, \ldots, s_d) = (k_1, \ldots, k_d)$, first subtree of $f_1 =$ first subtree of f_2, and second subtree of $f_1 <$ second subtree of f_2,
- or if $(s_1, \ldots, s_d) = (k_1, \ldots, k_d)$, first $d - 1$ subtrees of $f_1 =$ first $d - 1$ subtrees of f_2, and dth subtree of $f_1 < d$th subtree of f_2.

It is simple to check that this is a total order. Next, we present an algorithm that computes the subinterval corresponding to an input tree $f \in \mathcal{F}$ (see Algorithm 1).

This does exactly as intuitively described: it implements a depth-first search of the input tree f, and at each step refining the current interval based on the split of vertices among the root subtrees of the current node.

Now, we explain more precisely the procedures CALCULATESPLITPROBABILITY and CALCULATEINTERVALBEGIN. The former simply calculates the probability that a d-ary tree of size n has root subtrees of sizes $k_1, \ldots, k_d$ (giving the length of the next subinterval). This is illustrated in Figure 7.5.

The latter gives the probability that such a d-ary tree has a root subtree size tuple lexicographically less than $(s_1, \ldots, s_d)$. That is, it computes the expression

$$\sum_{\substack{(k_1, \ldots, k_d) \prec (s_1, \ldots, s_d) \\ k_1 + \ldots + k_d = n - 1}} \binom{n-1}{k_1, \ldots, k_d} \frac{g_{k_1} \cdots g_{k_d}}{g_n}.$$

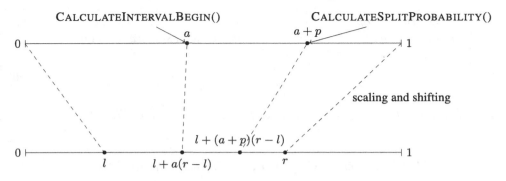

Figure 7.5 Visualization of lines $8 - 10$ in the Algorithm 1 listing.

Algorithm 1 Unlabeled d-ary Plane Tree Compression

1: **function** COMPRESSDTREE($f \in \mathcal{F}$) $\triangleright f$ tree to be compressed
2: $[a, b) \leftarrow$ EXPLORE(root of f, $[0, 1)$)
3: **return** first $\lceil -\log(b - a) \rceil + 1$ bits of $(a + b)/2$

4: **function** EXPLORE($v \in f$, $[l, r) \subseteq [0, 1)$)
5: $visited(v) \leftarrow true$
6: $n \leftarrow$ size of a subtree of f hanging from node v
7: $(s_1, \dots, s_d) \leftarrow$ sizes of subtrees of v
8: $a \leftarrow l + (r - l) \cdot$ CALCULATEINTERVALBEGIN($n, s_1, \dots, s_d$)
9: $p \leftarrow (r - l) \cdot$ CALCULATESPLITPROBABILITY($n, s_1, \dots, s_d$)
10: $I_{new} \leftarrow [a, a + p)$
11: **for all** u descendant of v **do**
12:   **if** not $visited(u)$ **then**
13:    $I_{new} \leftarrow$ EXPLORE(u, I_{new})
14: **return** I_{new}

15: **function** CALCULATESPLITPROBABILITY($n, k_1, \dots, k_d$)
16: **return** $\binom{n-1}{k_1,\dots,k_d} \frac{g_{k_1} \cdots g_{k_d}}{g_n}$

17: **function** CALCULATEINTERVALBEGIN($n, s_1, \dots, s_d$)
18: **return**

$$
\frac{1}{g_n} \sum_{i=1}^{d} \frac{(n-1)!}{s_1! \cdots s_{i-1}!} \left(\prod_{j=1}^{i-1} g_{s_j} \right) \cdot
$$
$$
\cdot \sum_{k=0}^{s_i - 1} \frac{g_k}{k!} \binom{n - 2 - k - \sum_{l=1}^{i-1} s_l + \frac{d-i}{d-1}}{\frac{1-i}{d-1}} (d - 1)^{n-1-k-\sum_{l=1}^{i-1} s_l}
$$

Observe that a naive implementation of this calculation generates all $\Theta(n^d)$ integer partitions with d parts of the number $n-1$ and calculates the split probability for each of them. To reduce the time complexity, we rewrite the sum as follows:

$$\sum_{\substack{(k_1,\ldots,k_d) \prec (s_1,\ldots,s_d) \\ k_1 + \cdots + k_d = n-1}} \binom{n-1}{k_1,\ldots,k_d} \frac{g_{k_1}\cdots g_{k_d}}{g_n}$$

$$= \frac{1}{g_n} \sum_{i=1}^{d} g_{s_1}\cdots g_{s_{i-1}} \sum_{k=0}^{s_i-1} \sum_{j_{i+1}+\cdots+j_d} \binom{n-1}{s_1,\ldots,s_{i-1},k,j_{i+1},\ldots,j_d} g_k g_{j_{i+1}}\cdots g_{j_d}.$$

For a given i, the ith term of the outermost sum gives the contribution of all tuples of the form $(s_1,\ldots,s_{i-1},k_i,k_{i+1},\ldots,k_d)$ with varying $k_i,\ldots,k_d$. We can, furthermore, write the multinomial coefficient as a product of two other multinomial coefficients, one of which can be brought outside the k sum. The kth term of the resulting sum can then be written as follows:

$$\frac{1}{(n-1-k-\sum_{l=1}^{i-1} s_l)!} \sum_{j_{i+1}+\cdots+j_d} \binom{n-1-k-\sum_{l=1}^{i-1} s_l}{j_{i+1},\ldots,j_d} g_{j_{i+1}}\cdots g_{j_d}$$

$$= \left[z^{n-1-k-\sum_{l=1}^{i-1} s_l}\right] (1-(d-1)z)^{-\frac{d-i}{d-1}}$$

$$= \binom{n-2-k-\sum_{l=1}^{i-1} s_l + \frac{d-i}{d-1}}{\frac{1-i}{d-1}} (d-1)^{n-1-k-\sum_{l=1}^{i-1} s_l}.$$

We thus finally find

$$\sum_{\substack{(k_1,\ldots,k_d) \prec (s_1,\ldots,s_d) \\ k_1 + \cdots + k_d = n-1}} \binom{n-1}{k_1,\ldots,k_d} \frac{g_{k_1}\cdots g_{k_d}}{g_n}$$

$$= \frac{1}{g_n} \sum_{i=1}^{d} \frac{(n-1)!}{s_1!\cdots s_{i-1}!} \left(\prod_{j=1}^{i-1} g_{s_j}\right)$$

$$\sum_{k=0}^{s_i-1} \frac{g_k}{k!} \binom{n-2-k-\sum_{l=1}^{i-1} s_l + \frac{d-i}{d-1}}{\frac{1-i}{d-1}} (d-1)^{n-1-k-\sum_{l=1}^{i-1} s_l}.$$

Observe that the resulting expression only requires to perform $O(n)$ calculations, where each of them is of the same order as the calculation of the split probability. An application of Algorithm 1 to a 3-tree is presented in Figure 7.6.

7.3 General Plane Trees

Finally we deal with (general) plane trees, where we do not put any restrictions on the node degree. In this context, we consider the following generation model of unlabeled plane trees (which is also known as the plane increasing tree model). Suppose that the process starts with the root node carrying a label 1. Then we add a child node with label 2 to the root. The next step is to attach a node with label 3. However, there are three possibilities: either

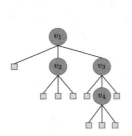

The following example describes algorithm COMPRESSDTREE in detail for a given 3-ary tree. From Equation (7.32), probability of the given tree equals to $\frac{4!}{g_4 4 \cdot 1 \cdot 2 \cdot 1} = \frac{1}{35}$. Moreover, consecutive calls of the EXPLORE procedure for the tree vertices outputs the following intervals: $v_1 \to \left[\frac{1}{7}, \frac{8}{35}\right)$, $v_2 \to \left[\frac{1}{7}, \frac{8}{35}\right)$, $v_3 \to \left[\frac{6}{35}, \frac{1}{5}\right)$, $v_4 \to \left[\frac{6}{35}, \frac{1}{5}\right)$. In the last step $\left\lceil -\log\left(\frac{1}{5} - \frac{6}{35}\right)\right\rceil + 1 = 7$ bits of the $\frac{1}{2}\left(\frac{6}{35} + \frac{1}{5}\right) = \frac{13}{70} = 0.001011111000101011111...$ is returned, i.e., 0010111.

Figure 7.6 Illustration to Algorithm 1.

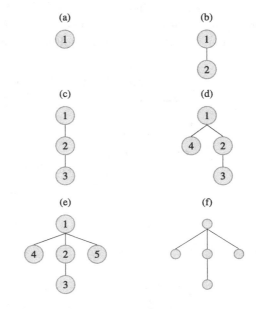

Figure 7.7 Example of the generation process that produces a labeled general plane tree of size 5 and its unlabeled counterpart.

add it to the root (as a left or right sibling of 2) or to the node with label 2. One proceeds further in the same way, as shown in Figure 7.7. At the end, we remove the labels from the nodes of the tree. Observe that if a node v already has out-degree $\text{outdeg}(v) = k$ (where the descendants are ordered), then there are $k + 1$ possible ways to add a new node (this time we do not distinguish between external and internal nodes). Hence, if a plane tree already has $j - 1$ nodes then there are $j - 2$ edges and precisely

$$\sum_v (\text{outdeg}(v) + 1) = (j - 2) + (j - 1) = 2j - 3$$

possibilities to attach the jth node (see Figure 7.7). For example, the probability of choosing a specific node of out-degree k equals $(k + 1)/(2j - 3)$. Here we define the size of the tree as the number of nodes.

7.3.1 Entropy of General Trees

In this section, we consider general plane trees as described (and illustrated in Figure 7.7). We only present the entropy analysis since the compression algorithm follows the same steps as for *d*-ary trees and is left as an exercise. In what follows, we will denote by $\mathcal{R}$ the set of rooted labeled plane trees, by $\mathcal{T}$, the set of rooted plane trees, and by $\mathcal{R}_n$ and $\mathcal{T}_n$ the corresponding subsets with *n* nodes.

Let $r_n = |\mathcal{R}_n|$, the number of labeled plane increasing trees with *n* nodes. Clearly, there are

$$r_n = \prod_{j=2}^{n-1}(2j - 3) = (2n - 3)!! = \frac{n!}{n2^{n-1}}\binom{2n - 2}{n - 1} \tag{7.41}$$

different labeled plane oriented increasing trees of size *n*. Alternatively, we could use the exponential generating function $R(z) = \sum_{n \geq 1} r_n z^n / n!$ that satisfies the differential equation

$$R'(z) = \frac{1}{1 - R(z)}, \tag{7.42}$$

which translates into the recurrence

$$r_n = \sum_{d \geq 1} \sum_{k_1 + \cdots + k_d = n-1} \binom{n - 1}{k_1, \ldots, k_d} r_{k_1} \cdots r_{k_d}.$$

Clearly, the differential equation (7.42) has the solution

$$R(z) = 1 - \sqrt{1 - 2z}$$

that leads to the explicit formula

$$r_n = (-1)^{n+1} n! 2^n \binom{\frac{1}{2}}{n} = \frac{n!}{n2^{n-1}}\binom{2n - 2}{n - 1}.$$

As in the case of the *d*-ary plane increasing trees, let [*t*] denote the subset of trees in $\mathcal{R}_n$ that have the same structure as a given unlabeled tree $t \in \mathcal{T}_n$ (i.e., [*t*] is the set of labeled *representatives* of *t*). Observe that

$$P(T_n = t) = \frac{|[t]|}{r_n}. \tag{7.43}$$

Suppose that the tree *t* of size *n* has *d* subtrees $t_1, \ldots, t_k$ of sizes $k_1, \ldots, k_d$. Then we have

$$P(T_n = t) = \binom{n - 1}{k_1, \ldots, k_d} \frac{r_{k_1} \cdots r_{k_d}}{r_n} \prod_{j=1}^{d} P(T_{k_j) = t_{k_j}}). \tag{7.44}$$

Observe that

$$\binom{n - 1}{k_1, \ldots, k_d} \frac{r_{k_1} \cdots r_{k_d}}{r_n}$$

is the probability that the root of a plane increasing tree of size *n* has degree equal to *d* and the root's subtrees are of sizes $k_1, \ldots, k_d$.

Let $\mathbf{W}_n$ be the random vector, where its *j*th component $W_{n,j}$ denotes the size of the *j*th subtree of a tree of size *n*. Clearly, $\mathbf{W}_n$ is concentrated on those vectors $(k_1, k_2, \ldots)$, where there exists $d \geq 0$ such that $k_1, \ldots, k_d > 0$, $k_1 + \cdots + k_d = n - 1$, and $k_{d+1} = k_{d+2} = \cdots = 0$. In particular, we have

$$P(\mathbf{W}_n = (k_1, k_2, \ldots)) = \binom{n-1}{k_1, \ldots, k_d} \frac{r_{k_1} \cdots r_{k_d}}{r_n}. \tag{7.45}$$

The initial conditions for the entropy are as follows. If $n = 1$, we have just a root node, so $H(T_1) = 0$. Similarly, if $n = 2$, we have one fixed tree, so $H(T_2) = 0$. We now give the recurrence for $n > 2$.

For $k = 1, \ldots, n-1$, let $q_{n,k}^{(d)}$ be defined as the probability that the root of a plane increasing tree has degree d and that one specified root subtree is of size k. Therefore, largely by the same reasoning as was used to derive the recurrence for d-ary plane trees,

$$H(T_n) = H(\mathbf{W}_n) + \sum_{d=1}^{n-1} d \sum_{k=1}^{n-d} H(T_k) q_{n,k}^{(d)}. \tag{7.46}$$

We need an expression for the probability $q_{n,k}^{(d)}$, which we present in the next lemma.

Lemma 7.25 *For $k = 1, \ldots, n - 1$, we have*

- $q_{n,n-1}^{(1)} = \frac{1}{2n-3}$ *and* $q_{n,k}^{(1)} = 0$ *if $k \neq n - 1$,*
- *for $d > 1$,*

$$q_{n,k}^{(d)} = 2^d \frac{d-1}{k(n-1-k)} \frac{\binom{2k-2}{k-1}\binom{2(n-1-k)-d}{n-2-k}}{\binom{2n-2}{n-1}}.$$

Proof If $d = 1$, then the root has only 1 subtree with all other nodes, so its size has to be equal to $n - 1$ and

$$q_{n,n-1}^{(1)} = \frac{r_{n-1}}{r_n} = \frac{1}{2n-3};$$

moreover, if $k \neq n - 1$: $q_{n,k}^{(1)} = 0$. In the case of $d > 1$, using (7.45), we can rewrite $q_n n, k$ as follows:

$$q_{n,k}^{(d)} = \frac{(n-1)! r_k}{k!(n-1-k)! r_n} \cdot \sum_{k_2 + \ldots + k_d = n-1-k} \binom{n-1-k}{k_2, \ldots, k_d} r_{k_2} \cdots r_{k_d}.$$

We use again the exponential generating function $R(z) = \sum_{n \geq 1} r_n \frac{z^n}{n!}$ and observe that

$$\sum_{k_2 + \cdots + k_d = n-1-k} \binom{n-1-k}{k_2, \ldots, k_d} r_{k_2} \cdots r_{k_d}$$

is the $(n - 1 - k)$th coefficient of the exponential generating function $R(z)^{d-1}$; that is,

$$\left[\frac{z^{n-1-k}}{(n-1-k)!} \right] R(z)^{d-1}.$$

Therefore,

$$q_{n,k} = \frac{(n-1)! r_k}{k! r_n} \left[z^{n-1-k} \right] R(z)^{d-1}.$$

We now use the fact that $R(z) = 1 - \sqrt{1 - 2z}$ is also the solution of the equation

$$R(z) = \frac{z}{1 - \frac{R(z)}{2}}.$$

Hence, by Lagrange's inversion formula, we obtain an explicit formula for

$$[z^{n-1-k}]R(z)^{d-1} = 2^{d-n+k} \frac{d-1}{n-1-k} \binom{2(n-1-k)-d}{n-2-k}.$$

This proves the desired result. ∎

The recurrence found in (7.46) is another one that we need to analyze. Its general solution is presented next.

Lemma 7.26 (Generalized entropy recurrence for unrestricted trees) *For given $y_1 = b_1$ and $y_2 = b_2$, the recurrence*

$$y_n = b_n + \sum_{d=1}^{n-1} d \sum_{k=1}^{n-d} q_{n,k}^{(d)} \cdot y_k, \qquad n > 2 \tag{7.47}$$

has the following solution for $n > 2$:

$$y_n = \frac{2(2n-1)}{3} b_1 + b_n + \frac{1}{2}\left(n - \frac{1}{2}\right) \sum_{j=2}^{n-1} \frac{b_j}{\left(j - \frac{1}{2}\right)\left(j + \frac{1}{2}\right)}.$$

Proof Using Lemma 7.25, for $n > 2$, we find

$$y_n = b_n + \frac{y_{n-1}}{2n-3} + \sum_{d=2}^{n-1} d(d-1)2^d \sum_{k=1}^{n-d} \frac{y_k}{k(n-1-k)} \frac{\binom{2k-2}{k-1}\binom{2n-2k-2-d}{n-k-2}}{\binom{2n-2}{n-1}}.$$

Multiplying both sides by $\frac{\binom{2n-2}{n-1}}{n}$ and substituting $\hat{y}_n = \frac{y_n\binom{2n-2}{n-1}}{n}$, $\hat{b}_n = \frac{b_n\binom{2n-2}{n-1}}{n}$, we find

$$\hat{y}_n = \hat{b}_n + \frac{2\hat{y}_{n-1}}{n(n-1)} + \frac{1}{n} \sum_{d=2}^{n-1} d(d-1)2^d \sum_{k=1}^{n-d} \frac{\hat{y}_k}{(n-1-k)} \binom{2n-2k-2-d}{n-k-2}.$$

Changing the order of summation gives us

$$\sum_{d=2}^{n-1} d(d-1)2^d \sum_{k=1}^{n-d} \frac{\hat{y}_k}{(n-1-k)} \binom{2n-2k-2-d}{n-k-2}$$

$$= \sum_{j=1}^{n-2} \frac{\hat{y}_j}{n-j-1} \sum_{s=0}^{n-j} s(s-1)2^s \binom{2n-2j-2-s}{n-j-2}.$$

Since for $N > 0$,

$$\sum_{s=0}^{N} s(s-1)2^s \binom{2N-2-s}{N-2} = (N-1)2^{2N-1},$$

we obtain

$$\hat{y}_n = \hat{b}_n + \frac{2\hat{y}_{n-1}}{n(n-1)} + \frac{1}{n}\sum_{j=1}^{n-2}\hat{y}_j 2^{2n-2j-1}.$$

Dividing both sides by 2^{2n} and substituting $\tilde{y}_n = \frac{\hat{y}_n}{2^{2n}}, \tilde{b}_n = \frac{\hat{b}_n}{2^{2n}}$, we find

$$\tilde{y}_n = \tilde{b}_n + \frac{1}{2n}\sum_{j=1}^{n-1}\tilde{y}_j.$$

Solving this recurrence relation by calculating $n\tilde{y}_n - (n-1)\tilde{y}_{n-1}$ leads to

$$\tilde{y}_n = b_1 \frac{\Gamma\left(n+\frac{1}{2}\right)}{\Gamma\left(\frac{5}{2}\right)n!} + \tilde{b}_n + \frac{\Gamma\left(n+\frac{1}{2}\right)}{n!}\sum_{j=2}^{n-1}\frac{\tilde{b}_j}{2j+1}\frac{j!}{\Gamma\left(j+\frac{1}{2}\right)}.$$

Substituting $\tilde{y}_n$ into y_n with $\tilde{y}_n = y_n \frac{\binom{2n-2}{n-1}}{n2^{2n}}$, we find the desired result.   ∎

This leads us to the following representation of the entropy $H(T_n)$.

Theorem 7.27 *The entropy of an unlabeled general plane tree, generated according to the model of plane increasing tree, is given by*

$$H(T_n) = H(\mathbf{W}_n) + \frac{1}{2}\left(n - \frac{1}{2}\right)\sum_{j=2}^{n-1}\frac{H(\mathbf{W}_j)}{\left(j-\frac{1}{2}\right)\left(j+\frac{1}{2}\right)}, \qquad (7.48)$$

where

$$H(\mathbf{W}_n) = -\sum_{k_1,k_2,\dots} P(\mathbf{W}_n = (k_1, k_2, \dots))\log P(\mathbf{W}_n = (k_1, k_2, \dots))$$

and the distribution of $\mathbf{W}_n$ is given in (7.45).

We conclude this section with the following result.

Corollary 7.28 *The entropy rate $h_3 = \lim_{n\to\infty} H(T_n)/n$ of unlabeled general plane trees, generated according to the model of plane increasing trees, is given by*

$$h_3 = \frac{1}{2}\sum_{j=2}^{\infty}\frac{H(\mathbf{W}_j)}{\left(j-\frac{1}{2}\right)\left(j+\frac{1}{2}\right)}. \qquad (7.49)$$

Proof From Theorem 7.27, we just need to prove that

$$H(\mathbf{W}_n) = o(n).$$

Let us recall that the random vector $\mathbf{W}_n$ describes the split at the root of a tree. Let D_n denote the number of subtrees of the root that has distribution

$$P(D_n = d) = \frac{(n-1)!}{r_n}[z^{n-1}]R(z)^d = \frac{d2^d}{n-1}\frac{\binom{2(n-1)-d-1}{n-2}}{\binom{2n-2}{n-1}}.$$

If we condition on the event $D_n = d$, then the image set of the random variable $(\mathbf{W}_n | D_n = d)$ is upper bounded by n^d. Consequently, we have

$$H(\mathbf{W}_n | D_n = d) \le \log(n^d) = d \log n,$$

which implies that

$$H(\mathbf{W}_n) = \sum_{d=1}^{n-1} P(D_n = d) H(\mathbf{W}_n | D_n = d)$$

$$\le \log n \sum_{d=1}^{n-1} d P(D_n = d).$$

Observe that $\mathbf{E}[D_n] = \sum_{d=1}^{n-1} d\, P(D_n = d)$ is the expected value of the general plane increasing tree root degree. In Exercise 7.14, we establish that $\mathbf{E}[D_n] = \sqrt{\pi n} + O(1)$, which gives us the desired result. ∎

Remark 7.29 Taking a closer look at $H(\mathbf{W}_n)$, we find that

$$H(\mathbf{W}_n | D_n = d) = \log \left(n \frac{r_n}{n!} \right) - d \sum_{k=1}^{n-d} q_{n,k}^{(d)} \log \left(\frac{r_k}{k!} \right).$$

This allows us to check numerically that the entropy rate of the unlabeled general plane trees, generated according to the model of plane increasing trees, is $h_3 \approx 1.68$.

7.4 Exercises

7.1 The arithmetic coding used for compressing trees runs as follows. The interval $[0, 1)$ is partitioned into subintervals $[a, b)$ such that every tree t of size n corresponds to one of these intervals and that $P(t) = b - a$. Then we associate to each interval $[a, b)$ a binary string, namely the first $\lceil - \log(b - a) \rceil + 1$ binary bits of the real number $(a + b)/2$. Show that this algorithm produces different codewords for different plane binary trees of size n.

7.2 Show that the worst case and the average case running time of the non-plane tree compression algorithms proposed in Section 7.1.5 satisfy (7.28) (see Magner et al. (2018)).

7.3 Analyze the m-ary search tree U_n built over n keys. In particular, prove that the entropy of m-ary search tree is given by

$$H(U_n) = c_m n + o(n),$$

where

$$c_m = 2\phi_m \sum_{k \ge 0} \frac{\log \binom{k}{m-1}}{(k+1)(k+2)};$$

$\phi_m = \frac{1}{2\mathcal{H}_m - 2}$ is called occupancy constant; $\mathcal{H}_m$ is the mth harmonic number; see Fill and Kapur (2005).

7.4 Using the functional equation (7.14), derive asymptotics of the Ottern trees for the uniform model (see Bona and Flajolet (2009)).

7.5 Let $b_n = [z^n]C(z)$, where $C(z)$ satisfies the Riccati differential equation (7.18). Prove that

$$b_n = \rho^n \left(6n - \frac{22}{5} + O(n^{-5}) \right) \tag{7.50}$$

where $\rho = 0.3183843834378459\ldots$ (see Chern et al. (2012)).

7.6 Derive (7.24).

7.7 First derive (7.25). Then design a compression algorithm of non-plane trees using the idea described around equation (7.25).

7.8 The entropy $h(s)$ is related to the Rényi entropy $h_1(t)$ of order 1 of non-plane trees. We define $h_1(t)$ as follows, if it exists,

$$h_1(t) = \lim_{n\to\infty} \frac{-\log \mathbf{E}[p(T_n)]}{n} = \lim_{n\to\infty} \frac{-\log \sum_{t_n \in \mathcal{T}_n} p(t_n)^2}{n}.$$

Note that for large n,

$$b_n = \sum_{t_n \in \mathcal{T}_n} p(t_n)^2 \sim \exp(-nh_1(t)).$$

By appealing to (7.50), prove that

$$b_n = \rho^n \left(6n - \frac{22}{5} + O(n^{-5}) \right),$$

where $\rho = 0.3183843834378459\ldots$. Thus $h_1(t) = -\log(\rho)$.

7.9 Prove (7.29) that gives a formula for the number of d-ary plane increasing trees.

7.10 Prove the hook formula (7.30).

7.11 Define the exponential generating function $G(z) = \sum_{n\geq 0} g_n \frac{z^n}{n!}$ with $g_0 = 1$ as in Section 7.2. Prove that

$$G(z) = (1 - (d-1)z)^{-\frac{1}{d-1}},$$

establishing (7.37).

7.12 Derive (7.41) that counts the number of general trees.

7.13 Design an optimal algorithm for compressing general trees following the steps presented for d-ary trees.

7.14 Consider general plane trees with n internal nodes. Show that the average degree D_n is

$$\mathbf{E}[D_n] = \sqrt{\pi n} + O(1)$$

(see Bergeron, Flajolet, and Salvy (1992)).

Bibliographical Notes

Trees are the most popular data structures and have been analyzed from algorithmic, probabilistic, and analytic points of view in many books. There are different types of trees: plane, non-plane, increasing, digital, and so forth. Here, we focus on analytic approaches to d-ary and general trees that are discussed in depth in Drmota (2009) and Bergeron et al. (1992) as well as Flajolet and Sedgewick (2008). See also Mahmoud (1992), Szpankowski (2001) and Jacquet and Szpankowski (2015).

There are a few scattered results for non-plane trees in a uniform model, for example, see Flajolet and Sedgewick (2008), Bona and Flajolet (2009), Drmota (2009). The non-plane trees in the binary search tree-like model were studied by analytic tools in Flajolet, Gourdon, and Martinez (1997) in a different context, and by a different method in Magner, Turowski, and Szpankowski (2016).

Symmetry in binary trees in the uniform model was first precisely analyzed Bona and Flajolet (2009). This was extended to a non-uniform model in Cichon et al. (2017). We should also point out that asymptotic analysis involved here is quite sophisticated and presented in Chern et al. (2012). However, to the best of our knowledge there is no study of symmetry for d-ary and general trees.

A more thorough studies on the compression of trees from an information-theoretic point of view can be found in Golebiewski, Magner, and Szpankowski (2018), Kieffer, Yang, and Szpankowski (2009), Magner et al. (2018), J. Zhang (2014). Zhang, Yang, and Kieffer (2014). For binary plane-oriented trees rigorous information-theoretic results were obtained in Magner et al. (2018). A universal grammar-based lossless coding scheme for trees was proposed in Zhang et al. (2014).

This chapter is based on Cichon et al. (2017), Golebiewski et al. (2018), and Magner et al. (2018). The hook formula can be found in Knuth (1998b) (page 47).

8

Graph and Structure Compression

Another class of advanced data structures that we study in this book is graphs. Unlike trees, graphs are a nonsequential data structure with no clear "beginning" and "end." However, just as trees graphs can come in two forms, graphs can be labeled or unlabeled. We often shall call the former simply graphs while the latter we will call unlabeled graphs, or better, *structures*.

Our basic question in this chapter is how many bits does one need to describe succinctly labeled graphs and structures? Formally, the labeled graph compression problem is as follows: fix a graph G_n or a distribution on (multi)graphs on n vertices. We would like to exhibit an efficiently computable *source code* (C_n, D_n) for G_n, where C_n is a function mapping graph in the support of G_n to bit strings, in such a way as to minimize the expected length of the output bit string when the input is a graph distributed according to G_n, and D_n inverts C_n and is efficiently computable. A related problem, and one focus of this chapter, seeks to compress graph structures: here, the encoding function C_n is presented with a multigraph G isomorphic to a sample from G_n, and $D_n(C_n(G))$ is only required to be a labeled multigraph isomorphic to G; that is, the labels are "discarded," leaving only the structural information. We again insist on a source code with the minimum possible expected code length that is given by the Shannon entropy of the distribution on unlabeled graphs induced by G_n, an often-nontrivial quantity to estimate; we call this the *structural entropy* of the model.

The structural compression problem is motivated by scenarios in which one only cares to transmit or store information about the isomorphism type of a graph (e.g., its degree sequence, number of occurrences of certain subgraphs, etc). In such scenarios, one *does not* care about labeled graph information, such as the fact that, say, vertex 2 connects to vertex 7. Taking advantage of this fact allows for a more compact description of the relevant information than would result if we naively encoded the labeled graph. More philosophically, structural compression allows to quantify and encode the information contained in the *shape* of graph-structured data. Structural compression may also answer questions like *how much information about the labels of a (random) graph is contained in its structure*?

As in the case of trees, graph and/or structural compression depends on the model of generations or on the graph distribution. However, because graphs are nonsequential models, governing the graph generation is very important. In this chapter, we focus on two models: Erdős–Rényi graphs and preferential attachment graphs. We also briefly discuss other graphs such as duplication graph generations.

8.1 Graph Generation Models

Let us here introduce two graph models. The first is the static Erdős–Rényi model $G(n,p)$ while the second is a dynamic *preferential attachment model* PA(n,m). We also briefly discuss the duplication-divergence model.

We start with the Erdős–Rényi model $G(n,p)$ with n nodes and parameter p. In such a model, given n nodes, one selects any pair of nodes and with probability p puts an edge. The probability $P(|E(G(n,p))| = k)$ of seeing a graph on k edges is

$$P(|E(G(n,p))| = k) = p^k(1 - p)^{\binom{n}{2}-k},$$

where $E(G(n,p))$ is a set of edges. The parameter p may depend on n, however, in most of the analysis in this chapter we assume that p is fixed.

Next we describe the preferential attachment model PA(n,m). We say that a multigraph G on vertex set $[n] = \{1, 2, \ldots, n\}$ is *m-left regular* if the only loop of G is at the vertex 1, and each vertex v, $2 \le v \le n$, has precisely m neighbors in the set $[v - 1]$. The *preferential attachment model* PA(n, m) is a dynamic model of network growth that gives a probability measure on the set of all m-left regular graphs on n vertices, proposed in Albert and Barabási (2002). More precisely, for a fixed integer parameter $m \ge 1$, we define the graph PA$(m; n)$ with vertex set $\{1, 2, \ldots, n\}$ using recursion on n in the following way: the graph $G_1 \sim$ PA$(1, m)$ is a single node with label 1 and m self-edges (these will be the only self-edges in the graph, and we will only count each such edge once in the degree of vertex 1). Inductively, we obtain a graph $G_{n+1} \in$ PA$(n + 1, m)$ from G_n by adding a vertex $n + 1$ and by connecting it to m randomly chosen (not necessarily different) vertices $v_1, \ldots, v_m$ of G_n such that for all vertices $w \le n$ in G_n,

$$P(v_i = w | G_n) = \frac{\deg_n(w)}{2mn},$$

where we denote by $\deg_n(w)$ the degree of vertex w in G_n (note that G_n has mn edges so that the sum of all degrees equals $2mn$).

There are many modifications and generalizations of the PA(n, m) model, but we focus here on the basic model with fixed m.

There are also graph models that are structurally different than preferential models. One such model is called a *duplication-divergence model*. It works as follows. Given an undirected, simple, seed graph G_{n_0} on n_0 nodes and a target number of nodes n, graph G_{k+1} with $k + 1$ nodes evolves from graph G_k using the following rules: a new vertex v is added to graph G_k, and then: (i) in the *duplication phase* a node u from G_k is selected uniformly at random and node v makes connections to all *neighbors* of u; (ii) in the *divergence phase* each of the newly made connections from v to neighbors of u are deleted with probability $1 - p$. Furthermore, for all nodes in G_k to which v is *not* connected, we create an extra edge from it to v independently with probability r/k for some $r \ge 0$.

8.2 Graphs versus Structures

For any graph G, we denote by $S(G)$ its unlabeled version (i.e., the equivalence class consisting of all labeled graphs isomorphic to G).

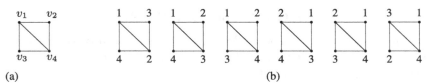

Figure 8.1 The six different labelings of a graph.

Our first concern will be to derive a fundamental lower bound on the expected code length for compression of unlabeled graphs. As usual, this is given by the *Shannon entropy* of the distribution on unlabeled graphs induced by a graph model. Thus, we need the entropy $H(G)$ of labeled graphs G and the structural entropy $H(S(G))$ of unlabeled graphs or structures $S(G)$.

By the chain rule for the conditional entropy, we have

$$H(G) = H(S(G)) + H(G|S(G)). \tag{8.1}$$

The second term, $H(G|S(G))$, measures our uncertainty about the labeled graph if we are given its structure. In some cases, for certain graph models (such as the Erdős–Rényi model and the preferential attachment model $PA(n, m)$), the conditional entropy $H(G|S(G))$ can be computed in terms of the size of the automorphism group $|Aut(G)|$ and another quantity $\Gamma(G)$, which is a subset of permutations that have positive probability of generation. Let us introduce these two quantities. We start with a graph automorphism $Aut(G)$. An *automorphism* of a graph G is an *adjacency preserving permutation* of the vertices of G. The collection $Aut(G)$ of all automorphisms of G is called *the automorphism group* of G. An automorphism is a measure of *symmetry* in a graph. Indeed, if two nodes have exactly the same view on the graph topology, then switching them does not change the adjacency matrix.

We illustrate it in the next example.

Example 8.1 In Figure 8.1(a), the graph G on four vertices $\{v_1, v_2, v_3, v_4\}$ has exactly four automorphisms; that is, in the usual cyclic permutation representation: $(v_1)(v_2)(v_3)(v_4)$, $(v_1)(v_4)(v_2 v_3)$, $(v_1 v_4)(v_2)(v_3)$, and $(v_1 v_4)(v_2 v_3)$. For example, $(v_1)(v_4)(v_2 v_3)$ stands for a permutation π such that $\pi(v_1) = v_1$, $\pi(v_4) = v_4$, $\pi(v_2) = v_3$, and $\pi(v_3) = v_2$. Thus, G has $4!/4 = 6$ different labelings as shown in Figure 8.1(b).

To count the number of *distinct* relabelings of a graph, we need one more parameter, namely, the set of *feasible permutations* $\Gamma(G)$. As usual, S_n denotes the set of all permutation on $\{1, 2, \ldots, n\}$.

Definition 8.2 Let G be a graph on n vertices. The set of *feasible permutations* $\Gamma(G)$ is a collection of permutations $\sigma \in S_n$ such that the graph $\sigma(G)$ has positive probability of generation (in the underlying probability model). Clearly, $\Gamma(G) \subseteq S_n$.

Obviously, the cardinality of $\Gamma(G)$ is upper bounded by $n!$; that is, $|\Gamma(G)| \leq n$ and the upper bound is achievable. For example, for Erdős–Rényi graphs $|\Gamma(G)| = n!$. But this is not true for preferential attachment graphs $PA(n, m)$ as illustrated in the following example.

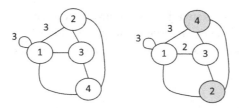

Figure 8.2 Preferential attachment graph PA(4, 3) before and after "illegal" permutation.

Example 8.3 Consider a preferential attachment model PA(4, 3) with $n = 4$ nodes and $m = 3$ as shown in Figure 8.2. In this case, the last node, node 4 must add three new edges as shown on the left of the figure. If we permute nodes 2 and 4, then, as shown on the right side of the figure, the last node 4 would have degree five, which is not allowed by the PA(4, 3) model, hence the probability of generating such a graph is zero.

Finally, we are able to define a set of *admissible graphs*.

Definition 8.4 The set of admissible graphs Adm(G) for G is defined as

$$\text{Adm}(G) := \{\sigma(G) : \ \sigma \in \Gamma(G)\}, \tag{8.2}$$

where $\Gamma(G)$ is the set of feasible permutations.

We observe that by the *orbit-stabilizer* property of groups we have the following relationship:

$$|\text{Adm}(G)| = \frac{|\Gamma(G)|}{|\text{Aut}(G)|}. \tag{8.3}$$

We are now able to prove the main result of this section, connecting the graph entropy $H(G)$ and $H(S(G))$, but only for graph models in which every labeled version of the same structure (unlabeled graph) has the same probability or, more precisely, in such models, graphs are invariant under isomorphism.

Lemma 8.5 *Consider a proper random graph model and assume that all positive probability labeled graphs G of the same structure $S(G)$ have the same probability. Then*

$$H(G) = H(S) + E[\log |Adm(G)|] \tag{8.4}$$
$$= H(S) + E[\log |\Gamma(G)|] - E[\log |\text{Aut}(G)|]. \tag{8.5}$$

Proof We recall the relation (8.1) saying that

$$H(G) = H(G, S) = H(S) + H(G|S).$$

Under our uniformity assumption (of all label graphs of the same structure), we have

$$P(G|S) = \frac{1}{|\text{Adm}(G)|} = \frac{|\text{Aut}(G)|}{|\Gamma(G)|},$$

hence, $H(G|S) = E[\log |\text{Adm}(G)|]$. The proof follows from this and (8.3). ∎

It is easy to see that Erdős–Rényi graphs are invariant under isomorphism. It is also true for the PA(m, n) model, however, it is harder to prove. We ask the reader to establish it in Exercise 8.5. We should also observe that this property does not hold for the duplication-divergence model.

8.3 Erdős–Rényi Graphs

We now focus on the structural compression of Erdős–Rényi graphs. Let us recall that in the Erdős–Rényi random graph model $G(n, p)$, graphs are generated randomly on n vertices with edges chosen independently with probability $0 < p < 1$. If a graph G in $G(n, p)$ has $|E(G(n, p))| = k$ edges, then

$$P(|E(G(n, p))| = k) = p^k q^{\binom{n}{2} - k},$$

where $q = 1 - p$.

It is clear that an Erdős–Rényi graph is uniquely represented by a memoryless 0-1-sequence of length $\binom{n}{2}$ that has entropy $\binom{n}{2} h(p)$. Thus, a (labeled) Erdős–Rényi graph can be encoded by 0-1-sequences of expected code length $\binom{n}{2} h(p) + O(1)$. For example, we could use a standard arithmetic encoding that has expected code length $< \binom{n}{2} h(p) + 2$. To recall the arithmetic encoder, that encodes a string x, computes an interval $I \subseteq [0, 1)$ of length $P(x)$, and takes then the first $\lfloor -\log P(x) \rfloor + 2$ binary digits of the mid-point of I. The intervals I form a partition of $[0, 1)$. For example, the first letter of x partitions $[0, 1)$ into two parts and so on. In the case of a memoryless source with parameter p, the length, of these two intervals are just p and $1 - p$.

Regarding the unlabeled version, or structure S of G, we first observe that $|\Gamma(G)| = n!$ so that every permutation is feasible. Hence, the cardinality $M(S) := |\text{Adm}(G)|$ of the admissible set is therefore $M(S) = n!/|\text{Aut}(G)|$ where $\text{Aut}(G)$ is the automorphism group of G. This further implies that the probability of a given structure S with k edges becomes

$$P(|E(S)| = k) = M(S) \cdot p^k (1 - p)^{\binom{n}{2} - k}.$$

The next aim is to estimate $M(S)$.

8.3.1 Structural Entropy

To compute the structural entropy $H(S(G))$ by Lemma 8.5, one needs to estimate the cardinality of $\text{Aut}(G)$ for randomly selected G from $G(n, p)$, which we do next. A graph is said to be *asymmetric* if its automorphism group does not contain any permutation other than the identity, that is, $|\text{Aut}(G)| = 1$; otherwise it is called *symmetric*.

Lemma 8.6 (Kim, Sudakov, and Vu, 2002) *For all p satisfying*

$$\frac{\log n}{n} \ll p \quad and \quad 1 - p \gg \frac{\log n}{n},$$

a random graph $G \in G(n, p)$ is symmetric with probability $O\left(n^{-w}\right)$ for any positive constant w; that is, $G \in G(n, p)$ is asymmetric with high probability.

Proof We follow here Kim, Sudakov, and Vu (2002). Let $G = (V, E)$ be a graph and let $\pi : V \rightarrow V$ be a permutation of the vertices of G. For a vertex $v \in V$, we define a *defect* of v with respect to π to be

$$D_\pi(v) = |N(\pi(v)) \, \Delta \, \pi(N(v))|,$$

where $N(v)$ is the set of neighbors of v and Δ denotes the symmetric difference of two sets; that is, $A \Delta B = (A \setminus B) \cup (B \setminus A)$ for two sets A and B. Similarly, we define a defect of G with respect to π to be

$$D_\pi(G) = \max_v D_\pi(v).$$

Finally, we define a *defect of a graph* G to be

$$D(G) = \min_{\pi \neq \text{identity}} D_\pi(G).$$

It is easy to see that a graph G is symmetric if and only if its graph defect equals zero; that is, $\exists_{\pi \neq \text{identity}} \forall_v D_\pi(v) = 0$. Thus we only need to show that $D(G) > 0$ for $G \in G(n, p)$ with high probability. But we shall next prove that $D(G)$ is at least $(2 - o(1))np(1 - p)$ with high probability.

Set $\varepsilon = \varepsilon(n, p)$ such that $\varepsilon = o(1)$ and $\varepsilon^2 np(1 - p) \gg \log n$. This is possible for all p's satisfying the conditions of the lemma (e.g., $\varepsilon = \Theta\left(\sqrt[4]{\frac{\log n}{np(1-p)}}\right)$). Fix an arbitrary $2 \leq k \leq n$, and let π be a permutation of vertices of G which fixes all but k vertices. Let U be the set of vertices $\{u | \pi(u) \neq u\}$ and

$$X = \sum_{u \in U} D_\pi(u).$$

By definition, $D_\pi(u)$ is a binomially distributed random variable with expectation either $2(n - 2)p(1 - p)$ or $2(n - 1)p(1 - p)$, depending on whether $\pi(\pi(u)) = u$ or not. Therefore,

$$\mathbf{E}[X] = \sum_{u \in U} \mathbf{E}[D_\pi(u)] = (2 - o(1))knp(1 - p).$$

We prove next that X is strongly concentrated around its mean, which implies that for some vertex $u \in U$, $D_\pi(u)$ is at least $\mathbf{E}[X]/k$ with high probability. Then we conclude that $D_\pi(G)$ is at least $\mathbf{E}[X]/k$ with high probability by the definition of $D_\pi(G)$. Finally, we shall prove that, for every possible permutation π, the minimum of $D_\pi(G)$ is still at least $\mathbf{E}[X]/k$ with high probability, which implies that $D(G)$ is at least $\mathbf{E}[X]/k$ with high probability by the definition of $D(G)$.

We start with the observation that X depends only on the edges of the graph adjacent to the vertices in U. Moreover, adding or deleting any such edge, say (u, v), can change only the values of at most four terms $D_\pi(u)$, $D_\pi(v)$, $D_\pi(\pi^{-1}(u))$, and $D_\pi(\pi^{-1}(v))$ in the sum, each by at most 1. Here, X can be seen as a random variable on a probability space generated by a finite set of mutually independent 0/1 choices, indexed by i. Let p_i be the probability that choice i is 1, and let c be a constant such that changing any choice i (keeping all other choices the same) can change X by at most c. Set $\sigma^2 = c^2 \sum_i p_i(1 - p_i)$. In Exercise 8.2, we ask the reader to show that for all positive $t < 2\sigma/c$,

$$P(|X - \mathbf{E}[X]| > t\sigma) \leq 2e^{-t^2/4}. \tag{8.6}$$

In this case, $c = 4$ and $\sigma^2 = 16(\binom{n}{2} - \binom{n-k}{2})p(1-p) = \Theta(knp(1-p))$. Therefore, for some positive constant α,

$$P(|X - \mathbf{E}[X]| > \varepsilon knp(1-p)) \leq e^{-\alpha\varepsilon^2 knp(1-p)}.$$

Thus, with probability at least $1 - e^{-\alpha\varepsilon^2 knp(1-p)}$, there is a vertex in U with defect at least

$$\frac{1}{k}(\mathbf{E}[X] - \varepsilon knp(1-p)) = (2 - o(1))np(1-p).$$

Therefore,

$$P(D_\pi(G) \leq (2 - \varepsilon)np(1-p)) \leq e^{-\alpha\varepsilon^2 knp(1-p)} = P_k.$$

Now we see that the number of permutations that fix $n-k$ vertices is at most $\binom{n}{k}k!$. Therefore, the probability that there exists a permutation such that the defect of G with respect to it is less than $(2 - \varepsilon)np(1-p)$ is at most

$$\sum_{k=2}^{n} \binom{n}{k}k!P_k \leq \sum_{k=2}^{n} n^k e^{-\alpha\varepsilon^2 knp(1-p)}$$

$$= \sum_{k=2}^{n} \left(e^{-\alpha\varepsilon^2 np(1-p)+\ln n}\right)^k$$

$$= O\left(e^{-\alpha\varepsilon^2 np(1-p)+\ln n}\right)^2$$

$$= O\left(e^{-\gamma \ln n+\ln n}\right)^2$$

$$= O\left(n^{1-\gamma}\right)^2 = O\left(n^{-w}\right)$$

for any positive constant w. We just have to choose $\gamma > 1$ and set $w = 2\gamma - 2$. Therefore, the probability that G is symmetric is at most $O\left(n^{-w}\right)$ for any positive constant w. ∎

Using Lemmas 8.5 and 8.6, we next present the structural entropy of $G(n,p)$ and establish the asymptotic equipartition property; that is, the typical probability of a structure S.

Theorem 8.7 *For large n and all p satisfying $\frac{\log n}{n} \ll p$ and $1 - p \gg \frac{\log n}{n}$, the following holds:*
(i) *The structural entropy $H(S)$ of the structure S generated by $G(n,p)$ is*

$$H(S) = \binom{n}{2}h(p) - \log n! + O\left(\frac{\log n}{n^\alpha}\right), \quad \text{for some } \alpha > 0.$$

(ii) *For every $\varepsilon > 0$,*

$$P\left(\left|-\frac{1}{\binom{n}{2}}\log P(S) - h(p) + \frac{\log n!}{\binom{n}{2}}\right| < \varepsilon\right) > 1 - 2\varepsilon, \tag{8.7}$$

where $h(p) = -p\log p - (1-p)\log(1-p)$ is the entropy rate of a binary memoryless source.

Proof Let us first compute the entropy $H(G)$ of $G(n,p)$. In $G(n,p)$, $m = \binom{n}{2}$ distinct edges are independently selected with probability p, and thus there are 2^m different labeled graphs.

That is, each graph instance can be considered as a binary sequence X of length m. Thus,

$$H(G) = -\mathbf{E}[\log P(X^m)] = -m\mathbf{E}[\log P(X)] = \binom{n}{2}h(p).$$

By Lemma 8.5,

$$H(S) = \binom{n}{2}h(p) - \log n! + A,$$

where

$$A = \sum_{S \in \mathcal{S}(n,p)} P(S) \log |\mathrm{Aut}(S)|$$

and $\mathcal{S}(n,p)$ denotes the structures that are generated by $G(n,p)$.

Now we show that $A = o(1)$ to prove part (i). By applying the upper bound $|\mathrm{Aut}(S)| \le n! \le n^n$ and Lemma 8.6 with some $w > 1$, we obtain

$$
\begin{aligned}
A &= \sum_{S \in \mathcal{S}(n,p) \text{ is symmetric}} P(S) \log |\mathrm{Aut}(S)| \\
&\quad + \sum_{S \in \mathcal{S}(n,p) \text{ is asymmetric}} P(S) \log |\mathrm{Aut}(S)| \\
&= \sum_{S \in \mathcal{S}(n,p) \text{ is symmetric}} P(S) \log |\mathrm{Aut}(S)| \\
&\le \sum_{S \in \mathcal{S}(n,p) \text{ is symmetric}} P(S) \cdot n \log n \\
&= O\left(\frac{\log n}{n^{w-1}}\right) \\
&= o(1).
\end{aligned}
$$

To prove part (ii), we define the *typical set* T_ε^n as the set of structures S on n vertices having the following two properties: (a) S is asymmetric; (b) for $G \sim S$,

$$2^{-\binom{n}{2}(h(p)+\varepsilon)} \le P(G) \le 2^{-\binom{n}{2}(h(p)-\varepsilon)}.$$

Let T_1^n and T_2^n be the sets of structures satisfying the properties (a) and (b), respectively. Then, $T_\varepsilon^n = T_1^n \cap T_2^n$. By the asymmetry of $G(n,p)$, we know that $P(T_1^n) > 1 - \varepsilon$ for large n. As explained, a labeled graph G can be viewed as a binary sequence of length $\binom{n}{2}$. Thus, by the property (b) and the asymptotic equidistribution property for binary sequences, we also know that $P(T_2^n) > 1 - \varepsilon$ for large n. Thus, $P(T_\varepsilon^n) = 1 - P(\overline{T_1^n} \cup \overline{T_2^n}) > 1 - 2\varepsilon$. Now let us compute $P(S)$ for S in T_ε^n. By the property (a), $P(S) = n!P(G)$ for any $G \cong S$. By this and the property (b), we can see that any structure S in T_ε^n satisfies the condition in (8.7). This completes the proof. ∎

8.3.2 *An Algorithm and Its Analysis*

Our algorithm, which we call SZIP (Structural ZIP), is a compression scheme for unlabeled graphs. In other words, given a labeled graph G, it compresses G into a codeword, from which one can reconstruct a graph S that is isomorphic to G. The algorithm consists of two stages: first it encodes G into two binary sequences (B_1 and B_2) and then it compresses them.

The main idea behind our algorithm is quite simple: we select a vertex, say v_1, and store the number of neighbors of v_1 in binary. Then we partition the remaining $n - 1$ vertices into two sets: the neighbors of v_1 and the nonneighbors of v_1. We continue by selecting a vertex, say v_2, from the neighbors of v_1 and store two numbers: the number of neighbors of v_2 among each of these two sets. Then we partition the remaining $n - 2$ vertices into four sets: the neighbors of both v_1 and v_2, the neighbors of v_1 that are nonneighbors of v_2, the nonneighbors of v_1 that are neighbors of v_2, and the nonneighbors of both v_1 and v_2. In each step we create a new child node if there is at least one graph vertex in that node. Similarly, in the ith step, we remove one graph vertex v_i from the (level-wise) leftmost node at level $i - 1$. If this removal makes the node empty, we remove the node. The other graph vertices at level $i-1$ move down to the left or to the right depending whether they are adjacent to v_i or not. We repeat these steps until all graph vertices are removed. During the construction, the number of neighbors of the selected vertex with respect to each set in the partition is appended either to the sequence B_1 or to the sequence B_2 where B_2 contains those numbers for singleton sets (i.e., we store either "0" when there is no neighbor or "1" otherwise). We then compress B_2 using, for example, an arithmetic encoder since it dominates the compression rate and can be viewed as generated by a memoryless source; see Lemma 8.9). The algorithm is illustrated in Figure 8.3.

It is an interesting exercise to reconstruct (decode) the structure of the graph from the lists B_1 and B_2 (see Exercise 8.1).

The main result of this section provides an asymptotic formula for the expected code length.

Theorem 8.8 *Let $L(S)$ be the length of the codeword generated by our algorithm for Erdős–Rényi graphs $G \in G(n,p)$ (with fixed p) isomorphic to a structure S. Then for large n,*

$$E[L(S)] = \binom{n}{2} h(p) - n \log n + (c + \Phi(\log n)) n + o(n),$$

where c is an explicitly computable constant, and $\Phi(x)$ is a periodic function.

Hence, the algorithm SZIP is close to an optimal one, since we certainly have

$$\mathbf{E}[L(S)] \geq H(S) = \binom{n}{2} h(p) - n \log n + \frac{n}{\ln 2} + O(\log n).$$

We also want to mention that the distribution of $L(S)$ has a kind of concentration around its expected value $\mathbf{E}[L(S)]$. In Exercise 8.3, we ask the reader to prove the following:

$$P(L(S) < \mathbf{E}[L(S)] + \varepsilon n \log n) = o(1) \tag{8.8}$$

for every $\varepsilon > 0$. Also, it is easy to see that our algorithm runs in time $O(n^2)$ in the worst case. We ask the reader to establish this in Exercise 8.2.

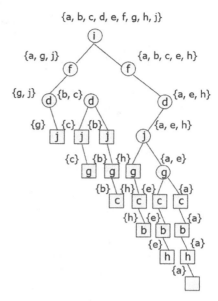

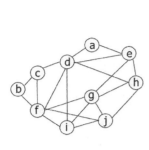

B1 = 0100110100001110101
B2 = 1001011000000101

Figure 8.3 Illustration of the Szip algorithm. On the left we show a graph that encodes to B_1 and B_2. The first vertex is chosen to be $v_1 = i$. So it is removed and the vertices $\{d, f, g, j\}$ are put to the left and the vertices $\{a, b, c, e, h\}$ to the right. In particular, the number of neighbor vertices of the root is $4 = (100)_2$. Thus, B_1 starts with 0100 (we use 4 digits since the maximum number of neighbors is 9 that need 4 digits). In the next step we choose the vertex $v_2 = f$ that is removed from the set $\{d, f, g, j\}$ and consider the neighbors/nonneighbors $\{d, g, j\}, \emptyset, \{b, c\}, \{a, e, h\}$. The neighbor numbers are $3 = (11)_2$ and $2 = (010)_2$. Thus, 11010 is appended to B_1. In this way we proceed further. In the third step, we choose $v_3 = d$ and in the fourth step, $v_4 = j$ etc. In the fourth step, there are the first singleton sets $\{g\}, \{c\}, \{b\}$, where only g is neighbor of j. Thus, B_2 starts with 1, 0, 0. Note also that in the fifth level the neighbor singleton set $\{g\}$ is removed since $v_5 = g$ (similar situations occur subsequently).

8.3.3 Proof of Theorem 8.8

We start with a description of two binary trees that better capture the progress of our algorithm. Recall that our algorithm runs as follows. Given a graph G on n vertices, a binary tree T_n is built as follows. At the beginning, the root node contains all n graph vertices, $V(G)$, that one can also visualize as n balls. In the first step, a graph vertex (ball) v is removed from the root node, and the other $n - 1$ graph vertices move down to the left or to the right depending whether they are adjacent vertices in G to v or not; adjacent vertices go to the left child node and the others go to the right child node. We create a new child node in T_n if there is at least one graph vertex in that node. After the first step, the tree is of height 1 with $n - 1$ graph vertices in the nodes at level 1. Similarly, in the ith step, we remove one graph vertex (ball) v from the (level-wise) leftmost node at level $i - 1$. If this removal makes the node empty, we remove the node. The other graph vertices at level $i - 1$ move down to the left or to the right depending whether they are adjacent to v or not. We repeat these steps until all graph vertices are removed (i.e., after n steps).

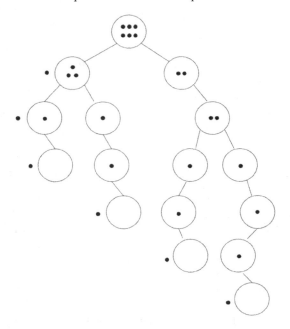

Figure 8.4 A $(6, 1)$-trie with six balls and $d = 1$, in which the deleted ball is shown next to the node from which it was removed.

The tree structure just described can be generalized to a tree that we call (n, d)-trie. In such a tree, the root contains n balls that are distributed between the left and the right subtrees according to the following rule. In each step, all balls independently move down to the left subtree (say with probability p) or the right subtree (with probability $1 - p$). A new node is created as long as there is at least one ball in that node. Furthermore, a nonnegative integer d is given, and at level d or greater one ball is removed from the leftmost node before the balls move down to the next level. These steps are repeated until all balls are removed (i.e., after $n + d$ steps). Observe that when $d = \infty$, our tree can be modeled as a *trie* that stores n independent sequences generated by a binary memoryless source with parameter p. Therefore, we coin the name (n, d)-tries for the tree just described, and to which we often refer simply as d-tries. This is illustrated in Figure 8.4.

Let N_x denote the number of graph vertices that pass through node x in T_n (excluding the graph vertex removed at x, if any). In Figure 8.3, for example, N_x is the number of graph vertices shown next to the node x. Our algorithm needs to encode, for each node x in T_n, the number of neighbors (of the removed graph vertex) among N_x vertices. This requires $\lceil \log(N_x + 1) \rceil$ bits. Let $L(B_1)$ and $L(B_2)$ be the lengths of sequences B_1 and B_2, respectively. By construction, these lengths are defined as

$$L(B_1) = \sum_{x \in T_n \text{ and } N_x > 1} \lceil \log(N_x + 1) \rceil,$$

$$L(B_2) = \sum_{x \in T_n \text{ and } N_x = 1} \lceil \log(N_x + 1) \rceil = \sum_{x \in T_n \text{ and } N_x = 1} 1.$$

In Figure 8.3(b), $L(B_1)$ and $L(B_2)$ are sums over all circle-shaped nodes and over all square-shaped nodes, respectively. Here we can observe an important property of B_2 presented next.

Lemma 8.9 *Given a graph from $G(n, p)$, the sequence B_2 constructed by our algorithm is probabilistically equivalent to a binary sequence generated by a memoryless source(p) with p being the probability of generating a "1."*

Proof Consider any bit $b \in B_2$. It represents the number of neighbors of a vertex u in a subset, which contains only one vertex, say v. Then the probability that $b = $"1" is the same as the probability that u and v are connected, which is p in the Erdős–Rényi model. Let us consider any two bits b_1 and b_2. Assume that b_i corresponds to vertices u_i and v_i (i.e., b_i corresponds to the potential edge between u_i and v_i). These two potential edges are chosen independently according to the Erdős–Rényi model. This shows the memoryless property. ∎

To set up precise recurrence relations for the analysis, we need to define a random binary tree $T_{n,d}$ for integers $n \geq 0$ and $d \geq 0$, which is generated similarly to T_n as follows. If $n = 0$, then it is just an empty tree. For $n > 0$, we create a root node, in which we put n balls. In each step, all balls independently move down to the left (with probability p) or right (with probability $1 - p$). We create a new node if there is at least one ball in that node. Thus, after the ith step, the balls will be at level i. If the balls are at level d or greater, then we remove one ball from the leftmost node before the balls move down to the next level. These steps are repeated until all balls are removed (i.e., after $n + d$ steps). We observe that, if T_n is generated by a graph from $G(n, p)$, T_n is nothing but the random binary tree $T_{n,0}$. Thus, by analyzing $T_{n,0}$, we can compute both $L(B_1)$ and $L(B_2)$.

Let us first estimate $L(B_1)$. Recall, N_x denotes the number of balls that pass through node x (excluding the ball removed at x, if any). Let

$$A_{n,d} = \sum_{x \in T_{n,d} \text{ and } N_x > 1} \lceil \log(N_x + 1) \rceil,$$

and $a_{n,d} = \mathbf{E}[A_{n,d}]$. Then $\mathbf{E}[L(B_1)] = a_{n,0}$. Clearly, $a_{0,d} = a_{1,d} = 0$ and $a_{2,0} = 0$. For $n \geq 2$ and $d = 0$, we observe that

$$a_{n+1,0} = \lceil \log(n + 1) \rceil + \sum_{k=0}^{n} \binom{n}{k} p^k q^{n-k} (a_{k,0} + a_{n-k,k}). \tag{8.9}$$

This follows from the fact that starting with $n + 1$ balls in the root node, and removing one ball, we are left with n balls passing through the root node. The root contributes $\lceil \log(n + 1) \rceil$. Then, those n balls move down to the left or right subtrees. Let us assume k balls move down to the left subtree (the other $n - k$ balls must move down to the right subtree, and this happens with probability $\binom{n}{k} p^k q^{n-k}$). At level one, one ball is removed from those k balls in the root of the left subtree. This contributes $a_{k,0}$. There will be no removal among $n - k$ balls in the right subtree until all k balls in the left subtree are removed. This contributes $a_{n-k,k}$. Similarly, for $d > 0$, we can see that

$$a_{n,d} = \lceil \log(n + 1) \rceil + \sum_{k=0}^{n} \binom{n}{k} p^k q^{n-k} (a_{k,d-1} + a_{n-k,k+d-1}). \tag{8.10}$$

This recurrence is quite complex. We start with the asymptotic behavior of the solution of the limit

$$a(n, \infty) = \lim_{d \to \infty} a_{n,d},$$

that satisfies the recurrence

$$a(n, \infty) = \lceil \log (n+1) \rceil + \sum_{k=0}^{n} \binom{n}{k} p^k q^{n-k} (a(k, \infty) + a(n-k, \infty)) \qquad (n \geq 2) \quad (8.11)$$

with initial conditions $a(0, \infty) = a(1, \infty) = 0$. It is not difficult to show that this limit actually exists. By induction it follows that $a_{n,d+1} \geq a_{n,d}$.

Lemma 8.10 *Let $a(n, \infty)$ be defined by the recurrence (8.11) with initial conditions $a(0, \infty) = a(1, \infty) = 0$.*
(i) If $\log p / \log q$ is irrational, then

$$a(n, \infty) = \frac{n}{h(p) \ln 2} A^*(-1) + o(n), \qquad (8.12)$$

where

$$A^*(-1) = \sum_{b \geq 2} \frac{\lceil \log(b+1) \rceil}{b(b-1)}. \qquad (8.13)$$

(ii) If $\log p / \log q = r/d$ (rational) with $\gcd(r, d) = 1$, then

$$a(n, \infty) = \frac{n}{h(p) \ln 2} \left(A^*(-1) + \Phi_1(\log_p n) \right) + o(n), \qquad (8.14)$$

where

$$\Phi_1(x) = \sum_{k \neq 0} A^*(-1 + 2k\pi r i / \log p) \exp(2k\pi r x i) \qquad (8.15)$$

is a periodic function, where

$$A^*(s) = \sum_{n \geq 2} \frac{\lceil \log (n+1) \rceil}{n!} \Gamma(n+s)$$

and $\Gamma(s)$ is the Euler gamma function.

Proof Define the exponential generating function (EGF) of $a(n, \infty)$ as

$$\hat{a}(z) = \sum_{n=0}^{\infty} a(n, \infty) \frac{z^n}{n!}$$

for complex z. Then, by setting $c_n = \lceil \log(n+1) \rceil$, we have for $n \geq 2$,

$$\frac{a(n,\infty)}{n!} z^n = \frac{c_n}{n!} z^n + \sum_{k=0}^{n} \frac{1}{k!}(zp)^k \frac{1}{(n-k)!}(zq)^{n-k}(a(k,\infty) + a(n-k,\infty))$$

$$= \frac{c_n}{n!} z^n + \sum_{k=0}^{n} \frac{a(k,\infty)}{k!}(zp)^k \frac{1}{(n-k)!}(zq)^{n-k}$$

$$+ \sum_{k=0}^{n} \frac{1}{k!}(zp)^k \frac{a(n-k,\infty)}{(n-k)!}(zq)^{n-k}.$$

Thus, using the fact that $a(0,\infty) = a(1,\infty) = c_0 = c_1 = 0$,

$$\sum_{n=0}^{\infty} \frac{a(n,\infty)}{n!} z^n = \sum_{n=0}^{\infty} \frac{c_n}{n!} z^n + \sum_{n=0}^{\infty} \sum_{k=0}^{n} \frac{a(k,\infty)}{k!}(zp)^k \frac{1}{(n-k)!}(zq)^{n-k}$$

$$+ \sum_{n=0}^{\infty} \sum_{k=0}^{n} \frac{1}{k!}(zp)^k \frac{a(n-k,\infty)}{(n-k)!}(zq)^{n-k}.$$

Finally, we arrive at

$$\hat{a}(z) = \hat{c}(z) + \hat{a}(zp)e^{zq} + \hat{a}(zq)e^{zp},$$

where $\hat{c}(z)$ is the EGF of c_n. The Poisson transform (see also Appendix C), defined as $\widetilde{A}(z) = \hat{a}(z)e^{-z}$, of the above equation satisfies, then

$$\widetilde{A}(z) = \widetilde{C}(z) + \widetilde{A}(zp) + \widetilde{A}(zq), \qquad (8.16)$$

where $\widetilde{C}(z) = \hat{c}(z)e^{-z}$.

At this stage, the analytic depoissonization result Theorem C.3 (of Appendix C) suggests that

$$a(n,\infty) \sim \widetilde{A}(n)$$

as $n \to \infty$. However, the conditions of Theorem C.3 cannot be directly checked, since it is not clear how $\widetilde{C}(z)$ behaves in the complex plane.

In order to overcome this technical problem, we can proceed as follows. For given $\varepsilon > 0$, we define $B(\varepsilon)$ such that

$$\sum_{b>B(\varepsilon)} \frac{\sqrt{b}}{b(b-1)} < \varepsilon.$$

We replace then the sequence $c_n = \lceil \log(n+1) \rceil$ by a lower and upper bound:

$$c_n^{(1)} = \begin{cases} c_n & \text{for } n \leq B(\varepsilon), \\ 0 & \text{for } n > B(\varepsilon), \end{cases} \qquad c_n^{(2)} = \begin{cases} c_n & \text{for } n \leq B(\varepsilon), \\ \sqrt{n} & \text{for } n > B(\varepsilon). \end{cases}$$

Since $c_n^{(1)} \leq c_n \leq c_n^{(2)}$, it follows that the corresponding solutions $a(n,\infty)^{(1)}$ and $a(n,\infty)^{(2)}$ satisfy $a(n,\infty)^{(1)} \leq a(n,\infty) \leq a(n,\infty)^{(2)}$. On the other hand, the corresponding Poisson transforms $\widetilde{C}^{(1)}(z)$ and $\widetilde{C}^{(2)}(z)$ satisfy the assumptions of Theorem C.3 (as we will show later). Hence, it follows that

$$a(n,\infty)^{(1)} \sim \widetilde{A}^{(1)}(n) \quad \text{and} \quad a(n,\infty)^{(2)} \sim \widetilde{A}^{(2)}(n).$$

If $\log p / \log q$ is irrational, we have (as for the sequence c_n)

$$\widetilde{A}^{(1)}(n) = \frac{n}{h(p)} \sum_{2 \le b \le B(\varepsilon)} \frac{\lceil \log(b+1) \rceil}{b(b-1)}$$

and

$$\widetilde{A}^{(2)}(n) = \frac{n}{h(p) \ln 2} \left(\sum_{2 \le b \le B(\varepsilon)} \frac{\lceil \log(b+1) \rceil}{b(b-1)} + \sum_{b > B(\varepsilon)} \frac{\sqrt{b}}{b(b-1)} \right).$$

Consequently it follows

$$\limsup_{n \to \infty} \frac{1}{n} \left| a(n, \infty) - \frac{n}{h(p) \ln 2} A^*(-1) \right| \le \frac{\varepsilon}{h(p) \ln 2}.$$

Since $\varepsilon > 0$ is arbitrary, it finally follows that

$$a(n, \infty) \sim \frac{n}{h(p) \ln 2} A^*(-1).$$

Similarly, we can argue in the rational case.

In order to solve asymptotically the functional equation (8.16), we apply the Mellin transform. The reader is referred to Appendix D for an in-depth discussion of the Mellin transform. In brief, the Mellin transform of a real-valued function $f(x)$ is defined as

$$f^*(s) = \int_0^\infty f(x) x^{s-1} dx.$$

It is defined in a strip $-\alpha < \Re(s) < -\beta$ when $f(x) = O(x^\alpha)$ for $x \to 0$ and $f(x) = O(x^\beta)$ for $x \to \infty$. Noting that the Mellin transform of the function $f(ax)$ is given by

$$a^{-s} f^*(s),$$

we transform the functional equation (8.16) into the following equation:

$$A^*(s) = C^*(s) + p^{-s} A^*(s) + q^{-s} A^*(s),$$

where $A^*(s)$ and $C^*(s)$ are the Mellin transforms of $\widetilde{A}(z)$ and $\widetilde{C}(z)$, respectively. This leads to

$$A^*(s) = \frac{C^*(s)}{1 - p^{-s} - q^{-s}}$$

for $-2 < \Re(s) < -1$, as is easy to see under our assumption on $a(0, \infty)$. Observe also that

$$C^*(s) = \int_0^\infty \widetilde{C}(z) z^{s-1} dz = \sum_{n \ge 2} \frac{c_n}{n} \int_0^\infty z^n e^{-z} z^{s-1} dz = \sum_{n \ge 2} \frac{c_n}{n} \Gamma(n+s), \qquad (8.17)$$

and for $c_n = \lceil \log(n+1) \rceil$ the series converges for $\Re(s) < 0$. The same holds for $c_n^{(1)}$. For $c_n^{(2)}$, we just have convergence for $\Re(s) < -\frac{1}{2}$.

In order to find asymptotics of $a(n, \infty)$ (as well as for $a(n, \infty)^{(1)}$ and $a(n, \infty)^{(2)}$, respectively), we first compute the inverse Mellin transform:

$$\widetilde{A}(z) = \frac{1}{2\pi i} \int_{c-i\infty}^{c+i\infty} A^*(s) z^{-s} ds, \qquad (8.18)$$

where $-2 < c < -1$ is a constant. The goal is to get asymptotics for $\widetilde{A}(n)$ as $n \to \infty$ (and then to apply the described depoissonization procedure). For this purpose we will shift the integral to the right. However, we have to take care of the zeros of $1 - p^{-s} - q^{-s}$. By Lemma D.7 (from Appendix D), we know that all zeros satisfy

$$-1 \le \Re(s) \le \sigma_0,$$

where σ_0 is a real positive solution of $1 + q^{-s} = p^{-s}$. Furthermore, for every integer k there uniquely exists a zero s_k with

$$(2k - 1)\pi / \ln(1/p) < \Im(s_k) < (2k + 1)\pi / \ln(1/p).$$

Furthermore, if $\log q / \log p = \ln q / \ln p$ is irrational, then $s_0 = -1$ and $\Re(s_k) > -1$ for all $k \ne 0$. If $\log q / \log p = r/d$ is rational, where $\gcd(r, d) = 1$ for integers $r, d > 0$, then $\Re(s_k) = -1$ if and only if $k \equiv 0 \bmod d$. In particular, $\Re(s_1), \dots, \Re(s_{d-1}) > -1$ and

$$s_k = s_{k \bmod d} + \frac{2(k - k \bmod d)\pi i}{\ln p};$$

that is, all zeros are uniquely determined by $s_0 = -1$ and by $s_1, s_2, \dots, s_{d-1}$, and their imaginary parts constitute an arithmetic progression.

To compute the integral (8.18) asymptotically, we apply the standard approach. We shift the integral to the right and collect the appearing residues at $s = s_k$ ($k \in \mathbb{Z}$). Due to the convergence properties of $C^*(s)$ (due to the Γ-factors in the representation (8.17)), it is easy to see that the residue theorem gives (for $\eta > 0$ sufficiently small)

$$\widetilde{A}(n) = \frac{1}{2\pi i} \int_{-\eta - i\infty}^{-\eta + i\infty} A^*(s) + \sum_{k \in \mathbb{Z}} \frac{n^{s_k} \log e}{-\log p \, p^{-s_k} - \log q \, q^{-s_k}} C^*(s_k).$$

If $\log p / \log q$ is irrational, then $\Re(s_k) > -1$ for all $k \ne 0$ and so we have

$$\sum_{k \in \mathbb{Z}} \frac{n^{s_k} \log e}{-\log p \, p^{-s_k} - \log q \, q^{-s_k}} C^*(s_k) = \frac{n \log e}{h(p)} C^*(-1) + o(n),$$

which gives

$$\widetilde{A}(n) \sim \frac{n \log e}{h(p)} C^*(-1) = \frac{n}{h(p) \ln 2} C^*(-1).$$

In the irrational case, we have a linear progression of k with $\Re(s_k) = -1$ that leads to the representation

$$\sum_{k \in \mathbb{Z}} \frac{n^{s_k} \log e}{-\log p \, p^{-s_k} - \log q \, q^{-s_k}} C^*(s_k) = \frac{n \log e}{h(p)} \left(C^*(-1) + \Phi_1(\log_p n) \right) + O(n^{1-\varepsilon})$$

for some $\varepsilon > 0$ and finally we find

$$\widetilde{A}(n) \sim \frac{n \log e}{h(p)} \left(C^*(-1) + \Phi_1(\log_p n) \right) = \frac{n}{h(p) \ln 2} \left(C^*(-1) + \Phi_1(\log_p n) \right).$$

All these computations can be done for $c_n = \lceil \log(n + 1) \rceil$ as well as for $c_n^{(1)}$ and $c_n^{(2)}$. As mentioned, this leads to asymptotic representations for $\widetilde{A}^{(1)}(n)$ and $\widetilde{A}^{(2)}(n)$.

At the next step, we recall that we want to apply depoissonization, in particular Theorem C.2, in order to obtain $a(n, \infty)^{(1)} \sim \tilde{A}^{(1)}(n)$ and $a(n, \infty)^{(2)} \sim \tilde{A}^{(2)}(n)$. For this purpose, we have to check that the functions $\tilde{C}^{(1)}(z)$ and $\tilde{C}^{(1)}(z)$ satisfy the conditions of Theorem C.2. Since

$$\tilde{C}^{(1)}(z) = e^{-z} \sum_{n \leq B(\varepsilon)} \frac{\lceil \log(n+1) \rceil}{n!} z^n$$

is only a finite sum, these conditions are trivially satisfied. Furthermore, $\tilde{C}^{(1)}(z)$ differs from

$$\tilde{D}(z) := e^{-z} \sum_{n \geq 0} \frac{\sqrt{n}}{n} z^n = \frac{\Gamma(3/2)}{2\pi i} \int_C e^{z(e^{-x}-1)}(-x)^{-3/2} \, dx$$

just by a finite sum; here C denotes a Hankel contour as in the Hankel integral representation of $1/\Gamma(s)$ (compare with Appendix C). It is an easy exercise that $\tilde{D}(z)$ satisfies the assumptions of Theorem C.2 (see Exercise 8.4).

This completes the proof of Lemma 8.10. ∎

The next step is to analyze the difference $\tilde{a}(n, d) = a(n, \infty) - a_{n,d}$. First we note that by definition we have $a_{n,1} = a_{n+1,0}$. We then obtain the (homogeneous) recurrence

$$\tilde{a}(n, d) = \sum_{k=0}^{n} \binom{n}{k} p^k q^{n-k} \left[\tilde{a}(k, d-1) + \tilde{a}(n-k, k+d-1) \right] \quad (n \geq 2, d \geq 1), \quad (8.19)$$

with the side and initial conditions

$$\tilde{a}(n+1, 0) - \tilde{a}(n, 1) = a(n+1, \infty) - a(n, \infty) \quad (n \geq 0)$$

and

$$\tilde{a}(0, d) = \tilde{a}(1, d) = 0 \quad (d \geq 0).$$

Lemma 8.11 *The following upper bound holds:*

$$\tilde{a}(n, d) \leq A_0 n^{\nu+\varepsilon} (p^2 + q^2)^d; \ n \geq 2, d \geq 0 \qquad (8.20)$$

where $\nu = \log(p^2 + q^2)/\log p > 0$.

Proof When $n = 2$, it is easy to see that we have (exactly)

$$\tilde{a}(2, d) = \left(\frac{1}{pq} - 2 \right) (p^2 + q^2)^{d-1},$$

so (8.20) clearly holds. Assuming that (8.20) holds for all (N, D) with $N + D < n + d$, we can estimate the first sum in the right-hand side of (8.19) by

$$\sum_{k=0}^{n-2} \binom{n}{k} p^k q^{n-k} \tilde{a}(k, d-1) \leq A_0 \sum_{k=0}^{n} k^{\nu+\varepsilon} (p^2 + q^2)^{d-1} p^k q^{n-k} \binom{n}{k}$$

$$\leq A_0 (np)^{\nu+\varepsilon} (p^2 + q^2)^{d-1}$$

$$= A_0 n^{\nu+\varepsilon} (p^2 + q^2)^d,$$

and the second sum (8.19) by

$$\sum_{k=0}^{n-2} \binom{n}{k} p^k q^{n-k} \widetilde{a}(n-k, k+d-1)$$

$$\leq A_0 \sum_{k=0}^{n} (n-k)^{\nu+\varepsilon} (p^2+q^2)^{k+d-1} p^k q^{n-k} \binom{n}{k}$$

$$\leq A_0 n^{\nu+\varepsilon} (p^2+q^2)^{d-1} \sum_{k=0}^{n} \binom{n}{k} \left[p(p^2+q^2) \right]^k q^{n-k}$$

$$= A_0 n^{\nu+\varepsilon} (p^2+q^2)^{d-1} \left[q + p(p^2+q^2) \right]^n,$$

which completes the proof of the lemma. ∎

In particular, we find

$$\sum_{k=0}^{n} \binom{n}{k} p^k q^{n-k} \widetilde{a}(n-k, d) \leq A_0 n^{\nu+\varepsilon} (p^2+q^2)^{d-1} \sum_{k=0}^{n} \binom{n}{k} p^k q^{n-k} (p^2+q^2)^k$$

$$= A_0 n^{\nu+\varepsilon} (p(p^2+q^2) + q)^{n+d-1}; \tag{8.21}$$

that is, the second part in the recurrence (8.19) is bounded by a term that is exponentially small in n and d. It it therefore convenient to study next the following recurrence:

$$a_*(n, d) = \sum_{k=0}^{n} \binom{n}{k} p^k q^{n-k} a_*(k, d-1) \quad (n \geq 2, \, d \geq 1),$$

with the side and initial conditions

$$a_*(n+1, 0) - a_*(n, 1) = a(n+1, \infty) - a(n, \infty) \quad (n \geq 0)$$

and

$$a_*(0, d) = a_*(1, d) = 0 \quad (d \geq 0).$$

The difference $a_{diff}(n, d) = \widetilde{a}(n, d) - a_*(n, d)$ then satisfies

$$a_{diff}(n, d) = \sum_{k=0}^{n} \binom{n}{k} p^k q^{n-k} a_{diff}(k, d-1) + \sum_{k=0}^{n} \binom{n}{k} p^k q^{n-k} \widetilde{a}(n-k, k+d-1) \tag{8.22}$$

and $a_{diff}(n+1, 0) = a_{diff}(n, 1)$. Note that $a_{diff}(n, d)$ is nonnegative.

Lemma 8.12 *We have the following upper bound:*

$$a_{diff}(n, d) \leq A_1 \tag{8.23}$$

for some constant A_1.

Proof Since $a_{diff}(n+1, 0) = a_{diff}(n, 1)$ and by (8.21) we have

$$a_{diff}(n+1, 0) = \sum_{k=0}^{n} \binom{n}{k} p^k q^{n-k} a_{diff}(k, 0) + O(\gamma^n)$$

for some $\gamma < 1$; this immediately shows that $a_{diff}(n, 0)$ is bounded.

Now we show by induction on d that $a_{diff}(n, d) \leq C_d$ for proper constants C_d that are uniformly bounded. By (8.22) and (8.21) we get

$$\sup_{n \geq 0} a_{diff}(n, d) \leq C_{d-1} + O((p^2 + q^2)^d).$$

Hence, it is clear that we can define inductively constants C_d by $C_d = C_{d-1} + O((p^2 + q^2)^d)$. Clearly, these constants are uniformly bounded. ∎

We finally need an upper bound for $a_*(n, d)$, which is presented next and proved in Section 8.3.5 since we need some additional results.

Lemma 8.13 *For every fixed d, the numbers $a_*(n, d)$ are bounded by*

$$a_*(n, d) = O((\log n)^2)$$

for large n.

Summing up, we have

$$
\begin{aligned}
\mathbb{E}[L(B_1)] &= a_{n,0} \\
&= a(n, \infty) - \widetilde{a}(n, 0) \\
&= a(n, \infty) - a_*(n, 0) - a_{diff}(n, 0) \\
&= a(n, \infty) + O((\log n)^2).
\end{aligned}
$$

Hence, together with Lemma 8.10, we have obtained the precise asymptotic behavior for $\mathbf{E}[L(B_1)]$.

Theorem 8.14 *For large n,*

$$\mathbf{E}[L(B_1)] = \frac{n}{h(p) \ln 2} (\beta + \Phi_1(\log n)) + o(n),$$

where

$$\beta = \sum_{b \geq 2} \frac{\lceil \log (b + 1) \rceil}{b(b - 1)} = 2.606 \cdots,$$

and $\Phi_1(\log n)$ is a periodic function for $\log p / \log q$ rational and zero otherwise.

Estimate of B_2. The next step is to estimate the average length of B_2. Let $S_{n,d}$ be the total number of nodes x in $T_{n,d}$ such that $N_x = 1$; that is,

$$S_{n,d} = \sum_{x \in T_{n,d} \text{ and } N_x = 1} 1 = \sum_{x \in T_{n,d} \text{ and } N_x = 1} N_x = \sum_{x \in T_{n,d}} N_x - \sum_{x \in T_{n,d} \text{ and } N_x > 1} N_x.$$

Let $B_{n,d} = \sum_{x \in T_{n,d}, N_x > 1} N_x$. We observe that

$$L(B_2) = S_{n,0} = \sum_{x \in T_{n,0}} N_x - B_{n,0} = \frac{n(n - 1)}{2} - B_{n,0}. \tag{8.24}$$

The last equality follows from the fact that the sum of N_x's for all x at level ℓ in $T_{n,0}$ is equal to $n - 1 - \ell$.

Let $b_{n,d} = \mathbf{E}[B_{n,d}]$. For our analysis, we only need $b_{n,0}$. Clearly, $b_{0,d} = b_{1,d} = 0$ and $b_{2,0} = 0$. For $n \geq 2$, we can find the following recurrence in a similar way to $a_{n,d}$:

$$b_{n+1,0} = n + \sum_{k=0}^{n} \binom{n}{k} p^k q^{n-k} (b_{k,0} + b_{n-k,k}), \tag{8.25}$$

$$\text{and} \quad b_{n,d} = n + \sum_{k=0}^{n} \binom{n}{k} p^k q^{n-k} (b_{k,d-1} + b_{n-k,k+d-1}) \quad \text{for } d > 0. \tag{8.26}$$

Instead of (8.25), we can just use the boundary condition

$$b_{n,1} = b_{n+1,0}, \quad \text{for } n \geq 0. \tag{8.27}$$

We should point out that this recurrence describes the path length in the (n,d)-trie discussed in the previous section. We just recall that in such a tree, the root contains n balls that are distributed between the left and the right subtrees. In each step, all balls independently move down to the left subtree (say with probability p) or the right subtree (with probability $1-p$). A new node is created as long as there is at least one ball in that node. Furthermore, a nonnegative integer d is given, and at level d or greater one ball is removed from the leftmost node before the balls move down to the next level. These steps are repeated until all balls are removed (i.e., after $n+d$ steps). Observe that when $d = \infty$, the above tree can be modeled as a *trie* that stores n independent sequences generated by a binary memoryless source with parameter p. This is illustrated in Figure 8.4.

We now study in detail recurrence (8.26), corresponding to the path length in an (n,d)-trie and show how much the path length of such a d-trie differs from that of regular tries (in which $d = \infty$).

If we let $d \to \infty$ in (8.26) and assume that $b_{n,d}$ tends to a limit that we denote as $b(n, \infty)$, then (8.26) becomes

$$b(n, \infty) = n + \sum_{k=0}^{n} \binom{n}{k} p^k q^{n-k} [b(k, \infty) + b(n-k, \infty)], \tag{8.28}$$

with $b(0, \infty) = b(1, \infty) = 0$. This is the same as the recurrence for the mean path length in a trie. We recall that the Poisson generating function $\widetilde{B}(z) = e^{-z} \sum_{n \geq 0} b(n, \infty) z^n / n!$ satisfies

$$\widetilde{B}(z) = z(1 - e^{-z}) + \widetilde{B}(pz) + \widetilde{B}(qz).$$

By inverting the Mellin transform of $\widetilde{B}(z)$, we obtain (similarly to before):

$$\widetilde{B}(z) = \frac{1}{2\pi i} \int_{-3/2-i\infty}^{-3/2+i\infty} z^{-s} \frac{\Gamma(s+1)}{1 - p^{-s} - q^{-s}} ds, \tag{8.29}$$

which holds for $-2 < \Re(s) < -1$. The integral certainly converges for z real and positive.

The asymptotic expansion of $b(n, \infty)$ as $n \to \infty$ can be obtained in the same way by shifting the integral in (8.29) to the right and by collecting the residues. The only difference to the above analysis is that the function $\Gamma(s+1)/(1-p^{-s}-q^{-s})$ has a double pole at $s = -1$. Hence, the residue of the integrand is then

$$\frac{1}{h(p)} n \log n + \frac{\gamma}{h(p)} + \frac{h_2(p)}{2h(p)^2},$$

where $h_2(p) = p \log^2 p + q \log^2 q$ and γ is the Euler constant. Together with the residues at $s = s_k$ and by applying the depoissonization theorem (Theorem C.2) we, thus, obtain

$$b(n, \infty) = \frac{1}{h(p)} n \log n + \frac{1}{h(p)} \left[\gamma + \frac{h_2(p)}{2h(p)} + \Phi_2(\log_p n) \right] n + o(n), \qquad (8.30)$$

where $\Phi_2(x)$ is the periodic function

$$\Phi_2(x) = \sum_{k=-\infty, k \neq 0}^{\infty} \Gamma\left(-\frac{2k\pi ir}{\log p}\right) e^{2k\pi rix},$$

provided that $\log p / \log q = r/s$ is rational, with r and s being integers with $\gcd(r, s) = 1$. If $\log p / \log q$ is irrational, then the term with Φ_2 is absent.

Our analysis requires, too, a two-term asymptotic estimate of the difference $b(n+1, \infty) - b(n, \infty)$, whose generating function may be represented, similarly to (8.30), as the inverse Mellin transform

$$\sum_{n \geq 0} [b(n+1, \infty) - b(n, \infty)] \frac{z^n}{n!} e^{-z} = \frac{1}{2\pi i} \int_{-3/2-i\infty}^{-3/2+i\infty} \frac{-s\Gamma(s+1)}{1 - p^{-s} - q^{-s}} z^{-s-1} ds. \qquad (8.31)$$

This integral has (again) a double pole at $s = -1$ and we can obtain a two-term approximation for $z \to \infty$:

$$b(n+1, \infty) - b(n, \infty) = \frac{1}{h(p)} \log n + \frac{1}{h(p)} \left(\gamma + 1 + \frac{h_2(p)}{2h(p)} \right) + \frac{1}{h(p)} \Psi_3(\log_p n) + o(1), \qquad (8.32)$$

where $\Psi_3(\cdot)$ is the periodic function in Theorem 8.15, which again appears only for rational $\log p / \log q$.

We next set

$$b_{n,d} = b(n, \infty) - \widetilde{b}(n, d) \qquad (8.33)$$

so that $\widetilde{b}(n, d) = b(n, \infty) - b_{n,d}$ measures how the path lengths in the d-trie differ from those in a trie. From (8.26) and (8.28), we then obtain

$$\widetilde{b}(n, d) = \sum_{k=0}^{n} \binom{n}{k} p^k q^{n-k} \left[\widetilde{b}(k, d-1) + \widetilde{b}(n-k, k+d-1) \right], \quad \text{for } n \geq 2, d \geq 1, \quad (8.34)$$

which, unlike (8.26), is a homogeneous recurrence. As before, we have the boundary condition

$$\widetilde{b}(n+1, 0) - \widetilde{b}(n, 1) = b(n+1, \infty) - b(n, \infty). \qquad (8.35)$$

We also have $\widetilde{b}(0, d) = \widetilde{b}(1, d) = 0$ for $d \geq 0$. As in Lemma 8.11, we get an a priori bound for $\widetilde{b}(n, d)$:

$$\widetilde{b}(n, d) \leq A_0 n^{\nu+\varepsilon} (p^2 + q^2)^d; \; n \geq 2, d \geq 0, \qquad (8.36)$$

where $\nu = \log(p^2 + q^2) / \log p > 0$.

We further define $b_*(n, d)$ to be the solution of

$$b_*(n, d) = \sum_{k=0}^{n} \binom{n}{k} p^k q^{n-k} b_*(k, d-1), \quad \text{for } n \geq 2, d \geq 1, \qquad (8.37)$$

and

$$b_*(n+1,0) - b_*(n,1) = b(n+1,\infty) - b(n,\infty). \tag{8.38}$$

Next set $b_{diff}(n,d) = \widetilde{b}(n,d) - b_*(n,d)$. Then (as before) we obtain from (8.34)–(8.38) that

$$b_{diff}(n,d) = \sum_{k=0}^{n}\binom{n}{k}p^k q^{n-k}b_{diff}(k,d-1) + \sum_{k=0}^{n}\binom{n}{k}p^k q^{n-k}\widetilde{b}(n-k,k+d-1) \tag{8.39}$$

with $b_{diff}(n+1,0) = b_{diff}(n,1)$. Using an inductive argument as in Lemma 8.12, we get that

$$b_{diff}(n,d) \le B_1 \tag{8.40}$$

for some constant B_1.

It remains to provide the asymptotic behavior of $b_*(n,d)$ from (8.38).

Lemma 8.15 *For* $n \to \infty$ *and* $d = O(1)$, *the sequence* $b_*(n,d)$ *is of order* $O(\log^2 n)$ *for* $n \to \infty$. *More precisely,*

$$b_*(n,d) = \frac{1}{2h\log(1/p)}\log^2 n - \frac{d}{h}\log n$$
$$+ \left[\frac{1}{2h} - \frac{1}{h\log p}\left(\frac{\gamma+1}{\ln 2} + \frac{h_2}{2h} + \Psi_3(\log_p n)\right)\right]\log n + o(\log n),$$

where $\Psi_3(\cdot)$ *is the periodic function*

$$\Psi_3(x) = \frac{1}{\ln 2}\sum_{k=-\infty, k\neq 0}^{\infty}\left[1 + \frac{2k\pi ir}{\ln p}\right]\Gamma\left(-\frac{2k\pi ir}{\ln p}\right)e^{2k\pi irx}$$

and $\log p/\log q = r/t$ *is rational. If* $\log p/\log q$ *is irrational, the term involving* Ψ_3 *is absent.*

Before proving Lemma 8.15 in Section 8.3.4, we just observed that

$$\begin{aligned}
\mathbf{E}[L(B_2)] &= \frac{n(n-1)}{2} - b_{n,0}\\
&= \frac{n(n-1)}{2} - b(n,\infty) + \widetilde{b}(n,0)\\
&= \frac{n(n-1)}{2} - b(n,\infty) + b_*(n,0) - b_{diff}(n,0)\\
&= \frac{n(n-1)}{2} - b(n,\infty) + O((\log n)^2).
\end{aligned}$$

This finally gives us a precise estimate for $\mathbf{E}[L(B_2)]$ leading to the following theorem.

Theorem 8.16 *For large* n,

$$\mathbf{E}[L(B_2)] = \frac{n(n-1)}{2} - \frac{n}{h(p)}\log n$$
$$- \frac{1}{h(p)}\left[\frac{\gamma}{\ln 2} + \frac{h_2(p)}{2h(p)} + \Phi_2(\log_p n)\right]n + o(n),$$

where $h_2(p) = p\log^2 p + q\log^2 q$, γ *is the Euler constant, and* $\Phi_2(x)$ *is a periodic function for* $\log p/\log q$ *rational and zero otherwise.*

8.3.4 Proof of Lemma 8.15

The goal is to analyze the recurrence (8.37). For this purpose, we introduce the exponential generating function

$$\widetilde{b}_d(z) = \sum_{n=2}^{\infty} b_*(n, d)\frac{z^n}{n!} \tag{8.41}$$

and the corresponding Poisson version

$$\widetilde{B}_d(z) = e^{-z}\widetilde{b}_d(z),$$

where $b_*(n, d)$ is defined from (8.37). We find that $\widetilde{b}_d(z) = \widetilde{b}_{d-1}(pz)e^{qz}$ or

$$\widetilde{B}_d(z) = \widetilde{B}_{d-1}(pz). \tag{8.42}$$

This can be solved by iteration to yield $\widetilde{B}_d(z) = \widetilde{B}_0(p^d z)$. Then setting

$$\widetilde{g}(z) = \sum_{n=2}^{\infty} b(n, \infty)\frac{z^n}{n!}$$

and noting that

$$\sum_{n=1}^{\infty} b_*(n + 1, 0)\frac{z^n}{n} = \frac{d}{dz}\widetilde{b}_0(z),$$

(8.38) leads to

$$\frac{d}{dz}\widetilde{b}_0(z) - \widetilde{b}_0(z) = -\widetilde{g}(z) + \widetilde{g}'(z). \tag{8.43}$$

If we set $\widetilde{G}(z) = e^{-z}\widetilde{g}(z)$, we also have

$$\widetilde{B}_0'(z) + \widetilde{B}_0(z) - \widetilde{B}_0(pz) = \widetilde{G}'(z). \tag{8.44}$$

We recall that by (8.29), the Mellin transform of $\widetilde{G}(z)$ is given by

$$\int_0^{\infty} \widetilde{G}(z)z^{s-1}dz = \frac{\Gamma(s + 1)}{1 - p^{-s} - q^{-s}}. \tag{8.45}$$

Furthermore, let $\mathcal{M}(s)$ denote the negative Mellin transform of $\widetilde{B}_0(z)$; that is,

$$\mathcal{M}(s) = -\int_0^{\infty} \widetilde{B}_0(z)z^{s-1}dz. \tag{8.46}$$

Then, by (8.44), we obtain the functional equation

$$-(s - 1)\mathcal{M}(s - 1) + (1 - p^{-s})\mathcal{M}(s) = \frac{(s - 1)\Gamma(s)}{1 - p^{1-s} - q^{1-s}}. \tag{8.47}$$

Next we set

$$\mathcal{M}(s) = \Gamma(s)\mathcal{N}(s) \tag{8.48}$$

with which (8.47) becomes

$$-\mathcal{N}(s - 1) + (1 - p^{-s})\mathcal{N}(s) = \frac{s - 1}{1 - p^{1-s} - q^{1-s}}. \tag{8.49}$$

To solve (8.49), we let

$$\mathcal{N}(s) = \prod_{k=0}^{\infty} \left[\frac{1 - p^{k+2}}{1 - p^{k-s}} \right] \mathcal{N}_1(s) \tag{8.50}$$

and then (8.49) becomes

$$\mathcal{N}_1(s) - \mathcal{N}_1(s-1) = \prod_{k=1}^{\infty} \left[\frac{1 - p^{k-s}}{1 - p^{k+1}} \right] \frac{s-1}{1 - p^{1-s} - q^{1-s}}. \tag{8.51}$$

Now, for $s \to -\infty$, the right side of (8.51) behaves as $(s-1) \prod_{k=1}^{\infty} (1 - p^{k+1})^{-1}$, with an exponentially small error. Letting

$$\mathcal{N}_1(s) = \frac{s(s-1)}{2} \prod_{k=1}^{\infty} \left(\frac{1}{1 - p^{k+1}} \right) + \mathcal{N}_2(s), \tag{8.52}$$

the equation for $\mathcal{N}_2(\cdot)$ becomes

$$\mathcal{N}_2(s) - \mathcal{N}_2(s-1) = \frac{s-1}{\prod_{k=1}^{\infty} \left(1 - p^{k+1} \right)} \left[\frac{1}{1 - p^{1-s} - q^{1-s}} \prod_{k=1}^{\infty} (1 - p^{k-s}) - 1 \right] \tag{8.53}$$

whose right-hand side is, unlike that of (8.51), exponentially small for $s \to -\infty$. The solution to (8.53) is

$$\mathcal{N}_2(s) = \mathcal{N}_2(-\infty) + \sum_{i=0}^{\infty} \left[\frac{\prod_{k=1}^{\infty}(1 - p^{k-s+i})}{1 - p^{1+i-s} - q^{1+i-s}} - 1 \right] \frac{s-1-i}{\prod_{k=1}^{\infty}(1 - p^{k+1})}. \tag{8.54}$$

From (8.41), we see that $\widetilde{B}_d(z) = O(z^2)$ as $z \to 0$ so that $\mathcal{M}(s)$ in (8.46) must be analytic at $s = -1$. From (8.48), we then conclude that $\mathcal{N}(-1) = 0$. From (8.50), we have $\mathcal{N}_1(-1) = 0$ and from (8.52) and (8.54) we obtain an expression for $\mathcal{N}_2(-\infty)$:

$$\mathcal{N}_2(-\infty) \prod_{k=1}^{\infty}(1 - p^{k+1}) + 1 - \sum_{i=0}^{\infty}(i+2) \left[\frac{\prod_{k=1}^{\infty}(1 - p^{k+i+1})}{1 - p^{2+i} - q^{2+i}} - 1 \right] = 0. \tag{8.55}$$

We have thus obtained the final expression for $\mathcal{M}(s)$ in (8.48) as

$$\mathcal{M}(s) = \frac{\Gamma(s)}{\prod_{L=0}^{\infty}(1 - p^{L-s})} \tag{8.56}$$

$$\cdot \left(\frac{s(s-1)}{2} + \beta + \sum_{i=0}^{\infty}(s-i-1) \left[\frac{\prod_{k=1}^{\infty}(1 - p^{k-s+i})}{1 - p^{1+i-s} - q^{1+i-s}} - 1 \right] \right),$$

where

$$\beta = \mathcal{N}_2(-\infty) \prod_{k=1}^{\infty}(1 - p^{k+1})$$

can be computed from (8.55). Inverting the transform in (8.46), we obtain

$$\widetilde{B}_d(z) = \frac{-1}{2\pi i} \int_{-3/2-i\infty}^{-3/2+i\infty} (p^d z)^{-s} \mathcal{M}(s) ds, \tag{8.57}$$

where we then set $z = n$. The function $\mathcal{M}(s)$ in (8.56) has a *triple pole* at $s = 0$, and there are other double poles on the imaginary s-axis if $1 - p^{1-s} - q^{1-s}$ has zeros there, which occurs only if $\log p / \log q$ is rational, say, r/t where r and t are integers. First we compute the contribution from $s = 0$. Using the expansion $\Gamma(s) = [1 - \gamma s + O(s^2)]/s$ as $s \to 0$, with γ being the Euler constant, (8.56) becomes

$$
\mathcal{M}(s) = \frac{1}{s}[1 - \gamma s + O(s^2)](1 - p^{-s})^{-1} \prod_{L=1}^{\infty}(1 - p^{L-s})^{-1}
$$

$$
\times \left(\frac{s-1}{1 - p^{1-s} - q^{1-s}} \prod_{k=1}^{\infty}(1 - p^{k-s}) - (s-1) + \frac{s(s-1)}{2} + \beta \right.
$$

$$
\left. + \sum_{i=1}^{\infty}(s-i-1)\left[\frac{\prod_{k=1}^{\infty}(1 - p^{k-s+i})}{1 - p^{1+i-s} - q^{1+i-s}} - 1 \right] \right). \tag{8.58}
$$

Now

$$
1 - p^{-s} = s \ln p - \frac{1}{2}s^2(\ln p)^2 + O(s^3)
$$

and

$$
1 - p^{1-s} - q^{1-s} = -hs \ln 2 - \frac{h_2 \ln^2 2}{2}s^2 + O(s^3).
$$

Also, using the expression in (8.55) to compute $\beta + 1$, the expansion of (8.58) for $s \to 0$ becomes

$$
\mathcal{M}(s) = \frac{1}{s^3}\frac{1 - \gamma s}{\ln p}\left[1 + \frac{s}{2}\ln p + O(s^2)\right]\left\{ \frac{1-s}{h \ln 2}\left[1 - \frac{h_2 \ln 2}{2h}s + O(s^2)\right] + O(s^2) \right\}
$$

$$
= \frac{1}{s^3}\frac{1}{h \ln p} + \frac{1}{s^2}\left[-\frac{\gamma}{h \ln 2 \ln p} - \frac{1}{h \ln p}\left(1 + \frac{h_2 \ln 2}{2h \ln 2}\right) + \frac{1}{2h}\right] + O\left(\frac{1}{s}\right). \tag{8.59}
$$

It follows that the integrand $p^{-ds}z^{-s}\mathcal{M}(s)$ in (8.57) has the residue

$$
\mathrm{res}\left(p^{-ds}z^{-s}\mathcal{M}(s), s = 0\right) = \frac{1}{2}\frac{\log^2 z}{h \log p} + \frac{d}{h}\log z \tag{8.60}
$$

$$
+ \log z \left[\frac{1}{\log p}\left(\frac{\gamma+1}{h \ln 2} + \frac{h_2}{2h^2}\right) - \frac{1}{2h}\right] + O(1),
$$

where the $O(1)$ refers to terms that are $O(1)$ for $z \to \infty$, and these can be evaluated by explicitly computing the $O(s^{-1})$ term(s) in (8.59). If $\log p / \log q$ is rational, we must also compute the contribution from the double poles along the imaginary axis at such points $p^{-s} = q^{-s} = 1$ and $p^{1-s} + q^{1-s} = 1$. These poles lead to the oscillatory terms in Lemma 8.15, as can be seen by computing their residues from (8.56).

Finally, we use the depoissonization Theorem C.2 (from Appendix C). We have already used (implicitly) the fact that the function $\widetilde{G}(z)$ satisfies the assumptions of Theorem C.2 (the proof of Theorem C.3 does precisely that); that is, $\widetilde{G}(z)$ is *JS*-admissible (see Appendix C). In particular, this property is inherited from the solution $\widetilde{B}_0(z)$ of the differential equation (8.44) (see again Appendix C). Hence, Theorem C.2 gives

$$b_*(n, d) \sim \widetilde{B}_d(n)$$

and completes the proof of Lemma 8.15. □

8.3.5 Proof of Lemma 8.13

We will apply Lemma 8.15 regarding $b_*(n, d)$, which establishes that $b_*(n, d) = O((\log n)^2)$, where $b_*(n, d)$ is defined by (8.37) and (8.38).

What remains is to show that $a_*(n, d) \leq b_*(n, d)$. Since they are defined by the same recurrence, we just have to check the initial and side conditions, in particular, the conditions

$$a_*(n + 1, 0) - a_*(n, 1) = a(n + 1, \infty) - a(n, \infty),$$
$$b_*(n + 1, 0) - b_*(n, 1) = b(n + 1, \infty) - b(n, \infty).$$

Thus, if we can show that

$$a(n + 1, \infty) - a(n, \infty) \leq b(n + 1, \infty) - b(n, \infty), \tag{8.61}$$

then we are done.

The differences $\Delta a(n, \infty) = a(n+1, \infty) - a(n, \infty)$ and $\Delta b(n, \infty) = b(n+1, \infty) - b(n, \infty)$ satisfy the recurrences

$$\Delta a(n, \infty) = \lceil \log(n + 2) \rceil - \lceil \log(n + 1) \rceil$$
$$+ \sum_{k=0}^{n} \binom{n}{k} p^k q^{n-k} \left(p \Delta a(k, \infty) + q \Delta a(n - k, \infty) \right),$$

$$\Delta b(n, \infty) = 1 + \sum_{k=0}^{n} \binom{n}{k} p^k q^{n-k} \left(p \Delta b(k, \infty) + q \Delta b(n - k, \infty) \right).$$

Since $\lceil \log(n + 2) \rceil - \lceil \log(n + 1) \rceil \leq 1$, it follows by induction that (8.61) holds. This completes the proof of the lemma.

Completion of the computes Proof of Theorem 8.8

We recall that the algorithms first computes two strings B_1 and B_2, where B_1 has expected length of order $\Theta(n)$ and B_2 has expected length of order $\binom{n}{2} - \Theta(n \log n)$. Furthermore, B_2 behaves as the initial part of a memoryless source (with parameter p). For B_1, we do not have such a property. Thus, it is not clear how much could be gained by a compression of B_1, and it would be only negligible compared to B_2. Conditioned on the length ℓ of B_2, B_2 is precisely a memoryless source with parameter p (all 2^ℓ strings appear). Thus, we should encode n (with $\Theta(\log n)$ digits), the ℓ of B_2 (with $\Theta(\log \ell)$ digits) and a compressed string $\widetilde{B}_2$. Conditioned on the length ℓ, the entropy of B_2 is $\ell h(p)$. Hence, if we use, for example, an arithmetic encoder to encode B_2, the expected code length is given by

$$\mathbf{E}[L(S)] = \mathbb{E}[L(B_1)] + O(\log n) + O\left(\sum_{\ell \geq 1} q_\ell \log \ell \right)$$
$$+ \sum_{\ell \geq 1} q_\ell \left(\ell h(p) + O(1) \right)$$
$$= \mathbf{E}[L(B_1)] + h(p)\mathbf{E}[L(B_2)] + O(\mathbf{E}[\log L(B_2)]) + O(\log n),$$

where $q_\ell = P[L(B_2) = \ell]$. By concavity of $\log x$ we have

$$\mathbf{E}[\log L(B_2)] \leq \log(\mathbf{E}[L(B_2)]) = O(\log n).$$

Hence, by applying Theorems 8.14 and 8.16, the asymptotic formula for $\mathbf{E}[L(S)]$ follows.

8.4 Preferential Attachment Graphs

In this section, we turn our attention to preferential attachment graphs $\mathrm{PA}(n, m)$ with n nodes and a fixed parameter m. Our ultimate goal is to find an (almost) optimal structural compression of $\mathrm{PA}(n, m)$. However, the problem is much more intricate than we encountered for Erdős–Rényi graphs.

Let us start by recalling Lemma 8.5, in which we proved a relation between graph entropy and structural entropy, namely,

$$H(S(G)) = H(G) + \mathbf{E}[\log |\Gamma(G)|] - \mathbf{E}[\log |\mathrm{Aut}(G)|], \qquad (8.62)$$

providing all relabelings of the underlying graph are *equally likely*. We recall that $\mathrm{Aut}(G)$ is the set of automorphisms of G and $\Gamma(G)$ is the set of feasible permutation. None of these quantities are trivial to evaluate, nor is the graph entropy $H(G)$. Therefore, in this section, we first give an overview of results regarding these parameters, ending with an asymptotically optimal algorithm for compressing a structure of $\mathrm{PA}(n, m)$.

However, before we start our journey we must assure that (8.62) holds; that is, all relabeling is equally likely. We prove it in the next lemma.

Lemma 8.17 *For any two graphs g_1, g_2 having the same structure (i.e., $g_2 \in \mathrm{Adm}(g_1)$), we have*

$$P(G = g_1) = P(G = g_2);$$

that is, they are equiprobable.

Proof This can be seen by deriving a formula for the probability assigned to a given graph g by the model and noting that it only depends on the structure and admissibility (a graph is said to be admissible if it is in $\mathrm{Adm}(S)$ for some unlabeled graph S). If g is not admissible, then there exists some $t \in [n]$ such that the degree of vertex t at time t is not equal to m. This has probability 0, so $P(G = g) = 0$.

Now, if g is an admissible graph on n vertices, then we can write $P(G = g)$ as a product over possible degrees of vertices at time n: let $\deg_g(v)$ denote the degree of vertex v in g. We consider the immediate ancestors (i.e., the parents, the vertices that chose to connect to v) of v in g, denoting the number of edges that they supply to v by $d_1(v), \ldots, d_{k(v)}(v)$, where $k(v)$ is the number of parents of v. We also denote by $K_g(v)$ the number of orders in which the parents of v could have arrived in the graph (which is only a function of its structure). Then we can write $P(G = g)$ as follows:

$$P(G = g) = \frac{\prod_{d \geq m} \prod_{v:\, \deg_g(v) = d} K_g(v) \prod_{j=1}^{k_g(v)} \binom{m}{j} [m + d_1(v) + \cdots + d_{j-1}(v)]^{d_j(v)}}{\prod_{i=1}^{n-1} (2mi)^m},$$

where each factor of the v product corresponds to the sequence of $d - m$ choices to connect to vertex v, which can be ordered in a number of ways determined by the structure of g. The innermost product gives the contribution of each such choice. Since this formula is only in terms of the degree sequence of the graph and its structure, two graphs that are admissible and have the same unlabeled DAG must have the same probability, which completes the proof. ∎

Now, knowing that (8.62) holds, we can estimate all its terms as a function of n and m.

8.4.1 Graph Entropy $H(G)$.

Our goal is to evaluate the graph entropy of G generated by the preferential attachment rule $PA(m; n)$. While it is easy to see that the leading term should behave like $nm \log n$, our goal is to find a more precise asymptotic behavior.

Theorem 8.18 *Suppose that $G \sim PA(m; n)$ for fixed $m \geq 1$. Then we have*

$$H(G) = mn \log n + mn \left(\log 2m - 1 - \log m! - A_m \right) + o(n), \tag{8.63}$$

where

$$A_m = \sum_{d=m}^{\infty} \frac{\log d}{(d+1)(d+2)}.$$

Proof We start by noting that, using the chain rule for entropy, we can write

$$H(G_n) = \sum_{t=1}^{n-1} H(v_{t+1} | G_t), \tag{8.64}$$

where we denote by v_{t+1} the multiset of connection choices of vertex $t + 1$ (i.e., a value for v_{t+1} takes the form of a multiset of m vertices $< t+1$). This follows because G_n corresponds precisely to exactly one n-tuple $(v_1, v_2, \ldots, v_n)$ of vertex choice multisets.

To calculate the remaining conditional entropy for each t, we note that it would be simpler if v_{t+1} were a sequence of vertex choices, rather than a multiset (i.e., an equivalence class of sequences). Let us denote by $\widetilde{v}_{t+1}$ the sequence of m choices made by vertex $t + 1$; that is, $\widetilde{v}_{t+1,1}$ is the first choice that it makes, and so on. Then we have the following observation:

$$H(\widetilde{v}_{t+1} | G_t) = H(\widetilde{v}_{t+1}, v_{t+1} | G_t) = H(v_{t+1} | G_t) + H(\widetilde{v}_{t+1} | v_{t+1}, G_t), \tag{8.65}$$

where the first equality is because v_{t+1} is a deterministic function of $\widetilde{v}_{t+1}$, and the second is by the chain rule for conditional entropy. We thus have

$$H(v_{t+1} | G_t) = H(\widetilde{v}_{t+1} | G_t) - H(\widetilde{v}_{t+1} | v_{t+1}, G_t). \tag{8.66}$$

We first compute $H(\widetilde{v}_{t+1} | G_t)$. By definition of conditional entropy,

$$H(\widetilde{v}_{t+1} | G_t) = \sum_{G \text{ on } t \text{ vertices}} P(G_t = G) H(\widetilde{v}_{t+1} | G_t = G).$$

Next, note that, conditioned on $G_t = G$, the m choices that vertex $t + 1$ makes are independent and identically distributed. So the remaining conditional entropy is just m times the conditional entropy of a single vertex choice made by $t + 1$. Using the definition of entropy (as a sum over all possible vertex choices, from 1 to t) and grouping together terms corresponding to vertices of the same degree, we get

$$H(\widetilde{v}_{t+1}|G_t) = m \sum_G P(G_t = G) \sum_{d=m}^{t} N_d(G) p_{t,d} \log(1/p_{t,d}), \tag{8.67}$$

where $N_d(G)$ denotes the number of vertices of degree d in the fixed graph G, and we recall $p_{t,d} = \frac{d}{2mt}$. Note that the d sum starts from $d = m$, since m is the minimum possible degree in the graph.

Next, we bring the G sum inside the d sum, and we note that

$$\sum_G P(G_t = G) N_d(G) = \mathbf{E}[N_d(G)] := \overline{N}_{t,d}.$$

Thus, we can express $H(\widetilde{v}_{t+1}|G_t)$ as

$$H(\widetilde{v}_{t+1}|G_t) = m \sum_{d=m}^{t} \overline{N}_{t,d} p_{t,d} \log(1/p_{t,d}). \tag{8.68}$$

Plugging this into (8.64), we find

$$H(G_n) + \sum_{t=1}^{n-1} H(\widetilde{v}_{t+1}|v_{t+1}, G_t) = m \sum_{t=1}^{n-1} \sum_{d=m}^{t} \overline{N}_{t,d} p_{t,d} \log(1/p_{t,d}). \tag{8.69}$$

Now, we split the inner sum into two parts:

$$H(G_n) + \sum_{t=1}^{n-1} H(\widetilde{v}_{t+1}|v_{t+1}, G_t) = m \sum_{t=1}^{n} \sum_{d=m}^{\lfloor t^{1/15} \rfloor} \overline{N}_{t,d} p_{t,d} \log(1/p_{t,d})$$

$$+ m \sum_{t=1}^{n-1} \sum_{d=\lfloor t^{1/15} \rfloor + 1}^{t} \overline{N}_{t,d} p_{t,d} \log(1/p_{t,d}). \tag{8.70}$$

The first part provides the dominant contribution, of order $\Theta(n \log n)$, and we will show that the second part is $o(n)$, due to the smallness of $\overline{N}_{t,d}$.

To estimate the contribution of the first sum, we apply the following estimate on $\overline{N}_{t,d}$, which we ask the reader to prove in Exercise 8.10: for $t \geq 1$ and $1 \leq d \leq t$ and for any fixed $m \geq 1$,

$$\left| \overline{N}_{t,d} - \frac{2m(m+1)t}{d(d+1)(d+2)} \right| \leq C \tag{8.71}$$

for some fixed $C = C(m) > 0$. This estimate is good for $d = o(t^{1/3})$. Furthermore, for $t \to \infty$, $d \geq t^{1/15}$, and fixed $m \geq 1$, we have (see Exercise 8.11)

$$\overline{N}_{t,d} = O\left(\frac{t}{d(d+1)(d+2)} \right) = O\left(\frac{t}{d^3} \right). \tag{8.72}$$

Now, with these estimates, we obtain

$$\sum_{t=1}^{n-1} \sum_{d=m}^{\lfloor t^{1/15} \rfloor} \overline{N}_{t,d} p_{t,d} \log(1/p_{t,d}) + \sum_{t=1}^{n-1} \sum_{d=m}^{\lfloor t^{1/15} \rfloor} \frac{Cd}{2mt} \log(2mt/d)$$

$$= 2m(m+1) \sum_{t=1}^{n-1} t \sum_{d=m}^{\lfloor t^{1/15} \rfloor} \frac{1}{d(d+1)(d+2)} \frac{d}{2mt} \log\left(\frac{2mt}{d}\right) + o(n)$$

$$= (m+1) \sum_{t=1}^{n-1} \sum_{d=m}^{\lfloor t^{1/15} \rfloor} \frac{d(\log t + \log 2m - \log d)}{d(d+1)(d+2)} + o(n).$$

Here, the second sum on the left-hand side is the error in approximation incurred by invoking (8.71). It is easily seen to be $o(n)$.

Now, the tail sum is

$$\sum_{t=1}^{n-1} \sum_{d=\lfloor t^{1/15} \rfloor + 1}^{\infty} \frac{d(\log t + \log 2m - \log d)}{d(d+1)(d+2)} \leq \sum_{t=1}^{n-1} \sum_{d=\lfloor t^{1/15} \rfloor + 1}^{\infty} \frac{O(\log d)}{(d+1)(d+2)} = o(n),$$

so we have

$$\sum_{t=1}^{n-1} \sum_{d=m}^{\lfloor t^{1/15} \rfloor} \overline{N}_{t,d} p_{t,d} \log(1/p_{t,d}) = \log n + (\log 2m - A_m) n + o(n),$$

where we define A_m as in the statement of Theorem 8.18.

Our next goal is now to show that the second sum of (8.70), which we denote by E, is $o(n)$. We apply (8.72) to upper bound $\overline{N}_{t,d}$, which yields

$$E \leq C \sum_{t=1}^{n-1} \sum_{d=\lfloor t^{1/15} \rfloor + 1}^{t} \frac{t}{d^3} \cdot \frac{d}{2tm} \log(2tm/d) \leq C' \sum_{t=1}^{n-1} \log t \sum_{d=\lfloor t^{1/15} \rfloor + 1}^{t} d^{-2},$$

where we canceled factors in the numerator and denominator of each term, and we upper bounded the expression inside the logarithm using the fact that $d > \lfloor t^{1/15} \rfloor$.

The inner sum is easily seen to be $O(t^{-1/15})$, so that, finally,

$$E \leq C' \sum_{t=1}^{n-1} t^{-1/15} \log t = o(n),$$

as desired. We thus end up with

$$\sum_{t=1}^{n-1} H(\widetilde{v}_{t+1} | G_t) = m \log n + m(\log 2m - A)n + o(n). \tag{8.73}$$

The final step is to estimate the contribution of $H(\widetilde{v}_{t+1} | v_{t+1}, G_t)$. Let C_t denote the set of multisets of m elements coming from $[t]$ having no repeated elements. Then we can write

$$H(\widetilde{v}_{t+1}|v_{t+1}, G_t) = \sum_{G,v \in \mathcal{C}_t} P(G_t = G, v_{t+1} = v)H(\widetilde{v}_{t+1}|v_{t+1} = v, G_t = G)$$

$$+ \sum_{G,v \notin \mathcal{C}_t} P(G_t = G, v_{t+1} = v)H(\widetilde{v}_{t+1}|v_{t+1} = v, G_t = G). \tag{8.74}$$

The first sum can be estimated as follows: we trivially upper bound $H(\widetilde{v}_{t+1}|v_{t+1} = v, G_t = G) \leq \log m!$ and take it outside the sum. This gives

$$\sum_{G,v \in \mathcal{C}_t} P(G_t = G, v_{t+1} = v)H(\widetilde{v}_{t+1}|v_{t+1} = v, G_t = G)$$

$$\leq \log m! \sum_{G,v \in \mathcal{C}_t} P(G_t = G, v_{t+1} = v)$$

$$= \log m P(v_{t+1} \in \mathcal{C}_t).$$

Now we can upper bound the remaining probability in this expression by noting that with high probability, the maximum degree in G_t is $O(\sqrt{t}(\log t)^2)$ as discussed in Frieze and Karoński (2016: p. 387). Using this fact, we have, for arbitrarily small fixed $\varepsilon > 0$,

$$P(v_{t+1} \in \mathcal{C}_t) = P(v_{t+1} \in \mathcal{C}_t, \text{max. degree of } G_t \leq Ct^{1/2+\varepsilon})$$

$$+ P(v_{t+1} \in \mathcal{C}_t, \text{max. degree of } G_t > Ct^{1/2+\varepsilon}). \tag{8.75}$$

The first term is at most

$$P(v_{t+1} \in \mathcal{C}_t, \text{max. degree of } G_t \leq Ct^{1/2+\varepsilon}) \leq 1 - \left(1 - \frac{Ct^{1/2+\varepsilon}}{2mt}\right)^{m-1}$$

$$= 1 - \left(1 - \Theta(t^{-1/2+\varepsilon}/m)\right)^{m-1}$$

$$= \Theta(t^{-1/2+\varepsilon}).$$

Now, the second term of (8.75) is at most

$$P(v_{t+1} \in \mathcal{C}_t, \text{max. degree of } G_t > Ct^{1/2+\varepsilon}) \leq P(\text{max. degree of } G_t > Ct^{1/2+\varepsilon})$$

$$= O(e^{-t^{\varepsilon}})$$

and is negligible compared to the first term. Thus, the first sum in (8.74) is at most

$$\sum_{G,v \in \mathcal{C}_t} P(G_t = G, v_{t+1} = v)H(\widetilde{v}_{t+1}|v_{t+1} = v, G_t = G) = O(t^{-1/2+\varepsilon}). \tag{8.76}$$

We will now show that the second sum in (8.74), over all multisets v of size m with no repeated elements, is $(1 + o(1)) \log m!$. This is trivial, since vertex $t + 1$ is equally likely to have chosen the elements of v in any order. Hence,

$$H(\widetilde{v}_{t+1}|v_{t+1} = v, G_t = G) = \log m!. \tag{8.77}$$

This implies that

$$\sum_{G,v \notin \mathcal{C}_t} P(G_t = G, v_{t+1} = v)H(\widetilde{v}_{t+1}|v_{t+1} = v, G_t = G) = \log m! \cdot P(v_{t+1} \notin \mathcal{C}_t)$$

$$= \log m(1 - O(t^{-1/2+\varepsilon})).$$

Thus,

$$H(\widetilde{v}_{t+1}|v_{t+1}, G_t) = \log m!(1 + O(t^{-1/2+\varepsilon})).$$

Summing over all t yields a total contribution of

$$-\sum_{t=1}^{n-1} H(\widetilde{v}_{t+1}|v_{t+1}, G_t) = -n \log m! + o(n). \tag{8.78}$$

From (8.69), (8.73), and (8.78), we arrive at

$$H(G_n) = mn \log n + m(\log 2m - 1 - A - \log m!)n + o(n), \tag{8.79}$$

where A is as in the statement of Theorem 8.18. ∎

8.4.2 Structural Entropy $H(S(G))$

The next goal is to discuss the structural entropy $H(S(G))$ for graphs in $\mathrm{PA}(n, m)$. By (8.62), it is sufficient to study the expected values $\mathbf{E}[\log |\Gamma(G)|]$ and $\mathbf{E}[\log |\mathrm{Aut}(G)|]$. Actually, by combining (8.62), Theorems 8.18, and the forthcoming Theorems 8.22 and 8.23, we arrive at an expression for the structural entropy.

Theorem 8.19 *Let $m \geq 3$ be fixed. Consider $G \sim \mathrm{PA}(n, m)$. We have*

$$H(S(G)) = (m - 1)n \log n + R(n), \tag{8.80}$$

where $R(n)$ satisfies

$$Cn \leq |R(n)| \leq O(n \log \log n)$$

for some nonzero constant $C = C(m)$.

The rest of this section is devoted to the proof of Theorem 8.19.

Evaluation of $\Gamma(G)$ First we turn our attention to the evaluation of the number of feasible permutations $|\Gamma(G)|$. We start by introducing a directed version of graph G that we denote as $\mathrm{DAG}(G)$. This is the directed multigraph defined on $[n]$, with an edge from w to the older node $v < w$ for each edge between v and w in G. We can partition the vertices of $\mathrm{DAG}(G)$ into *levels* inductively as follows: L_1 consists of the vertices with in-degree 0 (i.e., with total degree m). Inductively, L_j is the set of vertices incident on edges coming from vertices in L_{j-1}. Equivalently, a vertex w is an element of some level $\geq j$ if and only if there exist vertices $v_1 < \cdots < v_j$ such that $v_1 > w$ and the path $v_j v_{j-1} \cdots v_1 w$ exists in G. The *height* of $\mathrm{DAG}(G)$ is then defined to be the number of levels in this partition.

Then it is not too hard to see that any product of permutations that only permute vertices within levels is a member of $\Gamma(G)$. Thus, we have, with probability 1,

$$|\Gamma(G)| \geq \prod_{j \geq 1} |L_j|.$$

To continue, we will prove in Lemma 8.21 that almost all vertices lie in low levels of $\mathrm{DAG}(G)$. We define $X = X(\varepsilon, k)$ to be the number of vertices $w > \varepsilon n$ that are at level $\geq k$

in DAG(G). In other words, w is counted in X if there exist vertices $v_1 < v_2 < \cdots < v_k$ for which $w < v_1$ and the path $v_k \cdots v_1 w$ exists in DAG(G).

We have the following lemma bounding $\mathbf{E}[X]$.

Lemma 8.20 *For any $\varepsilon = \varepsilon(n) > 0$, there exists $k = k(\varepsilon)$ for which*

$$\mathbf{E}[X(\varepsilon, k)] \leq \varepsilon n.$$

In particular, we can take any k satisfying

$$k \geq 15 \frac{m}{\varepsilon^2} \ln(3/\varepsilon). \tag{8.81}$$

Proof Suppose that $w > \varepsilon n$. We want to upper bound the probability that there exist vertices $v_1 < \cdots < v_k$, with $w < v_1$, such that there is a path $v_k \cdots v_1 w$ in G. This probability is upper bounded by

$$\binom{n}{k} \cdot \frac{((5m/\varepsilon) \ln(3/\varepsilon))^k}{n^k} \leq \frac{e \left((5m/\varepsilon) \ln(3/\varepsilon)\right)^k}{k^k}.$$

Now, it is sufficient to show that we can choose k so that this is $\leq \varepsilon$. In fact, we can choose $k \geq 3 \cdot \frac{5m}{\varepsilon^2} \ln(3/\varepsilon)$. This completes the proof. ∎

Now, we define $Y = Y(k)$ to be the number of vertices $w \geq 1$ that are at level $\geq k$ in DAG(G). The variables X and Y are related by the following inequalities, which hold with probability 1:

$$X \leq Y \leq X + \varepsilon n.$$

Now, to get a bound on Y, we apply Markov's inequality:

$$P(Y \geq \delta n) \leq \frac{\mathbf{E}[Y]}{\delta n} \leq \frac{\mathbf{E}[X] + \varepsilon n}{\delta n},$$

and provided that (8.81) holds, we can further bound by

$$P(Y \geq \delta n) \leq 2\varepsilon/\delta$$

using Lemma 8.20. Then, selecting $\delta = \sqrt{2\varepsilon}$, we have shown that

$$P(Y \geq \delta n) \leq \delta.$$

This is summarized in the following lemma.

Lemma 8.21 *For any $\delta = \delta(n) > 0$, there exists $\ell = \ell(\delta)$ for which the number of vertices that are not in the first ℓ layers of DAG(G) is at most δn, with high probability. In particular, we can take*

$$\ell \geq \frac{15m}{2\delta^4} \ln(3/(2\delta^2)).$$

We now use Lemma 8.21 to finish our lower bound on $\mathbf{E}[\log|\Gamma(G)|]$. Fix

$$\varepsilon = \frac{1}{\ln^2 n}, \quad \delta = \sqrt{2\varepsilon} = \Theta(1/\ln n), \quad \ell = \frac{15m}{2\delta^4}\ln(3/(2\delta^2)).$$

Then, defining A to be the event that the number of vertices in layers $> \ell$ is at most $\delta n = \Theta(n/\log n)$, we have

$$\mathbf{E}[\log|\Gamma(G)|] \geq \mathbf{E}[\log|\Gamma(G)| \,|\, A]\,(1-\delta).$$

Among the ℓ layers, there are at most $\ell - 1$ that satisfy, say, $|L_i| < \log\log n$, since $\sum_{i=1}^{\ell} |L_i| \geq (1-\delta)n$. So we have the following:

$$\sum_{i=1}^{\ell} \log(|L_i|!) = O(\ell \log\log n \log\log\log n) + \sum_{i \in B}(|L_i|\log|L_i| + O(|L_i|)),$$

where $B = \{i \leq \ell: |L_i| \geq \log\log n\}$, and we used Stirling's formula to estimate the terms $i \in B$.

The sum $\sum_{i \in B} O(|L_i|) = O((1-\delta)n) = O(n)$, so it remains to estimate

$$\sum_{i \in B} |L_i|\log|L_i|.$$

Let $N = \sum_{i \in B} |L_i|$. Then, multiplying and dividing each instance of $|L_i|$ by N in the previous expression, it becomes

$$\sum_{i \in B} |L_i|\log|L_i| = N\sum_{i \in B} \frac{|L_i|}{N}\log\frac{|L_i|}{N} + N\sum_{i \in B} \frac{|L_i|}{N}\log N.$$

The first sum is simply $-NH(X)$, where X is a random variable distributed according to the empirical distribution of the vertices on the levels $i \in B$. Since $|B| \leq \ell$, we have that $|-NH(X)| \leq N\log\ell$. Thus, the first term in our expression is $O(N\log\ell) = O(n\log\log n)$. Meanwhile, the second term is $N\log N\sum_{i \in B} \frac{|L_i|}{N} = N\log N = n\log n - O(n\log\log n)$. Thus, in total, we have

$$\mathbf{E}[\log|\Gamma(G)|] \geq n\log n - O(n\log\log n).$$

Compare this with the trivial upper bound on $\mathbf{E}[\log|\Gamma(G)|]$:

$$\mathbf{E}[\log|\Gamma(G)|] \leq \log n! = n\log n - \frac{n}{\ln 2} + O(\log n).$$

This leads to our final estimate for $\mathbf{E}[\log|\Gamma(G)|]$.

Theorem 8.22 *For $G \sim \mathrm{PA}(n,m)$, we have the following bounds:*

$$n\log n - O(n\log\log n) \leq \mathbf{E}[\log|\Gamma(G)|] \leq n\log n - \frac{n}{\ln 2} + O(\log n) \tag{8.82}$$

as $n \to \infty$.

Asymmetry of $\mathrm{PA}(n,m)$. Next we have to discuss the asymmetry of $\mathrm{PA}(n,m)$. In what follows, we will focus on $m \geq 3$. In Exercise 8.12, we ask the reader to prove that $\mathrm{PA}(n,m)$ is symmetric for $m = 1$ and $m = 2$.

So from now on, suppose that $m \geq 3$. Let us define first two properties, $\mathfrak{A}$ and $\mathfrak{B}$ of $PA(m;n)$ which are crucial for our argument. Here and below we set $k = k(n) = n^{\Delta}$, $\tilde{k} = \tilde{k}(n) = n^{\Delta'}$, and $\tilde{k}' = \tilde{k}'(n) = n^{\Delta''}$ for some small enough $0 < \Delta < \Delta' < \Delta''$ to be chosen:

($\mathfrak{A}$) $PA(m;n)$ has property $\mathfrak{A}$ if no two vertices t_1, t_2, where $k < t_1 < t_2$, are adjacent to the same m neighbors from the set $[t_1 - 1]$.

($\mathfrak{B}$) $PA(m;n)$ has property $\mathfrak{B}$ if the degree of every vertex $s \leq \tilde{k}$ is unique in $PA(m;n)$; that is, for no other vertex s' of $PA(m;n)$ do we have $\deg_n(s) = \deg_n(s')$.

It is easy to see that

$$P(|\mathrm{Aut}(PA(m;n))| = 1) \geq P(PA(m;n) \in \mathfrak{A} \cap \mathfrak{B}), \tag{8.83}$$

and so

$$P(|\mathrm{Aut}(PA(m;n))| > 1) \leq P(PA(m;n) \notin \mathfrak{A}) + P(PA(m;n) \notin \mathfrak{B}). \tag{8.84}$$

Indeed, let us suppose that $PA(m;n)$ has both properties $\mathfrak{A}$ and $\mathfrak{B}$, and $\sigma \in \mathrm{Aut}(PA(m;n))$. Let us assume also that σ is not the identity, and let t_1 be the smallest vertex such that $t_2 = \sigma(t_1) \neq t_1$. Note that $\mathfrak{B}$ implies that for all $s \in [k]$, we have $\sigma(s) = s$, so that we must have $k < t_1 < t_2$. On the other hand, from $\mathfrak{A}$ it follows that t_1 and $t_2 = \sigma(t_1)$ have different neighborhoods in the set $[t_1 - 1]$ consists of fixed point of σ. This contradiction shows that σ is the identity, that is, $|\mathrm{Aut}(PA(m;n))| = 1$, which proves (8.83).

Theorem 8.23 *Let $G \sim PA(m;n)$ for fixed $m \geq 3$. Then, with high probability as $n \to \infty$,*

$$|\mathrm{Aut}(G)| = 1.$$

More precisely, for $m \geq 3$,

$$P(|\mathrm{Aut}(G)| > 1) = O(n^{-\delta}) \tag{8.85}$$

for some fixed $\delta > 0$ and large n.

In order to prove Theorem 8.23, it is enough to show that both probabilities $P(PA(m;n) \notin \mathfrak{A})$ and $P(PA(m;n) \notin \mathfrak{B})$ tend to 0 polynomially fast as $n \to \infty$.

We start with a number of results on the degree sequence of preferential attachment graphs that we will use in the proofs of Theorem 8.23.

First, we denote by $\deg_t(s)$ the degree of a vertex $s < t$ after time t (i.e., after vertex t has made its choices). We also define $\mathrm{dg}_t(s) = \deg_t(s) - m$.

Our first lemma gives a bound on the in-degree of each vertex at any given time.

Lemma 8.24 *For any v, w,*

$$P(\mathrm{dg}_v(w) = d) \leq \binom{m+d-1}{m-1} \left(1 - \sqrt{\frac{w}{v}} + O\left(\frac{d}{\sqrt{vw}} \right) \right)^d.$$

In particular,

$$P(\deg_v(w) = d) \leq (2m+d)^m \exp\left(-\sqrt{\frac{w}{v}} d + O\left(\frac{d^2}{\sqrt{vw}} \right) \right).$$

Proof We estimate this probability as follows. We set $t_{d+1} = mv + 1$.

$$P(\mathrm{dg}_v(w) = d) \leq \sum_{mw < t_1 < t_2 < \cdots < t_d \leq mv} \prod_{i=1}^{d} \frac{m+i-1}{2t_i} \prod_{j=t_i+1}^{t_{i+1}-1} \left(1 - \frac{m+i}{2j}\right)$$

$$\leq \sum_{mw < t_1 < t_2 < \cdots < t_d \leq mv} \frac{(m+d-1)!}{(m-1)!} \prod_{i=1}^{d} \frac{1 + O(d/t_i)}{2t_i} \exp\left(-\sum_{j=t_i}^{t_{i+1}-1} \frac{i}{2j}\right)$$

$$= \sum_{mw < t_1 < t_2 < \cdots < t_d \leq mv} \frac{(m+d-1)!}{(m-1)!} \prod_{i=1}^{d} \frac{1 + O(d/t_i)}{2t_i} \exp\left(-\sum_{j=t_i}^{mv} \frac{1}{2j}\right)$$

$$\leq \binom{d+m-1}{m-1} \left(\sum_{i=mw+1}^{mv} \frac{1 + O(d/t_i)}{2t_i} \exp\left(-\sum_{j=t}^{mv} \frac{1}{2j}\right)\right)^d.$$

Note that

$$\sum_{i=mw+1}^{mv} \frac{1 + O(d/t_i)}{2t_i} \exp\left(-\sum_{j=t_i}^{mv} \frac{1}{2j}\right)$$

$$\leq \sum_{i=mw+1}^{mv} \frac{1 + O(d/t_i)}{2t_i} \exp\left(-\frac{1}{2}\ln\frac{mv}{t_i} + O\left(\frac{1}{t_i}\right)\right)$$

$$\leq \sum_{i=mw+1}^{mv} \frac{1 + O(d/t_i)}{2\sqrt{mv t_i}}$$

$$\leq 1 - \sqrt{w/v} + O(d/\sqrt{vw}).$$

Thus, the assertion follows. ∎

The next result gives an upper bound on the probability that two given vertices are adjacent.

Corollary 8.25 *Let $w < v$. Then the probability that v is adjacent to w is bounded above by $5m\sqrt{1/(vw)}\ln(3v/w)$. In particular, each two vertices $v, w \geq \varepsilon n$ are adjacent with probability smaller than $(5m/\varepsilon)\ln(3/\varepsilon)/n$.*

Proof The probability that v and w are adjacent is bounded from above by

$$\sum_{d \geq 0} \frac{md}{2m(v-1)} P(\mathrm{dg}_{v-1}(w) = d - m).$$

When $d \leq d_0 = 8m\sqrt{v/w}\ln(3v/w)$, the above sum is clearly smaller than $d_0/2 = 4m\sqrt{1/vw}\ln(3v/w)$. If $d \geq d_0$, one can use Lemma 8.24 to estimate this sum by $m\sqrt{1/vw}\ln(3v/w)$. ∎

Recall that for $t > s$, the expectation of $\deg_t(s)$ is $O(\sqrt{t/s})$. We first state a simple tail bound to the right of this expectation that we asked the reader to prove in Exercise 8.13 (see also Frieze and Karoński (2016)).

Lemma 8.26 *Let $r < t$. Then*

$$P(\deg_t(r) \geq A e^m (t/r)^{1/2} (\ln t)^2) = O(t^{-A})$$

for any constant $A > 0$ and any t.

We now turn our attention to the left tail, which is much harder to establish. We prove a left-tail bound for the random variable $\deg_t(s)$ whenever $s \ll t$, as captured in the following lemma.

Lemma 8.27 *Let $v = O(T^{1-\varepsilon})$ as $T \to \infty$, for some fixed $\varepsilon \in (0, 1/2)$. Then there exist some $C, D > 0$ such that*

$$P\left(\deg_T(v) < C\left(\frac{T}{v}\right)^{(1-\varepsilon)^2/(2\pm 0.0001)}\right) \leq e^{-D\varepsilon^3 \ln(T)} = T^{-D\varepsilon^3}. \tag{8.86}$$

To prove this, we need the following coarser lemma.

Lemma 8.28 *Let $v < T^{1-\varepsilon}$, for some fixed $\varepsilon > 0$. Then there exist constants $C, D > 0$ independent of ε such that*

$$P(\deg_{vT^\varepsilon}(v) < C\varepsilon \ln T) \leq T^{-D\varepsilon} \tag{8.87}$$

for T sufficiently large.

Proof We observe the graph at exponentially increasing time steps: for some $\beta > 0$, let $t_0 = v$, $t_j = (1 + \beta)^j t_0$, $t_k = (1 + \beta)^k t_0 = vT^\varepsilon$ (so $k = \frac{\varepsilon \ln T}{\ln(1+\beta)}$). Note that $\deg_{t_0}(v) = \deg_v(v) = m$.

Let us upper bound the probability p_{j+1} that no connection to vertex v is made by any vertex in the subinterval $(t_j, t_{j+1}]$:

$$p_{j+1} \leq \left(1 - \frac{m}{2mt_{j+1}}\right)^{m(t_{j+1}-t_j)} = \left(1 - \frac{1}{2t_{j+1}}\right)^{m\beta t_j}, \tag{8.88}$$

which is at most some positive constant $\rho = \rho(m\beta)$, uniform in j, satisfying $\rho < 1$. This follows from the inequality $1 - x \leq e^{-x}$ for all real x. Thus, the total number of connections to vertex v in all subintervals can be stochastically lower bounded by a binomial random variable with number of trials $k = \Theta(\varepsilon \ln T)$ and success probability $\rho(m\beta)$: for any $d \geq 0$,

$$P(\deg_{t_k}(v) - m \geq d) \geq P\left(\binom{k}{1-\rho} \geq d\right). \tag{8.89}$$

In particular, as $T \to \infty$, this implies (using the Chernoff bound) that with probability $1 - T^{-D\varepsilon}$, the number of subintervals that contribute at least one new edge to v is at least $C\varepsilon \ln T$, for some C, so that $\deg_{vT^\varepsilon}(v) \geq C\varepsilon \ln T$, which completes the proof. ∎

With the previous lemma in hand, we now present the proof of our left tail bound; that is, Lemma 8.27. Similar to the proof of Lemma 8.28, we observe the graph at exponentially increasing times: fix a small $\alpha > 0$, and let $t_0 = vT^\varepsilon$, $t_j = (1 + \alpha)^j t_0$, $t_k = (1 + \alpha)^k t_0 = T$, so that $k = \frac{\ln(T/t_0)}{\ln(1+\alpha)}$. Denote by $d_j = \deg_{t_j}(v)$ and $\Delta_{j+1} = d_{j+1} - d_j$, for each j.

In the interval $(t_j, t_{j+1}]$, conditioned on the graph up to time t_j, Δ_{j+1} is stochastically lower bounded by a binomially distributed random variable with parameters $(t_{j+1} - t_j)m = \alpha t_j m$ and $p_{j+1} = \frac{d_j}{2mt_{j+1}}$. The former parameter is simply the interval length (in terms of number of vertex choices). The latter parameter comes from the fact that the degree of v at any point in the interval is at least d_j, and the total degree of the graph is at most $2mt_{j+1}$. Thus,

$$\Delta_{j+1} \mid G_{t_j} \succeq_{st} \text{Binomial}\left(m\alpha t_j, \frac{d_j}{2t_{j+1}m}\right), \tag{8.90}$$

where $\succeq_{st}$ denotes stochastic domination.

This suggests that we define the *bad* event $B_j = [\Delta_j < \alpha t_{j-1} m p_j (1 - \varepsilon)]$, for arbitrary $\varepsilon > 0$, and for $j \in [1, k]$. We further define $B_0 = [d_0 < C\varepsilon \ln T]$, for some constant $C > 0$.

Conditioning on all of the B_j (for $j \in \{0, \ldots, k\}$) failing to hold, we have

$$P\left(\bigcap_{j<k}\left[d_{j+1} \geq d_j\left(1 + \frac{(1-\varepsilon)\alpha}{2(1+\alpha)}\right)\right] \mid \bigcap_{j=0}^{k} \neg B_j\right) = 1, \tag{8.91}$$

recalling that $d_{j+1} = d_j + \Delta_{j+1}$, by definition. This in particular implies that (still under the same conditioning)

$$d_k \geq d_0 \cdot \left(1 + \frac{(1-\varepsilon)\alpha}{2(1+\alpha)}\right)^k = d_0 \exp\left(\ln(T/t_0)\frac{\ln(1 + \frac{(1-\varepsilon)\alpha}{2(1+\alpha)})}{\ln(1+\alpha)}\right). \tag{8.92}$$

Taking α close enough to 0, this becomes

$$d_k \geq d_0 \exp\left(\frac{1-\varepsilon}{2(1+o_{\alpha \to 0}(1))} \ln(T/t_0)\right) = d_0(T/t_0)^{\frac{1-\varepsilon}{2\pm 0.0001}}, \tag{8.93}$$

as in the statement of the lemma.

Now, it remains to lower bound the probability $P(\bigcap_{j=0}^{k} \neg B_j)$. We may write it as

$$P\left(\bigcap_{j=0}^{k} \neg B_j\right) = P(\neg B_0) \prod_{j=1}^{k} \mathbb{P}(\neg B_j \mid \neg B_0, \ldots, \neg B_{j-1})$$

$$\geq (1 - T^{-D\varepsilon}) \prod_{j=1}^{k} P(\neg B_j \mid \neg B_0, \ldots, \neg B_{j-1}),$$

where the inequality is by Lemma 8.28.

Now, by the stochastic domination (8.90), the conditioning, and the Chernoff bound, the jth factor of the product is lower bounded as follows:

$$P(\neg B_j \mid \neg B_0, \ldots, \neg B_{j-1}) \geq P(\text{Bin}(\alpha t_{j-1} m, p_j) \geq \alpha t_{j-1} m p_j (1 - \varepsilon) \mid \neg B_0, \ldots, \neg B_{j-1})$$

$$\geq 1 - \exp\left(-\frac{\varepsilon^2 \alpha d_{j-1}}{2(1+\alpha)}\right). \tag{8.94}$$

Under the conditioning, d_{j-1} is further lower bounded by

$$\left(1 + \frac{(1-\varepsilon)\alpha}{2(1+\alpha)}\right)^{j-1} C\varepsilon \ln T \geq \left(1 + \frac{\alpha}{4(1+\alpha)}\right)^{j-1} C\varepsilon \ln T$$

(using the fact that $\varepsilon < 1/2$), resulting in

$$P(\neg B_j | \neg B_0, \ldots, \neg B_{j-1}) \geq 1 - \exp\left(-C \frac{\varepsilon^3 \alpha}{2(1+\alpha)} \cdot \left(1 + \frac{\alpha}{4(1+\alpha)}\right)^{j-1} \ln(T)\right). \quad (8.95)$$

This implies

$$P\left(\bigcap_{j=0}^{k} \neg B_j\right) \geq P(\neg B_0) \quad (8.96)$$

$$\cdot \prod_{j=1}^{k}\left(1 - \exp\left(-C \frac{\varepsilon^3 \alpha}{2(1+\alpha)} \cdot \left(1 + \frac{\alpha}{4(1+\alpha)}\right)^{j-1} \ln(T)\right)\right). \quad (8.97)$$

For convenience, set $C' = C\frac{\alpha}{2(1+\alpha)}/D'$ and $D' = 1 + \frac{\alpha}{4(1+\alpha)}$. Note that $D' > 1$. So the product in (8.97) can be written (after some simple asymptotic analysis) as

$$\prod_{j=1}^{k}\left(1 - \exp\left(-\varepsilon^3 C' \cdot D'^j \ln(T)\right)\right) = 1 - \Theta(T^{-\varepsilon^3 C' D'}).$$

This implies, after combination with the lower bound on $P(\neg B_0)$, that we can write

$$P\left(\bigcap_{j=0}^{k} \neg B_j\right) \geq (1 - T^{-D\varepsilon})(1 - \Theta(-T^{-\varepsilon^3 C' D'})) \geq 1 - T^{-D''\varepsilon^3} \quad (8.98)$$

for some $D'' > 0$ (depending on α), as claimed. Combining this with (8.91) yields (8.93), with the claimed probability bound as follows:

$$P(d_k \geq d_0(T/t_0)^{\frac{1-\varepsilon}{2\pm 0.0001}}) \geq P\left(\bigcap_{j<k}\left[d_{j+1} \geq d_j\left(1 + \frac{(1-\varepsilon)\alpha}{2(1+\alpha)}\right)\right]\right)$$

$$\geq P\left(\bigcap_{j<k}\left[d_{j+1} \geq d_j\left(1 + \frac{(1-\varepsilon)\alpha}{2(1+\alpha)}\right)\right] \mid \bigcap_{j=0}^{k} \neg B_j\right) \cdot P\left(\bigcap_{j=0}^{k} \neg B_j\right)$$

$$\geq 1 \cdot (1 - T^{-D''\varepsilon^3}),$$

as required. ∎

Using Lemma 8.27, we can roughly lower bound the typical minimum degree of the collection of vertices before a given time.

Corollary 8.29 *Let $\Delta > 0$ be fixed. There exists some small enough $\delta > 0$ and positive constant D such that*

$$P\left(\bigcup_{w<T^\delta} \deg_T(w) < C\left(T^{1-\Delta}\right)^{1/2}\right) \leq T^{-D} \quad (8.99)$$

as $T \to \infty$.

The next result gives a bound on the probability that early vertices have the same degree needed to establish an upper bound on the probability of $\mathfrak{B}$.

Lemma 8.30 *There exist positive constants $\Delta < 1$ and c such that the probability that for some $s < s' < k^2 = n^{2\Delta}$ we have $\deg_n(s) = \deg_n(s')$ is $O(n^{-c})$.*

Proof Let $s < s' < k^2 = n^{2\Delta}$, for some $\Delta > 0$ to be chosen. We first estimate the probability that $\deg_n(s) = \deg_n(s')$. In order to do so, we set $n' = n^{0.6}$ and define

$$\deg'(s) = \deg_{n-n'}(s) \quad \text{and} \quad \deg''(s) = \deg_n(s) - \deg'(s).$$

Note that

$$P(\deg_n(s) = \deg_n(s')) \tag{8.100}$$

$$= \sum_{\underline{d},\underline{d}',\underline{d}'} P(\deg_n(s) = \deg_n(s')|\deg'(s) = \underline{d}, \deg'(s') = \underline{d}', \deg''(s') = \underline{d}')$$

$$\times P(\deg'(s) = \underline{d}, \deg'(s') = \underline{d}', \deg''(s') = \underline{d}')$$

$$= \sum_{\underline{d},\underline{d}',\underline{d}'} P(\deg''(s) = \underline{d}' + \underline{d}' - \underline{d}|\deg'(s) = \underline{d}, \deg'(s') = \underline{d}', \deg''(s') = \underline{d}')$$

$$\times P(\deg'(s) = \underline{d}, \deg'(s') = \underline{d}', \deg''(s') = \underline{d}'). \tag{8.101}$$

Observe that due to Lemma 8.27 (alternatively, Corollary 8.29) and Lemma 8.26, with probability $1 - O(n^{-c})$, for some appropriate $c > 0$ and small enough $k = n^\Delta$, a vertex $s \in [k^2]$ has degree e between $n^{0.488}$ and $n^{0.51}$ at any time in the interval $[n - n', n]$. Importantly, note that if this holds with probability $1 - O(n^{-c})$ for a given choice of Δ, then the same holds for all smaller choices of Δ, with the same value for c (this is a consequence of the fact that the probability bound in Lemma 8.27 is a function of ε and not of v).

Furthermore, one can estimate the random variable $\deg''(s)$ conditioned on $\deg'(s) = \underline{d}$ from above and below by binomial distributed random variables and use Chernoff bound to show that with probability at least $1 - O(n^{-c})$ we have

$$\left|\frac{dn'}{2mn} - \deg''(s)\right| = \left|0.5m^{-1}\underline{d}n^{-0.4} - \deg''(s)\right| \le \left(\frac{dn'}{2mn}\right)^{0.6} \le n^{0.08}. \tag{8.102}$$

Thus, in order to estimate $P(\deg_n(s) = \deg_n(s'))$, it is enough to bound

$$\rho(\underline{d}', \underline{d}', \underline{d}) = P(\deg''(s) = \underline{d}' + \underline{d}' - \underline{d}|\deg'(s) = \underline{d}, \deg'(s') = \underline{d}', \deg''(s') = \underline{d}')$$

for $n^{0.488} \le \underline{d}, \underline{d}' \le n^{0.51}$ and

$$|0.5\underline{d}n^{-0.4}/m - (\underline{d}' + \underline{d}' - \underline{d})| \le n^{0.08}.$$

In order to simplify the notation, set $\ell = \underline{d}' + \underline{d}' - \underline{d}$. Let us estimate the probability that $\deg''(s) = \ell$ conditioned on $\deg'(s) = \underline{d}$ and $\deg'(s') = \underline{d}'$. The probability that some vertex $v > n - n'$ is connected to s by more than one edge is bounded from above by

$$Cn'\left(\frac{m \deg_n(s)}{n - n'}\right)^2 \le n^{0.6} O(n^{-0.98}) = O(n^{-0.38})$$

so we can omit this case in further analysis. The probability that we connect a given vertex $v > n - n'$ with s is given by

$$\frac{m \deg_{v-1}(s)}{2m(v-1)} = \frac{d + O(dn^{-0.4})}{2(n - O(n'))} = \frac{d}{2n}\left(1 + O(n^{-0.4})\right). \tag{8.103}$$

Consequently, the probability that $\deg''(s) = \ell$ conditioned on $\deg'(s) = d$ and $\deg'(s') = d'$ is given by

$$\binom{n'}{\ell}\rho^{\ell}(1 - \rho)^{n'-\ell}\left(1 + O(n^{-0.4})\right)^{\ell}\left(1 + O(n^{-0.4}d/n)\right)^{n'-\ell},$$

where $\rho = d/2n$.

If we additionally condition on the fact that $\deg''(s') = d'$ (so that we now have conditioned on $\deg'(s) = d$, $\deg'(s') = d'$, and $\deg''(s') = d'$), it will result in an extra factor of the order $\left(1 + O(d/2n)\right)^{d'}$ since it means that some d' vertices already made their choice (and selected s' as their neighbor). Note however that, since $\ell, d' = O(dn'/n) = O(n^{0.11})$, we have

$$\left(1 + O(n^{-0.4})\right)^{\ell} = 1 + O(n^{-0.29}),$$

$$\left(1 + O(n^{-0.4}d/n)\right)^{n'-\ell} = 1 + O(n^{-0.29}),$$

$$\left(1 + O(d/2n)\right)^{d'} = 1 + O(n^{-0.48}).$$

Hence, the probability that $\deg''(s) = \ell$ conditioned on $\deg'(s) = d$, $\deg'(s') = d'$, and $\deg''(s') = d'$ is given by

$$\binom{n'}{\ell}\rho^{\ell}(1 - \rho)^{n'-\ell}\left(1 + O(n^{-0.29})\right),$$

and so it is well approximated by the binomial distribution. On the other hand, the probability that the random variable with binomial distribution with parameters n' and ρ takes a particular value is bounded from above by $O(1/\sqrt{n'\rho})$. Thus, for a given pair of vertices $s < s' < k^2 = n^{2\Delta}$, we have

$$P(\deg_n(s) = \deg_n(s')) = O(\sqrt{n/n'd}) + O(n^{-c}) = O(n^{-c}).$$

Hence, the probability that such a pair of vertices, $s < s' < k^2 = n^{2\Delta}$ exists is bounded from above by $O(k^4 n^{-c})$, and, as remarked at the beginning of the proof, $k = n^{\Delta}$ may be chosen small enough so that this yields a bound of the form $O(n^{-c'})$, for $c' > 0$. ∎

Proof of Theorem 8.23 Finally, we are ready to prove Theorem 8.23; that is, asymmetry of $\mathcal{P}(m, n)$ for $m \geq 3$. We recall that we need to prove that neither property $\mathfrak{A}$ nor properly $\mathfrak{B}$ defined in the previous section hold.

Let us study first the property $\mathfrak{A}$. Our task is to estimate from above the probability that there exist vertices t_1 and t_2 such that $k < t_1 < t_2$, which select the same m neighbors (which, of course, belong to $[t_1 - 1]$). Thus, we conclude

$$P(\text{PA}(m;n) \notin \mathfrak{A}) \leq \sum_{k<t_1<t_2} P(t_1, t_2 \text{ choose the same neighbors in } [t_1 - 1])$$

$$\leq \sum_{k<t_1<t_2} \sum_{1\leq r_1\leq r_2\ldots\leq r_m<t_1} P(t_1, t_2 \text{ choose } r_1, \ldots, r_m). \qquad (8.104)$$

The event in the last expression is an intersection of dependent events but, if we condition on the degrees $\deg_{t_\ell}(r_s)$ of the chosen vertices r_s at times t_1, t_2, then the choice events become independent.

Let us define $\mathfrak{D}$ as an event that for some $\ell = 1, 2$, and $s = 1, 2, \ldots, m$,

$$\deg_{t_\ell}(r_s) \leq \sqrt{t_\ell/r_s}(\ln t_\ell)^3.$$

Then from Lemma 8.26 it follows that

$$P(\text{PA}(m;n) \notin \mathfrak{D}) \leq t_1^{-10m/\Delta}.$$

Consequently, for $k < t_1 < t_2$ we get

$$P(t_1, t_2 \text{ choose } r_1, \ldots, r_m) \leq P(t_1, t_2 \text{ choose } r_1, \ldots, r_m | \mathfrak{D}) + P(\neg \mathfrak{D})$$

$$\leq \prod_{\ell=1}^{2} \prod_{s=1}^{m} \frac{\sqrt{t_\ell/r_s} \ln^3 t_\ell}{2t_\ell} + t_1^{-10m/\Delta}$$

$$\leq (\ln t_2)^{6m} \prod_{\ell=1}^{2} \prod_{s=1}^{m} \frac{1}{\sqrt{t_\ell r_s}} + n^{-10m}.$$

Thus, (8.104) becomes

$$P(\text{PA}(m;n) \notin \mathfrak{A}) \leq \sum_{k<t_1<t_2} (\ln t_2)^{6m} \sum_{1\leq r_1\leq r_2\cdots\leq r_m<t_1} \prod_{\ell=1}^{2}\prod_{s=1}^{m} \frac{1}{\sqrt{t_\ell r_s}} + n^{-1}$$

$$\leq \sum_{k<t_1<t_2} (t_1 t_2)^{-m/2}(\ln t_2)^{6m} \sum_{1\leq r_1\leq r_2\cdots\leq r_m<t_1} \prod_{s=1}^{m} \frac{1}{r_s} + n^{-1}$$

$$\leq \sum_{k<t_1} t_1^{-m+1}(\ln t_1)^{9m} + n^{-1}$$

$$\leq C(m)k^{2-m}(\ln k)^{9m} + n^{-1},$$

where $C(m)$ is some positive constant. Hence,

$$P(\text{PA}(m;n) \notin \mathfrak{A}) \leq n^{\Delta(2.0001-m)}, \qquad (8.105)$$

which is polynomially decaying since $m \geq 3$. We remark that this holds for *arbitrary* $\Delta > 0$.

Next we show that, with probability close to 1, the $\widetilde{k} = n^{\Delta'}$ oldest vertices of $\text{PA}(m;n)$ have unique degrees and so these are fixed points of every automorphism. The key ingredient of our argument is Lemma 8.30.

To estimate the probability that $\text{PA}(m;n) \notin \mathfrak{B}$, we reason as follows: from Lemma 8.30, we know that with probability at least $1 - O(n^{-c})$, for some positive constant c, the degrees of all vertices smaller than $\widetilde{k}^2 = n^{2\Delta''}$ are pairwise different, for some Δ'' small enough to satisfy Lemma 8.30.

Furthermore, using Corollary 8.29, one can deduce that we can choose $\Delta' > 0$ (playing the role of δ in the corollary) small enough so that, with probability at least $1 - O(n^{-c})$ (for another positive constant $c > 0$) all vertices $s < \widetilde{k} = n^{\Delta'}$ have degrees larger than those of all vertices $t > \widetilde{k}^2$ (in particular using the left tail bound to show that vertices $< \widetilde{k}$ all have high degree and the right tail bound to show that vertices $> \widetilde{k}^2$ have low degree with high probability). Let us be more precise here: we can choose Δ in Corollary 8.29 to be some very small constant (say, 0.00001). This ensures the existence of a choice for Δ' for which

$$P\left(\bigcap_{s<\widetilde{k}=n^{\Delta'}} \deg_n(s) \geq Cn^{(1-0.00001)/2}\right) \geq 1 - T^{-c}, \tag{8.106}$$

for some positive constant c. That is, with probability at least $1 - T^{-c}$, all vertices $< \widetilde{k}$ have degree larger than $Cn^{0.499995}$. Note that we can bring the exponent arbitrarily close to 0.5 by finding a small enough Δ'. We will require, in fact, that Δ' is small enough compared to Δ''.

Now, we can use Lemma 8.26 to show that all vertices $r > \widetilde{k}^2 = n^{2\Delta''}$ have low degree with high probability. In particular, in the lemma statement, we choose $t := n$ and arbitrary $r > \widetilde{k}^2$. This results, for arbitrary $A > 0$, in the bound

$$P\left(\bigcup_{r>\widetilde{k}^2} \deg_n(r) \geq Ae^m n^{(1-2\Delta'')/2}(\ln n)^2\right) \leq n \cdot O(n^{-A}) = O(n^{1-A}), \tag{8.107}$$

which is polynomially decaying if we set A sufficiently large (say, $A = 2$). Note that we have used the union bound, followed by Lemma 8.26. This shows that, with probability at least $1 - n^{-c}$ for some $c > 0$, *all* vertices $r > \widetilde{k}^2$ have degree at most $\widetilde{O}(n^{(1-2\Delta'')/2})$. Since Δ'' is some specific (small) constant, we may choose Δ' above so small that this is asymptotically smaller than the lower bound on the degrees of vertices $< \widetilde{k}$.

Consequently, with probability $1 - O(n^{-c})$, degrees of vertices from $[\widetilde{k}]$ are unique (i.e., $\text{PA}(m; n) \notin \mathfrak{B}$).

Finally, Theorem 8.23 follows directly from (8.84) and our estimates for $P(\text{PA}(m; n) \notin \mathfrak{A})$ and $P(\text{PA}(m; n) \notin \mathfrak{B})$, provided that we choose $\Delta < \Delta'$. This completes the proof.

8.4.3 A Structural Compression Algorithm

We now present an asymptotically optimal algorithm for compression of unlabeled graphs (see Theorem 8.33): that is, given an arbitrary labeled representative G isomorphic to $G' \sim \text{PA}(m; n)$, we construct a code from which $S(G')$ can be efficiently recovered. The algorithm can be run on general undirected graphs; our optimality guarantee is under the assumption that the input is generated by $\text{PA}(m; n)$.

We state our algorithm and analyze it in the case where the model is preferential attachment with m self-loops on the oldest vertex. Only simple tweaks are needed to generalize to the case where there are no self-loops (and hence where one cannot necessarily uniquely identify the oldest vertex).

Our algorithm starts with finding a certain orientation of the edges of the input graph G to produce a directed, acyclic graph D denoted as $\text{DAG}(G)$. In the case where G is isomorphic to a sample G' from $\text{PA}(m; n)$ (say, $G = \pi(G')$), we have $D = \pi(\text{DAG}(G'))$, and all vertices have out-degree m.

We accomplish this by a *peeling* procedure: at each step, consider the set D_{min} of minimum-degree as the graph. We orient the edges incident on those nodes away from them, and then recurse on the subgraph excluding the nodes in D_{min}. This procedure terminates precisely when there are no remaining vertices. For a general input graph G, which might not have arisen by preferential attachment, there may be edges between vertices in D_{min}. We orient edges from nodes with larger labels to those with smaller ones. In general, this yields a directed, acyclic graph (aside from self-loops) $D = \pi(\text{DAG}(G'))$.

Hence, we are free to apply our structural results (such as Theorem 8.31) on DAG(G'). We remark that it is not too hard to generalize our algorithm to tweaks of the model, since the only thing that is required is that the height of the resulting directed graph be at most $O(\log n)$; such an orientating on of the edges of G exists with high probability (this is granted by Theorem 8.31).

With this procedure in hand, the structural compression algorithm works as follows on input G:

1. Construct the directed version $D = \text{DAG}(G)$ by the peeling procedure just described.
2. Starting from the "bottom" vertex (i.e., the vertex with no out-edges except for self-loops), we will do a depth-first search (DFS) of D (following edges only from their destinations to their sources). To the jth vertex in this traversal, for $j = 1, \ldots, n$, we will associate a *backtracking number* B_j, which tells us how many steps to backtrack in the DFS process after visiting the jth node; for example, when there is at least one in-edge leading to an unvisited node (so that we do not backtrack), $B_j = 0$.

   Upon visiting vertex w from vertex v in the DFS, we do the following:

   (a) Denote by k the maximum out-degree of D (which can be determined in a preprocessing step, and which is equal to m if the input arises from preferential attachment). Using $\lceil \log k \rceil$ bits, encode the out-degree d_w of w (for preferential attachment, $d_w = m$, but we encode it for the sake of generality). Encode the names of the $d_w - 1$ vertex choices made by w, excluding one choice to connect to vertex v. Here, the *name* of a vertex is the binary expansion of its index in the DFS, which we can represent using exactly $\lceil \log n \rceil$ bits. These can be determined in a preprocessing step, by doing an initial DFS to label the nodes with their names.

   (b) We need to know what happens after we visit vertex w: do we go forward in the search, or is there nowhere left to go along the current route (i.e., do we need to backtrack)? Suppose w is the jth vertex to be visited. Then we output an encoding of B_j. We need to more precisely examine how we encode these numbers, since it would be suboptimal to simply encode them in $\Theta(\log n)$ bits. Lemma 8.32 tells us how to more efficiently perform this encoding; that is, in $O(\log \log n)$ bits as we will see.

3. For the purposes of decoding, we store (once, for the entire graph) the sequence of codewords for the code used for the backtracking numbers. This can be done in at most $O(n \log \log n)$ extra bits, at the beginning of the code. We also store k (the maximum out-degree), which can be done with at most $O(\log n)$ bits.

For the analysis of the algorithms, we need the following property on the height of DAG(G). (The proof is postponed to Section 8.4.4.)

Lemma 8.31 *Consider $G_n \sim \text{PA}(m; n)$ for fixed $m \geq 1$. Then, with probability at least $1 - o(n^{-1})$, the height of $\text{DAG}(G_n)$ is at most $Cm \ln n$, for some absolute positive constant C.*

With the help of Lemma 8.31, we obtain the following complexity bound.

Lemma 8.32 *The backtracking numbers $B_1, \ldots, B_n$ can be encoded using a total of $O(n \log \log n)$ bits on average.*

Proof Consider a random variable X whose distribution is given by the empirical distribution of the collection $B = \{B_1, \ldots, B_n\}$. That is,

$$P_X(x) = \frac{|\{j : B_j = x\}|}{n} \tag{8.108}$$

for each x. Note that this empirical distribution is itself a random variable. We will show that $\mathbf{E}[n \cdot H(X)] = O(n \log \log n)$. Denote by W the event that the number of levels in D is upper bounded by $O(\log n)$ (as considered in Lemma 8.31). Under conditioning on this event, X can take on at most $O(\log n)$ values, which implies that $H(X) = O(\log \log n)$. Then we have

$$\mathbf{E}[H(X)] \leq \mathbf{E}[H(X)|W] + (1 - P(W))\mathbf{E}[H(X)|\neg W]$$
$$\leq \mathbf{E}[H(X)|W] + (1 - P(W))\log n = O(\log \log n),$$

where we have used Lemma 8.31 to upper bound $1 - P(W)$.

We can thus construct a prefix code (once, for the entire graph) for the observed values of B_i, whose empirical average length is given by

$$\sum_{x \,:\, \exists j, B_j = x} \ell_x P_X(x) \leq H(X) + 1,$$

where ℓ_x denotes the length of the codeword for x. Now, recalling the definition of $P_X(x)$, this implies

$$\mathbf{E}\left[\sum_{x \,:\, \exists j, B_j = x} \ell_x |\{j \,:\, B_j = x\}| \right] \leq n\mathbf{E}[H(X)] + n = O(n \log \log n).$$

This completes the proof.   ∎

It is easy to show that the code for $S(G)$ is uniquely decodable. Furthermore, its expected length is at most $(m-1)n \log n + O(n \log \log n)$, which recovers the first term of the structural entropy and bounds the second. Construction of the Huffman code for the backtracking numbers takes time $O(n \log n)$, and each step of the DFS takes time at most $O(m \log n)$, so the running time is $O(mn \log n)$.

We have thus proved the following.

Theorem 8.33 *The algorithm given in this section, on input a graph G isomorphic to $G' \sim \text{PA}(m; n)$, runs in time $O(mn \log n)$ and outputs a code of expected length $(m-1)n \log n + O(n \log \log n)$ from which we can recover $S(G)$ in time $O(mn \log n)$. If self-loops are removed from G' and G (so that the first vertex is hard to identify), then the same code length can be achieved in time $O(mn^2 \log n)$.*

8.4.4 Proof Lemma 8.31

We start with the following, surprising at first sight, observation (which we ask the reader to verify in Exercise 8.14).

Fact 8.34 Let $w < v$. Then the degree $\deg_v(w)$ as well as the probability that v is adjacent to w does not depend on the structure of the graph induced by the first w vertices.

Let $p_m(n, k)$ denote the probability that $\mathrm{DAG}(G_n)$ contains a path of length k. From Fact 8.34 and Corollary 8.25, it follows that

$$p_m(n, k) \le \sum_{v_0 < v_1 < \cdots < v_k} \prod_{i=1}^{k} P(v_{i-1} \to v_i) \le \sum_{v_0 < v_1 < \cdots < v_k} \prod_{i=1}^{k} \frac{5m \ln(3v_i/v_{i-1})}{\sqrt{v_{i-1}v_i}}$$

$$\le \sum_{v_0=1}^{n-k} \frac{1}{\sqrt{v_0}} \prod_{i=1}^{k} \sum_{v_i=v_{i-1}+1}^{n-k-i} \frac{5m \ln(3v_i/v_{i-1})}{v_i}. \tag{8.109}$$

In order to estimate this sum we split all the vertices $v_1, \ldots, v_k$ of the path P into several classes. Namely, we say that a vertex v_i is of type t in P if t is the smallest natural number such that $v_i/v_{i-1} \le (1 + a)^t$, where a is a small constant to be chosen later; that is, $t = \lceil \ln(v_i/v_{i-1})/\ln(1 + a) \rceil$. Then, given v_{i-1}, the contribution of terms related to v_i can be estimated from above by

$$\sum_{v_i=v_{i-1}(1+a)^{t-1}}^{v_{i-1}(1+a)^t} \frac{5m \ln(3v_i/v_{i-1})}{v_i} \le 5m \ln[(1 + a)] \ln[3(1 + a)^t] \le \alpha t, \tag{8.110}$$

where, to simplify notation, we put $\alpha = 5m \ln(1 + a) \ln(3(1 + a))$. Let s_t denote the number of vertices of type t in P. Note that $\prod_{t \ge 2} \left[(1 + a)^{t-1} \right]^{s_t} \le n$ and

$$\sum_{t \ge 2} t s_t \le 2 \sum_{t \ge 2} (t - 1) s_t \le \frac{2 \ln n}{\ln(1 + a)}. \tag{8.111}$$

Let us set $J = 2 \ln n / \ln(1 + a)$. Thus, we arrive at the following estimate for $p_m(n, k)$:

$$p_m(n, k) \le \sum_{v_0=1}^{n-k} \frac{1}{\sqrt{v_0}} \binom{k}{s_1} \alpha^{s_1} \sum_{\sum_t s_t t \le J} \binom{k - s_1}{s_2, s_3, \ldots, s_k} \prod_{t \ge 2} (\alpha t)^{s_t}$$

$$\le 3\sqrt{n} \binom{k}{s_1} \alpha^{s_1} \sum_{\sum_t s_t t \le J} \binom{k - s_1}{s_2, s_3, \ldots, s_k} \exp \left(\sum_{t \ge 2} s_t \ln(\alpha t) \right)$$

$$\le 3\sqrt{n} \binom{k}{s_1} \alpha^{s_1} 2^{2J} \max_{\sum_t s_t t \le J} \exp \left(\sum_{t \ge 2} s_t \ln \left(\frac{e\alpha t(k - s_1)}{s_t} \right) \right).$$

In order to estimate the expression

$$\sigma(J, S) = \max_{\sum_t s_t t \le J} \exp \left(\sum_{t \ge 2} s_t \ln \left(\frac{e\alpha t S}{s_t} \right) \right)$$

where $S = \sum_{t \ge 2} s_t$, we split the set of all t's into two parts. Thus, let $T_1 = \{t : \ln(e\alpha t S/s_t) \le t\}$ and $T_2 = \{2, 3, \ldots, k\} \setminus T_1$. Then, clearly,

$$\max_{\sum_t s_t t \le J} \exp\left(\sum_{t \in T_1} s_t \ln\left(\frac{e\alpha t S}{s_t}\right)\right) \le \max_{\sum_t s_t t \le J} \exp\left(\sum_{t \in T_1} s_t t\right) \le \exp(J).$$

Observe that for every $t \in T_2$, we have $\ln(eS\alpha t/s_t) \ge t$ and so $s_t \le e\alpha t e^{-t} S$. It is easy to check then that $s_t \ln\left(\frac{e\alpha t S}{s_t}\right) \le 6 \cdot 2^{-t} S$, so

$$\max_{\sum_t s_t t \le J} \exp\left(\sum_{t \in T_2} s_t \ln\left(\frac{e\alpha t S}{s_t}\right)\right) \le \max_{\sum_t s_t t \le J} \exp\left(6S \sum_{t \in T_2} 2^{-t}\right) \le \exp(3S) \le \exp(3J).$$

Thus, $\sigma(J, S) \le \exp(4J)$, and, since $s_1 = k - S \ge k - J$,

$$p_m(n, k) \le 3\sqrt{n}\binom{k}{s_1}\alpha^{s_1} 2^{2J}\sigma(J, k - s_1) \le 3\sqrt{n}2^k\alpha^{k-J}\exp(6J)$$

$$\le 3\exp(\ln n + k + (k - J)\ln\alpha + 6J).$$

Since for $0 < a < 1$ we have $a/2 < \ln(1 + a) < a$, if we set $a = 1/(310m)$, then $\alpha < 1/61$ and $\ln\alpha < -4$. Now let us recall that $J = 2\ln n/\ln(1 + a)$ and $k = 5000m\ln n > 4J$. Thus,

$$p_m(n, k) \le 3\exp(\ln n + k + (k - J)\ln\alpha + 6J)$$

$$\le 3\exp(\ln n + k - 3k + 3k/2) = \exp(\ln n - k/2) = o(n^{-1}).$$

It is simple to show that with high probability the height is also lower bounded by $\Omega(\log n)$. Thus, the height is $\Theta(\log n)$ with high probability.

8.5 Exercises

8.1   Show that the structure of a graph can be uniquely reconstructed from the lists B_1 and B_2 that are generated by the algorithm SZIP.

8.2   Prove the algorithm SZIP runs in $O(n^2)$.

8.3   Prove the large deviation result (8.8) for SZIP (see Choi and Szpankowski (2012)).

8.4   Show that the function

$$\widetilde{D}(z) := e^{-z}\sum_{n \ge 0}\frac{\sqrt{n}}{n}z^n$$

satisfies the assumptions of Theorem C.2, that is, $\widetilde{a}(D) = O(|z|^\beta)$ uniformly as $|z| \to \infty$ and $|\arg(z)| \le \theta$, where $\beta > 0$ and $0 < \theta < \frac{\pi}{2}$, and $\widetilde{D}(z)e^z = O(e^{\alpha|z|})$ uniformly as $|z| \to \infty$ and $\theta \le |\arg(z)| \le \pi$, where $\alpha < 1$.

8.5   Show that preferential attachment graphs PA(m, n) are invariant under isomorphism; that is, every distinct relabeling of a graph has the same probability (see Lemma 8.17).

8.6   Prove by induction that (8.20) holds.

8.7   Design an efficient version of algorithm SZIP that runs in $O(n + e)$ time where n is the number of nodes and e is the number of edges.

8.8   Prove that the numbers $b(n, \infty)$ can be explicitly represented by

$$b(n, \infty) = \sum_{\ell=2}^{n}(-1)^\ell\binom{n}{\ell}\frac{\ell}{1 - p^\ell - q^\ell}. \tag{8.112}$$

Furthermore show that the Poisson transform $\widetilde{B}(z)$ can be represented by (8.29) (see also Jacquet and Szpankowski (2015)).

8.9   Consider a $G_t \in \mathrm{PA}(m, n)$ graph. Prove that the maximum degree is in G_t is $O(\sqrt{t})$ with high probability (see Frieze and Karoński (2016)).

8.10   Prove the following property regarding the average $\overline{N}_{t,d}$ number of vertices of degree d at time t for $\mathrm{PA}(n, m)$ graphs: we have, for $t \geq 1$ and $1 \leq d \leq t$ and for any fixed $m \geq 1$,

$$\left| \overline{N}_{t,d} - \frac{2m(m+1)t}{d(d+1)(d+2)} \right| \leq C$$

for some fixed $C = C(m) > 0$.

8.11   Prove the following property regarding the average $\overline{N}_{t,d}$ number of vertices of degree d at time t for $\mathrm{PA}(n, m)$ graphs: we have, for $t \to \infty$, $d \geq t^{1/15}$, and fixed $m \geq 1$,

$$\overline{N}_{t,d} = O\left(\frac{t}{d(d+1)(d+2)} \right) = O\left(\frac{t}{d^3} \right).$$

8.12   Prove that a preferential or uniform attachment graph is symmetric for $m = 1$ and $m = 2$. More precisely, prove the following theorem.

> **Theorem 8.35** (Symmetry behavior for $m = 1, 2$)   *Let $G \sim \mathrm{PA}(n, m)$. For $m = 1$,*
>
> $$P(|\mathrm{Aut}(G)| > \Omega(n)) \to 1.$$
>
> *For $m = 2$,*
>
> $$P(|\mathrm{Aut}(G)| > 1) > c$$
>
> *for some constant $c > 0$.*

8.13   Prove Lemma 8.26.

8.14   Prove Fact 8.34.

8.15   Consider the duplication-divergence model as discussed in Solé et al. (2002), Pastor-Satorras, Smith, and Solé (2003). In this mode, a new node first randomly and uniformly selects an existing node and then connects to all its neighbors with probability p. In addition, if the new node is the nth node, then it connects to nodes not selected in phase one with probability r/n.

For such a model, find the average degree of a node. Then derive a large deviation (see Frieze, Turowski, and Szpankowski (2020)).

8.16   For the duplication-divergence model discussed in Exercise 8.15, find the expected size of the automorphism group This seems to be an open problem.

8.17   Consider the following small-world-type model, similar to the one introduced in Watts and Strogatz (1998), Kleinberg (2000). It is defined as follows. Consider the vertex set $V = \{1, 2, \ldots, n\}$ arranged on the circle, with each vertex connected by an edge to its two nearest neighbors. For each one of the remaining $\binom{n}{2} - n$ pairs of vertices (u, v), we add an edge between them with probability $p(|u - v|)$, where $|u - v|$ is the discrete distance on the circle and $p_n(k) = c_n k^{-a}$, for some $a \in (0, 1)$ and with,

$$c_n = b_n(1 - a)\left(\frac{2}{n} \right)^{1-a},$$

where $\{b_n\}$ is a nondecreasing, unbounded sequence of positive real numbers, with $b_n = o(n^{1-a})$, as $n \to \infty$.

Prove that such a model is asymmetric as long as

$$b_n = o(n^{1-a}), \qquad \text{and} \qquad \frac{b_n}{\ln n} \to \infty, \qquad \text{as } n \to \infty$$

(see Kontoyiannis et al. (2021)).

Bibliographical Notes

There has been some work on compression of labeled graph and tree models in recent years in both information theory and computer science communities by Adler and Mitzenmacher (2001), Choi and Szpankowski (2012), Zhang et al. (2014), Abbe (2016), Asadi, Abbe, and Verdú (2017), Delgosha and Anantharam (2017). In 1990, Naor (1990) proposed an efficiently computable representation for unlabeled graphs (see Turan (1984)) that is optimal up to the first two leading terms of the entropy when all unlabeled graphs are equally likely. Naor's result is asymptotically a special case of Choi and Szpankowski (2012), where general Erdős–Rényi graphs were analyzed. In fact, Choi and Szpankowski (2012) seems to be the first article that dealt with structural compression and where graph automorphism was introduced in the context of graph compression. This was further extended to the compression of preferential attachment graphs in Luczak, Magner, and Szpankowski (2019b). Furthermore, in Mohri, Riley, and Suresh (2015) an automata approach was used to design an optimal graph compression scheme. Recently, the authors of Delgosha and Anantharam (2017, 2018, 2019) proposed a general universal scheme for lossless graph compression.

There also have been some heuristic methods for real-world graph compression including grammar-based compression for some data structures: see Peshkin (2007), Chierichetti et al. (2009), Maneth and Peternek (2018). Peshkin (2007) proposed an algorithm for a graphical extension of the one-dimensional SEQUITUR compression method. However, SEQUITUR is known not to be asymptotically optimal. A comprehensive survey of lossless graph compression algorithms can be found in Besta and Hoefler (2018).

It should be mentioned that there are other graph models such as the small-world model in Watts and Strogatz (1998) and Kleinberg (2000) and the duplication-divergence model in Solé et al. (2002) and Pastor-Satorras et al. (2003) that have not yet met with rigorous analysis, at least from the symmetry point of view. Some recent results in this context can be found in Hermann and Pfaffelhuber (2016), Jordan (2018), Turowski and Szpankowski (2019), Frieze et al. (2020), Frieze, Turowski, and Szpankowski (2021) (duplication-divergence model) and Kontoyiannis et al. (2021) (small-world model). More on graph dynamic models can be read in Frieze and Karoński (2016), van der Hofstad (2016).

Group automorphism for random graphs were discussed in several papers. Asymmetry of (unlabeled) Erdős–Rényi graphs was first proved in Bollobás (1982), and then strengthened in Kim Sudakov, and Vu (2002). Asymmetry of preferential attachment graphs were discussed and solved in Magner et al. (2014), Luczak, Magner, and Szpankowski (2019a). Asymmetry of the small-word model was proved recently in Kontoyiannis et al. 2021 (see also Exercise 8.17). However, symmetry behavior for the duplication-divergence model is unknown.

This chapter is mostly based on Choi and Szpankowski (2012) and Luczak et al. (2019a).

Part II

Universal Codes

9

Minimax Redundancy and Regret

In the second part of this book, we study universal coding, modeling, and learning. Universal coding and universal modeling are two driving forces of information theory, model selection, and statistical inference. In universal coding, we construct code for data sequences generated by an unknown source such that, as the length of the sequence increases, the average code length approaches the entropy of whatever processes in the family have generated the data. Universal codes are often characterized by the average *minimax* redundancy and regret, which are the excess over the *best* code from a class of decodable codes for the worst process in the family. In universal learning, however, we search for an unknown distribution so that one ignores the integer nature of universal coding, leading to some simplifications. In this chapter, we precisely define minimax redundancy and discuss some of its basic properties.

As pointed out by Rissanen (1996), over the years, universal coding evolved into *universal modeling*, where the purpose is no longer restricted to just coding but rather to finding optimal models. The central question of interest in universal modeling is how to achieve optimality for *individual* sequences. The burning question is how to measure it. The *worst-case* minimax redundancy and regret became handy since they measure the worst-case excess of the best code maximized over the processes in the family. Rissanen also admitted that the redundancy restricted to the first term cannot distinguish between codes over *large alphabets* and those that differ by a constant, however large.

In recent years, regrets become more popular in machine learning; in particular in online learning. Here, however, instead of code length we must learn model parameters from examples whose outcomes are already known to us. For example, in online setup, the training algorithm consumes data in rounds and the prediction algorithm incurs some loss that we try to estimate. The regret in online algorithm is defined as the excess loss it incurs over some value of a constant comparator that is used for prediction for the complete sequence. Often, one does the comparison through the so-called regression function.

The goal of this part of the book is to derive precise results for redundancy and regrets, whether in data compression or gambling or machine learning.

9.1 Minimax Redundancy and Regret

Before we proceed, let us recall some notation from Chapter 1. A code $C_n \colon \mathcal{A}^n \to \{0, 1\}^*$ is defined as an injective mapping from the set $\mathcal{A}^n$ of all sequences of length n over the finite alphabet $\mathcal{A}$ of size $m = |\mathcal{A}|$ to the set $\{0, 1\}^*$ of all binary sequences. A *probabilistic source* P is a probability measure on $\mathcal{A}^*$. For every n, this source induces a probability measure on $\mathcal{A}^n$ by setting

$$P(x^n) = P(\{y \in \mathcal{A}^* : y^n = x^n\}),$$

where $x^n \in \mathcal{A}^n$. We write X^n to denote a random variable representing a message of length n according to the probability measure P; that is, $P(X^n = x^n) = P(x^n)$. For a given code C_n, we let $L(C_n, x^n)$ be the code length for x^n.

Also, recall that the *pointwise redundancy* $R_n(C_n, P; x^n)$ and the *average redundancy* $\overline{R}_n(C_n, P)$ for a *given* source P are defined as

$$R_n(C_n, P; x^n) = L(C_n, x^n) + \log P(x^n),$$
$$\overline{R}_n(C_n, P) = \mathbf{E}[R_n(C_n, P; X^n)] = \mathbf{E}[L(C_n, X^n)] - H_n(P)$$
$$= \sum_{x^n} P(x^n) \left[L(C_n, x^n) + \log P(x^n) \right],$$

where $H_n(P) = -\mathbf{E} \log P(X^n)$ denotes the entropy of the probability distribution on the source sequences of length n. As pointed out above, the excess of the code length for *individual sequences* is a central issue for universal modeling, therefore we define the *maximal* or *worst case* redundancy as

$$R_n^*(C_n, P) = \max_{x^n} [L(C_n, x^n) + \log P(x^n)].$$

As observed in Chapter 1, while the pointwise redundancy can be negative, the maximal and the average redundancies cannot, by Kraft's inequality and Shannon's source coding theorem, respectively.

In practice, one can only hope to have some knowledge about a family of sources $\mathcal{S}$ that generates real data. For example, we may often be able to justify restricting our attention to memoryless sources (see Chapter 10) or Markov sources (see Chapter 11). Sometimes, however, we must consider a larger class of nonfinitely parameterized sources of unbounded memory such as renewal sources (see Chapter 12).

In several instances, we will represent the family of sources $\mathcal{S}$ by a parametrization $\mathcal{S} = \{P^\theta\}_{\theta \in \Theta}$; for example, m-ary memoryless sources can be parametrized by $\theta = (\theta_0, \ldots, \theta_{m-1}) = (p_0, \ldots, p_{m-1})$ with

$$\Theta = \{\theta : \theta_i \geq 0 \ (0 \leq i \leq m-1), \ \theta_0 + \cdots + \theta_{m-1} = 1\}$$

and

$$P^\theta(x^n) = \prod_{i=0}^{m-1} \theta_i^{k_i} = \prod_{i=0}^{m-1} p_i^{k_i},$$

where k_i is the number of symbol $i \in \mathcal{A}$ occurring in x^n.

We define the average minimax redundancy $\overline{R}_n(\mathcal{S})$ and the worst-case (maximal) minimax redundancy $R_n^*(\mathcal{S})$ for family $\mathcal{S}$ as follows:

$$\overline{R}_n(\mathcal{S}) = \min_{C_n \in \mathcal{C}} \sup_{P \in \mathcal{S}} \left(\sum_{x^n} P(x^n) \left[L(C_n, x^n) + \log P(x^n) \right] \right), \tag{9.1}$$

$$R_n^*(\mathcal{S}) = \min_{C_n \in \mathcal{C}} \sup_{P \in \mathcal{S}} \max_{x^n} \left[L(C_n, x^n) + \log P(x^n) \right], \tag{9.2}$$

where $\mathcal{C}$ denotes the set of all codes satisfying the Kraft inequality. In words, we search for the best code for the worst source on average and for individual sequences.

We should also point out that there are other measures of optimality for coding, learning, and prediction that are used in universal modeling and coding. We refer here to minimax *regret* functions defined as follows:

$$\bar{r}_n(\mathcal{S}) = \min_{C_n \in \mathcal{C}} \sup_{P \in \mathcal{S}} \sum_{x^n} P(x^n)[L(C_n, x^n) + \log \sup_{P \in \mathcal{S}} P(x^n)], \tag{9.3}$$

$$r_n^*(\mathcal{S}) = \min_{C_n \in \mathcal{C}} \max_{x^n}[L(C_n, x^n) + \log \sup_{P \in \mathcal{S}} P(x^n)], \tag{9.4}$$

and to the maxmin regret,

$$\underline{r}_n(\mathcal{S}) = \sup_{P \in \mathcal{S}} \min_{C_n \in \mathcal{C}} \sum_{x^n} P(x^n)[L(C_n, x^n) + \log \sup_{P \in \mathcal{S}} P(x^n)]. \tag{9.5}$$

We call $\bar{r}_n(\mathcal{S})$ the *average* minimax regret, $r_n^*(\mathcal{S})$ the worst-case (maximal) minimax regret, and $\underline{r}_n(\mathcal{S})$ the maxmin regret. Clearly, $\bar{R}_n(\mathcal{S}) \leq \bar{r}_n(\mathcal{S})$, and, as easy to establish,

$$r_n^*(\mathcal{S}) = R_n^*(\mathcal{S}).$$

Finally, we may link universal modeling and learning with game theory and statistics by ignoring the integer nature for the coding interpretations. Suppose nature picks up a distribution P from $\mathcal{S}$ and we try to find a distribution Q as the best guess for P. We may then reformulate our redundancy (average and maximal), as well as regrets, so that $L(C_n, x^n)$ is replaced by its continuous approximation, namely, $\log 1/Q(x^n)$. We denote these corresponding continuous redundancy and regret by placing a tilde over R or r. For example, $\widetilde{R}_n(\mathcal{S})$ and $\widetilde{R}_n^*(\mathcal{S})$ denote continuous approximations of the average and the worst-case minimax redundancies. They can be explicitly defined as

$$\widetilde{R}_n(\mathcal{S}) = \inf_{Q} \sup_{P \in \mathcal{S}} \left(\sum_{x^n} P(x^n) \log \frac{P(x^n)}{Q(x^n)} \right) = \inf_{Q} \sup_{P \in \mathcal{S}} D_n(P||Q), \tag{9.6}$$

$$\widetilde{R}_n^*(\mathcal{S}) = \inf_{Q} \sup_{P \in \mathcal{S}} \max_{x^n} \left[\log \left(P(x^n)/Q(x^n) \right) \right], \tag{9.7}$$

where $D_n(P||Q)$ is the Kullback–Leibler divergence between Q and P. The average minimax regret is defined in a similar manner, namely,

$$\widetilde{r}_n(\mathcal{S}) = \inf_{Q} \sup_{P \in \mathcal{S}} \left(\sum_{x^n} P(x^n) \log \frac{\sup_{P \in \mathcal{S}} P(x^n)}{Q(x^n)} \right).$$

Clearly, the continuous approximation of the redundancy and regrets are within one bit from the corresponding redundancy and regrets; that is,

$$\bar{R}_n(\mathcal{S}) \leq \widetilde{R}_n(\mathcal{S}) \leq \bar{R}_n(\mathcal{S}) + 1, \tag{9.8}$$

$$\bar{r}_n(\mathcal{S}) \leq \widetilde{r}_n(\mathcal{S}) \leq \bar{r}_n(\mathcal{S}) + 1. \tag{9.9}$$

Indeed, it suffices to consider the Shannon code for justifying these bounds.

9.2 Operational Expressions for Minimax Redundancy

In this section, we derive some useful representation for the average minimax $\bar{R}_n$ and the maximal minimax R_n^*.

9.2.1 Average Minimax Redundancy

The average minimax redundancy is almost entirely considered within the framework of the Bayes rule and parameterized family of distributions. Let now $\mathcal{S} = \{P^\theta\}_{\theta \in \Theta}$ be a parametrization for the source probability distributions. The average minimax problem is then reformulated as

$$\widetilde{R}_n(\Theta) = \inf_Q \sup_{\theta \in \Theta} D_n(P^\theta \| Q),$$

where we restrict P^θ to sequences of length n. Note that we use the (simplified) notation $\widetilde{R}_n(\Theta)$ instead of $\widetilde{R}_n(\{P^\theta\}_{\theta \in \Theta})$.

In the Bayesian framework, one assumes also a probability distribution w on Θ so that the parameter $\theta \in \Theta$ is generated according to this probability distribution. For fixed n, the mixture $M_n^w(x^n)$ is defined as

$$M_n^w(x^n) = \int_\Theta P^\theta(x^n) w(d\theta)$$

and is again a probability distribution on sequences of length n. Observe now

$$
\begin{aligned}
\inf_Q \mathbf{E}_w[D_n(P^\theta \| Q)] &= \inf_Q \int_\Theta D_n(P^\theta \| Q) dw(\theta) \\
&= \inf_Q \left(\sum_{x^n} M_n^w(x^n) \log \frac{1}{Q(x^n)} + \int_\Theta \sum_{x^n} P^\theta \log P^\theta dw(\theta) \right) \\
&\overset{(A)}{=} \sum_{x^n} M_n^w(x^n) \log \frac{1}{M_n^w(x^n)} + \int_\Theta \sum_{x^n} P^\theta \log P^\theta dw(\theta) \\
&= \int D_n(P^\theta \| M_n^w) dw(\theta) \\
&= I(\Theta; X^n),
\end{aligned}
$$

where $\mathbf{E}_w$ denotes the expectation with respect to w. The equality (A) follows from the fact

$$\min_Q \sum_i P_i \log \frac{1}{Q_i} = \sum_i P_i \log \frac{1}{P_i}, \tag{9.10}$$

and $I(\Theta, X^n)$ is the mutual information between the parameter space and the source output.

Lemma 9.1 *The following holds:*

$$\widetilde{R}_n(\Theta) = \inf_Q \sup_{\theta \in \Theta} D_n(P^\theta \| Q) = \sup_w \inf_Q \mathbf{E}_w[D_n(P^\theta \| Q)] \tag{9.11}$$

$$= \sup_w \int D(P^\theta \| M_n^w) dw(\theta) := C(\Theta, X^n), \tag{9.12}$$

that is, the continuous approximation of the average minimax redundancy is equal to the channel capacity $C(\Theta, X)$ between the parameter space and source output.

Proof As pointed out by Gallager (1968) (see Exercise 9.2) the minimax theorem of game theory entitles us to conclude (9.12) by replacing the minimax by maxmin. ∎

In view of this, the average minimax redundancy problem is reduced to finding the optimal prior distribution $w^*(\theta)$ for the Bayes rule. This was accomplished by Bernardo (1979) who proved that asymptotically $w^*(\theta)$ can be replaced by

$$\widetilde{w}^*(\theta) = \frac{\sqrt{\det \mathbf{I}(\theta)}}{\int \sqrt{\det \mathbf{I}(x)} dx}, \tag{9.13}$$

where $\mathbf{I}(\theta)$ is the Fisher information matrix

$$\mathbf{I}(\theta) = \left\{ -\mathbf{E} \left[\frac{\partial^2 w(\theta)}{\partial \theta_i \theta_j} \right] \right\}_{\theta_i, \theta_j \in \Theta}.$$

For example, for the binary memoryless source with one parameter θ,

$$I(\theta) = \frac{1}{\theta(1-\theta)}, \qquad \widetilde{w}^*(\theta) = \frac{1}{\pi \sqrt{\theta(1-\theta)}}. \tag{9.14}$$

This distribution, called also Jeffrey's prior, is a special case of the Dirichlet distribution that will find more applications in this book. To recall, for nonnegative integer $m > 1$, the Dirichlet's distribution is defined by

$$\mathrm{Dir}(x_1, \ldots, x_m; \alpha_1, \ldots, \alpha_m) = \frac{1}{B(\alpha_1, \ldots, \alpha_m)} \prod_{i=1}^{m} x_i^{\alpha_i - 1}, \tag{9.15}$$

where $\sum_{i=1}^{m} x_i = 1$ and

$$B(\alpha_1, \ldots, \alpha_m) = \frac{\Gamma(\alpha_1) \cdots \Gamma(\alpha_m)}{\Gamma(\alpha_1 + \cdots \alpha_m)}$$

is the beta function. For notational convenience, we write $\alpha = (\alpha_1, \ldots \alpha_m)$ and $\mathbf{x} = (x_1, \ldots x_m)$ with $\sum_{i=1}^{m} x_i = 1$. Finally, for

$$\mathcal{S} \subseteq \Theta = \{(\theta_1, \ldots, \theta_m) : \sum_{i=1}^{m} \theta_i = 1\},$$

we set

$$\mathrm{Dir}(\mathcal{S}; \alpha) = \frac{1}{B(\alpha)} \int_{\mathcal{S}} \mathbf{x}^{\alpha - 1} \, d\mathbf{x}.$$

Notice that $\mathrm{Dir}(\Theta, \alpha) = 1$.

We finally address the optimality of $\widetilde{w}^*$ defined in (9.13). As discussed, this may be only *asymptotic* optimality with respect to the leading term. It was Clarke and Barron (1990) who showed that under proper regularity conditions, such as the finiteness of the determinant of Fisher information and $\mathcal{S}$ being a compact subset of the interior of $\Theta = \{(p_0, \ldots, p_m) : p_j \geq 0, p_0 + \cdots + p_{m-1} = 1\}$, the following is true:

$$\lim_{n \to \infty} \left(\int_{\mathcal{S}} D(P^\theta \| M_n^{w^*}) dw^*(\theta) - \frac{m-1}{2} \log \frac{n}{2\pi e} \right)$$

$$= \lim_{n \to \infty} \left(\int_{\mathcal{S}} D(P^\theta \| M_n^{\widetilde{w}^*}) d\widetilde{w}^*(\theta) - \frac{m-1}{2} \log \frac{n}{2\pi e} \right) = \log \int_{\mathcal{S}} \sqrt{\det I(\theta)} \, d\theta.$$

This discussion leads us to the following notation of the *asymptotic average minimax redundancy*:

$$\widetilde{R}_n^{\text{asymp}}(\mathcal{S}) = \int_{\mathcal{S}} D(P^\theta \| M_n^{\widetilde{w}^*}) d\widetilde{w}^*(\theta).$$

We will use it in the next chapter to provide precise asymptotics for $\widetilde{R}_n^{\text{asymp}}(\mathcal{S})$, including the case when $\mathcal{S} \subset \Theta$, discussed in Section 10.3.1 (see also Section 10.1.3).

9.2.2 Maximal Minimax

We now present a new characterization of the maximal minimax. Let us define

$$D_n = D_n(\mathcal{S}) := \sum_{x^n} \sup_{P \in \mathcal{S}} P(x^n)$$

and

$$Q^*(x^n) := \frac{\sup_{P \in \mathcal{S}} P(x^n)}{D_n}. \tag{9.16}$$

The distribution Q^* is called the *maximum likelihood distribution*, while $\log D_n(\mathcal{S})$ is also know, as the *complexity* of $\mathcal{S}$.

We start with a simple result that decomposes the maximal minimax redundancy into two terms: the first one depends only on the underlying class of processes while the second one involves coding.

Lemma 9.2 *Let $\mathcal{S}$ be a set of probability distributions P on $\mathcal{A}^n$ and let Q^* be the maximum likelihood distribution defined by (9.16). Then*

$$R_n^*(\mathcal{S}) = R_n^*(Q^*) + \widetilde{R}_n^*(\mathcal{S}) = R_n^*(Q^*) + \log D_n(\mathcal{S}), \tag{9.17}$$

$$\widetilde{R}_n^*(\mathcal{S}) = \log D_n(\mathcal{S}), \tag{9.18}$$

where

$$R_n^*(Q^*) = \min_{C_n \in \mathcal{C}} \max_{x^n} [L(C_n, x^n) + \log Q^*(x^n)]$$

is the worst-case redundancy of a single source $\mathcal{S} = \{Q^*\}$.

Proof By definition and noting that max and sup commute, we have

$$R_n^*(\mathcal{S}) = \min_{C_n \in \mathcal{C}} \sup_{P \in \mathcal{S}} \max_{x^n} (L(C_n, x^n) + \log P(x^n))$$

$$= \min_{C_n \in \mathcal{C}} \max_{x^n} \left(L(C_n, x^n) + \sup_{P \in \mathcal{S}} \log P(x^n) \right)$$

$$= \min_{C_n \in \mathcal{C}} \max_{x^n} (L(C_n, x^n) + \log Q^*(x^n) + \log D_n)$$

$$= R_n^*(Q^*) + \log D_n,$$

which proves the lemma. If we assume that $L(C_n, x^n) = -\log Q(x^n)$ and set $Q^* = Q$, we establish (9.18). ∎

First, we observe that $R_n^*(Q^*)$ is the maximal redundancy for the known distribution Q^*. We studied this in Section 2.3 of Chapter 2 where we found in Theorem 2.13 a precise expression for a given source P. However, the maximal likelihood distribution Q^* needs extra care. We will come back to it in Chapter 10.

In passing, we observe an interesting property of the continuous part $\widetilde{R}_n^*(\mathcal{S})$ of the maximal minimax redundancy, namely that it is a *nondecreasing* function of n. In this context, we assume that $\mathcal{S}$ is a set of probability measures on infinite sequences. Of course, this naturally induces probability distributions for finite sequences by considering them as prefixes of infinite ones. Indeed, we have

$$
\widetilde{R}_n^*(\mathcal{S}) = \log \left(\sum_{x^n} \sup_{P \in \mathcal{S}} P(x^n) \right)
$$

$$
= \log \left(\sum_{x^n} \sup_{P \in \mathcal{S}} \sum_{z \in \mathcal{A}} \widetilde{P}(x^n z) \right)
$$

$$
\leq \log \left(\sum_{x^{n+1}} \sup_{\widetilde{P} \in \mathcal{S}} \widetilde{P}(x^{n+1}) \right) = \widetilde{R}_{n+1}^*(\mathcal{S});
$$

that is, $\widetilde{R}_n^*(\mathcal{S}) \leq \widetilde{R}_{n+1}^*(\mathcal{S})$.

9.3 Average and Maximal Minimax Relationships

In this section, we aim at finding relationships between maximal and average redundancy and regrets. For example, we would like to know under what conditions the following may hold:

$$
R_n^*(\mathcal{S}) \sim \overline{R}_n(\mathcal{S}) \sim \overline{r}_n(\mathcal{S}) \sim \underline{r}_n(\mathcal{S}). \tag{9.19}
$$

In the first attempt to answer this question, we restrict the class of sources to those for which the maximum likelihood distribution Q^* belongs to a convex hull of $\mathcal{S}$, where the convex hull of $\mathcal{S}$ is just the set of all finite convex combinations of elements of $\mathcal{S}$. (We assume no topology on the set of probability measures.) We formulate it as the following postulate.

(H) The maximum likelihood distribution Q^* can be represented as a linear combination of distributions from $\mathcal{S}$; that is, for $P_1, P_2, \ldots, P_N \in \mathcal{S}$,

$$
Q^* = \sum_{i=1}^{N} \alpha_i P_i, \tag{9.20}
$$

where $\alpha_i \geq 0$ and $\sum_{i=1}^{N} \alpha_i = 1$. In other words, Q^* can be represented as a mixture of the distributions of $\mathcal{S}$.

However, hypothesis (H) might be difficult, if possible at all, to verify. Therefore, we often relax and adopt another weaker hypothesis:

(H1) There exists a probability distribution $\widetilde{Q}$ in the convex hull of $\mathcal{S}$ such that

$$\max_{x^n} \left| \log \frac{Q^*(x^n)}{\widetilde{Q}(x^n)} \right| \leq C, \tag{9.21}$$

where C is a constant.

In Section 9.3.1, we prove the following crucial lemma that will allow us to establish some relationships between the maximal redundancy and the average redundancy and regrets.

Lemma 9.3 *Let $\mathcal{S}$ be a subset of probability distributions P on $\mathcal{A}^n$. Then for all probability distributions $\widetilde{Q}$ contained in the convex hull of $\mathcal{S}$ we have*

$$\inf_{Q} \sup_{P \in \mathcal{S}} \left(\sum_{x \in X} P(x) \log \frac{\widetilde{Q}(x)}{Q(x)} \right) = 0. \tag{9.22}$$

Now we are equipped with all the necessary tools to state and prove our first main result of this section. We recall that $D_n(\mathcal{S}) = \sum_{x^n} \sup_{P \in \mathcal{S}} P(x^n)$ and $\widetilde{R}_n^*(\mathcal{S}) = \log D_n(\mathcal{S})$.

Theorem 9.4 (i) [UPPER BOUND] *For any set of probability distributions $\mathcal{S}$ on $\mathcal{A}^n$, we have*

$$\widetilde{R}_n(\mathcal{S}) \leq \widetilde{R}_n^*(\mathcal{S}) - \inf_{P \in \mathcal{S}} \left(\sum_{x^n} P(x^n) \log \frac{\sup_{P \in \mathcal{S}} P(x^n)}{P(x^n)} \right). \tag{9.23}$$

(ii) [LOWER BOUND] *If hypothesis (H) holds, that is, if Q^* is contained in the convex hull of $\mathcal{S}$, then*

$$\widetilde{R}_n(\mathcal{S}) \geq \widetilde{R}_n^*(\mathcal{S}) - \sup_{P \in \mathcal{S}} \left(\sum_{x^n} P(x^n) \log \frac{\sup_{P \in \mathcal{S}} P(x^n)}{P(x^n)} \right). \tag{9.24}$$

If (H1) holds, then one finds the following weaker lower bound

$$\widetilde{R}_n(\mathcal{S}) \geq \widetilde{R}_n^*(\mathcal{S}) - C - \sup_{P \in \mathcal{S}} \left(\sum_{x^n} P(x^n) \log \frac{\sup_{P \in \mathcal{S}} P(x^n)}{P(x^n)} \right). \tag{9.25}$$

Proof For part (i), we just observe trivially

$$\widetilde{R}_n(\mathcal{S}) = \inf_{Q} \sup_{P \in \mathcal{S}} D(P||Q) \leq \sup_{P \in \mathcal{S}} D(P||Q^*)$$

$$= \log D_n(\mathcal{S}) - \inf_{P \in \mathcal{S}} \left(\sum_{x^n} P(x^n) \log \frac{\sup_{P \in \mathcal{S}} P(x^n)}{P(x^n)} \right).$$

For the lower bound (ii), we need to use Lemma 9.3. We have

$$\widetilde{R}_n(\mathcal{S}) = \inf_Q \sup_{P \in \mathcal{S}} D(P||Q)$$

$$= \log D_n(\mathcal{S}) + \inf_Q \sup_{P \in \mathcal{S}} \left(\sum_{x^n} P(x^n) \log \frac{Q^*(x^n)}{Q(x^n)} \right.$$

$$\left. - \sum_{x^n} P(x^n) \log \frac{\sup\limits_{P \in \mathcal{S}} P(x^n)}{P(x^n)} \right)$$

$$\geq \log D_n(\mathcal{S}) - \sup_{P \in \mathcal{S}} \left(\sum_{x^n} P(x^n) \log \frac{\sup\limits_{P \in \mathcal{S}} P(x^n)}{P(x^n)} \right),$$

provided (H) holds.

The proof of (9.25) (under condition (H1)) is a simple extension of the proof of (9.24). In fact, the maximal deviation can be bounded by

$$\sup_{P \in \mathcal{S}} \left| \sum_{x^n} P(x^n) \log \frac{Q^*(x^n)}{\widetilde{Q}(x^n)} \right| \leq C$$

and this completes the proof. ∎

In view of this, we notice that (9.19) holds if

$$c_n(\mathcal{S}) := \sup_{P \in \mathcal{S}} \left(\sum_{x^n} P(x^n) \log \frac{\sup\limits_{P \in \mathcal{S}} P(x^n)}{P(x^n)} \right) = o(\log D_n(\mathcal{S})). \tag{9.26}$$

We will verify these conditions for memoryless sources in Section 9.3.2; they also hold for Markovian sources (see Chapter 11).

Interestingly, we have a stronger result for the minimax regret $\bar{r}(\mathcal{S})$ that basically shows that the conjecture is true under postulate (H1).

Theorem 9.5 *Let hypothesis (H) hold. Then*

$$\widetilde{r}_n(\mathcal{S}) = \log D_n(\mathcal{S}) = \widetilde{R}_n^*(\mathcal{S}). \tag{9.27}$$

Under (H1) we have

$$\widetilde{R}_n^*(\mathcal{S}) - C \leq \widetilde{r}_n(\mathcal{S}) \leq \widetilde{R}_n^*(\mathcal{S}),$$

where C is the constant in (9.21).

Proof We start with an upper bound that actually holds without assumption (H). We have for any $\mathcal{S}$,

$$\widetilde{r}_n(\mathcal{S}) = \log D_n(\mathcal{S}) + \inf_Q \sup_{P \in \mathcal{S}} \left(\sum_{x^n} P(x^n) \log \frac{Q^*(x^n)}{Q(x^n)} \right)$$

$$\leq \log D_n(\mathcal{S}) + \sup_{P \in \mathcal{S}} \left(\sum_{x^n} P(x^n) \log \frac{Q^*(x^n)}{Q^*(x^n)} \right)$$

$$= \log D_n(\mathcal{S}).$$

For the lower bound, we need to use Lemma 9.3. We proceed as follows:

$$\tilde{r}_n(\mathcal{S}) = \log D_n(\mathcal{S}) + \inf_Q \sup_{P \in \mathcal{S}} \left(\sum_{x^n} P(x^n) \log \frac{Q^*(x^n)}{Q(x^n)} \right).$$

If (H) holds, then the second term is zero. Otherwise, under (H1), we can bound it by a constant C. This proves the theorem. ∎

Finally, for the maxmin regret $\underline{r}_n(\mathcal{S})$, we can also establish a precise result.

Theorem 9.6 *Let Q^* be defined in (9.16) and let $\overline{R}_n^H(P)$ be the average minimax redundancy of the Huffman code for the distribution P. Then*

$$\underline{r}_n(\mathcal{S}) = \log D_n(\mathcal{S}) + \sup_{P \in \mathcal{S}}(\overline{R}_n^H(P) - D(P||Q^*))$$

$$= \log D_n(\mathcal{S}) - \inf_{P \in \mathcal{S}} D(P||Q^*) + O(1)$$

$$= \sup_{P \in \mathcal{S}} \left(\sum_{x^n} P(x^n) \log \frac{\sup_{P \in \mathcal{S}} P(x^n)}{P(x^n)} \right) + O(1).$$

If $Q^* \in \mathcal{S}$, then $\underline{r}_n(\mathcal{S}) = \log D_n(\mathcal{S}) + O(1) = R_n^*(\mathcal{S}) + O(1)$.

Proof The calculations are straightforward:

$$\underline{r}_n(\mathcal{S}) = \sup_{P \in \mathcal{S}} \min_{C_n \in \mathcal{C}} \sum_{x^n} P(x^n)[L(C_n, x^n) + \log \sup_{P \in \mathcal{S}} P(x^n)]$$

$$= \log D_n(\mathcal{S}) + \sup_{P \in \mathcal{S}} \min_{C_n} \sum_{x^n} P(x^n)[L(C_n, x^n) + \log Q^*(x^n)]$$

$$= \log D_n(\mathcal{S})$$
$$\quad + \sup_{P \in \mathcal{S}} \min_{C_n} \sum_{x^n} P(x^n)[L(C_n, x^n) + \log Q^*(x^n) + \log P(x^n) - \log P(x^n)]$$

$$= \log \left(\sum_{x^n \in \mathcal{A}^n} \sup_{P \in \mathcal{S}} P(x^n) \right) + \sup_{P \in \mathcal{S}} \min_{C_n} \sum_{x^n} P(x^n)[L(C_n, x^n) + \log P(x^n)]$$
$$\quad - \sum_{x^n} P(x^n) \log \left(\frac{P(x^n)}{Q^*(x^n)} \right)$$

$$= \log D_n(\mathcal{S}) + \sup_{P \in \mathcal{S}}(\overline{R}_n^H(P) - D(P||Q^*))$$

$$= \log D_n(\mathcal{S}) - \inf_{P \in \mathcal{S}} D(P||Q^*) + O(1)$$

$$= \sup_{P \in \mathcal{S}} \left(\sum_{x^n} P(x^n) \log \frac{\sup_{P \in \mathcal{S}} P(x^n)}{P(x^n)} \right) + O(1),$$

which proves the desired result. ∎

In view of these results, we just proved that, under (H1),

$$\tilde{r}_n(\mathcal{S}) = R_n^*(\mathcal{S}) + O(1).$$

Furthermore, we have

$$\underline{r}_n(\mathcal{S}) = c_n(\mathcal{S}) \geq R_n^*(\mathcal{S}) - \overline{R}_n(\mathcal{S}) + O(1).$$

If $Q^* \in \mathcal{S}$, then $\underline{r}_n(\mathcal{S}) = R_n^*(\mathcal{S}) + O(1)$.

9.3.1 Proof of Lemma 9.3

Suppose that $P_1, \ldots, P_N$ are probability distributions on a finite set and $\widetilde{Q}$ is a convex combination of $P_1, \ldots, P_N$; that is,

$$\widetilde{Q} = \sum_{i=1}^N \alpha_i P_i$$

with $\alpha_i \geq 0$ and $\sum_{i=1}^N \alpha_i = 1$. We first show that for every $Q \neq \widetilde{Q}$,

$$\sum_{i=1}^N \alpha_i D(P_i \| \widetilde{Q}) \leq \sum_{i=1}^N \alpha_i D(P_i \| Q). \tag{9.28}$$

By using the definition of $D(P\|Q)$, it immediately follows that

$$\sum_{i=1}^N D(P_i \| Q) = \sum_{i=1}^N D(P_i \| \widetilde{Q}) + N D(\widetilde{Q} \| Q) > \sum_{i=1}^N D(P_i \| \widetilde{Q}).$$

Hence, (9.28) holds for α_i of the form $\alpha_i = 1/N$.

It is clear that the case of rational numbers $\alpha_i = M_i/M$ (with a common denominator M) can be reduced to this case. We just have to set $\beta_j = 1/M$ for $1 \leq M$ and $Q_j = P_i$ for $M_1 + \cdots + M_{i-1} + 1 \leq j \leq M_1 + \cdots + M_i$. Then

$$\sum_{i=1}^N \alpha_i D(P_i \| Q) = \sum_{j=1}^M \beta_j D(Q_j \| Q),$$

and the lemma is proved since α_i real can be viewed as a limit of the rational case.

We now prove (9.22). Obviously we have

$$\inf_Q \sup_{P \in \mathcal{S}} \left(\sum_{x \in X} P(x) \log \frac{\widetilde{Q}(x)}{Q(x)} \right) \leq 0.$$

(We only have to choose $Q = \widetilde{Q}$.)

The converse inequality can be proved indirectly. Let $\widetilde{Q}$ be contained in the convex hull of $\mathcal{S}$; that is, there are finitely many $P_1, \ldots, P_N \in \mathcal{S}$ such that $\widetilde{Q}$ is a convex combination of the form

$$\widetilde{Q} = \sum_{i=1}^N \alpha_i P_i.$$

Suppose that there exists Q such that for all P,

$$\sum_{x \in X} P(x) \log \frac{\widetilde{Q}(x)}{Q(x)} = D(P\|Q) - D(P\|\widetilde{Q}) < 0.$$

Then we also have

$$\sum_{i=1}^{N} \alpha_i D(P_i || Q) < \sum_{i=1}^{N} \alpha_i D(P_i || \tilde{Q}),$$

which is, of course, a contradiction to (9.28). Thus

$$\inf_{Q} \sup_{P \in \mathcal{S}} \left(\sum_{x \in X} P(x) \log \frac{\tilde{Q}(x)}{Q(x)} \right) \geq 0,$$

and this proves the lemma.   ∎

9.3.2 Hypothesis (H1) for Memoryless Sources

In what follows, we show that the boundedness of $c_n(\mathcal{S})$ as well as the condition (H1) are satisfied for memoryless sources. For more on memoryless sources, see Chapter 10.

Lemma 9.7 *Suppose that $m \geq 2$. Then we have uniformly for all $p_0, \ldots, p_{m-1} \geq 0$ with $p_0 + \cdots + p_{m-1} = 1$ and all $n \geq 1$,*

$$\sum_{k_0 + \cdots + k_{m-1} = n} \binom{n}{k_0 \cdots k_{m-1}} p_0^{k_0} \cdots p_{m-1}^{k_{m-1}} \ln \frac{\left(\frac{k_0}{n}\right)^{k_0} \cdots \left(\frac{k_{m-1}}{n}\right)^{k_{m-1}}}{p_0^{k_0} \cdots p_{m-1}^{k_{m-1}}} \leq m - 1.$$

Proof For notational convenience, we only consider the binary case $m = 2$, where we set $p_0 = p$ and $p_1 = 1 - p$. (The general case uses precisely the same ideas.)

By using the inequality $\ln x \leq x - 1$, we get

$$\ln \frac{\left(\frac{k}{n}\right)^k \left(1 - \frac{k}{n}\right)^{n-k}}{p^k (1-p)^{n-k}} = k \ln \frac{k/n}{p} + (n - k) \ln \frac{1 - k/n}{1 - p}$$

$$\leq k \left(\frac{k/n}{p} - 1 \right) + (n - k) \left(\frac{1 - k/n}{1 - p} - 1 \right)$$

$$= n \left(\frac{(k/n)^2}{p} + \frac{(1 - k/n)^2}{1 - p} - 1 \right).$$

Since

$$n \sum_{k=0}^{n} \binom{n}{k} p^k (1-p)^{n-k} \frac{(k/n)^2}{p} = np + (1 - p),$$

we find

$$n \sum_{k=0}^{n} \binom{n}{k} p^k (1-p)^{n-k} \left(\frac{(k/n)^2}{p} + \frac{(1 - k/n)^2}{1 - p} - 1 \right)$$

$$= np + 1 - p + n(1 - p) + p - n = 1,$$

which completes the proof of the lemma.   ∎

In view of this, we conclude that for memoryless sources $\mathcal{M}_0$,

$$c_n(\mathcal{M}_0) = \sup_{P \in \mathcal{S}} \left(\sum_{x_1^n} P(x_1^n) \log \frac{\sup_{P \in CM_0} P(x_1^n)}{P(x_1^n)} \right) = O(1).$$

In passing, we observe that we can be much more precise if we consider just p with $a \leq p \leq b$, where $0 < a < b < 1$. Here we have uniformly for $a \leq p \leq b$ as $n \to \infty$:

$$\sum_{k=0}^n \binom{n}{k} p^k (1-p)^{n-k} \log \frac{\left(\frac{k}{n}\right)^k \left(1 - \frac{k}{n}\right)^{n-k}}{p^k (1-p)^k} = \frac{1}{2 \ln 2} + O\left(n^{-1/2}\right).$$

Note that this relation is not true if $a = 0$ or $b = 1$.

Next we consider condition (H1), which states that Q^* belongs "almost" to the convex hull of $\mathcal{S}$. For technical reasons, we only consider the case $m = 2$.

Lemma 9.8 *Suppose that $m \geq 2$ and let $\mathcal{S}$ denote the set of all memoryless sources with parameters $p_0, \ldots, p_{m-1} \geq 0$ with $p_0 + \cdots + p_{m-1} = 1$. Let Q^* be the maximum likelihood distribution corresponding to $\mathcal{S}$, that is,*

$$Q^*(x^n) = \frac{k_0^{k_0} \cdots k_{m-1}^{k_{m-1}}}{\sum_{\ell_0 + \cdots + \ell_{k_{m-1}} = n} \ell_0^{\ell_0} \cdots \ell_{m-1}^{\ell_{m-1}}},$$

where $k_j = |\{1 \leq k \leq n \colon x_i = j\}|, j \in \{0, 1, \ldots, m - 1\}$. Then there exists a convex combination $\widetilde{Q}$ of $\mathcal{S}$ such that

$$\max_{x_n} \left| \log \frac{Q^*(x^n)}{\widetilde{Q}(x^n)} \right| = O(1)$$

as $n \to \infty$.

Proof We just consider the binary case $m = 2$. The general case can be handled in the same way. Our goal is to show that there exist positive numbers β_l such that the sums

$$s_k := \sum_{l=0}^n \beta_l l^k (n - l)^{n-k}$$

satisfy

$$\max_{0 \leq k \leq n} \left| \log \frac{s_k}{k^k (n - k)^{n-k}} \right| = O(1). \tag{9.29}$$

Then we just have to define $\widetilde{Q}$ by normalizing s_k.

We now show that we can use

$$\beta_k := \left(\sum_{l=0}^n \left(\frac{l}{k}\right)^k \left(\frac{n-l}{n-k}\right)^{n-k} \right)^{-1}.$$

Observe that the function $l \to l^k (n - l)^{n-k}$ has its maximum at $l = k$ and a local expansion of the form $(k + \delta)^k (n - k - \delta)^{n-k} \sim k^k (n - k)^{n-k} \exp\left(-\frac{n}{2k(n-k)} \delta^2\right)$. Thus, we obtain

$$\beta_k = \sqrt{\frac{n}{2\pi k(n - k)}} \left(1 + O\left(\frac{n}{k(n - k)}\right)\right)$$

and after some algebra

$$\frac{s_k}{k^k(n-k)^{n-k}} = \sum_{l=0}^{n} \beta_l \left(\frac{l}{k}\right)^k \left(\frac{n-l}{n-k}\right)^{n-k}$$

$$= 1 + \sum_{l=0}^{n} (\beta_l - \beta_k) \left(\frac{l}{k}\right)^k \left(\frac{n-l}{n-k}\right)^{n-k}$$

$$= 1 + O\left(\sqrt{\frac{n}{k(n-k)}}\right).$$

This proves (9.29).   ∎

In the binary case, it is also possible to cover the case $a \le p \le b$ with $0 < a < b < 1$. We have

$$\sup_{p \in [a,b]} p^k(1-p)^{n-k} = \begin{cases} a^k(1-a)^{n-k} & \text{for } 0 \le k < na, \\ \left(\frac{k}{n}\right)^k \left(1 - \frac{k}{n}\right)^{n-k} & \text{for } na \le k \le nb, \\ b^k(1-b)^{n-k} & \text{for } nb < k \le n. \end{cases}$$

Here we show that there exist positive numbers β_l ($an \le l \le bn$) such that the sum

$$s_k := \sum_{an \le l \le bn} \beta_l l^k (n-l)^{n-k}$$

satisfies

$$\max_{an \le k \le bn} \left| \log \frac{s_k}{k^k(n-k)^{n-k}} \right| = O(1), \tag{9.30}$$

$$\max_{0 \le k < an} \left| \log \frac{s_k}{(an)^k(n-an)^{n-k}} \right| = O(1), \tag{9.31}$$

and

$$\max_{bn < k \le n} \left| \log \frac{s_k}{(bn)^k(n-bn)^{n-k}} \right| = O(1). \tag{9.32}$$

We define β_k by

$$\beta_k := \begin{cases} 1/\sqrt{n} & \text{for } \lceil an \rceil < k < \lfloor bn \rfloor, \\ 1 & \text{for } k = \lceil an \rceil \text{ and } k = \lfloor bn \rfloor. \end{cases}$$

First, (9.31) follows from

$$(an)^k(n-an)^{n-k} \le (an)^k(n-an)^{n-k} + \frac{1}{\sqrt{n}} \sum_{l>an} l^k(n-l)^{n-k}$$

$$= O((an)^k(n-an)^{n-k})$$

if $k \le an$. Observe that (9.32) is just the symmetric case. Thus it remains to show (9.30).

It is clear that the mapping $l \mapsto \ell^k(n-\ell)^{n-k}$ attains its maximum for $\ell = k$. A local expansion (around this optimal value) shows that for every fixed $0 < a < b < 1$, there exist two positive constants c_1, c_2 such that

$$c_1 \sqrt{n} k^k(n-k)^{n-k} \le \sum_{an \le k \le bn} l^k(n-l)^{n-k} \le c_2 \sqrt{n} k^k(n-k)^{n-k}$$

for all k with $an \le k \le bn$. Thus, (9.30) follows.

9.4 Regret for Online Learning

Online learning is a popular sequential machine learning approach that has been used for such tasks as category classification, click-through-rate prediction, and risk assessment. In this case, a model consists of a set of features whose parameters represent their effect on some outcome. In an online setup, such a model is trained to learn these parameters from examples whose outcomes are already labeled. The training algorithm consumes data in rounds, where at each round t, it is allowed to predict the label based only on the labels it observed in the past $t - 1$ rounds. The prediction algorithm incurs some *loss* and updates its belief of the model parameters. The *regret* of an online algorithm is defined as the total (excess) loss it incurs over some value of a constant *comparator* that is used for prediction for the complete sequence.

More precisely, in machine learning, in particular, in online learning, the rounds of learning are denoted by t. We adopt it in this subsection. We denote by $\mathbf{x}_t = (x_{1,t}, \ldots, x_{d,t})$, a d-dimensional feature vector with $x_{i,t} \in \mathbb{R}$ for $i = 1, \ldots, d$ and $t = 1, \ldots, T$, and by $\mathbf{x}^T$ the $T \times d$ matrix with rows $\mathbf{x}_t$, $t = 1, \ldots, T$. The label binary vector is written as $y^T = (y_1, \ldots, y_T)$. We mostly consider linear predictors and by $\mathbf{w}_t = (w_{1,t}, \ldots, w_{d,t})$ we denote a d-dimensional vector of weights. Notice that T in this section plays the same role as n in previous sections.

We now phrase our learning problem in terms of a game between nature/environment and a learner. At each round, the learner obtains a d-dimensional input/feature vector $\mathbf{x}_t$ and makes prediction $\hat{y}_t$. Then nature reveals the true output/label y_t. Throughout we assume binary labels $y_t \in \mathcal{Y} = \{-1, 1\}$. We also assume that $\hat{y}_t \in \hat{\mathcal{Y}}$, which is usually some interval. Thus, at round t, the learner incurs some *loss*, which we denote as $\ell : \hat{\mathcal{Y}} \times \mathcal{Y} \mapsto \mathbb{R}$.

In online regret analysis, we are interested in comparing the accumulated loss of the learner with that of the best strategy within a predefined class of predictors (experts) denoted as $\mathcal{H}$. More precisely, $\mathcal{H}$ is a collection of prediction functions $h : \mathbb{R}^d \mapsto \hat{\mathcal{Y}}$, with input being $\mathbf{x}_t$ at each time t. Given a learner prediction function $g_t : \hat{\mathcal{Y}}^{t-1} \times \mathbb{R}^{td}$ and after T rounds with the realizations $(y_t, \mathbf{x}_t)_{t=1}^T$, the *pointwise regret* is defined as

$$R(g^T, y^T, \mathcal{H} | \mathbf{x}^T) = \sum_{t=1}^T \ell(\hat{y}_t, y_t) - \inf_{h \in \mathcal{H}} \sum_{t=1}^T \ell(h(\mathbf{x}_t), y_t),$$

where $\hat{y}_t = g_t(y^{t-1}, \mathbf{x}^t)$. The first and the second summations represent the accumulated loss of the learner and the best predictor in $\mathcal{H}$, respectively. There are two main perspectives on analyzing the regret, highlighted next.

Fixed Design This point of view studies the minimal regret for the worst realization of the label with the feature vector $\mathbf{x}^T$ known in advance. Let $g_t, t > 0$ be the strategy of the predictor. Then, the *fixed design minimax regret* is defined as

$$r_T^*(\mathcal{H} | \mathbf{x}^T) = \inf_{g^T} \sup_{y^T} R(g^T, y^T, \mathcal{H} | \mathbf{x}^T). \tag{9.33}$$

Further, the fixed design *maximal* minimax regret is given by

$$r_T^*(\mathcal{H}) = \sup_{\mathbf{x}^T} \inf_{g^T} \sup_{y^T} R(g^T, y^T, \mathcal{H} | \mathbf{x}^T). \tag{9.34}$$

Sequential Design In this point of view, the optimization on regret is performed at every time t without knowing $\mathbf{x}^T$ or y^T in advance. Then the *sequential minimax regret* is defined as

$$r_T^a(\mathcal{H}|\mathbf{x}^T) = \inf_{\hat{y}_1} \sup_{y_1} \cdots \inf_{\hat{y}_T} \sup_{y_T} R(\hat{y}^T, y^T, \mathcal{H}|\mathbf{x}^T). \tag{9.35}$$

Moreover, the *sequential maximal minimax regret* is

$$r_T^a(\mathcal{H}) = \sup_{\mathbf{x}_1} \inf_{\hat{y}_1} \sup_{y_1} \cdots \sup_{\mathbf{x}_T} \inf_{\hat{y}_T} \sup_{y_T} R(\hat{y}^T, y^T, \mathcal{H}|\mathbf{x}^T). \tag{9.36}$$

The sequential regret should be interpreted as follows. At round $t = 1$, the adversarial chooses a vector $\mathbf{x}_1 \in \mathbb{R}^d$ that gives the worst regret for the best choice of $\hat{y}_1$, for the worst choice of y_1, and for the interleaved worst, best, worst choices of $\mathbf{x}_t$, $h(\cdot)$ to compute $\hat{y}_t$ and y_t, respectively. Then, for the given $\mathbf{x}_1$, and subsequent worst/best choices, the player chooses $\hat{y}_1$, and the adversary chooses the worst choice of y_1 We ask the reader in Exercise 9.9 to compare $r_T(\mathbf{x}^T)$ to $r_T^a(\mathbf{x}^T)$ and see under what conditions they are equal.

More specifically, we consider a hypothesis (expert) class defined as follows:

$$\mathcal{H}_{p,\mathbf{w}} = \{h \colon \mathbb{R}^d \to \mathbb{R} : \ h(\mathbf{x}) = p(\langle \mathbf{w}, \mathbf{x} \rangle) : \mathbf{w}, \mathbf{x} \in \mathbb{R}^d\}, \tag{9.37}$$

where $\mathbf{w}$ is a d-dimensional weight vector with $\langle \mathbf{w}, \mathbf{x} \rangle$ being the scalar product, and $p(w)$ with $w = \langle \mathbf{w}, \mathbf{x} \rangle$ is a proper *probability function* defining the class $\mathcal{H}_p$. Often $p(w)$ is either the *logistic function* $p(w) = (1 + \exp(-w))^{-1}$ (see Section 10.5 in the next chapter) or the probit function $p(w) = \Phi(-w)$ where $\Phi(w)$ is distribution function of the normal distribution

In this book, we study only logarithmic loss as this is the most relevant for universal compression. For any $h \in \mathcal{H}$, we interpret $h(\mathbf{x}) = p(\langle \mathbf{w}, \mathbf{x} \rangle) \in [0, 1]$ as the conditional probability $P(-1|\mathbf{x}, \mathbf{w})$ assigned to $y = -1 \in \mathcal{Y}$; that is,

$$h(\mathbf{x}) = p(\langle \mathbf{w}, \mathbf{x} \rangle) = P(y = -1|\mathbf{x}, \mathbf{w}). \tag{9.38}$$

Similarly, we have $1 - p(\langle \mathbf{w}, \mathbf{x} \rangle) = P(y = 1|\mathbf{x}, \mathbf{w})$.

This should be seen in connection to the logarithmic loss function $\ell(p, y) = -\log|(1 + y)/2 - p|$ for $y \in \{-1, 1\}$ (often used in ML), which is related to $-\log P(y)$, also used to define the minimax regret in universal source coding. This is better justified in the following lemma.

Lemma 9.9 *Let $\ell \colon [0, 1] \times \{-1, 1\} \to \mathbb{R}^+$ be the logarithmic loss function defined as*

$$\ell(p, y) = -\log \left| \frac{1 + y}{2} - p \right|$$

for all $p \in [0, 1]$ and $y \in \{-1, 1\}$. Then,

$$\ell(p, y) = \begin{cases} -\log p & \text{for } y = -1, \\ -\log(1 - p) & \text{for } y = 1. \end{cases}$$

Proof If $y = -1$, then we have

$$\ell(p, -1) = -\log p,$$

whereas for $y = 1$,

$$\ell(p, 1) = -\log(1 - p)$$

as proposed. ∎

Hence, we can write

$$\sum_{t=1}^{T} \ell(h(\mathbf{x}_t), y_t) = -\sum_{t=1}^{T} \log P(y_t | \mathbf{x}_t, \mathbf{w}) = -\log P(y^T | \mathbf{x}^T, \mathbf{w}),$$

where $P(y^T | \mathbf{x}^T, \mathbf{w})$ abbreviates

$$P(y^T | \mathbf{x}^T, \mathbf{w}) = \prod_{t=1}^{T} P(y_t | \mathbf{x}_t, \mathbf{w}).$$

In a similar way, we interpret $\ell(\hat{y}_t, y_t) = \ell(g_t(y^{t-1}, \mathbf{x}^t), y)$ in terms of a conditional probability $Q(y_t | y^{t-1}, \mathbf{x}^t)$:

$$\ell(\hat{y}_t, y_t) = -\log Q(y_t | y^{t-1}, \mathbf{x}^t).$$

Hence,

$$\sum_{t=1}^{T} \ell(\hat{y}_t, y_t) = -\log Q(y^T | \mathbf{x}^T)$$

since

$$\prod_{t=1}^{T} Q(y_t | y^{t-1}, \mathbf{x}^t) = Q(y^T | \mathbf{x}^T),$$

where Q encodes the algorithmic learning distribution part up to T.

We should observe that the online learning can be viewed as a generalization of the universal source coding with side information $\mathbf{x}_t$. In this interpretation, $\mathcal{H}$ is represented by the class of sources $\mathcal{S}$ and Q can be viewed as a universal distribution.

In view of these definitions, we can now specifically rewrite the pointwise regret as

$$R_T(g^T, y^T | \mathbf{x}^T) = -\log Q(y^T | \mathbf{x}^T) + \sup_{\mathbf{w}} P(y^T | \mathbf{x}^T, \mathbf{w}) \tag{9.39}$$

and then the (maximal) minimax regret studied here is given by

$$r_T^*(\mathbf{x}^T) = \inf_{g^T} \max_{y^T} R_T(Q, y^T | \mathbf{x}^T) \tag{9.40}$$

$$= \inf_{Q} \max_{y^T} \left(-\log Q(y^T | \mathbf{x}^T) + \sup_{\mathbf{w}} P(y^T | \mathbf{x}^T, \mathbf{w}) \right).$$

As in universal source coding, in order to precisely study the minimax regret $r_T^*(\mathbf{x}^T)$ we need a more succinct and computationally manageable representation of it. This can be accomplished through a proper generalization of the Shtarkov sum:

$$D_T(\mathbf{x}^T) := \sum_{y^T} \sup_{\mathbf{w} \in \mathbb{R}^d} P(y^T | \mathbf{x}^T, \mathbf{w}). \tag{9.41}$$

If we define

$$P^*(y^T|\mathbf{x}^T) := \frac{\sup_{\mathbf{w}\in\mathbb{R}^d} P(y^T|\mathbf{x}^T, \mathbf{w})}{\sum_{v^T} \sup_{\mathbf{w}\in\mathbb{R}^d} P(v^T|\mathbf{x}^T, \mathbf{w})} \qquad (9.42)$$

as the *maximum-likelihood distribution*, then

$$\begin{aligned}
r_T^*(\mathbf{x}^T) &= \inf_Q \max_{y^T} \left(-\log Q(y^T|\mathbf{x}^T) + \sup_{\mathbf{w}} P(y^T|\mathbf{x}^T, \mathbf{w})) \right) \\
&= \inf_Q \max_{y^T} (-\log Q(y^T|\mathbf{x}^T) + \log P^*(y^T|\mathbf{x}^T)) \qquad (9.43) \\
&\quad + \log \sum_{y^T} \sup_{\mathbf{w}\in\mathbb{R}^d} P(y^T|\mathbf{x}^T, \mathbf{w}) \\
&= \log \sum_{y^T} \sup_{\mathbf{w}\in\mathbb{R}^d} P(y^T|\mathbf{x}^T, \mathbf{w}) = \log D_T(\mathbf{x}^T),
\end{aligned}$$

where the infimum is certainly attained for $Q(y^T, \mathbf{x}^T) = P^*(y^T|\mathbf{x}^T)$. Indeed, since Q and P^* are distributions, there is at least one y^T such that the first term in (9.43) is nonnegative if $Q \neq P^*$.

9.5 Exercises

9.1   Establish (9.10).

9.2   Justify that the minimax theorem of game theory can be used to prove (9.11).

9.3   Prove that the optimal prior (9.13) is asymptotically optimal (see Bernardo (1979)). Then for memoryless sources show that the Jeffrey's prior (9.14) are optimal.

9.4   Find an efficient algorithm to estimate the maximum likelihood distribution defined in (9.16).

9.5   ($\mathcal{MX}$) The (strongly) ψ-mixing source is defined as follows. Let $\mathcal{F}_m^n$ be a σ-field generated by X_m^n with $m \leq n$. The source is called *mixing*, if there exists a bounded function $\psi(g)$ such that for all $m, g \geq 1$ and any two events $A \in \mathcal{F}_1^m$ and $B \in \mathcal{F}_{m+g}^\infty$ the following holds:

$$(1 - \psi(g))P(A)P(B) \leq P(AB) \leq (1 + \psi(g))P(A)P(B). \qquad (9.44)$$

If, in addition, $\lim_{g\to\infty} \psi(g) = 0$, then the source is called *strongly* mixing.
In words, model $\mathcal{MX}$ postulates that the dependency between $X_{k=1}^m$ and $X_{k=m+g}^\infty$ is getting weaker and weaker as g becomes larger. The "quantity" of dependency is characterized by $\psi(g)$. We can write the ψ-mixing condition in an equivalent form as follows: there exist constants $c_1 \leq c_2$ such that

$$c_1 P(A)P(B) \leq P(AB) \leq c_2 P(A)P(B) \qquad (9.45)$$

for all $m, g \geq 1$. In some derivations, we shall require that $c_1 > 0$ which will impose further restrictions on the process. For mixing sources, determine whether postulates (H) and/or (H1) hold. Furthermore, estimate $c_n(\mathcal{MX})$ defined in (9.26).

9.6 Using the fact that $\Gamma(x+1) = x\Gamma(x)$, recover the well-known smoothed add-1/2 estimator also know as the Krichevsky–Trofimov estimator (see Krichevsky and Trofimov (1981)):

$$Q\left(y_t | y^{t-1}\right) = \frac{n_{t-1}\left(y_t\right) + 0.5}{t},$$

where $n_{t-1}\left(y_t\right)$ denotes the count of past occurrences of the label y_t in the $t-1$ initial labels.

9.7 Assume that $X = (X_1, \ldots, X_m)$ is distributed as Dirichlet distribution $\mathrm{Dir}(\mathbf{x}; \alpha)$ with parameters $\alpha_1, \ldots, \alpha_m$. Prove that

$$\mathbf{E}[\log X_i] = \Psi(\alpha_i) - \Psi\left(\sum_k \alpha_k\right),$$

where Ψ is the Euler psi function.

9.8 Prove that if X is distributed according to $\mathrm{Dir}(\mathbf{x}, \alpha)$, then the entropy $H(X)$ becomes

$$H(X) = \log B(\alpha) + (\alpha_0 - m)\Psi(\alpha_0) = \sum_{i=1}^{m}(\alpha_i - 1)\Psi(\alpha_j)$$

where $\alpha_0 = \sum_i \alpha_i$.

9.9 Compare $r_T(\mathbf{x}^T)$ defined in (9.33) and $r^a(\mathbf{x}^T)$ defined in (9.35) and establish under what conditions

$$r_T(\mathbf{x}^T) = r^a(\mathbf{x}^T)$$

for all $\mathbf{x}^T$ (see Wu et al. (2022)).

9.10 Consider the following one-dimensional logistic function:

$$\ell(w) = (1 + \exp(-w))^{-1}.$$

Find a good approximation of this function via the cumulative function $\Phi(x)$ of the standard normal distribution.

9.11 Consider a one-dimensional $d = 1$ logistic regret as in Section 9.4 with $x_t = 1$ for all t. Prove that

$$r_T^* = \frac{1}{2}\log T - \frac{1}{2}\log(2) + O(1/\sqrt{T}).$$

Bibliographical Notes

Universal coding can be traced back to the seminal works of Gallager (1968), Davisson (1973), Davisson and Leon-Garcia (1980), Krichevsky and Trofimov (1981), Rissanen (1984a,1984b), and Shtarkov (1987). Rissanen (1996) pointed out that universal coding evolved into universal modeling and learning. We should also mention the work of Kieffer (1978, 1991), on unified approach to weak universal coding.

The last 20 years have seen a resurgence of interest in redundancy rates for lossless coding: Wyner and Ziv (1989), Weinberger et al. (1994), Louchard and Szpankowski (1995), Weinberger, Rissanen, and Feder (1995), Csiszar and Shields (1996), Savari (1997), Wyner

(1997), Xie and Barron (1997), Barron, Rissanen, and Yu (1998), Szpankowski (1998), Drmota and Szpankowski (2004), Jacquet and Szpankowski (2004), Atteson (1999), Xie and Barron (2000), and more Ornstein and Shields (1990), Shields (1993, 1996), Orlitsky and Santhanam (2004), Orlitsky, Santhanam, and Zhang (2004), Shamir (2006a, 2006b, 2013). We shall discuss some of these references in a more detailed way in the next chapters. Some of them deal with finite alphabets while others such as Orlitsky et al. (2004), Orlitsky and Santhanam (2004), and Shamir (2006b, 2006a, 2013) consider unbounded alphabets or alphabets with some extra properties such as monotonicity condition.

Regret for logistic regression has been recently studied in Kakade and Ng (2005), Hazan, Agarwal, and Kale (2007), Hazan (2008), McMahan and Streeter (2012), Hazan, Koren, and Levy (2014), Foster et al. (2018), Shamir (2020). The adversarial regret is discussed in Ben-David, Pál, and Shalev-Shwartz (2009), Rakhlin, Sridharan, and Tewari (2010), Rakhlin and Sridharan (2014, 2015). See also Wu et al. (2022). Machine learning problems and techniques are discussed in many books, e.g., Shalev-Shwartz and Ben-David (2014), Mohri, Rostamizadeh, and Talwalker (2018).

This chapter is mainly based on Drmota and Szpankowski (2004).

10

Redundancy of Universal Memoryless Sources

In this chapter, we assume that an unknown source from the class $\mathcal{S} = \mathcal{M}_0$ of memoryless sources generates a sequence x^n over the alphabet $\mathcal{A} = \{0, \ldots, m - 1\}$. In other words, the empirical probability of x^n can be written as

$$P(x^n) = P^{\theta}(x^n) = \prod_{i=0}^{m-1} \theta_i^{k_i}, \tag{10.1}$$

where k_i is the number of symbol $i \in \mathcal{A}$ occurring in x^n, and θ_i is the *unknown* probability of generating symbol i.[1] Throughout we assume that $\theta = (\theta_0, \ldots, \theta_{m-1}) \in \Theta$, where

$$\Theta = \{\theta : \theta_i \geq 0 \ (0 \leq i \leq m - 1), \ \theta_0 + \cdots + \theta_{m-1} = 1\}.$$

In this chapter, in Section 10.1 and 10.2 we discuss the maximal minimax redundancy R_n^*, and then in Section 10.3, the average minimax $\overline{R}_n$. In Section 10.1, we assume that the alphabet size m is finite, while in Section 10.2, we deal with alphabets where the size $m = m(n)$ may depend on n and is not necessarily bounded. For finite alphabets, in Section 10.1.3 we analyze the case when the unknown probabilities θ are restricted to a subset $\mathcal{S} \in \Theta$ (for example, in the binary case we could postulate that $0 < a \leq \theta_0 \leq b < 1$).

10.1 Maximal Minimax Redundancy for Finite Alphabets

We now assume that the alphabet size m is finite and fixed (and does not depend on n) and the unknown probabilities $0 \leq \theta_i \leq 1$ are not constrained.

In Lemma 9.2 of Chapter 9, we derived a useful characterization of the maximal minimax R_n^*, namely,

$$R_n^* = R_n^*(Q^*) + \widetilde{R}_n^* = R_n^*(Q^*) + \log D_n,$$

where

$$D_n := \sum_{x^n} \sup_{P \in \mathcal{M}_0} P(x^n),$$

and

$$R_n^*(Q^*) = \min_{C_n \in \mathcal{C}} \max_{x^n} \left[L(C_n, x^n) + \log Q^*(x^n) \right]$$

---

[1] Throughout this chapter, we use the notation θ_i not p_i for the probability of the symbol i.

is the redundancy of the generalized Shannon code for distribution Q^*. We discussed the generalized Shannon code redundancy for a fixed distribution P in Section 2.3 of Chapter 2. We will use the term *coding redundancy* for $R_n^*(Q^*)$.

In Section 10.1.1, we derive precise asymptotics for the coding redundancy $R_n^*(Q^*)$. Then in Section 10.1.2, we deal with the main asymptotic terms of the maximal minimax redundancy, namely $\widetilde{R}_n^* = \log D_n$, finishing with Section 10.1.3, deriving the maximal minimax redundancy when the unknown probabilities θ_i are constrained.

10.1.1 Coding Contribution: Asymptotics of $R_n^*(Q^*)$

We now deal with $R_n^*(Q^*)$. Clearly, it is bounded between 0 and 1, however, we would like to have a more precise estimate.

In Chapter 2, we discussed the maximal redundancy $R_n^*(P)$ for a given distribution P. In particular, we proved in Theorem 2.14 that, in the case of a binary memoryless source, we have

$$R_n^*(P) = -\frac{\ln \ln 2}{\ln 2} + o(1),$$

provided that $\log(\theta_0/(1 - \theta_0))$ is irrational. In the rational case, $R_n^*(P)$ fluctuates as shown in (2.80). By the way, for an m-ary alphabet, we can prove in a similar way that

$$R_n^*(P) = \frac{\ln \left(\frac{1}{m-1} \ln m\right)}{\ln m} + o(1)$$

in the irrationally related case.

Surprisingly enough, we can show that $R_n^*(Q^*)$ behaves similarly. For the sake of brevity, we only present the binary case.

Theorem 10.1 *Consider a binary alphabet and fix two numbers a, b with $0 \le a < b \le 1$. Let S denote the set of binary memoryless sources with $a \le \theta = \theta_0 \le b$. Then, as $n \to \infty$,*

$$R_n^*(Q^*) = -\frac{\ln \ln 2}{\ln 2} + O\left(\frac{\log n}{n^{1/9}}\right). \tag{10.2}$$

We prove this theorem in the rest part of this section. We first recall that

$$\sup_{\theta \in [a,b]} \theta^k (1-\theta)^{n-k} = \begin{cases} a^k (1-a)^{n-k} & \text{for } 0 \le k < na, \\ \left(\frac{k}{n}\right)^k \left(1 - \frac{k}{n}\right)^{n-k} & \text{for } na \le k \le nb, \\ b^k (1-b)^{n-k} & \text{for } nb < k \le n, \end{cases} \tag{10.3}$$

and

$$Q^*(x^n) = \frac{\sup_{\theta \in [a,b]} \theta^k (1-\theta)^{n-k}}{D_n},$$

where $D_n = \sum_{x^n} \sup_{\theta \in [a,b]} \theta^k (1-\theta)^{n-k}$.

Next, we need to compute $R_n^*(Q^*)$, as we did in Chapter 2 for a *given* distribution. There, we reduced the evaluation of the redundancy $R_n^*(Q^*)$ to a verification of the Kraft inequality that in our case becomes

$$\sum_{x_1^n} Q^*(x_1^n) f_{s_0}(\langle -\log Q^*(x_1^n) \rangle),$$

where $f_{s_0}(x) = 2^{-\langle s_0 - x \rangle + s_0}$ for some $0 \le s_0 < 1$. Thus, the problem is to evaluate the following sum:

$$\sum_{k=0}^{n} \binom{n}{k} \frac{\sup_{\theta \in [a,b]} \theta^k (1-\theta)^{n-k}}{D_n} f_{s_0}\left(-\log\left(\sup_{\theta \in [a,b]} \theta^k (1-\theta)^{n-k}\right) + \log D_n\right)$$

$$= \frac{1}{D_n} \sum_{k < an} \binom{n}{k} a^k (1-a)^{n-k} f_{s_0}(-\log(a^k(1-a)^{n-k}) + \log D_n)$$

$$+ \frac{1}{D_n} \sum_{an \le k \le bn} \binom{n}{k} \left(\frac{k}{n}\right)^k \left(1 - \frac{k}{n}\right)^{n-k} f_{s_0}\left(-\log\left(\left(\frac{k}{n}\right)^k \left(1 - \frac{k}{n}\right)^{n-k}\right) + \log D_n\right)$$

$$+ \frac{1}{D_n} \sum_{k > bn} \binom{n}{k} b^k (1-b)^{n-k} f_{s_0}(-\log(b^k(1-b)^{n-k}) + \log D_n)$$

$$= S_1 + S_2 + S_3.$$

Since

$$D_n \ge \sum_{an \le k \le bn} \binom{n}{k} \left(\frac{k}{n}\right)^k \left(1 - \frac{k}{n}\right)^{n-k}$$

$$\sim \sum_{an \le k \le bn} \sqrt{\frac{n}{2\pi k(n-k)}}$$

$$\sim \frac{\sqrt{n}}{\sqrt{2\pi}} \int_a^b \frac{dx}{\sqrt{x(1-x)}}$$

and $f_{s_0}(x) = O(1)$, we directly find

$$S_1 = O(n^{-1/2}) \quad \text{and} \quad S_3 = O(n^{-1/2}).$$

Thus, it remains to study S_2.

We prove the following lemma.

Lemma 10.2 *Suppose that $0 \le a < b \le 1$. Then for every Riemann integrable function $f : [0,1] \to \mathbb{R}$ of bounded variation $V_0^1(f)$ and for every sequence $x_{n,k}$, $an \le k \le bn$, of the form*

$$x_{n,k} = k \log k + (n-k) \log(n-k) + c_n,$$

where c_n is an arbitrary sequence, we have

$$\frac{1}{D_n} \sum_{an \le k \le bn} \binom{n}{k} \left(\frac{k}{n}\right)^k \left(1 - \frac{k}{n}\right)^{n-k} f(\langle x_{n,k}\rangle) = \int_0^1 f(x)\, dx + O\left(V_0^1(f) \frac{\log n}{n^{1/9}}\right). \quad (10.4)$$

Proof We first show that $x_{n,k}$ is Q^*-u.d. sequence modulo 1 as defined and discussed in Chapter 2 and Appendix E. In particular, we will apply the Koksma–Hlawka inequality (Theorem E.7) to derive the error term in (10.4). For this purpose, we just have to obtain an upper bound for the discrepancy (see Theorem E.4 of Appendix E for a precise definition):

$$D_n^{(Q^*)}(x_k) = O\left(\frac{\log n}{n^{1/9}}\right).$$ (10.5)

By the Erdős–Turán–Koksma inequality (Theorem E.6) the discrepancy can be estimated with the help of exponential sums:

$$\widetilde{S}(h) := \sum_{an \leq k \leq bn} a_{n,k} e^{2\pi i h x_{nk}},$$

where h is an integer and

$$a_{n,k} = \binom{n}{k}\left(\frac{k}{n}\right)^k \left(1 - \frac{k}{n}\right)^{n-k}.$$

We have (for every integer $H \geq 1$)

$$D_n^{(Q^*)}(x_k) \leq \frac{3}{2(H+1)} + \frac{3}{A_n}\sum_{h=1}^{H}\frac{1}{h}\left|\widetilde{S}(h)\right|,$$

where

$$A_n = \sum_{an \leq k \leq bn} a_{n,k} \sim \frac{\sqrt{n}}{\sqrt{2\pi}}\int_a^b \frac{dx}{\sqrt{x(1-x)}}.$$

First, we consider the following exponential sum:

$$S := \sum_{an \leq k \leq cn} e^{2\pi i(h(k \log k + (n-k)\log(n-k))},$$

where $c \in [a, b]$, and h is an arbitrary nonzero integer. By van der Corput's method (see (E.1) from Appendix E), we know that

$$S = O\left(\frac{|F'(cn) - F'(an)| + 1}{\sqrt{\lambda}}\right),$$

where $\lambda = \min_{an \leq y \leq cn} |F''(y)| > 0$ and

$$F(y) = h(y \log y + (n-y)\log(n-y)).$$

Since $|F'(y)| \ll h \log n$, and $|F''(y)| \gg h/n$ (uniformly for $an \leq y \leq cn$), we immediately find

$$S = O\left(\log n\sqrt{hn}\right)$$

and consequently

$$\sum_{an \leq k \leq cn} e^{2\pi i h x_{nk}} = O\left(\log n\sqrt{hn}\right).$$

Note that all these estimates are uniform for $c \in [a, b]$.

Next we consider the exponential sum $\widetilde{S}(h)$. By elementary calculations, we obtain (uniformly for $an \leq k \leq bn$), $a_{n,k} \ll \min(k, n-k)^{-1/2}$ and

$$|a_{n,k+1} - a_{n,k}| \ll \min(k, n-k)^{-3/2}.$$

Thus, if $a > 0$ and $b < 1$, we have $a_{n,k} \ll n^{-1/2}$ and $|a_{n,k+1} - a_{n,k}| \ll n^{-3/2}$. Consequently, by partial summation,

$$
|\widetilde{S}(h)| \leq a_{n,bn} \left| \sum_{an \leq k \leq bn} e^{2\pi i h x_{n,k}} \right|
$$

$$
+ \sum_{an \leq k < bn} |a_{n,k+1} - a_{n,k}| \left| \sum_{an \leq \ell \leq k} e^{2\pi i h x_{n,\ell}} \right|
$$

$$
= O\left(n^{-1/2} \log n \sqrt{hn} + nn^{-3/2} \log n \sqrt{hn} \right)
$$

$$
= O\left(\sqrt{h} \log n \right).
$$

Note that the *shifting* sequence c_n does not change the absolute value of the exponential sums $\widetilde{S}(h)$.

Next suppose that $a = 0$ and $b < 1$. Set $\varepsilon = (h/n)^{1/4}$. Then

$$
|\widetilde{S}(h)| \leq \sum_{k \leq \varepsilon n} a_{n,k} + \left| \sum_{\varepsilon n \leq k \leq bn} a_{n,k} e^{2\pi i h x_{nk}} \right|
$$

$$
= O\left(\sqrt{\varepsilon n} + n^{-1/2} \log n \sqrt{hn} + n(\varepsilon n)^{-3/2} \log n \sqrt{hn} \right)
$$

$$
= O\left((\log n) h^{1/8} n^{3/8} \right).
$$

The case $b = 1$ is completely similar to handle.

If $0 < a < b < 1$, we set $H = n^{1/3}$ and find

$$
\frac{3}{2(H+1)} + \frac{3}{A_n} \sum_{h=1}^{H} \frac{1}{h} |\widetilde{S}(h)|
$$

$$
= O\left(\frac{1}{H+1} + \sum_{h=1}^{H} \frac{1}{h} \sqrt{h} \frac{\log n}{\sqrt{n}} \right)
$$

$$
= O\left(\frac{\log n}{n^{1/3}} \right).
$$

If $a = 1$ or $b = 1$, we choose $H = n^{1/9}$ and obtain the upper bound

$$
\frac{1}{H+1} + \sum_{h=1}^{H} \frac{1}{h} h^{1/8} \frac{\log n}{n^{1/8}} = O\left(\frac{\log n}{n^{1/9}} \right).
$$

Thus, in all cases, we obtain the upper bound (10.5) for the discrepancy. As mentioned, this proves the lemma. ∎

To complete the proof of Theorem 10.1, we note that we are now in a similar situation as in the proof of Theorem 2.13 of Chapter 2. We apply (10.4) with $f_{s_0}(x)$, which has variation $V_0^1(f_{s_0}) = 2$. We, thus, obtain

$$\sum_{\langle -Q^*(x^n)\rangle < s_0} Q^*(x^n) 2^{\langle -Q^*(x^n)\rangle} + \frac{1}{2} \sum_{\langle -Q^*(x^n)\rangle \geq s_0} Q^*(x^n) 2^{\langle -Q^*(x^n)\rangle}$$

$$= \frac{1}{D_n} \sum_{an \leq k \leq bn} a_{n,k} f_{s_0}(\langle x_{n,k}\rangle) + O\left(n^{-\frac{1}{2}}\right)$$

$$= \frac{2^{s_0-1}}{\log 2} + O\left(n^{-\frac{1}{2}}\right) + O\left(\frac{\log n}{n^{1/9}}\right)$$

$$= \frac{2^{s_0-1}}{\ln 2} + O\left(\frac{\log n}{n^{1/9}}\right).$$

This implies that t_0 (in the sense of Theorem 2.13) is given by

$$t_0 = 1 + \frac{\ln \ln 2}{\ln 2} + O\left(\frac{\log n}{n^{1/9}}\right)$$

and consequently (10.41) follows:

$$R^*(Q^*) = 1 - t_0 = -\frac{\ln \ln 2}{\ln 2} + O\left(\frac{\log n}{n^{1/9}}\right)$$

and this completes the proof of Theorem 10.1.

10.1.2 Unknown Statistics Contribution: Asymptotics of $\widetilde{R}_n^*$

We now deal with the main term of the maximal minimax redundancy; namely, with $\widetilde{R}_n^* = \log D_n$ where

$$D_n = \sum_{x_1^n} \sup_{P \in \mathcal{M}_0} P(x_1^n). \tag{10.6}$$

Observe that, with k_i being the number of times symbol $i \in \mathcal{A}$ occurs in a string of length n, we have

$$D_n = \sum_{x^n} \sup_{\theta_0 + \ldots + \theta_{m-1} = 1} \theta_0^{k_0} \cdots \theta_{m-1}^{k_{m-1}}$$

$$= \sum_{k_0 + \cdots + k_{m-1} = n} \binom{n}{k_0, \ldots, k_{m-1}} \sup_{\theta_0 + \ldots + \theta_{m-1} = 1} \theta_0^{k_0} \cdots \theta_{m-1}^{k_{m-1}}$$

$$= \sum_{k_0 + \cdots + k_{m-1} = n} \binom{n}{k_0, \ldots, k_{m-1}} \left(\frac{k_0}{n}\right)^{k_0} \cdots \left(\frac{k_{m-1}}{n}\right)^{k_{m-1}}.$$

We also set $D_0 = 1$.

In summary,

$$D_n = \sum_{k_0 + \cdots + k_{m-1} = n} \binom{n}{k_0, \ldots, k_{m-1}} \left(\frac{k_0}{n}\right)^{k_0} \cdots \left(\frac{k_{m-1}}{n}\right)^{k_{m-1}}, \tag{10.7}$$

which we can rewrite as

$$D_n = \frac{n!}{n^n} \sum_{k_0 + \cdots + k_{m-1} = n} \left(\frac{k_0}{n}\right)^{k_0} \cdots \left(\frac{k_{m-1}}{n}\right)^{k_{m-1}}.$$

This suggests we define the following so-called tree-like generating function

$$D(z) = \sum_{n=0}^{\infty} \frac{n^n}{n!} D_n z^n,$$

which becomes

$$D(z) = \sum_{n=0}^{\infty} z^n \sum_{k_0 + \cdots + k_{m-1} = n} \left(\frac{k_0}{n}\right)^{k_0} \cdots \left(\frac{k_{m-1}}{n}\right)^{k_{m-1}}.$$

In view of this, we conclude that $D(z)$ is the m-convolution of sequences like $k^k/k!$, thus we need to study the following tree-like generating function:

$$B(z) = \sum_{k=0}^{\infty} \frac{k^k}{k!} z^k. \tag{10.8}$$

But this generating function, in turn, satisfies (see Exercise 10.1)

$$B(z) = \frac{1}{1 - T(z)} \tag{10.9}$$

for $|z| < e^{-1}$, where $T(z)$ is the well-known *tree function* (that enumerates, for example, all rooted labeled trees), defined as

$$T(z) = \sum_{k=1}^{\infty} \frac{k^{k-1}}{k!} z^k, \tag{10.10}$$

which is also a solution to the implicit equation

$$T(z) = z e^{T(z)} \tag{10.11}$$

with $|T(z)| < 1$. In terms of the standard *Lambert-W* function, we have $T(z) = -W(-z)$ (see Appendix C).

In summary, we just established the following lemma.

Lemma 10.3 *The function $D(z)$ of $\frac{n^n}{n!} D_n$ satisfies, for $|z| < e^{-1}$,*

$$D(z) = B(z)^m = \frac{1}{(1 - T(z))^m}$$

and, consequently,

$$D_n = \frac{n!}{n^n} [z^n] B(z)^m. \tag{10.12}$$

Our next step is to derive asymptotic expansion for D_n. This requires to understand the singularities of $B(z)$ and $T(z)$. Since Euler, it is known that $T(z)$ has a singularity at $z = e^{-1}$, and around this point it has the following expansion (see Corless et al. (1996) for a full asymptotic expansion; the leading term follows also from Theorem C.7 from Appendix C and the functional equation $T = z e^T$):

$$T(z) = 1 - \sqrt{2(1 - ez)} + \frac{2}{3}(1 - ez) - \frac{11\sqrt{2}}{36}(1 - ez)^{3/2} + \frac{43}{135}(1 - ez)^2 + O((1 - ez)^{5/2}).$$

Then, $B(z)$ can also be expanded around $z = e^{-1}$ leading to

$$B(z) = \frac{1}{\sqrt{2(1 - ez)}} + \frac{1}{3} - \frac{\sqrt{2}}{24}\sqrt{(1 - ez)} + \frac{4}{135}(1 - ez)$$
$$- \frac{23\sqrt{2}}{1728}(1 - ez)^{3/2} + O((1 - ez)^2).$$

To extract the coefficients at z^n of $B(z)^m$ for *finite* m, we use the *transfer principle* of Lemma C.5 (from Appendix C), which allows us to compute separately the coefficients for every function involved in the asymptotic expansion.

By taking only the first two terms into account, we find

$$B(z)^m = (2(1 - ez))^{-\frac{m}{2}} + \frac{m}{3}(2(1 - ez))^{-\frac{m-1}{2}} + O\left((2(1 - ez))^{-\frac{m-2}{2}}\right)$$

and consequently

$$D_n = \frac{n!e^n}{n^n}\left(\frac{2^{-\frac{m}{2}}}{\Gamma\left(\frac{m}{2}\right)}n^{\frac{m}{2}-1} + \frac{m2^{-\frac{m-1}{2}}}{3\Gamma\left(\frac{m-1}{2}\right)}n^{\frac{m}{2}-\frac{3}{2}} + O\left(n^{\frac{m}{2}-2}\right)\right)$$
$$= \frac{\Gamma\left(\frac{1}{2}\right)^m}{\Gamma\left(\frac{m}{2}\right)}\left(\frac{n}{2\pi}\right)^{\frac{m-1}{2}}\left(1 + \frac{m\sqrt{2}\Gamma\left(\frac{m}{2}\right)}{3\Gamma\left(\frac{m-1}{2}\right)\sqrt{n}} + O(n^{-1})\right).$$

This leads directly to

$$\widetilde{R}_n^* = \log D_n = \frac{m-1}{2}\log\left(\frac{n}{2\pi}\right) + \log\frac{\Gamma\left(\frac{1}{2}\right)^m}{\Gamma\left(\frac{m}{2}\right)} + \frac{m\log e\,\sqrt{2}\Gamma\left(\frac{m}{2}\right)}{3\Gamma\left(\frac{m-1}{2}\right)\sqrt{n}} + O(n^{-1}).$$

Since we have (in principle) the full singular expansion of $B(z)$, we can be much more precise and obtain the following result.

Theorem 10.4 *Consider a class of memoryless sources $\mathcal{M}_0$ over the alphabet of fixed size m. Then we have the following asymptotic series expansion:*

$$\widetilde{R}_n^* \sim \frac{m-1}{2}\log\left(\frac{n}{2\pi}\right) + \log\frac{\Gamma\left(\frac{1}{2}\right)^m}{\Gamma\left(\frac{m}{2}\right)} + \frac{\Gamma\left(\frac{m}{2}\right)m}{3\ln 2\,\Gamma\left(\frac{m-1}{2}\right)}\cdot\frac{\sqrt{2}}{\sqrt{n}}$$
$$+ \left(\frac{3 + m(m-2)(2m+1)}{36} - \frac{\Gamma^2\left(\frac{m}{2}\right)m^2}{9\Gamma^2\left(\frac{m-1}{2}\right)}\right)\cdot\frac{1}{n}$$
$$+ \sum_{k=3}^{\infty}\frac{c_k}{n^{k/2}}, \tag{10.13}$$

where c_k are explicitly computable constants.

10.1.3 Redundancy for Constrained Distributions

Let us first consider the binary case, where we have now a complete picture. As before, we assume that $\theta_0 \in [a, b]$ for some $0 \le a < b \le 1$.

Theorem 10.5 *Let $0 < a < b < 1$ be given and let $\Theta^{a,b} = \{P : a \le \theta_0 \le b\}$. Then, as $n \to \infty$,*

$$R_n^*(\Theta^{a,b}) = \frac{1}{2} \log \left(\frac{n}{2\pi} \right) + \log \pi + \log C_{a,b} - \frac{\ln \ln 2}{\ln 2} + O\left(n^{-1/9} \log n \right), \qquad (10.14)$$

where

$$C_{a,b} = \frac{1}{\pi} \int_a^b \frac{dx}{\sqrt{x(1-x)}} = \frac{2}{\pi} (\arcsin \sqrt{b} - \arcsin \sqrt{a}).$$

Proof We already observed that

$$D_n(\Theta^{a,b}) = \sum_{k<na} \binom{n}{k} a^k (1-a)^{n-k} + \sum_{na \le k \le nb} \binom{n}{k} \left(\frac{k}{n} \right)^k \left(1 - \frac{k}{n} \right)^{n-k}$$

$$+ \sum_{k>nb} \binom{n}{k} b^k (1-b)^{n-k}$$

$$= \sqrt{\frac{n}{2\pi}} \int_a^b \frac{dx}{\sqrt{x(1-x)}} + O(1)$$

$$= 2\sqrt{\frac{n}{2\pi}} (\arcsin \sqrt{b} - \arcsin \sqrt{a}) + O(1),$$

which leads to

$$\widetilde{R}_n^*(\Theta^{a,b}) = \log D_n(\Theta^{a,b}) = \frac{1}{2} \log \left(\frac{n}{2\pi} \right) + \log \pi + \log C_{a,b} + O(n^{-1/2}).$$

By Theorem 10.1,

$$R_n^*(Q^*) = -\frac{\ln \ln 2}{\ln 2} + O\left(n^{-1/9} \log n \right)$$

and, by the general property,

$$R_n^*(\Theta^{a,b}) = \widetilde{R}_n^*(\Theta^{a,b}) + R_n^*(Q^*),$$

which completes the proof. ∎

Now we consider a general but finite alphabet of size m and study the (continuous) redundancy $\widetilde{R}_n^*$ in the constrained case $\mathcal{S} \ne \Theta$. In the unconstrained case, we know that

$$\sup \prod_{i=0}^{m-1} \theta_i^{k_i} = \prod_{i=0}^{m-1} (k_i/n)^{k_i};$$

that is, we know the optimal $\theta_i = k_i/n$. The situation is more complicated in the constrained case. For example, if we assume an interval restriction $a_i \le \theta_i \le b_i$, $i = 0, \ldots, m-2$, then for $k_i < na_i$ or $k_i > nb_i$ the optimal θ_i may be a_i or b_i, respectively. Fortunately, we are able to prove (see Exercise 10.2) that the main contribution to D_n comes from those $\mathbf{k} = (k_1, \ldots, k_m)$ for which $\mathbf{k}/n \in \mathcal{S}$. So we are led to analyze the following sum:

$$D_n^{(\mathcal{S})} = \sum_{\mathbf{k} \in n\mathcal{S}} \binom{n}{k_0, \cdots k_{m-1}} \prod_{i=0}^{m-1} \left(\frac{k_i}{n} \right)^{k_i},$$

which is of order $n^{\frac{m-1}{2}}$ as proved previously after Theorem 10.6. By a standard analysis, we find

$$
\begin{aligned}
D_n^{(S)} &= \frac{\sqrt{n}}{(2\pi)^{\frac{m-1}{2}}} \sum_{k/n \in S} \frac{1}{\sqrt{k_0 k_1 \cdots k_{m-1}}} \left(1 + O\left(\sum_{i=0}^{m-1} \frac{1}{k_i}\right)\right) \\
&= \left(\frac{n}{2\pi}\right)^{\frac{m-1}{2}} \int_S \frac{d\theta}{\sqrt{\theta_0 \theta_2 \cdots \theta_{m-1}}} \left(1 + O(1/\sqrt{n})\right) \\
&= \left(\frac{n}{2\pi}\right)^{\frac{m-1}{2}} C(S)B(1/2) \left(1 + O(1/\sqrt{n})\right),
\end{aligned}
$$

where $B(1/2)$ denotes the beta-function

$$
B(1/2) = B(1/2, \dots, 1/2) = \frac{\Gamma\left(\frac{1}{2}\right)^m}{\Gamma\left(\frac{m}{2}\right)}
$$

and $C(S)$ abbreviates

$$
C(S) = \mathrm{Dir}(S; 1/2) = \frac{1}{B(1/2)} \int_S \frac{d\mathbf{x}}{\sqrt{x_0 \cdots x_{m-1}}}, \tag{10.15}
$$

where $\mathrm{Dir}(S, ; \alpha)$ is defined in Section 9.2.1. The contribution of the remaining terms is only of order $O(n^{\frac{m-2}{2}})$, as we will argue presently.

With this notation, we can formulate the main result of this section.

Theorem 10.6 *Consider a memoryless constrained source on an alphabet of size $m \geq 2$ and $S \subset \Theta$ a convex polytope. Then the worst-case redundancy for S is*

$$
\widetilde{R}_n^*(S) = \frac{m-1}{2} \log \frac{n}{2\pi} - \log \frac{\Gamma(1/2)^m}{\Gamma(m/2)} + \log C(S) + O(1/\sqrt{n}), \tag{10.16}
$$

where $C(S)$ is defined above in (10.15).

To complete the proof, we must show

$$
\begin{aligned}
D_n - D_n^{(S)} &= \sum_{k \notin nS} \binom{n}{k_0, \cdots k_{m-1}} \sup_{\theta \in S} \prod_{i=0}^{m-1} \theta_i^{k_i} \\
&= O\left(n^{\frac{m}{2}-1}\right). \tag{10.17}
\end{aligned}
$$

Then we have $\log D_n = \log D_n^{(S)} + O(1/\sqrt{n})$ and (10.16) follows.

The proof of (10.17) is very involved (a full proof is given in Drmota, Shamir, and Szpankowski (2022)). We only give some heuristic arguments. First, it is not difficult to observe that the sum can be replaced by an integral over $n(\Theta \setminus S)$ so that all variables k_i are continuous. Second, by concavity of $\prod_{i=0}^{m-1} \theta_i^{k_i}$, it follows that the optimal choice $\theta_{\mathrm{opt}} = (\theta_{i,\mathrm{opt}})$ has to be on the boundary of S. Actually, all $\mathbf{k} = (k_i)$ that correspond to the same θ_{opt} are on a line. Set $\mathbf{k}_0 = n\theta_{\mathrm{opt}}$. We have then

$$\binom{n}{\mathbf{k}} \max_{\theta \in \partial H \cap \Theta} \prod_{i=0}^{m-1} \theta_i^{k_i} = \binom{n}{\mathbf{k}} \prod_{i=0}^{m-1} \theta_{i,\text{opt}}^{k_i}$$

$$= \binom{n}{\mathbf{k_0}} \prod_{i=0}^{m-1} \theta_{i,\text{opt}}^{k_{i,0}} \prod_{i=1}^{m} \frac{\Gamma(k_{i,0}+1)k_{i,0}^{k_i-k_{i,0}}}{\Gamma(k_i+1)},$$

where the last product can be upper bounded by

$$\prod_{i=1}^{m} \frac{\Gamma(k_{i,0}+1)k_{i,0}^{k_i-k_{i,0}}}{\Gamma(k_i+1)} = O\left(-c_1 \sum_{i=0}^{m-1} \frac{(k_i - k_{i0})^2}{k_{i,0}}\right)$$

for some constant $c_1 > 0$. Since all $\mathbf{k} \in n(\Theta \setminus \mathcal{S})$ with the same optimal choice θ_{opt} are one a line and all $k_{i,0}$ are proportional to n, the integral over this line can be upper bounded by $O(\sqrt{n})$. Finally, the integral over $\mathbf{k_0}$ on the (scaled) boundary $n\partial \mathcal{S}$ – recall that $\mathbf{k_0} = n\theta_{\text{opt}}$ – is upper bounded by

$$\int_{n\partial\mathcal{S}} \binom{n}{\mathbf{k_0}} \prod_{i=0}^{m-1} \theta_{i,\text{opt}}^{k_{i,0}} d\mathbf{k_0} = \int_{n\partial\mathcal{S}} \sqrt{\frac{n}{k_{1,0} \cdots k_{m,0}}} d\mathbf{k_0}$$

$$= O\left(n^{\frac{m-3}{2}}\right).$$

So the total contribution is of order $O(n^{\frac{m}{2}-1})$ as proposed.

10.2 Maximal Minimax Redundancy for Large Alphabets

Now we consider the maximal minimax redundancy when m grows with n. In this case, the expression (10.12) of Lemma 10.3 for the maximal minimax $\widetilde{R}_n^*$ still holds *but* the singularity analysis *does not* apply. Instead, the growth of the coefficient $[z^n] B^m(z)$ can be handled with the help of the saddle point method (see Appendix C).

Our main result of this section is presented next.

Theorem 10.7 *For the memoryless model family $\mathcal{M}_0$ over an m-ary alphabet, where $m \to \infty$ as n grows, the minimax pointwise redundancy $\widetilde{R}_n^*$ behaves asymptotically as follows:*

(i) *For $m = o(n)$,*

$$\widetilde{R}_n^* = \frac{m-1}{2} \log \frac{n}{m} + \frac{m}{2\ln 2} + \frac{m}{3\ln 2}\sqrt{\frac{m}{n}}$$
$$- \frac{1}{2} - \frac{\log e}{4}\sqrt{\frac{m}{n}} + O\left(\frac{m^2}{n} + \frac{1}{\sqrt{m}}\right). \tag{10.18}$$

(ii) *For $\alpha = m/n \in [a, b]$, where $a < b$ are positive constants,*

$$\widetilde{R}_n^* = n \log B_{m/n} - \log \sqrt{A_{m/n}} + O\left(\frac{1}{n}\right), \tag{10.19}$$

where

$$C_\alpha := \frac{1}{2} + \frac{1}{2}\sqrt{1 + \frac{4}{\alpha}}, \qquad A_\alpha := C_\alpha + \frac{2}{\alpha}, \qquad (10.20)$$

and

$$B_\alpha := \alpha C_\alpha^{\alpha+2} e^{-\frac{1}{C_\alpha}}. \qquad (10.21)$$

(iii) *For $n = o(m)$,*

$$\widetilde{R}_n^* = n \log \frac{m}{n} + \frac{3}{2 \ln 2} \frac{n(n-1)}{m} + O\left(\frac{1}{n} + \frac{n^3}{m^2}\right) \qquad (10.22)$$

for large m.

Before we prove Theorem 10.7, we offer some insights. The formulation of the scenario in which both n and m are large, as a sequence of problems where m varies with n, is easy to imagine. In a typical application of Theorem 10.7, for a *given* pair of values $n = n_0$ and $m = m_0$, which are deemed to fall in one of the three itemized cases, the formulas are used to approximate the minimax pointwise redundancy $\widetilde{R}_{n_0}^*$. The asymptotic expansion in (10.18) reveals that the error incurred by neglecting lower-order terms may be significant. Consider the example in which $n = 10^4$ and $m = 40$ (or, approximately, $m = n^{0.4}$). Then, the leading term in (10.3) is only 5.5 times larger than the second term, and 131 times larger than the third term. The error from neglecting these two terms is thus 15.4% (assuming all other terms are negligible). Even for $n = 10^8$ (and $m = 1600$), the error is still over 8%. It is interesting to notice that (10.18) is a "direct scaling" of (10.13): using Stirling's approximation to replace $\Gamma(x)$ in (10.13) by its asymptotic value $\sqrt{2\pi/x}(x/e)^x$, and further approximating $(1 + 1/x)^{(x+1)/2}$ with $\sqrt{e}(1 + 1/(4x))$, indeed yields exactly (10.18), up to the error terms. Thus, our results reveal that the first two terms of the asymptotic expansion for fixed m given by (10.13) are in fact a better approximation to $\widetilde{R}_n^*$ than the leading term of (10.18).

For the case $m = \Theta(n)$, the value of the constant, $\log B_\alpha$, where B_α is specified in (10.21) and (10.20), is plotted against α in Figure 10.1. It is easy to see that, when $\alpha \to 0$, $\log B_\alpha \approx (\alpha/2)\log(1/\alpha)$, in agreement with (10.3). Similarly, when $\alpha \to \infty$, $\log B_\alpha \approx \log \alpha$, in agreement with (10.22).

Observe that the second-order term in (10.18), which is $\Theta(m)$, dominates $-\log(n/m)$ whenever $m = \Omega(n^a)$ for some a, $0 < a < 1$. Hence, the leading term in the expansion is rather $(m/2)\log(n/m)$ than $(m-1)/2\log(n/m)$. In the numerical example given for this case, the choice of a growth rate $m = o(\sqrt{n})$ is due to the fact that, otherwise, the error term $O(m^2/n)$ may not even vanish, and it may dominate the constant, as well as the $\sqrt{m/n}$ terms. For any given growth rate $m = O(n^a)$, $0 < a < 1$, an expansion in which the error term vanishes can be derived; however, no expansion has this property for *every* possible value of a. The reason is that, as will become apparent in the proof of the theorem, any expansion will include an error term of the form $O(m(m/n)^{j/2})$ for some positive integer j. The same situation can be observed in (3.19), where one of the error terms becomes $O(n(n/m)^j)$ if a more accurate expansion is used.

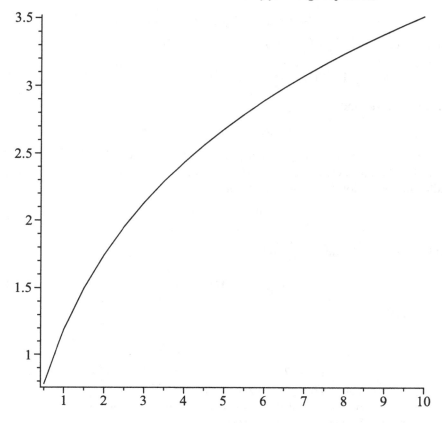

Figure 10.1 Value of the constant $\log B_\alpha$ in the $\Theta(n)$ term of $\widetilde{R}_n^*$ in case $m = \Theta(n)$.

We also want to mention that (10.19) can likewise be applied if $m = \alpha n + \ell(n)$ for some $\alpha > 0$ and $\ell(n) = o(n)$. We just observe that

$$\log B_{m/n} = \log B_\alpha + \log C_\alpha \frac{\ell(n)}{n} - \frac{1}{2\ln 2\, \alpha^2 A_\alpha} \frac{\ell(n)^2}{n^2} + O\left(\frac{\ell(n)^3}{n^3}\right)$$

and

$$\sqrt{2\pi A_{m/n}} = \sqrt{2\pi A_\alpha} + O\left(\frac{\ell(n)}{n}\right),$$

so that

$$\widetilde{R}_n^* = n\log B_\alpha + \ell(n)\log C_\alpha - \log\sqrt{2\pi A_\alpha}$$
$$- \frac{\log e}{2\alpha^2 A_\alpha} \frac{\ell(n)^2}{n} + O\left(\frac{\ell(n)^3}{n^2} + \frac{\ell(n)}{n} + \frac{1}{n}\right)$$

as long as $\ell(n) = o(1)$.

10.2.1 Proof of Theorem 10.7

We first describe a roadmap of our proof. Recall from (10.12) that

$$D_n = \frac{n!}{n^n}[z^n]B(z) = \frac{n!e^n}{n^n}[z^n][z^n][\beta(z)]^m = \frac{n!e^n}{n^n}\frac{1}{2\pi i}\oint e^{h(z)}dz, \tag{10.23}$$

where $\beta(z) = B(z/e)$ and

$$h(z) = m \ln \beta(z) - (n+1)\ln z. \tag{10.24}$$

We will now apply the saddle point methods, as discussed in depth in Appendix C. In particular, we first find an explicit *normalized* real root, $\bar{z}_0 = z_0/e$ (here z_0 is defined below) of the saddle point equation $h'(z) = 0$, which satisfies

$$\bar{z}_0 \frac{\beta'(\bar{z}_0)}{\beta(z_0)} = \frac{n+1}{m}. \tag{10.25}$$

Differentiating (10.11), and using (10.9), it is easy to see that

$$z\frac{\beta'(z)}{\beta(z)} = \beta(z)^2 - \beta(z). \tag{10.26}$$

Thus, (10.25) takes the form

$$\beta(\bar{z}_0)^2 - \beta(\bar{z}_0) = \frac{n+1}{m}. \tag{10.27}$$

By definition of the tree-function $T(z)$, the range of $\beta(z)$ for $0 \le z < 1$ is $[1, +\infty)$. The three cases (i)–(iii) discussed in Theorem 10.7 correspond to $\bar{z}_0$ close to 1 or inside the interval $(0, 1)$ or close to 0. As illustrated in Figure 10.2, when $m = o(n)$, the root $\bar{z}_0 \approx 1$; when $m = O(n)$, then $0 < \bar{z}_0 < 1$ and for $n = o(m)$ the root $\bar{z}_0 \approx 0$.

We now prove Theorem 10.7.

Case (ii) We start with the case (ii), where $m/n \in [a, b]$ for some positive constants a, b. In this case, we can directly apply (C.13) from Appendix C, a standard saddle point result. For notational convenience, we set $\alpha = m/n$. The essential observation is that the equation

$$\frac{z_0 B'(z_0)}{B(z_0)} = \frac{1}{\alpha} \tag{10.28}$$

has an explicit solution

$$z_0 = \frac{1}{e}\left(1 - \frac{1}{C_\alpha}\right)e^{1/C_\alpha},$$

where C_α is given by (10.20). Since $T(z)$ satisfies $T(z) = ze^{T(z)}$, the derivative is given by $T'(z) = T(z)/(z(1 - T(z)))$ and consequently

$$\frac{zB'(z)}{B(z)} = \frac{zT'(z)}{1 - T(z)} = \frac{T(z)}{(1 - T(z))^2}.$$

It is easy to check that $T(z) = 1 - 1/C_\alpha$ satisfies $T(z)/((1 - T(z))^2 = 1/\alpha$. Consequently, $T(z_0) = 1 - 1/C_\alpha$ and, thus,

$$z_0 = T(z_0)e^{-T(z_0)} = \frac{1}{e}\left(1 - \frac{1}{C_\alpha}\right)e^{1/C_\alpha},$$

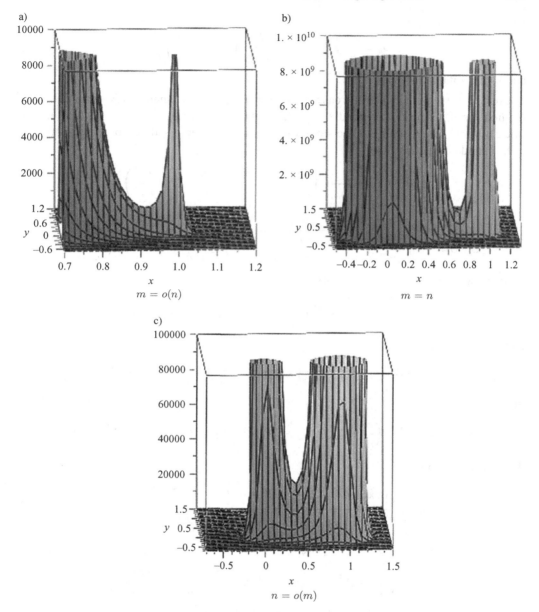

Figure 10.2 Illustration to locations of the saddle point $0 \le \bar{z}_0 \le 1$.

as proposed. (Note that $B(z_0) = C_\alpha$.) It also follows that

$$\frac{B(z_0)^\alpha}{z_0} = eB_\alpha$$

and

$$2\pi m \left(\frac{z_0^2 B''(z_0)}{B(z_0)} + \frac{1}{\alpha} - \frac{1}{\alpha^2} \right) = 2\pi n A_\alpha.$$

Hence,

$$D_n = \frac{n!}{n^n}[z^n] B(z)^m = \frac{B_\alpha^n}{\sqrt{A_\alpha}} \left(1 + O\left(\frac{1}{n}\right)\right),$$

and so we obtain (10.19).

Case (i) Next we consider the case (i), where $m = o(n)$. We again apply the saddle point method (as described in Appendix C). We consider λ as the pair (m, n) and the function $g(\lambda, z) = m \ln B(z) - n \ln z$. Of course, this leads to the same saddle point equation as in (10.28) and consequently to

$$z_0 = \frac{1}{e}\left(1 - \frac{1}{C_{m/n}}\right) e^{1/C_{m/n}} = \frac{1}{e}\left(1 - \frac{m}{n} + O\left(\frac{m^{3/2}}{n^{3/2}}\right)\right)$$

and

$$B(z_0) = C_{m/n} = \frac{1}{2} + \frac{1}{2}\sqrt{1 + \frac{4n}{m}} = \sqrt{\frac{n}{m}}\left(1 + \frac{1}{2}\sqrt{\frac{m}{n}} + \frac{1}{8}\frac{m}{n} + O\left(\frac{m^2}{n^2}\right)\right).$$

Notice that $z_0 = \bar{z}_0/e \approx 1/e$. This also gives

$$g(\lambda, z_0) = n + \frac{m}{2}\ln\frac{n}{m} + \frac{m}{2} + \frac{m}{3}\sqrt{\frac{m}{n}} + O\left(\frac{m^2}{n}\right)$$

as well as

$$g''(\lambda, z_0) = \frac{en}{z_0}\left(\frac{2n}{m} + C_{m/n}\right) = 2e^2\frac{n^2}{m}\left(1 + O\left(\sqrt{m/n}\right)\right)$$

and

$$g'''(\lambda, z_0) = \frac{nC_{m/n}}{z_0^3}\left(\frac{n}{m}(8C_{m/n} - 1) - 5C_{m/n} + 3\right) = 8e^3\frac{n^3}{m^2}\left(1 + O\left(\sqrt{m/n}\right)\right).$$

Therefore, we find

$$
\begin{aligned}
D_n &= \frac{n!}{n^n} \frac{\exp\left(n + \frac{m}{2}\ln\frac{n}{m} + \frac{m}{2} + \frac{m}{3}\sqrt{\frac{m}{n}} + O\left(\frac{m^2}{n}\right)\right)}{\frac{1}{e}\left(1 + O(\frac{m}{n})\right)\sqrt{4\pi e^2 \frac{n^2}{m}\left(1 + O\left(\sqrt{m/n}\right)\right)}} \\
&\quad \times \left(1 + O\left(1/\sqrt{m}\right)\right) \\
&= \sqrt{\frac{m}{2n}}\exp\left(n + \frac{m}{2}\ln\frac{n}{m} + \frac{m}{2} + \frac{m}{3}\sqrt{\frac{m}{n}} + O\left(\frac{m^2}{n}\right)\right) \\
&\quad \times \left(1 + O\left(\sqrt{m/n}\right) + O\left(1/\sqrt{m}\right)\right)
\end{aligned}
$$

leading to (10.18). Note that we can do slightly better by considering the fourth derivative which leads to an error term $O(1/m)$ instead of $O\left(1/\sqrt{m}\right)$. Furthermore, note that $\sqrt{m/n} = O(1/m + m/n^2)$.

Case (iii) Finally, we consider the case (iii), where $n = o(m)$. Here we proceed in completely the same way and obtain

$$z_0 = \frac{n}{m}\left(1 - 3\frac{n}{m} + O\left(\frac{n^2}{m^2}\right)\right) \approx 0$$

and

$$B(z_0) = 1 + \frac{n}{m} + 2\frac{n^2}{m^2} + O\left(\frac{n^3}{m^3}\right).$$

This leads (after some algebra) to (10.22). Note that $g''(z_0)$ is of order $\Theta(m^2/n)$, $g'''(z_0)$ of order $\Theta(m^3/n^2)$, and $g''''(z_0)$ of order $\Theta(m^4/n^3)$. Therefore, we obtain the error $O(1/n)$ in the saddle point approximation. (Of course, we can take even more terms into account and could find more precise error terms.)

10.3 Average Minimax Redundancy

We now turn to the average minimax $\widetilde{R}_n$. We first consider the case when the unknown symbol probabilities are constrained, and then we consider the unconstrained case but for $m = o(n)$.

10.3.1 Average Minimax with Constrained Distribution

Let $\mathcal{S} \subseteq \Theta = \{\theta = (\theta_0, \ldots, \theta_{m-1}): \theta_j \geq 0, \theta_0 + \cdots + \theta_{m-1} = 1\}$ in the memoryless case. We now slightly modify Lemma 9.1 to derive operational expression for the average minimax redundancy which we denote as $\widetilde{R}_n(\mathcal{S})$. By definition, we have

$$\widetilde{R}_n(\mathcal{S}) = \inf_{Q} \sup_{\theta \in \mathcal{S}} D_n(P^\theta \| Q)$$

where $D(P^\theta \| Q)$ is the Kullback–Leibler divergence.

We recall that

$$\widetilde{R}_n(\mathcal{S}) = \int_{\mathcal{S}} D(P^\theta \| M_n^{w^*}) dw^*(\theta), \tag{10.29}$$

where $w^*(\theta)$ is the maximizing prior distribution and

$$M_n^{w^+}(x^n) = \int_{\mathcal{S}} P^\theta(x^n) dw^*(\theta).$$

We already mentioned that Bernardo (1979) proved that asymptotically the maximizing density is proportional to the square root of the determinant of the Fisher information $I(\theta)$, the so-called Jeffrey prior. This leads to the density

$$\widetilde{w}^*(\theta) = \frac{1}{C(\mathcal{S}) \cdot B(1/2)} \frac{1}{\sqrt{\theta_1 \cdots \theta_m}}, \tag{10.30}$$

where $C(\mathcal{S})$ defined in (10.15) and is the probability that the Dirichlet distribution with $\alpha_i = 1/2$ falls into the subset $\mathcal{S}$.

Thus, we are led to consider the *asymptotic average minimax redundancy*

$$\widetilde{R}_n^{\text{asymp}}(\mathcal{S}) = \int_{\mathcal{S}} D(P^\theta \| M_n^{\widetilde{w}^*}) d\widetilde{w}^*(\theta).$$

The mixture distribution $M_n^{\widetilde{w}^*}(x^n)$ can be calculated as follows:

$$M_n^{\widetilde{w}^*}(x^n) = \frac{1}{C(\mathcal{S}) \cdot B(1/2)} \int_{\mathcal{S}} \prod_{i=1}^{m} \theta_i^{k_i - 1/2}$$

$$= \frac{1}{C(\mathcal{S}) \cdot B(1/2)} B(k_1 + 1/2, \cdots, k_m + 1/2)$$

$$\cdot \frac{1}{B(k_1 + 1/2, \cdots, k_m + 1/2)} \int_{\mathcal{S}} \prod_{i=1}^{m} \theta_i^{k_i - 1/2}$$

$$= \frac{1}{C(\mathcal{S}) \cdot B(1/2)} B(k_1 + 1/2, \cdots, k_m + 1/2) \cdot \mathrm{Dir}(\mathcal{S} : \mathbf{k} + \mathbf{1/2}).$$

Observe again that for the unconstrained case, $\mathrm{Dir}(\Theta; \mathbf{k} + 1/2) = 1$. In summary,

$$D_n(P^\theta \| M_n^{\widetilde{w}^*}) = \log\left(C(\mathcal{S})B(1/2)\right) \tag{10.31}$$

$$+ \sum_{\mathbf{k}} \binom{n}{\mathbf{k}} \prod_{i=1}^{m} \theta_i^{k_i} \log \frac{\prod_{i=1}^{m} \theta_i^{k_i}}{B(\mathbf{k} + 1/2)\mathrm{Dir}(\mathcal{S}; \mathbf{k} + 1/2)}. \tag{10.32}$$

The main result of this section is presented next.

Theorem 10.8 *Consider a memoryless constrained source $\mathcal{S} \subset \Theta$ with fixed but arbitrarily large $m \geq 2$, where $\mathcal{S}$ is a convex polytope. Then the asymptotic average minimax redundancy is*

$$\widetilde{R}_n^{asymp}(\mathcal{S}) = \frac{m-1}{2} \log \frac{2}{2\pi e} + \log \frac{\Gamma(1/2)^m}{\Gamma(m/2)} + \log C(\mathcal{S}) + O(1/\sqrt{n}), \tag{10.33}$$

where $C(\mathcal{S})$ is defined in (10.15).

We postpone the proof until Section 10.3.3 since we will use some ideas and calculations of the proof of the subsequent Theorem 10.9.

10.3.2 Unconstrained Case for $m = o(n)$

In Theorem 10.8, we assumed that m is fixed to avoid complications with constraints $\mathcal{S}_m$ that may depend on m. Now we do not impose any constrained on θ; that is, we assume that $\mathcal{S} = \Theta$.

Theorem 10.9 *Consider a memoryless unconstrained source Θ with $m = o(n)$. Then the unconstrained asymptotic average minimax redundancy becomes*

$$\widetilde{R}_n^{asymp}(\Theta) = \frac{m-1}{2} \log \frac{2}{2\pi e} + \log \frac{\Gamma(1/2)^m}{\Gamma(m/2)} + O(m^{3/2}/\sqrt{n}) \tag{10.34}$$

$$= \frac{m-1}{2} \log\left(\frac{n}{m}\right) + \frac{1}{2}(\log e - 1) + O(1/m) + O(m^{3/2}/\sqrt{n}).$$

Proof The starting point is

$$\widetilde{R}_n^{asymp}(\Theta) = \frac{1}{B(1/2)} \int_{\Theta} \sum_{\mathbf{k}} \binom{n}{\mathbf{k}} \theta^{\mathbf{k}-1/2} \log\left(\frac{\theta^{\mathbf{k}} B(1/2)}{B(\mathbf{k}+1/2)}\right), \tag{10.35}$$

where we write $\theta^{\mathbf{k}-1/2} := \prod_i \theta_i^{k_i-1/2}$. We need to estimate different parts of this sum. We first observe that

$$\sum_{\mathbf{k}} \binom{n}{\mathbf{k}} B(\mathbf{k}+1/2) = \int_{\Theta} \sum_{\mathbf{k}} \binom{n}{\mathbf{k}} \theta^{\mathbf{k}-1/2} d\theta$$
$$= \int_{\Theta} \theta^{-1/2} d\theta = B(1/2).$$

More importantly, we notice that

$$\int_{\Theta} \sum_{\mathbf{k}} \binom{n}{\mathbf{k}} \theta^{\mathbf{k}-1/2} \log \theta^{\mathbf{k}} d\theta = \sum_{\mathbf{k}} \binom{n}{\mathbf{k}} \sum_{i=1}^{m} k_i \int_{\Theta} \theta^{\mathbf{k}-1/2} \log \theta_i d\theta$$
$$= \sum_{\mathbf{k}} \binom{n}{\mathbf{k}} \sum_{i=1}^{m} \frac{k_i}{\ln 2} \frac{\partial}{\partial k_i} B(\mathbf{k}+1/2),$$

$$\int_{\Theta} \sum_{\mathbf{k}} \binom{n}{\mathbf{k}} \theta^{\mathbf{k}-1/2} \log B(\mathbf{k}+1/2) d\theta = \sum_{\mathbf{k}} \binom{n}{\mathbf{k}} B(\mathbf{k}+1/2) \log B(\mathbf{k}+1/2).$$

Thus,

$$\widetilde{R}_n^{\text{asymp}}(\Theta) = \log B(1/2) + \frac{1}{B(1/2)} \sum_{\mathbf{k}} \binom{n}{\mathbf{k}} \tag{10.36}$$
$$\cdot \left(\sum_{i=1}^{m} k_i \frac{\partial}{\partial k_i} B(\mathbf{k}+1/2) - B(\mathbf{k}+1/2) \log B(\mathbf{k}+1/2) \right).$$

To deal with sums like (10.36), we use the relation between the beta function, the gamma function, and the psi function. For example:

$$\frac{\partial}{\partial k_i} B(\mathbf{k}+1/2) = (\Psi(k_i+1/2) - \Psi(n+m/2)) B(\mathbf{k}+1/2),$$

where $\Psi(x) = \Gamma'(x)/\Gamma(x)$. Asymptotically, we have

$$\Psi(x+1/2) = \ln x + 1/(12x) + O(1/x^3),$$
$$\Psi(x+m/2) = \ln x + (m-1)/(2x) + O(1/x^2).$$

Using this and Stirling's formula, we finally find

$$\ln \Gamma(x+1/2) = x \ln x - x + \ln \sqrt{2\pi} - \frac{1}{24x} + O(1/x^2),$$
$$\ln \Gamma(x+m/2) = x \ln x - x + \frac{m-1}{2} \ln(x+m/2)$$
$$+ \ln \sqrt{2\pi} + \left(\frac{1}{12} - \frac{m^2}{8} \right) \frac{1}{x} + O(m^3/x^2)$$

leading to

$$\sum_{i=1}^{m} \frac{k_i}{\ln 2} \frac{\partial}{\partial k_i} B(\mathbf{k} + 1/2) - B(\mathbf{k} + 1/2) \log B(\mathbf{k} + 1/2)$$

$$= B(\mathbf{k} + 1/2) \left(\frac{m-1}{2} (\log(n + m/2) - 1 - \log(2\pi)) \right.$$

$$\left. + O\left(m^2/n + \sum_i (k_i + 1)^{-1} \right) \right).$$

It is involved but not very difficult to show that (see Exercise 10.4)

$$\sum_{\mathbf{k}} \binom{n}{\mathbf{k}} \frac{B(\mathbf{k} + 1/2)}{k_i + 1} = O\left(\frac{\sqrt{m} B(1/2)}{\sqrt{n}} \right). \tag{10.37}$$

In summary, we arrive at

$$\widetilde{R}_n^{\text{asmp}}(\Theta) = \frac{m-1}{2} \log(n/2\pi e) + \log \frac{\Gamma^m(1/2)}{\Gamma(m/2)} + O(m^{3/2}/\sqrt{n}). \tag{10.38}$$

We now use Stirling's formula for $\Gamma(m/2)$ and complete the proof. ∎

10.3.3 Proof of Theorem 10.8

To prove the second statement of Theorem 10.8, the starting point for the asymptotic average redundancy is (10.31); however, we rewrite it in terms of $\mathcal{S} \subseteq \Theta$ as follows:

$$\widetilde{R}_n^{\text{asympt}}(\mathcal{S}) = \frac{1}{B_{\mathcal{S}}(1/2)} \int_{\mathcal{S}} \sum_{\mathbf{k}} \binom{n}{\mathbf{k}} \theta^{\mathbf{k}-1/2} \log \left(\frac{\theta^{\mathbf{k}} B_{\mathcal{S}}(1/2)}{B_{\mathcal{S}}(\mathbf{k} + 1/2)} \right), \tag{10.39}$$

where we use the short hand notation

$$B_{\mathcal{S}}(\alpha) = \int_{\mathcal{S}} \theta^{\alpha - 1} \, d\theta = \text{Dir}(\mathcal{S}; \alpha) B(\alpha).$$

As in the proof of Theorem 10.9, we obtain

$$\overline{R}_n^{\text{asympt}}(\mathcal{S}) = \log B_{\mathcal{S}}(1/2)$$

$$+ \frac{1}{B_{\mathcal{S}}(1/2)} \sum_{\mathbf{k}} \binom{n}{\mathbf{k}} \left(\sum_{i=1}^{m} \frac{k_i}{\ln 2} \frac{\partial}{\partial k_i} B_{\mathcal{S}}(\mathbf{k} + 1/2) - B_{\mathcal{S}}(\mathbf{k} + 1/2) \log B_{\mathcal{S}}(\mathbf{k} + 1/2) \right).$$

Again, we split the summation over $\mathbf{k}$ into several parts. If $\mathbf{k}/n \in \mathcal{S}^-$, where $\mathcal{S}^-$ denotes all points in the interior of $\mathcal{S}$ with distance $\geq n^{-1/2+\varepsilon}$ to the boundary (for some $\varepsilon > 0$), then the saddle point $\theta_i = k_i/n$ of the integrand $\theta^{\mathbf{k}}$ of the integral of $B_{\mathcal{S}}(\mathbf{k}+1/2)$ or $\frac{\partial}{\partial k_i} B_{\mathcal{S}}(\mathbf{k}+1/2)$, respectively, is contained in $\mathcal{S}^-$. The precise statement is as follows.

Lemma 10.10 *Suppose that* $\mathbf{k}/n \in \mathcal{S}^-$, *then for every fixed integer* $L \geq 0$ *we have*

$$B_{\mathcal{S}}(\mathbf{k} + 1/2) = B(\mathbf{k} + 1/2) \left(1 + O\left(\sum_{i=1}^{m} k_i^{-L-1} \right) \right)$$

and

$$\sum_{i=1}^{m} \frac{k_i}{\ln 2} \frac{\partial}{\partial k_i} B_S(\mathbf{k} + 1/2) - B_S(\mathbf{k} + 1/2) \log B_S(\mathbf{k} + 1/2)$$

$$= \sum_{i=1}^{m} \frac{k_i}{\ln 2} \frac{\partial}{\partial k_i} B(\mathbf{k} + 1/2) - B(\mathbf{k} + 1/2) \log B(\mathbf{k} + 1/2) + O\left(B(\mathbf{k} + 1/2) \sum_{i=1}^{m} k_i^{-L-1}\right)$$

for large n.

Before we start with the proof of Lemma 10.10, we comment on the relation between the beta and gamma function:

$$B(\mathbf{k} + 1/2) = \frac{\Gamma\left(k_1 + \frac{1}{2}\right) \cdots \Gamma\left(k_m + \frac{1}{2}\right)}{\Gamma\left(k_1 + \cdots + k_m + \frac{m}{2}\right)}.$$

First, this formula follows from the following substitution on m-dimensional integrals:

$$\Gamma\left(k_1 + \cdots + k_m + \frac{m}{2}\right) B(\mathbf{k} + 1/2) = \int_0^\infty e^{-z} z^{k_1 + \cdots + k_m + -\frac{m}{2}} z^{m-1} \, dz$$

$$\cdot \int_\Theta \prod_{i=1}^{m} \theta_i^{k_i - \frac{1}{2}} \, d\theta$$

$$= \int_0^\infty \int_\Theta \prod_{i=1}^{m} \left(e^{-z\theta_i} (z\theta_i)^{k_i - \frac{1}{2}}\right) z^{m-1} \, dz \, d\theta$$

$$= \prod_{i=1}^{m} \int_0^\infty e^{-z_i} z_i^{k_i - \frac{1}{2}} \, dz_i,$$

where θ_m abbreviates $\theta_m = 1 - (\theta_1 + \cdots + \theta_{m-1})$ and the substitution

$$z_i = z\theta_i \quad (1 \le i \le m - 1), \quad z_m = z(1 - (\theta_1 + \cdots + \theta_{m-1})$$

has determinant z^{m-1}.

Second, we can use Stirling's formula to obtain the asymptotic formula

$$B(\mathbf{k} + 1/2) = \frac{(2\pi)^{\frac{m-1}{2}}}{n^{\frac{m-1}{2}}} \prod_{i=1}^{m} \left(\frac{k_i}{n}\right)^{k_i} \left(1 + O\left(\sum_{i=1}^{m} \frac{1}{k_i + 1}\right)\right).$$

Note that we only have to work with the integral that represents the gamma function and that can be asymptotically evaluated as

$$\Gamma(k + 1/2) = \int_0^\infty e^{-z} z^{k - \frac{1}{2}} \, dz$$

$$= \int_{|z-k| \le c k^{\frac{1}{2}+\varepsilon}} e^{-z} z^{k - \frac{1}{2}} \, dz + O\left(e^{-k} k^k e^{-c^2 k^{2\varepsilon}/2}\right)$$

$$= \sqrt{2\pi} e^{-k} k^k \left(1 + \sum_{\ell=1}^{L} c_\ell k^{-\ell} + O(k^{-L-1})\right)$$

for every given integer $L \geq 0$, for every $\varepsilon > 0$, and for every constant $c > 0$, and where c_ℓ are certain real constants. We just have to use the saddle point $z_0 = k$ of the function $e^{-z}z^k$ and the local expansion

$$e^{-z}z^{k-\frac{1}{2}} = e^{-k}k^{k-\frac{1}{2}}e^{-(z-k)^2/(2k)}\left(1 - \frac{z-k}{2k} + \frac{(z-k)^3}{3k^2} + \cdots\right).$$

In particular, it is sufficient to consider the integral on the interval $[k - c\,k^\varepsilon, k + c\,k^\varepsilon]$. The remaining part of the integral is negligible.

Proof of Lemma 10.10 By using the same substitution as before, we have

$$\Gamma\left(k_1 + \cdots + k_m + \frac{m}{2}\right)B_{\mathcal{S}}(\mathbf{k}+1/2) = \int_0^\infty e^{-z}z^{k_1 + \cdots + k_m + -\frac{m}{2}}z^{m-1}\,dz$$

$$\cdot \int_{\mathcal{S}}\prod_{i=1}^m \theta_i^{k_i - \frac{1}{2}}\,d\theta$$

$$= \int_0^\infty \int_{\mathcal{S}}\prod_{i=1}^m\left(e^{-z\theta_i}(z\theta_i)^{k_i-\frac{1}{2}}\right)z^{m-1}\,dz\,d\theta$$

$$= \int_{\text{cone}(\mathcal{S})}\prod_{i=1}^m e^{-z_i}z_i^{k_i-\frac{1}{2}}\,dz_1\cdots dz_m, \qquad (10.40)$$

where

$$\text{cone}(\mathcal{S}) = \{z\theta : z \geq 0, \theta \in \mathcal{S}\}.$$

By assumption, $\mathbf{k}/n \in \mathcal{S}^-$, which implies (for a properly chosen constant $c > 0$) that

$$\prod_{i=1}^m\left[k_i - c\,n^{\frac{1}{2}+\varepsilon}, k_i + c\,n^{\frac{1}{2}+\varepsilon}\right] \subseteq \text{cone}(\mathcal{S}).$$

Since $k_i \leq n$, it also follows that

$$\prod_{i=1}^m\left[k_i - c\,k_i^{\frac{1}{2}+\varepsilon}, k_i + c\,k_i^{\frac{1}{2}+\varepsilon}\right] \subseteq \text{cone}(\mathcal{S}).$$

This implies that

$$\Gamma\left(k_1 + \cdots + k_m + \frac{m}{2}\right)B_{\mathcal{S}}(\mathbf{k}+1/2) = \Gamma\left(k_1 + \cdots + k_m + \frac{m}{2}\right)B(\mathbf{k}+1/2)$$

$$+ O\left(e^{-k_1-\cdots-k_m}\prod_{i=1}^m k_i^{k_i} \cdot \sum_{i=1}^m k_i^{-L-1}\right)$$

and consequently

$$B_{\mathcal{S}}(\mathbf{k}+1/2) = B(\mathbf{k}+1/2) + O\left(n^{-\frac{m-1}{2}}\prod_{i=1}^m\left(\frac{k_i}{n}\right)^{k_i}\sum_{i=1}^m k_i^{-L-1}\right)$$

$$= B(\mathbf{k}+1/2)\left(1 + O\left(\sum_{i=1}^m k_i^{-L-1}\right)\right).$$

This proves the first part of Lemma 10.10.

It remains to consider the second part of Lemma 10.10. We start with the integral representation (10.40) for

$$\Gamma\left(k_1 + \cdots + k_m + \frac{m}{2}\right) B_{\mathcal{S}}(\mathbf{k} + 1/2)$$

and consider the derivative with respect to k_i. By the product rule, this leads to an integral representation for

$$\frac{\partial}{\partial k_i} B_{\mathcal{S}}(\mathbf{k} + 1/2) = \frac{1}{\Gamma\left(n + \frac{m}{2}\right)} \frac{\partial}{\partial k_i} \left(\Gamma\left(k_1 + \cdots + k_m + \frac{m}{2}\right) B_{\mathcal{S}}(\mathbf{k} + 1/2) \right)$$

$$- \frac{\Gamma'\left(n + \frac{m}{2}\right)}{\Gamma\left(n + \frac{m}{2}\right)^2} \Gamma\left(n + \frac{m}{2}\right) B_{\mathcal{S}}(\mathbf{k} + 1/2)$$

$$= \frac{1}{\Gamma\left(n + \frac{m}{2}\right)} \int_{\text{cone}(\mathcal{S})} \ln z_i \prod_{i=1}^{m} e^{-z_i} z_i^{k_i - \frac{1}{2}} \, dz_1 \cdots dz_m$$

$$- \frac{\Gamma'\left(n + \frac{m}{2}\right)}{\Gamma\left(n + \frac{m}{2}\right)^2} \int_{\text{cone}(\mathcal{S})} \prod_{i=1}^{m} e^{-z_i} z_i^{k_i - \frac{1}{2}} \, dz_1 \cdots dz_m.$$

Next, we consider

$$\sum_{i=1}^{m} \frac{k_i}{\ln 2} \frac{\partial}{\partial k_i} B_{\mathcal{S}}(\mathbf{k} + 1/2) - B_{\mathcal{S}}(\mathbf{k} + 1/2) \log B_{\mathcal{S}}(\mathbf{k} + 1/2),$$

where we replace $\log B_{\mathcal{S}}(\mathbf{k} + 1/2)$ by

$$\log B(\mathbf{k} + 1/2) + O\left(\sum_{i=1}^{m} k_i^{-L-1}\right).$$

The appearing integrals over cone($\mathcal{S}$) can be safely replaced by integrals over $[0, \infty)^m$ since the dominating part of the integral is (again) contained in $\mathcal{S}$. This means that we can switch between $\mathcal{S}$ and Θ without changing the leading asymptotic behavior. Actually the error term from the integration can be upper bounded by

$$O\left(B(\mathbf{k} + 1/2) \exp\left(-c^2 \sum_{k=1}^{m} k_i^{\varepsilon}\right)\right).$$

Together with the error from the approximation of $\log B_{\mathcal{S}}(\mathbf{k} + 1/2)$ by $\log B(\mathbf{k} + 1/2)$, which is of the form

$$O\left(B(\mathbf{k} + 1/2) \sum_{i=1}^{m} k_i^{-L-1}\right),$$

we obtain the proposed relation. This completes the proof of Lemma 10.10. ∎

Note that $\mathbf{k}/n \in \mathcal{S}^-$ implies that $k_i \geq c \, n^{\frac{1}{2}+\varepsilon}$ for some constant $c > 0$ and all $i = 1, \ldots, m$. Thus, the error term can be also stated in terms of negative powers of n. With the help of Lemma 10.10, we obtain, for any large $L' > 0$,

$$\sum_{\mathbf{k}/n \in \mathcal{S}^-} \binom{n}{\mathbf{k}} \left(\sum_{i=1}^{m} \frac{k_i}{\ln 2} \frac{\partial}{\partial k_i} B_{\mathcal{S}}(\mathbf{k}+1/2) - B_{\mathcal{S}}(\mathbf{k}+1/2) \log B_{\mathcal{S}}(\mathbf{k}+1/2) \right)$$

$$= \sum_{\mathbf{k}/n \in \mathcal{S}^-} \binom{n}{\mathbf{k}} \left(\sum_{i=1}^{m} \frac{k_i}{\ln 2} \frac{\partial}{\partial k_i} B(\mathbf{k}+1/2) - B(\mathbf{k}+1/2) \log B(\mathbf{k}+1/2) \right) + O(n^{-L'})$$

$$= \sum_{\mathbf{k}/n \in \mathcal{S}^-} \binom{n}{\mathbf{k}} B(\mathbf{k}+1/2) \cdot \left(\frac{m-1}{2} \log \frac{n}{2\pi e} + O\left(\sum_{i=1}^{m} 1/(k_i+1) \right) \right) + O(n^{-L'})$$

$$= \left(\frac{m-1}{2} \log \frac{n}{2\pi e} + O\left(1/\sqrt{n} \right) \right) B_{\mathcal{S}}(1/2).$$

Finally, to simplify our presentation, we now explain the other parts of the summation over $\mathbf{k}$ only for $m = 2$ and $\mathcal{S} = \{(\theta, 1-\theta) : \theta \in [a,b]\}$. Suppose that $|k_1 - nb| \le n^{1/2+\varepsilon}$; that is, $(k_1/n, 1 - k_1/n)$ is at distance $\le n^{-1/2+\varepsilon}$ from the boundary of $\mathcal{S}$. Here we have

$$B_{\mathcal{S}}(k_1 + 1/2, n - k_1 + 1/2)$$

$$= \sqrt{\frac{2\pi}{n}} \left(\frac{k_1}{n} \right)^{k_1} \left(\frac{n-k_1}{n} \right)^{n-k_1} \left(\Phi\left(\frac{nb-k_1}{\sqrt{nb(1-b)}} \right) + O(1/\sqrt{n}) \right),$$

where $\Phi(u)$ denotes the normal distribution function. A similar representation holds for the derivatives $\frac{\partial}{\partial k_i} B_{\mathcal{S}}(\mathbf{k}+1/2)$. A standard analysis yields

$$\sum_{|k_1 - nb| \le n^{1/2+\varepsilon}} \binom{n}{\mathbf{k}} \left(\sum_{i=1}^{2} \frac{k_i}{\ln 2} \frac{\partial}{\partial k_i} B_{\mathcal{S}}(\mathbf{k}+1/2) - B_{\mathcal{S}}(\mathbf{k}+1/2) \cdot \log B_{\mathcal{S}}(\mathbf{k}+1/2) \right)$$

$$= O(1/\sqrt{n}).$$

The summation for $nb + n^{1/2+\varepsilon} < k_1 \le n$ is much easier to handle.

For dimension $m > 2$, one has deal with multivariate Gaussian approximations. This is just technical and more involved but there is no substantial problem (see Exercise 10.6. Therefore, we just add some comments on this case. If $\mathbf{k}/n \notin \mathcal{S}^-$, we can distinguish two cases. The first is when $\mathbf{k}/n$ is not contained in $\mathcal{S}$ and has distance $\ge n^{-\frac{1}{2}+\varepsilon}$ to $\mathcal{S}$. In this case, the box

$$Q := \prod_{i=1}^{m} \left[k_i - c\, n^{\frac{1}{2}+\varepsilon}, k_i + c\, n^{\frac{1}{2}+\varepsilon} \right]$$

is not contained in $\mathrm{cone}(\mathcal{S})$, which implies that

$$B_{\mathcal{S}}(\mathbf{k}+1/2) = O\left(B(\mathbf{k}+1/2) \exp\left(-c^2 \sum_{k=1}^{m} k_i^{\varepsilon} \right) \right).$$

Second, if $\mathbf{k}/n$ has distance $\le n^{-\frac{1}{2}+\varepsilon}$ to the boundary of $\mathcal{S}$, then the *Gaussian integral*

$$\int_{Q \cap \mathrm{cone}(\mathcal{S})} \prod_{i=1}^{m} e^{-z_i} z_i^{k_i - \frac{1}{2}}\, dz_1 \cdots dz_m$$

$$\sim e^{-n} \prod_{i=1}^{m} k_i^{k_i - \frac{1}{2}} \int_{Q \cap \mathrm{cone}(\mathcal{S})} \exp\left(-\sum_{i=1}^{m} \frac{(z_i - k_i)^2}{2k_i} \right) dz_1 \cdots dz_m$$

can be expressed in terms of the distribution function Φ of the standard normal distribution, provided that the boundary of S is (locally) a hyperplane. Since we only need upper bounds in this case, the general case can be reduced to this one.

Summing up, in all cases, the remainder is of order $O(1/\sqrt{n})$. This completes the proof of Theorem 10.8.

10.4 Learnable Information and Minimax Redundancy

One of the fundamental questions of information theory and statistical inference probes how much "useful or learnable information" one can actually extract from a given dataset. In this section, we connect useful information to the minimax redundancy.

Let us fix n, the length of a sequence $x^n = x_1 \ldots x_n$ given to us. We would like to understand how much useful information, structure, regularity, or summarizing properties are in x^n. For example, for a binary sequence, the number of ones is a regularity property; the positions of ones is not. Let S be such a summarizing property. We can describe it in two parts. First, we describe the set S, and then the location of x^n in S. We denote by $I(S)$ the learnable/useful information of S; clearly $\log |S|$ bits are needed to point out a particular location in S. Usually, S can be described in many ways, however, one should choose S so that it extracts all relevant information and nothing else. This means we need S that minimizes $I(S)$. We denote such a set $\hat{S}$ and call it *I-sufficient statistics*. It makes sense to call $I(\hat{S})$ the *learnable information* ($\log |S|$ is rather a measure of complexity of S).

Let us consider two possible measures of learnable information. If we describe $\hat{S}$ as the shortest program on a universal Turing machine (i.e., Kolmogorov complexity), then $I(\hat{S})$ becomes *Kolmogorov information* $K(\hat{S})$, and $K(x^n) = K(\hat{S}) + \log |\hat{S}|$. For example, if x^n is a binary sequence, we first describe the *type* of x^n (number of ones; see Chapter 11) that requires $\log n$ bits (and can be improved to $\frac{1}{2} \log n$), and then the location of x^n within the type that requires $\log \binom{n}{k} \approx nH(k/n)$ bits where $H(k/n)$ is the empirical entropy. While this sounds reasonable, in general, Kolmogorov information is not computable, so we need another approach.

We now turn our attention to *computable* learnable information contained in a sequence x^n generated by a source belonging to a class of parameterized distributions $\mathcal{M}(\Theta) = \{P_\theta : \theta \in \Theta\}$. Let $\hat{\theta}(x^n)$ be the ML estimator; that is,

$$\hat{\theta}(x^n) = \arg\max_{\theta \in \Theta} P_\theta(x^n).$$

Observe that for a given sequence x^n, produced either by θ or by θ', we can use $\hat{\theta}(x^n)$ to decide which model generates the data with a small error probability, *provided* these two parameters are far apart in some distance. If these two models, θ and θ', are too close to each other, they are virtually indistinguishable, and thus do not introduce any additional useful information. In view of this, it is reasonable to postulate that learnable information about x^n is summarized in the number of *distinguishable distributions* (models). In summary, if there are $C_n(\Theta)$ such distinguishable distributions according to some distance, it is natural to call

$$I_n(\Theta) = \log C_n(\Theta)$$

the *useful information*. See Figure 10.3 for an illustration.

$C_n(\theta)$ *balls* ; $\log C_n(\theta)$ *useful bits*

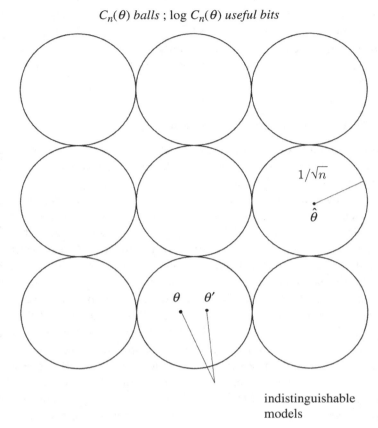

Figure 10.3 Illustration to "learnable information."

Let us estimate $C_n(\Theta)$ for the memoryless case. As a distance between distributions/models, we first adopt the Kullback–Leibler (KL) divergence. Using Taylor expansion around $\hat{\theta}$, we find

$$D(P_{\hat{\theta}}||P_\theta) := \mathbf{E}[\log P_{\hat{\theta}}(X^n)] - \mathbf{E}[\log P_\theta(X^n)] = \frac{1}{2}(\theta - \hat{\theta})^T I(\hat{\theta})(\theta - \hat{\theta}) + o(||\theta - \hat{\theta}||^2), \quad (10.41)$$

where $I(\theta) = [I_{ij}(\theta)]_{ij}$ is the *Fisher information matrix* defined as

$$I_{ij}(\theta) = -\mathbf{E}\left[\frac{\partial^2}{\partial\theta_i\partial\theta_j}\log P_\theta(X)\right].$$

In fact, another related distance is more useful for us, namely, the so-called Mahalanobis distance defined as

$$d_I(\theta, \theta_0) = \sqrt{(\theta - \hat{\theta})^T I(\hat{\theta})(\theta - \hat{\theta})}.$$

This is a rescaled version of Euclidean distance, and in Exercise 10.5 we ask the reader to show that (see also (9.14))

$$d_I(\theta, \theta_0) = O(\sqrt{D(\theta||\theta_0)}). \quad (10.42)$$

One property of the d_I distance is that the volume V of a ball (ellipsoid) at center θ and radius ε is

$$V(B_I(\theta, \varepsilon)) = 1/\sqrt{\det I(\theta)} V(B(\varepsilon)), \tag{10.43}$$

where $B(\varepsilon)$ is the regular Euclidean ball of radius ε and $\det I(\theta)$ is the determinant of $I(\theta)$.

To proceed, we need to specify the error probability and distinguishibility. Let

$$B_{KL}(\theta_0, \varepsilon) = \{\theta : \ D(\theta || \theta_0) \le \varepsilon\}$$

be the KL ball or radius ε around θ_0. Observe that the KL ball $B_{KL}(\theta, \varepsilon)$ becomes a $B_I(\theta, \sqrt{\varepsilon})$ ball in the d_I distance. The distinguishibility of models depends on the error probability that can be estimated as follows for some $\theta \in \Theta_0$:

$$P_\theta(\hat\theta \ne \theta) = P_\theta(\arg \min_{\theta \in \Theta_0} D(\hat\theta(X^n) || \theta) \ne \theta) \tag{10.44}$$

$$\approx P_\theta(\theta(X) \notin B_{KL}(\theta, \varepsilon/n)) \sim 1 - O(\varepsilon^{k/2}) \tag{10.45}$$

for some small $\varepsilon > 0$, where we use the fact that for memoryless sources (more generally, exponential family of distributions),

$$\log \frac{P_{\hat\theta}(x^n)}{P_\theta(x^n)} = n \mathbf{E}_{\hat\theta}\left[\log \frac{P_{\hat\theta}(X)}{P_\theta(X)}\right] = n D(\hat\theta || \theta).$$

We conclude that the number of distinguishable distributions $C_n(\Theta)$ is approximately equal to the *volume* $V_I(\Theta)$ of Θ under distance d_I divided by the volume of the ball size $B_I(\theta, \sqrt{\varepsilon/n})$. In Exercise 10.7 we ask the reader to prove that

$$V_I(\Theta) = \int_\Theta \sqrt{\det I(\theta)} d\theta \tag{10.46}$$

and $V(B_I(\theta, \sqrt{\varepsilon}) \approx O(\varepsilon^{k/2}/\sqrt{\det I(\theta)})$.

Setting up the error probability at level $O(1/\sqrt{n})$ as indicated, we conclude that the number of distinguishable distributions $C_n(\Theta)$ (i.e., the number of centers of the balls $B_I(\theta, \sqrt{\varepsilon})$) is

$$C_n(\Theta) = \left(\frac{n}{2\pi}\right)^{k/2} \int_\Theta \sqrt{\det I(\theta)} d\theta + O(1) \tag{10.47}$$

$$= \sum_{x^n} \sup_{\theta \in \Theta} P_\theta(x^n) = \inf_{\theta \in \Theta} \max_{x^n} \log \frac{P_{\hat\theta}}{P_\theta}$$

$$= \inf_{\theta \in \Theta} D(P_{\hat\theta} || P_\theta) + O(1)$$

$$= R_n^* + O(1) = \overline{R}_n + O(1). \tag{10.48}$$

In summary, average or maximal minimax redundancy can be viewed as a measure of learnable or useful information. Unlike entropy, minimax redundancy provides information about regularity properties of a sequence.

10.5 Minimax Regret for Online Logistic Regression

In Section 9.4, we introduced online regression and its minimax regret. We shall analyze precisely the regret for the specific class $\mathcal{H}_{p,\mathbf{w}}$ of functions $h(\mathbf{x}) = p(\langle \mathbf{x}, \mathbf{w} \rangle)$ with the so-called *logistic function* $p(w) = (1 + \exp(-w))^{-1}$, where $w = \langle \mathbf{x}, \mathbf{w} \rangle$ is the scalar product of $\mathbf{x}$ and $\mathbf{w}$. Using machine learning convention, we write T for n.

We adopt all the notation from Section 9.4. Thus $\mathbf{x}_t = (x_{1,t}, \ldots, x_{d,t})$ is a d-dimensional feature vector such that $\|\mathbf{x}_t\| \le 1$ for some norm $\|\cdot\|$. We also assume that the set $\mathbf{x}_t$ spans $\mathbb{R}^d$. The label binary vector is denoted as $y^T = (y_1, \ldots, y_T)$ with $y_t \in \{-1, 1\}$ and the prediction is $\hat{y}_t \in [0, 1]$. As already defined in Section 9.4, $\mathbf{w}_t = (w_{1,t}, \ldots, w_{d,t})$ is a d-dimensional vector of weights.

Our goal is to precisely estimate the minimax regret with the logarithmic loss for the logistic regression, thus we set $\ell(y_t | \mathbf{x}_t, \mathbf{w}_t) = \log(1 + \exp(-y_t \langle \mathbf{x}_t, \mathbf{w}_t \rangle))$. Observe that for the logistic regression,

$$P(y_t | \mathbf{x}^t, \mathbf{w}^t) = p(y_t \langle \mathbf{x}_t, \mathbf{w}_t \rangle) = \frac{1}{1 + \exp(-y_t \langle \mathbf{x}_t, \mathbf{w}_t \rangle)}$$

is the probability of seeing label y_t, and thus

$$\ell(y_t | \mathbf{x}_t, \mathbf{w}_t) = -\log P(y_t | \mathbf{x}^t, \mathbf{w}^t).$$

Finally, in (9.43) we established that the (fixed-designed) minimax regret $r_T^*(\mathbf{x}^T)$ can be computed through the Shtarkov sum; that is,

$$r_T^*(\mathbf{x}^T) = \log D_T(\mathbf{x}^T)$$

where

$$D_T(\mathbf{x}^T) = \sum_{y^T} \sup_{\mathbf{w}} P(y^T | \mathbf{x}^T, \mathbf{w}) \tag{10.49}$$

and $P(y^T | \mathbf{x}^T, \mathbf{w})$ abbreviates

$$P(y^T | \mathbf{x}^T, \mathbf{w}) = \prod_{j=1}^{T} P(y_t | \mathbf{x}^t, \mathbf{w}). \tag{10.50}$$

In order to make our analysis simpler, we assume that the feature vector $\mathbf{x}_t$ takes only finite number of (vector) values; that is, there is a finite set $\mathcal{A} = \{\mathbf{a}_1, \ldots, \mathbf{a}_N\}$ of vectors such that $\mathbf{x}_t \in \mathcal{A}$ for all t. By T_j; we denote the number of t such that $\mathbf{x}_t = \mathbf{a}_j$ so that

$$T_1 + \cdots + T_N = T.$$

Furthermore, also write $\alpha_j = T_j / T$ so that $\alpha_1 + \cdots + \alpha_N = 1$.

Next, given $y^T \in \{-1, 1\}^T$, we denote by k_j the number of t with $\mathbf{x}_t = \mathbf{a}_j$ and $y_t = 1$. Then (10.50) simplifies to

$$P(y^T | \mathbf{x}^T, \mathbf{w}) = \prod_{j=1}^{N} p(\langle \mathbf{a}_j, \mathbf{w} \rangle)^{k_j} q(\langle \mathbf{a}_j, \mathbf{w} \rangle)^{T_j - k_j}$$

$$= \frac{1}{\prod_{j=1}^{N}(1 + e^{\langle \mathbf{a}_j, \mathbf{w} \rangle})^{T_j}} \cdot \exp\left(\sum_{j=1}^{N} k_j \langle \mathbf{a}_j, \mathbf{w} \rangle\right).$$

Under these restrictions, we prove the following result in Section 10.5.1. Recall that $p(w) = (1 + e^{-w})^{-1}$ and $q(w) = 1 - p(w) = p(-w)$.

Theorem 10.11 *Suppose that d and $N > d$ are fixed positive integers and that $\mathcal{A} = \{\mathbf{a}_1, \ldots, \mathbf{a}_N\}$ is a finite set of d-dimension real vectors with norms $\|\mathbf{a}_j\| \leq 1$ that span $\mathbb{R}^d$. Let $\mathbf{x}_t \in \mathcal{A}$ for $t = 1, \ldots, T$ and denote by T_j the number of t with $\mathbf{x}_t = \mathbf{a}_j$. Furthermore, suppose that there exists $\eta > 0$ such that $T_j \geq \eta T$ for $j = 1, \ldots, N$. Then the maximal minimax regret becomes asymptotically, as $T \to \infty$,*

$$r^*(\mathbf{x}^T) = \frac{d}{2} \log T - \frac{d}{2} \log 2\pi + \log \left(\int_{\mathbb{R}^d} \sqrt{\det(\widetilde{\mathbf{B}}_d(\mathbf{w}))} dw_1 \cdots dw_d \right) + O(1/\sqrt{T}), \quad (10.51)$$

where $\widetilde{\mathbf{B}}_d(\mathbf{w})$ is a $d \times d$ matrix computed as follows:

$$\widetilde{\mathbf{B}}_d(\mathbf{w}) = \sum_{i=1}^{N} \alpha_i p(\langle \mathbf{a}_i, \mathbf{w} \rangle) q(\langle \mathbf{a}_i, \mathbf{w} \rangle) \mathbf{a}_i \cdot \mathbf{a}_i^\tau,$$

where $\alpha_j = T_j/T$ and A^τ denotes the transpose of a matrix A.

We expect that the asymptotic relation (10.51) should hold in a much more general context, in particular when the vectors $\mathbf{x}_t$ are not restricted to a finite set and d varying with T. In this context, the matrix $\widetilde{\mathbf{B}}_d(\mathbf{w})$ is to be replaced by

$$\mathbf{B}(\mathbf{w}, \mathbf{x}^T) = \frac{1}{T} \sum_{t=1}^{T} p(\langle \mathbf{x}_t, \mathbf{w} \rangle) q(\langle \mathbf{x}_t, \mathbf{w} \rangle) \mathbf{x}_t \cdot \mathbf{x}_t^\tau. \quad (10.52)$$

In such a case, we can study the behavior of $\mathbf{B}(\mathbf{w}, \mathbf{x}^T)$ when the vectors $\mathbf{x}_t$ are generated randomly by an iid process. By the law of large numbers, we find (almost surely)

$$\mathbf{B}(\mathbf{w}, \mathbf{x}^T) \to \overline{\mathbf{B}}(\mathbf{w}) := \mathbf{E} \left(p(\langle \mathbf{X}, \mathbf{w} \rangle) q(\langle \mathbf{X}, \mathbf{w} \rangle) \mathbf{X} \cdot \mathbf{X}^\tau \right).$$

We present an asymptotic analysis of $\overline{\mathbf{B}}(\mathbf{w})$ when the feature vector $\mathbf{x}_t$ are generated uniformly on the d-dimensional unit sphere $\mathcal{S}_d$. In this case,

$$\overline{\mathbf{B}}(\mathbf{w}) = \frac{1}{s_d} \int_{\mathcal{S}_d} p(\langle \mathbf{x}, \mathbf{w} \rangle) q(\langle \mathbf{x}, \mathbf{w} \rangle) \mathbf{x} \cdot \mathbf{x}^\tau \, d\mathbf{x},$$

where s_d is the area of the sphere of dimension d and radius 1; that is,

$$s_d = 2\pi^{(d+1)/2} / \Gamma \left(\frac{d+1}{2} \right).$$

In Section 10.5.2, we prove the following result.

Proposition 10.12 *In the case of uniform distribution on the d-dimensional sphere we have, as $d \to \infty$,*

$$\int_{\mathbb{R}^d} \sqrt{\det(\overline{\mathbf{B}}(\mathbf{w}))} d\mathbf{w} = (\pi/8)^{d/4} e^{3/8} (d/4)^{-d/2} \left(1 + O(1/d) \right). \quad (10.53)$$

We observe that when features $\mathbf{x}_t$ are uniformly distributed inside the d-dimensional unit ball, we need an extra factor

$$\left(\frac{d}{d-1} \right)^{d/2} \left(\frac{d-1}{d+1} \right)^{\frac{d-1}{2}}$$

leading to

$$\int_{\mathbb{R}^d} \sqrt{\det(\overline{\mathbf{B}}(\mathbf{w}))}d\mathbf{w} = (\pi/8)^{d/4}e^{-1/8}(d/4)^{-d/2}\left(1 + O(1/d)\right). \qquad (10.54)$$

10.5.1 Proof of Theorem 10.11

In what follows, we sketch the proof of Theorem 10.11. The first step is to understand the behavior of the following optimization problem:

$$\sup_{\mathbf{w}} P(y^T|\mathbf{x}^T, \mathbf{w}).$$

It is easy to see that there is a uniquely defined weight vector $\mathbf{w}^*$ with

$$\max_{\mathbf{w}} P(y^T|\mathbf{x}^T, \mathbf{w}) = P(y^T|\mathbf{x}^T, \mathbf{w}^*)$$

that satisfies the relation

$$\sum_{j=1}^{N} \mathbf{a}_j p(\langle \mathbf{a}_j, \mathbf{w}^* \rangle) T_j = \sum_{j=1}^{N} \mathbf{a}_j k_j. \qquad (10.55)$$

Actually, the matrix

$$\sum_{j=1}^{N} p(\langle \mathbf{a}_j \mathbf{w} \rangle) q(\langle \mathbf{a}_j, \mathbf{w} \rangle) T_j \mathbf{a}_j \cdot \mathbf{a}_j^{\tau}$$

is positive definite (since the vectors $\mathbf{a}_j$ span $\mathbb{R}^d$) and so we have a convex optimization problem.

Next we rewrite the Shtarkov sum (10.49) as

$$D_T(\mathbf{x}^T) = \sum_{k^N} \prod_{j=1}^{N} \binom{T_j}{k_j} \sup_{\mathbf{w}} P(y^T(k^N)|\mathbf{x}^T, \mathbf{w}), \qquad (10.56)$$

where k^N denotes $k^N = (k_1, \ldots, k_N) \in [0, T_1] \times \cdots \times [0, T_N]$ and $y^T(k^N)$ denotes the corresponding binary vector. We then have

$$P(y^T(k^N)|\mathbf{x}^T, \mathbf{w}^*) = \prod_{j=1}^{N} p(\langle \mathbf{a}_j, \mathbf{w}^* \rangle)^{k_j} q(\langle \mathbf{a}_j, \mathbf{w}^* \rangle)^{T_j - k_j},$$

where $\mathbf{w}^* = \mathbf{w}^*(k^N)$ satisfies (10.55). Let now

$$B(k^N, \mathbf{w}^*) := \prod_{j=1}^{N} \binom{T_j}{k_j} p(\langle \mathbf{a}_j, \mathbf{w}^* \rangle)^{k_j} q(\langle \mathbf{a}_j, \mathbf{w}^* \rangle)^{T_j - k_j}$$

for real $k_j \in [0, T_j]$. We just replace $k_j!$ and $(T_j - k_j)!$ by $\Gamma(k_j + 1)$ and $\Gamma(T_j - k_j + 1)$, respectively, and determine $\mathbf{w}^* = \mathbf{w}^*(k^N)$ by the equation (10.55) for real-valued k_j. With the help of Stirling's formula, $B(k^N, \mathbf{w}^*)$ can be approximated by

$$B(k^N, \mathbf{w}^*) \sim \frac{1}{\prod_j \sqrt{2\pi p(\langle \mathbf{a}_j, \mathbf{w}^* \rangle) q(\langle \mathbf{a}_j, \mathbf{w}^* \rangle) T_j}}$$

$$\cdot \exp\left(-\sum_j \frac{(k_j - k_j(w))^2}{2p(\langle \mathbf{a}_j, \mathbf{w}^* \rangle) q(\langle \mathbf{a}_j, \mathbf{w}^* \rangle) T_j} \right)$$

where $k_j(\mathbf{w}^*) = p(\langle \mathbf{a}_j, \mathbf{w}^* \rangle)^{k_j} T_j$ and we assume that $|k_j - k_j(\mathbf{w}^*)| \leq c_j \sqrt{T_j} \log T_j$ for proper constants c_j. By setting

$$\mathbf{D}(\mathbf{w}^*) = \text{diag}\left(\frac{1}{p(\langle \mathbf{a}_1, \mathbf{w}^* \rangle) q(\langle \mathbf{a}_1, \mathbf{w}^* \rangle) T_1}, \ldots, \frac{1}{p(\langle \mathbf{a}_N, \mathbf{w}^* \rangle) q(\langle \mathbf{a}_N, \mathbf{w}^* \rangle) T_N} \right)$$

with $k^N(\mathbf{w}^*) = (k_1(\mathbf{w}^*), \ldots, k_N(\mathbf{w}^*))$, we find

$$B(k^N(w), \mathbf{w}^*) \sim \sqrt{\det(\mathbf{D}(\mathbf{w}^*)/(2\pi))} \tag{10.57}$$

$$\cdot \exp\left(-\frac{1}{2}(k^N - k^N(\mathbf{w}^*))^\tau \mathbf{D}(w)(k^N - k^N(\mathbf{w}^*)) \right).$$

We ask the reader in Exercise 10.13 to show that the sum (10.56) can be approximated by the integral (note that it will also make use of the Gaussian approximations (10.57).

$$\hat{D}_T(\mathbf{x}^T) := \int_{\prod[0, T_j]} \prod_{j=1}^N \binom{T_j}{k_j} p(\langle \mathbf{a}_j, \mathbf{w}^*(k^N) \rangle)^{k_j} q(\langle \mathbf{a}_j, \mathbf{w}^*(k^n) \rangle)^{T_j - k_j}; \tag{10.58}$$

that is, $D_T(\mathbf{x}^T) \sim \hat{D}_T(\mathbf{x}^T)$ as $T \to \infty$.

We next consider the map that assigns to $\mathbf{w}^* \in \mathbb{R}^d$ the vector

$$\mathbf{w}^* \mapsto A(\mathbf{w}^*) := \sum_{j=1}^N \mathbf{a}_j p(\langle \mathbf{a}_j \mathbf{w}^* \rangle) T_j.$$

Furthermore, let $\overline{\mathcal{A}}$ denote the image of the set $A(\mathbb{R}^d)$. This map is bijective and has a strictly positive Jacobian determinant

$$J(\mathbf{w}^*) = \det\left(\sum_{j=1}^N p(\langle \mathbf{a}_j \mathbf{w}^* \rangle) q(\langle \mathbf{a}_j \mathbf{w}^* \rangle) T_j \mathbf{a}_j \cdot \mathbf{a}_j^\tau \right)$$

$$= \det\left(T \widetilde{\mathbf{B}}_d(\mathbf{w}) \right).$$

We further denote by $\mathcal{H}(\mathbf{w}^*)$, the set of $k^N = (k_1, \ldots, k_N) \in \prod_{j=1}^N [0, T_j]$ with

$$A(\mathbf{w}^*) = \sum_{j=1}^N \mathbf{a}_j k_j.$$

Note that

$$k^N(\mathbf{w}^*) = (p(\langle \mathbf{a}_1, \mathbf{w}^* \rangle) T_1, \ldots, p(\langle \mathbf{a}_N, \mathbf{w}^* \rangle) T_N) \in \mathcal{H}(\mathbf{w}^*).$$

Next we replace the integral $\hat{D}_T(\mathbf{x}^T)$ into an integral over $\overline{\mathcal{A}}$ and an $(N - d)$-dimensional integrals over $\mathcal{H}(\mathbf{w}^*)$; that is, k^N is mapped to

$$\sum_{j=1}^{N} \mathbf{a}_j k_j \times \widetilde{\mathcal{H}},$$

where $\widetilde{\mathcal{H}}$ denotes the $(N - d)$-dimensional subspace

$$\widetilde{\mathcal{H}} = \left\{ \mathbf{z} = (z_1, \ldots, z_N) \in \mathbb{R}^N : \sum_{j=1}^{N} \mathbf{a}_j z_j = 0 \right\},$$

where we apply just the $(N - d)$-dimensional Lebesgue measure. Actually, this is a linear mapping with determinant

$$\sqrt{\det(\mathbf{A} \cdot \mathbf{A}^\tau)},$$

where $\mathbf{A} = (\mathbf{a}_1, \ldots, \mathbf{a}_N)$.

In the second step, we apply the substitution $A(\mathbf{w}^*) = \mathbf{a}$ to the first component $\mathbf{a} = \sum_{j=1}^{N} \mathbf{a}_j k_j$. Since this substitution has determinant $J(\mathbf{w}^*)$, we find

$$\hat{D}_T(\mathbf{x}^T) \sim \int_{\mathbb{R}^d} \frac{J(\mathbf{w}^*)}{\sqrt{\det(\mathbf{A} \cdot \mathbf{A}^\tau)}}$$
$$\times \int_{\widetilde{\mathcal{H}}} \sqrt{\det(\mathbf{D}(\mathbf{w}^*)/(2\pi))} \exp\left(-\frac{1}{2}\mathbf{z}^\tau \mathbf{D}(w)\mathbf{z}\right) d\mathbf{z}_{N-d} \, d\mathbf{w}^*.$$

Let us denote by $I(\mathcal{H}, \mathbf{D})$ the following Gaussian integral:

$$I(\widetilde{\mathcal{H}}, \mathbf{D}) = \sqrt{\det(\mathbf{D}/2\pi)} \int_{\widetilde{\mathcal{H}}} \exp\left(-\frac{\langle \mathbf{z}^\tau \mathbf{D}\mathbf{z} \rangle}{2}\right) d\mathbf{z}, \qquad (10.59)$$

where we can assume more generally that $\mathbf{D}$ is a positive definite symmetric matrix.

In order to make the following computations more transparent, we assume that $d = 1$; that is, the vectors $\mathbf{a}_j$ are just real numbers a_j. We also denote by $\mathbf{u}$ the normalized N-dimensional vector

$$\mathbf{u} = \frac{1}{\sqrt{\sum_{j=1}^{N} a_j^2}} (a_1, \ldots, a_N)^\tau.$$

We know that the integral on the whole space equals 1, since the integrand is a Gaussian density with $\mathbf{D}^{-1}$ as the covariance matrix. By slicing the whole space into a folio of hyperplanes parallel to $\widetilde{\mathcal{H}}$ we find

$$\sqrt{\det(\mathbf{D}/2\pi)} \int_{-\infty}^{+\infty} dt \int_{\widetilde{\mathcal{H}}} \exp\left(-\frac{\langle (\mathbf{z} + t\mathbf{u})^\tau \mathbf{D}(\mathbf{z} + t\mathbf{u}) \rangle}{2}\right) d\mathbf{z} = 1.$$

Let $\mathbf{u} = p(\mathbf{u}) + \mathbf{v}$ where $p(\mathbf{u})$ is the projection of $\mathbf{u}$ on $\widetilde{\mathcal{H}}$, according to the metric induced by $\mathbf{D}$. Thus, in the integrand, we have

$$\langle (\mathbf{z} + t\mathbf{u})^\tau \mathbf{D}(\mathbf{z} + t\mathbf{u}) \rangle = \langle (\mathbf{z} + tp(\mathbf{u}))^\tau \mathbf{D}(\mathbf{z} + tp(\mathbf{u})) \rangle + t^2 \langle \mathbf{v}^\tau \mathbf{D}\mathbf{v} \rangle.$$

For a given t, after a simple change of variable, we find

$$\int_{\widetilde{\mathcal{H}}} \exp\left(-\frac{\langle(\mathbf{z} + tp(\mathbf{u}))^\tau \mathbf{D}(\mathbf{z} + tp(\mathbf{u}))\rangle}{2}\right) d\mathbf{z} = \int_{\widetilde{\mathcal{H}}} \exp\left(-\frac{\langle \mathbf{z}^\tau \mathbf{D} \mathbf{z}\rangle}{2}\right) d\mathbf{z}.$$

Thus,

$$I(\widetilde{\mathcal{H}}, \mathbf{D}) \int_{-\infty}^{\infty} \exp(-t^2 \langle \mathbf{v}^\tau \mathbf{D} \mathbf{v}\rangle / 2) dt = 1$$

and therefore,

$$I(\widetilde{\mathcal{H}}, \mathbf{D}) = \sqrt{\frac{\langle \mathbf{v}^\tau \mathbf{D} \mathbf{v}\rangle}{2\pi}}.$$

In order to determine $\mathbf{v}$, we notice that if $\mathbf{v}$ is orthogonal to $\mathcal{H}$ with metric $\mathbf{D}$, then $\mathbf{D}\mathbf{v}$ is orthogonal to $\widetilde{\mathcal{H}}$ with classic metric. Thus, $\mathbf{D}\mathbf{v}$ is colinear with $\mathbf{u}$, or equivalently $\mathbf{D}^{-1}\mathbf{u}$ is colinear with $\mathbf{v}$. Since $\mathbf{u} - \mathbf{v}$ must belong to $\widetilde{\mathcal{H}}$, then $\langle \mathbf{u}^\tau (\mathbf{u} - \mathbf{v})\rangle = 0$ and

$$\mathbf{v} = \frac{1}{\langle \mathbf{u}^\tau \mathbf{D}^{-1} \mathbf{u}\rangle} \mathbf{D}^{-1} \mathbf{u},$$

and consequently $\langle \mathbf{v}^\tau \mathbf{D} \mathbf{v}\rangle = \frac{1}{\langle \mathbf{u}^\tau \mathbf{D}^{-1} \mathbf{u}\rangle}$. Finally, we arrive at

$$I(\widetilde{\mathcal{H}}, \mathbf{D}) = \sqrt{\frac{1}{2\pi \langle \mathbf{u}^\tau \mathbf{D}^{-1} \mathbf{u}\rangle}}$$

$$= \frac{\sqrt{2\pi \sum_{j=1}^{N} a_j^2 p(a_j w) q(a_j w) T_j}}{\sqrt{\sum_{i=1}^{N} a_i^2}},$$

which gives then

$$D_T(\mathbf{x}^T) \sim \int_{-\infty}^{\infty} \sqrt{2\pi \sum_{j=1}^{N} a_j^2 p(a_j w) q(a_j w) T_j} \, dw$$

$$= \sqrt{2\pi N} \int_{-\infty}^{\infty} \sqrt{\det(\widetilde{\mathbf{B}}_1(w))} \, dw$$

as desired. The general case $d \geq 1$ can be worked out in a similar fashion (we ask the reader to do this in Exercise 10.14).

10.5.2 Proof of Proposition 10.12

We recall that we consider the case for which the feature $\mathbf{x}_t$ is uniformly distributed on the d-dimensional unit sphere. We aim at computing the integral (10.53) asymptotically.

We first need the following lemma.

Lemma 10.13 *Let $f(x) = p(x)q(x) = [(1 + e^{-x})(1 + e^x)]^{-1}$ and $\mathbf{u} = \mathbf{w}/||\mathbf{w}||$.*
(i) Then $\overline{\mathbf{B}}(w)$ can be represented as

$$\overline{\mathbf{B}}(\mathbf{w}) = \lambda(\mathbf{w})\mathbf{u} \cdot \mathbf{u}^\tau + \mu(\mathbf{w})(\mathbf{I}_d - \mathbf{u} \cdot \mathbf{u}^\tau), \tag{10.60}$$

where $\mathbf{I}_d$ *is the identity matrix and*

$$\lambda(\mathbf{w}) = \frac{s_{d-1}}{s_d} \int_0^\pi \cos(\theta)^2 \sin(\theta)^{d-2} f(\cos(\theta)\|\mathbf{w}\|) d\theta \qquad (10.61)$$

and

$$\mu(\mathbf{w}) = \frac{s_{d-1}}{s_d} \int_0^\pi \frac{\sin(\theta)^d}{d-1} f(\cos(\theta)\|\mathbf{w}\|) d\theta \qquad (10.62)$$

are the eigenvalues of $\overline{\mathbf{B}}(w)$ *with multiplicities* 1 *and* $d - 1$, *respectively.*

(ii) *Furthermore,* $\det \overline{\mathbf{B}}(\mathbf{w}) = \lambda(\mathbf{w}) \cdot \mu^{d-1}(\mathbf{w})$ *and both* $\lambda(\mathbf{w})$ *and* $\mu(\mathbf{w})$ *are of order* $O(\|\mathbf{w}\|^{-3})$, *thus* $\det(\mathbf{B}(\mathbf{w}))$ *is* $O(\|\mathbf{w}\|^{-3d})$. *More precisely,*

$$\det(\mathbf{B}(\mathbf{w})) = 2 \left(\frac{s_{d-1}}{3 s_d} \pi^2 \|\mathbf{w}\|^{-3} (1 + O(\|\mathbf{w}\|^{-2})) \right)^d \qquad (10.63)$$

as $\|\mathbf{w}\| \to \infty$.

Proof We start with part (i). Let θ be the angle between $\mathbf{a}$ and $\mathbf{u}$. We have the decomposition $\mathbf{a} = \cos(\theta)\mathbf{u} + \mathbf{b}$ with $\mathbf{b} \in \sin\theta \mathcal{S}_{d-1}(\mathbf{u})$ where $\mathcal{S}_{d-1}(\mathbf{u})$ is the unit hypersphere orthogonal to $\mathbf{u}$. Since $\mathbf{a}$'s have a spheric symmetry in their distribution, so it is the case for the $\mathbf{b}$'s in $\sin\theta \mathcal{S}_{d-1}(\mathbf{u})$ for any given angle θ. Thus,

$$\begin{aligned}
\overline{\mathbf{B}}(\mathbf{w}) &= \frac{1}{s_d} \int_0^\pi f(\|\mathbf{w}\| \cos\theta) d\theta \int_{\sin\theta \mathcal{S}_{d-1}(\mathbf{u})} (\mathbf{b} + \cos\theta \mathbf{u}) \cdot (\mathbf{b} + \cos\theta \mathbf{u})^\tau d\mathbf{b} \\
&= \frac{1}{s_d} \int_0^\pi f(\|\mathbf{w}\| \cos\theta) d\theta \int_{\sin\theta \mathcal{S}_{d-1}(\mathbf{u})} (\mathbf{b} \cdot \mathbf{b}^\tau + (\cos\theta)^2 \mathbf{u} \cdot \mathbf{u}^\tau) d\mathbf{b} \\
&\quad + \frac{1}{s_d} \int_0^\pi f(\|\mathbf{w}\| \cos\theta) d\theta \int_{\sin\theta \mathcal{S}_{d-1}(\mathbf{u})} \cos\theta (\mathbf{b} \cdot \mathbf{u}^\tau + \mathbf{u} \cdot \mathbf{b}^\tau) d\mathbf{b}.
\end{aligned}$$

Again, due to the spheric symmetry of $\mathbf{b}$, we also have $\int_{\sin\theta \mathcal{S}_{d-1}(\mathbf{u})} \mathbf{b} = 0$ leading to

$$\begin{aligned}
\overline{\mathbf{B}}(\mathbf{w}) &= \frac{1}{s_d} \int_0^\pi f(\|\mathbf{w}\| \cos\theta) d\theta \int_{\sin\theta \mathcal{S}_{d-1}(\mathbf{u})} (\mathbf{b} \cdot \mathbf{b}^\tau + (\cos\theta)^2 \mathbf{u} \cdot \mathbf{u}^\tau) d\mathbf{b} \\
&= \frac{1}{s_d} \int_0^\pi f(\|\mathbf{w}\| \cos\theta)(\sin\theta)^{d-1} d\theta \\
&\quad \int_{\mathcal{S}_{d-1}(\mathbf{u})} ((\sin\theta)^2 \mathbf{b} \cdot \mathbf{b}^\tau + (\cos\theta)^2 \mathbf{u} \cdot \mathbf{u}^\tau) d\mathbf{b}. \qquad (10.64)
\end{aligned}$$

The $(\sin\theta)^{d-1}$ factor arises from the change of integration domain from $\sin\theta \mathcal{S}_{d-1}(\mathbf{u})$ to $\mathcal{S}_{d-1}(\mathbf{u})$.

The quantity

$$\int_{\mathcal{S}_{d-1}(\mathbf{u})} \mathbf{b} \cdot \mathbf{b}^\tau d\mathbf{b}$$

is the $(d-1) \times (d-1)$ matrix whose (i, j) coefficient is $\int_{\mathcal{S}_{d-1}} b_i b_j d\mathbf{b}$. Clearly, by spheric symmetry of the $\mathbf{b}$ vectors

$$\int_{\mathcal{S}_{d-1}} b_i b_j d\mathbf{b} = 0$$

when $i \neq j$. We also have for all $i = j$,

$$\int_{\mathcal{S}_{d-1}} (b_i)^2 \, d\mathbf{b} = \int_{\mathcal{S}_{d-1}} (b_j)^2 \, d\mathbf{b} = \frac{1}{d-1} \int_{\mathcal{S}_{d-1}} \|\mathbf{b}\|^2 \, d\mathbf{b} = \frac{s_{d-1}}{d-1}.$$

Thus,

$$\int_{\mathcal{S}_{d-1}(\mathbf{u})} \mathbf{b} \cdot \mathbf{b}^\tau \, d\mathbf{b} = \frac{s_{d-1}}{d-1} \mathbf{I}_{d-1}(\mathbf{u})$$

and similarly

$$\int_{\mathcal{S}_{d-1}(\mathbf{u})} \mathbf{u} \cdot \mathbf{u}^\tau \, d\mathbf{b} = s_{d-1} \mathbf{u} \cdot \mathbf{u}^\tau,$$

which completes the proof of part (i) of the lemma.

Now we move to part (ii) of Lemma 10.13. Both $\lambda(\mathbf{w})$ and $\mu(\mathbf{w})$ are functions of $w = \|\mathbf{w}\|$. We write $\lambda(w) = \lambda(\|\mathbf{w}\|)$ and $\mu(w) = \mu(\|\mathbf{w}\|)$. To capture the asymptotics of these functions we apply the Mellin transform discussed in Appendix D.

The Mellin transforms $\lambda^*(s)$ and $\mu^*(s)$ of $\lambda(w)$ and $\mu(w)$ are defined, respectively, as

$$\lambda^*(s) = \int_0^\infty \lambda(w) w^{s-1} \, dw, \qquad \mu^*(s) = \int_0^\infty \mu(w) w^{s-1} \, dw.$$

Observe now that

$$\lambda(w) = 2 \frac{s_{d-1}}{s_d} \int_0^{\pi/2} f(\cos(\theta)w) \cos^2(\theta) \sin^{d-2}(\theta) d\theta$$

$$= \frac{2s_{d-1}}{s_d} \int_0^1 y^2 (1 - y^2)^{(d-3)/2} f(yx) dy$$

via the change of variable $y = \cos(\theta)$. Thus, we find

$$\lambda^*(s) = \frac{2s_{d-1}}{s_d} \int_0^1 (1 - y^2)^{(d-3)/2} y^2 dy \int_0^\infty f(yx) x^{s-1} dx$$

$$= \frac{2s_{d-1}}{s_d} f^*(s) \int_0^1 (1 - y^2)^{(d-3)/2} y^{2-s} dy$$

$$= 2 \frac{s_{d-1}}{s_d} f^*(s) \beta_1^*(3 - s),$$

where $f^*(s)$ is the Mellin transform of $f(x) = p(x)q(x)$ and $\beta_1(s)$ is the Mellin transform of the function $(1 - y^2)^{(d-3)/2}$ defined over $[0, 1]$.

The Mellin transform $\beta_1^*(s)$ exists for $\Re(s) > 0$ and can be written in terms of the beta-function (after applying a substitution $y^2 = z$):

$$\beta_1^*(s) = \frac{1}{2} B((d-1)/2, s/2) = \frac{\Gamma((d-1)/2)\Gamma(s/2)}{2\Gamma((d+s-1)/2)}.$$

Clearly, $\beta_1^*(s)$ has poles on the negative even integers (by the way they also correspond to the Taylor expansion of $(1 - y^2)^{(d-3)/2}$).

The Mellin transform $f^*(s)$ of function $f(x)$ also exists for $\Re(s) > 0$. We furthermore consider the Mellin transform $h^*(s)$ of the function $h(x) = \log(1 + e^{-x})$ (which exists for $\Re(s) > 0$ too) and is given by

$$h^*(s) = (1 - 2^{-s})\zeta(s + 1)\Gamma(s),$$

where $\zeta(s)$ is the Riemann zeta-function. By applying partial integration twice, we get for $\Re(s) > 2$,

$$h^*(s - 2) = \frac{1}{(s - 1)(s - 2)}f^*(s)$$

or

$$f^*(s) = (s - 1)(s - 2)h^*(s - 2).$$

Note that the poles of $h^*(s - 2)$ at $s = 1$ and $s = 2$ are canceled so that this identity actually holds for $\Re(s) > 0$.

Summing up, the product $\beta_1(2 - s)f^*(s)$ (and, thus, $\lambda^*(s)$) is defined for $\Re(s) \in (0, 3)$. At $s = 3$, there is a pole that has the residue $-\zeta(2)\Gamma(3) = -\pi^2/3$.

We can make a similar analysis for $\mu^*(s)$ and we arrive at

$$\mu^*(s) = 2\frac{s_{d-1}}{(d - 1)s_d}\beta_2^*(1 - s)f^*(s),$$

where $\beta_2^*(s)$ is the Mellin transform of the function $(1 - y^2)^{(d-1)/2}$. Similarly to the Mellin transform, $\mu^*(s)$ is also defined on $\Re(s) \in (0, 3)$ and has a simple pole at $s = 3$ with residue

$$-\zeta(2)\Gamma(3)\frac{d - 1}{2} = -\frac{\pi^2(d - 1)}{6}.$$

For both $\lambda^*(s)$ and $\mu^*(s)$, the next pole is at $s = 5$.

We now apply the inverse Mellin transform,

$$\lambda(w) = \frac{1}{2\pi i}\int_{1-i\infty}^{1+i\infty}\lambda^*(s)w^{-s}ds, \qquad \mu(w) = \frac{1}{2\pi i}\int_{1-i\infty}^{1+i\infty}\mu^*(s)w^{-s}ds,$$

to extract asymptotics of $\lambda(w)$ and $\mu(w)$ for $w \to \infty$. By moving the integration path over the simple poles at $s = 3$ and $s = 5$ and catching the residues, we finally obtain

$$\lambda(w) = 2\frac{s_{d-1}}{3s_d}\pi^2 w^{-3} + O(w^{-5}),$$

$$\mu(w) = \frac{s_{d-1}}{3s_d}\pi^2 w^{-3} + O(w^{-5})$$

for $w \to \infty$. In conclusion,

$$\det(\overline{\mathbf{B}}(\mathbf{w})) = 2\left(\frac{s_{d-1}}{3s_d}\pi^2\|\mathbf{w}\|^{-3}(1 + O(\|\mathbf{w}\|^{-2}))\right)^d \tag{10.65}$$

when $\|\mathbf{w}\| \to \infty$. This completes the proof of Lemma 10.13. ∎

It is now easy to complete the proof of Proposition 10.12. We have to evaluate the quantities $\lambda(\mathbf{w})$ and $\mu(\mathbf{w})$, the eigenvalues of matrix $\overline{\mathbf{B}}(\mathbf{w})$ for large d. The main contribution of both integrals is for θ around $\frac{\pi}{2}$. For $\theta = \frac{\pi}{2} + \sqrt{\frac{2}{d}}x$, we have

$$\sin(\theta)^{d-2} = \exp\left(-\frac{d-2}{d}(x^2 + O(x^4))\right),$$

$$\cos(\theta)^2 = \frac{2}{d}x^2 - 4/(3d^2)x^4 + O(x^6/d^3),$$

$$f(\cos(\theta)\|\mathbf{w}\|) = \frac{1}{4}\exp\left(-\frac{\|\mathbf{w}\|^2}{2d}x^2\right) \cdot (1 + O(w^4x^4/d^2)),$$

leading to (after dropping the error term, which is easy to estimate)

$$\int_0^\pi \sin(\theta)^{d-2}\cos(\theta)^2 f(\cos(\theta)\|\mathbf{w}\|)d\theta$$

$$\sim (2/d)^{3/2}\int_{-\infty}^{+\infty}\exp\left(-(1+\frac{\|\mathbf{w}\|^2 - 4}{2d})x^2\right)x^2\,dx$$

$$= (2/d)^{3/2}\frac{\sqrt{\pi}}{2}\left(1 + \frac{\|\mathbf{w}\|^2 - 4}{2d}\right)^{-3/2}$$

and

$$\int_0^\pi \sin(\theta)^d f(\cos(\theta)\|\mathbf{w}\|)d\theta \sim (2/d)^{1/2}\int_{-\infty}^{+\infty}\exp\left(-(1+\frac{\|\mathbf{w}\|^2}{2d})x^2\right)dx$$

$$= (2/d)^{1/2}\sqrt{\pi}\left(1 + \frac{\|\mathbf{w}\|^2}{2d}\right)^{-1/2}.$$

In summary,

$$\det(\mathbf{B}(\mathbf{w})) \sim \left(\frac{s_{d-1}}{s_d}\right)^d (2/d)^{d/2}\frac{1}{d}\frac{1}{(d-1)^{d-1}}\pi^{d/2}\exp\left(-\frac{\|\mathbf{w}\|^2}{4}\right).$$

To complete the derivation, we need to integrate $\sqrt{\det(\mathbf{B}(\mathbf{w}))}$ over the vectors $\mathbf{w}$. This leads to

$$\int \sqrt{(\det(\mathbf{B}(\mathbf{w})))}d\mathbf{w} \sim \frac{1}{2^d}\left(\frac{s_{d-1}}{s_d}\right)^{d/2}(2/d)^{d/4}\frac{1}{\sqrt{d}}\frac{1}{\sqrt{d-1}^{d-1}}\pi^{d/4}(2\sqrt{2\pi})^d. \tag{10.66}$$

The final touch is to estimate of the ratio $\frac{s_{d-1}}{s_d}$. But

$$\frac{s_{d-1}}{s_d} = \sqrt{\pi}\frac{\Gamma(d/2)}{\Gamma((d-1)/2)}, \qquad \frac{\Gamma(d/2)}{\Gamma((d-1)/2)} = \sqrt{\frac{d}{2} - \frac{1}{4}} + O(1/d)$$

so that

$$\int \sqrt{(\det(\mathbf{B}(\mathbf{w})))}d\mathbf{w} \sim (\pi/8)^{d/4}e^{3/8}(d/4)^{-d/2}, \tag{10.67}$$

which completes the proof.

10.6 Exercises

10.1 Prove (10.9) using the definitions of $T(z)$ and $B(z)$; that is, prove that

$$B(z) = \frac{1}{1 - T(z)}$$

for all $z < e^{-1}$.

10.2   Prove (10.17); that is,

$$S_n - S_n^{(\mathcal{S})} = O\left(n^{\frac{m}{2}-1}\right).$$

10.3   Consider the binary constrained case as discussed in Section 10.3. Prove that in this case the KT-estimator (see Krichevsky and Trofimov (1981)) can be computed as

$$M(x_{n+1}|x^n) = \frac{N_{x_{n+1}}(x^n) + 1/2}{n+1} + (2x_{n+1} - 1)\frac{a_1^{N_1(x^n)+1/2}(1 - a_1 N_0(x^n)) + 1/2}{C(\mathcal{S})(n+1)}$$
$$- (2x_{n+1} - 1)\frac{b_1^{N_1(x^n)+1/2}(1 - b_1 N_0(x^n)) + 1/2}{C(\mathcal{S})(n+1)}$$

where $C(\mathcal{S})$ is defined in (10.15).

10.4   Prove the estimate (10.37; that is,

$$\sum_k \binom{n}{k} \frac{B(k+1/2)}{k_i+1} = O\left(\frac{\sqrt{m}B(1/2)}{\sqrt{n}}\right)$$

uniformly for all m and n.

10.5   Prove (10.42) and (10.43).

10.6   Complete the proof of Theorem 10.8 for $m > 2$ by providing rigorous derivations.

10.7   Prove (10.46) (see Balasubramaniam (1997), Grunwald (2007)).

10.8   Consider the following recurrence that is related to the maximal minimax redundancy of memoryless sources. Under some initial conditions, a sequence x_n^m satisfies for $n \geq 1$ and $m \geq 1$:

$$x_n^m = a_n + \sum_{i=0}^{n} \binom{n}{i} \left(\frac{i}{n}\right)^i \left(1 - \frac{i}{n}\right)^{n-i} (x_i^{m-1} + x_{n-i}^{m-1}), \qquad (10.68)$$

where a_n is a given sequence (the so-called *additive* term), and m is an additional parameter. Prove that the following tree-generating functions

$$X_m(z) = \sum_{k=0}^{\infty} \frac{k^k}{k!} z^k x_k^m, \qquad A(z) = \sum_{k=0}^{\infty} \frac{k^k}{k!} z^k a_k$$

satisfy the following functional equation:

$$X_m(z) = A(z) + 2B(z)X_{m-1}(z),$$

where $B(z)$ is defined in (10.8).

10.9   Consider a memoryless unconstrained source Θ with $m = o(n)$. Using *elementary* asymptotics (without complex analysis), prove the following:

$$R_n^*(\Theta) = \frac{m-1}{2} \log\left(\frac{en}{m}\right) + \frac{1}{2}(1 - \log 2)$$
$$+ O(1/m) + O(m^{3/2}/\sqrt{n})$$

for large n.

10.10 Consider the midfield model $\mathcal{M}_0$ denoted as $\widetilde{\mathcal{M}}_0$. In this model, family $\widetilde{\mathcal{M}}_0$ assumes an alphabet $\mathcal{A} \cup \mathcal{B}$, where $|\mathcal{A}| = m$ and $|\mathcal{B}| = M$. The probabilities of symbols in $\mathcal{A}$, denoted by $p_1, \ldots, p_m$, are allowed to vary (unknown), while the probabilities $q_1, \ldots, q_M$ of the symbols in $\mathcal{B}$ are fixed (known). Furthermore, $q = q_1 + \cdots + q_M$ and $p = 1 - q$. We assume that $0 < q < 1$ is fixed (independent of the sequence length n). To simplify our notation, we also write $\mathbf{p} = (p_1, \ldots, p_m)$ and $\mathbf{q} = (q_1, \ldots, q_M)$. The output sequence is denoted $x := x_1^n \in (\mathcal{A} \cup \mathcal{B})^n$.
Let $\widetilde{R}^*_{n,m,M}(\widetilde{\mathcal{M}}_0)$ denote the redundancy of the model $\widetilde{\mathcal{M}}_0$. Prove the following:

$$\widetilde{R}^*_{n,m,M} = \sum_{k=0}^{n} \binom{n}{k} p^k (1-p)^{n-k} \widetilde{R}^*_{n,m}(\mathcal{M}_0),$$

where $\widetilde{R}^*_{n,m}(\mathcal{M}_0)$ is the minimax redundancy of the original $\mathcal{M}_0$.

10.11 Consider the model $\widetilde{\mathcal{M}}_0$ defined in Exercise 10.10. Prove the following theorem established in Szpankowski and Weinberger (2012).

Theorem 10.14 *Consider a family of memoryless models $\widetilde{\mathcal{M}}_0$ over the $(m + M)$-ary alphabet $\mathcal{A} \cup \mathcal{B}$, with fixed probabilities $q_1, \ldots, q_M$ of the symbols in $\mathcal{B}$, such that $q = q_1 + \ldots + q_M$ is bounded away from 0 and 1. Let $p = 1 - q$. Then, the minimax pointwise redundancy $d_{n,m,M}$ takes the form:*
(i_0) *If m is fixed, then*

$$\widetilde{R}^*_{n,m,M} = \frac{m-1}{2} \log\left(\frac{np}{2}\right) + \log\left(\frac{\sqrt{\pi}}{\Gamma(\frac{m}{2})}\right) + O\left(\frac{1}{\sqrt{n}}\right). \qquad (10.69)$$

(i) Let $m_n \to \infty$ as n grows, with $m_n = o(n)$. Assume:

(a) $m(x) := m_x$ is a continuous function, as well as its derivatives $m'(x)$ and $m''(x)$.

(b) denote $\Delta_n := m_{n+1} - m_n = O(m'(n))$, $m'(n) = O(m/n)$, and $m''(n) = O(m/n^2)$, where $m'(n)$ and $m''(n)$ are derivatives of $m(x)$ at $x = n$.

If $m_n = o(\sqrt{n}/\log n)$, then

$$\widetilde{R}^*_{n,m,M} = \frac{m_{np} - 1}{2} \log\left(\frac{np}{m_{np}}\right) + \frac{m_{np}}{2} \log e$$
$$- \frac{1}{2} + \frac{m_{np}}{3} \log e \sqrt{\frac{m_{np}}{np}} + O\left(\frac{1}{\sqrt{m_n}} + \frac{m_n^2 \log^2 n}{n}\right).$$

Otherwise,

$$\widetilde{R}^*_{n,m,M} = \frac{m_{np}}{2} \log\left(\frac{np}{m_{np}}\right) + \frac{m_{np}}{2} \log e$$
$$+ \frac{m_{np}}{3} \log e \sqrt{\frac{m_{np}}{np}} + O\left(\log n + \frac{m_n^2}{n} \log^2 \frac{n}{m_n}\right).$$

(ii) Let $m_n = \alpha n + \ell(n)$, where α is a positive constant and $\ell(n)$ is a monotonic function such that $\ell(n) = o(n)$. Then,

$$\widetilde{R}^*_{n,m,M} = n \log \left(B_\alpha p + 1 - p \right)$$
$$- \log \sqrt{A_\alpha} + O\left(\ell(n) + \frac{1}{\sqrt{n}} \right)$$

where A_α and B_α are defined in Theorem 10.7(ii).

(iii) Let $n = o(m_n)$ and assume m_k/k is a nondecreasing sequence. Then,

$$\widetilde{R}^*_{n,m,M} = n \log \left(\frac{p m_n}{n} \right) + O\left(\frac{n^2}{m_n} + \frac{1}{\sqrt{n}} \right) \qquad (10.70)$$

for large n.

10.12 Prove rigorously (10.44).

10.13 Prove that the sum (10.56) is asymptotically equal to the integral (10.58) as $T \to \infty$.

10.14 Calculate the integral (10.59) for any dimensions $1 \leq d < N$.

10.15 Suppose that the N vectors $\mathbf{a}_1, \dots, \mathbf{a}_N \in \mathbb{R}^d$ span $\mathbb{R}^d$ and suppose that $\alpha_j > 0, 0 \leq j \leq N$. Prove that the integral

$$\int_{\mathbb{R}^d} \sqrt{\det \left(\sum_{i=1}^N \alpha_i p(\langle \mathbf{a}_i \mathbf{w} \rangle) q(\langle \mathbf{a}_i \mathbf{w} \rangle) \mathbf{a}_i \cdot \mathbf{a}_i^\tau \right)} \, dw_1 \cdots dw_d$$

is finite.

Bibliographical Notes

Redundancy and regret for memoryless sources are analyzed in many papers. The leading term of the minimax redundancy was already known to Rissanen (1984b). A better estimate was provided by Clarke and Barron (1990), and then Xie and Barron (1997, 2000). The precise asymptotic expansion for $\widetilde{R}^*_n$ was presented in Szpankowski (1998), while the coding part $R^*_n(Q^*)$ was derived in Drmota and Szpankowski (2004). Finally, the constrained distribution was first discussed in Drmota and Szpankowski (2004) for the binary case while the sequential algorithm for this case was presented in Shamir, Tjalkens, and Willems (2008). It was recently extended to nonbinary alphabets in Drmota et al. (2022).

Minimax redundancy for large alphabets was tackled in Gyorfi, Pali, and der Meulen (1994) (see also Kieffer (1978)), but then significantly extended in Orlitsky, Santhanam, and Zhang (2004), Orlitsky and Santhanam (2004), Shamir (2006b, 2006a), Boucheron, Garivier, and Gassiat (2009). The leading terms of the asymptotic expansions in Theorem 10.7 for $m = o(n)$ and $n = o(m)$ were also derived in Orlitsky and Santhanam (2004). The precise maximal minimax redundancy was for the time established in Szpankowski and Weinberger (2012).

The precise maximal minimax redundancy for finite alphabets presented in Section 10.1 is based on Drmota and Szpankowski (2004), while minimax redundancy for large alphabets discussed in Section 10.2 follows Szpankowski and Weinberger (2012). The average minimax redundancy described in Section 10.3 come from Drmota et al. (2022). Section 10.4

follows Balasubramaniam (1997), Grunwald (2007), Rissanen (2007). Finally Section 10.5 is based on Jacquet et al. (2021) (see also Foster et al. (2018), Shamir (2020)).

Properties of the Lambert W function and tree function $T(z)$ are discussed in depth in Corless et al. (1996).

11

Markov Types and Redundancy for Markov Sources

In this chapter, we study Markov sources $\mathcal{M}_r$ of order r, however, we usually assume that they are of order 1. Our goal to is derive precise estimates for the minimax redundancy and regrets, where our main focus is on the maximal (worst-case) minimax R_n^*.

However, in order to address the minimax redundancy, we must understand Markov types; that is, the number of *distinct* distributions and the number of sequences generated by a Markov source of the same distribution type. We shall discuss Markov types in this chapter too.

11.1 Some Preliminaries

In Lemma 9.2, we showed that the maximal minimax can be partitioned into the coding part $R_n^*(Q^*)$ and the part $\widetilde{R}_n^*$ that represents the class of sources. That is,

$$R_n^* = R_n^*(Q^*) + \widetilde{R}_n^*$$

where $\widetilde{R}_n^* = \log D_n$ with

$$D_n = \sum_{x^n} \sup_{P \in \mathcal{M}_r} P(x^n).$$

Here, x^n is generated by an unknown Markov source from $\mathcal{M}_r$ with empirical distribution $P(x^n)$ where $P \in \mathcal{M}_r$.

Let now $P \in \mathcal{M}_1$, where $\mathcal{M}_1$ is a Markov source of order 1. Assume that the alphabet is $\mathcal{A} = \{0, 1, \dots, m-1\}$, and the unknown transition probabilities are p_{ij} for $i, j \in \mathcal{A}$. Then we can write

$$P(x^n) = P(x_0) \prod_{i,j \in \mathcal{A}} p_{ij}^{k_{ij}},$$

where k_{ij} is the number of (consecutive) pairs $(i,j) \in \mathcal{A}^2$ in x^n. For example,

$$P(0101100) = P(0)p_{00}p_{01}^2 p_{10}^2 p_{11}.$$

Clearly, we have

$$\sum_{1 \leq i,j \leq m} k_{ij} = n - 1.$$

The matrix $\mathbf{k} = [k_{ij}]_{i,j \in \mathcal{A}}$ is called the frequency matrix and plays a crucial role in the Markov analysis. It satisfies the so-called *conservation law*, which asserts that the number of pairs

(j, i) that ends with symbol i must be equal (with the possible exception of the first and last symbols) to the number of pairs (i, j) that start with symbol i (see (11.6).

In order to analyze the maximal minimax redundancy, we need to find $\sup P(x^n)$ and $D_n(\mathcal{M})$. Since

$$\sup_P P(x^n) = \sup_{p_{ij}} \prod_{ij} p_{ij}^{k_{ij}} = \left(\frac{k_{00}}{k_0}\right)^{k_{00}} \cdots \left(\frac{k_{m-1,m-1}}{k_{m-1}}\right)^{k_{m-1,m-1}},$$

where $k_i = \sum_{j=1}^m k_{ij}$, one finds

$$D_n(\mathcal{M}) = \sum_{\mathbf{k}} M_{\mathbf{k}} \left(\frac{k_{00}}{k_0}\right)^{k_{00}} \cdots \left(\frac{k_{m-1,m-1}}{k_{m-1}}\right)^{k_{m-1,m-1}}, \tag{11.1}$$

where $M_{\mathbf{k}}$ is the number of x^n generated over $\mathcal{A}$ having k_{ij} pairs (i, j) in x^n. It is known as the *frequency count* but in fact it is the number of Markov sequences of a given *type*, as we shall define precisely in the next section.

Thus, in order to study the minimax redundancy R_n^*, in Section 11.2.1, we first discuss Markov types. Then in Theorem 11.14 we present precise asymptotics for the maximal minimax redundancy leading to

$$\widetilde{R}_n^* \sim \frac{m^r(m-1)}{2} \log n$$

for Markov of order r.

11.2 Markov Types

The underlying idea of types is that two sequences x^n, y^n of the same type should have the same probabilities: $P(x^n) = P(y^n)$. This could be used as a definition of types. However, we use a combinatorial approach.

Suppose that $\mathbf{k} = [k_{ij}]_{i,j \in \mathcal{A}}$ is a frequency matrix of a sequence x^n (for some $n \geq 0$). Then the type $\mathcal{T}(\mathbf{k})$ is the set of sequences with the frequency matrix $\mathbf{k}$. Sometimes we will also use the notation $\mathcal{T}(x^n)$. Clearly we have

$$\bigcup_{x^n} \mathcal{T}(x^n) = \mathcal{A}^n.$$

Furthermore we denote the set of all types of sequences of length n over an alphabet of size m as $\mathcal{Q}_n(m)$.

So our goal is to find asymptotic expressions for the number of (first order) Markov types $|\mathcal{Q}_n(m)|$ and number of sequences of type x^n; that is, $|\mathcal{T}(x^n)|$.

Example 11.1 For a memoryless source over the alphabet $\mathcal{A} = \{0, 1, \ldots, m-1\}$ we can consider the vector $\mathbf{k} = (k_i)_{i \in \mathcal{A}}$ of frequencies of the appearing symbols; that is, a sequence x^n is of type $\mathbf{k}$ if the symbol i appears k_i times in x^n, $0 \leq i < m$. Since

$$P(x^n) = \prod_{i \in \mathcal{A}} p_i^{k_i}$$

it follows that two sequences x^n, y^n of the same type satisfy $P(x^n) = P(y^n)$. From a more combinatorial point of view we consider nonnegative integers k_i, $i \in \mathcal{A}$, with $k_0 + \cdots + k_{m-1} = n$.

The corresponding type class $\mathcal{T}(\mathbf{k})$ is then fully described. Accordingly we denote by $\mathcal{Q}_n(m)$ the set of all types of sequences of length n. By elementary combinatorial considerations we have

$$|\mathcal{T}(\mathbf{k})| = \binom{n}{k_1, \ldots, k_m} \quad \text{and} \quad |\mathcal{Q}_n(m)| = \binom{n+m-1}{m-1}.$$

Let us now return to Markovian types. We recall that

$$P(x^n) := P(x_0) \prod_{i,j \in \mathcal{A}} p_{ij}^{k_{ij}}, \tag{11.2}$$

where k_{ij} is the number of consecutive occurrences of the pair $(i, j) \in \mathcal{A}^2$ in x^n. The matrix $\mathbf{k} = [k_{ij}]_{i,j \in \mathcal{A}}$ is the *frequency matrix*, that defines the Markov *type class*. We already mentioned that the frequency matrix $\mathbf{k}$ is an integer matrix satisfying two important properties:

$$\sum_{i,j \in \mathcal{A}} k_{ij} = n - 1, \tag{11.3}$$

and additionally for any $i \in \mathcal{A}$,

$$\sum_{j=1}^{m} k_{ij} = \sum_{j=1}^{m} k_{ji} + \delta(x_1 = i) - \delta(x_n = i), \quad i \in \mathcal{A}, \tag{11.4}$$

where $\delta(A) = 1$ when A is true and zero otherwise. The last property is called the *flow conservation property* and is a consequence of the fact that the number of pairs starting with symbols $i \in \mathcal{A}$ must be equal to the number of pairs ending with symbol $i \in \mathcal{A}$ with the possible exception of the first and last pairs.

In a first step we will *neglect* this exception by considering artificially the so-called *cyclic* sequences in which the first element x_1 follows formally the last symbol x_n. If we associate to a cyclic sequence x^n the *cyclic frequency matrix* $\mathbf{k} = [k_{ij}]$ then these integer matrices $\mathbf{k} = [k_{ij}]$ satisfy the following two properties

$$\sum_{i,j \in \mathcal{A}} k_{ij} = n, \tag{11.5}$$

$$\sum_{j=1}^{m} k_{ij} = \sum_{j=1}^{m} k_{ji}, \quad i \in \mathcal{A}. \tag{11.6}$$

We will call such integer matrices $\mathbf{k}$ also *balanced frequency matrices* or simply balanced matrices. We shall call (11.6) the *conservation law* equation or the *balanced boundary condition* (BBC). We denote by $\mathcal{F}_n(m)$ the set of nonnegative integer solutions of (11.5) and (11.6).

Accordingly we define cyclic Markov types. Two cyclic sequences have the same (cyclic) Markov type if they are related to the same balanced frequency matrix. We denote by $\mathcal{P}_n(m)$ the set of cyclic Markov types.

We first study these cyclic Markov types $\mathcal{P}_n(m)$. They are more natural from a combinatorial point of view and they can be handled in an elegant way. They are also related to other interesting combinatorial objects (e.g., counting the number of integer solutions of some system of linear equations). In a second step we will relate them to non-cyclic Markov types.

Figure 11.1 A frequency matrix and its corresponding Eulerian graph.

Example 11.2 Consider a binary Markov source over $\mathcal{A} = \{0, 1\}$. A balanced frequency matrix is of the form

$$\mathbf{k} = \begin{bmatrix} k_{00} & k_{01} \\ k_{10} & k_{11} \end{bmatrix}$$

where the nonnegative integers k_{ij} satisfy

$$k_{00} + k_{01} + k_{10} + k_{11} = n \quad \text{and} \quad k_{01} = k_{10}.$$

Equivalently we have

$$k_{00} + 2k_{01} + k_{11} = n. \tag{11.7}$$

The number of nonnegative integer solutions of (11.7) is obviously

$$|\mathcal{F}_n(2)| = \sum_{k_{01}=0}^{\lfloor \frac{n}{2} \rfloor} (n - 2k_{01} + 1)$$

$$= \left(\left\lfloor \frac{n}{2} \right\rfloor + 1 \right) (n - \left\lfloor \frac{n}{2} \right\rfloor + 1) = \frac{n^2}{4} + O(n). \tag{11.8}$$

In general, it is easy to show that the elements of $\mathcal{F}_n(m)$ can be parametrized by the $m^2 - m$ variables k_{ij}, $0 \le i \le m-1$, $0 \le j \le m-2$. The remaining frequencies $k_{i,m-1}$, $0 \le i \le m-1$, are then uniquely given by the balance conditions and the condition $\sum_{i,j} k_{ij} = n$.

As mentioned, there are close connections between (cyclic) Markov types and other combinatorial objects. The most prominent examples are Eulerian graphs. For example, consider the balanced frequency matrix over $\mathcal{A} = \{0, 1\}$ given by $k_{00} = 1$, $k_{01} = k_{10} = 2$, and $k_{11} = 2$, so that $n = 7$. This matrix can be related to a directed multigraph on the vertex set $\mathcal{A}$ as depicted in Figure 11.1, where here k_{ij} denotes the number of directed edges from i to j. Observe that due to the balance property of the frequency matrix $\mathbf{k}$, the number of edges leaving a node must be equal to the number of edges coming in. But this defines an Eulerian graph. With that in mind, we observe that the number of cyclic types is equal to the number of Eulerian graphs on $|\mathcal{A}|$ nodes (see next section and Figure 11.2), while the number of Eulerian paths gives us the number of cyclic sequences of type $\mathbf{k}$ (see Section 11.2.3).

In the next example, we show that the number of Markov types $|\mathcal{P}_n(m)|$ is not necessarily equal to the number of nonnegative integer solutions $|\mathcal{F}_n(m)|$ of (11.5) and (11.6).

Example 11.3 Suppose that $m = 3$. The balanced frequency matrix has nine elements $\{k_{ij}\}_{i,j \in \{0,1,2\}}$, and they satisfy

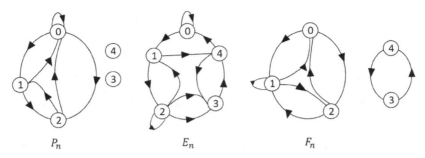

Figure 11.2 Examples of graphs belonging to $\mathcal{P}_7(5)$, $\mathcal{E}_{11}(5)$, and $\mathcal{F}_9(5)$ sets.

$$k_{00} + k_{01} + k_{02} + k_{10} + k_{11} + k_{12} + k_{20} + k_{21} + k_{22} = n,$$
$$k_{01} + k_{02} = k_{10} + k_{20},$$
$$k_{01} + k_{21} = k_{10} + k_{12},$$
$$k_{02} + k_{12} = k_{20} + k_{21}.$$

It is not quite obvious how many integer solutions such a system has. Nevertheless, we show later (see the proof of Theorem 11.6) that it is asymptotically $n^6/(12 \cdot 6!)$. However, we observe that not every solution of this system of equations leads to a legitimate sequence x^n. Consider the following example with $n = 5$:

$$k_{00} = 2, \quad k_{01} = k_{02} = 0,$$
$$k_{10} = 0, \quad k_{11} = 0, \quad k_{12} = 1,$$
$$k_{20} = 0, \quad k_{21} = k_{22} = 1.$$

There is no sequence of length five that can satisfy these conditions. Such a cyclic sequence would have to consist of five elements and contain the substrings 12, 21, 22, and two 00 or one 000, which is impossible. Observe that the underlying multigraph consists of two connected components that do not communicate.

11.2.1 Number of Types

We now deal with the set $\mathcal{P}_n(m)$ of cyclic Markov types of length n over an alphabet $\mathcal{A}$ of size m.

We first relate the counting problem of cyclic Markov types with the number of special connected Eulerian digraphs $G = (V(G), E(G))$ such that $V(G) \subseteq \mathcal{A}$ and $|E(G)| = n$, where the number of (directed) edges between the ith node and jth node in G is equal to k_{ij}, and $\mathbf{k} = [k_{ij}]_{i,j \in \mathcal{A}}$ is a balanced frequency matrix satisfying the balance property (11.6). Clearly, the balance property assures that the graphs are Eulerian; that is, the number of incoming edges to node i is equal to the number of outgoing edges from node i.

Note that G may be defined over a *subset* of $\mathcal{A}$, as shown in the first example in Figure 11.2 (i.e., there may be some isolated vertices).

We denote by $\mathcal{E}_n(m)$ the set of (connected) Eulerian digraphs on $\mathcal{A}$; the middle of Figure 11.2 shows an example of a graph in this set. Finally, the set $\mathcal{F}_n(m)$ can be viewed as the set of digraphs G with $V(G) = \mathcal{A}$, $|E(G)| = n$ and satisfying the flow conversation property (in-degree equals out-degree). We call such graphs conservative digraphs. Observe that a graph in $\mathcal{F}_n(m)$ may consist of several connected (not communicating) Eulerian digraphs, as shown in the third example in Figure 11.2.

There is a simple relation between $|\mathcal{E}_n(m)|$ and $|\mathcal{P}_n(m)|$. Indeed,

$$|\mathcal{P}_n(m)| = \sum_k \binom{m}{k} |\mathcal{E}_n(k)|, \tag{11.9}$$

since there are $\binom{m}{k}$ ways to choose $m - k$ isolated vertices in $\mathcal{P}_n(m)$. This implies

$$|\mathcal{P}_n(m)| \geq |\mathcal{E}_n(m)|.$$

Indeed, it is certainly true since every Eulerian graph on $\mathcal{A}$ with $k \leq m$ (by definition it must be strongly connected and satisfy the flow-conservation law) belongs to $\mathcal{P}_n(m)$. In fact, by the same reasoning, we can expand this inequality to obtain for any n and m:

$$|\mathcal{F}_n(m)| \geq |\mathcal{P}_n(m)| \geq |\mathcal{E}_n(m)|. \tag{11.10}$$

Our goal is to find an asymptotic relation between the number of digraphs $|\mathcal{P}_n(m)|$ and the number of solutions $|\mathcal{F}_n(m)|$ of the flow conservation equations (11.5)–(11.6); that is, the number of conservative digraphs.

As a direct consequence of our definition, a conservative digraph may have several connected components. Each connected component is either a connected Eulerian digraph or an isolated node without an edge. This leads to

$$|\mathcal{F}_n(m)| = |\mathcal{E}_n(m)| + \sum_{i=1}^{m-1} \sum_{\mathcal{A}=\mathcal{A}_0\cup\cdots\cup\mathcal{A}_i} \sum_{n_0+\cdots+n_i=n} \prod_{j=0}^{i} |\mathcal{E}_{n_j}(\mathcal{A}_j)|, \tag{11.11}$$

where the sum is over all (unordered) set partitions $\mathcal{A} = \mathcal{A}_0 \cup \cdots \cup \mathcal{A}_i$ into $i \geq 1$ (nonempty) parts with n_j edges in each di-subgraph $\mathcal{E}_{n_j}(\mathcal{A}_j)$ over $\mathcal{A}_j$ vertices. Observe that every set partition $\mathcal{A} = \mathcal{A}_0 \cup \cdots \cup \mathcal{A}_i$ with $|\mathcal{A}_j| = m_j > 0$ is a partition of $\mathcal{A}$ into i distinguished subsets of cardinality m_j. Notice that there are $\binom{m}{m_0\ldots m_i}$ ways of dividing m into $i+1$ subsets of size m_i when permuting the subsets does not lead to a new distinct permutation. For example, for $\mathcal{A} = \{0, 1, 2, 3\}$ and $m_0 = m_1 = 2$, we have the following partition of $\mathcal{A}$:

$$\{0, 1\}, \{2, 3\}; \quad \{0, 2\}, \{1, 3\}; \quad \{1, 2\}, \{0, 3\}.$$

But there are three additional partitions included in the count $\binom{4}{2,2} = 6$; namely,

$$\{2, 3\}, \{0, 1\}; \quad \{1, 3\}, \{0, 2\}; \quad \{0, 3\}, \{1, 2\},$$

that follow by permuting equal subsets. In general, permuting two subsets of equal size does not lead to a new partition, as seen her. As a consequence of this, we can write (11.11) as

$$|\mathcal{F}_n(m)| \leq |\mathcal{E}_n(m)| + \sum_{i=i}^{m-1} \sum_{m_0+\cdots+m_i=m} \sum_{n_0+\cdots+n_i=n} \binom{m}{m_1\ldots m_i} \prod_{j=0}^{i} |\mathcal{E}_{n_j}(m_j)|. \tag{11.12}$$

Furthermore, since by (11.10), $|\mathcal{E}_n(m)| \leq |\mathcal{F}_n(m)|$ for all $n, m \geq 0$, we finally arrive at

$$|\mathcal{F}_n(m)| \leq |\mathcal{E}_n(m)| + \sum_{i=1}^{m-1} \sum_{m_0+\cdots+m_i=m} \sum_{n_0+\cdots+n_i=n} \binom{m}{m_0\ldots m_i} \prod_{j=0}^{i} |\mathcal{F}_{n_j}(m_j)|. \tag{11.13}$$

In the proof of Theorem 11.6 we shall show that $|\mathcal{F}_n(m)| = O(n^{m^2-m})$ (and that is actually the correct order or magnitude). By using just this property, we will obtain an upper bound for the difference between $|\mathcal{F}_n(m)|$ and $|\mathcal{E}_n(m)|$; see Lemma 11.4. Together with Theorem 11.6, the relation (11.10), and the upper bound from Lemma 11.4, it directly follows that, as $n \to \infty$,

$$|\mathcal{P}_n(m)| \sim |\mathcal{F}_n(m)| \sim |\mathcal{E}_n(m)|.$$

Lemma 11.4 *If $m \geq 2$ is fixed, then we have for $n \to \infty$,*

$$|\mathcal{F}_n(m)| - |\mathcal{E}_n(m)| = O(n^{m^2-3m+3}). \tag{11.14}$$

Proof Our starting point is (11.13), where we denote the sum on the right-hand side by $A(m,n)$; that is,

$$A(m,n) = \sum_{i=1}^{m-1} \sum_{m_0+\cdots+m_i=m} \sum_{n_0+\cdots+n_i=n} \binom{m}{m_0 \ldots m_i} \prod_{j=0}^{i} |\mathcal{F}_{n_j}(m_j)|.$$

Since $|\mathcal{F}_n(m)| - |\mathcal{E}_n(m)| \leq A(m,n)$, it is sufficient to show

$$A(n,m) = O(m^3 n^{m^2-3m+3}). \tag{11.15}$$

In the proof of Theorem 11.6, we shall prove that $|\mathcal{F}_n(m)| = O(n^{m^2-m})$; thus,

$$\prod_{j=0}^{i} |\mathcal{F}_{n_j}(m_j)| = O(n^{m_0^2+\cdots+m_i^2-m}).$$

For $m_j \geq 1$, we have

$$\sum_{j=0}^{i} m_j^2 = m^2 - \sum_{j=0}^{i} m_j(m-m_j) \leq m^2 - \sum_{j=0}^{i}(m-1) = m^2 - i(m-1),$$

and consequently

$$A(m,n) \ll \sum_{i=1}^{m-1} \sum_{m_0+\cdots+m_i=m} \sum_{n_0+\cdots+n_i=n} \binom{m}{m_0 \ldots m_i} n^{m^2-i(m-1)-m}$$

$$= n^{m^2-m} \sum_{i=1}^{m-1} n^{-i(m-1)} \sum_{n_0+\cdots+n_i=n} \sum_{m_0+\cdots+m_i=m} \binom{m}{m_0 \ldots m_i}$$

$$= n^{m^2-m} \sum_{i=1}^{m-1} n^{-i(m-1)} \sum_{n_0+\cdots+n_i=n} i^m$$

$$\ll n^{m^2-m} \sum_{i=1}^{m-1} n^{-i(m-1)} i^m n^{i-1}$$

$$\ll n^{m^2-m-1} \sum_{i=1}^{m-1} n^{-i(m-2)} i^m$$

$$\ll n^{m^2-m-1} m^2 \sum_{i=1}^{m-1} \left(\frac{i}{n^i}\right)^{m-2}$$

$$\ll n^{m^2-3m+3},$$

where the last line follows from the fact that $i/n^i \leq 2/n^2$ for $i \geq 2$. This completes the proof. ∎

In the sequel, we concentrate on estimating $|\mathcal{F}_n(m)|$. For this purpose, we introduce certain generating functions over matrices. In general, let $g_{\mathbf{k}}$ be a sequence of scalars indexed by integer matrices $\mathbf{k}$ and consider the generating function

$$G(\mathbf{z}) = \sum_{\mathbf{k}} g_{\mathbf{k}} \mathbf{z}^{\mathbf{k}},$$

where the summation is over all nonnegative $m \times m$ integer matrices $\mathbf{k}$ and $\mathbf{z} = [z_{ij}]_{i,j \in \mathcal{A}}$ is an $m \times m$ matrix that we often denote simply as $\mathbf{z} = [z_{ij}]$ (assuming the indices i and j run from 0 to $m-1$). Here, $\mathbf{z}^{\mathbf{k}} = \prod_{i,j} z_{ij}^{k_{ij}}$.

We associate to $G(\mathbf{z})$ the generating function

$$\mathcal{F}G(\mathbf{z}) = \sum_{\mathbf{k} \in \mathcal{F}} g_{\mathbf{k}} \mathbf{z}^{\mathbf{k}} = \sum_{n \geq 0} \sum_{\mathbf{k} \in \mathcal{F}_n(m)} g_{\mathbf{k}} \mathbf{z}^{\mathbf{k}} \tag{11.16}$$

over matrices $\mathbf{k} \in \mathcal{F}_n(m)$ satisfying the balance equations (11.5) and (11.6).

The following useful lemma relates $G(\mathbf{z})$ and $\mathcal{F}G(\mathbf{z})$. We use the following shorthand notation. Let $[z_{ij}\frac{x_i}{x_j}]$ be the matrix $\Delta^{-1}(x)\mathbf{z}\Delta(x)$ where $\Delta(x) = \text{diag}(x_0, \ldots, x_{m-1})$ is a diagonal matrix with elements $x_0, \ldots, x_{m-1}$; that is, the element z_{ij} in $\mathbf{z}$ is replaced by $z_{ij}x_i/x_j$. Similarly, we set $[z_{ij}\exp(\theta_j - \theta_i)] = \exp(-\Delta(\theta))\mathbf{z}\exp(\Delta(\theta))$.

Lemma 11.5 *Let $G(z) = \sum_{\mathbf{k}} g_{\mathbf{k}} \mathbf{z}^{\mathbf{k}}$ be given. Then*

$$\mathcal{F}G(z) := \sum_{n \geq 0} \sum_{\mathbf{k} \in \mathcal{F}_n} g_{\mathbf{k}} \mathbf{z}^{\mathbf{k}} = \left(\frac{1}{2\pi i}\right)^m \oint \frac{dx_0}{x_0} \cdots \oint \frac{dx_{m-1}}{x_{m-1}} G\left(\left[z_{ij}\frac{x_j}{x_i}\right]\right) \tag{11.17}$$

$$= \frac{1}{(2\pi)^m} \int_{-\pi}^{\pi} d\theta_1 \cdots \int_{-\pi}^{\pi} d\theta_m G([z_{ij}\exp((\theta_j - \theta_i)i)]) \tag{11.18}$$

$$= [x_1^0 \cdots x_m^0] G\left(\left[z_{ij}\frac{x_j}{x_i}\right]\right). \tag{}$$

Proof Observe that

$$G(\Delta^{-1}(x)\mathbf{z}\Delta(x)) = G\left(\left[z_{ij}\frac{x_j}{x_i}\right]\right) = \sum_{\mathbf{k}} g_{\mathbf{k}} \mathbf{z}^{\mathbf{k}} \prod_{i=1}^{m} x_i^{\sum_j k_{ji} - \sum_j k_{ij}}. \tag{11.19}$$

Therefore, $\mathcal{F}G(\mathbf{z})$ is the coefficient of $G([z_{ij}\frac{x_j}{x_i}])$ at $x_1^0 x_2^0 \cdots x_m^0$ since $\sum_j k_{ji} - \sum_j k_{ij} = 0$ for matrices $\mathbf{k} \in \mathcal{F}$. We write it in short as

$$\mathcal{F}G(\mathbf{z}) = [x_1^0 \cdots x_m^0] g\left(\left[z_{ij}\frac{x_j}{x_i}\right]\right).$$

The result follows from Cauchy's formula (see Appendix B). ∎

We consider the number of solutions to (11.5) and (11.6). For this purpose, we start with the generating function:

$$F_m(z) = \sum_{\mathbf{k}} \mathbf{z}^{\mathbf{k}} = \prod_{ij} (1 - z_{ij})^{-1}.$$

Then applying Lemma 11.5 with $z_{ij} = zx_i/x_j$, we conclude that the generating function $F_m^*(z)$ of $|\mathcal{F}_n(m)|$ is

$$F_m^*(z) = \sum_{n \geq 0} |\mathcal{F}_n(m)| z^n = \frac{1}{(1-z)^m} [x_1^0 x_2^0 \cdots x_m^0] \prod_{i \neq j} \left[1 - z \frac{x_i}{x_j} \right]^{-1}. \qquad (11.20)$$

Thus, by Cauchy's formula,

$$|\mathcal{F}_n(m)| = [z^n] F_m^*(z) = \frac{1}{2\pi i} \oint \frac{F_m^*(z)}{z^{n+1}} dz.$$

We will use this representation to obtain an asymptotic formula for $|\mathcal{F}_n(m)|$. As mentioned, this leads to a corresponding asymptotic formula for the number of cyclic types $|\mathcal{P}_n(m)|$ as stated in our main theorem (the proof will be given in the next subsection).

Theorem 11.6 *For fixed m and $n \to \infty$, the number of cyclic Markov types is*

$$|\mathcal{P}_n(m)| = d(m) \frac{n^{m^2 - m}}{(m^2 - m)!} + O(n^{m^2 - m - 1}), \qquad (11.21)$$

where $d(m)$ is a constant that also can be expressed by the following integral:

$$d(m) = \frac{1}{(2\pi)^{m-1}} \underbrace{\int_{-\infty}^{\infty} \cdots \int_{-\infty}^{\infty}}_{(m-1)-fold} \prod_{j=1}^{m-1} \frac{1}{1 + \phi_j^2} \cdot \prod_{k \neq \ell} \frac{1}{1 + (\phi_k - \phi_\ell)^2} d\phi_1 d\phi_2 \cdots d\phi_{m-1}. \quad (11.22)$$

Remark 11.7 It is easy to count the number of matrices **k** satisfying *only* equation (11.5); that is, $\sum_{ij} k_{ij} = n$. Indeed, it coincides with the number of integer solution of (11.5), which turns out to be the number of combinations with repetitions (the number of ways of selecting m^2 objects from n):

$$\binom{n + m^2 - 1}{n} = \binom{n + m^2 - 1}{m^2 - 1} \sim \frac{n^{m^2 - 1}}{(m^2 - 1)!}.$$

Thus, the conservation law equation (6.1) decreases the above by the factor $\Theta(n^{m-1})$.

The evaluation of the integral (11.22) is quite cumbersome (see next section), but for small values of m, we computed it to find that

$$|\mathcal{P}_n(2)| \sim \frac{1}{2} \frac{n^2}{2!}, \qquad (11.23)$$

$$|\mathcal{P}_n(3)| \sim \frac{1}{12} \frac{n^6}{6!}, \qquad (11.24)$$

$$|\mathcal{P}_n(4)| \sim \frac{1}{96} \frac{n^{12}}{12!}, \qquad (11.25)$$

$$|\mathcal{P}_n(5)| \sim \frac{37}{34560} \frac{n^{20}}{20!} \qquad (11.26)$$

for large n. The coefficients of $n^{m^2 - m}$ are rational numbers since $F^*(z)$ is a rational generating function.

We now compare the coefficient at $n^{m^2 - m}$ for fixed m in (11.21), shown in Table 11.1. We observe extremely small values of these constants even for relatively small m.

Table 11.1 *Constants at n^{m^2-m} for fixed m*

m	constant in (11.21)
2	$2.500000000 \ 10^{-1}$
3	$1.157407407 \ 10^{-5}$
4	$2.174662186 \ 10^{-11}$
5	$4.400513659 \ 10^{-22}$

Proof of Theorem 11.6

In this section, we prove Theorem 11.6. Our starting formula is (11.20), which we repeat here:

$$F_m^*(z) = \frac{1}{(1-z)^m} [x_1^0 x_2^0 \cdots x_m^0] \prod_{i \neq j} \left[1 - z \frac{x_i}{x_j} \right]^{-1}. \tag{11.27}$$

Clearly, we just have to provide an asymptotic representation for $\mathcal{F}_n(m)$ of the form (11.21). By Lemma 11.4, we, thus, obtain the corresponding asymptotic representation for $\mathcal{P}_n(m)$.

We first compute asymptotic expansions for $\mathcal{F}_n(m)$ (and equivalently for $\mathcal{P}_n(m)$) explicitly for $m = 2, 3, 4, 5$ as summarized in Table 11.1.

For $m = 2$, we have

$$F_2^*(z) = \frac{1}{(1-z)^2} [x_0^0 x_1^0] \left[\frac{1}{1 - z \, x_0/x_1} \frac{1}{1 - z \, x_1/x_0} \right]. \tag{11.28}$$

Let us set $A = x_0/x_1$ so we need the coefficient of A^0 in $(1 - Az)^{-1}(1 - z/A)^{-1}$. This can be seen at a formal level as the product of two (formal) geometric series or also from an analytic point of view. In the latter case, we just have to assume that $|z| < |A| < |1/z|$.

Now, by using a partial fractions expression in A, we have

$$\frac{1}{1 - Az} \frac{1}{1 - z/A} = \frac{1}{1 - z^2} \left[\frac{1}{1 - Az} + \frac{z}{A - z} \right].$$

Recall that $|z| < |A| < |1/z|$, so that the coefficient of A^0 in $(1 - Az)^{-1}$ is one and that in $z(A-z)^{-1}$ is zero. Hence,

$$F_2^*(z) = (1-z)^{-2}(1-z^2)^{-1} = (1+z)^{-1}(1-z)^{-3}$$

and consequently

$$|\mathcal{F}_n(2)| = [z^n] \frac{1}{1+z} \frac{1}{(1-z)^3}$$

$$= \frac{n^2}{4} + n + \frac{3}{4} + \frac{1}{8}[1 + (-1)^n] = \frac{1}{2} \frac{n^2}{2!} + O(n), \tag{11.29}$$

which agrees with (11.8) of Example 11.1.

For $m \geq 3$, we use recursive partial fractions expansions. When $m = 3$, we set $x_0/x_1 = A$, $x_0/x_2 = B$ so that we wish to compute

$$[A^0 B^0] \left(\frac{1}{1 - zA} \frac{1}{1 - z/A} \frac{1}{1 - Bz} \frac{1}{1 - z/B} \frac{1}{1 - Az/B} \frac{1}{1 - Bz/A} \right). \tag{11.30}$$

First, we do a partial fractions expansion in the A variable, for fixed B and z. Thus the factor inside the parentheses in (11.30) becomes

$$
\frac{1}{1-zA}\frac{1}{1-z^2}\frac{1}{1-Bz}\frac{1}{1-z/B}\frac{1}{1-1/B}\frac{1}{1-Bz^2}
$$
$$
+\frac{1}{1-z/A}\frac{1}{1-z^2}\frac{1}{1-Bz}\frac{1}{1-z/B}\frac{1}{1-z^2/B}\frac{1}{1-B}
$$
$$
+\frac{1}{1-Az/B}\frac{1}{1-B}\frac{1}{1-z^2/B}\frac{1}{1-B/z}\frac{1}{1-z/B}\frac{1}{1-z^2}
$$
$$
+\frac{1}{1-Bz/A}\frac{1}{1-Bz^2}\frac{1}{1-1/B}\frac{1}{1-Bz}\frac{1}{1-z/B}\frac{1}{1-z^2}. \tag{11.31}
$$

The coefficient of A^0 in the first term in (11.31) is

$$
\frac{1}{1-z^2}\frac{1}{1-Bz}\frac{1}{1-z/B}\frac{1}{1-1/B}\frac{1}{1-Bz^2}, \tag{11.32}
$$

and that in the third term is

$$
\frac{1}{1-B}\frac{1}{1-z^2/B}\frac{1}{1-Bz}\frac{1}{1-z/B}\frac{1}{1-z^2}, \tag{11.33}
$$

while the coefficients of A^0 are zero in the second and fourth terms. Combining (11.32) and (11.33), we must now compute

$$
[B^0]\left(\frac{1+z^2}{1-z^2}\frac{1}{1-Bz}\frac{1}{1-z/B}\frac{1}{1-Bz^2}\frac{1}{1-z^2/B}\right). \tag{11.34}
$$

Now expanding (11.34) by a partial fractions expansion in B leads to

$$
\frac{1+z^2}{1-z^2}[B^0]\left(\frac{1}{1-Bz}\frac{1}{1-z^2}\frac{1}{1-z}\frac{1}{1-z^2}+\frac{1}{1-z/B}\frac{1}{1-z^2}\frac{1}{1-z^3}\frac{1}{1-z}\right.
$$
$$
\left.+\frac{1}{1-1/z}\frac{1}{1-z^3}\frac{1}{1-Bz^2}\frac{1}{1-z^4}+\frac{1}{1-z^3}\frac{1}{1-1/z}\frac{1}{1-z^4}\frac{1}{1-z^2/B}\right)
$$
$$
=\frac{1+z^2}{1-z^2}\left[\frac{1}{1-z^2}\frac{1}{1-z}\frac{1}{1-z^3}+\frac{-z}{(1-z)}\frac{1}{1-z^3}\frac{1}{1-z^4}\right]
$$
$$
=\frac{1-z+z^2}{(1-z)^4(1+z)^2(1+z+z^2)}.
$$

Hence,

$$
F_3^*(z)=\frac{1-z+z^2}{(1-z)^7(1+z)^2(1+z+z^2)}.
$$

For $z\to 1$, $F_3^*(z)\sim\frac{1}{12}(1-z)^{-7}$ so that

$$
|\mathcal{F}_n(3)|=\frac{1}{12}\frac{n^6}{6!}+O(n^5),\qquad n\to\infty. \tag{11.35}
$$

Table 11.2 *Poles and their orders for various m*

$m \backslash$ root	1	-1	$e^{\pm 2\pi i/3}$	$\pm i$	$e^{\pm 2\pi i/5}$	$e^{\pm 4\pi i/5}$
2	3	1	–	–	–	–
3	7	2	1	–	–	–
4	13	5	2	1	–	–
5	21	8	4	2	1	1

In the same way, it follows that $F_m^*(z)$ can be represented as a linear combination of functions of the form

$$\frac{z^r}{(1-z)^m} \prod_{i=1}^{L} \frac{1}{1-z^{\ell_i}}$$

for some $r \geq 0, L \geq 0$, and $\ell_i \geq 1$. Actually, a more careful look shows that $L = m^2 - 2m + 1$. Hence, it follows that $F_m^*(z)$ has a pole of order $\leq m^2 - m + 1$ at $z = 1$ and other polar singularities at roots of unity that are of order $\leq L$. (For $2 \leq m \leq 5$, these poles and their orders are given in Table 11.2.)

In order to show that the order of the pole $z = 1$ is actually $m^2 - m + 1$, we consider the limit

$$d(m) = \lim_{z \to 1}[(1-z)^{m^2-m+1} F_m^*(z)].$$

We will show that this limit actually exists and that it is positive. Consequently,

$$|\mathcal{F}_n(m)| = d(m)\frac{n^{m^2-m}}{(m^2-m)!} + O(n^{m^2-m-1}). \tag{11.36}$$

However, it seems that there is no simple formula for the sequence of constants $d(m)$. We just characterize $d(m)$ as an $(m-1)$-fold integral.

First consider the simple case $m = 2$. Setting $A = e^{i\Phi}$ and using a Cauchy integral, we have

$$[A^0] \frac{1}{1-z/A} \frac{1}{1-Az} = \frac{1}{2\pi} \int_{-\pi}^{\pi} \frac{d\Phi}{1 - 2z\cos\Phi + z^2}.$$

Now set $z = 1 - \delta$ and expand the integral for $z \to 1$. The major contribution will come from where $\delta \approx 0$, and scaling $\Phi = \delta\phi$ and using the Taylor expansion $1 - 2(1 - \delta)\cos(\delta\phi) + (1-\delta)^2 = \delta^2[1 + \phi^2] + O(\delta^3)$, we find that

$$F_2^*(z) \sim \frac{1}{\delta^2} \frac{1}{2\pi} \int_{-\infty}^{\infty} \frac{\delta}{\delta^2[1+\phi^2]} d\phi = \frac{1}{2} \frac{1}{\delta^3} = \frac{1}{2}(1-z)^{-3},$$

as $z \to 1$.

When $m = 3$, we use (11.30) and Cauchy's formula with $A = e^{i\Phi}$ and $B = e^{i\Psi}$ to get

$$\frac{1}{(2\pi)^2} \int_{-\pi}^{\pi} \int_{-\pi}^{\pi} \frac{1}{1 - 2z\cos\Phi + z^2} \cdot \frac{1}{1 - 2z\cos\Psi + z^2} \cdot \frac{1}{1 - 2z\cos(\Phi - \Psi) + z^2} d\Phi d\Psi.$$

Again, expanding for $z = 1 - \delta \to 1$ and $\Phi = \delta\phi = O(\delta)$, $\Psi = \delta\psi = O(\delta)$, we obtain the leading order approximation

$$\frac{1}{\delta^4} \frac{1}{(2\pi)^2} \int_{-\infty}^{\infty} \int_{-\infty}^{\infty} \frac{1}{1+\phi^2} \frac{1}{1+\psi^2} \frac{1}{1+(\phi-\psi)^2} d\phi d\psi = \frac{1}{\delta^4} \cdot \frac{1}{12}.$$

Thus, as $z \to 1$, $F_3^*(z) \sim \frac{1}{12}\delta^{-7} = \frac{1}{12}(1-z)^{-7}$, which follows also from the exact generating function.

For general m, a completely analogous calculation shows that as $\delta = 1 - z \to 0$, $F_m^*(z) \sim \delta^{m-m^2-1} d(m)$, where

$$d(m) = \frac{1}{(2\pi)^{m-1}} \underbrace{\int_{-\infty}^{\infty} \cdots \int_{-\infty}^{\infty}}_{(m-1)-fold} \prod_{j=1}^{m-1} \frac{1}{1+\phi_j^2} \cdot \prod_{k<\ell} \frac{1}{1+(\phi_k-\phi_\ell)^2} d\phi_1 d\phi_2 \cdots d\phi_{m-1}. \quad (11.37)$$

Note that $d(m)$ always exists and that $d(m) > 0$.

We recall that the upper bound $|\mathcal{F}_n(m)| = O(n^{m^2-m})$ was used in Lemma 11.4 to prove that $|\mathcal{P}_n(m)| = |\mathcal{F}_n(m)| + O(n^{m^2-3m+3})$, which finally completes the proof of Theorem 11.6.

We remark that there are other representations for the constant $d(m)$. For example, if we directly start with the representation (11.13), rewrite it into an m-fold Cauchy integral, and apply the substitutions $x_i = e^{i\vartheta_i}$, we obtain

$$F_m^*(z) = \frac{\delta^{-m}}{(2\pi)^m} \int_{-\pi}^{\pi} \cdots \int_{-\pi}^{\pi} \prod_{i \neq j} \frac{1}{1-(1-\delta)e^{i(\vartheta_i-\vartheta_j)}} d\vartheta_0 \cdots d\vartheta_{m-1}$$

$$\sim \frac{\delta^{m^2-m-1}}{(2\pi)^m} \int_{-\infty}^{\infty} \cdots \int_{-\infty}^{\infty} \prod_{i \neq j} \frac{1}{1+i(\theta_i-\theta_j)} d\theta_0 \cdots d\theta_{m-1},$$

where we used the substitutions $\vartheta_i = \delta\theta_i$. Thus, we also have the representation

$$d(m) = \frac{1}{(2\pi)^m} \int_{-\infty}^{\infty} \cdots \int_{-\infty}^{\infty} \prod_{i \neq j} \frac{1}{1+i(\theta_i-\theta_j)} d\theta_0 \cdots d\theta_{m-1} \quad (11.38)$$

for any $m \geq 2$.

11.2.2 Counting Noncyclic Markov Types

Finally, we address the issue of Markov types over cyclic strings versus non-cyclic or linear strings. Recall that $\mathcal{Q}_n(m)$ denotes the set of Markov types over noncyclic (linear) strings. It turns out that there is a simple relation between $|\mathcal{Q}_n(m)|$ and $|\mathcal{P}_n(m)|$.

Let $a \in \mathcal{A}$ and define $\mathcal{P}_n(a, \mathcal{A})$ as the set of cyclic types of strings of length n that contain at least one occurrence of symbol a. Clearly,

$$|\mathcal{P}_n(a, \mathcal{A})| = |\mathcal{P}_n(m)| - |\mathcal{P}_n(m-1)|,$$

and therefore

$$|\mathcal{P}_n(a, \mathcal{A})| = |\mathcal{P}_n(m)|(1 - O(n^{-2m}))$$

by Theorem 11.6.

In the same spirit, let $\mathcal{Q}_n(a)$ be the set of types over linear strings starting with symbol a, and $\mathcal{Q}_n(a, b)$ be the set of (noncyclic) types over strings of length n that start with symbol a

and end with symbol b. Certainly, $\mathcal{Q}_n(a,a) = \mathcal{P}_{n-1}(a, \mathcal{A})$ and noticing that $\bigcup_{a \in \mathcal{A}} \mathcal{P}_n(a, \mathcal{A}) = \mathcal{P}_n(m)$, we conclude that

$$\mathcal{Q}_n(m) = \bigcup_{\substack{(a,b) \in \mathcal{A}^2 \\ a \neq b}} \mathcal{Q}_n(a,b) \cup \bigcup_{a \in \mathcal{A}} \mathcal{P}_{n-1}(a, \mathcal{A}) \tag{11.39}$$

$$= \bigcup_{\substack{(a,b) \in \mathcal{A}^2 \\ a \neq b}} \mathcal{Q}_n(a,b) \cup \mathcal{P}_{n-1}(m).$$

Observe also that $\mathcal{Q}_n(a,b)$ are disjoint for $a \neq b$ and for every $a \neq b$ the set $\mathcal{Q}_n(a,b)$ is disjoint from $\mathcal{P}_n(a, \mathcal{A})$. Furthermore, the cardinality of $\mathcal{Q}_n(a,b)$ is the same for all pairs (a,b) with $a \neq b$. In summary, by (11.39), we conclude that (for $a \neq b$),

$$|\mathcal{Q}_n(m)| = |\mathcal{P}_{n-1}(m)| + (m^2 - m)|\mathcal{Q}_n(a,b)|. \tag{11.40}$$

Next we estimate the cardinality of $\mathcal{Q}_n(a,b)$ by proving the following inequalities:

$$|\mathcal{P}_{n-2}(a, \mathcal{A})| \leq |\mathcal{Q}_n(a,b)|, \tag{11.41}$$

$$|\mathcal{Q}_n(a,b)| \leq |\mathcal{P}_n(a, \mathcal{A})|. \tag{11.42}$$

Indeed, for (11.41), we observe that if $\mathbf{k} \in \mathcal{P}_{n-2}(a, \mathcal{A})$, then $\mathbf{k} + \mathbf{e}_{ab} \in \mathcal{Q}_n(a,b)$, where $\mathbf{e}_{ab}$ is a matrix with all 0's, except at position (a,b) where it contains a 1. This implies (11.41). For (11.42), we notice that if $\mathbf{k} \in \mathcal{Q}_n(a,b)$, then $\mathbf{k} + \mathbf{e}_{ba} \in \mathcal{P}_n(a, \mathcal{A})$ and the inequality follows.

Consequently, since $|\mathcal{P}_{n-2}(m)| \sim |\mathcal{P}_{n-1}(m)| = |\mathcal{P}_n(m)|(1 - O(n^{-m^2}))$, we have $|\mathcal{Q}_n(a,b)| = |\mathcal{P}_n(m)|(1 - O(n^{-2m}))$, which by (11.40) leads to the following conclusion (where we also apply Theorem 11.6).

Corollary 11.8 *The number of (noncyclic) Markov types* $|\mathcal{Q}_n(m)|$ *of strings of length n satisfies*

$$|\mathcal{Q}_n(m)| = (m^2 - m + 1)|\mathcal{P}_n(m)|(1 - O(n^{-2m}))$$

$$= d(m) \frac{m^2 - m + 1}{(m^2 - m)!} n^{m^2 - m} + O(n^{m^2 - m - 1})$$

for large n and finite m.

11.2.3 Number of Sequences of a Given Type

In this section, we tackle a harder problem: we count the number of Markov sequences of a given type $\mathbf{k}$; that is, we estimate $|\mathcal{T}_n(\mathbf{k})|$. In other words, we shall enumerate the number of Eulerian paths in the digraph as introduced in the previous section (see Figure 11.1).

We start by introducing the following quantity:

$$B_{\mathbf{k}} = \prod_{i \in \mathcal{A}} \frac{k_i!}{\prod_{j \in \mathcal{A}} k_{i,j}!} = \binom{k_0}{k_{00} \cdots k_{0,m-1}} \cdots \binom{k_{m-1}}{k_{m-1,0} \cdots k_{m-1,m-1}}, \tag{11.43}$$

where $k_i = \sum_j k_{ij}$. We will use the concept of the matrix generating functions as already discussed. Recall that $\mathbf{z} = \{z_{ij}\}_{ij=1}^m$ denotes a complex $m \times m$ matrix, $\mathbf{k}$ an integer matrix, and that we write $\mathbf{z^k} = \prod_{ij \in \mathcal{A}^2} z_{ij}^{k_{ij}}$. In particular, we have (see Exercise 11.5)

$$B(\mathbf{z}) = \sum_{\mathbf{k}} B_{\mathbf{k}} \mathbf{z}^{\mathbf{k}} = \prod_{a \in \mathcal{A}} (1 - \sum_{b \in \mathcal{A}} z_{a,b})^{-1}. \tag{11.44}$$

However, we really need to compute the generating function

$$\mathcal{F}B(\mathbf{z}) = \sum_{\mathbf{k} \in \mathcal{F}} B_{\mathbf{k}} \mathbf{z}^{\mathbf{k}}$$

as defined in (11.16). We first prove the following lemma.

Lemma 11.9 *We have*

$$\mathcal{F}B(\mathbf{z}) = (\det(\mathbf{I} - \mathbf{z}))^{-1},$$

where $\mathbf{I}$ is the identity $m \times m$ matrix.

Proof Setting $g_{\mathbf{k}} = B_{\mathbf{k}}$ in Lemma 11.5 and denoting $\mathbf{a}(\mathbf{z}) = (a_{ij}(\mathbf{z})) = \mathbf{I} - \mathbf{z}$, we find

$$\mathcal{F}B(\mathbf{z}) = \left(\frac{1}{2\pi i}\right)^m \oint dx_1 \cdots \oint dx_m \prod_i \left(\sum_j a_{ij}(\mathbf{z}) x_j\right)^{-1}.$$

By applying the linear change of variables $y_i = \sum_j a_{ij}(\mathbf{z}) x_j$, we obtain

$$\left(\frac{1}{2\pi i}\right)^m \oint dx_1 \cdots \oint dx_m \prod_i \left(\sum_j a_{ij}(\mathbf{z}) x_j\right)^{-1}$$

$$= (\det(\mathbf{a}(\mathbf{z})))^{-1} \left(\frac{1}{2\pi i}\right)^m \oint \frac{dy_1}{y_1} \cdots \oint \frac{dy_m}{y_m}$$

$$= (\det(\mathbf{a}(\mathbf{z})))^{-1},$$

which completes the proof since we can assume that the matrix $\mathbf{a}(\mathbf{z})$ is not singular. ■

Throughout, we also write $B_{\mathcal{A}}(\mathbf{z}) = \mathcal{F}_{\mathcal{A}} B(\mathbf{z})$ to simplify the notation; the subscript $\mathcal{A}$ indicates that the underlying alphabet is $\mathcal{A}$. In particular, from the Corollary 11.8, we conclude that

$$B_{\mathcal{A}-\{a\}}(\mathbf{z}) = (\det_{aa}(\mathbf{I} - \mathbf{z}))^{-1},$$

where $\det_{ij}(\mathbf{a})$ is the determinant of a matrix with the ith row and the jth column of $\mathbf{a}$ deleted.

For a given (cyclic) type $\mathbf{k} \in \mathcal{F}_n$, we defined the *frequency counts* $N_{\mathbf{k}}$, $N_{\mathbf{k}}^a$, and $N_{\mathbf{k}}^{ba}$ as follows:

- The frequency count $N_{\mathbf{k}}$ is the number of cyclic strings of type $\mathbf{k}$;
- $N_{\mathbf{k}}^a$ is the number of cyclic strings of type $\mathbf{k}$ starting with a symbol $a \in \mathcal{A}$;
- $N_{\mathbf{k}}^{b,a}$ is the number of cyclic strings of type $\mathbf{k}$ starting with a pair of symbols $ba \in \mathcal{A}^2$.

These quantities satisfy the following properties.

Theorem 11.10 *Let $\mathbf{k} \in \mathcal{F}_n$ for $n \geq 1$.*
(i) *The number $N_{\mathbf{k}}^a$ of cyclic strings of type $\mathbf{k}$ starting with symbol a is*

$$N_{\mathbf{k}}^a = [\mathbf{z}^{\mathbf{k}}] B(\mathbf{z}) \cdot \det_{aa}(\mathbf{I} - \mathbf{z}). \tag{11.45}$$

(ii) *The number N_k^{ba} of cyclic strings (of type k) starting with the pair of symbols ba is*

$$N_k^{ba} = [z^k] z_{ba} B(z) \cdot \det_{bb}(I - z). \tag{11.46}$$

(iii) *N_k^{ba} is asymptotically given by*

$$N_k^{b,a} = \frac{k_{ba}}{k_b} B_k \cdot \det_{bb}(I - k^*) + O\left(B_k \left(\min k_{ij}\right)^{-1}\right), \tag{11.47}$$

where k^* is the matrix whose ijth element is k_{ij}/k_i; that is, $k^* = [k_{ij}/k_i]$.

The remaining part of this section is devoted to the proof of Theorem 11.10. We prove Theorem 11.10(i). We recall that $B_{\mathcal{A}}(z) = \mathcal{F}B(z)$ with $B(z)$ defined in (11.44). By Lemma 11.9, we also know that

$$\mathcal{F}_{\mathcal{A}-\{a\}}B(z) = B_{\mathcal{A}-\{a\}}(z) = \det_{aa}^{-1}(I - z),$$

where $\det_{aa}(I - z)$ is the determinant of the matrix $(I - z)$ with row a and column a deleted.

We want to prove that N_k^a is the coefficient at z^k of $B(z)/B_{\mathcal{A}-\{a\}}(z)$, which leads then directly to (11.45):

$$N_k^a = [z^k] \frac{B(z)}{B_{\mathcal{A}-\{a\}}(z)} = [z^k] B(z) \cdot \det_{aa}(I - z).$$

The proof proceeds via the enumeration of Euler cycles (paths) in a directed multigraph $\mathcal{G}_m$ over m vertices defined in the previous section. We recall that in such a graph, vertices are labeled by symbols from the alphabet $\mathcal{A}$ with the edge multiplicity given by the matrix k: there are k_{ij} edges from vertex $i \in \mathcal{A}$ to $j \in \mathcal{A}$. The number of Eulerian paths starting from vertex $a \in \mathcal{A}$ in such a multigraph is equal to N_k^a.

For a given vertex i of $\mathcal{G}_m$ with $k_i = k_{i,0} + \cdots + k_{i,m-1}$, there are

$$\frac{k_i!}{k_{i,0}! \cdots k_{i,m-1}!} = \binom{k_i}{k_{i,0} \cdots k_{i,m-1}} \tag{11.48}$$

ways of departing from i. Clearly, (11.48) is the number of permutations with repetitions. Furthermore, B_k defined in (11.43) is the product of (11.48) for $i = 1, \ldots, m$. Let us define a *coalition* a set of m such permutations, one permutation per vertex, corresponding to a combination of the edges that depart from a vertex. There are B_k coalitions.

Observe that for a given string, when scanning its symbols, we trace an Eulerian path in $\mathcal{G}_m$. However, we are interested in an "inverse" problem: given an initial symbol $a \in \mathcal{A}$ and a matrix k satisfying the flow property (with a nonzero weight for symbol a, $k_a > 0$), does a coalition of paths correspond to a string x_1^n; that is, does it trace an Eulerian path? The problem is that such a trace may end prematurely at symbol $a \in \mathcal{A}$ (by exhausting all edges departing from a) without visiting all edges of $\mathcal{G}_m$ (i.e., the length of the traced string is shorter than n). For example, in Figure 11.1 the following path 001010 of length six leaves edges 11 and 11 unvisited. Let k' be the matrix composed of the remaining nonvisited edges of the multigraph (the matrix $k - k'$ has been exhausted by the trace). Notice that matrix k' satisfies the flow property but the row and column corresponding to symbol a contain only zeros.

Given that k and k' are members of $\mathcal{F}_*$, let $N_{k,k'}^a$ be the number of ways matrix k is transformed into another matrix k' when the Eulerian path starts with symbol a. Notice that $k_a' = 0$. We have $N_{k,[0]}^a = N_k^a$, but also the following:

$$N^a_{\mathbf{k},\mathbf{k'}} = N^a_{\mathbf{k}-\mathbf{k'}} \times B_{\mathbf{k'}}, \quad k'_a = 0.$$

Summing over all matrices $\mathbf{k'}$, we obtain $\sum_{\mathbf{k'}} N^a_{\mathbf{k},\mathbf{k'}} = B_{\mathbf{k}}$, thus,

$$B_{\mathbf{k}} = \sum_{\mathbf{k'}, k'_a = 0} N^a_{\mathbf{k}-\mathbf{k'}} \times B_{\mathbf{k'}}.$$

Multiplying by $\mathbf{z^k}$ and summing now over all $\mathbf{z^k}$ such that $k_a \neq 0$, it yields

$$\sum_{\mathbf{k}\in\mathcal{F}_*, k_a\neq 0} B_{\mathbf{k}}\mathbf{z^k} = \left(\sum_{\mathbf{k}} N^a_{\mathbf{k}}\mathbf{z^k}\right) \times \left(\sum_{\mathbf{k}\in\mathcal{F}_*, k_a=0} B_{\mathbf{k}}\mathbf{z^k}\right). \tag{11.49}$$

Denoting $N^a(\mathbf{z}) = \sum_{\mathbf{k}\in\mathcal{F}_*} N^a_{\mathbf{k}}\mathbf{z^k}$, we arrive at

$$B_{\mathcal{A}}(\mathbf{z}) - B_{\mathcal{A}-\{a\}}(\mathbf{z}) = N^a(\mathbf{z})B_{\mathcal{A}-\{a\}}(\mathbf{z}).$$

We observe that for any generating functions $g(\mathbf{z})$ and $h(\mathbf{z})$, we have $\mathcal{F}(g\mathcal{F}h)(\mathbf{z}) = \mathcal{F}g(z)$ $\mathcal{F}h(\mathbf{z})$. Consequently, $\mathcal{F}(\frac{1}{g})(\mathbf{z}) = \frac{1}{\mathcal{F}g(\mathbf{z})}$. Since $\mathcal{F}B(\mathbf{z}) = B_{\mathcal{A}}(\mathbf{z})$ and $\mathcal{F}B_{\mathcal{A}-\{a\}}(\mathbf{z}) = B_{\mathcal{A}-\{a\}}(\mathbf{z})$, for all $\mathbf{k} \in \mathcal{F}_*$, we obtain

$$[\mathbf{z^k}]\frac{B_{\mathcal{A}}(\mathbf{z})}{B_{\mathcal{A}-\{a\}}(\mathbf{z})} = [\mathbf{z^k}]\frac{\mathcal{F}B(\mathbf{z})}{B_{\mathcal{A}-\{a\}}(\mathbf{z})}$$
$$= [\mathbf{z^k}]\mathcal{F}\left(\frac{B}{B_{\mathcal{A}-\{a\}}}\right)(\mathbf{z})$$
$$= [\mathbf{z^k}]\frac{B(\mathbf{z})}{B_{\mathcal{A}-\{a\}}(\mathbf{z})},$$

which is the last step needed to complete the proof.

Knowing $N^a_{\mathbf{k}}$, we certainly can compute the frequency count $N_{\mathbf{k}}$ as

$$N_{\mathbf{k}} = [\mathbf{z^k}]B(\mathbf{z})\sum_{a\in\mathcal{A}}(B_{\mathcal{A}-\{a\}}(\mathbf{z}))^{-1} = [\mathbf{z^k}]B(\mathbf{z})\sum_{a\in\mathcal{A}}\det{}_{aa}(\mathbf{I}-\mathbf{z}).$$

Next we establish Theorem 11.10 (ii); that is, we prove that for $n \geq 1$ and $\mathbf{k} \in \mathcal{F}_n$,

$$N^{ba}_{\mathbf{k}} = [\mathbf{z^k}]\frac{B(\mathbf{z})z_{b,a}}{B_{\mathcal{A}-\{b\}}(\mathbf{z})} = z_{ba}B(\mathbf{z})\cdot\det{}_{bb}(\mathbf{I}-\mathbf{z}).$$

The proof proceeds in the same way as in the previous proof except that we have to consider a coalition with the first edge departing from b to a. We let $B^{ba}_{\mathbf{k}}$ be the number of such coalitions. Observe that $B^{ba}_{\mathbf{k}} = B_{\mathbf{k}}\frac{k_{ba}}{k_b} = B_{\mathbf{k}-[\delta_{ba}]}$, where $[\delta_{ba}]$ is the matrix with all zeros except the bath element, which is set to be one. Let $\mathbf{k} \in \mathcal{F}_*$. Then, using the same approach as before, we arrive at the following recurrence:

$$B^{ba}_{\mathbf{k}} = \sum_{\mathbf{k'}, k'_b=0} N^{ba}_{\mathbf{k}-\mathbf{k'}} \times B_{\mathbf{k'}}, \quad k'_b = 0. \tag{11.50}$$

Computing the generating function, we find

$$\sum_{\mathbf{k}\in\mathcal{F}, k_{ba}\neq 0} B^{ba}_{\mathbf{k}}\mathbf{z^k} = \left(\sum_{\mathbf{k}} N^{ba}_{\mathbf{k}}\mathbf{z^k}\right) \times \left(\sum_{\mathbf{k}\in\mathcal{F}_*, k_b=0} B_{\mathbf{k}}\mathbf{z^k}\right).$$

In other words,

$$\sum_{\mathbf{k}\in\mathcal{F}_*, k_{ba}\neq 0} B_{\mathbf{k}}^{ba}\mathbf{z}^{\mathbf{k}} = N^{ba}(\mathbf{z})B_{\mathcal{A}-\{a\}}(\mathbf{z}),$$

where $N^{ba}(\mathbf{z}) = \sum_{\mathbf{k}} N_{\mathbf{k}}^{ba}\mathbf{z}^{\mathbf{k}}$. Using the fact that

$$\sum_{\mathbf{k}\in\mathcal{F}_*, k_{ba}\neq 0} B_{\mathbf{k}}^{ba}\mathbf{z}^{\mathbf{k}} = \mathcal{F}B^{ba}(\mathbf{z}),$$

where

$$B^{ba}(\mathbf{z}) = \sum_{\mathbf{k}, k_{ba}>0} B_{\mathbf{k}}^{ba}\mathbf{z}^{\mathbf{k}} = \sum_{\mathbf{k}, k_{ba}>0} B_{\mathbf{k}-[\delta_{ba}]}\mathbf{z}^{\mathbf{k}} = B(\mathbf{z})z_{ba},$$

we complete the proof.

Finally, we prove Theorem 11.10 (iii). We recall that $B_{\mathbf{k}}$ is explicitly given by (11.43). Furthermore, for every (fixed) integer matrix $\mathbf{a} = [a_{ij}]$, we have

$$[\mathbf{z}^{\mathbf{k}}]\,\mathbf{z}^{\mathbf{a}}B(\mathbf{z}) = B_{\mathbf{k}-\mathbf{a}} = (\mathbf{k}^*)^{\mathbf{a}}B_{\mathbf{k}} + O\left(B_{\mathbf{k}}\left(\min k_{ij}\right)^{-1}\right).$$

Consequently, if $P(\mathbf{z})$ is a polynomial in $\mathbf{z} = [z_{ij}]$, we have

$$[\mathbf{z}^{\mathbf{k}}]\,P(\mathbf{z})B(\mathbf{z}) = P(\mathbf{k}^*)B_{\mathbf{k}} + O\left(B_{\mathbf{k}}\left(\min k_{ij}\right)^{-1}\right).$$

This immediately implies (11.47). $\qquad\square$

11.3 Minimax Redundancy for Markov Sources

As discussed in the Chapter 9, the maximal minimax redundancy R_n^* has two components: the coding part $R_n^*(Q^*)$ and the noncoding part $\widetilde{R}_n^*$, which is governed by the statistics of the underlying class of distributions.

we first estimate $\widetilde{R}_n^*$ for Markov sources of order 1, then we generalize to any order $r \geq 1$, and finally we deal with the coding part $R_n^*(Q^*)$.

11.3.1 Asymptotics of $\widetilde{R}_n^*$

In this section, we consider the worst-case minimax redundancy for Markov sources $\mathcal{M}_1$ (of order 1) over a finite alphabet $\mathcal{A}$. We recall that $\widetilde{R}_n^* = \log D_n(\mathcal{M}_1)$ is given by (11.1). First, we observe that $D_n(\mathcal{M})_1 = mD_n^a(\mathcal{M}_1)$, where $D_n^a(\mathcal{M}_1)$ denotes the minimax redundancy restricted to all strings starting with symbol a. Second, we recall that $N_{\mathbf{k}}^{ba}$ represents the number of cyclic strings with frequency matrix $\mathbf{k}$, starting with $a \in \mathcal{A}$ and ending with $b \in \mathcal{A}$. But $N_{\mathbf{k}}^{ba}$ is also the number of (regular) strings starting with $ba \in \mathcal{A}^2$ and with frequency matrix equal to $\mathbf{k} - [\delta_{ba}]$.

We can now rewrite formula (11.1) for the redundancy of (regular) strings of length n in terms of cyclic strings. Equation (11.1) rewrites to

$$D_n(\mathcal{M}_1) = m\sum_{b\in\mathcal{A}}\sum_{\mathbf{k}\in\mathcal{F}_n, k_{ba}>0} N_{\mathbf{k}}^{ba}(\mathbf{k}-[\delta_{ba}])^{\mathbf{k}-[\delta_{ba}]}(k_b-1)^{-k_b+1}\prod_{i\neq b}(k_i)^{-k_i}. \qquad (11.51)$$

This formula is the starting point of our asymptotic analysis. In particular we obtain the following result.

Theorem 11.11 *Let $\mathcal{M}_1$ be the class of Markov sources of order 1 over a finite alphabet $\mathcal{A}$ of size m. Then $D_n(\mathcal{M}_1)$ is asymptotically given by*

$$D_n(\mathcal{M}_1) = \left(\frac{n}{2\pi}\right)^{m(m-1)/2} A_m \times \left(1 + O\left(\frac{1}{\sqrt{n}}\right)\right) \tag{11.52}$$

with

$$A_m = m \int_{\mathcal{K}(1)} \sum_{b \in \mathcal{A}} \det{}_{bb}(1 - \mathbf{y}^*) \prod_{i \in \mathcal{A}} \frac{\sqrt{\sum_{j \in \mathcal{A}} y_{ij}}}{\prod_{j \in \mathcal{A}} \sqrt{y_{ij}}} \prod_{ij \in \mathcal{A}^2} d\mathbf{y},$$

where

$$\mathcal{K}(1) = \left\{ y_{ij} : y_{ij} \geq 0,\ \sum_{ij} y_{ij} = 1, \forall i : \sum_j y_{ij} = \sum_j y_{ji} \right\}.$$

and $\mathbf{y}^*$ is the matrix $[y_{ij}/\sum_{j'} y_{ij'}]$. Consequently, the worst-case minimax redundancy is asymptotically given by

$$\widetilde{R}_n^*(\mathcal{M}_1) = \log D_n(\mathcal{M}_1) = \frac{m(m-1)}{2} \log \frac{n}{2\pi} + \log A_m + O\left(\frac{1}{\sqrt{n}}\right).$$

We note that the set $\mathcal{K}(1)$ is actually an $(m^2 - m)$-dimensional linear subset of the m^2-dimensional space that can be parametrized by the $m^2 - m$ variables y_{ij}, $0 \leq i \leq m-1$, $0 \leq j \leq m-2$. Hence, an integral of the form $\int_{\mathcal{K}(1)} F(\mathbf{y})d\mathbf{y}$ has to interpreted accordingly.

Furthermore, we also want to note that the constant A_m can be evaluated for some small values of m. In particular, for a binary alphabet ($m = 2$), we have

$$A_2 = 2 \int_{\mathcal{K}(1)} (\det{}_{00}(\mathbf{I} - \mathbf{y}^*) + \det{}_{11}(\mathbf{I} - \mathbf{y}^*)) \frac{\sqrt{y_0}}{\sqrt{y_{00}}\sqrt{y_{01}}} \frac{\sqrt{y_1}}{\sqrt{y_{10}}\sqrt{y_{11}}} d\mathbf{y}. \tag{11.53}$$

Since $\det{}_{00}(\mathbf{I} - \mathbf{y}^*) = \frac{y_{10}}{y_1}$ and $\det{}_{11}(\mathbf{I} - \mathbf{y}^*)$ by symmetry, and since the condition $\mathbf{y} \in \mathcal{K}(1)$ means $y_0 + y_1 = 1$ and $y_{01} = y_{10}$, we arrive, after the change of variable $x = \sin^2(\theta)$, at

$$A_2 = 4 \int_{y_{00}+2y_{01}+y_{11}=1} \frac{1}{\sqrt{y_{00}}\sqrt{y_0}\sqrt{y_{11}}\sqrt{y_1}} d\mathbf{y}.$$

Therefore,

$$\begin{aligned}
A_2 &= 4 \int_0^1 \frac{dx}{\sqrt{(1-x)x}} \int_0^{\min\{x,1-x\}} \frac{dy}{\sqrt{(1-x-y)(x-y)}} \\
&= 8 \int_0^{1/2} \frac{\ln(1-2x) - \ln(1 - 2\sqrt{(1-x)x})}{\sqrt{(1-x)x}} dx \\
&= 16 \int_0^{\pi/4} \ln\left(\frac{\cos(2\theta)}{1 - \sin(2\theta)}\right) d\theta \\
&= 16 \cdot G,
\end{aligned}$$

where G is the Catalan constant defined as

$$G = \sum_{i \geq 0} \frac{(-1)^i}{(2i+1)^2} \approx 0.915965594.$$

In the rest of this section, we prove Theorem 11.11. We start with a continuous version of Lemma 11.5. Let $\mathcal{K}(x)$ be the set of matrices $\mathbf{y} = [y_{ij}]$ with nonnegative *real* coefficients that satisfy the conservation flow property and the condition $\sum_{i,j} y_{ij} = x$. Observe that $\mathcal{F}_n$ is the set of nonnegative integer matrices $\mathbf{k}$ that belongs to $\mathcal{K}(n)$. Let $a(x)$ be the $(m^2 - m)$-dimensional volume of $\mathcal{K}(x)$. The reader is asked in Exercise 11.6 to prove the following.

Lemma 11.12 *Let $g(x)$ be a function of real $m \times m$ matrices x. Let $G(t)$ be the Laplace transform of $g(\cdot)$, that is,*

$$G(t) = \int_{\mathbf{R}_{\geq 0}^{m^2}} g(x) \exp\left(-\sum_{ij} t_{ij} x_{ij} \right) dx,$$

and let

$$\widetilde{G}(t) = \int_0^\infty dy \int_{\mathcal{K}(y)} g(x) \exp\left(-\sum_{ij} t_{ij} x_{ij} \right) dx.$$

Then we have

$$\widetilde{G}(t) = \frac{1}{(2\pi i)^m} \int_{-i\infty}^{+i\infty} \cdots \int_{-i\infty}^{+i\infty} G([t_{ij} + \theta_i - \theta_j]) d\theta_0 \cdots d\theta_{m-1}, \tag{11.54}$$

where $[t_{ij} + \theta_i - \theta_j]$ is a matrix whose the ijth coefficient is $t_{ij} + \theta_i - \theta_j$.

Next, we compare the size of $|\mathcal{F}_n(m)|$, that is, the number of matrices $\mathbf{k}$ satisfying (11.5)–(11.6), with $a(n)$, the $(m^2 - m)$-dimensional volume of $\mathcal{K}(n)$.

Lemma 11.13 *We have, as $n \to \infty$,*

$$|\mathcal{F}_n(m)| = a(n)\left(1 + O(1/n)\right).$$

Proof Since the asymptotic behavior of $|\mathcal{F}_n(m)|$ is known (see the proof of Theorem 11.6), it is sufficient to evaluate $a(n)$. By definition we have

$$a(y) = y^{m^2 - m} a(1). \tag{11.55}$$

Next, by setting $g(\mathbf{x}) = 1$ in Lemma 11.12, we find

$$\int_0^\infty a(y) e^{-ty} dy = \widetilde{G}(t[1]),$$

where $[1]$ is the matrix with all coefficients equal to 1. In particular, by setting $t = 1$ and by using (11.55), we find

$$\widetilde{G}([1]) = a(1) \int_0^\infty y^{m^2 - m} e^{-y} dy = a(1)(m^2 - m)!.$$

Since $g(\mathbf{x}) = 1$, we get explicitly

$$G(\mathbf{t}) = \int \exp(-\sum_{ij} t_{ij} x_{ij}) d\mathbf{x} = \prod_{ij} \frac{1}{t_{ij}}.$$

Therefore, by (11.54) and (11.38), we obtain

$$\widetilde{G}([1]) = \frac{1}{(2\pi i)^m} \int_{-i\infty}^{+i\infty} \cdots \int_{-i\infty}^{+i\infty} G([1 + \theta_i - \theta_j]) d\theta_0 \cdots d\theta_{m-1}$$

$$= \frac{1}{(2\pi)^m} \int_{-\infty}^{\infty} \cdots \int_{\infty}^{\infty} \prod_{i \neq j} \frac{1}{1 + i(\theta_i - \theta_j)} d\theta_0 \cdots d\theta_{m-1}$$

$$= d(m).$$

Consequently,

$$a(n) = a(1)n^{m^2-m} = \frac{d(m)}{(m^2-m)!} n^{m^2-m}.$$

This completes the proof. ∎

Now we can return to the proof of Theorem 11.11. It suffices to calculate the partial redundancy $D_n^a(\mathcal{M}_1)$ restricted to all strings starting with a symbol a since $D_n(\mathcal{M}_1) = mD_n^a(\mathcal{M}_1)$. We have from (11.51),

$$D_n^a(\mathcal{M}_1) = \sum_{b \in \mathcal{A}} \sum_{\mathbf{k} \in \mathcal{F}_n, k_{ba} > 0} N_{\mathbf{k}}^{ba}(\mathbf{k} - [\delta_{ba}])^{\mathbf{k} - [\delta_{ba}]} (k_b - 1)^{-k_b+1} \prod_{i \neq b} (k_i)^{-k_i}$$

$$= \sum_{b \in \mathcal{A}} \sum_{\mathbf{k} \in \mathcal{F}_n, k_{ba} > 0} \frac{k_{ba}}{k_a} \det_{bb}(\mathbf{I} - \mathbf{k}^*) B_{\mathbf{k}}(\mathbf{k} - [\delta_{ba}])^{\mathbf{k} - [\delta_{ba}]} (k_b - 1)^{k_b-1}$$

$$\prod_{i \neq b} (k_i)^{-k_i} \times \left(1 + O(1/\min k_{ij})\right).$$

Recall that $B_{\mathbf{k}}$ is defined in (11.43). Hence, by Stirling's formula, we obtain for $\mathbf{k} \in \mathcal{F}_n(m)$,

$$\frac{k_{ba}}{k_b} B_{\mathbf{k}}(\mathbf{k} - [\delta_{ba}])^{\mathbf{k} - [\delta_{ba}]} (k_b - 1)^{-k_b+1} \prod_{i \neq b} (k_i)^{-k_i} = \prod_i \frac{\sqrt{2\pi k_i}}{\prod_j \sqrt{2\pi k_{ij}}} \left(1 + O(1/\min k_{ij})\right),$$

and this yields

$$D_n^a(\mathcal{M}_1) = \sum_{\mathbf{k} \in \mathcal{F}_n} F_m(\mathbf{k}^*) \prod_i \frac{\sqrt{2\pi k_i}}{\prod_j \sqrt{2\pi k_{ij}}} \left(1 + O(1/\min k_{ij})\right),$$

where $F_m(\mathbf{x}) = \sum_{b \in \mathcal{A}} \det_{bb}(\mathbf{I} - \mathbf{x}^*)$ and $\mathbf{x}^*$ is the matrix whose (i,j)th entry is x_{ij}/x_i, with $x_i = \sum_{j'} x_{ij'}$.

Using standard tools, this sum can be approximated by an integral. We recall that $\mathcal{F}_n(m)$ can by parametrized by the $m^2 - m$ variables k_{ij}, $0 \leq i \leq m-1, 0 \leq j \leq m-2$. This leads to

$$D_n(\mathcal{M}_1) = \frac{|\mathcal{F}_n(m)|}{a(n)} \int_{\mathcal{K}(n)} F_m(\mathbf{y}) \prod_i \frac{\sqrt{2\pi \sum_j y_{ij}}}{\prod_j \sqrt{2\pi y_{ij}}} d\mathbf{y} \left(1 + O\left(\frac{1}{\sqrt{n}}\right)\right). \tag{11.56}$$

By applying the change of variables $\mathbf{y}' = \frac{1}{n}\mathbf{y}$, and since $F_m(\frac{1}{n}\mathbf{y}) = F_m(\mathbf{y})$ (indeed, $y_{ij}/y_i = y'_{ij}/y'_i$), we find

$$\int_{\mathcal{K}(n)} F_m(\mathbf{y}) \prod_i \frac{\sqrt{2\pi \sum_j y_{ij}}}{\prod_j \sqrt{2\pi y_{ij}}} d\mathbf{y} = \left(\frac{n}{2\pi}\right)^{(m-1)m/2} \int_{\mathcal{K}(1)} F_m(\mathbf{y}') \prod_i \frac{\sqrt{\sum_j y'_{ij}}}{\prod_j \sqrt{y'_{ij}}} d\mathbf{y}'.$$

Since $|\mathcal{F}_n|/a(n) = 1 + O(1/n)$, we obtain our final result; that is,

$$D_n(\mathcal{M}_1) = \left(\frac{n}{2\pi}\right)^{(m-1)m/2} A_m \left(1 + O\left(\frac{1}{\sqrt{n}}\right)\right).$$

This proves Theorem 11.11.

11.3.2 Higher-Order Markov Sources

Next, we extend Theorem 11.11 to Markov sources of order r.

Theorem 11.14 *Let $\mathcal{M}_r$ be the class of Markov sources of order r over a finite alphabet $\mathcal{A}$ of size m. Then we have asymptotically as $n \to \infty$,*

$$D_n(\mathcal{M}_r) = \left(\frac{n}{2\pi}\right)^{m^r(m-1)/2} A_m^{(r)} \times \left(1 + O\left(\frac{1}{\sqrt{n}}\right)\right) \tag{11.57}$$

with

$$A_m^{(r)} = m^r \int_{\mathcal{K}_r(1)} F_m^{(r)}(\mathbf{y}) \prod_{w \in \mathcal{A}^r} \frac{\sqrt{y_w}}{\prod_j \sqrt{y_{w,j}}} d\mathbf{y},$$

where $\mathcal{K}_r(1)$ is the convex set of $m^r \times m$ matrices $\mathbf{y}$ with nonnegative coefficients such that $\sum_{w,j} y_{w,j} = 1$, $w \in \mathcal{A}^r$. Furthermore,

$$F_m^{(r)}(\mathbf{y}_r) = \sum_w \det_{ww}(\mathbf{I} - \mathbf{y}_r^*),$$

where $\mathbf{y}_r^*$ is the $m^r \times m^r$ matrix whose (w, w') coefficient is equal to $y_{w,a}/\sum_{i \in \mathcal{A}} y_{wi}$ if there exist a in $\mathcal{A}$ such that w' is a suffix of wa, otherwise the (w, w')th coefficient is equal to 0. Consequently, the worst-case minimax redundancy satisfies, as $n \to \infty$,

$$\widetilde{R}_n^*(\mathcal{M}_r) = \log D_n(\mathcal{M}_r) = \frac{m^r(m-1)}{2} \log \frac{n}{2\pi} + \log A_m^{(r)} + O\left(\frac{1}{\sqrt{n}}\right).$$

Proof We only sketch the proof following the steps of the proof of Theorem 11.11 for $r = 1$. For Markov sources of order r, we define the frequency matrix $\mathbf{k}$ as an $m^r \times m$ matrix whose $k_{w,j}$th coefficient ($w \in \mathcal{A}^r$) is the number of times the string w is followed by symbol $j \in \mathcal{A}$ in the string x_1^n. We can also view $\mathbf{k}$ as a $m^r \times m^r$ matrix indexed by $w, w' \in \mathcal{A}^r \times \mathcal{A}^r$ with the convention that nonzero elements of $\mathbf{k}$ are for $w' = w_2 \ldots w_r j, j \in \mathcal{A}$; that is, when w' is constructed from w by deleting the first symbol and adding symbol $j \in \mathcal{A}$ at the end. Then,

$$\sup_{P \in \mathcal{M}_r} P(x_1^n) = \prod_{w,j \in \mathcal{A}^{r+1}} \left(\frac{k_{w,j}}{k_w}\right)^{k_{w,j}},$$

where $k_w = \sum_j k_{w,j}$.

The main combinatorial result that we need is the enumeration of types; that is, how many strings of length n have type corresponding to the matrix $\mathbf{k}_{w,w'}$, $w, w' \in \mathcal{A}^r$ with w' as defined here. As in the previous section, we focus on cyclic strings in which the last symbol is followed by the first. To enumerate cyclic strings of type $\mathbf{k}_{w,w'}$, we build a multigraph on m^r vertices with edges labeled by symbols from the alphabet $\mathcal{A}$. The number of Eulerian paths is equal to the number $N_{\mathbf{k}}$ of strings of type $\mathbf{k}$.

We recall that $B_{\mathbf{k}}^{(r)}$ is the number of permutations with repetitions; that is,

$$B_{\mathbf{k}}^{(r)} = \prod_{w \in \mathcal{A}^r} \binom{k_w}{k_{w1} \cdots k_{wm}}.$$

Its generating function is

$$B^{(r)}(\mathbf{z}) = \prod_{w \in \mathcal{A}^r} (1 - \sum_{j \in \mathcal{A}} z_{w,j})^{-1},$$

while its $\mathcal{F}$ generating function of $B_{\mathbf{k}}^{(r)}$ is

$$\mathcal{F}B_r(\mathbf{z}) = (\det(\mathbf{I} - \mathbf{z}_r))^{-1},$$

where $\mathbf{z}_r$ is an $m^r \times m^r$ matrix whose (w, w') coefficient is equal to $z_{w,a}$ if there exist $a \in \mathcal{A}$ such that w' is a suffix of wa; otherwise the (w, w') coefficient is equal to 0 (as discussed). Finally, we need to estimate $N_{\mathbf{k}}^{w,w'}$, the number of strings of type $\mathbf{k}$ starting with $ww' \in \mathcal{A}^{2r}$. As in Theorem 11.10(ii), we find that

$$N_{\mathbf{k}}^{w,w'} = [\mathbf{z}^{\mathbf{k}}] \left(B_r(\mathbf{z}) \det_{w,w}(\mathbf{I} - \mathbf{z}_r) \prod_{i=1}^{r} z_{(ww')_i^{i+r}} \right),$$

where $w_i^j = w_i w_{i+1} \ldots w_j$ $(i \leq j)$. The rest follows the footsteps of our previous analysis. ∎

11.3.3 Coding Contribution to the Redundancy

In this section, we consider the coding part of the redundancy, namely $R_n^*(Q^*)$. As in the memoryless case, we expect that for Markov sources $\mathcal{M}_r$ of order r over an alphabet $\mathcal{A}$ of size m,

$$R_n^*(Q^*) = -\frac{\ln \frac{1}{m-1} \ln m}{\ln m} + o(1) \tag{11.58}$$

as $n \to \infty$.

However, for the sake of brevity, we only present the binary case of Markov sources of order 1.

Theorem 11.15 *For a Markov source of order* 1 *over a binary alphabet, we have*

$$R_n^*(Q^*) = -\frac{\ln \ln 2}{\ln 2} + o(1) \tag{11.59}$$

as $n \to \infty$.

The proof runs very similarly to the proof of Theorem 10.1. The main step is to provide upper bounds for exponential sums; see Lemma 11.16. In order to simplify our considerations, we only consider (binary) strings of length n that start and end with 0. Then the corresponding (noncyclic) types $\mathbf{k} = (k_{00}, k_{01}, k_{10}, k_{11})$ are characterized by the equations

$$k_{00} + k_{01} + k_{10} + k_{11} = n - 1, \quad k_{01} = k_{10}$$

or just by

$$k_{00} + 2k_{01} + k_{11} = n - 1.$$

These types can be parametrized by k_{00} and k_{01} by considering

$$0 \leq k_{01} \leq \left\lfloor \frac{n-1}{2} \right\rfloor, \quad 0 \leq k_{00} \leq n - 1 - 2k_{01},$$

where

$$k_{10} = k_{01} \quad \text{and} \quad k_{11} = n - 1 - k_{00} - 2k_{01}.$$

We also recall that $N_{\mathbf{k}}^{00}$ is asymptotically given by

$$N_{\mathbf{k}}^{00} = \frac{k_{01}}{k_{01} + k_{11}} \binom{k_{00} + k_{01}}{k_{00}} \binom{k_{01} + k_{11}}{k_{11}} \left(1 + O\left(\frac{1}{\min k_{ij}}\right)\right)$$

and that Q^* can be represented as (note that we consider noncyclic strings)

$$Q^*(\mathbf{k}) = \frac{1}{D_n} \left(\frac{k_{00}}{k_{00} + k_{01}}\right)^{k_{00}} \left(\frac{k_{01}}{k_{00} + k_{01}}\right)^{k_{01}} \left(\frac{k_{10}}{k_{10} + k_{11}}\right)^{k_{10}} \left(\frac{k_{11}}{k_{10} + k_{11}}\right)^{k_{11}},$$

where

$$D_n = \frac{A_2}{2\pi} n + O(\sqrt{n}).$$

In particular, it follows (if all k_{ij} are nonzero) that

$$N_{\mathbf{k}}^{00} Q^*(\mathbf{k}) = \frac{1}{2\pi D_n} \sqrt{\frac{k_{00} + k_{01}}{(k_{10} + k_{11})k_{00}k_{11}}} \left(1 + O\left(\frac{1}{\min k_{ij}}\right)\right).$$

However, note that the estimate holds too, if some of the $k_{ij} = 0$ and we interpret $1/k_{ij}$ as 1. In what follows, we will use this *convention* to simplify the notation and to avoid several case studies.

Setting

$$a_{n,k_{00},k_{01}} = \sqrt{\frac{k_{00} + k_{01}}{(n - 1 - k_{00} - k_{01})k_{00}(n - 1 - k_{00} - 2k_{01})}},$$

we have

$$N_{\mathbf{k}}^{00} Q^*(\mathbf{k}) = \frac{1}{2\pi D_n} a_{n,k_{00},k_{01}} \left(1 + O\left(\frac{1}{\min k_{ij}}\right)\right).$$

Since

$$\sum_{\mathbf{k}} a_{n,k_{00},k_{01}} \frac{1}{\min k_{ij}} = O\left(\sqrt{n}\right) = O\left(\frac{D_n}{\sqrt{n}}\right),$$

it is sufficient to consider just $a_{n,k_{00},k_{01}}$ and to neglect the error term.

As already mentioned, we need proper estimates for exponential sums.

Lemma 11.16 *We have uniformly for nonzero integers h with $|h| \leq n/16$,*

$$\widetilde{S} = \sum_{\mathbf{k}} a_{n,k_{00},k_{01}} e^{2\pi i h \log Q^*(\mathbf{k})} = O\left(|h|^{1/4} n^{3/4} \log n\right). \tag{11.60}$$

With the help of Lemma 11.16 (and analogue properties for strings that start with 0 and end at 1 or start with 1 and end with 0 or 1), we can then proceed in the same way as for the proof of Theorem 10.1. The reader is asked to fill in these details in Exercise 11.10.

Proof In a first step, we consider the exponential sums

$$S = \sum_{a \le k_{00} \le b} e^{2\pi i h \log Q^*(\mathbf{k})},$$

where $a \ge 0$ and $b \le n$. We also set

$$\begin{aligned}
F(k_{00}, k_{01}) = &\ k_{00} \log k_{00} - (k_{00} + k_{01}) \log(k_{00} + k_{01}) + 2k_{01} \log k_{01} \\
&+ (n - 1 - k_{00} - 2k_{01}) \log(n - 1 - k_{00} - 2k_{01}) \\
&- (n - 1 - k_{00} - k_{01}) \log(n - 1 - k_{00} - k_{01}).
\end{aligned}$$

Then $Q^*(\mathbf{k}) = e^{F(k_{00}, k_{01})}/D_n$ and, thus, S and

$$S' = \sum_{a \le k_{00} \le b} e^{2\pi i h \log F(k_{00}, k_{01})}$$

have the same absolute value.

By van der Corput's method (see (E.1) from Appendix E), we know that

$$S = O\left(\frac{|h| \, |F_{k_{00}}(b, k_{01}) - F_{k_{00}}(a, k_{01})| + 1}{\sqrt{\lambda}} \right),$$

where $\lambda = \min_{a \le y \le b} |h| \, |F_{k_{00} k_{00}}(y, k_{01})| > 0$ (and where $F_{k_{00}}$ denotes the derivative with respect to k_{00}). Since

$$\begin{aligned}
|F_{k_{00}}(y, k_{01})| = &\ \log(y) - \log(y + k_{01}) \\
&+ \log(n - 1 - y - k_{01}) - \log(n - 1 - y - 2k_{01}) \\
\ll &\ \log n
\end{aligned}$$

and

$$\begin{aligned}
\ln 2 \, |F_{k_{00} k_{00}}(y, k_{01})| = &\ \frac{1}{y} - \frac{1}{y + k_{01}} \\
&- \frac{1}{n - 1 - y - k_{01}} + \frac{1}{n - 1 - y - 2k_{01}} \\
= &\ \frac{k_{01}}{y(y + k_{01})} + \frac{k_{01}}{(n - 1 - y - k_{01})(n - 1 - y - 2k_{01})} \\
\gg &\ \frac{1}{n}
\end{aligned}$$

uniformly for $a \le y \le b$, we immediately find

$$S = O\left(\sqrt{|h| n} \log n \right).$$

In a next step, we will use the following upper bounds (that follow directly from the definition):

$$a_{n, k_{00}, k_{01}} \ll \frac{1}{\sqrt{k_{00} k_{11}}} + \frac{1}{\sqrt{k_{01} k_{11}}}$$

and

$$\left| a_{n,k_{00}+1,k_{01}} - a_{n,k_{00},k_{01}} \right| \ll \frac{1}{\sqrt{k_{00}^3 k_{11}}} + \frac{1}{\sqrt{k_{00} k_{11}^3}} + \frac{1}{\sqrt{k_{01}^3 k_{11}}},$$

where k_{11} abbreviates $k_{11} = n - 1 - k_{00} - 2k_{01}$.

We will split the sum in $\widetilde{S}$ into several parts, where we use a parameter $K \leq n/4$ that will be fixed later. First, we suppose that

$$\frac{n}{2} - K \leq k_{01} \leq \frac{n-1}{2}.$$

In this case, we only use trivial upper bounds for the corresponding part of the sum $\widetilde{S}$; that is, we apply the relation $|e^{2\pi i x}| = 1$. Thus, we consider the sum

$$\widetilde{S}_1 = \sum_{\frac{n}{2}-K \leq k_{01} \leq \frac{n-1}{2}} \sum_{0 \leq k_{00} \leq n-1-2k_{01}} a_{n,k_{00},k_{01}}$$

$$\ll \sum_{\frac{n}{2}-K \leq k_{01} \leq \frac{n-1}{2}} \sum_{0 \leq k_{00} \leq n-1-2k_{01}} \left(\frac{1}{\sqrt{k_{00} k_{11}}} + \frac{1}{\sqrt{k_{01} k_{11}}} \right).$$

Since

$$\sum_{0 \leq k_{00} \leq n-1-2k_{01}} \frac{1}{\sqrt{k_{00}(n-1-2k_{01}-k_{00}}} \ll 1$$

and

$$\sum_{0 \leq k_{00} \leq n-1-2k_{01}} \frac{1}{\sqrt{k_{01}(n-1-2k_{01}-k_{00}}} \ll \frac{\sqrt{n-1-2k_{01}}}{\sqrt{n}},$$

it immediately follows that

$$\widetilde{S}_1 \ll K + \frac{K^{3/2}}{\sqrt{n}}.$$

Second, we consider the case where $0 \leq k_{01} \leq \frac{n}{2} - K$ and

$$k_{00} \leq K.$$

Here we use again trivial upper bounds and arrive at

$$\widetilde{S}_2 = \sum_{k_{01} \leq \frac{n}{2}-K} \sum_{0 \leq k_{00} \leq K} a_{n,k_{00},k_{01}}$$

$$\ll \sum_{k_{01} \leq \frac{n}{2}-K} \sum_{0 \leq k_{00} \leq K} \left(\frac{1}{\sqrt{k_{00} k_{11}}} + 1 \sqrt{k_{01} k_{11}} \right)$$

$$\ll K^{1/2} \sum_{k_{01} \leq \frac{n}{2}-K} \frac{1}{\sqrt{n-1-2k_{01}-K}}$$

$$+ K \sum_{k_{01} \leq \frac{n}{2}-K} \frac{1}{\sqrt{k_{01}(n-1-2k_{01}-K)}}$$

$$\ll \sqrt{Kn} + K.$$

In a similar way we can handle the case, where $0 \leq k_{01} \leq \frac{n}{2} - K$ and

$$k_{11} = n - 1 - 2k_{01} - k_{00} \leq K.$$

Here we obtain

$$\widetilde{S}_3 = \sum_{k_{01} \leq \frac{n}{2} - K} \sum_{n-1-2k_{01}-K \leq k_{00} \leq n-1-2k_{01}} a_{n,k_{00},k_{01}}$$

$$\ll \sum_{k_{01} \leq \frac{n}{2} - K} \sum_{n-1-2k_{01}-K \leq k_{00} \leq n-1-2k_{01}} \left(\frac{1}{\sqrt{k_{00}k_{11}}} + \frac{1}{\sqrt{k_{01}k_{11}}} \right)$$

$$\ll K^{1/2} \sum_{k_{01} \leq \frac{n}{2} - K} \frac{1}{\sqrt{n-1-2k_{01}-K}}$$

$$+ K^{1/2} \sum_{k_{01} \leq \frac{n}{2} - K} \frac{1}{\sqrt{k_{01}}}$$

$$\ll \sqrt{Kn}.$$

It remains to consider the case where $0 \leq k_{01} \leq \frac{n}{2} - K$, $k_{00} \geq K$, and $k_{11} = n - 1 - 2k_{01} - k_{00} \geq K$. Here we apply partial summation for the following exponential sum:

$$\sum_{K \leq k_{00} \leq n-1-2k_{01}-K} a_{n,k_{00},k_{01}} e^{2\pi i h F(h_{00},h_{01})}$$

$$\leq a_{n,K,k_{01}} \left| \sum_{K \leq k_{00} \leq n-1-2k_{01}-K} e^{2\pi i h F(h_{00},h_{01})} \right|$$

$$+ \sum_{K \leq k_{00} < n-1-2k_{01}-K} |a_{n,k_{00}+1,k_{01}} - a_{n,k_{00},k_{01}}| \left| \sum_{K \leq y \leq n-1-2k_{01}-K} e^{2\pi i h F(y,h_{01})} \right|$$

$$\ll \sqrt{|h|n} \log n \left(\frac{1}{\sqrt{K(n-1-2k_{01}-K)}} + \frac{1}{\sqrt{k_{01}(n-1-2k_{01}-K)}} \right)$$

$$+ \sqrt{|h|n} \log n \sum_{K \leq k_{00} < n-1-2k_{01}-K} \left(\frac{1}{\sqrt{k_{00}^3 k_{11}}} + \frac{1}{\sqrt{k_{00}k_{11}^3}} + \frac{1}{\sqrt{k_{01}^3 k_{11}}} \right)$$

$$\ll \sqrt{|h|n} \log n \left(\frac{1}{\sqrt{K(n-1-2k_{01}-K)}} + \frac{1}{\sqrt{k_{01}(n-1-2k_{01}-K)}} \right)$$

$$+ \sqrt{|h|n} \log n \left(\frac{1}{\sqrt{K(n-2k_{01}-K)}} + \frac{1}{\sqrt{Kk_{01}}} \right).$$

Finally, by summing over $k_{01} \leq \frac{n}{2} - K$, it follows that the remaining sum $\widetilde{S}_4$ is upper bounded by

$$\widetilde{S}_4 \ll \sqrt{|h|n} \log n \sqrt{\frac{n}{K}} = \frac{\sqrt{|h|} n}{\sqrt{K}} \log n.$$

Summing up, we finally arrive at

$$\widetilde{S} \ll K + \frac{K^{3/2}}{\sqrt{n}} + \sqrt{KN} + \frac{\sqrt{|h|}\,n}{\sqrt{K}} \log n,$$

and by choosing $K = \sqrt{|h|n}$ we finally obtain (11.60), which completes the proof of Lemma 11.16. ∎

11.4 Exercises

11.1 Compute explicitly the number of types in Example 11.3.

11.2 Provide details of the derivation (11.37) of $d(m)$.

11.3 Using similar recursive partial fractions expansions as in Section 11.2.1, prove that for $m = 4$ and $m = 5$,

$$F_4^*(z) = \frac{z^8 - 2z^7 + 3z^6 + 2z^5 - 2z^4 + 2z^3 + 3z^2 - 2z + 1}{(1-z)^{13}(1+z)^5(1+z^2)(1+z+z^2)^2} \tag{11.61}$$

and

$$F_5^*(z) = \frac{Q(z)}{(1-z)^{21}(1+z)^8(1+z^2)^2(1+z+z^2)^4(1+z+z^2+z^3+z^4)}, \tag{11.62}$$

where

$$\begin{aligned}
Q(z) = z^{20} &- 3z^{19} + 7z^{18} + 3z^{17} + 2z^{16} + 17z^{15} + 35z^{14}\\
&+ 29z^{13} + 45z^{12} + 50z^{11}\\
&+ 72z^{10} + 50z^9 + 45z^8 + 29z^7 + 35z^6\\
&+ 17z^5 + 2z^4 + 3z^3 + 7z^2 - 3z + 1.
\end{aligned}$$

By expanding (11.61) and (11.62) near $z = 1$, prove then that as $n \to \infty$,

$$|\mathcal{P}_n(4)| \sim \frac{1}{96} \frac{n^{12}}{12!}, \qquad |\mathcal{P}_n(5)| \sim \frac{37}{34560} \frac{n^{20}}{20!}. \tag{11.63}$$

11.4 Prove the following asymptotic extension of Theorem 11.6. When $m \to \infty$, we find that

$$|\mathcal{P}_n(m)| \sim \frac{\sqrt{2}m^{3m/2}e^{m^2}}{m^{2m^2}2^m\pi^{m/2}} \cdot n^{m^2-m}, \tag{11.64}$$

provided that $m^4 = o(n)$.

11.5 Prove (11.44); that is,

$$B(\mathbf{z}) = \sum_k B_{\mathbf{k}}\mathbf{z}^{\mathbf{k}} = \prod_{a \in \mathcal{A}}(1 - \sum_{b \in \mathcal{A}} z_{a,b})^{-1}.$$

11.6 Prove Lemma 11.12.

11.7 Establish (11.49), providing all details.

11.8 Derive the recurrence (11.50).

11.9   Prove the following:

$$\sum_{k=0}^{n} \binom{n}{k} p^k (1-p)^{n-k} \log \frac{\left(\frac{k}{n}\right)^k \left(1 - \frac{k}{n}\right)^{n-k}}{p^k (1-p)^k} = \frac{1}{2} + O\left(n^{-1/2}\right)$$

for large n.

11.10   Deduce Theorem 11.15 from Lemma 11.16 (and from corresponding properties for strings that start with 0 and end at 1, or start with 1 and end with 0 or 1).

Bibliographical Notes

The method of types is quite a popular and useful technique in information theory and combinatorics. The essence of the method of types was known for some time in probability and statistical physics, but it was only in the 1970s that Csiszár and his group developed a general method and made it a basic tool of information theory of discrete memoryless systems; see Csiszar and Korner (1981). However, earliest works for Markov types are by Goodman (1958) and Billingsley (1968); see also Biza (1971). Markov types were studied in Whittle (1955), Weinberger et al. (1994), Jacquet and Szpankowski (2004), Martin, Seroussi, and Weinberger (2007). Types for tree models were discussed in Martin et al. (2007) and further developed in Whittle (1955), Cover and Thomas (1991), Weinberger et al. (1994), Csiszar (1998), Drmota and Szpankowski (2004), Jacquet and Szpankowski (2004), Seroussi (2006), Martin et al. (2007). Non-Markovian types were developed by Seroussi (2006); see also Knessl and Szpankowski (2005).

The minimax redundancy for Markov sources was first discussed in Atteson (1999), Rissanen (1996), Shields (1993), which was later further improved in Jacquet and Szpankowski (2004).

Our exposition in this chapter follows Whittle (1955), Jacquet, Knessl, and Szpankowski (2012) and Jacquet and Szpankowski (2004).

12

Non-Markovian Sources: Redundancy of Renewal Processes

In this chapter, we discuss sources with unbounded memory. In the last two chapters, we showed that the maximal and average minimax redundancy and regret grow as

$$\frac{d}{2} \log n + O(1),$$

where d is the dimension (number of unknown parameters). For sources over alphabet of size m, we have $d = m - 1$. Here, we focus on the so-called *renewal sources* introduced by Csiszar and Shields (1996). Such a process generates binary sequences as follows. Starting with a 1, there is a run of 0 of length governed by a distribution over nonnegative integers. At the end of the run, we put a 1, and repeat the scheme until we generate a sequence of length n. Clearly, such a source is not Markovian (unless the distribution of the run has some extra constraints).

There are a few interesting challenges. How does the minimax redundancy grow? Is it still true that the average minimax redundancy is within $O(1)$ away from the maximal minimax redundancy? We address these questions in this chapter.

12.1 Renewal Source

We start with a precise definition of class $\mathcal{R}_0$ of a nonstationary renewal process and its associated sources. Let $T_1, T_2 \ldots$ be a sequence of i.i.d. positive-integer-valued random variables with common distribution $Q(j) = P(T_1 = j)$. Throughout we assume that $\mathbf{E}[T_1] < \infty$. The process $T_1, T_1 + T_2, \ldots$ is called the (nonstationary) renewal process. With such a renewal process there is an associated *binary renewal sequence* in which the 1's occur exactly at the renewal epochs $T_1, T_1 + T_2$, etc. Accordingly, we start the renewal sequence with a 1 put at the zeroth position. Then we put $T_1 - 1$ run of 0s following by a 1. We repeat the process until the sequence is of length $n + 1$ (with the zeroth symbol being a 1). We denote such a source as $\mathcal{R}_0$.

In order to estimate the maximal minimax redundancy $\widetilde{R}_n^* := \widetilde{R}_n^*(\mathcal{R}_0)$, we need to compute the probabilities $P(x^n)$ and analyze $\sup_P P(x^n)$, which we discuss next. Observe that the nonstationary renewal sequence $x_0^n = 1x_1^n$ can be represented as

$$x_n = 10^{\alpha_1} 1 \cdots 10^{\alpha_l} 1 \underbrace{0 \cdots 0}_{k^*},$$

where $0 \leq \alpha_i \leq n$ for $i = 1, \ldots, l \leq n$ and k^* is the length of the last "unfinished" run. Let k_m be the number of i such that $\alpha_i = m$, where $m = 0, 1, \ldots, n - 1$; that is, k_m is the number of runs of zeros of length m. Then,

$$P(x^n) = Q(1)^{k_0} Q(2)^{k_1} \cdots Q(n)^{k_{n-1}} P\{T_1 > k^*\}, \tag{12.1}$$

subject to $Q(1) + Q(2) + \cdots + Q(n) \leq 1$ and

$$k_0 + 2k_1 + \cdots + nk_{n-1} + k^* = n. \tag{12.2}$$

To simplify somewhat the next presentation, we set $q_i = Q(i + 1)$; that is, q_i describes the distribution of the number of zeros between two renewals. (By definition, we set $q_{-1} = Q(0) = 0$.) In Exercise 12.1, we ask the reader to show that $P(x^n)$ is a distribution; that is,

$$\sum_{x^n} P(x^n) = 1.$$

Our goal is to estimate

$$\widetilde{R}_n^* = \log \sum_{x_n} \sup_P P(x^n)$$

(see Lemma 9.2). For this purpose, we define a sequence r_m as follows (by convention here $0^0 = 1$):

$$r_m = \sum_{k=0}^{m} r_{m,k},$$

$$r_{m,k} = \sum_{\mathcal{P}(m,k)} \binom{k}{k_0 \cdots k_{m-1}} \left(\frac{k_0}{k}\right)^{k_0} \cdots \left(\frac{k_{m-1}}{k}\right)^{k_{m-1}}, \tag{12.3}$$

where $\mathcal{P}(m, k)$ denotes the set of partitions of m into k summands; that is, the collection of tuples of nonnegative integers $(k_0, k_1, \ldots, k_{m-1})$ satisfying

$$m = k_0 + 2k_1 + \cdots + mk_{m-1}, \tag{12.4}$$

$$k = k_0 + k_1 + \cdots + k_{m-1}. \tag{12.5}$$

We first establish the following bounds on the maximal minimax redundancy $\widetilde{R}_n^*$.

Lemma 12.1 *For all $n \geq 0$,*

$$r_{n+1} - 1 \leq \sum_{x_n} \sup_P P(x^n) \leq \sum_{m=0}^{n} r_m, \tag{12.6}$$

where r_n is defined in (12.3)–(12.5).

Proof Let, as before, $q_i = Q(i + 1) = P(T = i + 1)$. By (12.1), we have

$$P(x_1^n) = q_0^{k_0} q_1^{k_1} \cdots q_{n-1}^{k_{n-1}} (1 - q_0 - q_1 - \cdots - q_{k^*-1}), \tag{12.7}$$

subject to $q_0 + \cdots + q_{n-1} \leq 1$, $k^* \geq 0$, and

$$k_0 + 2k_1 + \cdots + nk_{n-1} \leq n. \tag{12.8}$$

Observe that in (12.8) we have $\leq n$ instead of $= n$ (cf. (12.4) where m is replaced by n). We denote such a set of partitions (i.e., satisfying (12.8) and (12.5) in which m is replaced by n) as $\mathcal{P}_{\leq}(n, k) = \bigcup_{m \leq n} \mathcal{P}(m, k)$.

For the proof of the upper bound, we proceed as follows. Suppose that $k_0, \ldots, k_{n-1}$ satisfy $\mathcal{P}_{\leq}(n, k)$. Then we have

$$\sup_{q} \; q_0^{k_0} q_1^{k_1} \cdots q_{n-1}^{k_{n-1}} (1 - q_0 - q_1 - \cdots - q_{k^*-1})$$

$$\leq \sup_{q} q_0^{k_0} q_1^{k_1} \cdots q_{n-1}^{k_{n-1}}$$

$$= \left(\frac{k_0}{k}\right)^{k_0} \cdots \left(\frac{k_{n-1}}{k}\right)^{k_{n-1}}. \tag{12.9}$$

The last line of (12.9) follows from solving a simple optimization problem with the constraints $q_0 + q_1 + \cdots + q_{n-1} \leq 1$. It follows that

$$\frac{q_i}{q_j} = \frac{k_i}{k_j} \quad \text{for } 0 \leq i, j \leq n-1$$

maximizes the product $q_0^{k_0} q_1^{k_1} \cdots q_{n-1}^{k_{n-1}}$. Thus, (12.9) is established. Since $\mathcal{P}_{\leq}(n,k) = \bigcup_{i=0}^{n} \mathcal{P}(n-i,k)$, we finally get the upper bound for $\widetilde{R}_n^*$.

The lower bound is more intricate. We first observe that the last term of the probability $P(x_1^n)$ can be estimated as

$$(1 - q_0 - \cdots - q_{k^*-1}) = P\{T > k^*\} \geq P\{T = k^* + 1\} = q_{k^*}.$$

In other words, we add an additional 1 at the end of the sequence (making it of length $n + 1$), but then the last k^* zeros fall into the same distribution as the previous ones, and can be handled by the same optimization technique as in the upper bound case. A simple calculation reveals that

$$\sup_{q} \; q_0^{k_0} q_1^{k_1} \cdots q_{k^*}^{k^*+1} \cdots q_{n-1}^{k_{n-1}}$$

$$= \left(\frac{k_0}{k+1}\right)^{k_0} \cdots \left(\frac{k_{k^*}+1}{k+1}\right)^{k^*+1} \cdots \cdots \left(\frac{k_{n-1}}{k+1}\right)^{k_{n-1}}.$$

In Exercise 12.3, we ask the reader to prove the following:

$$\widetilde{R}_n^* \geq \sum_{k=0}^{n} \sum_{\mathcal{P}(n+1,k+1)} \binom{k+1}{k_0 \cdots} \left(\frac{k_0}{k+1}\right)^{k_0} \left(\frac{k_1}{k+1}\right)^{k_1} \cdots$$

$$= r_{n+1} - 1. \tag{12.10}$$

This proves the lower bound and Lemma 12.1. ∎

12.2 Maximal Minimax Redundancy

By Lemma 12.1, it follows that

$$\log(r_{n+1} - 1) \leq \widetilde{R}_n^* \leq \log\left(\sum_{m=0}^{n} r_m\right).$$

Thus, in order to get bounds for $\widetilde{R}_n^*$, we need some asymptotic information on the sequence r_n. A difficulty of finding such asymptotics stems from the factor $k!/k^k$ present in the definition (12.3) of $r_{n,k}$. We circumvent this problem by analyzing a related pair of sequences, namely s_n and $s_{n,k}$, that are defined as

$$s_n = \sum_{k=0}^{n} s_{n,k},$$
$$s_{n,k} = e^{-k} \sum_{\mathcal{P}(n,k)} \frac{k_0^{k_0}}{k_0!} \cdots \frac{k_{n-1}^{k_{n-1}}}{k_{n-1}!}.$$

(12.11)

The translation from s_n to r_n is most conveniently expressed in probabilistic terms. Introduce the random variable K_n whose probability distribution is $s_{n,k}/s_n$; that is,

$$P(K_n = k) = \frac{s_{n,k}}{s_n}.$$

(12.12)

Then Stirling's formula yields

$$\frac{r_n}{s_n} = \sum_{k=0}^{n} \frac{r_{n,k}}{s_{n,k}} \frac{s_{n,k}}{s_n} = \sum_{k=0}^{n} k! k^{-k} e^{-k} P(K_n = k)$$
$$= \mathbf{E}[(K_n)! K_n^{-K_n} e^{K_n}] = \mathbf{E}[\sqrt{2\pi K_n}] + O(\mathbf{E}[K_n^{-\frac{1}{2}}]).$$

(12.13)

Thus, the problem of finding r_n reduces to asymptotic evaluations of s_n, $\mathbf{E}[\sqrt{K_n}]$ and $\mathbf{E}[K_n^{-\frac{1}{2}}]$. The following lemma provides asymptotic information on s_n, $\mathbf{E}[K_n]$, and $\mathbf{Var}\,(K_n)$. (The proof of the lemma is given in the next subsection.)

Lemma 12.2 *Let* $\mu_n = E[K_n]$ *and* $\sigma_n^2 = \mathbf{Var}\,(K_n)$, *where* K_n *has the distribution defined in (12.12). The following hold:*

$$s_n = \exp\left(2\sqrt{cn} - \frac{7}{8}\ln n + d + O(n^{-\frac{1}{4}+\varepsilon})\right),$$

(12.14)

$$\mu_n = \frac{1}{4}\sqrt{\frac{n}{c}}\ln\frac{n}{c} + o(\sqrt{n}),$$

(12.15)

$$\sigma_n^2 \sim \frac{\pi^2}{12c}n = o(\mu_n^2),$$

(12.16)

where $\varepsilon > 0$, $c = \pi^2/6 - 1$, $d = -\ln 2 + \frac{3}{8}\ln c - \frac{3}{4}\ln\pi$.

Once the estimates of Lemma 12.2 are granted, the moments of order $\pm\frac{1}{2}$ of K_n follow by a standard argument based on concentration of the distribution of K_n.

Lemma 12.3 *For large n,*

$$E[\sqrt{K_n}] = \mu_n^{1/2}(1 + o(1)),$$

(12.17)

$$E[K_n^{-\frac{1}{2}}] = o(1),$$

(12.18)

where $\mu_n = E[K_n]$.

Proof The upper bound $\mathbf{E}[\sqrt{K_n}] \le \sqrt{\mathbf{E}[K_n]}$ follows from concavity of the function $\sqrt{x}$ and from Jensen's inequality. The lower bound follows from concentration of the distribution. Chebyshev's inequality and (12.16) of Lemma 12.2 entail, for any arbitrarily small $\varepsilon > 0$,

$$P(|K_n - \mu_n| > \varepsilon\mu_n) \le \frac{\mathbf{Var}\,[K_n]}{\varepsilon^2\mu_n^2} = \frac{\delta(n)}{\varepsilon^2}$$

where $\delta(n) = O(1/(\ln n)^2)$ as $n \to \infty$. Then,

$$\mathbf{E}[\sqrt{K_n}] \geq \sum_{k \geq (1-\varepsilon)\mu_n} \sqrt{k} P(K_n = k)$$

$$\geq (1 - \varepsilon)^{\frac{1}{2}} \mu_n^{1/2} P(K_n \geq (1 - \varepsilon)\mu_n)$$

$$\geq (1 - \varepsilon)^{\frac{1}{2}} \left(1 - \frac{\delta(n)}{\varepsilon^2}\right) \mu_n^{1/2}.$$

Hence, by setting $\varepsilon = (\ln n)^{-\frac{2}{3}}$, we obtain $\mathbf{E}[\sqrt{K_n}] > \mu_n^{1/2} \left(1 + O(\ln n)^{-\frac{2}{3}}\right)$, provided n is large enough.

Finally, the upper bound (12.18) follows from

$$\mathbf{E}[K_n^{-\frac{1}{2}}] \leq (\mu_n(1 - \varepsilon))^{-\frac{1}{2}} + P(K_n \leq \mu_n(1 - \varepsilon)) \leq (\mu_n(1 - \varepsilon))^{-\frac{1}{2}} + \frac{\delta(n)}{\varepsilon^2}.$$

By setting $\varepsilon = \frac{1}{2}$, we, thus, obtain $\mathbf{E}[K_n^{-\frac{1}{2}}] = O(1/(\ln n)^2)$. This completes the proof. ∎

In summary, r_n and s_n are related by

$$r_n = s_n \left(\mathbf{E}[\sqrt{2\pi K_n}](1 + o(1)) + o(1)\right) = s_n \sqrt{2\pi \mu_n}(1 + o(1)),$$

by virtue of (12.13) and Lemma 12.3. This leads to

$$\log r_n = \log s_n + \frac{1}{2} \log \mu_n + \log \sqrt{2\pi} + o(1). \tag{12.19}$$

At this point, it suffices to apply the estimates provided by Lemma 12.2 to present our main result.

Theorem 12.4 *Consider the class $\mathcal{R}_0$ of nonstationary renewal sources. Then the minimax redundancy $\widetilde{R}_n^*(\mathcal{R}_0)$ satisfies*

$$\frac{2}{\ln 2} \sqrt{cn} - \frac{5}{8} \log n + \frac{1}{2} \log \ln n \tag{12.20}$$

$$\leq \widetilde{R}_n^*(\mathcal{R}_0) \leq \frac{2}{\ln 2} \sqrt{cn} - \frac{1}{8} \log n + \frac{1}{2} \log \ln n,$$

where

$$c = \frac{\pi^2}{6} - 1 \approx 0.645.$$

Numerical verifications suggest the claim that the lower bound of Theorem 12.4 is an accurate asymptotic expansion up to a constant term. Indeed, let

$$\varphi(n) = \frac{2}{\ln 2} \sqrt{\left(\frac{\pi^2}{6} - 1\right) n} - \frac{5}{8} \log n + \frac{1}{2} \log \ln n + K,$$

where

$$K = \frac{1}{8} \ln \left(\frac{\pi^2/6 - 1}{2^{12}\pi^2}\right) \approx -1.99197. \tag{12.21}$$

In the following table, show a sample of the differences $\Delta(n) = \widetilde{R}_n^* - \varphi(n)$:

n:	3	5	10	20	50	100
$\Delta(n)$:	0.223	0.026	0.128	0.055	0.002	-0.010

In view of this, we feel confident to put forward the following conjecture.

Conjecture 12.5 *The maximal minimax redundancy* $\widetilde{R}_n^*$ *becomes asymptotically*

$$\widetilde{R}_n^* = \varphi(n) + o(1) = \frac{2}{\ln 2}\sqrt{\left(\frac{\pi^2}{6} - 1\right)n} - \frac{5}{8}\log n + \frac{1}{2}\log\ln n + K + o(1),$$

where K is defined in (12.21).

12.2.1 Proof of Lemma 12.2 and Theorem 12.4

The main part of the proof of Theorem 12.4 is the proof of Lemma 12.2, which requires complex analytic tools.

The heart of the proof is precise asymptotic estimates for the quantity s_n and for moments of the distribution K_n as expressed in (12.15) and (12.16) of Lemma 12.2. It turns out that the quantities $s_{n,k}$ and s_n have generating functions $S(z, u)$ and $S(z, 1)$, respectively, which are infinite products involving the tree function defined in (10.10) of Chapter 10. The corresponding coefficient asymptotics are dictated by the behavior at the singularity of greatest weight (in the case at hand, the positive real singularity $z = 1$) so that we start by investigating asymptotics of $S(z, 1)$ as $z \to 1$. This itself requires a dedicated analysis by means of the Mellin transform. Once the dominant singular behavior of $S(z, 1)$ near $z = 1$ has been found, it remains to extract information on the coefficients s_n. This task involves an appeal to the saddle point method; actually, we can apply Hayman's method (see Appendix C). Proceeding in this way, the estimate (12.14) of s_n in Lemma 12.2 is established. Finally, the method adapts to moment estimates, yielding the other two estimates (12.15), (12.16) of Lemma 12.2.

Generating Functions The expression of $s_{n,k}$ in (12.11) involves quantities of the form $k^k/k!$. We recall from Section 10.1.2, the tree function $T(z)$, defined as the solution of

$$T(z) = ze^{T(z)}$$

that is analytic at 0. Next we consider the function

$$\beta(z) = B(ze^{-1}) = \frac{1}{1 - T(ze^{-1})}$$

that has the power series expansion

$$\beta(z) = \sum_{k=0}^{\infty} \frac{k^k}{k!}e^{-k}z^k.$$

The quantities s_n and $s_{n,k}$ of (12.11) have generating functions,

$$S_n(u) = \sum_{k=0}^{\infty} s_{n,k}u^k, \qquad S(z, u) = \sum_{n=0}^{\infty} S_n(u)z^n.$$

Then, since equation (12.22) involves convolutions of sequences of the form $k^k/k!$, we have

$$S(z, u) = \sum_{\mathcal{P}(n,k)} z^{1k_0 + 2k_1 + \cdots} \left(\frac{u}{e}\right)^{k_0 + \cdots + k_{n-1}} \frac{k_0^{k_0}}{k_0!} \cdots \frac{k_{n-1}^{k_{n-1}}}{k_{n-1}!}$$

$$= \prod_{i=1}^{\infty} \beta(z^i u). \tag{12.22}$$

We also need access to the first moment $\mu_n = \mathbf{E}[K_n]$ and the second factorial moment $\mathbf{E}[K_n(K_n - 1)]$. They are obtained as

$$s_n = [z^n] S(z, 1),$$

$$\mu_n = \frac{[z^n] S'_u(z, 1)}{[z^n] S(z, 1)},$$

$$\mathbf{E}[K_n(K_n - 1)] = \frac{[z^n] S''_{uu}(z, 1)}{[z^n] S(z, 1)},$$

where $S'_u(z, 1)$ and $S''_{uu}(z, 1)$ represent the first and the second derivative of $S(z, u)$ at $u = 1$.

In a first step, we show that $S(z, 1)$ is *Hayman admissible*; that is, the two relations (C.9) and (C.10) hold. We then can apply (C.11) to obtain an asymptotic relation for s_n. In order to check (C.9) and (C.10), we need the following two lemmas. (Note that the two lemmas cover the whole range.)

Lemma 12.6 *We have, as $z \to 1$ with $|\arg(1 - z) < \frac{\pi}{2} - \varepsilon$,*

$$S(z, 1) = a(1 - z)^{\frac{1}{4}} \exp\left(\frac{c}{1 - z}\right)\left(1 + O(|1 - z|^{\frac{1}{2} - \varepsilon})\right), \tag{12.23}$$

where $\varepsilon > 0$, $c = \frac{\pi^2}{6} - 1$, and $a = \exp(-\frac{1}{4}\ln \pi - \frac{1}{2}c)$.

Proof We consider first positive real $z < 1$ and set $z = e^{-t}$. Then, with the help of the local expansion

$$\beta(z) = \frac{1}{\sqrt{2(1 - z)}} + \frac{1}{3} - \frac{\sqrt{2}}{24}\sqrt{(1 - z)} + O(1 - z)$$

for $\beta(z)$ (as $z \to 1$), it follows that the function

$$L(t) = \ln \beta(e^{-t})$$

has the expansion

$$L(t) = -\frac{1}{2}\ln t - \frac{1}{2}\ln 2 + O(\sqrt{t})$$

as $t \to 0$. Consequently the Mellin transform

$$\Lambda(s) = \int_0^{\infty} L(t) t^{s-1}\, dt = \int_0^{\infty} \ln \beta(e^{-t}) t^{s-1}\, dt$$

exists as an absolute convergent integral for $\Re(s) > 0$. Since $\ln \beta(e^{-t}) = O(e^{-t})$, the integral $\int_1^{\infty} \ln \beta(e^{-t}) t^{s-1}\, dt$ represents an entire function. Furthermore, the integrals

$$\int_0^1 \ln t \, t^{s-1} \, dt = -\frac{1}{s^2} \quad \text{and} \quad \int_0^1 t^{s-1} \, dt = \frac{1}{s}$$

have meromorphic extensions to $\mathbb{C} \setminus \{0\}$. Finally, the integral $\int_0^1 O(\sqrt{t}) t^{s-1} \, dt$ is analytic for $\Re(s) > -\frac{1}{2}$. Hence, the function $\Lambda(s)$ has a meromorphic extension to $\Re(s) > -\frac{1}{2}$ with a polar singularity of order 2 at $s = 0$.

Next, we use the scaling property

$$\int_0^\infty f(at) t^{s-1} \, dt = a^{-s} \int_0^\infty f(t) t^{s-1} \, dt$$

of the Mellin transform to represent the Mellin transform of $L(t) = \ln S(e^{-t}, 1)$ as

$$L^*(s) = \sum_{k \geq 1} \int_0^\infty \ln \beta(e^{-kt}) t^{s-1} \, dt$$

$$= \sum_{k \geq 1} k^{-s} \int_0^\infty \ln \beta(e^{-t}) t^{s-1} \, dt$$

$$= \zeta(s) \Lambda(s)$$

that exists for $\Re(s) > 1$ and where $\zeta(s)$ denotes the Riemann zeta function (see Appendix C). We recall that $\zeta(s)$ has a meromorphic extension to $\mathbb{C} \setminus \{1\}$. The zeta function has a pole of order 1 and residue 1 at $s = 1$. Furthermore, the local expansion at $s = 0$ is given by

$$\zeta(s) = -\frac{1}{2} - s \ln \sqrt{2\pi} + O(s^2).$$

Consequently, $L^*(s) = \zeta(s) \Lambda(s)$ has a meromorphic extension to $\Re(s) > -\frac{1}{2}$, with a polar singularity of order 1 and residue $\Lambda(1)$ at $s = 1$ and a polar singularity of order 2 at $s = 0$ with a singular behavior of the form

$$L^*(s) = -\frac{1}{4s^2} - \frac{\ln \pi}{4s} + O(1).$$

By the inverse Mellin transform (see Appendix D), it follows that for every $s_0 > 0$,

$$L(t) = \frac{1}{2\pi i} \int_{s_0 - i\infty}^{s_0 + i\infty} \frac{L^*(s)}{s} t^{-s} \, ds.$$

(Note that we have absolute convergence.) Hence, after shifting the line of integration to the left to $\Re(s) = -\frac{1}{2} + \varepsilon$ and by collecting the corresponding residues at $s = 1$ and $s = 0$, we obtain

$$L(t) = \mathrm{res}\left(L^*(s) t^{-s}/s, 1\right) + \mathrm{res}\left(L^*(s) t^{-s}/s, 0\right) + \frac{1}{2\pi i} \int_{-\frac{1}{2} + \varepsilon - i\infty}^{-\frac{1}{2} + \varepsilon + i\infty} \frac{L^*(s)}{s} t^{-s} \, ds$$

$$= \frac{\Lambda(1)}{t} + \frac{1}{4} \ln t - \frac{1}{4} \ln \pi + O(t^{1/2 - \varepsilon}), \tag{12.24}$$

where $\varepsilon > 0$. (Note that we have used implicitly proper – well known – estimates for $\zeta(s + it)$ which implies that the integral of the inverse Mellin transform is absolutely convergent.)

By using the substitution $z = e^{-t} = 1 - t + O(t^2)$, this translates to

$$L(z) = \frac{\Lambda(1)}{1 - z} + \frac{1}{4} \ln(1 - z) - \frac{1}{4} \ln \pi - \frac{1}{2} \Lambda(1) + O(|1 - z|^{1/2 - \varepsilon}). \tag{12.25}$$

We note that $\Lambda(1)$ can be explicitly computed:

$$\Lambda(1) = -\int_0^1 \ln(1 - T(x/e)) \frac{dx}{x}$$

$$= -\int_0^1 \ln(1-t) \frac{(1-t)}{t} dt \qquad (x = te^{1-t})$$

$$= \frac{\pi^2}{6} - 1.$$

This proves (12.23) for real z. However, the formula (12.24), on which (12.23) rests, holds for *complex t* only constrained in such a way that $-\frac{\pi}{2} + \varepsilon \le \arg(t) \le \frac{\pi}{2} - \varepsilon$, for any $\varepsilon > 0$. The reason is that (12.24) relies on residues of the inverse Mellin integral that still converges when t is restricted to such a wedge. Thus, the expansion (12.23) actually holds true as $z \to 1$ in a sector. ∎

To continue with the Hayman method, we need the following technical lemma.

Lemma 12.7 *Consider the ratio*

$$q(z) = \prod_{j=1}^{\infty} \left| \frac{\beta(z^j)}{\beta(|z|^j)} \right| = \left| \frac{S(z,1)}{S(|z|,1)} \right|.$$

Then, there exist constants $c_0, c_1 > 0$ such that

$$q(re^{i\theta}) = O\left(e^{-c_0(1-r)^{-1}} \right),$$

uniformly, for $\frac{1}{2} \le r < 1$ and $c_1(1-r) \le |\theta| \le \pi$.

Proof First, by the triangular inequality, a function like $\beta(z)$ that has nonnegative Taylor coefficients attains its maximum modulus on the positive real axis. More precisely, one has

$$\sup_\theta |\beta(re^{i\theta})| = \beta(r).$$

Furthermore, by the converse triangular inequality, the maximum is uniquely attained on $|z| = r$ as soon as the function is aperiodic, which means the following: there is no $\widehat{\beta}(z)$ analytic at 0 such that $\beta(z) = z^a \widehat{\beta}(z^b)$ for integers a, b and $b \ge 2$. This condition is obviously satisfied here since $\beta(z) = 1 + e^{-1}z + 2(e^{-1}z)^2 + \cdots$.

Fix some small angle parameter ϕ_0, for instance, $\phi_0 = \frac{1}{10}$, and define

$$\sigma(r) = \sup_{|\theta| \ge \phi_0} \left| \frac{\beta(re^{i\theta})}{\beta(r)} \right|. \tag{12.26}$$

Then $\sigma(r)$ is continuous on the open interval $(0, 1)$ where it satisfies $\sigma(r) < 1$ while it tends to zero when r tends to 1. Actually, we have $\sigma(r) = O(\sqrt{1-r})$ for $r \to 1-$. As a consequence, for each $\delta > 0$, there exists an $A_\delta < 1$ such that

$$\sigma(r) < A_\delta \qquad \text{for all } r \text{ satisfying } \delta \le r < 1. \tag{12.27}$$

Consider the case where $z = re^{i\theta}$ with $r \to 1$. Set $r = e^{-\tau}$. The powers z^j form a discrete set of points on a logarithmic spiral that winds about 0. The number of such powers that have modulus larger than δ is

$$J = \frac{\ln \delta^{-1}}{\tau} + O(1).$$

The essential observation is now that for $2\pi/J \le |\theta| \le \pi$, a positive fraction will lie outside the region $|\arg(z^j)| < \phi_0 = \frac{1}{10}$; that is,

$$\#\{1 \le j \le J : |\arg(z^j)| = \lfloor j\theta \bmod 2\pi \rfloor \ge \phi_0\} \ge c_2 J$$

for some $c_2 > 0$. Hence, (12.27) immediately implies

$$q(re^{i\theta}) \le A_\delta^{c_2 J} = O(e^{-c_3/\tau}) = O(e^{-c_4/(1-r)}) \tag{12.28}$$

for some positive constants c_3, c_4. This proves the lemma. ∎

We are now ready to show that $S(z, 1)$ is Hayman admissible; that is, it satisfies (C.9), (C.10), and $b(r) \to \infty$ as $r \to R = 1$, where we set $\theta(r) = (1 - r)^{17/12}$.

First, by Lemma 12.6, we get

$$a(r) = \frac{rS'(r, 1)}{S(r, 1)} = \frac{cr}{(1-r)^2} + \frac{r}{4(1-r)} + O\left(|1 - z|^{-\frac{1}{2}+\varepsilon}\right) \tag{12.29}$$

and

$$b(r) = ra'(r) = \frac{2cr^2}{(1-r)^3} + \frac{cr}{(1-r)^2} + \frac{r^2}{4(1-r)^2} + O\left(|1 - z|^{-\frac{3}{2}+\varepsilon}\right).$$

Clearly, we have $b(r) \to \infty$ as $r \to 1$. Furthermore, by using the representation $S(z, 1) = e^{L(t)}$, where $t = \ln(1/z) = \ln(1/r) - i\theta$, and asymptotic expansion (12.24) for $L(t)$, we obtain for $|\theta| = O(\ln(1/r)) = O(1 - r)$,

$$S(re^{i\theta}, 1) = S(r, 1)e^{i\theta a(r) - \frac{1}{2}\theta^2 b(r) + O(\theta^3/(1-r)^4)}. \tag{12.30}$$

If $|\theta| \le (1 - r)^{17/12}$, the error term $O(\theta^3/(1 - r)^4) = O((1 - r)^{1/4})$ is negligible. This verifies (C.9).

Second, (12.30) also proves that

$$S(re^{i\theta}, 1) = O\left(S(r, 1)e^{-c\theta^2/(1-r)^3}\right)$$

for $|\theta| \le (1 - r)$ and some constant $c > 0$. Hence, if $(1 - r)^{17/12} \le |\theta| \le (1 - r)$, it follows that

$$S(re^{i\theta}, 1) = O\left(S(r, 1)e^{-c(1-r)^{-\frac{1}{6}}}\right) = o\left(\frac{S(r, 1)}{\sqrt{b(r)}}\right).$$

Finally, if $(1 - r) \le |\theta| \le \pi$, we can apply Lemma 12.7 and obtain

$$S(re^{i\theta}, 1) = O\left(S(r, 1)e^{-c_0(1-r)^{-1}}\right) = o\left(\frac{S(r, 1)}{\sqrt{b(r)}}\right).$$

Hence, we find the asymptotic expansion

$$s_n = [z^n]S(z, 1) = \frac{S(r_n, 1)}{r_n^n\sqrt{2\pi b(r_n)}}\left(\exp\left(-\frac{(a(r_n) - n)^2}{2b(r_n)}\right) + o(1)\right),$$

where we choose r_n as

$$r_n = 1 - \sqrt{\frac{c}{n}}.$$

In particular, we obtain

$$a(r_n) = n + O\left(n^{\frac{1}{2}}\right),$$

$$b(r_n) = \frac{2}{\sqrt{c}} n^{3/2} \left(1 + O(n^{-1/2})\right),$$

$$S(r_n, 1) = a\left(\frac{c}{n}\right)^{\frac{1}{8}} e^{\sqrt{nc}} \left(1 + O(n^{-\frac{1}{4} + \frac{\varepsilon}{2}})\right),$$

$$r_n^{-n} = e^{\sqrt{cn} + 2c + O(n^{-1/2})},$$

which gives

$$s_n \sim \frac{ac^{\frac{3}{8}}}{2\sqrt{\pi}} n^{-\frac{7}{8}} e^{2\sqrt{cn} + \frac{c}{2}} = e^{2\sqrt{cn} - \frac{7}{8}\ln n + d}.$$

We can do slightly better by taking the integration error explicitly into account, which gives (in our case)

$$s_n = [z^n]S(z, 1) = \frac{S(r_n, 1)}{r_n^n \sqrt{2\pi b(r_n)}} \left(\exp\left(-\frac{(a(r_n) - n)^2}{2b(r_n)}\right) + O(n^{-1/4})\right)$$

$$= \frac{S(r_n, 1)}{r_n^n \sqrt{2\pi b(r_n)}} \left(1 + O(n^{-1/4})\right).$$

This finally leads to (12.14) of Lemma 12.2.

Moments In order to complete the proof of Lemma 12.2, it remains to evaluate μ_n and σ_n^2 asymptotically. We follow the same principles as before. For $\mu_n = \mathbf{E}[K_n]$, it is necessary to estimate $[z^n]S'_u(z, 1)$ with

$$S'_u(z, 1) = S(z, 1) \sum_{k=0}^{\infty} z^k \frac{\beta'(z^k)}{\beta(z^k)}. \tag{12.31}$$

Set

$$D_1(z) = \sum_{k=0}^{\infty} \alpha(z^k), \qquad \text{where} \qquad \alpha(z) = z\frac{\beta'(z)}{\beta(z)}.$$

We again use Mellin transform techniques. Since $\alpha(e^{-t})$ behaves (for $t \to 0+$) as

$$\alpha(e^{-t}) = \frac{1}{2t} - \frac{\sqrt{2}}{6}\frac{1}{\sqrt{t}} - \frac{1}{18} + O(\sqrt{t}),$$

it follows that the Mellin transform,

$$\alpha^*(s) = \int_0^\infty \alpha(e^{-t})t^{s-1}\,ds,$$

that converges for $\Re(s) > 1$, has a meromorphic continuation to $\Re(s) > -\frac{1}{2}$ with simple polar singularities at $s = 0$, $s = \frac{1}{2}$, and $s = 1$. The Mellin transform of $D_1(e^{-t})$ is, thus, given by

$$D_1^*(s) = \int_0^\infty \sum_{k=0}^\infty \alpha(e^{-kt})t^{s-1}\,ds = \zeta(s)\alpha^*(s)$$

and has (again) a meromorphic extension to $\Re(s) > -\frac{1}{2}$ (with a double pole at $s = 1$). By inverting the Mellin transform (and by shifting the integral to the left and after collecting residues), we derive (as before) the asymptotic behavior of $D_1(e^{-t})$ as $t \to 0$ that rewrites to (as $z \to 1$)

$$D_1(z) = \frac{1}{2}\frac{1}{1-z}\ln\frac{1}{1-z} + \frac{1}{2}\frac{\gamma}{1-z}$$
$$- \frac{1}{6}\frac{\sqrt{2}\zeta(\frac{1}{2})}{\sqrt{1-z}} - \frac{1}{4}\ln\frac{1}{1-z} + O(1),$$

where $\gamma = 0.577\ldots$ denotes the Euler constant. As before, this asymptotic expansion can be extended to complex z.

Combining this representation with that of $S(z, 1)$ in (12.23), yields

$$S'_u(z, 1) \underset{z \to 1}{\sim} \frac{1}{2}a \exp\left(\frac{c}{1-z} + \frac{3}{4}\ln\frac{1}{1-z} + \ln\ln\frac{1}{1-z}\right), \qquad (12.32)$$

where a is the same constant as in (12.23). As for $S(z, 1)$, we can directly check that $S'_u(z, 1)$ is Hayman admissible. Actually, we can use the same value r_n as before and obtain an asymptotic expansion for

$$[z^n]S'_u(z, 1) = \mu_n s_n = \frac{S(r_n, 1)D_1(r_n)}{r_n^n\sqrt{2\pi\overline{b}(r_n)}}\left(\exp\left(-\frac{(\overline{a}(r_n) - n)^2}{2\overline{b}(r_n)}\right) + O(n^{-\frac{1}{4}})\right),$$

where $\overline{a}(r)$ and $\overline{b}(r)$ are the corresponding functions for $S'_u(z, 1)$. Note that $\overline{a}(r_n) = a(r_n) + O(\sqrt{n}) = n + O(\sqrt{n})$ and $\overline{b}(r_n) = b(r_n) + O(n)$. This directly proves the asymptotic relation

$$\mu_n = \mathbf{E}[K_n] = D_1(r_n)\left(1 + O(n^{-\frac{1}{4}+\frac{\varepsilon}{2}})\right)$$

and, thus, proves (12.15) of Lemma 12.2.

Finally, we need to justify (12.16) that represents a bound on the variance of K_n. The computations follow the same steps as before, so we only sketch them briefly. One needs to estimate a second derivative,

$$S''_{uu}(z, 1) = S(z, 1)\left(D_2(z) + D_1^2(z)\right),$$

where

$$D_2(z) = \sum_{k=0}^{\infty} z^{2k}\frac{\beta''(z^k)}{\beta(z^k)} - \left(\frac{z^k\beta'(z^k)}{\beta(z^k)}\right)^2.$$

The sum $D_2(z)$ is (again) amenable to Mellin transform techniques, with the result that

$$D_2(z) = \frac{\zeta(2)}{2}\frac{1}{(1-z)^2} + O((1-z)^{-3/2}).$$

Furthermore, the function $S''_{uu}(z, 1)$ is Hayman admissible and so we obtain

$$\frac{[z^n]S''_{uu}(z, 1)}{s_n} = \mathbf{E}[K_n(K_n - 1)] = (D_1(r_n)^2 + D_2(r_n))\left(1 + O(n^{-\frac{1}{4}+\frac{\varepsilon}{2}})\right).$$

Consequently,

$$\sigma_n^2 = \mathbf{E}[K_n(K_n - 1)] + \mathbf{E}[K_n] - \mathbf{E}[K_n]^2$$
$$= \frac{\zeta(2)}{2c} n + O\left(n^{\frac{3}{4}+\varepsilon}\right).$$

Since $\zeta(2) = \pi^2/6$, this establishes the second moment estimate (12.16) of Lemma 12.2.

To complete the proof of Theorem 12.4, we must show how to obtain the asymptotics for the upper bound on $\widetilde{R}_n^*$; that is, $r_n^U = \sum_{i=0}^n r_i$. We follow the footsteps of the analysis for r_n; that is, we define s_n^U and observe that its generating function is

$$S^U(z, u) = \frac{S(z, u)}{1 - z}.$$

In particular, (12.23) implies

$$S^U(z, 1) = e^{L(z)} = a(1 - z)^{-\frac{3}{4}} \exp\left(\frac{c}{1 - z}\right)(1 + o(1)).$$

Thus,

$$\ln s_n^U = 2\sqrt{cn} - \frac{3}{8}\ln n + O(1).$$

To establish $\ln \mu_n^U$ (where μ_n^U is the corresponding quantity to μ_n defined in Lemma 12.2), we just repeat the calculations leading to (12.32), which yield

$$\ln \mu_n^U = \frac{1}{2}\ln n + \ln\ln n + O(1).$$

This establishes the desired upper bound and proves the main result.

12.2.2 Average vs Maximal Redundancy

Finally, we comment on the average minimax redundancy $\widetilde{R}_n$. Clearly,

$$\widetilde{R}_n \le \widetilde{R}_n^* \le C_2\sqrt{n},$$

where

$$C_2 = \frac{2}{\ln 2}\sqrt{\frac{\pi^2}{6} - 1} = 2.317\ldots.$$

Furthermore, Csiszar and Shields (1996) proved that $\widetilde{R}_n \ge C_1\sqrt{n}$. The question is whether $C_1 = C_2$, and hence $\widetilde{R}_n \sim \widetilde{R}_n^*$. This is still an open problem; however, we conjecture that $C_1 < C_2$. We leave this as an open problem.

12.3 Exercises

12.1 Prove that the $P(x_0^n)$ is a probability distribution; that is, $\sum_{x_0^n} P(x_0^n) = 1$. In other words, prove that for any z, the following holds:

$$\sum_{n=0}^{\infty} z^n \sum_{x_0^n} P(x_0^n) = \frac{1}{1 - z}$$

for $|z| < 1$.

12.2   It can also be observed that the quantity r_m has an intrinsic meaning of its own. Let $\mathcal{W}_m$ denote the set of all m^m sequences of length m over the alphabet $\{0, \ldots, m-1\}$. For a sequence w, take k_j to be the number of letters j in w. Then each sequence w carries a "maximum likelihood probability" $\pi_{ML}(w)$ (given by (12.9)): this is the probability that w gets assigned in the Bernoulli model that makes it most likely. Prove that

$$r_m = \sum_{w \in \mathcal{W}_m} \pi_{ML}(w).$$

12.3   Prove (12.10).

12.4   Consider strongly mixing sources defined in Exercise 9.5. Try to establish redundancy rates that may depend on the function ψ defined in (9.44).

12.5   Consider the r-order renewal process in which the renewal sequence $T_1, T_2, \ldots$ for an r-order Markov process. We call such a process $\mathcal{R}_r$. Prove that for such processes,

$$\widetilde{R}_n^*(\mathcal{R}_r) = \Theta(n^{\frac{r-1}{r}}).$$

Find the constant in front of $n^{\frac{r-1}{r}}$.

12.6   Consider the average minimax redundancy $\overline{R}_n(\mathcal{R}_r)$ and give a precise asymptotic expression for it.

Bibliographical Notes

Shields (1993) proved that there are no universal rates for redundancy for stationary ergodic processes. Therefore, Csiszar and Shields (1996) introduced a restricted class of sources, such as renewal sources, where they also derived to the rate of growth $\Theta(\sqrt{n})$. The current presentation is based on Flajolet and Szpankowski (2002).

Analysis of redundancy or regret for non-Markovian sources is very scarce. We mention here Boucheron, Garivier, and Gassiat (2009) and Shamir (2013).

In this chapter, we used various tools from analytic number theory and analytic combinatorics. For integer partition, we refer Andrews (1984). Mellin transform is well explained in Flajolet, Gourdon, and Martinez (1997) and Flajolet and Sedgewick (2008). The saddle point method used in this chapter is discussed in Appendix C; see also Wright (1997) and Odlyzko (1995).

Appendices

Appendix A

Probability

In this appendix, we collect facts about probability that are used in this book.

A.1 Preliminaries

A probability space (Ω, S, P) consists of a nonempty sample space Ω, a system S of events that constitutes a σ-algebra, and a probability measure $P \colon S \to [0, 1]$. Recall that a system S is a σ-algebra on Ω if $\Omega \in S$, if $A \in S$ implies that its complement $\Omega \setminus A \in S$, too, and if for every countable system $A_i \in S$ $(i \in \mathbb{N})$ the union $\bigcup_{i \in N} A_i)$ belongs to S. Furthermore, a probability measure P satisfies $P(\Omega) = 1$ and $P\left(\bigcup_{i \in N} A_i\right) = \sum_{i \in \mathbb{N}} P(A_i)$ for pairwise disjoint sets $A_i \in S$.

A typical example in the context of coding theory is the space $\Omega = \{0, 1\}^{\mathbb{N}}$ of 0-1-sequences $x = x_1 x_2 \dots$. The system S is the σ-algebra that is generated by the sets $\{x = x_1 x_2 \dots \in \Omega \colon x_1 = b_1, \dots, x_n = b_n\}$ $(n \geq 1, b_j \in \{0, 1\})$, and the probability measure P is defined by

$$P\left(\{x = x_1 x_2 \dots \in \Omega \colon x_1 = b_1, \dots, x_n = b_n\}\right) = p^k (1 - p)^{n-k},$$

where

$$k = \#\{1 \leq j \leq n \colon b_j = 0\},$$

and $p \in (0, 1)$ is a given number. Usually we denote this probability space as a memoryless source (with parameter p).

A.2 Random Variables

A real random variable X is a measurable function $X \colon \Omega \to \mathbb{R}$; that is, all preimages $X^{-1}(-\infty, a) = \{\omega \in \Omega \colon X(\omega) < a\} \in S$. (This implies that all preimages of Lebesgue-measurable sets $A \subseteq \mathbb{R}$ satisfy $X^{-1}(A) \in S$.) The probability distribution P of X is then given by

$$P(X \in A) := P(X^{-1}(A)) = P(\{\omega \in \Omega : X(\omega) \in A\}).$$

The distribution function F_X is defined by

$$F_X(x) = P(X \leq x) = P(\{\omega \in \Omega : X(\omega) \leq x\}).$$

The distribution of X has a density $f_X(t)$ if we have

$$F_X(x) = \int_{-\infty}^{x} f_X(t)\, dt;$$

that is, the distribution of X is absolutely continuous with respect to the Lesbegue measure.

There is a natural generalization of random variables X with values in the so-called Polish space. (A Polish space is a separable completely metrizable topological space; that is, a space homeomorphic to a complete metric space that has a countable dense subset.) Of course, $\mathbb{R}$ is a Polish space, $\mathbb{R}^n$ for every $n \geq 1$, as well as any separable Banach spaces. This notion naturally includes n-dimensional random vectors as well as stochastic processes.

Moments Let $f \colon \mathbb{R} \to \mathbb{R}$ be a measurable function and X a real random variable. Then the expected value $\mathbf{E}[f(X)]$ of $f(X)$ is defined by the integral

$$\mathbf{E}[f(X)] = \int_{\Omega} f(X(\omega))\, dP(\omega) = \int_{\mathbb{R}} f(x)\, dF_X(x),$$

if it exists. In particular, the expected value of X is given by $\mathbf{E}[X]$ and the kth moments of X by

$$\mathbf{E}[X^k].$$

The variance $\mathbb{V}\mathrm{ar}[X]$ of a random variable X is given by

$$\mathbb{V}\mathrm{ar}[X] = \mathbf{E}[(X - \mathbf{E})^2] = \mathbf{E}[X^2] - (\mathbf{E}[X])^2.$$

Characteristic and Moment Generating Functions. The characteristic function $\varphi_X(t)$ is defined by

$$\varphi_X(t) = \mathbf{E}[e^{itX}]$$

and the moment generating function $m_X(t)$ by

$$m_X(t) = \mathbf{E}[e^{tX}].$$

Since e^{itx} is absolutely bounded, the characteristic function is always well defined. This is not necessarily the case for the moment generating function. However, if the moment generating function exists for $|t| \leq \delta$ for some $\delta > 0$, then we certainly have $\varphi_X(t) = m_X(it)$ and

$$m_X(t) = \sum_{k \geq 0} \frac{\mathbf{E}[X^k]}{k} t^k.$$

Inequalities There are several inequalities related to moments. The most basic one is Markov's inequality, which says that for every nonnegative random variable X and for every $a > 0$,

$$P(X \geq a) \leq \frac{\mathbf{E}[X]}{a}.$$

This inequality is easy to establish since

$$\mathbf{E}X \geq \mathbf{E}[X \cdot \mathbf{1}_{[X \geq a]}] \geq a\, \mathbf{E}[\mathbf{1}_{[X \geq a]}] = a\, P(X \geq a).$$

A similar inequality is Chebyshev's inequality:

$$P(|X - \mathbf{E}X| \geq a) \leq \frac{\mathbb{V}\mathrm{ar}[X]}{a^2}.$$

Of course, this is just a restatement of Markov's inequality applied to the random variable $(X - \mathbf{E}X)^2$.

Both inequalities can be used to establish estimates for the tail of a distribution. Actually these tail estimates can be (usually) improved by using the moment generating function. This leads to Chernoff's inequality (which is another application of Markov's inequality):

$$P(X \geq a) = P(e^{tX} \geq e^{ta}) \leq m_X(t)e^{-ta}.$$

This inequality can be optimized by choosing t appropriately.

Independent random variables Suppose that X and Y are real-valued random variables (that are defined on the same probability space). We say that X and Y are independent if for all measurable functions $f, g \colon \mathbb{R} \to \mathbb{R}$, we have

$$\mathbf{E}[f(X)g(Y)] = \mathbf{E}[f(X)] \cdot \mathbf{E}[g(Y)].$$

For example, if $f = \mathbf{1}_A$ is the indicator function of a set A and $g = \mathbf{1}_B$ the indicator function of a set B, this rewrites to

$$P(X \in A \text{ and } Y \in B) = P(X \in A) P(Y \in B).$$

If $f(x) = g(x) = e^{itx}$, then our relation for independent random variables X, Y rewrites to a product relation for the characteristic functions of X, Y, and $X + Y$:

$$\varphi_{X+Y}(t) = \mathbf{E}[e^{it(X+Y)}] = \mathbf{E}[e^{itX}e^{itY}] = \varphi_X(t)\,\varphi_Y(t).$$

Of course, the same holds for the moment generating functions: $m_{X+Y}(t) = m_X(t)m_Y(t)$.

Similarly to the notion for random variables here, we say that two events $A, B \in \mathcal{S}$ are independent if

$$P(A \cap B) = P(A)P(B).$$

In general, if we have two events $A, B \in \mathcal{S}$ with $P(B) > 0$, we define the conditional probability $P(A|B)$ by

$$P(A|B) = \frac{P(A \cap B)}{P(B)}.$$

Of course, A and B are independent if and only if $P(A|B) = P(A)$.

Entropy Suppose that Ω is a finite set and $\mathcal{S}$ consists of all subsets of Ω. Then P is characterized by $P(\omega) := P(\{\omega\})$, $\omega \in \Omega$. The entropy $H(P)$ of the probability distribution P is then defined by

$$H(P) = -\sum_{\omega \in \Omega} P(\omega) \log P(\omega),$$

where log usually denotes the binary logarithm. Similarly, the entropy of a random variable $X \colon \Omega \to \mathbb{R}$ is given by the probability distribution of X; recall that $P(X = a) = P(X^{-1}(\{a\}))$:

$$H(X) = -\sum_{a \in X(\Omega)} P(X = a) \log P(X = a).$$

We note that the image set $H(\Omega)$ is finite, too, in this context. Of course, this definition can be extended to all random variables with finite image.

The entropy is a kind of *uncertainty measure*. For example, if the distribution P is concentrated at one value, that is, $P(\omega_0) = 1$ for some $\omega_0 \in \Omega$, then $H(P) = 0$. On the other hand, if every value in Ω (of size N) is equally likely, that is, $P(\omega) = 1/N$ for all $\omega \in \Omega$, then $H(P) = \log N$. In all other cases, the entropy satisfies $0 < H(P) < \log N$.

The entropy has many properties. The most important ones are listed in Chapter 1 (see also the Exercises in Chapter 1).

A.3 Convergence of Random Variables

A sequence $X_1, X_2, \ldots$ of random variables converges weakly (or in distribution) to a random variable X if

$$\lim_{n \to \infty} F_{X_n}(x) = F_X(x)$$

for all continuity points of the distribution function F_X. In this case, we write

$$X_n \overset{d}{\to} X.$$

By Lévy's theorem, weak convergence can be checked with the help of the characteristic functions. If $X_n \overset{d}{\to} X$, then

$$\lim_{n \to \infty} \varphi_{X_n}(t) = \varphi_X(t)$$

for all real t. Conversely if $\varphi_{X_n}(t)$ converges for every real t to a function $\varphi(t)$ that is continuous at 0, then $\varphi(t)$ is the characteristic function of a random variable X and we have $X_n \overset{d}{\to} X$.

Note that weak convergence can be defined for arbitrary sequences of random variables that need not be defined on the same probability space. However, for all other notions of convergence, we assume that the sequence of random variables $X_1, X_2, \ldots$ as well as the (potential) limit X are defined on the same space.

We say that a sequence of random variables $X_1, X_2, \ldots$ converges in probability to a random variable X and this is denoted by $X_n \overset{P}{\to} X$ if

$$\lim_{n \to \infty} P(|X_n - X| > \varepsilon) = 0 \qquad \text{for all } \varepsilon > 0.$$

Similarly, we say that a sequence of random variables $X_1, X_2, \ldots$ converges almost surely to a random variable X and this is denoted by $X_n \overset{a.s.}{\longrightarrow} X$ if

$$\lim_{n \to \infty} P\left(\lim_{n \to \infty} X_n = X\right) = 1.$$

Equivalently, we can define it as

$$\lim_{N \to \infty} P\{\sup_{n \geq N} |X_n - X| < \varepsilon\} = 1$$

for any $\varepsilon > 0$.

Finally, we say that a sequence of random variables $X_1, X_2, \ldots$ converges in L^p to a random variable X (for some $p \geq 1$) if the absolute moments $\mathbf{E}[|X_j|^p], j \geq 1$, and $\mathbf{E}[|X|^p]$ exist and if

$$\lim_{n \to \infty} \mathbf{E}[|X_n - X|^p] = 0.$$

In this case, we write

$$X_n \xrightarrow{L^p} X.$$

Of course, in this case, we also have $\mathbf{E}[|X_n|^p] \to \mathbf{E}[|X|^p]$.

There are several relations between these notions of convergence that we list here.

Theorem A.1 *Let $X_1, X_2, \ldots$ and X random variables that are defined on the same probability space. Then the following relations hold:*

1. $X_n \xrightarrow{P} X$ *implies* $X_n \xrightarrow{d} X$. *If X is constant, then the converse implication is also true.*
2. $X_n \xrightarrow{a.s.} X$ *implies* $X_n \xrightarrow{P} X$.
3. $X_n \xrightarrow{L^p} X$ *implies* $X_n \xrightarrow{P} X$.

Normal random variables We say that a random variable X is normally distributed (or Gaussian) $N(\mu, \sigma)$ with mean μ and variance $\sigma^2 > 0$ if the distribution of X has a density of the form

$$f(x) = \frac{1}{\sqrt{2\pi\sigma^2}} e^{-(x-\mu)^2/(2\sigma^2)}.$$

Clearly, we then have

$$\mathbf{E}[X] = \mu, \quad \mathbb{V}\mathrm{ar}[X] = \sigma^2, \quad \varphi_X(t) = e^{it\mu - t^2\sigma^2/2}.$$

Sometimes it is convenient to add the case of zero variance; that is, the distribution $N(\mu, 0)$ is concentrated at $x = \mu$.

The standard normal distribution is just $N(0, 1)$, the normal distribution with mean 0 and variance 1. Clearly, if X is $N(\mu, \sigma)$-distributed then the normalized random variable $(X - \mu)/\sigma$ is $N(0, 1)$-distributed. The density and the distribution function of the standard normal distribution are given by

$$f_X(x) = \frac{1}{\sqrt{2\pi}} e^{-x^2/2}, \quad \Phi(x) = \frac{1}{\sqrt{2\pi}} \int_{-\infty}^{x} e^{-t^2/2} \, dt.$$

If $X_1, \ldots, X_n$ are independent $N(\mu_j, \sigma_j^2)$-distributed, $1 \leq j \leq n$. Then the sum $Y = X_1 + \cdots + X_n$ is $N(\mu, \sigma^2)$-distributed with

$$\mu = \mu_1 + \cdots + \mu_n \quad \text{and} \quad \sigma^2 = \sigma_1^2 + \cdots + \sigma_n^2.$$

Let $\mu = (\mu_1, \ldots, \mu_d)$, a d-dimensional vector, and Σ a $d \times d$-dimensional semi-positive definite matrix. Then a d-dimensional random vector $\mathbf{X} = (X_1, \ldots, X_d)$ is normally distributed with mean μ and covariance matrix Σ if every projection $Y = \mathbf{a} \cdot \mathbf{X} = a_1 X_1 + \cdots + a_d X_d$ is $N(\mathbf{a} \cdot \mu, \mathbf{a}^t \cdot \Sigma \cdot \mathbf{a})$-distributed.

The importance of the normal distribution is that it universally appears as the scaling limit of sums of independent random variables.

Theorem A.2 (Central Limit Theorem) *Let $X_1, X_2, \ldots$ be a sequence of identically distributed and independent random variables with mean value $\mathbf{E}[X_j] = \mu$ and variance $\mathbb{V}ar[X_j] = \sigma^2$. Set $S_n = X_1 + \cdots + X_n$. Then the normalized random variable converges weakly to the standard normal distribution:*

$$\frac{S_n - \mu n}{\sqrt{\sigma^2 n}} \xrightarrow{d} N(0, 1).$$

Special distributions Let X be a random variable with image set $\{0, 1\}$; that is, we have $P(X = 1) = p \in [0, 1]$ and $P(X = 0) = q = 1 - p$. A random variable Y has a binomial distribution $Bi(n, p)$ if the distribution of Y is the same as the distribution of $X_1 + \cdots + X_n$, where X_i, $1 \leq i \leq n$, are independent copies of X. The probability distribution is given by

$$P(Y = k) = \binom{n}{k} p^k (1 - p)^{n-k} \qquad (0 \leq k \leq n).$$

Expected value, variance and characteristic function are given by

$$\mathbf{E}[Y] = np, \quad \mathbb{V}ar[Y] = np(1 - p), \quad \varphi_Y(t) = (pe^{it} + (1 - p))^n.$$

Clearly, the central limit theorem implies

$$\frac{Y - np}{\sqrt{np(1 - p)}} \xrightarrow{d} N(0, 1).$$

The Poisson distribution $Po(\lambda)$ with parameter $\lambda > 0$ is defined on the nonnegative integers by

$$P(k) = \frac{\lambda^k}{k!} e^{-\lambda}.$$

If a random variable X is $Po(\lambda)$-distributed, then expected value, variance and characteristic function are given by

$$\mathbf{E}[X] = \mathbb{V}ar[X] = \lambda, \quad \varphi_X(t) = e^{\lambda(e^{it} - 1)}.$$

If X_j, $1 \leq j \leq n$, are independent random variables that are $Po(\lambda_j)$-distributed, then the sum $Y = X_1 + \cdots + X_n$ is $Po(\lambda_1 + \cdots + \lambda_n)$-distributed. In particular, if we apply this property for $\lambda_j = \lambda$ for all j, it follows that a $Po(n\lambda)$-distribution can be approximated by a normal distribution with mean and variance $n\lambda$. More generally, $Po(\lambda)$ is approximated by a normal distribution with mean and variance λ if $\lambda \to \infty$.

The exponential distribution $Exp(\lambda)$ (with a parameter $\lambda > 0$) is a continuous distribution with density

$$f(x) = \lambda e^{-\lambda x}, \quad x \geq 0.$$

Hence, if a random variable X is $Exp(\lambda)$-distributed, then $P(X \geq x) = e^{-\lambda x}$; that is, the distribution function is $F_X(x) = 1 - e^{-\lambda x}$ (for $x \geq 0$). Expected value, variance and characteristic function are given by

$$\mathbf{E}[X] = \frac{1}{\lambda}, \quad \mathbb{V}ar[X] = \frac{1}{\lambda^2}, \quad \varphi_X(t) = \frac{\lambda}{\lambda - it}.$$

An important property of the exponential distribution is that it is memoryless in the following sense:

$$P(X \geq x + t | X \geq x) = P(X \geq t).$$

Another interesting property is that the minimum $\min(X_1, \ldots, X_n)$ is $Exp(\lambda_1 + \cdots + \lambda_n)$-distributed if the random variables X_j are independent and $Exp(\lambda_j)$-distributed, $1 \leq j \leq n$.

Bibliographical Notes

There are many good books on probability, in particular discrete probability. For example, Billingsley (1968), Feller (1970), Chung (1974), Durrett (1991).

Appendix B

Generating Functions

In this Appendix, we recall some facts about generating functions. Generating functions are not only useful tools to count combinatorial objects but also analytic objects that can be used to obtain asymptotics. They can be used to encode the distribution of random variables that are related to counting problems. Furthermore, asymptotic methods can be applied to obtain probabilistic limit theorems like central limit theorems.

B.1 Generating Functions

The *ordinary generating function* (ogf) of a sequence $(a_n)_{n \geq 0}$ (of complex numbers) is the formal power series

$$a(x) = \sum_{n \geq 0} a_n x^n. \tag{B.1}$$

Similarly, the *exponential generating function* (egf) of the sequence $(a_n)_{n \geq 0}$ is given by

$$\hat{a}(x) = \sum_{n \geq 0} a_n \frac{x^n}{n!}. \tag{B.2}$$

We use the notation

$$[x^n]a(x) = a_n$$

to *extract* the coefficient of x^n in a generating function.

Example B.1 Let b_n denote the number of different binary trees with n internal vertices (and $n + 1$ external vertices). Then we have $b_0 = 1$ and the following recurrence relation

$$b_{n+1} = \sum_{k=0}^{n} b_k b_{n-k}. \tag{B.3}$$

If a binary tree has $n + 1$ internal nodes, then the left and right subtrees are also binary trees (with k and $n - k$ internal nodes, where $0 \leq k \leq n$). Thus, by summing up all such possible combinations, we get the total number b_{n+1}.

This recurrence can be solved using the generating function:

$$b(x) = \sum_{n \geq 0} b_n x^n.$$

Table B.1 *Basic relations between sequences and their generating functions*

	sequence	ogf
sum	$c_n = a_n + b_n$	$c(x) = a(x) + b(x)$
product	$c_n = \sum_{k=0}^{n} a_k b_{n-k}$	$c(x) = a(x)b(x)$
partial sums	$c_n = \sum_{k=0}^{n} a_k$	$c(x) = \frac{1}{1-x} a(x)$
marking	$c_n = n a_n$	$c(x) = x a'(x)$
scaling	$c_n = \gamma^n a_n$	$c(x) = a(\gamma x)$

	sequence	egf
sum	$c_n = a_n + b_n$	$\hat{c}(x) = \hat{a}(x) + \hat{b}(x)$
product	$c_n = \sum_{k=0}^{n} \binom{n}{k} a_k b_{n-k}$	$\hat{c}(x) = \hat{a}(x)\hat{b}(x)$
binomial sums	$c_n = \sum_{k=0}^{n} \binom{n}{k} a_k$	$\hat{c}(x) = e^x \hat{a}(x)$
marking	$c_n = n a_n$	$\hat{c}(x) = x \hat{a}'(x)$
scaling	$c_n = \gamma^n a_n$	$\hat{c}(x) = \hat{a}(\gamma x)$

By (B.3), we find the relation

$$b(x) = 1 + xb(x)^2 \tag{B.4}$$

and consequently an explicit representation of the form

$$b(x) = \frac{1 - \sqrt{1 - 4x}}{2x}. \tag{B.5}$$

In summary, we find

$$
\begin{aligned}
b_n &= [x^n]\frac{1 - \sqrt{1 - 4x}}{2x} \\
&= -\frac{1}{2}[x^{n+1}](1 - 4x)^{\frac{1}{2}} \\
&= -\frac{1}{2}\binom{\frac{1}{2}}{n + 1}(-4)^{n+1} \\
&= \frac{1}{n + 1}\binom{2n}{n}.
\end{aligned}
$$

It is clear that certain algebraic operations on sequences have their counterpart on the level of generating functions. Table B.1 collects some of them.

B.2 Combinatorial Structures

A useful observation is that generating functions can be viewed as a power series generated by certain *combinatorial objects*, which we discuss next.

Let C be a (countable) set of objects; for example, a set of graphs, and

$$|\cdot| : C \to \mathbb{N}$$

a *weight function* that assigns to every element $c \in C$ a weight or size $|c|$. We assume that the sets

$$C_n := |\cdot|^{-1}(\{n\}) = \{c \in C : |c| = n\} \qquad (n \in \mathbb{N})$$

are all finite. Set $c_n = |C_n|$. Then the ordinary generating function $c(x)$ of the pair $(C, |\cdot|)$, which we also call *combinatorial structure*, is given by

$$c(x) = \sum_{c \in C} x^{|c|} = \sum_{n \geq 0} c_n x^n,$$

and the exponential generating function $\hat{c}(x)$ by

$$\hat{c}(x) = \sum_{c \in C} \frac{x^{|c|}}{|c|!} = \sum_{n \geq 0} c_n \frac{x^n}{n!}.$$

The choice of ordinary generating functions or exponential generating functions depends on the problem at hand. As a rule, unlabeled (or unordered) structures should be counted with the help of ordinary generating functions and labeled (or ordered) structures with exponential generating functions.

For example, the ogf of binary trees, where the weight is the number of internal nodes, is given by

$$b(x) = \frac{1 - \sqrt{1 - 4x}}{2x}.$$

On the other hand the egf of permutations of finite sets, where the weight is the size of the finite set, is given by

$$\hat{p}(x) = \sum_{n \geq 0} n! \frac{x^n}{n!} = \frac{1}{1 - x}.$$

Combinatorial Constructions. One major aspect in the use of generating functions is that certain combinatorial constructions have their counterparts in relations of the corresponding generating functions.

We again use the notation $A, B, C, \ldots$ for sets of combinatorial objects with corresponding size functions $|\cdot|$. First, suppose that the objects that we consider are (in some sense) unlabeled or unordered. We have the following basic operations:

1. If A and B are disjoint then $C = A + B = A \cup B$ denotes the union of A and B.
2. $C = A \times B$ denotes the Cartesian product. The size function of a pair $c = (a, b)$ is given by $|c| = |a| + |b|$.
3. Suppose that A contains no object of size 0 and that the sets $A, A \times A, A \times A \times A, \ldots$ are disjoint. Then

$$C = A^* := \{\varepsilon\} + A + A \times A + A \times A \times A + \cdots$$

is the set of (finite) sequences of elements of A (ε denotes the empty object of size zero).

Table B.2 *Combinatorial structures and their corresponding generating functions*

combinat. constr.	ogf
$C = A + B$	$c(x) = a(x) + b(x)$
$C = A \times B$	$c(x) = a(x)b(x)$
$C = A^*$	$c(x) = \frac{1}{1-a(x)}$
$C = \mathcal{P}_{\mathrm{fin}}(A)$	$c(x) = e^{a(x) - \frac{1}{2}a(x^2) + \frac{1}{3}a(x^3) \mp \cdots}$
$C = \mathcal{M}_{\mathrm{fin}}(A)$	$c(x) = e^{a(x) + \frac{1}{2}a(x^2) + \frac{1}{3}a(x^3) + \cdots}$
$C = A(B)$	$c(x) = a(b(x))$

4. Let $C = \mathcal{P}_{\mathrm{fin}}(A)$ denote the set of all finite subsets of A. The size of a subset $\{a_1, a_2, \ldots, a_k\} \subseteq A$ is given by $|\{a_1, a_2, \ldots, a_k\}| = |a_1| + |a_2| + \cdots + |a_k|$.

5. Let $C = \mathcal{M}_{\mathrm{fin}}(A)$ denote the set of all finite multisets $\{a_1^{j_1}, a_2^{j_2}, \ldots, a_k^{j_k}\}$ of A; that is, the element a_i is taken j_i times ($1 \le i \le k$). Its size is given by $|\{a_1^{j_1}, a_2^{j_2}, \ldots, a_k^{j_k}\}| = j_1|a_1| + j_2|a_2| + \cdots + j_k|a_k|$.

6. Suppose that B has no object of zero size. Then the composition $C = A(B)$ of A and B is given by

$$C = A(B) := A_0 + A_1 \times B + A_2 \times B \times B + \cdots,$$

where $A_n = \{a \in A \mid |a| = n\}$. The size of $(a, b_1, b_2, \ldots, b_n) \in A_n \times B \times B \times \cdots \times B$ is defined by $|b_1| + |b_2| + \cdots + |b_n|$. The combinatorial interpretation of this construction is that an element $a \in A$ of size $|a| = n$ is substituted by an n-tuple of elements of B.

As already indicated, these combinatorial constructions have counterparts in relations of generating functions shown in Table B.2.

For example, the relation

$$b(x) = 1 + xb(x)^2,$$

for the generating function of binary trees, can be seen as the *translation* of the recursive description of binary trees. A binary tree is either just one (external) vertex or an (internal) root, where two binary trees are attached.

Labeled Combinatorial Constructions There are similar constructions of the so-called labeled or ordered combinatorial objects with corresponding relations for their exponential generating functions. We call a combinatorial object c of size n labeled if it is formally of the form $c = \widetilde{c} \times \pi$, where $\pi \in \mathfrak{S}_n$ is a permutation. For example, we can think of a graph $\widetilde{c}$ of n vertices and the permutation π represents a labeling of its nodes. We list some of the combinatorial constructions where we have to take care of the permutations involved.

1. If A and B are disjoint, then $C = A + B = A \cup B$ denotes the union of A and B.

2. The *labeled product* $C = A * B$ of two labeled structures is defined as follows. Suppose that $a = \widetilde{a} \times \pi \in A$ has size $|a| = k$ and $b = \widetilde{b} \times \sigma \in B$ has size $|b| = m$. Then we define $a * b$ as the set of objects $((\widetilde{a}, \widetilde{b}), \tau)$, where $\tau \in \mathfrak{S}_{k+m}$ runs over all permutations that are consistent with π and σ in the following way: there is a partition $\{j_1, j_2, \ldots, j_k\}, \{\ell_1, \ell_2, \ldots, \ell_m\}$ of $\{1, 2, \ldots, k + m\}$ with $j_1 < j_2 < \cdots < j_k$ and

Table B.3 *Combinatorial labeled structures and their corresponding exponential generating functions*

combinat. constr.	egf
$C = A + B$	$\hat{c}(x) = \hat{a}(x) + \hat{b}(x)$
$C = A * B$	$\hat{c}(x) = \hat{a}(x)\hat{b}(x)$
$C = A^*$	$\hat{c}(x) = \dfrac{1}{1 - \hat{a}(x)}$
$C = e^A$	$\hat{c}(x) = e^{\hat{a}(x)}$
$C = A(B)$	$\hat{c}(x) = \hat{a}(\hat{b}(x))$

$\ell_1 < \ell_2 < \cdots < \ell_m$ such that

$$\tau(1) = j_{\pi(1)}, \ \tau(2) = j_{\pi(2)}, \ldots, \tau(k) = j_{\pi(k)} \quad \text{and}$$
$$\tau(k+1) = \ell_{\sigma(1)}, \ \tau(k+2) = \ell_{\sigma(2)}, \ldots, \tau(k+m) = \ell_{\sigma(m)}.$$

Finally we set

$$A * B = \bigcup_{a \in A, \, b \in B} a * b.$$

The size of $((\widetilde{a}, \widetilde{b}), \tau)$ is given by $|((\widetilde{a}, \widetilde{b}), \tau)| = |a| + |b|$.

3. Suppose that A contains no object of size 0 and that the sets $A, A * A, A * A * A, \ldots$ are disjoint. Then

$$C = A^* := \{\varepsilon\} + A + A * A + A * A * + \cdots$$

is the set of (finite labeled) sequences of elements of A.

4. Similarly we define unordered labeled sequences by

$$C = e^A = \{\varepsilon\} + A + \frac{1}{2!}A * A + \frac{1}{3!}A * A * A + \cdots,$$

where the shorthand notation $\frac{1}{n!}A * A * \cdots * A$ means that we do not take care of the order of the n elements in the sequence $A * A * \cdots * A$.

5. Suppose that B has no object of size zero. Then the composition $C = A(B)$ of A and B is given by

$$C = A(B) := A_0 + A_1 \times B + A_2 \times B \times B + \cdots,$$

where $A_n = \{a \in A \mid |a| = n\}$.

The corresponding relations for the exponential generating functions are listed in Table B.3.

The only case that has to be explained is the labeled product $C = A * B$. If $|a| = k$ and $|b| = m$, then there are exactly $\binom{k+m}{k}$ possible ways to partition $\{1, 2, \ldots, k+m\}$ into two sets of size k and m. Thus $a * b$ has size $\binom{k+m}{k}$ and consequently

$$\hat{c}(x) = \sum_{a \in A, b \in B} \binom{|a| + |b|}{|a|} \frac{x^{|a| + |b|}}{(|a| + |b|)!} = \sum_{a \in A} \frac{x^{|a|}}{|a|!} \cdot \sum_{b \in B} \frac{x^{|b|}}{|b|!} = \hat{a}(x) \cdot \hat{b}(x).$$

Lagrange Inversion Formula Next we present a very powerful tool for generating function. Let $a(x) = \sum_{n \geq 0} a_n x^n$ be a power series with $a_0 = 0$ and $a_1 \neq 0$. The *Lagrange inversion formula* provides an explicit representation of the coefficients of the inverse power series $a^{[-1]}(x)$, which is defined by $a(a^{[-1]}(x)) = a^{[-1]}(a(x)) = x$.

Theorem B.2 *Let $a(x) = \sum_{n \geq 0} a_n x^n$ be a formal power series with $a_0 = 0$ and $a_1 \neq 0$. Let $a^{[-1]}(x)$ be the inverse power series and $g(x)$ an arbitrary power series. Then the nth coefficient of $g(a^{[-1]}(x))$ is given by*

$$[x^n]g(a^{[-1]}(x)) = \frac{1}{n}[u^{n-1}]g'(u)\left(\frac{u}{a(u)}\right)^n \qquad (n \geq 1).$$

The following variant is usually more appropriate for combinatorial problems.

Theorem B.3 *Let $\Phi(x)$ be a power series with $\Phi(0) \neq 0$ and $y(x)$ the (unique) power series solution of the equation*

$$y(x) = x\Phi(y(x)).$$

Then $y(x)$ is invertible and the nth coefficient of $g(y(x))$ (where $g(x)$ is an arbitrary power series) is given by

$$[x^n]g(y(x)) = \frac{1}{n}[u^{n-1}]g'(u)\Phi(u)^n \qquad (n \geq 1).$$

Theorems B.2 and B.3 are equivalent. If $a(x) = x/\Phi(x)$, then $a^{[-1]}(x) = y(x)$, where $y(x)$ satisfies the equation $y(x) = x\Phi(y(x))$.

Example B.4 We give an immediate application of Theorem B.3. We have already observed that the generating function $b(x)$ of binary trees satisfies the functional equation (B.4). If we set $\widetilde{b}(x) = b(x) - 1$ then

$$\widetilde{b}(x) = x(1 + \widetilde{b}(x))^2.$$

By Theorem B.3 with $\Phi(x) = (1 + x)^2$ we obtain (for $n \geq 1$)

$$b_n = [x^n]\widetilde{b}(x) = \frac{1}{n}[u^{n-1}](1 + u)^{2n}$$

$$= \frac{1}{n}\binom{2n}{n-1} = \frac{1}{n+1}\binom{2n}{n}.$$

Bibliographical Notes

Generating functions are discussed in many textbooks. We mention here the classic monograph by Flajolet and Sedgewick (2008). See also Drmota (2009) and Szpankowski (2001).

Appendix C

Complex Asymptotics

In this appendix, we present some powerful asymptotic methods that use complex analysis. In particular, after some introductory remarks about complex functions, we shall discuss special functions, the saddle point method, polar asymptotics, and the singularity analysis.

C.1 Analytic Functions

Let $G \subseteq \mathbb{C}$ be an open set. A function $f: G \to \mathbb{C}$ is an *analytic* or *holomorphic function* if for every $z_0 \in G$ there exists $R > 0$ such that $f(z)$ can be represented for $|z - z_0| < R$ as a power series:

$$f(z) = \sum_{n \geq 0} a_n(z - z_0)^n. \tag{C.1}$$

A function is called *entire* if it is analytic in $\mathbb{C}$. For example, polynomials or e^z are entire; power series are analytic inside the circle of convergence.

A very important property of analytic functions is that they are differentiable in the sense that the complex derivative

$$f'(z_0) = \lim_{z \to z_0} \frac{f(z) - f(z_0)}{z - z_0} \tag{C.2}$$

exists for all $z_0 \in G$. Actually, from (C.1), we get the power series of the derivative:

$$f'(z) = \sum_{n \geq 0} (n + 1)a_{n+1}(z - z_0)^n.$$

Hence, $f'(z)$ is also analytic in G. In the same way, it follows that f is infinitely often differentiable. The coefficients in (C.1) are then given by

$$a_n = \frac{f^{(n)}(z_0)}{n!}$$

and are unique.

Similarly, we can define an analytic function $F: C \to \mathbb{C}$ with $F'(z) = f(z)$. We just note that the corresponding power series are

$$F(z) = F(z_0) + \sum_{n \geq 0} \frac{a_n}{n + 1}(z - z_0)^{n+1}.$$

In order to be more precise, we consider complex contour integrals:

$$\int_C f(z)\,dz = \int_C (u\,dx - v\,dy) + i\int_C (v\,dx + u\,dy),$$

where $z = x + iy$, $u = u(x,y) = \Re(f(x+iy))$, and $v = v(x,y) = \Im(f(x+iy))$, and C is a path in $\mathbb{C}$. However, since $f(z)$ is differentiable in the sense (C.2), we have the following relations for u and v (Cauchy–Riemann differential equations):

$$\frac{\partial u}{\partial x} = \frac{\partial v}{\partial y}, \quad \frac{\partial u}{\partial y} = -\frac{\partial v}{\partial x}.$$

To see this, we take the limit in (C.2) parallel to the real axis and parallel to the imaginary axis and compare the results: $f' = \frac{\partial u}{\partial x} + i\frac{\partial v}{\partial x} = \frac{\partial v}{\partial y} - i\frac{\partial u}{\partial y}$. In particular, it follows by Green's theorem that the integrals $\int_C (u\,dx - v\,dy)$ and $\int_C (v\,dx + u\,dy)$ only depend on the starting and endpoints of the path C. Hence, the same is true for complex contour integrals over analytic functions. Hence, it makes sense to define the function

$$F(z) = \int_{z_0 \to z} f(w)\,dw,$$

which has (as in the real case) the following property:

$$F'(z) = f(z).$$

Cauchy Formula Now let γ be a closed path (in G) with winding number 1 around z_0. Then, for every analytic function $f\colon G \to \mathbb{C}$, we have

$$\int_\gamma \frac{f(z) - f(z_0)}{z - z_0}\,dz = 0,$$

since the function $g(z) = (f(z) - f(z_0))/(z - z_0)$ for $z \neq z_0$ and $g(z_0) = f'(z_0)$ is also analytic. Since

$$\int_\gamma \frac{dz}{z - z_0} = 2\pi i,$$

we obtain the representation

$$f(z_0) = \frac{1}{2\pi i} \int_\gamma \frac{f(z)}{z - z_0}\,dz. \tag{C.3}$$

Now, suppose that γ also has winding number 1 around 0 and that $|z| > |z_0|$ for all $z \in \gamma$. Then by replacing $1/(z - z_0)$ by $\sum_n z_0^n/z^{n+1}$, we further obtain

$$f(z_0) = \frac{1}{2\pi i} \int_\gamma \sum_{n \geq 0} \frac{z_0^n}{z^{n+1}} f(z)\,dz = \sum_{n \geq 0} \left(\frac{1}{2\pi i} \int_\gamma \frac{f(z)}{z^{n+1}}\,dz \right) z_0^n.$$

This is precisely *Cauchy's formula* that states that the coefficients a_n in the power series expansion of $f(z) = \sum_n a_n z^n$ are given by

$$a_n = \frac{1}{2\pi i} \int_\gamma \frac{f(z)}{z^{n+1}}\,dz. \tag{C.4}$$

At this stage, we drop the, conditions on γ since the integral on the right-hand side does not depend on γ. We just have to make sure that the winding number around 0 is 1.

The representation (C.3) has another striking application. Suppose that $f_k\colon G \to \mathbb{C}$ is a sequence of analytic functions that converges uniformly to a function $f\colon G \to \mathbb{C}$ for all bounded and closed sets $K \subseteq G$. Then the limit f is analytic too.

This property applies to several special functions discussed in Section C.2. For example, for the Riemann zeta-function $\zeta(s) = \sum_{n \geq 1} n^{-s}$ that is uniformly convergent in the half-spaces, $\Re(s) \geq 1 + \eta$ (for every $\eta > 0$). Another example is the gamma function $\Gamma(s) = \int_0^\infty t^{s-1} e^{-t}\, dt$, $\Re(s) > 0$. Here we have to apply this concept in two steps, first to integrals over the finite intervals $[1/k, k]$ (with Riemann sums) and then the limit $k \to \infty$.

Residue Theorem Before we start with complex asymptotic methods, we also mention the *residue theorem*. We say that an analytic function $f: G \setminus \{z_0\} \to \mathbb{C}$ (where $z_0 \in G$) has a *polar singularity* if there exists a natural number $K \geq 1$ such that the function $g(z) = (z - z_0)^K f(z)$ has an analytic continuation to G. In particular, $g(z)$ has a power series expansion at $z = z_0$. This implies that $f(z) = (z - z_0)^{-K} g(z)$ can be locally represented as

$$f(z) = \frac{a_{-K}}{(z - z_0)^K} + \frac{a_{-K+1}}{(z - z_0)^{K-1}} + \cdots + \frac{a_{-1}}{z - z_0} + a_0 + a_1(z - z_0) + \cdots.$$

The coefficient a_{-1} is called *residue*

$$a_{-1} = \mathrm{res}(f(z), z_0)$$

and the smallest possible K is the order of the polar singularity.

Suppose now that γ is a closed path (contained in G) and that $z_1, \ldots, z_m$ are polar singularities of a function $f: G \setminus \{z_1, \ldots, z_m\} \to \mathbb{C}$ such that the winding number of γ around z_j is 1 for all $j = 1, \ldots, m$; that is, γ *goes around* $z_1, \ldots, z_m$ once. Then the *residue theorem* says that

$$\int_\gamma f(z)\, dz = 2\pi i \sum_{j=1}^m \mathrm{res}(f(z), z_j). \tag{C.5}$$

The proof follows (up to proper shifts of the path of integration) from

$$\int_\gamma \frac{dz}{z - z_0} = 2\pi i, \quad \text{and} \quad \int_\gamma (z - z_0)^k\, dz = 0, \quad k \neq -1$$

if γ just goes around z_0.

C.2 Special Functions

In this section, we collect some results on special functions such as Euler, gamma, and beta functions, the Riemann zeta function, and the Lambert function.

Gamma Function The *gamma function* $\Gamma(s)$ is defined for complex s with $\Re(s) > 0$ by the integral

$$\Gamma(s) = \int_0^\infty t^{s-1} e^{-t}\, dt$$

and is an analytic function there. For example, $\Gamma(1) = 1$ or $\Gamma(\frac{1}{2}) = \sqrt{\pi}$. Partial integration leads to the functional equation:

$$\Gamma(s + 1) = s\Gamma(s) \qquad (\Re(s) > 0), \tag{C.6}$$

which gives

$$\Gamma(n + 1) = n! \qquad (n \geq 0).$$

Furthermore, the functional equation (C.6) can be used to extend $\Gamma(s)$ meromorphically to $\mathbb{C} \setminus \{0, -1, -2, \ldots\}$. For $s = -n$ ($n = 0, 1, 2, \ldots$), this meromorphic extension has simple polar singularities with residues

$$\text{res}(\Gamma(s), -n) = \frac{(-1)^n}{n!}.$$

By separating the integral from 0 to 1 and from 1 to ∞, one obtains the representation

$$\Gamma(s) = \sum_{n=0}^{\infty} \frac{(-1)^n}{n!} \frac{1}{s+n} + \int_1^{\infty} t^{s-1} e^{-t} dt$$

that is valid for all $s \in \mathbb{C} \setminus \{0, -1, -2, \ldots\}$. Other important relations are Euler's reflection formula

$$\Gamma(s) \cdot \Gamma(1 - s) = \frac{\pi}{\sin(\pi s)}$$

and the multiplication theorem

$$\Gamma\left(\frac{s}{n}\right) \cdot \Gamma\left(\frac{s+1}{n}\right) \cdots \Gamma\left(\frac{s+n-1}{n}\right) = \frac{(2\pi)^{(n-1)/2}}{n^{s-1/2}} \cdot \Gamma(s),$$

which is valid for all integers $n \geq 1$.

We also note that $\Gamma(s)$ has no zeros, so the reciprocal function $1/\Gamma(s)$ is an entire function (with zeros at $s = 0, -1, 2, \ldots$). Furthermore, the reciprocal function can be represented by the so-called Hankel integral representation:

$$\frac{1}{\Gamma(s)} = -\frac{1}{2\pi i} \int_C (-t)^{s-1} e^{-t} \, dt,$$

where C starts at $i + \infty$, goes around 0 in the positive sense, and terminates at $-i + \infty$ so that the positive real line is not crossed.

It is well known that $n!$ is asymptotically given $n^n e^{-n} \sqrt{2\pi n}$. Actually, such an asymptotic relation is also true for the Γ-function. For every $\delta > 0$, we have uniformly

$$\Gamma(s) = \sqrt{2\pi} \, s^{s-\frac{1}{2}} e^{-s} \left(1 + O(s^{-1})\right)$$

as $|s| \to \infty$ and $0 \leq |\arg(s)| \leq \pi - \delta$ (that is, one has to avoid a cone that contains the negative real axis).

Beta Function The *beta function* $B(x, y)$, which is defined by

$$B(x, y) = \int_0^1 t^{x-1}(1 - t)^{y-1} \, dt \qquad (\Re(x) > 0, \Re(y) > 0),$$

is closely related to the Γ-function:

$$B(x, y) = \frac{\Gamma(x)\Gamma(y)}{\Gamma(x + y)}.$$

This formula can also be used to extend $B(x, y)$ meromorphically to $\mathbb{C} \setminus \{0, -1, -2, \ldots\}$ or to obtain asymptotic relations as $x, y \to \infty$.

Similarly one defines the *multiple beta function* $B(x_1, x_2, \ldots, x_n)$ (with $n \geq 2$) by

$$B(x_1, x_2, \ldots, x_n) = \int_\Delta t_1^{x_1-1} t_1^{x_2-1} \cdots t_n^{x_n-1} d\mathbf{t},$$

where

$$\Delta = \{\mathbf{t} = (t_1, t_2, \ldots, t_n) \in \mathbb{R}^n : t_1 \geq 0, \ldots, t_n \geq 0, t_1 + t_2 + \cdots + t_n = 1\}.$$

The multiple beta function is also related to the Γ-function:

$$B(x_1, x_2, \ldots, x_n) = \frac{\Gamma(x_1)\Gamma(x_2)\cdots\Gamma(x_n)}{\Gamma(x_1 + x_2 + \cdots + x_n)}.$$

Multinomial Coefficient The multinomial coefficients are defined by

$$\binom{k_1 + k_2 + \cdots + k_m}{k_1, k_2, \ldots, k_m} = \frac{(k_1 + k_2 + \cdots + k_m)!}{k_1! k_2! \cdots k_m!}$$

and generalize the binomial coefficients $\binom{n}{k} = \binom{n}{k, n-k} = n!/(k!(n-k)!)$. They appear naturally as coefficients of the multinomial

$$(x_1 + x_2 + \cdots + x_m)^n = \sum_{k_1 + \cdots + k_m = n} \binom{n}{k_1, k_2, \ldots, k_m} x_1^{k_1} x_2^{k_2} \cdots x_m^{k_m}.$$

Clearly, m^n is an upper bound,

$$\binom{n}{k_1, k_2, \ldots, k_m} \leq m^n \qquad (n = k_1 + k_2 + \cdots + k_m),$$

that is actually quite tight if all k_j are the same. By Stirling's approximation formula we have

$$\binom{n}{k_1, k_2, \ldots, k_m} \sim \frac{1}{(2\pi)^{\frac{m-1}{2}}} \left(\frac{n}{k_1 k_2 \cdots k_m}\right)^{\frac{1}{2}} e^{n\sum_{j=1}^{m} \frac{k_j}{n} \ln \frac{n}{k_j}} \left(1 + O\left(\sum_{j=1}^{m} \frac{1}{k_j}\right)\right).$$

Riemann Zeta Function. A function that appears frequently with the Γ-function is the *Riemann zeta function* that is defined by

$$\zeta(s) = \sum_{n \geq 1} \frac{1}{n^s} \qquad (\Re(s) > 1)$$

and represents an analytic function. It turns out that $\zeta(s)$ can be meromorphically extended to $\mathbb{C} \setminus \{1\}$. At $s = 1$, it has a simple pole with $\mathrm{res}(\zeta(s), 1) = 1$.

The connection between $\zeta(s)$ and $\Gamma(s)$ is established in the functional equation

$$\zeta(s) = 2^s \pi^{s-1} \sin\left(\frac{\pi s}{2}\right) \Gamma(1-s) \zeta(1-s),$$

which is fundamental in analytic number theory.

Special values of $\zeta(s)$ are

$$\zeta(2n) = \frac{(-1)^{n+1} B_{2n} (2\pi)^{2n}}{2(2n)!} \qquad (n \geq 1)$$

and

$$\zeta(-n) = (-1)^n \frac{B_{n+1}}{n+1} \qquad (n \geq 0),$$

where B_n denote the Bernoulli numbers defined by the series

$$\sum_{n \geq 0} B_n \frac{x^n}{n!} = \frac{x}{e^x - 1}.$$

For example, we have $B_0 = 1$, $B_1 = -\frac{1}{2}$, $B_2 = \frac{1}{6}$, and $B_{2k+1} = 0$ for $k \geq 1$.

More generally, if c_n, $n \geq 1$ is a complex sequence, the corresponding *Dirichlet series* is given by

$$C(s) = \sum_{n \geq 1} \frac{c_n}{n^s}.$$

There exists always an *abscissas of convergence* $\sigma_c \in [-\infty, \infty]$ with the property that $C(s)$ is convergent for $\Re(s) > \sigma_c$, where $C(s)$ is an analytic function. On the other hand, the series representing $C(s)$ is divergent for $\Re(s) < \sigma_c$ (compare also with Appendix D).

Lambert Function A function of completely different type, the *Lambert W function* is defined by the relation

$$W(z)e^{W(z)} = z.$$

The Lambert function has infinitely many branches, $W_k(z)$. However, if z is real, it is sufficient to consider only two branches: $W_0(z)$ and $W_{-1}(z)$ that can only be solved for $z \geq -1/e$. More precisely, the branch $W_0(z)$ exists for all $z \geq -1/e$, it is monotonely increasing, and it satisfies $W_0(0) = 0$. The other branch, $W_{-1}(z)$, exists only for $-1/e \leq z < 0$ and is strictly decreasing with $\lim_{z \to 0-} W_{-1}(z) = -\infty$.

Asymptotically, we have

$$W_0(z) = \ln z - \ln \ln z + O\left(\frac{\ln \ln z}{\ln z}\right)$$

as $z \to \infty$.

All branches of the Lambert function satisfy the differential equation:

$$zW'(1 + W) = W \qquad (w \neq -1/e),$$

and for the integral we have

$$\int W(z)\,dz = z\left(W(z) - 1 + \frac{1}{W(z)}\right) + C,$$

where C is a constant.

The principal branch $W_0(z)$ has an explicit series expansion at $z = 0$:

$$W_0(z) = \sum_{n \geq 0} (-1)^{n-1} \frac{n^{n-1}}{n!} z^n.$$

Moreover, for all integers r, we have

$$W_0(z)^r = \sum_{n \geq r} (-1)^{n-r} \frac{r n^{n-r}}{(n-r)!} z^n.$$

Both formulas can be easily deduced from Lagrange's inversion theorem (Theorem B.3).

The principal branch of the Lambert function is directly related to the *tree function* $T(z)$, which is the power series solution of the function equation:

$$T(z) = ze^{T(z)}.$$

Clearly, we have

$$T(z) = -W_0(-z) = \sum_{n \geq 0} \frac{n^{n-1}}{n!} z^n.$$

The numbers n^{n-1} count rooted labeled trees with n vertices.

The *generalized Lambert* $W_r(z)$ function is defined as a solution of

$$W_r(z)e^{W_r(z)} + r = z.$$

To simplify the notation, by $W_r(z)$ we mean the main branch for z real. It is known that

$$W_r(x) = \frac{x}{r+1} + O(x^2), \quad x \to 0, \quad \text{and} \quad W_r(x) = \ln x + O(\ln \ln(x)) \quad x \to \infty.$$

C.3 Asymptotic Methods: Saddle Point

Complex contour integrals are used to obtain *asymptotic expansions* of sequences and functions. In what follows, we collect some standard methods.

Example C.1 In a first example, we use Cauchy's formula in order to obtain asymptotically the nth coefficient $1/n!$ or the exponential function $e^z = \sum_n z^n/n!$:

$$\frac{1}{n!} = \frac{1}{2\pi i} \int_\gamma \frac{e^z}{z^{n+1}} \, dz,$$

where γ is a closed path with winding number 1 around 0. More precisely, we will use a circle of radius R for γ and the substitution $z = Re^{it}$, $-\pi < t \leq \pi$:

$$\frac{1}{n!} = \frac{1}{2\pi} \int_{-\pi}^{\pi} \frac{e^{Re^{it}}}{(Re^{it})^n} \, dt = \frac{e^R}{R^n} \frac{1}{2\pi} \int_{-\pi}^{\pi} e^{R(e^{it}-1)-int} \, dt.$$

It turns out that $R = n$ is a proper choice for R. The reason is simply that for $R = n$, we get the minimum value:

$$\frac{e^n}{n^n} = \min_{R>0} \frac{e^R}{R^n}.$$

Thus, is remains to handle the integral:

$$\frac{1}{2\pi} \int_{-\pi}^{\pi} e^{(e^{it}-1-it)n} \, dt.$$

We now distinguish between the interval $I_1 = [-n^{-1/3}, n^{1/3}]$ and the remaining part $(-\pi, \pi] \setminus I_1$. For $t \in I_1$, we have

$$e^{it} - 1 - it = -\frac{t^2}{2} + O(t^3)$$

and consequently

$$\int_{I_1} e^{(e^{it}-1-it)n}\,dt = \int_{I_1} e^{-nt^2/2}\left(1+O(n|t|^3)\right)\,dt$$

$$= \int_{\mathbb{R}} e^{-nt^2/2}\,dt - \int_{\mathbb{R}\setminus I_1} e^{-nt^2/2}\,dt + O\left(\int_{\mathbb{R}} e^{-nt^2/2}n|t^3|\,dt\right)$$

$$= \frac{\sqrt{2\pi}}{\sqrt{n}} + O\left(e^{-n^{1/3}/2}/\sqrt{n}\right) + O\left(\frac{1}{n}\right).$$

Since $\Re(e^{it}-1-it) = -(1-\cos(t)) \le -ct^2$ for some $c>0$, we also get

$$\int_{(-\pi,\pi]\setminus I_1} e^{(e^{it}-1-it)n}\,dt = O\left(e^{-cn^{1/3}/2}\right),$$

which leads to

$$\frac{1}{n!} = \frac{e^n}{n^n}\frac{1}{\sqrt{2\pi n}}\left(1+O(n^{-1/2})\right)$$

or

$$n! = n^n e^{-n}\sqrt{2\pi n}\left(1+O(n^{-1/2})\right).$$

This is precisely *Stirling's approximation formula* for $n!$. By the way, with a slightly more careful analysis, the error term improves to $\left(1+O(n^{-1})\right)$.

This method was a direct application of the *saddle point method*. The saddle point method applies generally to integrals of the form

$$I(\lambda) = \int_C e^{g(\lambda,z)}h(z)\,dz,$$

where C is a proper path of integration (that can be adapted because of the path independence property) and $g(\lambda, z)$ is an analytic function in z that depends also on a parameter λ (that will tend to ∞), and $h(z)$ is an analytic function. In Example C.6, we had

$$g(\lambda, z) = z - \lambda \ln z \quad \text{and} \quad h(z) = \frac{1}{2\pi i z}.$$

The *saddle point* $z_0(\lambda)$ is now defined by the relation

$$g'(\lambda, z_0(\lambda)) = 0,$$

where g' denotes the derivative with respect to z. We next suppose that the path C (that will also depend on λ), is parametrized by the curve $C(t)$, $0 \le t \le 1$, such that for some t_0,

$$C(t_0) = z_0(\lambda), \qquad g'(\lambda, z_0(\lambda))C'(t_0)^2 < 0,$$

and

$$\left|e^{g(\lambda,C(t))}\right| < \left|e^{g(\lambda,z_0(\lambda))}\right|, \quad (0 \le t \le 1).$$

We also assume that

$$\frac{g'''(\lambda, z_0(\lambda))}{g''(\lambda, z_0(\lambda))^{3/2}} \to 0 \qquad (\lambda \to \infty).$$

From the local expansion

$$g(\lambda, z) = g(\lambda, z_0) + \frac{1}{2}g''(\lambda, z_0)(z - z_0)^2 + \frac{1}{6}g'''(\lambda, z_0)(z - z_0)^3 + \cdots,$$

it follows that we can expect that the integral $I(\lambda)$ can be approximated by

$$I(\lambda) = \int_0^1 e^{g(\lambda, C(t))} h(C(t)) C'(t)\, dt$$

$$\sim e^{g(\lambda, z_0(\lambda))} h(z_0(\lambda)) C'(t_0) \int_{-\infty}^{\infty} e^{-\frac{1}{2}g''(\lambda, z_0(\lambda)) C'(t_0)^2 (t - t_0)^2}\, dt$$

$$= e^{g(\lambda, z_0(\lambda))} h(z_0(\lambda)) \sqrt{\frac{2\pi}{|g''(\lambda, z_0(\lambda))|}}$$

as $\lambda \to \infty$.

In order to make this calculation completely rigorous, we have to check that the appearing error terms (as in Example C.6) are actually negligible. Usually this is an easy task and leads to the following expression:

$$I(\lambda) = e^{g(\lambda, z_0(\lambda))} h(z_0(\lambda)) \sqrt{\frac{2\pi}{|g''(\lambda, z_0(\lambda))|}} \left(1 + O\left(\frac{g'''(\lambda, z_0(\lambda))}{g''(\lambda, z_0(\lambda))^{3/2}} \right) \right). \qquad \text{(C.7)}$$

By taking higher-order terms into account and observing that $\int_{-\infty}^{\infty} e^{-v^2/2} v^3\, dv = 0$, the error term can be (usually) replaced by

$$O\left(\frac{g''''(\lambda, z_0(\lambda))}{g''(\lambda, z_0(\lambda))^2} \right). \qquad \text{(C.8)}$$

Of course, we have to require that this term tends to 0 for $\lambda \to \infty$ (and that all *other parts* are negligible).

As a second example, we take the Γ-function $\Gamma(s) = \int_0^{\infty} t^{s-1} e^{-t}\, dt$. Here the parameter is s and we take $g(s, t) = s \ln t - t$ and $h(t) = 1/t$. The saddle point $t_0(s)$ is then $t_0(s) = s$ and $g''(s, t_0(s)) = -1/s$. Thus, we directly obtain

$$\Gamma(s) \sim e^{s \ln s - s} \frac{1}{s} \sqrt{2\pi s} = \sqrt{2\pi} s^{s - \frac{1}{2}} e^{-s} \qquad (s \to \infty).$$

Hayman Method We now consider an analytic function $f(z)$ and we seek the asymptotic behavior of the coefficients a_n or the power series expansion

$$f(z) = \sum_n a_n z^n$$

at $z_0 = 0$. By Cauchy's formula (C.4), we know that a_n can be represented by a proper complex integral. We apply a special approach called the *Hayman method* to streamline the saddle point calculations.

We define *Hayman-admissible functions* as analytic functions $f(z)$, $|z| < R$, with the property that there exists a function $\theta(r)$ such that

$$f(re^{it}) \sim f(r) e^{ita(r) - \frac{1}{2}t^2 b(r)} \qquad \text{(C.9)}$$

uniformly for $|t| \leq \theta(r)$ as $r \to R$ and

$$f(re^{it}) = o\left(\frac{f(r)}{\sqrt{b(r)}}\right) \tag{C.10}$$

uniformly for $\theta(r) \leq |t| \leq \pi$ as $r \to R$, where

$$a(r) = \frac{rf'(r)}{f(r)}, \qquad b(r) = ra'(r),$$

and $b(r)$ satisfies $b(r) \to \infty$ as $r \to R$. By applying the saddle point method with $g(n, z) = \ln f(z) - n \ln z$ and $h(z) = 1/(2\pi iz)$ and saddle point $z_0(n)$ that is given by the equation

$$a(z_0(n)) = n,$$

we immediately get, as $n \to \infty$,

$$a_n \sim \frac{f(z_0(n))}{z_0(n)^n \sqrt{2\pi b(z_0(n))}}. \tag{C.11}$$

More generally, we have uniformly for all n and $z_0 \to R$,

$$a_n = \frac{f(z_0)}{z_0^n \sqrt{2\pi b(z_0)}} \left(\exp\left(-\frac{(a(z_0) - n)^2}{2b(z_0)}\right) + o(1)\right). \tag{C.12}$$

Of course, if z_0 is chosen in a way that $a(z_0) = n$, then this is precisely (C.11). The advantage of (C.12) is that we can use an approximation z_0 for $z_0(n)$ and also obtain precise information on the asymptotic behavior of a_n. Note that due to (C.12) it is not necessary to solve the equation $a(z_0) = n$ exactly. We have control over the error.

Functions like $e^{P(z)}$ with a polynomial $P(z)$ with nonnegative coefficient or functions like $e^{(1-z)^{-\alpha}}$ (with some $\alpha > 0$) are Hayman admissible. Furthermore, products of Hayman-admissible functions are Hayman admissible, as well as $e^{f(z)}$ if $f(z)$ is Hayman admissible.

C.4 Analytic Depoissonization

As we have seen in the last section, it is not always necessary to choose the *exact saddle point*. This also applies if we have a multiplicative factor $A(z)$ of *modest* growth. More precisely, we can expect (under suitable assumptions on $A(z)$) that

$$[z^n]A(z)F(z) \sim A(z_0(n))[z^n]F(z),$$

where $z_0(n)$ is the saddle point of $F(z)$; that is, $z_0(n)F'(z_0(n))/F(z_0(n)) = n$. A very powerful application of this concept is the so-called analytic depoissonization.

The *Poisson transform* $\widetilde{a}(z)$ of a sequence a_n is defined by

$$\widetilde{a}(z) = \sum_{n \geq 0} a_n \frac{e^{-z}z^n}{n!}.$$

It can be interpreted as the expected value of the random variable a_X, where X has a Poisson distribution with parameter z: $P(X = n) = e^{-z}z^n/n!$. On the other hand, $\widetilde{a}(z)$ can be also seen as an analytic function in z; more precisely, it equals the exponential generating function $f(z) = \sum_{n \geq 0} a_n z^n/n!$ times e^{-z}.

We are interested in the asymptotic expansion of

$$a_n = \left[\frac{z^n}{n!}\right] f(z) = \left[\frac{z^n}{n!}\right] \tilde{a}(z) e^z.$$

We already know that the saddle point method applies to the exponential function e^z with saddle point $z_0(n) = n$. If $\tilde{a}(z)$ is of *modest* growth compared to e^z (for an example of polynomial growth, see Theorem C.2 for a precise statement), then we can expect that

$$a_n \sim \tilde{a}(n) \left[\frac{z^n}{n!}\right] e^z = \tilde{a}(n),$$

where $\tilde{a}(n)$ is equal to $\tilde{a}(z)$ for $z = n$. This principle is called *analytic depoissonization*. There are various sufficient conditions on $\tilde{a}(z)$ that assures this principle holds; see Jacquet and Szpankowski (1998). We cite here just a slightly extended basic version (theorem 1 of Jacquet and Szpankowski (1998)).

Theorem C.2 *Suppose that $\tilde{a}(z) = \sum_{n \geq 0} a_n \frac{e^{-z} z^n}{n!}$ is the Poisson transform of the sequence a_n that represents an entire function in z. Suppose that*

1. *$\tilde{a}(z) = O(|z|^\beta)$ uniformly as $|z| \to \infty$ and $|\arg(z)| \leq \theta$, where $\beta > 0$ and $0 < \theta < \frac{\pi}{2}$.*
2. *$\tilde{a}(z) e^z = O(e^{\alpha|z|})$ uniformly as $|z| \to \infty$ and $\theta \leq |\arg(z)| \leq \pi$, where $\alpha < 1$.*

Then, as $n \to \infty$,

$$a_n = \tilde{a}(n) - \frac{n}{2} \tilde{a}''(n) + O(n^{\beta-2}).$$

We mention that it is also possible to obtain a more precise asymptotic series expansion for a_n and there are certain closure properties for functions that satisfy the assumptions of Theorem C.2 (this also leads to the notion of JS-admissible functions).

A typical application of Theorem C.2 is the following situation (theorem 10 of Jacquet and Szpankowski (1998)).

Theorem C.3 *Suppose that $\tilde{a}(z)$ is the Poisson transform of the sequence a_n that represents an entire function in z and satisfies the functional equation:*

$$\tilde{a}(z) = \gamma_1(z) \tilde{a}(pz) + \gamma_2(z) \tilde{a}((1-p)z) + t(z),$$

where $0 < p < 1$. Furthermore, suppose that the following conditions are satisfied:

1. *$|\gamma_1(z)| p^\beta + |\gamma_2(z)| q^\beta \leq 1 - \eta$ and $|t(z)| = O(|z|^\beta)$ uniformly for $|\arg(z)| \leq \theta$ and $|z| \geq R$, where $\beta > 0$, $R > 0$, and $0 < \theta < \frac{\pi}{2}$.*
2. *$|\gamma_1(z)| e^{q\Re(z)} \leq \frac{1}{3} e^{\alpha|z|q}$, $|\gamma_2(z)| e^{p\Re(z)} \leq \frac{1}{3} e^{\alpha|z|p}$, and $|t(z)| e^{\Re(z)} \leq \frac{1}{3} e^{\alpha|z|}$ uniformly as $|z| \geq R$ and $\theta \leq |\arg(z)| \leq \pi$, where $\alpha < 1$.*

Then, Theorem C.2 applies; that is, we have, as $n \to \infty$,

$$a_n = \tilde{a}(n) - \frac{n}{2} \tilde{a}''(n) + O(n^{\beta-2}).$$

Therefore – in this context – it is sufficient to study the asymptotic behavior of $\tilde{a}(z)$ as $z \to \infty$.

Large Powers Another application of the saddle point method are *powers of analytic functions*. Set $f(z)^k = \sum_n a_{n,k} z^n$ then

$$a_{n,k} = \frac{1}{2\pi i} \int_\gamma \frac{f(z)^k}{z^{n+1}} \, dz.$$

Suppose that the coefficients a_n of $f(z) = \sum_n a_n z^n$ are aperiodic; that is, $f(z)$ cannot be represented as $f(z) = z^r F(z^q)$ for some natural number r, q, where $q > 1$, and some analytic function $F(z)$. Furthermore, suppose that k is proportional to n, say, $k = \alpha n$ for some $\alpha > 0$. Then we can apply the saddle point method with $g(z) = k \ln f(z) - n \ln z$ and $h(z) = 1/(2\pi i z)$ and obtain

$$a_{n,k} = \frac{f(z_0)^k}{z_0^n \sqrt{2\pi k \left(\frac{z_0^2 f''(z_0)}{f(z_0)} + \frac{z_0 f'(z_0)}{f(z_0)} - \frac{z_0^2 f'(z_0)^2}{f(z_0)^2} \right)}} \left(1 + O\left(\frac{1}{n} \right) \right) \tag{C.13}$$

as $n \to \infty$, where the saddle point z_0 is given by the equation

$$\frac{z_0 f'(z_0)}{f(z_0)} = \frac{n}{k} = \frac{1}{\alpha}.$$

Note that the aperiodicity condition implies that $|f(re^{it})| \le f(r) e^{-ct^2}$ for some $c > 0$ and $|t| \le \pi$. Furthermore, we have used the error term (C.8) (the error term in (C.7) gives only $O(1/\sqrt{n})$).

C.5 Polar and Algebraic Singularities

The saddle point method applies to Cauchy's formula usually for entire functions $f(z)$ or if a function has an essential singularity (such as $e^{1/(1-z)}$). However, if $f(z)$ has a polar singularity or a singularity of an algebraic nature, then we use the concept of *singularity analysis*.

Polar Singularities The first result into this direction is quite simple (but still quite powerful).

Theorem C.4 *Suppose that $f(z) = \sum_n a_n z^n$ is analytic for $G = \{z \in \mathbb{C} : |z| < R\} \setminus \{z_0\}$ such that z_0 is a simple polar singularity with residue $\mathrm{res}(f(z), z_0) = A$. Then*

$$a_n = -\frac{A}{z_0} z_0^{-n} + O(r^{-n})$$

for every $r < R$.

Proof Clearly,

$$g(z) = f(z) - \frac{A}{z - z_0}$$

is analytic for $|z| < R$ and, thus, for every fixed $r < R$, the corresponding Cauchy integral can be estimated by

$$\left| \frac{1}{2\pi i} \int_{|z|=r} \frac{g(z)}{z^{n+1}} \, dz \right| \le r^{-n} \max_{|z|=r} |g(z)| = O(r^{-n}).$$

Since

$$\frac{A}{z - z_0} = -\frac{A}{z_0} \sum_{n \geq 0} z_0^{-n} z^n,$$

it follows that

$$a_n = -\frac{A}{z_0} z_0^{-n} + O(r^{-n})$$

as needed.   ∎

Since we can choose r such that $|z_0| < r < R$, it follows that a_n is (up to a constant) asymptotically z_0^{-n}. In other words, the contribution of the term $A/(z - z_0)$ determines the leading asymptotic behavior. Of course, this method can be extended to finitely many polar singularities (and also to higher-order poles). We just mention that

$$\frac{1}{(z - z_0)^K} = \frac{(-z_0)^{-k}}{(1 - z/z_0)^k} = (-z_0)^{-k} \sum_{n \geq 0} \binom{n + k - 1}{k - 1} z_0^{-n} z^n.$$

Singularity Analysis The situation is very similar if there is an singularity of the form $(z - z_0)^\alpha$ for some complex α different from a natural number. Here the central observation is the following one.

Lemma C.5 (Flajolet and Odlyzko, 1990) *Suppose that $f(z) = (1 - z)^\alpha$, where $\alpha \in \mathbb{C} \setminus \{0, 1, 2, \ldots\}$. Then $f(z)$ is analytic on $\mathbb{C} \setminus [1, \infty)$ and we have*

$$[z^n] f(z) = \binom{\alpha}{n} = \frac{n^{-\alpha - 1}}{\Gamma(-\alpha)} \left(1 + O(n^{-1})\right) \qquad (n \to \infty).$$

Furthermore, suppose that $f(z)$ is analytic in a so-called delta-domain

$$\Delta = \{z \in \mathbb{C} : |z| < 1 + \varepsilon, \; |\arg(z - 1)| > \eta\}$$

for some $\varepsilon > 0$ and some $0 < \eta < \pi/2$ such that

$$f(z) = O\left((1 - z)^{\Re(\alpha)}\right) \qquad (z \in \Delta),$$

then

$$[z^n] f(z) = O\left(n^{-\Re(\alpha) - 1}\right).$$

Example C.6 As a first application, let us consider the generating function $b(z) = \sum_n b_n z^n$ of the Catalan numbers $b_n = \frac{1}{n+1}\binom{2n}{n}$ that is given by

$$b(z) = \frac{1 - \sqrt{1 - 4z}}{2z} = 2 - 2\sqrt{1 - 4z} + 2(1 - 4z) + O\left((1 - 4z)^{3/2}\right)$$

for $z \in \{z \in \mathbb{C} : |z| < 1/2\} \setminus [\frac{1}{4}, \frac{1}{2}]$ (see Appendix B). The polynomial part $2 + 2(1 - 4z)$ does not contribute for $n \geq 2$. Thus, we automatically get

$$\begin{aligned}
b_n &= [z^n] b(z) \\
&= -2\frac{4^n}{\Gamma(-\frac{1}{2})} n^{-3/2} \left(1 + O(n^{-1})\right) + O\left(4^n n^{-5/2}\right) \\
&= \frac{4^n}{\sqrt{\pi n}} n^{-3/2} \left(1 + O(n^{-1})\right).
\end{aligned}$$

Recall that $\Gamma(-\frac{1}{2}) = -2\sqrt{\pi}$. Clearly this asymptotic expansion could be also derived from Stirling's formula applied to the explicit representation $b_n = \frac{1}{n+1}\binom{2n}{n}$. However, in order to obtain just the asymptotic expansion, this is not needed. We just need the local behavior of $b(z)$ around its singularity $z_0 = \frac{1}{4}$.

We want to add that singularities of square-root type (as for $b(z)$) that lead to an asymptotic leading term $c\,z_0^{-n} n^{-3/2}$ appear very frequently. The reason is the following *folklore theorem*.

Theorem C.7 *Suppose that $F(z,y)$ is an analytic function in z,y around $z = y = 0$ such that $F(0,y) = 0$ and that all Taylor coefficients of F around 0 are real and nonnegative. Then there exists a unique analytic solution $y = y(z)$ of the functional equation*

$$y = F(z,y), \tag{C.14}$$

with $y(0) = 0$ that has nonnegative Taylor coefficients around 0.

If the region of convergence of $F(z,y)$ is large enough such that there exist positive solutions $z = z_0$ and $y = y_0$ of the system of equations

$$y = F(z,y),$$
$$1 = F_y(z,y)$$

with $F_z(z_0,y_0) \neq 0$ and $F_{yy}(z_0,y_0) \neq 0$, then $y(z)$ is analytic for $|z| < z_0$ and there exist functions $g(z)$, $h(z)$ that are analytic around $z = z_0$ such that $y(z)$ has a representation of the form

$$y(z) = g(z) - h(z)\sqrt{1 - \frac{z}{z_0}} \tag{C.15}$$

locally around $z = z_0$. We have $g(z_0) = y(z_0)$ and

$$h(z_0) = \sqrt{\frac{2z_0 F_z(z_0,y_0)}{F_{yy}(z_0,y_0)}}.$$

Moreover, (C.15) provides a local analytic continuation of $y(z)$ (for $\arg(z - z_0) \neq 0$).

If we assume that $[z^n]y(z) > 0$ for $n \geq n_0$, then $z = z_0$ is the only singularity of $y(z)$ on the circle $|z| = z_0$ and we obtain an asymptotic expansion for $[z^n]y(z)$ of the form

$$[z^n]y(z) = \sqrt{\frac{z_0 F_z(z_0,y_0)}{2\pi F_{yy}(z_0,y_0)}}\, z_0^{-n}\, n^{-3/2} \left(1 + O(n^{-1})\right). \tag{C.16}$$

We recall that the generating function $b(z)$ satisfies the functional equation $b(z) = 1 + zb(z)^2$ (see Appendix B). If we set $y(z) = b(z) - 1$ and

$$F(z,y) = z(y + 1)^2,$$

we can apply Theorem C.7 directly.

Bibliographical Notes

There are many good books on complex analysis and analytic function. We mention here Henrici (1977) and Remmert (1983).

Complex asymptotics are discussed in DeBruijn (1958), Flajolet and Sedgewick (2008), Drmota (2009), Szpankowski (2001), Wong (1989). Hayman (1956) introduced the Hayman's method, while the singularity analysis was designed by Flajolet and Odlyzko (1990). The folklore theorem C.7 goes back to Bender (1973), Canfield (1977) and Meir and Moon (1978), Bender and Richmond (1983).

Special functions are discussed in many classical books. We mention here Abramowitz and Stegun (1964) and Bateman (1955). The Lambert function is covered in depth in Corless et al. (1996) while the generalized Lambert function was introduced in Mezo and Baricz (2017).

Appendix D

Mellin Transforms and Tauberian Theorems

In this appendix, we collect facts about Mellin transforms and Tauberian theorems that we use throughout the book.

D.1 Mellin Transforms

Let $c(v)$, $v > 0$, be a complex valued function of bounded variation. Then the *Mellin transform*

$$c^*(s) := \mathcal{M}[c(v); s]$$

of $c(v)$ is defined by the integral

$$c^*(s) = \int_0^\infty c(v)v^{s-1}dv.$$

There is a strip $a < \Re(s) < b$, where $c^*(s)$ converges and represents an analytic function in s. The most prominent example is the Mellin transform of the exponential function e^{-v},

$$\int_0^\infty e^{-v}v^{s-1}dv = \Gamma(s),$$

namely the Γ-function ($\Re(s) > 0$); see also Appendix C.

A nice property of the Mellin transform is that there is a simple rule for scaled versions. For every $a > 0$, we have

$$\int_0^\infty c(av)v^{s-1}dv = \frac{1}{a^s}\int_0^\infty c(v)v^{s-1}dv = \frac{1}{a^s}c^*(s).$$

Example D.1 Let $c(v) = 1/(e^v - 1)$. Together with the linearity of the Mellin transform, it follows that the Mellin transform of $c(v)$ is given by

$$c^*(v) = \int_0^\infty \frac{1}{e^v - 1}v^{s-1}dv$$

$$= \int_0^\infty \frac{e^{-v}}{1 - e^{-v}}v^{s-1}dv$$

$$= \int_0^\infty \sum_{n \geq 1} e^{-nv}v^{s-1}dv$$

$$= \sum_{n \geq 1} \int_0^\infty e^{-nv} v^{s-1} dv$$

$$= \sum_{n \geq 1} \frac{1}{n^s} \int_0^\infty e^{-v} v^{s-1} dv$$

$$= \zeta(s)\Gamma(s),$$

where $\zeta(s) = \sum_{n \geq 1} n^{-s}$, $\Re(s) > 1$ is the Riemann ζ-function. (Note that in all steps we have absolute convergence if $\Re(s) > 1$.)

One important property is that $c(v)$ can be reconstructed from the Mellin transform. We have the *inverse Mellin transform*

$$\frac{1}{2}(c(v-) + c(v+)) = \frac{1}{2\pi i} \lim_{T \to \infty} \int_{s_0 - iT}^{s+iT} c^*(s) v^{-s} \, ds$$

for every s_0 such that $a < \Re(s_0) < b$.

Mellin–Stieltjes Transform A variant of the Mellin transform is the *Mellin–Stieltjes transform* of a function $\bar{c}(v)$, $v > 0$, of bounded variation with $\bar{c}(v) = 0$ for $0 < v < 1$:

$$C(s) = \int_0^\infty v^{-s} d\bar{c}(v),$$

where we assume that for all (complex) s for which the integral converges,

$$\lim_{v \to \infty} \bar{c}(v) v^{-s} = 0.$$

There is always a half-plane $\Re(s) > a$, where the Mellin–Stieltjes transform converges.

By partial integration, we immediately observe that the Mellin–Stieltjes transform equals the mirrored Mellin transform times a factor s:

$$C(s) = \int_0^\infty v^{-s} d\bar{c}(v) = s \int_0^\infty \bar{c}(v) v^{s-1} dv = s \, c^*(-s).$$

It is suboptimal that there are these two different conventions that lead to $C(s) = s \, c^*(-s)$. However, it is standard to use the above definitions.

In this appendix, we mainly focus on the Mellin–Stieltjes transform. Of course, all results have their counterparts for the Mellin transform.

We note that by applying the inverse Mellin transform we have

$$\frac{1}{2\pi i} \lim_{T \to \infty} \int_{s_0 - iT}^{s_0 + iT} \frac{C(s)}{s} v^s \, ds = \frac{1}{2}(\bar{c}(v-) + \bar{c}(v+))$$

for every s_0 with $\Re(s_0) > a$.

Dirichlet Series For any complex-valued sequence c_n, we define the *Dirichlet series* as

$$C(s) = \sum_{n \geq 1} \frac{c_n}{n^s}.$$

Again, these kind of series converge in a half plane $\Re(s) > a$ and represent analytic functions there (see Appendix C).

Actually, there is an intimate relation between Dirichlet series and the Mellin–Stieltjes transform (and consequently to the Mellin transform). If we set

$$\bar{c}(v) = \sum_{n \le v} c_n,$$

then we actually have

$$C(s) = \sum_{n \ge 1} c_n n^{-s} = \int_{1-}^{\infty} v^{-s} \, d\bar{c}(v).$$

Thanks to the last relation, we use the same notation $C(s)$ for the Dirichlet series and Mellin–Stieltjes transform.

D.2 Tauberian Theorems

The analytic properties of the Mellin–Stieltjes transform (as well as those of the Mellin transform or the Dirichlet series) can be used to recover asymptotic properties of $\bar{c}(v)$ and $c(v)$, respectively. The Wiener–Ikehare Tauberian theorem is one of the key properties in this context.

Theorem D.2 (Wiener–Ikehara) *Let $\bar{c}(v)$, $v > 0$, be nonnegative and nondecreasing with $\bar{c}(v) = 0$ for $0 < v < 1$ such that the Mellin–Stieltjes transform*

$$C(s) = \int_{1-}^{\infty} v^{-s} \, d\bar{c}(v) = s \int_{1}^{\infty} \bar{c}(v) v^{-s-1} \, dv$$

exists for $\Re(s) > 1$. Suppose that for some constant $A_0 > 0$, the analytic function

$$F(s) = \frac{1}{s} C(s) - \frac{A_0}{s - 1} \qquad (\Re(s) > 1)$$

has a continuous extension to the closed half-plane $\Re(s) \ge 1$. Then

$$\bar{c}(v) \sim A_0 v$$

as $v \to \infty$.

Theorem D.2 is quite flexible. For example, it is sufficient to assume that $\bar{c}(v)(\ln v)^b$ is nondecreasing for some real b (and $v \ge 2$). Furthermore, it is clear that it generalizes directly to the case when $C(s)$ converges for $\Re(s) > s_0$ and has a continuous extension to the closed half-plane $\Re(s) \ge s_0$ (for $s_0 \ge 0$). It also applies if $C(s)$ behaves like a pole of higher order for $s \to s_0$, however, the asymptotic result has to be adjusted accordingly.

Theorem D.3 *Let $\bar{c}(v)$ be nonnegative and nondecreasing on $[1, \infty)$ such that the Mellin–Stieltjes transform $C(s)$ exists for $\Re(s) > s_0$ for some $s_0 \ge 0$ and suppose that there exist real constants $A_0, \ldots, A_K$ (with $A_K > 0$) such that*

$$\tilde{F}(s) = \frac{1}{s} C(s) - \sum_{j=0}^{K} \frac{A_j}{(s - s_0)^{j+1}} \tag{D.1}$$

has a continuous extension to the closed half-plane $\Re(s) \ge s_0$. Then,

$$\bar{c}(v) \sim \frac{A_K}{K!} (\ln v)^K v^{s_0} \qquad (v \to \infty). \tag{D.2}$$

Note that corresponding theorems hold for the Mellin transform $c^*(s)$. For example, if $c(v)$, $v > 0$, is nonnegative and nondecreasing such that the Mellin transform exists for $a < \Re(s) < b$ and that the function

$$F(s) = c^*(s) - \frac{A_0}{b-s}$$

has a continuous extension to the region $a < \Re(s) \le b$, then we have

$$c(v) \sim A_0 v^{-b} \qquad (v \to \infty).$$

The advantage of a Tauberian theorem of this form is that it is very easy to apply. It is only necessary to show that a proper function defined for $\Re(s) > s_0$ can be continuously extended to the closed half-plane $\Re(s) \ge s_0$. However, in many cases we know much more.

For example, let us consider the Dirichlet series with coefficients:

$$c_n = n^\sigma (\ln n)^\alpha.$$

It is clear that the Dirichlet series $C(s) = \sum_{n \ge 1} c_n n^{-s}$ converges (absolutely) for complex s with $\Re(s) > \sigma + 1$. Interestingly, there are analytic continuations for $C(s)$.

Theorem D.4 *Suppose that σ and α are real numbers and let $C(s)$ be the Dirichlet series*

$$C(s) = \sum_{n \ge 2} n^\sigma (\ln n)^\alpha n^{-s}.$$

(i) *If α is not a negative integer, then $C(s)$ can be represented as*

$$C(s) = \frac{\Gamma(\alpha + 1)}{(s - \sigma - 1)^{\alpha+1}} + G(s),$$

where $G(s)$ is an entire function.
(ii) *If $\alpha = -k$ is a negative integer, then*

$$C(s) = \frac{(-1)^k}{(k-1)!}(s - \sigma - 1)^{k-1} \ln(s - \sigma + 1) + G(s),$$

where $G(s)$ is an entire function.

Note that the theorem is quite flexible. A variant applies to sequences of the form $c_n = a_{n+2} - a_{n+1}$, where $a_n = n^a (\ln n)^b$.

Theorem D.5 *Suppose that $a_n = n^a (\ln n)^b$, where a and b are real numbers, and let $\widetilde{A}(s)$ be the Dirichlet series*

$$\widetilde{A}(s) = \sum_{n \ge 1} \frac{a_{n+2} - a_{n+1}}{n^s}.$$

(i) *If b is not a negative integer, then $\widetilde{A}(s)$ can be represented as*

$$\widetilde{A}(s) = a\frac{\Gamma(b+1)}{(s-a)^{b+1}} + \frac{\Gamma(b+1)}{(s-a)^b} + G(s),$$

where $G(s)$ is analytic for $\Re(s) > a - 1$.

(ii) *If $b = -k$ is a negative integer, then we have*

$$\widetilde{A}(s) = a\frac{(-1)^k}{(k-1)!}(s-a)^{k-1}\ln(s-a)$$

$$+ \frac{k(-1)^k}{(k-1)!}(s-a)^k\ln(s-a) + G(s),$$

where $G(s)$ is analytic for $\Re(s) > a - 1$.

These two theorems show that we can usually expect more than just continuous extension to the closed half-plane $\Re(s) \geq s_0$. Actually, if we can assume analytic continuation to a larger half plane, then we can also obtain error terms and can handle uniformity questions if an additional parameter is involved. Furthermore, it is not necessary to assume positivity or monotonicity assumptions.

Theorem D.6 *Suppose that the Mellin–Stieltjes transform $C(s)$ of a function $\overline{c}(v)$ exists for $\Re(s) > s_0$ and that the function*

$$F(s) = \frac{1}{s}C(s) - \frac{A_0}{s-s_0}$$

can be analytically continued to the half plane $\Re(s) > s_0 - \eta$ for some $\eta > 0$ such that

$$\lim_{T \to \infty} \sup_{s_0 - \eta < \sigma < s_0 + \eta} |F(\sigma \pm iT)| = 0 \tag{D.3}$$

and that the integral

$$I(\sigma) = \int_{-\infty}^{\infty} |F(\sigma + it)|\, dt \tag{D.4}$$

exists for $s_0 - \eta < \sigma < s_0 + \eta$. Then we have for all $\sigma \in (s_0 - \eta, s_0)$,

$$\left| \frac{1}{2}(\overline{c}(v-) + \overline{c}(v+)) - A_0 v^{s_0} \right| \leq \frac{I(\sigma)}{2\pi} v^\sigma.$$

Proof Clearly the function $A_0 s/(s - s_0)$ is the Mellin–Stieltjes transform of the function $A_0 v^{s_0}$, $v > 1$. Consequently, $sF(s)$ is the Mellin–Stieltjes transform of the function

$$\overline{c}(v) - A_0 v^{s_0}$$

and, thus, we have for all $v > 1$ and for all $\sigma < s_0$,

$$\frac{1}{2}(\overline{c}(v-) + \overline{c}(v+)) - A_0 v^{s_0} = \frac{1}{2\pi i} \lim_{T \to \infty} \int_{\sigma - iT}^{\sigma + iT} F(s) v^s\, ds.$$

By (D.4), the integral on the right-hand side is absolutely convergent for $s_0 < \sigma < s_0 + \eta$. Furthermore, F can be analytically continued and by (D.3) and (D.4) we can shift the line of integration to $\Re(s) = \sigma$ with $s_0 - \eta < \sigma < s_0$:

$$\frac{1}{2}(\overline{c}(v-) + \overline{c}(v+)) - A_0 v^{s_0} = \frac{1}{2\pi i} \int_{\sigma - i\infty}^{\sigma + i\infty} F(s) v^s\, ds.$$

The integral on the right-hand side is bounded by

$$\left| \frac{1}{2\pi i} \int_{\sigma-i\infty}^{\sigma+i\infty} F(s) v^s \, ds \right| \leq \frac{I(\sigma)}{2\pi} v^\sigma,$$

which proves the theorem.   ∎

D.3 A Recurrence

Finally, we discuss a slightly more involved example. Let the function $\bar{c}(v)$ be given by $\bar{c}(v) = 0$ for $0 < v \leq 1$ and by the *recurrence*

$$\bar{c}(v) = 1 + R(\bar{c}(pv) + \bar{c}(qv)) \qquad (v > 0), \tag{D.5}$$

where $R > \frac{1}{2}, 0 < p < 1$ and $0 < q < 1$ are real numbers. By a direct computation, it follows that the Mellin–Stieltjes transform $C(s)$ is given by

$$C(s) = \int_0^\infty v^{-s} \, d\bar{c}(v) = \frac{1}{1 - R(p^s + q^s)} \qquad (\Re(s) > s_0),$$

where $s_0 > 0$ is the unique solution of the equation

$$R(p^{s_0} + q^{s_0}) = 1. \tag{D.6}$$

(Note that $R > \frac{1}{2}$ implies $s_0 > 0$. We can also consider the case $0 < R \leq \frac{1}{2}$ but then the analysis is slightly different.)

First we observe that the equation (D.6) has actually more (complex) solutions than $s = s_0$. The following lemma will be used several times in this book. Note that the case $p = q$ reduces to the exponential function, where are the zeros are periodically lined up parallel to the imaginary axis.

Lemma D.7 *Suppose that $0 < p < q < 1$ and $R > 0$. Let*

$$\mathcal{Z}(R) = \{s \in \mathbf{C} : R(p^{s_0} + q^{s_0}) = 1\}.$$

(i) *All $s \in \mathcal{Z}(R)$ are simple zeros and satisfy*

$$\sigma_0(R) \leq \Re(s) \leq s_0(R),$$

where $s_0(R)$ is the (unique) real solution of $p^s + q^s = 1/R$ and $\sigma_0(R) < s_0(R)$ is the (unique) real solution of $1/R + q^s = p^s$. Furthermore, for every integer k there uniquely exists $s_k(R) \in \mathcal{Z}(R)$ with

$$(2k - 1)\pi / \ln p < \Im(s_k(R)) < (2k + 1)\pi / \ln p$$

and consequently $\mathcal{Z}(R) = \{s_k(R) : k \in \mathbf{Z}\}$.

(ii) *If $\ln q / \ln p$ is irrational, then $\Re(s_k(R)) < \Re(s_0(R))$ for all $k \neq 0$ and for all real intervals $[R_1, R_2]$, we have*

$$\min_{R \in [R_1, R_2]} (\Re(s_0(R)) - \Re(s_k(R))) > 0. \tag{D.7}$$

(iii) *If $\ln q / \ln p = r/d$ is rational, where $\gcd(r, d) = 1$ for integers $r, d > 0$, then we have $\Re(s_k(R)) = \Re(s_0(R))$ if and only if $k \equiv 0 \bmod d$. In particular, $\Re(s_1(R)), \ldots, \Re(s_{d-1}(R)) < \Re(s_0(z))$ and*

$$s_k(R) = s_{k \bmod d}(R) + \frac{2(-k \bmod d)\pi i}{\ln p};$$

that is, all $s \in \mathcal{Z}(R)$ are uniquely determined by $s_0(R)$ and by $s_1(R), s_2(R), \ldots, s_{d-1}(R)$, and their imaginary parts constitute an arithmetic progression.

In particular, it follows that we have to distinguish two cases: the irrational case and the rational case.

In the irrational case, the it follows that $C(s)$ has a meromorphic extension to the complex plane, where on the line $\Re(s) = s_0(R)$ there is only one polar singularity, namely $s_0(R)$. Furthermore there are no singularities in the half plane $\Re(s) > s_0(R)$, and this actually is the region where $C(s)$ converges. Hence, by the Wiener–Ikehara theorem D.3 it follows that for every fixed $R > \frac{1}{2}$ we have

$$\bar{c}(v) \sim \frac{1}{s_0(R)R \left(p^{s_0(R)} \ln \frac{1}{p} + q^{s_0(R)} \ln \frac{1}{q} \right)} v^{s_0(R)}. \tag{D.8}$$

In the rational case, that is, $\ln(1/p) = n_0 L$ with L being a real number and $\ln(1/q) = n_1 L$ for coprime integers n_0, n_1, we just have to analyze the recurrence

$$G_n = 1 + G_{n-n_0} + G_{n-n_1}, \tag{D.9}$$

where G_n abbreviates $C(e^{Ln})$. Equivalently, we have $\bar{c}(v) = G(\lfloor \ln v \rfloor / L)$ (see Chapter 3). By setting

$$G(z) = \sum_{n \geq 0} G_n z^n,$$

we obtain from (D.9) the relation

$$G(z) = \frac{1}{(1-z)(1 - z^{n_0} - z^{n_1})}.$$

This rational function has a dominant simple polar singularity at $z_0 = e^{-L} < 1$. Since n_0 and n_1 are coprime, there are no other polar singularities on the circle $|z| = e^{-L}$. Thus, from the representation

$$G(z) = \frac{1}{(1 - z_0)(n_0 z_0^{n_0} + n_1 z^{n_1})} \frac{1}{1 - z/z_0} + H(z),$$

where $H(z)$ is analytic for $|z| < z_0 + \kappa$ for some $\kappa > 0$, we directly find

$$G_n = \frac{1}{(1 - e^{-L})(n_0 e^{-n_0 L} + n_1 e^{-n_1 L})} e^{Ln} + O(e^{Ln(1-\eta)})$$

for some $\eta > 0$ and consequently,

$$\bar{c}(v) = \frac{L e^{-L\langle \ln v/L \rangle}}{(1 - e^{-L})} \frac{v}{h} + O(v^{(1-\eta)}) \tag{D.10}$$

where $h = p \ln \frac{1}{p} + q \ln \frac{1}{q}$ is formally related to the entropy.

This analysis is quite simple and direct if R is fixed. However, if we want to obtain asymptotic relations that are uniform in the parameter R when R varies (e.g., in an interval $[R_1, R_2]$), the process is much more sophisticated. Actually, the rational case can be directly adapted. We only have to observe that κ and η can be chosen uniformly if $R \in [R_1, R_2]$ varies. However, this is immediate since zeros of polynomial depend continuously on the coefficients. Thus, (D.10) holds also uniformly for $R \in [R_1, R_2]$, where $R_1 > \frac{1}{2}$.

Unfortunately, uniformity is not that immediate when we apply a Tauberian theorem like the Wiener–Ikehara theorem. In order to overcome this problem, we apply the inverse Mellin transform and observe that

$$\frac{1}{2}(\overline{c}(v-) + \overline{c}(v+)) = \frac{1}{2\pi i} \lim_{T \to \infty} \int_{\sigma-iT}^{\sigma+iT} \frac{1}{s(1 - R(p^s + q^s))} v^s \, ds,$$

where $\sigma > s_0(R)$. The idea is to shift the integral to the left and to add up the contributions coming from the polar singularities (with the help of the residue theorem). The only problem with this method is that the integral on the right hand is not absolutely convergent since the integrand is only of order $1/s$.

In order to overcome this problem, we apply a so-called smoothing argument. Instead of $\overline{c}(v)$, we consider the integral

$$\overline{c}_1(v) = \int_0^v \overline{c}(t) \, dt.$$

The Mellin–Stieltjes transform of $\overline{c}_1(v)$ is then given by

$$C_1(s) = \frac{1}{s-1}C(s-1) = \frac{1}{(s-1)(1 - R(p^{s-1} + q^{s-1}))}$$

and consequently,

$$\overline{c}_1(v) = \frac{1}{2\pi i} \int_{\sigma-i\infty}^{\sigma+i\infty} \frac{1}{s(s-1)(1 - R(p^{s-1} + q^{s-1}))} v^s \, ds,$$

where $\sigma > s_0(R) + 1$. Note that the integral on the right-hand side is now absolutely convergent. With the help of the residue theorem, we can shift the integral to the left and obtain for $\sigma'(R) = \frac{1}{2}(s_0(R) + \sigma_0(R))$ (see Lemma D.7),

$$\overline{c}_1(v) = \sum_{\Re(s_k) > \sigma'(R)} \frac{-v^{s_k(R)+1}}{s_k(R)(s_k(R) + 1)R(p^{s_k(R)} \ln p + q^{s_k(R)} \ln q)}$$

$$+ \frac{1}{2\pi i} \int_{\sigma'(R)+1-i\infty}^{\sigma'(R)+1+i\infty} \frac{1}{s(s-1)(1 - R(p^{s-1} + q^{s-1}))} v^s \, ds.$$

Note that we have to be careful if there are $k \neq 0$ with $\sigma'(R) - \kappa \leq \Re s_k(R) \leq \sigma'(R)$, where $\kappa > 0$ is chosen such that $\kappa \leq \frac{1}{4}(s_0(R) - \sigma_0(R))$ for all $R \in [R_1, R_2]$. In this case, we *bypass* the polar singularity with a small half cycle of radius κ from the right and assure that we do not interfere with other zeros $s_k(R) + 1$ (this is possible due to the properties listed in Lemma D.7). In particular, if $\sigma'(R) \leq \Re(s_k) \leq s_0(R)$, we also have that

$$\left| p^{s_k(R)} \ln p + q^{s_k(R)} \ln q \right| \geq \eta$$

uniformly for $R \in [R_1, R_2]$ for some $\eta > 0$. Hence, the infinite sum as well as the remaining integral are absolutely convergent. Furthermore, the last integral can be trivially estimated by $O(v^{\sigma'(R)+1+\kappa}) = O(v^{s_0(R)+1-\kappa})$. Recall that $s_0(R) > \Re(s_k(R))$ for all $k \neq 0$ and consequently $v^{s_k(R)+1} = o(v^{s_0(R)+1})$ for all $k \neq 0$.

Now suppose that $\varepsilon > 0$ is given. By the properties of $s_k(R)$ stated in Lemma D.7, it is possible to find an integer $K = K(\varepsilon)$ such that uniformly for all $v \geq 1$ and for all $R \in [R_1, R_2]$,

$$\sum_{\Re(s_k) > \sigma'(R),\, |k| \geq K} \frac{-v^{s_k(R)+1}}{s_k(R)(s_k(R)+1)R(p^{s_k(R)}\ln p + q^{s_k(R)}\ln q)} \leq \varepsilon v^{s_0(R)+1}.$$

Now, if $0 < |k| < K$, we have

$$\min_{R_1 \leq R \leq R_2} (s_0(R) - \Re(s_k(R))) > 0.$$

Hence, there exists v_0 such that for all $v \geq v_0$ and all $R \in [R_1, R_2]$,

$$\sum_{\Re(s_k) > \sigma'(R),\, 1 \leq |k| < K} \frac{-v^{s_k(R)+1}}{s_k(R)(s_k(R)+1)R(p^{s_k(R)}\ln p + q^{s_k(R)}\ln q)} \leq \varepsilon v^{s_0(R)+1}.$$

Summing up, it follows that for $v \geq v_0$ and all $R \in [R_1, R_2]$,

$$\left| \bar{c}_1(v) + \frac{v^{s_0(R)+1}}{s_0(R)(s_0(R)+1)R(p^{s_0(R)}\ln p + q^{s_0(R)}\ln q)} \right| \leq C_1 \varepsilon v^{s_0(R)+1} + C_2 v^{s_0(R)+1-\kappa}$$

for certain positive constants C_1, C_2. This implies that

$$\bar{c}_1(v) \sim \frac{1}{(s_0(R)+1)s_0(R)R\left(p^{s_0(R)}\ln\frac{1}{p} + q^{s_0(R)}\ln\frac{1}{q}\right)} v^{s_0(R)+1}, \tag{D.11}$$

which holds uniformly for $R \in [R_1, R_2]$.

We finally have to show that (D.11) also implies (D.8) uniformly for $R \in [R_1, R_2]$. For this purpose, we use the following property.

Lemma D.8 *Suppose that $f(v, \lambda)$ is a nonnegative increasing function in $v \geq 0$, where λ is a real parameter with $\lambda \in \Lambda$, where Λ is a closed and bounded interval that does not contain -1. Assume that*

$$F(v, \lambda) = \int_0^v f(w, \lambda)\, dw$$

has the asymptotic expansion

$$F(v, \lambda) = \frac{v^{\lambda+1}}{\lambda+1}(1 + \lambda \cdot o(1))$$

as $v \to \infty$ and uniformly for $\lambda \in \Lambda$. Then

$$f(v, \lambda) = v^\lambda(1 + |\lambda|^{\frac{1}{2}} \cdot o(1))$$

as $v \to \infty$ and again uniformly for $\lambda \in \Lambda$.

Proof By assumption,

$$\left| F(v, \lambda) - \frac{v^{\lambda+1}}{\lambda+1} \right| \leq \varepsilon|\lambda| \frac{v^{\lambda+1}}{\lambda+1}$$

for $v \geq v_0$ and all $\lambda \in \Lambda$. Set $v' = (\varepsilon|\lambda|)^{1/2}v$. By monotonicity, we obtain (for $v \geq v_0$)

$$f(v, \lambda) \le \frac{F(v + v', \lambda) - F(v, \lambda)}{v'}$$

$$\le \frac{1}{v'} \left(\frac{(v + v')^{\lambda+1}}{\lambda + 1} - \frac{v^{\lambda+1}}{\lambda + 1} \right) + \frac{2}{v'} \varepsilon |\lambda| \frac{(v + v')^{\lambda+1}}{\lambda + 1}$$

$$= \frac{1}{v'(\lambda + 1)} \left(v^{\lambda+1} + (\lambda + 1)v^\lambda v' + O(v^{\lambda-1}(v')^2) - v^{\lambda+1} \right)$$

$$+ O\left(\frac{\varepsilon |\lambda| v^{\lambda+1}}{v'} \right)$$

$$= v^\lambda + O\left(v^\lambda \varepsilon^{\frac{1}{2}} |\lambda|^{\frac{1}{2}} \right) + O\left(\frac{\varepsilon |\lambda| v^{\lambda+1}}{v'} \right) = v^\lambda + O\left(v^\lambda \varepsilon^{\frac{1}{2}} |\lambda|^{\frac{1}{2}} \right).$$

In a similar way, when we find the corresponding lower bound (for $v \ge v_0 + v_0^{1/2}$), the result follows. ∎

In order to complete our considerations, we just have to apply Lemma D.8 for $\lambda = s_0(R)$ and

$$f(v, \lambda) = \frac{\overline{c}(v)}{s_0(R)R \left(p^{s_0(R)} \ln \frac{1}{p} + q^{s_0(R)} \ln \frac{1}{q} \right)}$$

and obtain (D.8) uniformly for $R \in [R_1, R_2]$.

Bibliographical Notes

The Mellin transform was introduced by Finnish mathematician Hjalman Mellin (1854–1933). In the analysis of algorithms, it seems that it was used for the first time by D. E. Knuth under the name "gamma methods" (Knuth, 1998b), but it was systematically developed and popularized by P. Flajolet. The best account on Mellin transform can be found in Flajolet, Gourdon, and Dumas (1995). See also Flajolet and Sedgewick (2008) and Szpankowski (2001).

An excellent summary and exposition of Tauberian theorems can be found in Korevaar (2002).

Dirichlet series are standard tools, especially in the analytic number theory and analysis of algorithms. Theorem D.4 is from Grabner and Thuswaldner (1996).

Recurrence (D.5) was discussed in depth in Drmota et al. (2006) and Drmota et al. (2010). Lemma D.7 was first mentioned in Jacquet's Ph.D. thesis and fully proved in Schachinger (2001).

Appendix E

Exponential Sums and Uniform Distribution mod 1

E.1 Exponential Sums

Let $e(x)$ denote the exponential function $e(x) = e^{2\pi i x}$; that is, for real x we have $|e(x)| = 1$ and $e(x + 1) = e(x)$. An *exponential sum* is a finite sum of the form

$$S = \sum_{k \in K} c_k e(x_k),$$

where c_k is (usually) a sequence of positive real numbers and x_k a real sequence. Sometimes one only considers the case $c_k = 1$. An exponential sum is *trivial* if x_k are integers; that is, $e(x_k) = 1$ and consequently $S = \sum_k c_k$. Usually one is interested in *nontrivial estimates* for exponential sums, which means that

$$\sum_{k \in K} c_k e(x_k) = o\left(\sum_{k \in K} c_k\right)$$

as the cardinality of K tends to infinity.

The most prominent exponential sum is when $x_k = \alpha k$ for all k; that is,

$$S = \sum_{k=0}^{K-1} e(\alpha k) = \frac{e(\alpha K) - 1}{e(\alpha) - 1},$$

which can be estimated by

$$\left|\sum_{k=0}^{K-1} e(\alpha k)\right| \leq \min\left(K, \frac{1}{|\sin(\pi\alpha)|}\right).$$

If α is an integer, then this exponential sum is trivial, whereas if α is not an integer, then we get a nontrivial estimate (observe that $2/|e(\alpha) - 1| = 1/|\sin(\pi\alpha)|$).

A very general method for handling exponential sums is due to van der Corput (see theorem 2.7 from Kuipers and Niederreiter (1974)), which applies to exponential sums of the form

$$S = \sum_{k=A}^{B} e(f(n)),$$

where f is twice differentiable on $[A, B]$. Here we have

$$|S| \leq (|f'(B) - f'(A)| + 2)\left(\frac{4}{\sqrt{\lambda}} + 3\right) \tag{E.1}$$

335

with

$$\lambda = \min_{A \leq x \leq B} |f''(x)|.$$

Example E.1 Let $f(x) = x \ln x$. Here we have $f'(x) = \ln x + 1$ and $f''(x) = 1/x$ and, thus,

$$\sum_{k=1}^{K} e(k \ln k) = O(\sqrt{K} \ln K).$$

Case $x_k = ky$. If x_k is of the form $x_k = ky$, then exponential sums can be considered as finite Fourier series in the variable y. By the Weierstrass theorem we know that every continuous periodic function can be uniformly approximated by finite Fourier sums. Unfortunately, the functions we want to approximate are usually not continuous; for example, indicator functions. There is, however, a very strong theorem by Vaaler (1985) that allows to approximate such discontinuous functions by finite Fourier series, where the error term is (again) a proper Fourier series.

For $0 < \alpha < 1$, we denote by $\chi_\alpha(y)$ the indicator function of the interval $[0, \alpha)$, which is periodically extended with period 1. Furthermore, we recall that $\langle y \rangle = y - \lfloor y \rfloor$ denotes the fractional part of y.

Theorem E.2 (Vaaler, 1985) *For every $0 < \alpha < 1$ and for every integer $H \geq 1$, there exist finite Fourier series*

$$A_{\alpha,H}(y) = \sum_{|h| \leq H} a_h(\alpha, H) e(hy), \quad B_{\alpha,H}(y) = \sum_{|h| \leq H} b_h(\alpha, H) e(hy),$$

where the coefficients $a_h(\alpha, H), b_h(\alpha, H)$ satisfy

$$a_0(\alpha, H) = \alpha, \quad |a_h(\alpha, H)| \leq \min\left(\alpha, \frac{1}{\pi |h|}\right), \quad |b_h(\alpha, H)| \leq \frac{1}{H+1}$$

and (for real y)

$$|\chi_\alpha(y) - A_{\alpha,H}(y)| \leq B_{\alpha,H}(y). \tag{E.2}$$

Furthermore, (for every integer $H \geq 1$) there exist finite Fourier series

$$C_H(y) = \sum_{|h| \leq H} c_h(H) e(hy), \quad D_H(y) = \sum_{|h| \leq H} c_h(H) e(hy),$$

where the coefficients $c_h(H), d_h(H)$ satisfy

$$c_0(\alpha, H) = \frac{1}{2}, \quad |c_h(H)| \leq \frac{1}{2\pi |h|}, \quad |d_h(H)| \leq \frac{1}{2H+2}$$

and (for real y)

$$|\langle y \rangle - C_H(y)| \leq D_H(y). \tag{E.3}$$

As a first application of this property, we state the following general relation.

Lemma E.3 *Suppose that $p_{n,k}$ are positive real numbers with*

$$\sum_{k=0}^{n} p_{n,k} = 1$$

and suppose that x_k is a real sequence such that for all integers $h \neq 0$,

$$\sum_{k=0}^{n} p_{n,k} e(h x_k) = o(1)$$

as $n \to \infty$. Then we have uniformly for all $0 < \alpha < 1$ and for all real sequences δ_n,

$$\lim_{n \to \infty} \sum_{k=0}^{n} p_{n,k} \chi_\alpha(x_k + \delta_n) = \alpha$$

and (also uniformly for all real sequences δ_n)

$$\lim_{n \to \infty} \sum_{k=0}^{n} p_{n,k} \langle x_k + \delta_n \rangle = \frac{1}{2}.$$

Proof We present the proof of the second case. The proof of the first case is analogue. By (E.3) we have

$$C_H(y) - D_H(y) \leq \langle y \rangle \leq C_H(y) + D_H(y)$$

and consequently

$$\langle y \rangle \leq \frac{1}{2} + \sum_{0 \neq |h| \leq H} c_h(H) e(hy) + \sum_{|h| \leq H} d_h(H) e(hy).$$

(We just consider the upper bound. The corresponding lower bound can be handled similarly.) Hence, we obtain

$$\sum_{k=0}^{n} p_{n,k} \langle x_k + \delta_n \rangle \leq \frac{1}{2} + \sum_{0 \neq |h| \leq H} c_h(H) e(h\delta_n) \sum_{k=0}^{n} p_{n,k} e(h x_k)$$

$$+ d_0 + \sum_{0 \neq |h| \leq H} d_h(H) e(h\delta_n) \sum_{k=0}^{n} p_{n,k} e(h x_k).$$

By assumption, we know that the exponential sums on the right-hand side converge to 0. This implies that

$$\limsup_{n \to \infty} \sum_{k=0}^{n} p_{n,k} \langle x_k + \delta_n \rangle \leq \frac{1}{2} + \frac{1}{2H + 2}.$$

Since H can be arbitrarily chosen, it also follows that the lim sup is upper bounded by $\frac{1}{2}$. By using the corresponding lower bound it follows that the lim inf is lower bounded by $\frac{1}{2}$ too. Thus, the limit exists and equals $\frac{1}{2}$. Note that this limit is uniform in the sequence δ_n. ∎

E.2 Uniformly Distributed Sequences mod 1

The most prominent case, where this concept applies, is the *Theory of Uniformly Distributed Sequences mod 1*. Here $p_{n,k} = \frac{1}{n}$. By defining the *discrepancy* $D_n(x_k)$ of a real sequence (x_k) by

$$D_n(x_k) = \sup_{0<\alpha<1} \left| \frac{1}{n} \sum_{k=0}^{n} \chi_\alpha(x_k) - \alpha \right|, \tag{E.4}$$

we say that a sequence (x_k) is *uniformly distributed mod 1* if $D_n(x_k) \to 0$ as $n \to \infty$. Informally, this means that the number of $k \le n$ with x_k mod $1 \in [0, \alpha)$ is asymptotically αn. Lemma E.3 then says that the exponential sum condition

$$\sum_{k=1}^{n} e(hx_k) = o(n)$$

(for nonzero integers h) implies that the sequence (x_k) is uniformly distributed mod 1. Actually, the two conditions are equivalent and the exponential sum condition is called the *Weyl criterion.*

We make this precise in a more general context.

Theorem E.4 *Suppose that $p_{n,k}$ are positive real numbers with*

$$\sum_{k=0}^{n} p_{n,k} = 1$$

and suppose that x_k is a real sequence. Then the following three properties are equivalent:

1. For all integers $h \ne 0$,

$$\sum_{k=0}^{n} p_{n,k} e(hx_k) = o(1) \tag{E.5}$$

as $n \to \infty$.

2. The discrepancy

$$D_n^{(p_{n,k})}(x_k) = \sup_{0<\alpha<1} \left| \sum_{k=0}^{n} p_{n,k} \chi_\alpha(x_k) - \alpha \right|$$

satisfies

$$D_n^{(p_{n,k})}(x_k) = o(1) \tag{E.6}$$

as $n \to \infty$.

3. For all Riemann integrable periodic function $f(y)$ (with period 1), we have

$$\lim_{n \to \infty} \sum_{k=0}^{n} p_{n,k} f(x_k + \delta_n) = \int_0^1 f(y)\, dy \tag{E.7}$$

uniformly for all real sequences δ_n.

Proof We prove (E.7). Next suppose that (E.6) holds and that f is a Riemann integrable periodic function $f(y)$ (with period 1). Then for every $\varepsilon > 0$, there are two periodic step functions $S_1(y), S_2(y)$ with

$$S_1(y) \le f(y) \le S_2(y) \quad \text{and} \quad \int_0^1 (S_2(y) - S_1(y))\, dy < \varepsilon.$$

Next we observe that step functions $S(y)$ are just finite linear combinations of χ_α functions. Since $\int_0^1 \chi_\alpha(y)\, dy = \alpha$, it follows from (E.6) that for all step functions $S(y)$,

$$\lim_{n \to \infty} \sum_{k=0}^{n} p_{n,k} S(x_k) = \int_0^1 S(y)\, dy.$$

Consequently,

$$\limsup_{n \to \infty} \left| \sum_{k=0}^{n} p_{n,k} f(x_k) - \int_0^1 f(y)\, dy \right| \le \varepsilon.$$

Since this holds for all $\varepsilon > 0$, we also obtain (E.7). Note everything is uniform in possible shifts δ_n.

Finally, we apply (E.7) for $f(y) = \cos(2\pi h y)$ and $f(y) = \sin(2\pi h y)$ for nonzero integers h. Since they have zero integral, we immediately obtain (E.5). ∎

Example E.5 We provide a second application (that is also used in Chapter 2). Suppose that $0 < p < 1$ is given and that $p_{n,k}$ are defined by

$$p_{n,k} = \binom{n}{k} p^k (1 - p)^{n-k}.$$

Suppose further that $x_k = \alpha k$ for some real number α. Then the corresponding exponential sums can be directly computed with the help of the binomial theorem:

$$\sum_{k=0}^{n} \binom{n}{k} p^k (1 - p)^{n-k} e(h\alpha k) = (pe(h\alpha) + 1 - p)^n.$$

Clearly, if $h\alpha$ is an integer, then $(pe(h\alpha) + 1 - p)^n = 1$. However, if $h\alpha$ is not an integer, then $|pe(h\alpha) + 1 - p| < 1$ and it follows that $(pe(h\alpha) + 1 - p)^n \to 0$ as $n \to \infty$.

Erdős–Turán–Koksma inequality In the theory of uniformly distributed sequences there are two fundamental inequalities, the Erdős–Turán–Koksma inequality and the Koksma–Hlawka inequality. We close this part of the Appendix with the presentation of these results.

Let $d \ge 1$ be a fixed integer and $\mathbf{x}_0, \mathbf{x}_1, \ldots, \mathbf{x}_n$ be points in the d-dimensional space $\mathbb{R}^d$, and $p_{n,k}$ be positive numbers with $\sum_{k=0}^{n} p_{n,k} = 1$. Then the d-dimensional discrepancy with respect to $p_{n,k}$ is defined by

$$D_n^{(p_{n,k})}(\mathbf{x}_k) = \sup_{0 < \alpha_1, \ldots, \alpha_d < 1} \left| \sum_{k=0}^{n} p_{n,k} \chi_{(\alpha_1, \ldots, \alpha_d)}(\mathbf{x}_k) - \alpha_1 \cdots \alpha_d \right|,$$

where $\chi_{(\alpha_1, \ldots, \alpha_d)}(y_1, \ldots, y_d) = \prod_{j=1}^{d} \chi_{\alpha_j}(x_j)$.

Theorem E.6 (Erdős–Turán–Koksma inequality) *Let* $\mathbf{x}_0, \mathbf{x}_1, \ldots, \mathbf{x}_n$ *be points in the d-dimensional space* $\mathbb{R}^d$ *and* H *an arbitrary positive integer. Then*

$$D_n^{(p_{n,k})}(\mathbf{x}_k) \le \left(\frac{3}{2} \right)^d \left(\frac{2}{H+1} + \sum_{0 < \|\boldsymbol{h}\|_\infty \le H} \frac{1}{r(\mathbf{h})} \left| \sum_{k=0}^{n} p_{n,k} e(\mathbf{h} \cdot \mathbf{x}_k) \right| \right), \tag{E.8}$$

where $r(\mathbf{h}) = \prod_{i=1}^{d} \max\{1, |h_i|\}$ *for* $\mathbf{h} = (h_1, \ldots, h_d) \in \mathbb{Z}^d$.

This theorem is a quantitative version of the major part of Theorem E.4 (even in a d-dimensional version).

In order to state the Koksma–Hlawka inequality, we need the notation of the variation of a function (in d variables). By a partition P of $[0, 1]^d$ we mean a set of d finite sequences $\eta_i^{(0)}, \ldots, \eta_i^{(m_i)}$, $i = 1, \ldots, d$, with $0 = \eta_i^{(0)} \le \eta_i^{(1)} \le \cdots \le \eta_i^{(m_i)} = 1$. In connection with such a partition we define for each $i = 1, \ldots, d$ an operator Δ_i by

$$\Delta_i f(x_1, \ldots, x_{i-1}, \eta_i^{(j)}, x_{i+1}, \ldots, x_d) = f(x_1, \ldots, x_{i-1}, \eta_i^{(j+1)}, x_{i+1}, \ldots, x_d) \qquad \text{(E.9)}$$
$$- f(x_1, \ldots, x_{i-1}, \eta_i^{(j)}, x_{i+1}, \ldots, x_d)$$

for $0 \le j < m_i$. Operators with different subscripts obviously commute and $\Delta_{i_1, \ldots, i_l}$ will stand for $\Delta_{i_1} \cdots \Delta_{i_l}$.

For a function $f : [0, 1]^d \to \mathbb{R}$ we set

$$V^{(d)}(f) = \sup_P \sum_{j_1=0}^{m_1-1} \cdots \sum_{j_k=0}^{m_d-1} \left| \Delta_{1,\ldots,k} f(\eta_1^{(j_1)}, \ldots, \eta_k^{(j_d)}) \right|,$$

and

$$V(f) = \sum_{l=0}^{d-1} \sum_{F_\ell} V^{(k-\ell)}(f|_{F_\ell}),$$

where the $(d - \ell)$-dimensional faces F_ℓ of the form $x_{i_1} = \cdots = x_{i_\ell} = 1$.

We say that f is of bounded variation in the sense of Hardy and Krause if $V(f) < \infty$. For example, if the partial derivative

$$\frac{\partial^l f|_{(F_l)}}{\partial x_{i_1} \cdots \partial x_{i_l}}$$

is continuous on the $(d - \ell)$-dimensional face F_ℓ of $[0, 1]^d$, defined by $x_{i_1} = \cdots = x_{i_\ell} = 1$, the variation can be computed by the integral

$$V^{(d-\ell)}(f|_{(F_\ell)}) = \int_{F_\ell} \left| \frac{\partial^\ell f|_{(F_l)}}{\partial x_{i_1} \cdots \partial x_{i_\ell}} \right| dx_{i_1} \cdots dx_{i_\ell}.$$

Theorem E.7 (Koksma–Hlawka inequality) *Let f be of bounded variation on $[0, 1]^d$ in the sense of Hardy and Krause. Then we have for all sequences $\mathbf{x}_0, \mathbf{x}_1, \ldots, \mathbf{x}_n \in [0, 1)^d$,*

$$\left| \sum_{k=0}^n p_{n,k} f(\mathbf{x}_k) - \int_{[0,1]^d} f(\mathbf{x}) \, d\mathbf{x} \right| \le V(f) D_n^{(p_{n,k})}(\mathbf{x}_k)$$

for every n.

Bibliographical Notes

Exponential sums and uniform distributions mod 1 (including the Erdős–Turán–Koksma inequality etc.) are discussed in depth in Walfisz (1963), Kuipers and Niederreiter (1974), Korobov (1992), Niederreiter (1992), Huxley (1996), Drmota and Tichy (1997), Kowalski (2021). Theorem E.2 is proved in Vaaler (1985).

Appendix F

Diophantine Approximation

In this appendix, we collect some facts about Diophantine approximations of irrational numbers through continued fractions and some facts about geometry of numbers.

F.1 Dirichlet's Approximation Theorem

Let α be a real number. Clearly α can be approximated by rational numbers:

$$\left| \alpha - \frac{p}{q} \right| < \varepsilon$$

to arbitrary precision $\varepsilon > 0$. A slightly stronger question is, whether we can find integers $p, q,\, q \neq 0$, such that

$$|q\alpha - p| < \varepsilon$$

for every given $\varepsilon > 0$. The answer is actually yes, and moreover this question can be answered in an optimal way.

Theorem F.1 (Dirichlet's Approximation Theorem) *Let α be a real number. Then for every integer $N \geq 1$, there exist integers p, q with $1 \leq q \leq N$ and*

$$|q\alpha - p| < \frac{1}{N}.$$

Proof Consider the $N + 1$ numbers:

$$x_k = k\alpha - \lfloor k\alpha \rfloor = \langle k\alpha \rangle \in [0, 1), \qquad 0 \leq k \leq N.$$

Next we partition the unit interval $[0, 1)$ into N subintervals $I_j = [j/N, (j+1)/N)$, $j = 0, \dots, N - 1$. By the pigeon principle there exist j_0 and $k_1 < k_2$ (with $0 \leq k_1, k_2 \leq N$) such that $x_{k_1}, x_{k_2} \in I_{j_0}$. Since the length of I_{j_0} equals $1/N$, we also have $|x_{k_2} - x_{k_1}| < 1/N'$ or

$$|(k_2 - k_1)\alpha - (\lfloor k_2\alpha \rfloor - \lfloor k_1\alpha \rfloor)| < \frac{1}{N}.$$

Setting $q = k_2 - k_1$ (that satisfies $1 \leq q \leq N$) and $p = \lfloor k_2\alpha \rfloor - \lfloor k_1\alpha \rfloor$ completes the proof of the lemma. $\blacksquare$

A direct consequence of Dirichlet's Approximation Theorem is the following property.

Lemma F.2 *Suppose that α is an irrational number. Then there are infinitely many coprime integer pairs p, q with $q > 0$ and*

$$|q\alpha - p| < \frac{1}{q}.$$

Proof Suppose that there are only finitely many integer pairs p, q with this property and set

$$\mu = \min |q\alpha - p|,$$

where the minimum is taken over this finite set of integer pairs. Since α is irrational, this minimum μ is positive. Now choose an integer $N > 1/\mu$ and apply Theorem F.1. Then we have $|Q\alpha - P| < \frac{1}{N}$ for integers P, Q with $1 \leq Q \leq N$. Without loss of generality we can assume that P, Q are coprime. Since $Q \leq N$, we also have

$$|Q\alpha - P| < \frac{1}{Q}.$$

However, $|Q\alpha - P| < \frac{1}{N} < \mu$, which leads to a contradiction. This proves the lemma. ∎

F.2 Continued Fractions

With the help of the continued fraction expansion of an irrational number α it is easy to find, explicitly, an infinite sequence of integer pairs p, q with $|q\alpha - p| < \frac{1}{q}$.

A finite *continued fraction expansion* is a rational number of the form

$$a_0 + \cfrac{1}{a_1 + \cfrac{1}{a_2 + \cfrac{1}{\ddots + \frac{1}{a_n}}}},$$

where a_0 is an integer and a_j are positive integers for $j \geq 1$. We denote this rational number as

$$[a_0, a_1, \ldots, a_n].$$

Such continued fractions appear naturally in the context of the Euclidean algorithm.

Example F.3 If we start with the integers 25 and 7, we have

$$\frac{25}{7} = 3 + \frac{4}{7}, \quad \frac{7}{4} = 1 + \frac{3}{4}, \quad \frac{4}{3} = 1 + \frac{1}{3}$$

or

$$\frac{25}{7} = 3 + \frac{1}{\frac{7}{4}} = 3 + \frac{1}{1 + \frac{3}{4}} = 3 + \frac{1}{1 + \frac{1}{1 + \frac{1}{3}}}.$$

In other words,

$$\frac{25}{7} = [3, 1, 1, 3].$$

More generally this procedure shows that every rational number can be represented as a (finite) continued fraction.

Furthermore, if a_j is a given sequence of integers (that are positive for $j > 0$) then we can consider the sequence of rational numbers

$$r_n = \frac{p_n}{q_n} = [a_0, a_1, \ldots, a_n].$$

It follows easily by induction that the numerators $p_n = p_n(a_0, a_1, \ldots, a_n)$ and denominators $q_n = q_n(a_0, a_1, \ldots, a_n)$ satisfy the recurrences

$$p_n = a_n p_{n-1} + p_{n-2}, \quad q_n = a_n q_{n-1} + q_{n-2}. \tag{F.1}$$

Furthermore, we have the relation

$$p_n q_{n-1} - q_n p_{n-1} = (-1)^{n-1}.$$

In particular, the pairs p_n, q_n are coprime, they grow exponentially, and we have

$$r_n - r_{n-1} = \frac{p_n q_{n-1} - q_n p_{n-1}}{q_n q_{n-1}} = \frac{(-1)^{n-1}}{q_n q_{n-1}}.$$

Thus, the sequence r_n is a Cauchy sequence and has a limit. This limit denotes an *infinite continued fraction expansion*:

$$[a_0, a_1, a_2, \ldots] = \lim_{n \to \infty} [a_0, a_1, \ldots, a_n].$$

Actually, every real number α has a finite or infinite continued fraction expansion that is (essentially) unique. If α is rational, then its continued fraction is finite (and unique up to the last entry; for example, $\frac{25}{7} = [3, 1, 1, 3] = [3, 1, 1, 2, 1]$). Conversely, if α is irrational then we recursively set

$$\alpha_0 = \alpha, \quad a_j = \lfloor \alpha_j \rfloor, \quad \alpha_{j+1} = 1/(\alpha_j - a_j),$$

and obtain recursively

$$\alpha = a_0 + \cfrac{1}{a_1 + \cfrac{1}{a_2 + \cfrac{1}{\ddots + \cfrac{1}{a_{n-1} + \frac{1}{\alpha_n}}}}} = [a_0, a_1, \ldots, a_{n-1}, \alpha_n].$$

Note that $a_n \le \alpha_n < a_n + 1$. Thus, it immediately follows that

$$\alpha = [a_0, a_1, a_2, \ldots]$$

and it is another simple observation that this continued fraction expansion is unique.

The corresponding finite continued fraction expansions

$$\frac{p_n}{q_n} = [a_0, a_1, \ldots, a_n]$$

are called *convergents* of α.

For example, it is an easy exercise to show the following two relations for (infinite) continued fraction expansion hold:

$$\frac{\sqrt{5} + 1}{2} = [1, 1, 1, \ldots], \quad \sqrt{2} = [1, 2, 2, 2, \ldots].$$

These are very easy examples of numbers with a so-called *periodic continued fraction expansion*. It is nice to observe (but this is not completely trivial) that an irrational number α has an ultimately periodic continued fraction expansion if and only if α is a quadratic irrational number (that is, a root of an integer polynomial $Ax^2 + Bx + C$, where $AC \neq 0$ and $B^2 \neq 4AC$).

Similarly to the recurrences of p_n and q_n, it follows that

$$\alpha = [a_0, a_1, \ldots, a_{n-1}, \alpha_n] = \frac{\alpha_n p_{n-1} + p_{n-2}}{\alpha_n q_{n-1} + q_{n-2}}$$

and

$$(\alpha_n p_{n-1} + p_{n-2}) q_{n-1} - (\alpha_n q_{n-1} + q_{n-2}) p_{n-1} = (-1)^n.$$

Hence,

$$\alpha - \frac{p_{n-1}}{q_{n-1}} = \frac{(\alpha_n p_{n-1} + p_{n-2}) q_{n-1} - (\alpha_n q_{n-1} + q_{n-2}) p_{n-1}}{q_{n-1}(\alpha_n q_{n-1} + q_{n-2})} = \frac{(-1)^{n-1}}{q_{n-1}(\alpha_n q_{n-1} + q_{n-2})}.$$

Since $\alpha_n \geq a_n$, we also have $\alpha_n q_{n-1} + q_{n-2} \geq a_n q_{n-1} + q_{n-2} = a_n$ and consequently

$$\left| \alpha - \frac{p_{n-1}}{q_{n-1}} \right| < \frac{1}{q_{n-1} q_n} < \frac{1}{q_{n-1}^2}.$$

This means that the pairs p_n, q_n form an infinite sequence of integer pairs p, q with $|q\alpha - p| < \frac{1}{q}$.

It turns out that the approximation of the kind $|q\alpha - p| < \frac{1}{q}$ cannot be sharpened in general. An irrational number α is called *badly approximable* if there exists a constant $c > 0$ such that

$$|q\alpha - p| \geq \frac{c}{q}$$

holds for all integers p, q with $q > 0$.

With the help of continued fraction expansions, badly approximable number can be classified.

Lemma F.4 *An irrational number α is badly approximable if and only if its continued fraction expansion*

$$\alpha = [a_0, a_1, a_2, \ldots]$$

is bounded; that is, there exists $C > 0$ with $a_j \leq C$ for all $j \geq 1$.

It turns out that the condition that the continued fraction expansion is bounded is quite restrictive. Of course, there are many examples with this property (for example quadratic irrational numbers), however, from a *global perspective* there are only very few numbers with this property. It turns out that the set of badly approximable real numbers has zero Lebesgue measure. In other words, almost all real numbers are not badly approximable. These lead us to the question of which approximation behavior we can typically expect.

For this purpose, we introduce the following notation. Suppose that Ψ is a nonincreasing positive function on the positive integers. We say that a real number α is Ψ-approximable if there exist infinitely many integer pairs p, q with $q > 0$ and

$$|q\alpha - p| < \Psi(q).$$

The following theorem by Khinchin provides a complete answer to whether or not such a situation is typical.

Theorem F.5 (Khinchin) *Suppose that* Ψ *is a nonincreasing positive function on the positive integers. If the series* $\sum_q \Psi(q)$ *diverges, then almost all real numbers (in the sense of Lebesgue) are* Ψ*-approximable. Conversely, if the series* $\sum_q \Psi(q)$ *converges, then almost all real numbers are not* Ψ*-approximable.*

We apply this theorem for $\Psi(q) = 1/q^{1+\varepsilon}$ for some $\varepsilon > 0$. Then the series $\sum_q \Psi(q)$ converges. Thus, for almost all real numbers the inequality

$$|q\alpha - p| < \frac{1}{q^{1+\varepsilon}}$$

has only finitely many solutions. Consequently there exists a constant $c > 0$ such that

$$|q\alpha - p| \geq \frac{c}{q^{1+\varepsilon}} \tag{F.2}$$

holds in all cases. If we replace ε by 0 this is not true anymore. This means that *typically* we have (F.2), whereas the inequality $|q\alpha - p| < 1/q$ has infinitely many solutions.

Khinchin's theorem is the start of a whole theory, namely *metric Diophantine approximation*. This is highly nontrivial if several real numbers shall be approximated simultaneously.

F.3 Geometry of Numbers

A complete lattice Γ of the space $\mathbb{R}^n$ is the linear image $A(\mathbb{Z}^n)$ of the integer points $\mathbb{Z}^n$, where A is an invertible $n \times n$-matrix; that is,

$$\Gamma = \{k_1 \mathbf{a}_1 + \cdots + k_n \mathbf{a}_n : k_1, \ldots, k_n \in \mathbb{Z}\},$$

where the (basis) vectors $\mathbf{a}_1, \ldots, \mathbf{a}_n \in \mathbb{R}^n$ are linearly independent. (Actually they form the columns of the matrix A.) Note that the matrix A is not unique. We can replace A by $A' = CA$, where C is an integer matrix with $\det C = \pm 1$.

The set

$$D = \{x_1 \mathbf{a}_1 + \cdots + x_n \mathbf{a}_n : x_1, \ldots, x_n \in [0, 1)\}$$

is called fundamental domain of Γ related to the lattice basis $\mathbf{a}_1, \ldots, \mathbf{a}_n$. Note that $D + \Gamma = \mathbb{R}^n$. The volume of D

$$d(\Gamma) = \text{Vol}(D) = |\det A|$$

is independent of the choice of the basis and called the lattice constant.

If B is any (measurable) set of $\mathbb{R}^n$ then it is expected that B contains $\text{Vol}(B)/d(G)$ lattice points of Γ; however, in general it is not granted that B contains any lattice points. Nevertheless, if K is convex and centrally symmetric then Minkowski's first theorem gives an answer.

Theorem F.6 (Minkowski's First Theorem) *Suppose that* Γ *is a complete lattice in* $\mathbb{R}^n$ *and* K *a convex and centrally symmetric body. If*

$$\text{Vol}(K) > 2^n d(\Gamma),$$

then K *contains a nonzero element of* Γ.

For example, Minkowski's theorem implies the Dirichlet approximation theorem. Suppose that $\alpha \in (0,1)$ is a real number and $N \geq 1$ is an integer. Consider the convex and centrally symmetric body

$$K = \{(x,y) \in \mathbb{R}^2 : |x| \leq N + 1/2, \ |\alpha x - y| \leq 1/N\}$$

with volume $\mathrm{Vol}(K) = 2(2N+1)/N > 2^2$. Hence, K contains a nonzero integer point (q,p) in $\Gamma = \mathbb{Z}^n$. Clearly we have $|q| \leq N$ and $|\alpha q - p| \leq 1/N$.

Minkowski's First Theorem has a very important generalization. Suppose again that K is a convex and centrally symmetric body. Then the so-called successive minima $\lambda_k = \lambda_k(K)$, $1 \leq k \leq n$, with respect to a complete lattice Γ are defined by

$$\lambda_k = \inf\{\lambda > 0 : \lambda K \text{ contains } k \text{ linearly independent lattice points of } \Gamma\}.$$

Theorem F.7 (Minkowski's Second Theorem) *Suppose that Γ is a complete lattice in $\mathbb{R}^n$, K a convex and centrally symmetric body, and $\lambda_k = \lambda_k(K)$, $1 \leq k \leq n$, the successive minima of K with respect to Γ. Then we have*

$$\frac{2^n}{n!}d(\Gamma) \leq \lambda_1 \cdots \lambda_n \mathrm{Vol}(K) \leq 2^n d(\Gamma).$$

In order to show that Minkowski's second theorem implies the first one, we consider a convex and centrally symmetric body K with $\mathrm{Vol}(K) > 2^n d(\Gamma)$. Since $\lambda_1 \leq \lambda_2 \leq \cdots \leq \lambda_n$, it follows that

$$2^n d(\Gamma) < \mathrm{Vol}(K) \leq (2/\lambda_1)^n d(\Gamma)$$

and consequently $\lambda_1 \leq 1$. Thus K contains (by definition of λ_1) a nonzero lattice point.

Bibliographical Notes

Diophantine approximations are discussed in Allouche and Shallit (2008), Beck (2014), Bernik and Dodson (1999), Bugeaud (2012), Schmidt (1980, 1991), Sprindzuk (1979).

References

Abbe, E. (2016). Graph compression: The effect of clusters. In *Proceedings of the 54th Annual Allerton Conference on Communication, Control, and Computing* (Allerton), Monticello, IL, USA, 2016, pp. 1–8.

Abrahams, J. (2001). Code and parse trees for lossless source encoding, *Communications in Information and Systems*, *1*, 113–146.

Abramowitz, M. and Stegun, I. (1964). *Handbook of Mathematical Functions*. New York: Dover.

Adler, M. and Mitzenmacher, M. (2001). Towards compressing web graphs. In *Proceedings of the Data Compression Conference*, DCC '01, pp. 203–212. Washington, DC: IEEE Computer Society.

Akra, M. and Bazzi, L. (1998). On the solution of linear recurrence equations, *Computational Optimization and Applications*, pp. *10*, 195–201.

Albert, R. and Barabási, A.-L. (2002). Statistical mechanics of complex networks, *Reviews of Modern Physics*, *74*, 47–97.

Aldous, D. J. and Ross, N. (2014). Entropy of some models of sparse random graphs with vertex-names, *Probability in the Engineering and Informational Sciences*, *28*(2), 145–168.

Allouche, J. and Shallit, J. (2008). *Automatic Sequences*. Cambridge: Cambridge University Press.

Alon, N. and Orlitsky, A. (1994). A Lower bound on the expected length of one-to one codes, *IEEE Transactions on Information Theory*, *40*(5), 1670–1672.

Andrews, G. E. (1984). *The Theory of Partitions*. Cambridge: Cambridge University Press.

Apostol, T. (1976). *Introduction to Analytic Number Theory*. New York: Springer.

Asadi, A. R., Abbe, E., and Verdú, S. (2017). Compressing data on graphs with clusters. *2017 IEEE International Symposium on Information Theory (ISIT)*, Aachen, Germany, pp. 1583–1587.

Atteson, K. (1999). The asymptotic redundancy of Bayes rules for Markov chains, *IEEE Transactions on Information Theory*, *45*(6), 2104–2109.

Baker, R. C. (1978). Dirichlet's theorem on diophantine approximation, *Cambridge Philosophical Society*, *83*(1), 37–59.

Balasubramaniam, V. (1997). Statistical inference, Occam's razor, and statistical mechanics on the space of probability distributions, *Natural Computation*, *9*, 349–368.

Barron, A. (1985). Logically smooth density estimation, Ph.D. thesis, Stanford University Stanford, CA.

Barron, A., Rissanen, J., and Yu, B. (1998). The minimum description length principle in coding and modeling, *IEEE Transactions on Information Theory*, *44*(6), 2743–2760.

Bateman, H. (1955). *Higher Transcendental Functions*. New York: McGraw-Hill.

Beck, J. (2014). *Probabilistic Diophantine Approximation: Randomness in Lattice Point Counting*. Springer Monogr. Math. Cham: Springer.

Ben-David, S., Pál, D., and Shalev-Shwartz, S. (2009). Agnostic online learning. In the 22nd Conference on Learning Theory (COLT), vol. 3, p. 1.

Bender, E. (1973). Central and local limit theorems applied to asymptotic enumeration *Journal of Combinatorial Theory*, *15*, 91–111.

Bender, E. and Richmond, B. (1983). Central and local limit theorems applied to asymptotic enumeration II: Multivariate generating functions, *Journal of Combinatorial Theory*, *34*, 255–265.

Bergeron, F., Flajolet, P., and Salvy, B. (1992). Varieties of increasing trees. In J. C. Raoult (ed.), *CAAP '92, Lecture Notes in Computer Science*, vol. 581, Berlin: Springer. pp. 24–48.

Bernardo, J. (1979). Reference posterior distributions for Bayesian inference, *Journal of the Royal Statistical Society, B, 41*(2), 113–147.

Bernik, V. and Dodson, M. (1999). *Metric Diophantine Approximation on Manifolds*. Cambridge: Cambridge University Press.

Besta, M. and Hoefler, T. (2018). Survey and taxonomy of lossless graph compression and space-efficient graph representations. *arXiv:1806.01799*.

Billingsley, P. (1968). *Convergence of Probability Measures*. New York: John Wiley and Sons.

Bollobás, B. (1982). The asymptotic number of unlabelled regular graphs, *Journal of the London Mathematical Society*, *26*, 201–206.

Bona, M. and Flajolet, P. (2009). Isomorphism and symmetries in random phylogenetic trees, *Journal of Applied Probability*, *46*(4), 1005–1019.

Boncelet, C. (1993). Block arithmetic coding for source compression, *IEEE Transactions on Information Theory*, *39*(5), 1546–1554.

Boucheron, S., Garivier, A., and Gassiat, E. (2009). Coding on countably infinite alphabets, *IEEE Transactions on Information Theory*, *55*(1), 358–373.

Boza, L. B. (1971). Asymptotically optimal tests for finite Markov chains, *Annals of Mathematical Statistics*, *42*(6), 1992–2007.

Bugeaud, Y. (2012). *Distribution Modulo One and Diophantine Approximation*, vol. 193 of Cambridge Tracts in Mathematics. Cambridge: Cambridge University Press.

Bugeaud, Y., Drmota, M., and Szpankowski, W. (2008). On the construction of (explicit) Khodak's code and its analysis, *IEEE Transactions on Information Theory*, *54*(1), 5073–5086.

Campbell, L. (1965). A coding theorem and Rényi's entropy, *Information and Control*, *8*, 423–429.

Canfield, E. R. (1977). Central and local limit theorems for the coefficients of polynomials of binomial type, *Journal of Combinatorial Theory*, *23*, 275–290.

Capocelli, E. and de Santis, A. (1989). Tight upper bounds on the redundancy of Huffman codes, *IEEE Transactions on Information Theory*, *35*, 1084–1091.

Capocelli, E. and de Santis, A. (1991). New bounds on the redundancy of Huffman codes, *IEEE Transactions on Information Theory*, 37, 1095–1104.

Cassels, J. W. S. (1957). *An Introduction to Diophantine Approximation*. Cambridge: Cambridge University Press.

Chern, H.-H., Fernandez-Camacho, M., Hwang, H.-K., and Martinez, C. (2012). Psi-series method for equality of random trees and quadratic convolution recurrences, *Random Structures & Algorithms*, 44, 67–108.

Cheung, Y., Flajolet, P., Golin, M., and Lee, C. (2008). Multidimensional divide-and-conquer and weighted digital sums. In *Proceedings of the Workshop on Analytic Algorithmics and Combinatorics* (ANALCO), SIAM, pp. 58–65.

Chierichetti, F., Kumar, R., Lattanzi, S. et al. (2009). On compressing social networks, *Proceedings of the 15th ACM SIGKDD International Conference on Knowledge Discovery and Data Mining*, KDD '09, pp. 219–228. New York: ACM.

Choi, V. and Golin, M. J. (2001). Lopsided trees I: Analyses, *Algoritmica*, 31, pp. 240–290.

Choi, Y. and Szpankowski, W. (2012). Compression of graphical structures: Fundamental limits, algorithms, and experiments, *IEEE Transactions on Information Theory*, 58(2), 620–638.

Chung, K. L. (1974). *A Course in Probability Theory*. 2nd ed. New York: Academic Press.

Cichon, J. and Golebiewski, Z. (2012). On the Bernoulli sums and Bernstein polynomials. In *23rd International Meeting on Probabilistic, Combinatorial, and Asymptotic Methods in the Analysis of Algorithms* (AofA'12), 2012, Montreal. pp. 179–190.

Cichon, J., Magner, A., Turowski, K., and Szpankowski, W. (2017). On symmetries of non-plane trees in a non-uniform model, *Proceedings of the Workshop on Analytic Algorithmics and Combinatorics* (ANALCO), SIAM, pp. 156–163.

Clarke, B. and Barron, A. (1990). Information-theoretic asymptotics of Bayes methods, *IEEE Transactions on Information Theory*, 36(3), 453–471.

Corless, R., Gonnet, G., Hare, D., Jeffrey, D., and Knuth, D. (1996). On the Lambert *W* function, *Advances in Computational Mathematics*, 5, 329–359.

Cormen, T., Leierson, C., and Rivest, R. (1990). *Introduction to Algorithms*. Cambridge, MA: MIT Press.

Cover, T. M. and Thomas, J. A. (1991). *Elements of Information Theory*, Hoboken, NJ: John Wiley and Sons.

Csiszar, I. (1998). The method of types, *IEEE Transactions on Information Theory*, 44(6), 2505–2523.

Csiszar, I. and Korner, J. (1981). *Information Theory: Coding Theorems for Discrete Memoryless Systems*. Boston: Academic Press.

Csiszar, I. and Shields, P. (1996). Redundancy rates for renewal and other processes, *IEEE Transactions on Information Theory*, 42(6), 2065–2072.

Davisson, L. (1973). Universal noiseless coding, *IEEE Transactions on Information Theory*, 19(6), 783–795.

Davisson, L. and Leon-Garcia, A. (1980). A source matching approach to finding minimax codes, *IEEE Transactions on Information Theory*, 26(2), 166–174.

DeBruijn, N. G. (1958). *Asymptotic Methods in Analysis*. New York: Dover.

Delange, H. (1954). Généralisation du théorème de Ikehara, *Annales Scientifiques de l'Ecole Normale Superieure*, 71, 213–242.

Delange, H. (1975). Sur la fonction sommatoire de la fonction "Somme des Chiffres,", *Enseignement Mathématique*, *21*, 31–47.

Delgosha, P. and Anantharam, V. (2017). Universal lossless compression of graphical data. 2017 *IEEE International Symposium on Information Theory*, pp. 1578–1582. *arXiv:1909.09844*.

Delgosha, P. and Anantharam, V. (2022). Distributed Compression of Graphical Data, *IEEE Transactions on Information Theory*, *68*(3), 1412–1439.

Dembo, A. and Kontoyiannis, I. (1999). The asymptotics of waiting times between stationary processes allowing distortion, *Annals of Applied Probability*, *9*(2), 413–429.

Dembo, A. and Kontoyiannis, I. (2001). Critical behavior in lossy coding, *IEEE Transactions on Information Theory*, *47*(3), 1230–1236.

Dembo, A. and Kontoyiannis, I. (2002). Source coding, large deviations, and approximate pattern matching, *IEEE Transactions on Information Theory*, *48*(6), 1590–1615.

Dickinson, H. and Dodson, M. M. (2000). Extremal manifolds and Hausdorff dimension, *Duke Mathematical Journal*, *101*(2), 271–281.

Drmota, M. (2009). *Random Trees: An Interplay between Combinatorics and Probability*. New York: Springer.

Drmota, M., Hwang, H. K., and Szpankowski, W. (2002). Precise average redundancy of an idealized arithmetic coding, *Proceedings DCC Data Compression Conference, Snowbird*, UT, USA, pp. 222–231.

Drmota, M., Reznik, Y., Savari, S., and Szpankowski, W. (2006). Precise asymptotic analysis of the Tunstall code, *2006 International Symposium on Information Theory*, pp. 2334–2337.

Drmota, M., Reznik, Y., and Szpankowski, W. (2010). Tunstall code, Khodak variations, and random walks, *IEEE Transactions on Information Theory*, *56*(6), 2928–2937.

Drmota, M., Shamir, G. I., and Szpankowski, W. (2022). Sequential universal compression for non-binary sequences with constrained distributions, *Communications in Information and Systems*, *22*(1), 1–38.

Drmota, M. and Szpankowski, W. (2002). Generalized Shannon code minimizes the maximal redundancy, In *LATIN'02*, pp. 306–318.

Drmota, M. and Szpankowski, W. (2004). Precise minimax redundancy and regrets, *IEEE Transactions on Information Theory*, *50*(11), 2686–2707.

Drmota, M. and Szpankowski, W. (2007). On the exit time of a random walk with the positive drift, *2007 Conference on Analysis of Algorithms, Juan-les-Pins, France, and Discrete Mathematics and Theoretical Computer Science DMTCS Proceedings*, vol. AH, pp. 291–302.

Drmota, M. and Szpankowski, W. (2013). A master theorem for discrete divide and conquer recurrences, *Journal of the ACM*, 60(3), 16:1–16:49.

Drmota, M. and Tichy, R. (1997). *Sequences Discrepancies and Applications*. Berlin: Springer.

Durrett, R. (1991). *Probability: Theory and Examples*. Wadsworth, Belmont.

Erdős, P., Hildebrand, A., Odlyzko, A., Pudaite, P., and Reznick, B. (1987). The asymptotic behavior of a family of sequences, *Pacific Journal of Mathematics*, *126*, 227–241.

Fabris, F. (1992). Variable-length-to-variable-length source coding: A greedy step-by-step algorithm, *IEEE Transactions on Information Theory*, 38(5), 1609–1617.

Feller, W. (1970). *An Introduction to Probability Theory and Its Applications*, vol. I. New York: John Wiley and Sons

Fill, J. A. and Kapur, N. (2005). Transfer theorems and asymptotic distributional results for m-ary search trees, *Random Structures & Algorithms*, 26(4), 359–391.

Flajolet, P. (1999). Singularity analysis and asymptotics of Bernoulli sums, *Theoretical Computer Science*, 215(1), 371–381.

Flajolet, P. and Golin, M. (1954). Mellin transforms and asymptotics: The Mergesort recurrence, *Acta Informatica*, *31*, 673–696.

Flajolet, P., Gourdon, X., and Dumas, P. (1995). Mellin transforms and asymptotics: Harmonic sums, *Theoretical Computer Science*, *144*(1), 3–58.

Flajolet, P., Gourdon, X., and Martinez, C. (1997). Patterns in random binary search trees, *Random Structures & Algorithms*, *11*, 223–244.

Flajolet, P. and Odlyzko, A. M. (1990). Singularity analysis of generating functions, SIAM *Journal on Discrete Mathematics*, 3(2), 216–240.

Flajolet, P. and Sedgewick, R. (2008). *Analytic Combinatorics*. Cambridge: Cambridge University Press.

Flajolet, P. and Szpankowski, W. (2002). Analytic variations on redundancy rates of renewal processes, *IEEE Transactions on Information Theory*, 48(11), 2911–2921.

Foster, D. J., Kale, S., Luo, H., Mohri, M., and Sridharan, K. (2018). Logistic regression: The importance of being improper. *Proceedings of Machine Learning Research* (PMLR), 75, 167–208.

Freeman, G. H. (1993). Divergence and the construction of variable-to-variable-length lossless codes by source-word extensions, *Proceedings Data Compression Conference*, Snowbird, UT, USA, pp. 79–88.

Frieze, A. and Karoński, M. (2016). *Introduction to Random Graphs*. Cambridge: Cambridge University Press.

Frieze, A., Turowski, K., and Szpankowski, W. (2020). Degree distribution for duplication-divergence graphs: Large deviations. In *WG2020: Algorithms and Complexity*, LNCS 12301, 226–237.

Frieze, A., Turowski, K., and Szpankowski, W. (2021). The concentration of the maximum degree in the duplication-divergence models. *COCOON Proceedings*, pp. 413–424.

Gallager, R. (1968). *Information Theory and Reliable Communications*. New York: Wiley.

Gallager, R. (1978). Variations on the theme by Huffman, *IEEE Transactions on Information Theory*, *24*(6), 668–674.

Gallager, R. and van Voorhis, D. (1975). Optimal source codes for geometrically distributed integer alphabets, *IEEE Transactions on Information Theory*, 21(2), 228–230.

Golebiewski, Z., Magner, A., and Szpankowski, W. (2018). Entropy and optimal compression of some general trees, *ACM Transaction on Algorithms*, 15, 1–23.

Golomb, S. (1996). Run-length coding, *IEEE Transactions on Information Theory*, pp. 399–401.

Goodman, L. (1958). Exact probabilities and asymptotic relationships for some statistics from m-th order markov chains, *Annals of Mathematical Statistics*, *29*(2), 476–490.

Grabner, P. and Hwang, H. K. (2005). Digital sums and divide-and-conquer recurrences: Fourier expansions and absolute convergence, *Constructive Approximation*, *21*, 149–179.

Grabner, P. and Thuswaldner, J. M. (1996). Analytic continuation of a class of Dirichlet series, *Abhandlungen aus dem Mathematischen Seminar der Universität Hamburg*, *66*, 281–287.

Grunwald, P. (2007). *The Minimum Description Length Principle*. Cambridge: MIT Press.

Gyorfi, L., Pali, I., and Van der Meulen, E. C. (1994). There is no universal source code for an infinite source alphabet, *IEEE Transactions on Information Theory*, 40 (1), 267–271.

Hayman, W. K. (1956). A generalization of Stirling's formula, *Journal für die reine und angewandte Mathematik*, *196*, 67–95.

Hazan, E. (2008). Extracting certainty from uncertainty: Regret bounded by variation in costs, In *Machine Learning*, *80*(2), 165–188.

Hazan, E., Agarwal, A., and Kale, S. (2007). Logarithmic regret algorithms for online convex optimization, *Machine Learning*, *69*, 169–192.

Hazan, E., Koren, T., and Levy, K. Y. (2014). Logistic regression: Tight bounds for stochastic and online optimization, In *The 27th Conference on Learning Theory, Proceedings of Machine learning Research* (PMLR), pp. 197–209. Cambridge: MIT Press.

Henrici, P. (1977). *Applied and Computational Complex Analysis*. New York: John Wiley.

Hermann, F. and Pfaffelhuber, P. (2016). Large-scale behavior of the partial duplication random graph, *ALEA, Latin American Journal of Probability and Mathematical Statistics*, *13*(2), 687–710.

Hofstad, R. van der (2016). *Random Graphs and Complex Networks: vol. 1*. Cambridge: Cambridge University Press.

Huffman, D. (1952). A method for the construction of minimum redundancy codes, *Proceedings of the IRE*, *40*(9), 1089–1101.

Huxley, M. N. (1996). *Area, Lattice Points, and Exponential Sums*, vol. 13 of Lond. Math. Soc. Monogr. Oxford: Clarendon Press.

Hwang, H. K. (2000). Distribution of the number of factors in random ordered factorizations of integers, *Journal of Number Theory*, *81*, 61–92.

Hwang, H. K. and Janson, S. (2011). A central limit theorem for random ordered factorizations of integers, *Electronic of Probability*, *16*, 347–361.

Jacquet, P., Knessl, C., and Szpankowski, W. (2012). Counting Markov types, balanced matrices, and Eulerian graphs, *IEEE Transactions on Information Theory*, 58(7), 4261–4272.

Jacquet, P., Milioris, D., and Szpankowski, W. (2020). Joint string complexity for Markov Sources: Small data matters, *Theoretical Computer Science*, *844*, 46–80.

Jacquet, P., Shamir, G., and Szpankowski, W. (2021). Precise minimax regret for logistic regression with categorical feature values, *Proceedings of Machine Learning Research* (PMLR), 132, 1–17.

Jacquet, P. and Szpankowski, W. (1995). Asymptotic behavior of the Lempel–Ziv parsing scheme and digital search trees, *Theoretical Computer Science*, *144*(1–2), 161–197.

Jacquet, P. and Szpankowski, W. (1998). Anaylytical depoissonization and its applications, *Theoretical Computer Science*, *201*(1–2), 1–62.

Jacquet, P. and Szpankowski, W. (1999). Entropy computations via analytic depoissonization, *IEEE Transactions on Information Theory*, *45*(4), 1072–1081.

Jacquet, P. and Szpankowski, W. (2004). Markov types and minimax redundancy for Markov sources, *IEEE Transactions on Information Theory*, *50*(7), 1393–1402.

Jacquet, P. and Szpankowski, W. (2015). *Analytic Pattern Matching: From DNA to Twitter*. Cambridge: Cambridge University Press.

Janson, S. (1986). Moments for first passage and last exit times the minimum and related quantities for random walks with positive drift, *Advances in Applied Probability*, *18*(4), 865–879.

Jelinek, F. and Schneider, K. S. (1972). On variable-length-to-block coding, *IEEE Transactions on Information Theory*, *18*(6), 765–774.

Jordan, J. (2018). The connected component of the partial duplication graph, *ALEA – Latin American Journal of Probability and Mathematical Statistics*, *15*, 1431–1445.

Kakade, S. M. and Ng, A. Y. (2005). Online bounds for Bayesian algorithms, In Saul, L. K., Weiss, Y., and Bottou, L. (eds.), *Advances in Neural Information Processing Systems 17*, pp. 641–648. Cambridge: MIT Press.

Katona, G. and Tusnady, G. (1967). The principle of conservation of entropy in a noiseless channel, *Studia Scientiarum Mathematicarum Hungarica*, *2*, 29–35.

Khodak, G. L. (1969). Connection between redundancy and average delay of fixed-length coding, *All-Union Conference on Problems of Theoretical Cybernetics*, Novosibirsk, USSR, 12 (in Russian).

Khodak, G. L. (1972). Bounds of redundancy estimates for word-based encoding of sequences produced by a Bernoulli source, *Problemy Peredachi Informacii*, 8, 21–32.

Kieffer, J. C. (1978). A unified approach to weak universal source coding, *IEEE Transactions on Information Theory*, *24*(6), 340–360.

Kieffer, J. C. (1991). Sample converses in source coding theory, *IEEE Transactions on Information Theory*, *37*(2), 263–268.

Kieffer, J. C., Yang, E., and Szpankowski, W. (2009). Structural complexity of random binary trees, *IEEE International Symposium on Information Theory*, pp. 635–639.

Kim, J. H., Sudakov, B., and Vu, V. (2002). On the asymmetry of random regular graphs and random graphs, *Random Structures & Algorithms*, *21*(3–4), 216–224.

Kleinberg, J. (2000). Navigation in a small world, *Nature*, *406*(6798), 845–845.

Knessl, C. and Szpankowski, W. (2005). Enumeration of binary trees, Lempel–Ziv '78 parsings and universal types, *Proceedings of Analytic Algorithms and Combinatorics* (ALENEX/ANALCO), Vancouver: SIAM, pp. 222–229.

Knuth, D. E. (1997). *The Art of Computer Programming: Fundamental Algorithms*, 3rd ed. Reading MA: Addison-Wesley.

Knuth, D. E. (1998a). *The Art of Computer Programming: Seminumerical Algorithms*, 3rd ed. Reading MA: Addison-Wesley.

Knuth, D. E. (1998b). *The Art of Computer Programming: Sorting and Searching*, 2nd ed. Reading MA: Addison-Wesley.

Kontoyiannis, I. (1999). An implementable lossy version of the Lempel–Ziv algorithm – Part I: Optimality for memoryless sources, *IEEE Transactions on Information Theory*, *45*(7), 2285–2292.

Kontoyiannis, I. (2000). Pointwise redundancy in lossy data compression and universal lossy data compression, *IEEE Transactions on Information Theory*, 46(1), 136–152.

Kontoyiannis, I. (2001). Sphere-covering, measure concentration, and source coding, *IEEE Transactions on Information Theory*, 47(4), 1544–1552.

Kontoyiannis, I., Lim, Y., Papakonstantinopoulou, K., and Szpankowski, W. (2021). Compression and symmetry of small-world graphs and structures, *Communication in Information and Systems*, 2, 275–302.

Kontoyiannis, I. and Verdu, S. (2014). Optimal lossless data compression: Non-asymptotics and asymptotics, *IEEE Transactions on Information Theory*, 60(2), 777–795.

Korevaar, J. (2002). A century of complex tauberian theory, *Bulletin of the American Mathematical Society*, 39(4), 475–531.

Korobov, N. M. (1992). *Exponential Sums and Their Applications*. Transl. from the Russian by Yu. N. Shakhov, vol. 80 Mathematics and Its Applications. Dordrecht: Kluwer Academic Publishers.

Kosut, O. and Sankar, L. (2017). Asymptotics and non-asymptotics for universal fixed-to-variable source coding, *IEEE Transactions on Information Theory*, 63(6), 3757–3772.

Kowalski, E. (2021). *An Introduction to Probabilistic Number Theory*, vol. 192 of Camb. Stud. Adv. Math. Cambridge: Cambridge University Press.

Krichevsky, R. (1994). *Universal Compression and Retrieval*. Dordrecht: Kluwer.

Krichevsky, R. and Trofimov, V. (1981). The performance of universal coding, *IEEE Transactions on Information Theory*, 27(2), 199–207.

Kuipers, L. and Niederreiter, H. (1974). *Uniform Distribution of Sequences*, New York: John Wiley and Sons.

Linder, T., Lugosi, G., and Zeger, K. (1995). Fixed-rate universal lossy source coding and rates of convergence for memoryless sources, *IEEE Transactions on Information Theory*, 41(3), 665–676.

Louchard, G. and Szpankowski, W. (1995). Average profile and limiting distribution for a phrase size in the Lempel-Ziv parsing algorithm, *IEEE Transactions on Information Theory*, 41(2), 478–488.

Luczak, T., Magner, A., and Szpankowski, W. (2019a). Asymmetry and structural information in preferential attachment graphs, *Random Structures & Algorithms*, 55(3), 696–718.

Luczak, T., Magner, A., and Szpankowski, W. (2019b). Compression of preferential attachment graphs, *IEEE International Symposium on Information Theory*, pp. 1697–1701,

MacMillan, B. (1956). Two inequalities implied by unique decipherability, *IEEE Transactions on Information Theory*, 2, 115–116.

Magner, A., Janson, S., Kollias, G., and Szpankowski, W. (2014). On symmetries of uniform and preferential attachment graphs, *Electronic Journal of Combinatorics*, 21(3), #P3.32.

Magner, A., Turowski, K., and Szpankowski, W. (2016). Lossless compression of binary trees with correlated vertex names, *IEEE International Symposium on Information Theory*, Barcelona, Spain, pp. 1217–1221.

Magner, A., Turowski, K., and Szpankowski, W. (2018). Lossless compression of binary trees with correlated vertex names, *IEEE Transactions on Information Theory*, 64(9), 6070–6080.

Mahmoud, H. (1992). *Evolution of Random Search Trees*. New York: John Wiley and Sons.

Maneth, S. and Peternek, F. (2018). Grammar-based graph compression, *Information Systems*, *76*, 19–45.

Manstetten, D. (1980). Tight upper bounds on the redundancy of Huffman codes, *IEEE Transactions on Information Theory*, *38*, 220–222.

Martin, A., Seroussi, G., and Weinberger, M. (2007). Type classes of tree models, *IEEE International Symposium on Information Theory*, Nice, France, pp 886–890.

Massey, J. (1983). The entropy of a rooted tree with probabilities, *Proceedings of the IEEE International Symposium on Information Theory*.

McMahan, H. B. and Streeter, M. J. (2012). Open problem: Better bounds for online logistic regression, *Proceedings of Machine Learning Research (PMLR)* 44.1–44.3.

Meir, A. and Moon, J. (1978). On the altitude of nodes in random trees, *Canadian Journal of Mathematics*, *30*, 997–1015.

Merhav, N. and Neuhoff, D. (1992). Variable-to-fixed length codes provided better large Deviations performance than fixed-to-variable codes, *IEEE Transactions on Information Theory*, *38*(1), 135–140.

Merhav, N., Seroussi, G., and Weinberger, M. (2000). Optimal prefix codes for sources with two-sided geometric distributions, *IEEE Transactions on Information Theory*, *46*(1), 121–135.

Merhav, N. and Szpankowski, W. (2013). Average redundancy of the Shannon code for Markov sources, *IEEE Transactions on Information Theory*, *59*(11), 7186–7193.

Mezo, I. and Baricz, A. (2017). On the generalization of the Lambert W function, *Transactions of the American Mathematical Society*, *369*(11), 7917–7934. *arXiv:1408.3999v2*.

Mohri, M., Riley, M., and Suresh, A. T. (2015). Automata and graph compression, *IEEE International Symposium on Information Theory* (ISIT).

Mohri, M., Rostamizadeh, A., and Talwalker, A. (2018). *Foundation of Machine Learning*. 2nd ed. Cambridge, MA: MIT Press.

Naor, M. (1990). Succinct representation of general unlabeled graphs, *Discrete Applied Mathematics*, *28*, 303–307.

Nath, P. (1975). On a coding theorem connected with Rényi's entropy, *Information and Control*, *29*, 234–242.

Niederreiter, H. (1992). *Random Number Generation and Quasi-Monte Carlo Methods*, vol. 63 of CBMS-NSF Reg. Conf. Ser. Appl. Math. Philadelphia, PA: SIAM.

Noble, R. and Johnson, C. (1985). *Matrix Analysis*. Cambridge: Cambridge University Press.

Odlyzko, A. (1995). Asymptotic enumeration, in R. L. Graham et al,, ed., *Handbook of Cominatorics*, Amsterdam: Elsevier, 1063–1229.

Orlitsky, A. and Santhanam, P. (2004). Speaking of infinity, *IEEE Transactions on Information Theory*, *50*(10), 2215–2230.

Orlitsky, A., Santhanam, P., and Zhang, J. (2004). Universal compression of memoryless sources over unknown alphabets, *IEEE Transactions on Information Theory*, *50*(10), 1469–1481.

Ornstein, D. and Shields, P. (1990). Universal almost sure data compression, *Annals of Probability*, *18*(2), 441–452.

Park, G., Hwang, H., Nicodeme, P., and Szpankowski, W. (2009). Profile in tries, *SIAM Journal of Computing*, *38*(5), 1821–1880.

Parker, D. S. (1980). Conditions for optimality of the Huffman algorithm, *SIAM Journal of Computing*, *9*, 470–489.

Pastor-Satorras, R., Smith, E., and Solé, R. V. (2003). Evolving protein interaction networks through gene duplication, *Journal of Theoretical Biology*, *222*(2), 199–210.

Peshkin, L. (2007). Structure induction by lossless graph compression, In *Data Compression Conference*, pp. 53–62.

Rakhlin, A. and Sridharan, K. (2014). Online nonparametric regression with general loss function, *Proceedings of Machine learning* (PMLR), *35*, 1–33.

Rakhlin, A. and Sridharan, K. (2015). Sequential probability assignment with binary alphabets and large classes of experts, *arXiv preprint arXiv:1501.07340*.

Rakhlin, A., Sridharan, K., and Tewari, A. (2010). Online learning: Random averages, combinatorial parameters, and learnability, *Advances in Neural Information Processing Systems*, *23*, 1984–1992.

Remmert, R. (1983). *Theory of Complex Functions*. New York: Springer.

Rissanen, J. (1984a). Complexity of strings in the class of Markov sources, *IEEE Transactions on Information Theory*, *32*(4), 526–532.

Rissanen, J. (1984b). Universal coding and information and prediction and estimation, *IEEE Transactions on Information Theory*, *30*(4), 629–636.

Rissanen, J. (1996). Fisher information and stochastic complexity, *IEEE Transactions on Information Theory*, 42(1), 40–47.

Rissanen, J. (2003). *Complexity and Information Data*. Princeton, NJ: Princeton University Press.

Rissanen, J. (2007). *Information and Complexity in Statistical Modeling*. New York: Springer.

Roura, S. (2001). Improved master theorems for divide-and-conquer recurrences, *Journal of the ACM*, *48*, 170–205.

Savari, S. A. (1997). Redundancy of the Lempel–Ziv incremental parsing rule, *IEEE Transactions on Information Theory*, *43*(1), 9–21.

Savari, S. A. (1998). Variable-to-fixed length codes for predictable sources, *Proceeding of the DCC '98 Data Compression Conference*, Snowbird, UT, pp. 481–490.

Savari, S. A. (1999). Variable-to-fixed length codes and the conservation of enthropy, *IEEE Transactions on Information Theory*, 45(5), 1612–1620.

Savari, S. A. and Gallager, R. (1997). Generalized Tunstall codes for sources with memory, *IEEE Transactions on Information Theory*, 43(2), 658–668.

Schachinger, W. (2001). Limiting distributions for the costs of partial match retrievals in multidimensional tries, *Random Structures and Algorithms*, *17*, 428–459.

Schalkwijk, J. (1972). An algorithm for source coding, *IEEE Transactions on Information Theory*, 18(3), 395–399.

Schmidt, W. M. (1980). *Diophantine Approximation*. New York: Springer.

Schmidt, W. M. (1991). *Diophantine Approximations and Diophantine Equations*, vol. 1467 of Lecture Notes in Mathematics. Berlin: Springer-Verlag.

Seroussi, G. (2006). On universal types, *IEEE Transactions on Information Theory*, 52(1), 171–189.

Shalev-Shwartz, S. and Ben-David, S. (2014). *Understanding Machine Learning: From Theory to Algorithms*. Cambridge: Cambridge University Press.

Shamir, G. I. (2006a). On the MDL principle for i.i.d. sources with large alphabets, *IEEE Transactions on Information Theory*, 52(5), 1939–1955.

Shamir, G. I. (2006b). Universal lossless compression with unknown alphabets: The average case, *IEEE Transactions on Information Theory*, 52(1), 4915 – 4944.

Shamir, G. I. (2013). Universal source coding for monotonic and fast decaying monotonic distributions, *IEEE Transactions on Information Theory*, 59(11), 7194–7211.

Shamir, G. I. (2020). Logistic regression regret: What's the catch?, *Proceedings of Machine Learning* (PMLR), *125*, 1–14.

Shamir, G. I. and Szpankowski, W. (2021a). A general lower bound for regret in logistic regression, *IEEE International Symposium on Information Theory* (ISIT), pp. 2507–2512.

Shamir, G. I. and Szpankowski, W. (2021b). Low complexity approximate bayesian logistic regression for sparse online learning, *ArXiv: http://arxiv.org/abs/2101.12113*.

Shamir, G. I., Tjalkens, T., and Willems, F. (2008). Low-complexity sequential probability estimation and universal compression for binary sequences with constrained distributions, *IEEE International Symposium on Information Theory*, pp. 995–999.

Shannon, C. (1948). A mathematical theory of communication, *Bell System Technical Journal*, 27, 379–423, 623–656.

Shields, P. (1993). Universal redundancy rates do not exist, *IEEE Transactions on Information Theory*, 39(2), 520–524.

Shields, P. (1996). *The Ergodic Theory of Discrete Sample Path*. Providence, RI: American Mathematical Society.

Shtarkov, Y. (1987). Universal sequential coding of single messages, *Problems of Information Transmission*, 23(3), 3–17.

Solé, R., Pastor-Satorras, R., Smith, E., and Kepler, T. (2002). A model of large-scale proteome evolution, *Advances in Complex Systems*, 5(01), 43–54.

Sprindzuk, V. G. (1979). *Metric Theory of Diophantine Approximations*. Wiley.

Stubley, P. (1994). On the redundancy of optimum fixed-to-variable length codes, *Proceedings of IEEE Data Compression Conference*, Snowbird, UT, 90–97.

Szpankowski, W. (1998). On asymptotics of certain recurrences arising in universal coding, *Problems of Information Transmission*, 34, 142–146.

Szpankowski, W. (2000). Asymptotic redundancy of Huffman (and other) block codes, *IEEE Transactions on Information Theory*, 46(7), 2434–2443.

Szpankowski, W. (2001). *Average Case Analysis of Algorithms on Sequences*. New York: Wiley.

Szpankowski, W. (2008). A one-to-one code and its anti-redundancy, *IEEE Transactions on Information Theory*, 54(10), 4762–4766.

Szpankowski, W. (2012). Algorithms, combinatorics, information, and beyond, *IEEE Information Theory Society Newsletter*, *62*, 5–20.

Szpankowski, W. and Verdu, S. (2011). Minimum expected length of fixed-to-variable lossless compression without prefix constraints, *IEEE Transactions on Information Theory*, 57(7), 4017–4025.

Szpankowski, W. and Weinberger, M. (2012). Minimax pointwise redundancy for memoryless models over large alphabets, *IEEE Transactions on Information Theory*, 58(7), 4094–4104.

Tjalkens, T. and Willems, F. (1992). A universal variable-to-fixed length source code based on Lawrence's algorithm, *IEEE Transactions on Information Theory*, 38(2), 247–253.

Tunstall, B. P. (1967). Synthesis of noiseless compression codes, Ph.D. dissertation, Georgia Tech.

Turan, G. (1984). On the succinct representation of graphs, *Discrete Applied Mathematics*, 8, 289–294.

Turowski, K. and Szpankowski, W. (2019). Towards degree distribution of duplication graph models, *Electronic Journal on Combinatorics, 28*(1), P1.18

Vaaler, J. D. (1985). Some extremal functions in Fourier analysis, *Bulletin of the American Mathematical Society, 12*, 183–216.

Visweswariah, K., Kulkurani, S., and Verdu, S. (2001). Universal variable-to-fixed length source codes, *IEEE Transactions on Information Theory*, 47(4), 1461–1472.

Walfisz, A. (1963). Weylsche Exponentialsummen in der neueren Zahlentheorie, Mathematische Forschungsberichte. 16. Berlin: VEB Deutscher Verlag der Wissenschaften. 231 S. (1963).

Watts, D. and Strogatz, S. (1998). Collective dynamics of 'small-world' networks, *Nature*, *393*(6684), 440–442.

Weinberger, M., Merhav, N., and Feder, M. (1994). Optimal sequential probability assignments for individual sequences, *IEEE Trans. Information Theory*, 40(2), 384–396.

Weinberger, M., Rissanen, J., and Feder, M. (1995). A universal finite memory source, *IEEE Transactions on Information Theory*, 41(3), 643–652.

Whittle, P. (1955). Some distribution and moment formulae for Markov chain, *Journal of the Royal Statistical Society, Series B, 17(2)*, pp. 235–242.

Wong, R. (1989). *Asymptotic Approximations of Integrals*. Boston: Academic Press.

Wright, E. M. (1997). The coefficients of certain power series, *J. London Mathematical Society, 43*, 1439–1465.

Wu, C., Heidari, M., Grama, A., and Szpankowski, W. (2022). Sequential vs fixed design regrets in online learning, *IEEE International Symposium on Information Theory* (ISIT), pp. 438–443.

Wyner, A. D. and Ziv, J. (1989). Some asymptotic properties of the entropy of a stationary ergodic data source with applications to data compression, *IEEE Transactions on Information Theory*, 35(6), 1250–1258.

Wyner, A. D. (1972). An upper bound on the entropy series, *Information and Control*, 20(2), 176–181.

Wyner, A. J. (1997). The redundancy and distribution of the phrase lengths of the fixed-database Lempel–Ziv algorithm, *IEEE Transactions on Information Theory*, 43(5), 1439–1465.

Xie, Q. and Barron, A. (1997). Minimax redundancy for the class of memoryless souces, *IEEE Transactions on Information Theory*, 43(2), 647–657.

Xie, Q. and Barron, A. (2000). Asymptotic minimax regret for data compression and gambling and prediction, *IEEE Transactions on Information Theory*, 46(2), 431–445.

Yang, E. H. and Kieffer, J. (1998). On the performance of data compression algorithms based upon string matching, *IEEE Transactions on Information Theory*, 44(1), 47–65.

Zhang, J., Yang, E.-H., and Kieffer, J. C. (2014). A universal grammar-based code for loss-less compression of binary trees, *IEEE Transactions on Information Theory*, 60(3), 1373–1386.

Ziv, J. (1990). Variable-to-fixed length codes are better than fixed-to-variable length codes for Markov sources, *IEEE Transactions on Information Theory*, 36(4), 861–863.

Index

Printed in the United States
by Baker & Taylor Publisher Services